PENGUIN BOOKS

THE LIONS' CAGE

John Clive is one of those instantly recognizable faces one knows from more than a hundred film and television appearances. His films include *The Italian Job*, *Clockwork Orange*, *Great Expectations* and *Carry On Abroad*. On television he has appeared notably in *The Sweeney*, *How Green was My Valley*, *Rising Damp*, *The History of Mr Polly*, *The Government Inspector* and last year for the BBC in *Lady Windermere's Fan*. This picked up the Ace Award for Excellence in Hollywood for 'Best Theatrical Special'. As well as his acting career, there is a growing awareness of his work as an author. He has won high praise for his novels, the first of which, *KG 200*, sold over a million copies in Britain and America alone. His other books are *The Last Liberator*, *Barossa*, *Broken Wings* and, with Nicolas Head, *Ark*, which is published in Penguin.

Reviews for John Clive's previous book *Ark*:

'Fiction based on fact makes for breathless reading . . . Exciting and moving' – Kati Nicholl in *Today*

'If you're for a book to send you to sleep after reading a few pages, don't buy John Clive and Nicolas Head's novel *Ark*. The book is a classic wartime suspense thriller which will have you riveted to your seat after the first chapter. More important, the story, set in Beirut, depicts the horror, chaos and futility of the conflict in that war-torn city with an impact no news bulletin could achieve . . . an experience both vivid and disturbing . . . the tale is not one a reader is likely to forget' – *Daily News*

'Gripping . . . our own Ross Benson and photographer John Downing were among tho[se] . . . "Thank you for taking us from hell to heaven, . . . [auth]or in the *Daily Express*

THE LIONS' CAGE

JOHN CLIVE

PENGUIN BOOKS

PENGUIN BOOKS

Published by the Penguin Group
27 Wrights Lane, London w8 5tz, England
Viking Penguin Inc., 40 West 23rd Street, New York, New York 10010, USA
Penguin Books Australia Ltd, Ringwood, Victoria, Australia
Penguin Books Canada Ltd, 2801 John Street, Markham, Ontario, Canada l3r 1b4
Penguin Books (NZ) Ltd, 182–190 Wairau Road, Auckland 10, New Zealand

Penguin Books Ltd. Registered Offices: Harmondsworth, Middlesex, England

First published by Viking 1987
Published in Penguin Books 1988

Made and printed in Great Britain by
Richard Clay Ltd, Bungay, Suffolk
Filmset in Monophoto Bembo

For Anita,
who came to me in Ireland and
told me a story about a brave
and extraordinary woman who had
lived in Antwerp as the tides of
war swept through . . .
And for Max,
who once made a promise to Joe,
when they were young and callow
and living each day as though it were
their last.
Max died last year

To Anita and Max, I dedicate this book

The tides of war flow up the beach and at their ebb they leave behind tales, countless as the drying grains of sand, tales that must be told.

Anon.

The woman sat quietly, resting; her brown-leather sensible shoes were dusty from the hard-baked roads. The sun continued to pour down on her, but this far away she could not hear the sounds of the refugee column moving slowly in the distance.

It all seemed strangely peaceful and serene, the heat haze shimmering across ripe Belgian fields in the full flush of late summer. She had left the column only fifteen minutes before, but already it seemed an age away, a different time. The harsh cries of thirsty babies, the whining of children becoming accustomed to the brutalities of war. They were hungry and tired.

All the earlier excitement of travelling from their familiar surroundings in the city, many of them seeing the countryside for the first time, all this had evaporated. They were exhausted; the roads were hot and crowded with thousands like themselves fleeing, as hosts to a war they had not invited and knew nothing of, until first the German and now the Allied armies advanced across their country.

The column crept along, agonizingly slowly beyond the hedgerows that bounded the narrow lane. To the woman they seemed from this distance like an elongated, humpbacked caterpillar, moving in gentle waves. Curiously silent and inhuman.

How could this be, she thought?

It was as if she were in a dream. A slipping, flowing nightmare, set in an incredibly peaceful countryside. The shifting beams of sunlight made it even more unreal.

Yesterday, only yesterday, her life had had a pattern, some meaning. Then Manfred had gone to face an ordeal much worse than her own, to confront an enemy that had crept ominously closer to the borders of Belgium as the summer of her life had slipped too swiftly by.

It was the day she had feared most of all, and it had come, just as she always knew it would. They had been too happy. It was not possible that it could have lasted. She had sensed that from the start.

Before Manfred had left he'd warned her to get out of the city, away from the Cinéac in Antwerp where her connection with the occupying authorities as manager of the cinema might make her a target for those who harboured a grudge.

But Hauser had come back and told her Manfred was dead. She didn't believe him, she couldn't. She would find him. Manfred had come this way; she knew he was alive. Yet now she was caught in the open, trapped by the refugees jamming the roads, inextricably mixed with the German columns trying to close with the advancing Allied armies and stop them. Her cinema seemed a long way away. A cool, pleasant place of images on a silver screen that had flickered through her working life. How she ached to return to that safe dark world – dull and routine perhaps, but secure. What price her security now?

She lay back in the warm, long grass on the shallow slope of the hill that rose gently behind her. She closed her eyes, trying to shut out her chaotic, paralysing thoughts, trying to imagine it was just another sunny Sunday, a trip to the country. The insects still hummed reassuringly around her, the grass still smelt as sweet. In the distance she could hear faintly the bark of a dog.

It wasn't true, she reasoned. None of this had happened. She would wake in a moment and find it was all inspired by some melodramatic, cinematic trailer from across the sea. Please, God, she mouthed silently to herself, help us survive this horror, save us all. She felt a tear slide from beneath her closed lids and trickle slowly down her left cheek. She drew her arm across her face, wiping it away, shutting off the light from the sun.

From beyond the hill behind her she heard the murmur of a tractor, its steady note beating the air drowsily. It grew louder, more intense. Her eyes opened wide, frightened. She sat up, staring at the sky. She knew that sound. She'd heard it before. Now it came closer, suddenly slipping into a high-pitched whine as the fighter plane dived from the cloudless blue sky.

She watched, horrified, as the tiny, antlike people in the distance scattered like grains of corn before a wind. The plane gleamed dark and deadly, spreading its message of death, splattering the helpless column with its shower of lead. Killing, terrifying, it dived and swooped several times over the defenceless horses that had been left standing in the middle of the country road. They fell, milling and screaming soundlessly amongst their harnesses, their legs pumping the air until finally they were still.

As quickly as it had appeared the fighter plane rolled over gracefully and pirouetted back up into the sky, leaving its spreading pools of red sinking into the dusty road.

The woman screamed hysterically and turned face down on her stomach, clutching the grass in her fists, pounding the earth in her fear and rage, the sun still hot on her back. Lissette felt sick, sick and terribly frightened . . .

CHAPTER ONE

The valley was silent, unnaturally so. The sun, already warm, dappled the thick woods that dipped steeply down to the green bottom land. Yet there were no cries from the birds to greet the early morning. The narrow valley was still, as though in suspense, waiting for something to happen.

A road twisted along one side, serving the well laid-out houses and vast gardens that sectioned the floor of the valley. The houses were empty now, some blown apart by the shelling, all of them damaged either by blast or by machine-gun fire. The green lawns of the gardens were torn and brown, pockmarked by shell and mortar fire, the holes gradually filling with water. The only sound was that of the brook that snaked the length of the valley, tucked into the foot of the hill opposite the road.

The valley seemed deserted, but Joe continued to watch unblinkingly, waiting for the slightest movement that might betray the position of a sniper. His eyes followed the contours of the landscape. In a field between the trees on the opposite side of the valley he saw five figures sprawled untidily beside a machine-gun emplacement. He needed no second look to know they were dead. The German gunners had commanded a fine view of the ground below and of the only road. But it was too fine, too obvious a spot not to be seen by experienced infantry. It had received a direct hit, probably by mortar fire. Joe couldn't be sure.

He made no effort to use the binoculars strapped to his belt. The sun streaming in through the shattered roof of the house was in line with his view and it might have reflected the light from the lens, betraying his position. He had no intention of dying, not now. Not as his life was just beginning.

Still the valley brooded, empty of life. But Joe didn't believe it. He accepted nothing on face value – he never had. He eased himself slowly away from the window and crawled back into the bedroom until he could not be seen from outside, then he stood up.

It had obviously been a child's room; the expensive wallpaper hung in strips from the walls, the pictures of white rabbits decorating it ripped by the blast. A brown bear lay beside the overturned cot, its stuffing scattered around it, only its beady eyes undamaged. Frozen, they stared up through the hole in the roof at the blue sky above. There was nothing here for him. He descended the stairs, keeping his feet close to the wall, making no sound. The house had been stripped of all its valuables. Only the furnishings remained and Joe wasn't interested in them.

From the open back door the ground dropped sharply away to the flat land between the house and the brook. Joe moved swiftly into the cover of a tall row of evergreen bushes that marked the boundary between this and the next house up the valley. His feet made no sound on the soft bottom ground, and he crossed the brook in a single leap, ignoring the decorative little bridge that was still, incongruously, in one piece. The trees closed around him and he felt safer. He began to ascend the steep hill, moving as quietly as he could towards the clearing.

It was much cooler beneath the trees. They were close together and cut off most of the light. Just the occasional patch of sunshine spilled on to the brown earth. Insects fluttered in its glow, their wings translucent in its beam. Joe stayed in the shadows, darting silently from tree to tree, sometimes stopping and listening intently. Nothing disturbed the faint sounds of the wood.

The light began to grow stronger as the trees thinned. Between them he could see the patch of green that formed the clearing. He stopped and studied carefully the sprawled figures of the dead men around the gun emplacement. He waited for his eyes to adjust to the increased light and was about to step from the cover of the trees when something moved. He flattened himself, motionless, against the trunk of a tree and stared at the woods almost directly opposite.

Gradually he perceived the outline of a man sitting slumped against a fallen tree. The man rubbed his eyes. That was the movement Joe had caught before. He was wearing the field-grey of a German soldier. Joe began to move silently, carefully, skirting the edge of the clearing, working himself into a position behind the soldier. There was a predatory implacability about his progress as he slipped from one cover to the next, always drawing closer to the man with his back to the fallen tree trunk.

As he drew closer to the soldier Joe heard something. At first he could not identify it, then he realized that the German was crying, rubbing his eyes, his face in his hands. Joe paused and slowly pulled from his battledress tunic pocket a round brass shellcase-end about three inches in diameter. When that was safely in one hand he took another from the other pocket, holding one in each palm. When he was about ten feet from the back of the soldier he stopped moment-arily and studied the ground between himself and his quarry, noting anything that might betray his presence.

The soldier was no longer crying. He sat quietly, staring sightlessly out across the sunlit clearing at the dead bodies of his former comrades. He breathed a long, juddering sigh.

Instinctively Joe sensed that the soldier was about to stir. He moved swiftly across the intervening space between them, and in one blurring movement he smashed the two brass shellcase-ends against the German's ears with immense force. There was a sickening sound as the imploding concussion killed the soldier instantly. He slumped sideways to the ground, a dark-brown stain spreading across the green of the grass beneath the side of his head.

Joe casually wiped the brass ends against his trousers, then put them back, one into each tunic pocket. That way they made no sound. Joe preferred them to a knife; they were just as silent and not as messy. Blood was sticky, difficult to remove, and Joe was a fastidious man about some things.

He stood quite still, listening. Nothing seemed to have changed. The normal pattern of sounds continued on the tree line. Beyond, past the clearing, the valley remained empty of life. The battle had moved elsewhere.

Joe knelt down beside the body and, using a wickedly sharp-bladed penknife sawed the insignia from the soldier's uniform. Then he went methodically through the man's pockets until he found his pay book. He transferred that and anything of value that he could find into the khaki haversack that he carried on his shoulder.

He slipped the rings from the man's fingers. They came off easily. His hands were already going cold. There were no personal weapons. Satisfied, Joe trod softly across the grass of the clearing and proceeded to strip the bodies of the gun-emplacement crew of everything that he could find, having first taken all their insignia and identification. He also secured a Luger automatic from one of them; it would fetch a good price when the GIs came down the line looking for mementoes. When he was sure he had everything he disappeared into the cover of the woods, melting through them, a vague, indistinct shadow retracing his steps the way he had come.

The town was crowded, overflowing; staff cars and trucks jostled for position in front of Joe's jeep, trying to force their way through the narrow, twisting street that was the main road. A wrecked Sherman tank partially blocked it, its turret almost blown off, the barrel of its gun leaning drunkenly down on to the pavement. Children were using it as a slide, their legs wrapped around it as they slid from the turret to the ground.

It reminded Joe of a long banister down which he had cheerfully slid, risking life and limb, when he was a kid. But *he* had done it because the money was right; he'd won a lot of bets that way. Most of the time he had got away with it, though he suffered if members of staff caught him, which they did, occasionally. Not that Joe had minded. The punishment didn't worry him and he enjoyed the notoriety – the institution had never really contained him.

Slowly the traffic began to edge forward again, avoiding the tank and the ruins of a building that had collapsed beside it, spilling its masonry into the road.

Joe turned the jeep off the street and manoeuvred it through a pair of huge, trellised iron gates set into a long blank wall that dominated the right side of the road. Inside was a courtyard that formed the inner well of an old stone building that had once been a monastery, until first the Germans and now the British occupied it as a barracks. Joe parked the jeep next to the trucks that belonged to his transportation unit and climbed stiffly out of the vehicle after switching off the engine.

He felt tired. He'd had no sleep for nearly thirty-six hours. The smell of frying bacon wafted across from the temporary cookhouse and he suddenly felt very hungry. The cobblestones were still damp in the shadows of the courtyard where the sun would not reach until later in the day. They were slippery under his rubber soled boots and he trod carefully.

Eddie Pearce stared at the officer's ludicrous Adam's apple. He couldn't take his eyes off it. Every time the officer spoke it bobbed up and down convulsively, and the Irishman fought desperately not to smile. It was the custom, when being upbraided by a superior, to gaze at a point somewhere just above the officer's head, thus avoiding any eyeball-to-eyeball contact. But for Eddie this was difficult.

He was small, and the officer was tall and angular. Eddie knew that if he tried to raise his eyes from the comic protuberance wobbling alarmingly before him, there was a chance he might see the silly bugger's face and burst out laughing. He concentrated all his efforts on keeping a straight face.

'Well?' the voice said sharply, demanding an explanation.

Eddie took a deep breath. 'Well, sir, I was just nipping into the cookhouse behind me to get meself a hot drink. And I thought, surely I don't need me cap because it's not going to rain, and it is such a short distance, sir.'

Second Lieutenant Glanville stared down at the diminutive Irishman, irritated by the apparent logic of his answer. He was about to tear him off a further strip when he sensed the presence of someone behind him. He turned and stared at the unkempt figure of Joe Porter. Dried mud clung to the knees of his khaki trousers, and the sleeveless leather jerkin that covered his tunic was a mess. 'What on earth . . .?'

Porter cut across him. 'Excuse me, sir.' He tried to push past the officer in the narrow confines of the half covered passage that bordered the courtyard.

Glanville poked his baton hard into Joe's chest, halting him. 'Just a minute!'

Porter stared at the officer without expression, but Glanville felt an uncontrollable shiver of apprehension trace a pattern down his back as he gazed into Porter's basilisk eyes. He swallowed hard, his Adam's apple leaping up and down. He raised his nose and affected an anger he couldn't quite sustain.

'Do you usually ignore officers when you pass them?'

Joe studied the lieutenant carefully. He was new. The uniform had been tailored, edges neatly stitched and creases sharply pressed – but it was not just the uniform. He was trying too hard to be hard, and the slapping of his baton on his leg betrayed his nervousness.

Joe was tempted to be sarcastic, but he was tired and hungry and he had succeeded in doing what he had set out to do – diverting the lieutenant's attention away from Eddie, who had quietly faded into the cookhouse. 'No, sir,' he said politely. 'From the back I couldn't tell you were an officer.'

Glanville was at first inclined to accept the explanation. But the soldier's eyes worried him. They were startlingly green, yet, oddly, it was not just the colour. There was something else, something he could not quite pin down. Instinctively he responded to his own uncertainty. 'You haven't shaved!' he shouted. It sounded ridiculous even to his own ears. His voice seemed to echo round the closed courtyard, mocking him. 'Why not?' he said.

Joe released his breath slowly. He knew he was not going to get out of this. The smell of bacon from the cookhouse smelt delicious, tempting him. He tried again. 'I'm sorry, sir. I didn't have time.'

'Time!' Glanville thundered. 'Why not? I've shaved. I had time.'

Joe stared at the officer's face. The nose was long and pointed, and the chin sloped back, almost from the bottom lip, into a thin neck in which the Adam's apple continued to swallow ridiculously. He weighed his answer carefully. 'Well, you haven't as much chin to shave as I have, sir.'

The officer's baton slapped agitatedly against his leg. Joe's answer had struck a nerve. The lieutenant was well aware of the jibes – they had pursued him relentlessly, mostly out of earshot and behind his back from the ranks, ever since he had been commissioned. But never had he been so overtly put down to his face, whatever its lack of chin.

For a moment he felt bewildered. He looked around quickly to see if anyone else was watching, and he felt a hot flush of embarrassment rise from beneath his collar. The soldier continued to stare at him, the green eyes expressionless, waiting for his reaction. His manner was neither arrogant nor subdued.

The young officer wanted to ignore him, to turn and walk away.

17

This soldier unnerved him, but he knew he had to see it through. It had gone too far and he had to deal with it.

'Your name?'

'Porter,' Joe said resignedly. 'Private Porter.'

The lieutenant's eyes flicked over the dirty uniform and focused on the haversack on Porter's shoulder. 'What have you got there?'

'Where?' Joe asked innocently.

'In the haversack, man,' Glanville snapped. 'Give it to me.'

Joe gazed at him silently for a moment. The officer shifted uncomfortably. The eyes were cold now and he suddenly felt frightened.

'I can't do that, sir,' Joe said softly.

He knew he was not going to get his breakfast.

Eddie Pearce knocked once on the solid oak door, lifted the latch and poked his head inside. Rainy Day Robinson looked up from his well thumbed *Picture Post*. He'd been dubbed 'Rainy Day' because of his penchant for clichés and his constant and morose grumbling about the foul weather that had pursued them ever since they had gone under canvas in Norfolk.

Eddie smiled quickly and indicated Joe, who was slumped on a wooden bench in the corner of the small room. 'Mind if I have a word with him, sarge?'

Robinson stared at him suspiciously. 'Why not? Nobody else will.'

He looked at Porter with undisguised animosity, then added with some satisfaction, 'He's in bloody trouble again. There's an officer in there,' he nodded towards the CO's door, 'who doesn't like your soddin' friend at all.'

Eddie shook his head in apparent dismay. 'Yeah, I heard, sarge.' He glanced at Joe, who hadn't moved, and raised his voice. 'You've missed your breakfast, you know.' Then he added quickly, 'It was bacon and eggs today.'

Joe sighed. 'I know, I could smell it.'

Eddie crossed the room and leaned on a window ledge facing Porter. He spoke quietly, under his breath, his back to the sergeant. 'Thanks for getting me out of trouble.' He grinned. 'But you're in it now.'

Joe looked up at the Irishman. 'That's right.'

Eddie sensed that beneath his poker-faced exterior, Joe was laughing at him, almost as if he derived some satisfaction from the mayhem that constantly surrounded him. Maybe he did.

'How bad is it this time?' he asked.

Joe allowed himself a faint smile. 'Depends.' He tapped the haversack. 'Depends on whether the CO prefers my information to the chinless bastard's who's playing silly buggers in there.'

A pained look crossed Eddie's face, and he glanced apprehensively at the sergeant who had half risen from his chair behind the desk.

'That's enough of that, Porter, unless you want something else added to the charge.'

Joe didn't answer and Eddie dashed quickly into the yawning, dangerous silence. 'I'm sure Joe didn't mean anything, sergeant. All that new Sandhurst mob are trying to make a name for themselves.' He turned quickly back to Joe. 'What happened after I left?'

Porter slowly unfastened his eyes from the sergeant and looked at Eddie. 'Not a lot. I just forgot to salute, that's all.'

Eddie could see he was tired and grim-faced. 'Did you find anything?'

'Yes. The valley is clear now. We can get the transport through.'

Eddie was concerned. He knew Joe in this mood and he knew the damage he could cause himself – in a way Eddie felt responsible. Ever since they had shared the same train compartment on that interminable journey to Gallowgate Barracks, Joe had somehow managed to protect him. Eddie was small physically, and there were always those who tried to intimidate the smallest and weakest. It didn't help that he was from Ireland, the southern part, and that had remained firmly neutral. But Joe had quickly and brutally put a stop to the bullying. In return Eddie tried to extricate Joe from his constant war with authority. He leaned forward and lifted his boot on to the bench where Joe was sitting and pretended to tie his lace. 'Fancy a nice cup of tea?' he said quietly enough for the sergeant not to hear. Joe looked at him and nodded imperceptibly. Eddie winked. 'Leave it to me.'

He finished tying the lace and walked casually over to the sergeant. 'I've just made a fresh pot in the mess, sarge. Would you like a cup?'

Robinson's eyes lifted from the month-old magazine and he almost smiled. 'Why not? Two sugars and plenty of milk.'

Eddie grinned. 'Right, sarge. Your wish is my command.' He glanced at Joe. 'I'll be right back.' He sprang to mock attention and clicked his heels at the sergeant, then affected his best Teutonic. '*Auf wiedersehen*,' he said gutterally and just managed to restrain the Nazi salute.

This time even Rainy Day Robinson managed to find what passed for a smile.

Eddie left.

Major Matthews ran his fingers through his close-cropped, thinning hair and rubbed the back of his neck. The muscles felt stiff and tight and he tried to knead some of the tension from them. His eyes were deep-set, their rims slightly reddened, revealing his tiredness. He looked older than his forty-seven years, the lines drawn into his face. Yet his appearance was deceptive. He was a professional soldier to his fingertips and he operated efficiently, and with some imagination, whatever the conditions.

He stared at the door that had just shut behind a highly indignant Second Lieutenant Glanville and wondered what the hell he was going to do. His desk, laden untidily with forms – vouchers and passes, all in triplicate – mocked him with their weight and numbers. Moving vital supplies up from the mulberry harbours through the chaos of the *bocage* country to the front-line troops was a task not made any easier by the paperwork demanded by his superiors.

Matthews breathed in deeply, mentally squaring his shoulders, then called out sharply, 'Sergeant!'

Robinson opened the door with a flourish. He had been expecting the call and stood smartly in the entrance. 'Sir!'

'Get Porter and send him in.'

'Sir,' the sergeant repeated and made to leave.

'Oh, and sergeant –'

Robinson halted, the door half closed. 'Yes, sir?'

'Send him in by himself, will you? I don't think I could stand you banging about in those heavy boots this morning. I'll deal with the matter. I just want Porter, all right?'

The sergeant's face betrayed no expression, though privately he strongly disapproved. Not just of his CO's action but also of Private Porter – nothing about Porter pleased him at all. But he had been in the army a long time, and sergeants choose their moments carefully before attempting to sway events with their superiors. This was not one of them.

'Yes, sir,' was all that Sergeant Robinson would allow himself. He left, and Major Matthews found himself staring blankly at the door again. He shook his head. This would not do. He dug deeply into his pocket and extracted his pipe, then chewed the end reflectively. It helped him to think, and he found it comforting.

That Private Porter had suddenly, from being a thorn in his side, become an asset there was no doubt. It was strange how being in action and facing the enemy had changed everything. He'd checked Porter's record thoroughly. From the moment he had been conscripted into the Green Howards at Gallowgate in June '43 at the tender age of eighteen, Porter had totally resisted authority. Twice he had been placed into custody. First he had gone absent without leave. He'd been picked up by the MPs en route to London. Then, while under guard, he had brutally assaulted a sergeant with a shovel when on a work detail, though there had been some element of physical provocation. Those two charges would have been enough to see him permanently in the glasshouse for several years – and there he would undoubtedly have remained but for Operation Overlord.

Men were needed for D-Day, all kinds of men, and the Honorary Colonel-in-Chief of the regiment, King Haakon of Norway, had issued a full pardon to all ranks on charges in the Green Howards. Whether Joe felt he was lucky to swop the inside of a cell for Gold Beach had not been recorded; nor had the major inquired.

The Green Howards had suffered heavy casualties in the initial assault. It was then that Joe's gory predilection for scavenging from the dead had emerged. He was not alone in that, though for most men in that inferno simply staying alive had been enough. What brought Porter to the edge of a court martial for desertion was his disappearance from his unit for hours, on one occasion for nearly a day and a night. It was in this respect that his usefulness had finally emerged. Porter was unique, and in combat the information he brought back was beyond price.

There was a sharp knock on the door, and it swung open to admit Porter as he was ushered in by an impressively correct Sergeant

Robinson. The difference in attitude and demeanour of the two men could hardly have been more pronounced. Porter was not insolent or even deliberately provocative. Nevertheless, the provocation was distinct perhaps because it was not at all deliberate.

The sergeant was not the only one who felt its challenge. 'Private Porter, sir,' he announced.

'Thank you, sergeant.'

Robinson left without stamping his feet, and the door closed quietly. The major was grateful. He glanced briefly at the dishevelled figure in front of him. Unlike Lieutenant Glanville, Matthews detected beneath the apparent slovenliness a combat garb that would serve Porter well on his brutally efficient operations. Without haste the officer began to fill his pipe with tobacco from a tin that he took from his pocket. He thumbed the tobacco tightly down into the bowl, enjoying the familiar ritual and ignoring Porter who stood impassively in front of him. Matthews filled the silence with his preparations, then struck a match and took a long pull at the pipe until the tobacco glowed red. Slowly he blew out the smoke.

'You know, Porter, you'd find life much easier if you didn't antagonize your superiors quite so blatantly.'

'I don't try to antagonize them, sir.'

The major took another puff before answering. 'Perhaps not. Fact is, you succeed without even trying. And on this occasion you've outdone yourself.'

Porter did not reply.

The major glanced up at him. 'Well?' he demanded.

'Well, sir, all I said was that I had more chin to shave than he did.' He paused, then added, 'Sir,' as an afterthought.

The major was not without a sense of humour and he found it difficult to prevent the corners of his mouth from twitching. He took another pull at his pipe to disguise his amusement. 'Look, Porter, it's not for you to comment on the chin or lack of it in our junior officers. The freedom of movement that I grant you is dependent upon a number of things. I certainly do not want you attracting attention to yourself, otherwise your usefulness to me disappears. Is that clear?'

Porter nodded his assent. 'Yes, sir.'

One of the things that irritated the major most of all about Porter was his own inability to judge whether or not the point had been absorbed. Porter's replies, when they came, were perfunctory and without emphasis.

'Let me make this crystal-clear. If it becomes known to any of the brass that I allow you the freedom to go wherever you want, no matter what information you bring back, I will have a hard time explaining it. So no more "incidents", Porter. Now what have you got for me?'

Joe grinned suddenly. 'The valley was clear, sir. No sign of anything. We can move the transportation up through there any time.'

'And Jerry?'

'Nothing, sir. Just a machine-gun emplacement that had already been knocked out. They were all dead, bar one.'

'Did you bring him in for questioning?'

Porter shook his head slowly. 'No. He got in the way, sir.'

The major knew the man was lying, but he didn't want to inquire too deeply into what motivated Porter's blood-lust.

'I've got this, sir,' Porter said, patting his haversack.

Matthews glanced at it. That was what had caused all the bloody trouble with Glanville.

'I'm not interested in your spoils,' he said irritably. 'Just the information.'

Porter's eyes clouded over, and the major averted his gaze. They were absolutely devoid of any feeling, and Matthews busied himself with his pipe.

Porter reached down into the haversack and pulled out the insignia and identification of the dead German soldiers. He flung them on to the desk in front of the officer.

Matthews picked them up and examined them briefly. He realized that he had made a mistake. The insignia would provide valuable information as to the deployment of German forces in the area. The major apologized in the only way he could. 'Thank you, Porter. I'll get these down to intelligence right away.'

There was an uncomfortable silence that vaguely annoyed Matthews. Goddam the man. Why did he make him feel so guilty? He dismissed the soldier gruffly. 'You'd better go and get some breakfast . . . and get yourself cleaned up.'

Porter came to attention and turned to leave. As he reached the door he stopped and faced the major. 'I'd like to go in ahead of that supply column, sir.'

Matthews smiled. 'All right, Porter. I don't see why not, since you know the terrain.'

Joe tried not to let his satisfaction show. The major watched the door close behind him and slowly let out a sigh of relief. He couldn't fathom the man, but he was glad he was on his side.

Then came the next thought, crowding in almost at once. Was he? And if he was not on his side, then whose side did he favour?

The major suspected he already knew the answer to that . . .

CHAPTER TWO

Manfred Kepner walked, perhaps a shade unsteadily, through the small back streets behind the railway station in Antwerp. He had enjoyed his lunch and the unexpected bottle of German white wine. It had been fruity and cold, just the way he liked it. He was a tall man, about six feet two, with a boyish shock of brown hair that refused to lie down. Even under his Luftwaffe cap it sprang strongly to attention, giving him a slightly comic appearance.

He reached the busier central areas of the city. They had not suffered too badly in the raids as yet, though the docks were taking a pounding. The air raids were growing steadily more intense as the Allies broke free from their beachhead in France. The Luftwaffe seemed to have disappeared. They were told that the interception points were concentrated on the approaches over the North Sea, but it was hard for his overworked flak unit to believe this when the Allied bomber raids arrived seemingly unopposed. Just a single dogfight would have improved morale – they needed to know that the Luftwaffe existed. The enemy dominated the skies above them.

The programme had changed at the Cinéac, and he stopped to have a look at the stills outside before making his way up to the flat roof of the cinema, where the 20-millimetre Flakvierling had been placed. This week it was *The Hunchback of Notre Dame*, starring the English actor Charles Laughton as the grotesque Quasimodo. How strange, he thought, that he should be engaged in a war against the English, yet here was one of his favourite actors playing in a cinema above which his unit would be trying desperately to bring down any British aircraft that ventured in the skies above them.

He stared, fascinated, at the stills; they had done a magnificent job in transforming the pleasant, rotund Laughton into the hunchback.

25

One eye had somehow been raised higher than the other, and the horribly misshapen features of the actor made Manfred shiver in spite of the warm early afternoon sunshine.

He turned away and was about to go inside to reach the roof of the cinema when he felt someone tugging at the tunic of his uniform. He looked down; it was a small, grubby-faced boy about seven or eight years old. He looked up pleadingly at the German and held out a small silver Belgian coin. He said something that Manfred could not quite understand and pointed at the cinema. Manfred did not need to comprehend the request fully; the boy's intention was clear. Years ago he himself had many times asked such a question outside his local fleapit: 'Please, sir, would you take me in?'

He smiled cheerfully at the boy and accepted his money, taking the dirty hand and leading him inside the cool foyer. The boy's eyes gleamed with excitement, and although Manfred could not stay to see the film himself, he bought two tickets.

The young girl in the box office had seen him before and knew his duties – he ought to be going up to the roof, not in to see the film. But she did not refuse him. They went through the foyer. The usherette took the tickets and tore them in half before leading them into the darkened cinema. Manfred and the boy followed her down the aisle, and sat dutifully where she indicated with her flashlight.

Manfred waited until she had gone, then leaned over and whispered quietly to the boy. '*Auf wiedersehen*.'

He saw the boy's pale face looking at him, surprised. He winked in the darkness, then slipped out of his seat, making his way back up a different aisle towards the foyer once more. He emerged quietly from the gloom of the auditorium and glanced quickly along to the other entrance. The usherette, evidently bored, was leaning against the wall examining her fingernails.

He slipped as noiselessly as he could along the heavily carpeted passage, then turned sharply up the stairs that led to the circle and eventually through a door and up an iron staircase to the roof. A woman coming down from the circle stopped impassively in front of him, barring his progress. She eyed him coldly and he shifted his weight uncomfortably from one foot to the other.

'Herr Kepner, I have already asked you on more than one occasion not to use the circle stairway to reach your emplacement on the roof. I do not want my customer's curiosity piqued by your creeping through doors where they are not allowed to go. If they find there is a gun up there, they may not want to come into the cinema.'

Manfred could not dispute the logic of her argument, and he already felt guilty enough about sneaking the boy in. He held up his hands placatingly. 'You are quite right, *Fräulein*. I'm afraid it was such a lovely afternoon I quite forgot. Please accept my humblest apologies.'

Was he laughing at her? She could not be sure. His blue eyes looked blandly into hers without the trace of a twinkle. She cleared her throat and moved aside to allow him to pass. 'All right, but I do not want to see you in uniform on these stairs again, Herr Kepner.'

He moved up past her, then looked back. 'Thank you, Lissette,' he said, using her first name for the first time. 'I promise next time you see me I will not wear these clothes at all.'

He smiled at her and this time she did detect the laughter in his eyes. She wanted to smile herself but instead tightened her lips and turned away to continue her descent.

'Make sure you do,' was all she could think of to say.

The bouquet of flowers was beautiful, a vivid kaleidoscope of blue, white and green, prettily encased in a long box. It rested squarely in the middle of her desk, the celluloid glinting in the sunlight from her office window.

Lissette stared at the card, astonished, then sat down suddenly in her chair. Her legs felt ridiculously weak. She must pull herself together – after all, it was only a bouquet of flowers – but her throat was constricted and she would have cried had she not swallowed hard and resisted the tears.

They'd come from the German, the one she had spoken to so sharply only yesterday. Lissette had never received flowers, certainly not from a man, not from anyone. She knew she was not beautiful. Apart from her eyes she was even plain, and she did not attract men. They sensed her fear. She had been frightened of them ever since . . . She cut off the thought sharply. Men did not play a part in her life and it was useless and stupid to get emotional about it.

She read the card again: *May I send you these as a peace offering?*

No more a state of war, Lissette. I promise not to enter ever again through your lovely foyer. Manfred.

She glanced at her watch. It was nearly ten o'clock and he would already be on duty. He'd probably put the flowers on her desk when he took over from the night watch earlier this morning. She did not know what to do. She felt confused, but she knew she could not ignore them.

She filled an empty vase with water from the tap in the anteroom and tenderly lifted the flowers from the box. They were lovely. She arranged them carefully so that all of them caught the light. She looked around the office for a place to put the vase and decided finally that they should sit on the end of her desk.

They smelt beautiful and reminded her of the tiny garden at the back of her mother's house where she used to play as a child. The memory clouded her face. Wallflowers. Wallflowers that crept upwards behind her, smothering her face, as her mother pinned her to the wall, her eyes wild, her voice hysterical, holding a small, nickel-plated pistol to her head, demanding to know what had happened.

Lissette had shaken her head, tears blinding her eyes. She could see the jealous rage in her mother's face, and she knew she could never tell her. She could never tell anyone . . .

She stood up abruptly, trying to compose herself. This would not do. It was silly, and there was her work. But first she had to see the German.

She left her office and looked down into the foyer below, empty at this time in the morning except for a middle-aged lady slowly pushing a Hoover over the heavy carpet. The woman returned her 'Good morning' with a wan smile and withdrew into her own thoughts, her face devoid of expression.

Lissette crossed the circle lobby, then walked through a door marked 'private' and up some functional iron steps to a doorway at the top that opened on to the flat roof.

The sunlight blinded her momentarily after the dark of the iron stairs and she stood quite still, shading her eyes until they adjusted to the light. In the middle of the roof a gun pointed ominously at the sky. Then she saw the three men.

They were all lying on grey blankets, stripped to the waist, enjoying the sunshine that made the concrete warm beneath her feet. She suddenly felt quite apprehensive, as though she were invading some private male ritual, and she turned to slip quietly away. At that moment the door that had been slowly closing behind her clicked shut.

Manfred lifted himself up on one elbow and, seeing her, grinned, rising slowly. 'Hello.' His voice was friendly and she hesitated, facing them. The others turned around to look at her and Manfred said something to them in German. They lay back and continued to sunbathe, trying to hide their smiles. Manfred picked up his shirt and pulled it on as he crossed the roof towards her. 'I'm sorry,' he said without embarrassment. 'We were enjoying the sunshine.'

Lissette shook her head. 'That's all right. You might as well – who knows how long it will last?'

He stopped in front of her, his shadow falling across her face.

She tilted her head back, looking up at him directly. 'Thank you for the flowers, Herr Kepner . . .'

'Please, call me Manfred,' he said, interrupting her.

She paused, caught off balance. His words rather spoilt the flow of the little speech she had prepared.

'Yes, of course. Manfred, thank you for them. They are lovely, but you really should not have spent so much of your money. I don't wish to be officious, but when you are on duty you must use those outside stairs. I'm sorry. It's just that we seem to have got off on the wrong foot somehow.'

He stood awkwardly in front of her, and Lissette suddenly felt as though she had been mean and ungracious. She crossed the roof, walking slowly towards the parapet. 'It's nice up here on a day like this.' She looked over the edge at the traffic in the street down below. It seemed small and incredibly far away.

He nodded affably. 'Yes. As you can see, we shall soon be nicely brown. I'm glad the summer's come. I think it could be uncomfortable in winter.'

She glanced at him. 'Do you expect to be here very long?'

Manfred shrugged his shoulders eloquently. 'I do not know. We are here. It is not of my doing. I would sooner be back home.' He stopped, as if unwilling to reveal too much of his feelings.

She was curious. 'Where is your home?'

He stared out over the rooftops, not answering, and she thought that he hadn't heard her question. Then he held out his arm, pointing. 'That way, towards the east. Frankfurt-am-Main,' he said quietly.

She realized he had already worked out in which direction his home lay long before she had asked the question. He must be very homesick. She remembered doing much the same thing when the nuns had looked after her as a child.

Manfred hadn't moved. He continued to stare sightlessly over the city. The faint sounds of the traffic below hardly permeated this quiet, solitary world.

Lissette felt cut off, suspended, and in a sudden rush of emotion she realized that she had spoken to Manfred. He was looking at her, surprised by the invitation.

'Yes, yes, I do like the theatre, though I seldom go, for some reason.'

She stared at him aghast. Had she really invited him?

'Yes, I would be delighted, but only if you will allow me to buy you dinner afterwards.' He paused and laughed. 'However, I think you'd better select the restaurant. I have not been in Antwerp long enough to know a good one.'

She was astonished. How had this happened? But, curiously, she did not feel afraid of this big, tall man. There was a vulnerability, a boyishness, about him to which she responded. She held out her hand. 'Then let me arrange it. I assume you will remain on duty during the days this week?'

'Yes, until next Tuesday, when we take over night duties.'

Lissette's hand trembled slightly in his. 'In that case I will fix it for this week, and I'll let you know the date and time.' Unconsciously, in her nervousness, she had fallen back on the jargon of business language.

Manfred seemed unperturbed. He smiled, releasing her hand. 'Thank you, Lissette, I look forward to it enormously.'

They broke away from the parapet and crossed the roof to the doorway. He opened it for her and she paused momentarily, wanting to say something, but she didn't speak.

Manfred looked at her and in his eyes she sensed an understanding. She wasn't sure. She turned and descended the dark stairs. Manfred continued to hold the door open, letting the light spill down them until she reached the bottom.

'All right, Lissette?' His voice echoed back from the concrete walls.

'All right,' she called back softly.

The light cut off as the door closed above her. She stood quietly in the gloom, trying to compose herself before opening the door to the circle.

The jeep bounced unerringly into a pothole cleverly disguised as a puddle, and Joe cursed as the hard seat jarred up into his spine. Avoiding the bloody things was almost impossible in the wet. They caused more damage to transportation than enemy action; the repairs went on continuously, and he was glad he had no tradesman's skills that could have collected him a mechanic's job.

The jeep climbed the last rise from the valley. As he rounded the bend, Joe braked and slowly brought the vehicle to a halt. The road twisted gently downwards from this point on to a wide plain dotted with small clumps of woods and fields, swaying heavily with growing wheat and barley.

The woods were large enough to conceal a small company or give cover to sniper fire. Out there somewhere on the flat lands were American infantry who had finally broken through the *bocage* country behind him. This road, though potholed and difficult, was too vital to go completely undefended. The German infantry may well have pulled back from this area, but they would have mined the road and made use of the cover the trees provided. Joe sensed their presence on the ground below. Far away in the distance he gradually became aware of a fast-moving object. It was too far away to identify, just a tiny speck occasionally disappearing into a clump of trees, then emerging with a rush on the other side.

Joe grabbed the binoculars from the dashboard and focused them on the traveller. Slowly the figure took shape as he adjusted the lens. It was a motorbike with a single rider, moving at speed. As it grew closer to the rolling foothills of the valley Joe was able to see he was an American. The infantry gaiters and olive-green jacket were unmistakable, though he wasn't wearing a helmet A pair of goggles covered his eyes.

But it was the bike that attracted Joe's interest. Even in the fitful sunshine between the grey clouds, it shone and sparkled. No colourless camouflage on this; it was painted bright red and the polished chromium glinted as it weaved its way towards him.

Joe stepped from the jeep into the road and waited. He could hear the roar of its engine growing louder as it rapidly closed the distance between them. The machine took the hill without changing gear and roared up the last stretch. Joe caught a glimpse of the face below the dark goggles, which prevented him from seeing the eyes. A shock of fair hair blew in the slipstream, and the head was turned slightly, looking at him. Then, without slowing down, bike and rider sped past him in a powerful rush, disappearing round the bend in the road. The sound of the engine rapidly diminished. Just the whiff of the exhaust hanging on the air signified its brief appearance.

Joe stood listening, hands on hips, head cocked slightly to one side. As far as he could tell, the rider had survived the pothole. He grinned to himself. It would have been sod's law if the Yank had come unstuck on a French pothole, having safely run the gauntlet of the plain below. Pity. A bike like that would have been extremely useful. Maybe he would come back.

Joe climbed reflectively back into the jeep and released the brake. If the Yank could get through, maybe he could.

He drove slowly down the incline, trying to absorb as much as he could of the terrain below. Once on to the plain, his view would be restricted. The ripening corn rippled like water beneath the grey clouds, surging before the gusty wind in waves from one field to the next. It would rain soon. Joe could smell it.

He kept the engine in top gear, moving as quietly as he could. All his senses alert, he looked for the tell-tale passage of battle that must have occurred somewhere along this country road. It did not follow a straight line, though it was not the landscape that dictated its course. Property and ownership had forced it to meander this way and that.

Joe steered round a long curve, and ahead of him the road dipped below the overhanging branches of a copse of trees. This was where the rider had re-emerged after disappearing briefly from his sight.

He eased the gears down, moving cautiously into the gloom. He reached forward under the dashboard and unclipped the Thompson sub-machine gun, resting it across his knees. The American infantry out on the plain ahead of him somewhere should have cleared this area, but you could never be sure. Assumptions could be lethal.

There was no sign of fighting, no debris, human or otherwise. The wood was quiet, just the usual sounds: the cry of a lone bird, the rustle of the trees as they moved beneath the breeze.

A circle of light ahead of him marked the position where the road emerged on the other side and Joe moved up through the gears, increasing his speed as he cleared the edge of the wood. He reached forward to clip the Thompson back under the dashboard. As he did so, the near-side rear wheel bumped over a pothole and slid fractionally to the right, catching the side of the mine a glancing blow. It erupted, throwing the jeep upwards and forwards. Joe's head crashed against the dashboard. For a moment he had the sickening impression of the earth reaching up to meet him – then darkness, oblivion.

He was asleep. It was a dream, he knew it was a dream – yet he could not move. If he could only open his eyes. He tried, but they stayed shut. The effort was too much. He was sweating. The rider approached the bed on which he was lying, standing at the foot, watching him. He bent down over Joe's body, his fair hair flopping down over his forehead, but Joe could see nothing behind the goggles, just two black, empty holes staring down at him. Joe tried to reach up to tear them from the rider's face, but his arms would not move – it was as if he were paralysed.

The rider smiled at him, then slowly his hands reached down, elongated, towards Joe's throat. He was going to strangle the life from his body and there was nothing Joe could do.

The hands disappeared below the bottom of the bed, gripping it. Slowly they began to lift it upwards, and Joe felt the bed fold in the centre. He tried to pull his legs back into his body. In an agony of effort and sweat he managed to bring his legs up to his chest.

The bed was folding up and over him, crushing and suffocating him within its soft covers. The rider smiled once more, mirthlessly, before pushing the foot of the bed hard down over his head, blotting out the light and the air.

He could not breathe or move. The bed was squeezing his life from him, pressing him like a butterfly between the pages of a book, enveloping him like clinging cotton wool. He gasped for air, but there was none.

He had to move, to break open this cocoon of suffocating softness. His knees were drawn up across his chest and he pushed his feet into the folds. The blood pounded in his head. His mouth was open, gasping for air. With all the strength he had left he pushed upwards with his legs, forcing his body to straighten.

The bed sprang open as if it were on a hinge. Suddenly he could breathe again and there was light, yet the pounding would not go from his head. Then, gradually, the texture of the noise changed and he knew it was an engine, a motorcycle engine, and it was drawing closer. It got louder, pounding like a sledge hammer, reaching a crescendo as if it were on top of him. Then his eyes opened and he was conscious.

The gleaming motorbike swept by the overturned jeep, the rider hardly giving it a glance. Dust filtered down over Joe and he realized he was lying in a ditch. The jeep was on its side, resting, poised perilously above him on the bank. The seat was heavy across his body, still partially over his face, the cause of his frenzied nightmare.

Joe understood instantly what had happened and cursed himself for his stupidity. Because the motorbike had traversed the road safely, he had assumed that the jeep would. Moments before the mine exploded he had congratulated himself on making no assumptions. He was lucky to be alive, though how long he would remain so was uncertain. At any minute the jeep above him could roll over into the ditch where he lay.

He made no sudden moves – he did not know how badly he might have been injured. He could feel blood wet on his face. Carefully he raised an arm. It worked. He gripped the seat that had broken free from the vehicle and eased himself from below it. He felt no violent pains – so far so good. He lifted his head and looked down at his feet. The bonnet had also detached itself from the wrecked jeep and lay partially over his legs. Gingerly he eased himself backwards. The vehicle groaned as though in pain itself and tipped slowly towards him.

He froze, watching it, fascinated. Gradually it stopped reaching the point of balance, then slid back until it was still again. Joe expelled a long sigh of relief, then, still on his back, not taking his eyes off the jeep balanced so finely above him, he began to pull himself gently by the elbows through the sticky mud of the ditch. His progress was slow, inch by painful inch, each movement threatening to bring the vehicle down on top of him. At last he was clear, and he allowed himself the luxury of hauling himself up the bank, out of the stinking mud that had cushioned his fall and probably saved his life.

Nothing seemed to be broken. He stood up in the road and reached for the Thompson that had fallen beside the jeep. He stared malevolently at the vehicle that had threatened to crush him, then put his foot against the exposed, rusting underside and pushed. It tipped, paused, then rolled down into the ditch where he had lain a moment before, the mud squelching obscenely beneath it.

Joe turned away and looked down the road where the American rider had disappeared. Faint particles of dust still hung in the air, slowly settling after his swift, noisy passage. He glanced at the crater left in the road by the explosion of the mine, shouldered the automatic and, staying on the grass verge, began to walk down the road after the American.

The grey clouds began to break. Joe watched a patch of sunlight creep across the fields towards him. The low hill that he had climbed was as good a vantage point as he was going to find in this flat terrain; it was situated about half a mile from the road he had left and was of no strategic value, except that it did offer him a fine view of a farmhouse beyond another patch of woodland. The sound of the Spandau was oddly delayed at this distance, and he saw its effects before he heard its distinctive ripping burst of fire as it shredded the undergrowth and foliage of the wood.

The German infantry had chosen a sound position to hold up the advance. The farmhouse commanded the ground immediately surrounding it, as well as the road as it emerged from the trees. The Spandau had already taken its toll. Joe could see some bodies lying in the road. They were American.

The Spandau was on the upper floor of the two-storey brick building. The ground around the farmhouse had been cleared of any cover. The GIs had a difficult task, and Joe didn't envy them. He transferred his gaze to the small group deployed on the edge of the trees nearest to him.

The motorcycle shone red and chrome as the patch of sunlight slowly crossed the road. It was parked against a tree on the grass verge, the goggles of the rider hanging from the handlebars; the rider was presumably one of the group. He focused his glasses on them. They were huddled around an officer who was poring over a map, but Joe could see no sign of the motorcyclist. He waited.

The group broke up and, following a command from the officer, the men spread out and began to infiltrate the wood. Joe glanced at his watch. A drop of rain splattered on to the dial, distorting the image. He wiped it against his sleeve. He would give them five minutes.

The rain began to fall steadily. His clothes clung to him; they were curiously warm and sticky. The distant sound of the automatic fire was deadened by the faint hiss of the rain on the cornfields.

Joe crawled down the rise in the ground, keeping the low hill between himself and the engagement around the farmhouse. Crouching low, he began to move through the rapidly ripening corn directly towards the road. The field provided good cover. No one could see him from the wood or the farmhouse, though there would be little protection if he were spotted.

The flattened swathe of corn that marked his progress grew longer as he approached the narrow lane. A hedgerow lined the verge separating it from the field. Joe crouched behind it and peered up and down the lane. It was deserted. No sign of movement, but the rattle of gunfire was louder here and Joe could smell the cordite on the damp air.

The bike stood, dripping, against the tree that marked the edge of the wood. Joe stayed in the field behind the hedgerow, keeping as much cover as he could between himself and the dark maw of the trees where the road disappeared. Now he was level. He ran his eyes over the machine, making sure it had not been padlocked. As far as he could see, it simply rested against the tree waiting for its owner to return.

Joe checked the Thompson. The rain had made the metal surfaces slippery, and he banged the magazine clip to make sure it was firmly engaged. A sudden burst of fire, louder than the rest, emanated from the wood and Joe heard a man screaming. He waited no longer; his footsteps made no sound as he leapt through a gap in the hedge. He moved fast but carefully, his senses alert, ready for friend or foe. In combat, troops becoming aware of an unexpected uniform infiltrating behind their position were likely to fire first and ask questions later.

Joe reached the bike and slung the Thompson over his shoulder. He pulled it upright and heaved a sigh of relief; nothing restrained it. The rider might need to use it quickly, so he had gambled. Joe grinned to himself. The bastard had lost.

He grabbed the goggles from the handlebars and wiped the moisture from them with his sleeve, then he changed his mind and stuffed them into his pocket. In the rain they would be more of a hindrance than a help.

Joe gripped the handlebars and turned the bike so that it faced down the road away from the wood. He slung his leg over the machine; the seat was wet but it made no impression on him. He was already soaked to the skin.

Now came the moment of maximum danger. He had to start the bike with his weapon slung. If the engine did not fire quickly, the sound would warn anyone nearby and he would be defenceless. He kicked at the starter. It burst immediately into life. It was marvellously tuned and Joe felt the power surge through the machine as he slowly released the clutch. He crouched over the handlebars and glanced back towards the wood. There was nothing, no sign of the rider. He threw back his head and laughed exultantly, the rain bouncing off his face. He increased the speed, drawing swiftly away from the crackle of gunfire behind him. No one could stop him now. The red machine was his.

The small restaurant was crowded and very busy. It seemed to Lissette that the Allied invasion of Normandy had hardly affected trade at all. In fact, neither the war nor the invasion had deprived this particular establishment of anything except the best. And as long as the German officers continued to favour it with their presence, it would remain a privileged venue.

The usual Friday-night people were there, mainly after-theatre diners like themselves. But, significantly perhaps, there seemed fewer Germans present. Indeed, Manfred was the only non-commissioned officer in the place and that seemed to worry him at first. Lissette persuaded him to order the wine immediately. Her experience with business lunches confirmed her impression that a little alcohol removed the barriers most quickly.

Manfred ate the last remains of the main course enthusiastically, then sat back with a sigh of satisfaction. 'Ah, Lissette, that was fantastic. I cannot think when I have enjoyed a meal more.' His pleasure was infectious and Lissette smiled.

'It's not over yet. The sweets here are marvellous – I get fat just looking at them.'

He shook his head. 'I don't believe you. You are so small, like a schoolgirl. I don't believe you will ever be fat.'

'Well,' she said ruefully, 'I hope you are right.' She watched a slim, fair-haired woman make her way through the tables to a grand piano in the corner. 'I think we are about to have some entertainment.' She indicated the woman.

Manfred turned slightly to see her. She was wearing an ivory satin dress. It was long and clinging, emphasizing her full breasts, and it was abundantly clear she had nothing on beneath it.

'She is very beautiful,' Lissette said quietly.

It was as if she had read his thoughts, and Manfred turned quickly back to her, smiling. 'Yes, perhaps she is, but I am enjoying our evening more, and this restaurant is perfect.'

The woman began to sing. Inevitably it was 'Lili Marlene', but she had a pleasant, deep voice with a nice timbre to it, slightly husky. She sang very well and the patrons of the restaurant listened attentively until she had finished, then applauded warmly, particularly the small contingent of German officers.

Manfred gazed reflectively at the plain tablecloth, turning a small spoon between his fingers. Lissette did not break the intimate silence. She sipped some wine twisting her glass in her hand, the light from the candle on the table making it seem almost incandescent. 'What did you do before the war?' she asked.

'Mmm?' he said. He seemed lost in thought.

She laughed. 'I do believe you are getting drunk, Manfred.'

He pretended to be shocked. 'Nonsense! I have drunk only three glasses of wine.'

Lissette looked at him, astonished. 'Three glasses! Manfred, this is our second bottle of wine.'

'Well,' he said diplomatically, 'maybe four. Besides,' he added, 'I never get drunk until I have had my sweet. But I will admit I feel pleasantly relaxed.'

He waved to the waiter authoritatively, as if to prove it, and asked to see the sweet trolley. It creaked across the floor laden with a crystallized apple tart, fruit salad, figs and profiteroles oozing with cream, but Manfred ordered the Black Forest *gâteau* while Lissette contented herself with figs and cream.

'Aha!' he exclaimed. 'Figs and cream. I'll bet you are a Libra.'

'Why should figs and cream make me a Libra?'

'Because,' he said mysteriously, tapping the side of his nose, 'I once knew someone who always ate figs and cream and she was a Libra.'

Lissette nodded sagely. 'Of course, I should have known.'

'Well?' he said.

'What?' She looked puzzled.

'Are you?'

She sighed deeply. 'I'm afraid your method has come unstuck Manfred. I am a Scorpio.'

'Aha!' he said again.

'You keep saying "Aha!" What now?' Lissette feigned exasperation. She was enjoying his company more than she realized.

'Allow me to read your palm,' he said. He took her hand and studied it with elaborate seriousness. 'Mmm,' he muttered again, like a witch doctor brewing some incredible potion.

Lissette played out the charade. 'All right, I give in. What does it say?'

He looked up from her palm, his eyes gleaming with excitement. 'Lissette, your palm tells me a great deal. It says that you will meet a tall handsome stranger who is climbing right to the top — not, of course,' he added quickly, 'up the circle staircase.'

Lissette giggled and two German officers at a near-by table looked at them disapprovingly.

'I'm sorry,' she confided, straightfaced. 'I must control myself.'

'Ignore them,' he whispered. 'I have it on the highest authority, namely your palm, that they are in fact British spies. The fat one holding the cigar is, I believe, Winston Churchill.'

Lissette began to giggle again, she shook her head. 'Come on, what does it say?'

He studied her palm carefully. 'It says . . .,' he began, then stopped.

'Go on,' she said impatiently.

He looked up, suddenly serious. 'It says that you have had much pain, Lissette.' He paused, looking at her intently. 'But that now you are happy.' He took her hand between both of his and lifted it to his lips, kissing her palm. 'I hope it is true. I hope you are happy now, Lissette.'

Touched by his concern, she felt a lump rise in her throat. She closed her hand over his. 'Oh, Manfred, you are a sweet man and I think it is true. I know I'm enjoying this evening enormously.' She gazed at him quietly for a moment. 'Who knows, maybe you can read palms after all.'

Afterwards they walked slowly through the late-night streets. It was close and very quiet. The city was dark beneath its blackout, and there was hardly any traffic. Their footsteps seemed loud, almost intrusive, in the pervasive silence, Lissette's high heels tip-tapping along beside Manfred. His arm slipped down from her shoulders to her waist, his hand just brushing her breast as it fell. She could feel her nipples harden beneath her soft blouse, and she leaned against him, slipping her arm around his waist, pulling him close.

They stopped in the shelter of a doorway. Manfred cupped her face in his hands and kissed her tenderly for the first time. She held him tight, nestling her head against his chest, feeling his erection harden against her stomach.

He pulled away from her slightly, aware of what was happening, realizing that she might not want to go any further and conscious of the open street, knowing that anyone could see them. He didn't want to cheapen the evening.

Lissette was sensitive to his reaction and she instinctively understood his reasons. She knew then that she wanted him . . .

Her apartment was small, only four rooms, but nicely situated at the top of an old-fashioned block with a creaky, groaning lift that caused them both a good deal of amusement before it reached her floor. They were both slightly intoxicated by the wine and by the evening, and ready to laugh at almost anything. The lift was a joy, a ludicrously mad ascent, almost the crowning glory of the evening.

Lissette opened the door to her apartment, not switching on the light. She stood silently in the small vestibule, facing him. He could see the pale oval of her face outlined by the faint light from the lift glowing slightly behind him.

He entered and walked slowly towards her. She didn't move. He gripped the collar of her jacket in both his hands, pulling her to him. Lissette held her face up for Manfred to kiss her and slid her arms around his waist.

His lips closed over hers and she kissed him passionately, squirming loose from her jacket and allowing it to drop to the floor. She led him into her bedroom and they parted briefly to remove the rest of their clothing. Lissette sat down on the edge of the bed and was suddenly afraid.

Manfred felt the tenseness of her body as he slipped, naked into the bed, pulling her down beside him. He leaned on his elbow, gazing down at her face. Her hair had spread out over the pillow and she was looking into his eyes as though she were searching for something.

42

He touched the side of her face with his hand. 'What is it?'

The words were spoken so quietly, so tenderly, that she knew at once that her instinctive fear was groundless. Manfred was young, unlike her mother's obscene lover who had taken her so brutally when she was merely a child. Manfred was seeking nothing she didn't want to give – she needed him. The tension evaporated, and she swallowed convulsively.

'Manfred . . .' She paused, not knowing quite how to say it.

'Yes?'

'I don't want to be silly –'

'Why not?' he interrupted. 'I like you best when you're silly.'

She felt herself giggling again and playfully slapped his bare shoulder. 'Stop it,' she said. 'How can I talk when you keep making me want to laugh?'

He brushed a hair from her face. 'I don't want you to talk, Lissette. I want to love you.'

She blinked, feeling the tears behind her eyes. 'Oh, Manfred,' she said, pulling him down on top of her. 'It's been so long.'

He buried his face in her hair, kissing her neck and ears until his lips were on hers. She kissed him back, hard, all her fears draining from her, straining her body up against the flat muscles in his stomach, feeling his penis press against the inside of her thigh.

His hand cupped her breast and he pulled himself down her body until his tongue caressed a nipple, circling it as his hand slipped down between her legs.

'Now,' she whispered to him. 'Please, Manfred, now.'

He pulled his arm from beneath her and slid over her body. Lissette placed his heavy penis into her then felt it slowly slide up, filling her body.

He felt so hard, pushing her legs apart. She lifted herself towards him, wanting to feel him press up inside her as far as he could go. She felt no pain. Although she had never made love to a man before, she was not a virgin. That had been taken from her, but she knew that it no longer mattered.

He began to thrust himself into her, slowly at first but gradually increasing his tempo. She grasped his sweaty shoulders, pulling him tight, loving the heavy weight of his body arching up and down.

Then she felt the convulsive pumping motion as he came, flooding inside her, hot and wet. She moaned, feeling her own first incredible release.

He lay on top of her for a long time, supporting the weight of his body with his elbows, kissing her eyes and face, saying nothing. Then suddenly she looked up and smiled.

'What is it?' he asked.

She turned her head aside, as though too embarrassed to say.

He shook her shoulders gently. 'Come, tell me.'

She grinned. 'It's getting smaller,' she said impishly.

He groaned, collapsing on her. 'What do you expect, madam? It comes and goes, if you see what I mean.'

Lissette laughed, pushing him away. He rolled over on to his back. 'My God, woman, you're shameless.'

She lifted herself above him, trying to plaster his damp hair down, but it continued to spring up. 'I'm not shameless,' she protested. 'I just think I like it, that's all.'

'Good,' he said, frowning ominously. 'At least we are agreed on something.'

Lissette didn't answer him. She ran the palm of her hand down the side of his cheek, feeling the stubble of his beard. 'How often do you shave?'

'Once a day, in the morning.'

She gazed at him, her eyes wide and loving, rubbing his chin. 'I think I like it better like this.' He was about to say something, but she put her finger across his lips. 'Manfred, please don't think I'm foolish, but there's something I want you to know.' She kissed the end of his nose. 'Today has been the best day of my life.' She could not stop her tears this time.

He lifted his head, holding her face between his hands and kissed the salty tears away. 'Don't cry, Lissette,' he whispered softly. 'There is no need. This is only our first day. We have all the rest of our lives.'

It didn't seem possible; she could hardly believe it had happened, and she cried herself quietly to sleep in his arms. But when she awoke his body was still warm against hers, his arms around her. Only then did she think it might be true.

Joe had often seen the cheering crowds, the overwhelming receptions that the forward liberating columns received, but he had never envied them or the perks that were theirs: the drinking parties, the food and the grateful population. Crowds slowed him down, made it impossible for him to operate, and he found them oppressive. He preferred the open road, the surprise that might await him round the next corner.

Today he was wearing a parachutist's smock over his uniform. It served a dual purpose in that it was impossible to detect his rank, and the brown boots he wore gave him the opportunity, should he need it, of posing as an officer; it was a ploy he had used before to his advantage. It also concealed the Colt 1911a automatic pistol that rested comfortably under his belt. The Thompson was clipped to the handlebars.

His route was well away from the direct path that the Guards Armoured Division were pursuing as the Germans fell back after the carnage of the Falaise Gap. The red Harley-Davidson purred quietly along the country road, the peaceful scene belying the conflict that surrounded this pocket of apparent tranquillity. The only sound that broke the calm was that of a distant high-altitude bomber group as they hummed faintly, like a swarm of bees, towards their targets.

He rounded the bend and saw the old lady immediately. She was sitting on a fold-up canvas chair just inside the entrance to a drive on the right. Joe slowed down and slid his hand under the smock, resting it on the Colt. The old woman seemed to be waiting, but she raised herself slowly to her feet as the machine came to a halt beside her.

Joe supported the weight of the bike, his legs splayed out either side, his feet on the dusty road. The old woman smiled warmly. Joe noticed her teeth. They were in surprisingly good condition. She was clearly delighted to see him and touched his arm, almost as if to reassure herself of his presence.

'*Bonjour*,' she said, and then again, '*bonjour*.'

She bit her lip, trying to retain her composure. Joe thought for a moment that she was going to fling her arms around him, and he drew back slightly, holding out his hands apologetically.

'I'm sorry, I don't speak French.'

She smiled again. 'That is all right, *monsieur*. I am happy to speak English at last.' She gestured up the drive behind her. 'You are welcome to some food and wine. The *château* is only about half a kilometre.'

He eyed her curiously. Her manner was not subservient; there was a dignity about her, and she spoke as if she were used to being obeyed. There was something else too that he couldn't identify. But the *château* sounded interesting.

'Are you by yourself?'

She shook her head. 'No, there are my two granddaughters. I look after them now,' she added enigmatically.

Joe did not question the remark. There were personal tragedies in abundance, and he saw no reason to reopen what might be an old wound. He pointed up the drive. 'That way?'

'Yes. Follow the path to the house. I will come shortly.'

He thought of offering her a lift, then dismissed the idea. She was too old to be riding pillion – besides, he might need to move fast. He gunned the engine gently and started off along the narrow, gravelled road. It wound through some high shrubbery, then straightened out between two rows of poplars, and he saw the *château* for the first time.

The house was old and shuttered. There were some outbuildings that looked like stables, and a couple of cows grazing in a field, the first live ones he'd seen in France for a long time. A few half-circular steps led up to a pair of double front doors. They were open and he saw two young women emerge and walk down on to the drive in front of the *château*.

Even at this distance, it was clear they were sisters: both had the same long, dark hair and wide, oval face. One was slightly younger than the other – they were about seventeen and nineteen, Joe guessed. They were bare-legged, wearing sandals and plain cotton dresses. But it was the way they moved that fascinated Joe. There was an animal, almost feline, grace about their movements as they walked down the drive towards him.

He smiled to himself. He was pleased. He had reason to be. When the old lady had mentioned two granddaughters, he had imagined two schoolchildren. They were anything but that. The older one's beckoning smile indicated a good deal more carnal knowledge than any schoolgirl was likely to possess, even in wartime France. He continued to ride slowly towards them and didn't stop the machine until the front mudguard was almost touching the skirt of her summer dress.

She studied him from beneath lowered eyes, but there was a boldness in the way she stood that belied her look.

Joe grinned. 'I saw your grandmother back there. She said I was welcome to some food and wine.'

She shrugged. 'Why not? We have plenty.'

Her sister stayed close behind her. The older one had noticed his look at her sister, and she half turned, indicating her.

'This is Annette.'

The younger one smiled shyly, remaining firmly behind her sister.

'And my name is Maria.'

Joe nodded briefly to Annette, then held out his hand to Maria. 'I'm Joe Porter.'

She ignored his outstretched hand and leaned forward, gripping his shoulders, kissing him on each cheek. As she stepped back she said quietly, and without emphasis, 'Thank you for coming. We have waited a long time for you.' She looked at the red machine admiringly. 'It is beautiful. You must be very proud of it.'

Joe shifted awkwardly, not sure how to respond. Maria ran her fingers along the chromium-plated handlebars, touching his hand lightly as she did so.

'Will you give me a ride?'

Joe eyed her quizzically. 'Why not? Hop on.'

She laughed excitedly, brazenly lifted her dress, exposing her brown legs, and leapt on to the back. Joe sat down into the saddle and Maria put her arms around his waist, clinging to him, her fingers sliding down his chest and touching his stomach. He felt an immediate arousal and pushed her hands higher before throttling up the engine and turning the bike in a half circle back down the drive.

She shouted above the roar of the engine. 'Take me further. I want to go fast.'

Joe shook his head. The heart of enemy occupied territory was no place for a joyride with Maria. 'Later,' he said, and gunned the bike down the drive until he met the old woman, struggling a little with her canvas chair. He braked to a sharp halt in a cloud of dust and ordered Maria off the pillion. 'Help her.'

Maria pouted. She didn't want to get off the bike, but the look on her grandmother's face quelled her objection. She dismounted, shaking her dress down from around her thighs. Then she snatched the chair with ill grace from the old woman, while Joe watched impassively. He could see the sweat on the old woman's wrinkled face.

'Are you all right?' he asked.

She shrugged dispassionately. 'The young have no manners any more, but I can walk to the house.'

She strode past him, ignoring Maria.

Joe turned the bike and rode slowly up to the front door where Annette was waiting. He switched off the engine and dismounted, kicking down the support stand, then turned towards the younger girl and stood beside her, waiting for the others to catch up with him.

He glanced at Annette. 'How old are you?'

'Seventeen,' she said.

Joe ticked that one off. He'd guessed right.

The grandmother came up the drive and walked past them, leading the way into the house. The vestibule opened up into a large, spacious hallway that was dominated by an oak staircase, which curved gently down to face the double front doors. The carpets were faded but of good quality, and the interior vaguely reminded Joe of something. At first he couldn't place it.

Maria paused on the bottom step, leaning against the banister, then Joe remembered the children sliding down the barrel of the

Sherman tank and the institute of his own childhood. This place had the air of an institution. It seemed too big for just the old woman and her two granddaughters.

They led him into the kitchen and sat him at a long wooden table. The ceiling was low. Cooking implements hung on the walls, and it smelt deliciously of toast and coffee. He suddenly realized how hungry he was, and the coffee that Annette poured into the mug in front of him was surprisingly good, not a bit like the tasteless muck they served up in the mess. He drained it all in one swallow.

Annette took the empty mug from him. 'Would you like some more?'

He looked up into her face and she quickly averted her eyes. It was the second time she had done that. She seemed tense, uneasy. Joe nodded. 'Please.'

She refilled the mug from the pot on the range in the corner, then put it in front of him again, standing just behind him with her back to the wall. Joe shifted his chair slightly so that he could see her.

The old woman fussed around him, preparing some bread and cheese, while Maria just watched him quietly from the other side of the kitchen.

He sipped some more of the coffee, then addressed himself directly to Annette. 'The lavatory – could you show me where it is?'

She looked confused for an instant, glancing apprehensively at her grandmother, who placed the bread and cheese in front of Joe.

'Show him Annette. This can wait.'

Though she had spoken quietly, Joe detected an edge in her voice, a steeliness that brooked no dissent. He stood up from the table and smiled at the girl. He could see her fingers were clenched tight.

She did not reply to her grandmother but led him from the kitchen and through the hall to the stairs. She pointed upwards to the next floor.

'Up there,' she said. 'The door at the end of the passage is the bathroom.' She turned to go back to the kitchen, but Joe gripped her tightly around the waist, clamping his other hand over her mouth and dragging her back into the well of the staircase so that they could not be seen.

He put his mouth close to her ear. 'You're coming upstairs with me – I want you to show me every room. We will search them together.'

He felt Annette stiffen in his arms. He was right, there was something they were hiding. But he didn't want to alarm the other two women in the kitchen, not yet. He would deal with them later.

He spoke soothingly to Annette. 'There is no need to be frightened. I won't hurt you. I just want to be sure we are all safe in this house.'

He glanced around him quickly. He could hear the faint murmur of voices from the kitchen.

'I'm going to take my hand from your mouth. I don't want you to make any noise – I don't want your grandmother to know.'

That seemed to work. She relaxed slightly; he slowly removed his hand. She turned her head and looked at him, her eyes wide with fear.

'It's all right,' he whispered. He indicated the stairs. 'Let's go.'

She led the way up ahead of him, glancing back occasionally. Joe held the Colt beneath his smock. From the landing a passage ran the length of the house. In all about ten rooms led off from it. He began to check them methodically, one by one.

The bedrooms were well furnished with traditional, heavy pieces offering some room for concealment. It was a warm, humid afternoon. There was no breeze to ruffle the trees outside; the curtains were all pulled right back and the windows were open to allow what little air there was to circulate.

Joe held tightly on to Annette's arm, never releasing it. As they came to a large double bedroom he felt a tiny tremor run through her. The door had been left ajar and he pushed it gently open with his foot.

It creaked slightly as it swung open, revealing a huge oak bed, neatly made up, an old-fashioned dressing table with a high oval mirror standing between two windows, and a stone washbasin and jug in the corner. Towels were folded over a wooden rack to air. It smelt faintly of toilet water and Joe suspected it was the grandmother's room. It seemed to be empty.

Joe pushed Annette in ahead of him, bringing up the automatic pistol from beneath his smock. She felt his movement and turned, seeing the gun for the first time. She clenched her hand and held it to her mouth, suppressing a reaction. At that moment her grandmother called loudly from downstairs, her voice shrill, apprehensive.

'Annette, where are you?'

Before Joe could stop her, the girl opened her mouth and screamed, 'Up here, Grandmama – in your bedroom.'

There was no reply, but Joe could sense the shocked silence, then heard the old woman's footsteps on the stairs.

Annette was staring at the gun, horrified yet fascinated. He pulled her towards him savagely, his fingers digging into her flesh.

'Where is he?'

Annette could feel his breath on her face. His green eyes seemed luminous, frightening. She could not answer. Joe shook her, his hand, vice-like, on her forearm.

'Tell me!'

'I can't,' she whispered, but her eyes betrayed her, shifting momentarily to the heavy wooden wardrobe standing in the far corner of the room. Joe pushed her from him, almost knocking her over. He levelled the gun at the door.

'Come out now,' he shouted. He yelled the command again, louder. Even if the bastard didn't speak English he'd know what he meant.

There was no sound in the room except the heavy, hysterical breathing of the girl, then the old woman called again. She had reached the top of the stairs.

'Wait, please wait, *monsieur*. I can explain.'

Joe was going to wait for no one. He'd seen too many die because they had hesitated. He cocked the pistol. Annette covered her ears with her hands and screamed. Joe fired five times, stitching the wardrobe across the door and down. The explosions were shattering in the confined space of the room, and the cordite fumes hung heavily in the still, humid air.

There was a thud from inside, and the wardrobe shook as the body fell against the door before sliding to the floor. Joe heard a gasp from behind him, but he did not take his eyes off his target. The old woman stared at the five holes that had splintered the front of the wardrobe; blood began to seep from beneath the door. She crossed the room slowly, not looking at Joe. He moved slightly to one side so that his view was unimpaired. She grasped the handle of the door and paused for a moment, frightened of what she might find, then pulled it open.

The weight of the body was lying against the door, and it sprang back the moment she released the handle. The German soldier fell so that he lay half in, half out of the wardrobe, his mouth open and his sightless eyes staring up at the ceiling. The old woman knelt down beside him and raised his head on to her lap, heedless of the blood that stained her clothing. Holding him tenderly, she brushed the hair from his face and pulled his eyelids shut with her fingertips, then wiped the blood from his mouth with the corner of her dress. She looked at Joe uncomprehendingly, her eyes blinded with tears.

'He was only a boy. He would not have harmed you. I hid him here. He was frightened. He did not want to fight.'

Her gaze shifted slightly, looking behind him. Joe swivelled round quickly. It was Maria. She stared at the body curiously, not reacting, keeping her feelings under control. She flicked back her hair, then looked at Joe haughtily.

'There is no need for you to be sorry.'

Joe shrugged his shoulders. 'I'm not.'

Maria glanced at her grandmother. 'She was going to kill you – she wanted your clothes for him. I know, I watched her wait at the gate for someone like you to come along. For her,' she looked at the German this time, 'he was like a son. He has lived here with the others since the occupation.'

Joe began to reload the pistol. 'Others?'

'Yes, this place, this house, it was used by them as a boarding house . . . a brothel . . .' She stopped, looking at her sister.

Annette leapt forward, raising her arm to strike Maria. Joe grabbed her quickly and pinned her arms to her sides. She struggled wildly, trying to free herself.

'You bitch!' she screamed. 'It's not true, it's not true, not to me.'

Joe bundled her to the door and pushed her outside, shutting it against her. For a while she continued to scream, pounding it with her fists. They waited, saying nothing, until the helpless rage subsided. Then Annette began to sob quietly in the passage.

Joe looked at Maria. 'Is that all?' he said.

She turned on him bitterly. 'All? No, of course it isn't all, but there is nothing more I wish to tell you.'

Maria looked down at her grandmother, who was still nursing the dead soldier in her lap, rocking him from side to side. She knelt beside the old woman and gently stroked her hair.

Joe felt confused. One minute Maria seemed to be siding with him, the next she was screaming him down. Only occasionally did he reveal his lack of years. Now he was wise enough to remain silent.

Maria squeezed her grandmother's arm. 'Come,' she said, 'we will put him on the bed.'

The old woman stared at her granddaughter blankly for a moment, then looked absently at the huge bed.

'Yes, that is good. We must put him there.'

Maria lifted the soldier, slipping her hands under his arms, pulling him free of the wardrobe. Joe moved in to help her. The old woman stood up quickly, facing him, her eyes full of hate.

'Leave him. Leave him to us. You have done enough!'

Joe stopped and looked at Maria, who shook her head fractionally. He shrugged his shoulders, turned away and opened the bedroom door. Annette was slumped against the wall, staring in front of her. Joe pushed the Colt back into his waistband and lifted her to her feet as gently as he could, putting one arm around her waist to support her. He led her away from the bedroom to the top of the stairs.

'Go down to the kitchen and make some tea.'

She looked at him for a moment, then, still in a daze, she descended the stairs.

He searched the house thoroughly after that. He didn't intend to take any more chances. The *château* had obviously been of considerable value to the Germans, and not just because of the attraction of the two sisters.

In the basement he found a printing press. There was also a vast collection of maps. Maybe one of the units had set up shop here. There was a lot he was not being told – not that he gave a shit what this family had been up to. But he might be able to find a use for the printing press . . .

He'd drunk too much of the wine, he knew that. The episode with the old woman had really pissed him off. She didn't understand: he'd had to kill the German. You just couldn't take that kind of risk, not if you were going to continue, and Joe intended to outlive this war. There were too many things he hadn't done yet, too much to taste, to experience. The privation of his childhood, starved of everything except competition to survive, had prepared him better than most for this newer, wider conflict.

The soldier hiding in the wardrobe had had his chance; all he had to do was fire through the woodwork at the sound of Joe's voice, and it might have been him lying on that old woman's bed upstairs. And what if what Maria had said was true? Maybe the old crone *had* lured him here for his uniform to help that shitty little deserter to escape. Joe smiled sardonically and helped himself to some more of the wine. The bastard had deserved it.

Maria was a strange one. He studied her across the room, sitting sideways in an old armchair, her bare brown legs dangling over the padded arm, sipping at the wine and watching him over the edge of her glass. She had only one thought on her mind and Joe was very willing to oblige. Maria seemed totally unaffected by the death of the German and Joe warmed to that. In her he saw something of himself.

He looked around the kitchen. 'Where is your sister?'

She smiled at him suggestively and did not answer immediately. She took another sip of the wine. 'Why do you want to know? Do you prefer the company of two to one?'

Joe hadn't actually thought about that, though it had crossed his mind that he would need to keep an eye on Annette. He grinned back. 'Now that's not a bad idea.'

Maria regarded him calculatingly. 'My sister is, shall we say, a little shy. But if she knew that she and Grandmama were safe in this house, then I might be able to persuade her.'

'Safe? You mean from me? Of course.'

Maria smiled. 'No, not from you, Joe.' She ran her fingers round the lip of the glass. 'I do not regard you as a threat.'

Joe shrugged his shoulders. 'So?'

Maria uncrossed her legs and lifted them from the arm of the chair on to the floor, allowing Joe a tantalizing glimpse of the future. She went over to the kitchen window and gazed at the garden.

'Why do you think the German was hiding here?'

The question was rhetorical, so he made no response.

'And why do you suppose we have so much food and wine?' She turned and faced him, answering her own question. 'Because they used to come here, sometimes for me,' she paused briefly, 'sometimes for Annette. They used this place as a kind of club. They'd bring their girlfriends and their food. When the village is liberated, when your friends arrive, there will be those who will want their revenge on us for having had it so easy.'

She laughed bitterly, then crossed the kitchen and placed her hands on the table in front of him, leaning down until her face was level with his. 'Can you protect us from them, Joe?' She took his hand and placed it on her breast. 'If not, then the answer is no.'

Joe traced a pattern around her nipple with his fingers. He felt it rise and harden and he smiled into her eyes.

'Your future is safe, Maria. The only hard time you will get is from me.'

She laughed and slid on to his lap, squirming her bottom into him. 'I think it is beginning already, Joe.'

He pulled her back into the crook of his arm, pushing his hand up under her dress until it pressed between her legs. He kissed her hard on the lips, his fingers caressing her. He waited until he knew she wanted him, then he stood up abruptly, dropping her on to the floor of the kitchen.

She looked up at him, her face a mixture of surprise, desire and frustration.

Joe laughed. 'Not yet, *ma cherie*. Remember our bargain. Your safety in exchange for both of you.'

Maria angrily pulled her dress down over her legs and sprang to her feet. Her eyes glittered with rage.

'You pig. I'll make you pay for this.'

Joe adjusted his trousers and patted himself suggestively. 'I look forward to it, my innocent little Maria.' He smiled insolently, turned on his heel and left her fuming.

The American strolled casually past the wrecked tank. One of the children playing on the barrel spotted him and leapt off, running alongside him. He got in front, then back-pedalled furiously, grinning from ear to ear. In atrocious English he parroted what he'd been taught, what he'd learnt to say over and over: 'Got any gum, chum?'

The American pulled out a packet and gave a piece to the kid, then, before he was besieged by his friends, he threw the rest in their direction and crossed the road, darting between the traffic, leaving the still-yelling children behind.

He stopped beside the open wrought-iron gates that led into the courtyard. Inside were a number of trucks and a jeep. Just beneath the windscreen of the jeep was the supply units identification. He pulled out the back of a cigarette pack and checked it against the number he had scribbled down. They were the same.

He stood there for a few moments, contemplating the temporary headquarters and wondering if he should go inside. He decided against it. He moved over to the high wall so that he could not be seen, then leaned against it, lit a cigarette and waited.

Eddie Pearce was thirsty. The roads had been long and dusty, and he didn't fancy the hot, sweet tea of the mess. He walked quickly through the gates and down the crowded French street. Business had resumed almost at once. Broken shop windows that could not be repaired had been boarded up, and what little food was available would not last long.

The bar, Eddie knew, had lost most of its furniture in the fighting. The owner had simply covered some wooden boxes with cloths and used them as makeshift tables. Eddie was lucky. He found one of the few remaining bar stools and ordered himself a beer. It was American, of course, stolen from a PX and sold at inflated prices to the bars and hotels, but at least it was cold. Eddie put it down in one long swallow. He immediately ordered another. Then someone moved into the seat beside him.

'I'll take one of those as well.' Eddie glanced at the Yank. 'You'll recognize the label. It's one of yours.'

'In that case, maybe I'll have another.'

'No, you'd better wait until you've had one. I like it, but I'm so thirsty I can't even taste it.'

The barman pushed the can that he had punctured along the counter and the American raised it to his lips and took an experimental swallow before putting it down again and delivering his verdict.

'Not bad. It's the real thing too.' He stuck out his hand. 'Hillier,' he said, by way of an introduction. 'Nick Hillier.'

Eddie grasped it and returned the compliment.

The Yank indicated the can of beer in front of him. 'Do you carry much of this stuff?'

'No, we don't load beer. I don't think they trust us.' He paused, puzzled. 'Wait a minute, how did you know I was a driver?'

Hillier took another drink at the beer and wiped his mouth with the back of his hand. 'I saw you come out of the courtyard down the road. There were a few trucks inside, so I guess I just assumed it.'

Eddie waved a hand dismissively. 'I drive them out full, then drive them back empty. It may not be any red-ball express, but we get there eventually, and at least they are glad to see us.'

They both took a pull at their drinks. A comfortable silence developed between them as the beer eased Eddie's thirst.

'You on rest leave or just going up front?'

'The first. My outfit got pretty mashed up in a wood. They laid a neat little ambush, holed up in a farmhouse the other side. We walked straight into it.' Eddie belched. 'This GI beer always gives me wind.'

Hillier grinned. 'It's our secret weapon.'

He shook his can until it frothed, then poured it down his throat.

Eddie grinned. 'Aw, Christ, don't spoil it. That stuff costs a fortune in this bar.'

The American banged the counter. 'In that case, the rest is on me.' He ordered two more and slid one across to Eddie.

Eddie raised it. 'Here's long life to you, Yank, and no flats for me.'

Hillier took another gulp of beer and looked at the Irishman reflectively. 'Do you lose many trucks in those convoys?'

Eddie shrugged his shoulders. 'A few. Mostly due to mechanical failure, but also the mines.'

Hillier paused, waiting. This was the moment.

'Yeah, I think I saw one of your jeeps upside-down in a ditch close to where we came unstuck.'

Eddie looked at him curiously. 'How do you know it was ours?'

'I noticed the identification numbers, same as those in the courtyard.'

Eddie thought about it for a while, his mind slightly befuddled by the drink. 'Yeah, we did lose one. That must have been where Joe copped it.'

Hillier tried not to sound too interested. 'Joe?'

Eddie nodded. 'Joe Porter.'

He took another swallow of his beer, then laughed suddenly.

'Lucky bastard. Got turned over by a bloody mine, then came back with a fuckin' red motorbike.'

The American let out his breath slowly and stared into the long mirror behind the bar. Joe Porter. Now the thief had a name. He was getting closer.

It was the smell that woke Joe up. Stemming from the kitchen, drifting deliciously through the hall, then wafting up the stairs and into the bedroom, it rippled above his head like a breath from the Bisto ad, tempting him from his slumber.

He rolled over – at least he attempted to do so, but Maria lay half across his hip, pinning him to the mattress. He eased himself from beneath her and stared at the strange ceiling. He'd been dreaming about food and his stomach rumbled, reminding him. God, he was so hungry. He glanced at Maria, who hadn't stirred, then slid from beneath the sheets and dressed swiftly.

He stood at the top of the long, curving staircase, listening. It was quiet, just the sound of someone bustling around the kitchen. Sunlight filtered into the hall below, dappling the old timbers of the house but exposing the threadbare carpet on the stairs. Yet it was clean and well cared for. The long balustrade gleamed from the years of polishing and Joe could not resist its mute challenge. He tucked the pistol into the back of his waistband and threw his leg over the banister, then slid triumphantly down to the foot of the stairs. He swept off the end and landed with a thump on the polished floor as his feet slipped from beneath him.

Annette heard the thud and rushed to the door of the kitchen. Joe was still sitting on the floor, staring up at the stairs with an expression of huge satisfaction on his face. She walked towards him.

'Are you all right?'

Joe smiled at her concern. 'Fine. I just wondered if I could still do it.'

Annette grabbed his arm and helped him to his feet. 'Do what?'

Joe rubbed his arse and grimaced. 'Slide down the banisters, love.' He put his hands on her shoulder and pulled her into his arms, kissing her lightly on the nose. '*Bonjour, mon petite une.*'

She looked up at him shyly, then cuddled her head into his chest. He held her tightly for a moment.

She heard his stomach rumble and broke away from him, laughing. 'Come,' she said, 'your stomach is giving me messages.'

They walked arm in arm to the kitchen and Joe sat down at the table while Annette prepared his breakfast. He found himself enjoying her supple movements as she bent over the range whisking the eggs in the pan. Here in a familiar environment she worked with an absence of inhibition that he found faintly erotic. She became aware of his eyes on her and flushed slightly, pulling loose her blouse, which was sticking to her in the warmth of the kitchen. Joe smiled to himself. Her innocence was beguiling, yet last night in bed there had been an abandonment, a healthy lust, that even now aroused him.

He noticed a cluttered tray, some of the food half eaten but most of it left. He realized that Annette had been up for some time.

'How is your grandmother?'

She shook her head, not looking at him. 'The soldier is still on the bed. I think she slept in the armchair.' She turned and faced Joe. 'You must help me to get him out.'

She stared at him for a moment, then picked up the hot plate, protecting her hands with a cloth, and carried the bacon and eggs to the table. She put the plate down in front of him.

Joe could see she was concerned. There was a vulnerability about her that he found difficult to resist. He patted his lap and she sat down, putting her head on his shoulder.

'It's all right,' he said soothingly. 'Don't worry about your grandmother. I will deal with it before I go.'

She pushed herself away and gazed tearfully at him.

'Please stay, at least for a while. They will come from the village for us because of the Germans who were here.'

Joe wiped the tears away with the palm of his hand. 'No, they won't. I'll deal with them. Now, please, do you think I could have a cup of coffee?'

She rubbed her eyes dry and stood up. She fetched the pot and poured it out for him. Joe tucked into the bacon and scrambled eggs. He would have to do something about the dead soldier, but first he needed to eat.

Joe wrapped the German soldier's body in a sheet. It was already stiffening and it was more difficult than he had anticipated to carry it downstairs.

The old woman, supported by Maria and Annette, followed him slowly. She seemed finally to have accepted his death and was much calmer now. Joe was sweating. It had taken him nearly an hour to dig a suitable grave in the back garden. He had chosen a spot behind some shrubbery which was unlikely to be found. One missing German soldier was hardly likely to raise any questions in the present situation, but Joe wanted him out of the way quickly.

He lowered the body into the grave and at once began to cover it with earth before the three women could reach the spot. By the time the grandmother had negotiated the stairs and the walk through the shrubbery he was almost through. They stood silently watching him work. He was stripped to the waist, his body streaked with dirt and sweat; he didn't slow down until he had finished.

He flattened the earth with the shovel, trying to make the ground look as undisturbed as possible. The old woman, suddenly aware of what he was doing, protested in French, shaking her head. She tried to take the shovel from him. Maria and Annette held on to her, placing themselves between the old woman and Joe, and spoke to her soothingly, as to a child.

Joe stopped. He leaned on the shovel, breathing heavily. 'Tell her I have to do this. The grave can't be marked. Someone might find it and ask awkward questions. Perhaps later, when the war is over . . .'

He tailed off. She wasn't listening. The words sounded hollow even to his own ears. He covered the grave with dead leaves, then put on his shirt and battledress.

The old woman was crying, Annette was close to tears herself. Joe looked from one to the other. Something seemed to be expected of him and he felt a surge of irritation. He didn't know what to do. He wasn't a priest. Annette appealed to him mutely with her eyes, and Joe attempted to brush some of the dirt from his trousers. He pushed his hair back from his face and wiped the sweat from his forehead with the back of his hand, leaving a streak of dirt. Then he lowered his head and said the only prayer he knew.

'Our father, which art in heaven . . .'

The old woman stopped crying and gazed at him through her

tears, surprised. The prayer, though in English, was not unfamiliar to her. Yet, coming as it did from this strange young British soldier who had so callously killed the German she had grown fond of, it was curiously affecting in her sunlit garden. She closed her eyes and lowered her head too, drawing some comfort from the words.

Joe came to the end. He opened his eyes. The old woman was looking at him; she seemed more composed now and stronger. Firmly yet gently, she disengaged herself from the support of her two granddaughters, then took one pace towards him.

'Merci, monsieur.' She said it quietly but clearly. She paused for a moment, staring at his face as though imprinting it on her memory, then she turned and slowly left the garden, the sisters following automatically behind.

Joe waited until they had gone, then took the pistol from the pocket of his smock and pushed it under his waistband. He slung the smock over his shoulder and picked up the shovel, glancing down at the grave. It was the best he could do. No one was likely to find it unless they were looking. He walked wearily back to the house and waited in the kitchen.

Annette eventually came in and rushed into his arms, pushing herself inside his open battledress. She didn't mind his sweat.

'Oh, Joe,' she said.

He lifted her head and kissed her, then held her at arm's length. 'Now,' he said matter-of-factly, 'I want a piece of white cardboard I can write on, a pencil – a red one if you've got it – and, please, how about something to drink?'

Annette smiled, amused in spite of herself. 'I shall do the best I can.'

He grinned suggestively. 'You always do.'

Joe wrote carefully and laboriously. The cardboard was thick and heavy, and it would last some time. The pencil would not run if it rained. He tried to make his words look as official as possible. The sisters were curious, but he shielded the message from their gaze. He didn't want them to see it yet.

He stood up, tucking the cardboard under his arm. 'Come on,' he said mysteriously.

He led them out of the house to the front door, then took the piece of cardboard and pinned it firmly in the middle, banging the nail in with the butt of his pistol. When he had finished he stood back and surveyed his handiwork. 'There,' he said, pleased with himself, 'that should do the trick.'

Maria and Annette read it and exchanged a look before bursting into uproarious laughter. Joe held out his arms and they both hugged him. He crushed them to him, kissing their hair, then stepped back. It was time to go.

He pulled the motorbike off its stand, pushing it up with his foot until it sprang back into position, then slung his leg over the machine and kicked the starter twice before it fired. He adjusted the mixture until the engine was turning over nicely and sat down into the saddle.

The two sisters had watched his preparations, but there was no sign of the grandmother. Joe wasn't surprised. He looked from one girl to the other.

Maria came to him first and kissed him firmly on each cheek. 'You bastard,' she breathed quietly into his ear. 'I'd cut off your cock if it wasn't so nice.' She stepped back, smiling, and pushed Annette towards him. 'Go on,' she commanded, 'kiss your man goodbye, but make sure he comes back.'

Annette leaned over the bike holding on to him tightly. She kissed him once on the lips and lingered for a moment before returning to her sister's side.

Joe pulled the goggles down over his eyes, blew them a kiss then gunned the red machine swiftly down the drive and out into the road. The sound of the engine gradually faded, but the two young sisters stood there for a long time before they went inside, past the sign Joe had nailed to the door. It read:

THIS HOUSE, ITS CONTENTS AND THE
PEOPLE WHO LIVE IN IT ARE UNDER
THE PROTECTION OF THE BRITISH
ARMY.
NO ENTRANCE!

Signed,   J. Porter
        Brigerdear

CHAPTER
SIX

It was still dark when the American heard the roar of the Harley-Davidson burst into life. The hum of the well tuned engine as it settled down was unmistakable. He would have recognized the sound of his machine anywhere. Only for the moment, he was not on it. It was in the hands of a thief.

The Irishman had said his name was Porter. Hillier smiled grimly to himself. Well, Mr Porter, you'd better get back on your train pretty damn quick. That bike is mine. I've made it into something special and no Limey son of a bitch is gonna keep it from me.

But Porter was good. Hillier had been unable to get anywhere near the machine. He'd not even been able to spot it, but he'd known it was there. Now he could hear it, and the sweet sound of its engine was music to his ears.

He waited silently in the darkness for the sound to fade as it turned towards the outskirts of the town, then Hillier gave his own bike a quick thrust with his foot. The engine started immediately. It was muted, the smaller engine capacity muffled by the heavy wadding he had wrapped around the exhaust. He had made his preparations and thought them through.

Quietly he manoeuvred the machine out past the high wall of the British barracks, following the faint sound from the Harley-Davidson through the blacked-out streets, keeping himself well out of earshot. The built-up areas quickly slipped behind him, and they were enveloped by the dark, empty countryside.

The sky gradually lightened low down on the horizon, and Porter drove carefully through the winding country lanes. He couldn't afford a spill, not with the explosive charges he had carefully wrapped and placed in the dispatch bag slung over the rear mudguard.

The roads were still damp from the heavy overnight dew, but they would soon dry out as the day warmed up. He didn't expect any trouble. The area he was visiting had been cleared forty-eight hours earlier. But Joe didn't take any unnecessary risks. He was alert, watching the road ahead, scanning the hedgerows for any sign of movement.

But all was peaceful, inviting him to relax, drop his guard, enjoy the heavy scents of summer. The war seemed to have faded from this spot.

He knew his route. He'd come back this way the day before. The village had been interesting, one shop particularly. Joe's French was still practically non-existent, but the sign had intrigued him. It looked like 'Coffee and Dames'. The possibility of a French brothel would have been warmly welcomed – and not just by him. He could have extracted a high price for such valuable information, but it had proved to be far from erotic. A puzzled local had explained in broken English that the shop was a ladies' hairdressers. '*Coiffeur des dames*,' he'd said, staring slightly mystified at Joe's regulation short back and sides.

But it was the other building that had brought him back to the village. Joe throttled the H-D down as he entered the single main street. It was still very early and the place was deserted. There was not even a sign of smoke from a chimney to indicate that anyone was awake.

That pleased Joe.

He switched off the engine and freewheeled the rest of the way to the front of the building. It looked as formidable and respectable as it had the day before – but Joe was prepared this time.

He pushed the bike out of sight behind the square structure and carefully slid the explosive charges from the dispatch bag. Then he unclipped the submachine-gun from its position on top of the handlebars and carried it loosely in his other hand.

The back door of the building was as he had left it, hanging from its hinges. He stepped just inside the door and looked round the gloomy interior. The sun wasn't yet high enough to throw much light through the wide windows.

Joe made his way past the counter and into the manager's office. In the corner stood the safe. It was huge, heavy and impregnable. So far it had resisted Joe's puny efforts without a scratch.

He gazed at it malevolently and held up the charge in front of its securely fastened door. 'This is going to see you off, you ugly bastard. It's going to rip you wide open like a tin can,' he murmured.

The French safe said nothing. It just squatted in its corner sneering at him.

Joe set to work. He'd never blown a safe before, but this one had upset him, got beneath his skin. He'd tried everything the day before – fiddling delicately with the combination unavailingly, then battering it with a pick-axe. But the goddam thing hadn't budged. He hadn't even dented it. Joe didn't care what was in it anymore, he just had to get it open.

He set the explosive, sticking the plastic charge around the combination mechanism and then forcing as much as he could behind the safe and the wall. He'd read somewhere that the back was the weakest point. He used up all the explosive. It didn't matter what was in the safe. He would totally destroy the bloody thing.

Delicately he inserted the fixing pins, then rewound the wires back into the main part of the bank. He set up the plunger behind one of the counters and attached the wires to the points.

He was ready.

He went back into the manager's office and checked out everything. As far as he could see, he'd done it all correctly. He patted the top of the safe with his hand and gazed at it for a minute.

'You ready?' he inquired.

The safe sat still and impassive in its corner. Joe turned and strode quickly back to the detonator. He crouched down behind the counter and grasped the plunger. He paused for a second, then shoved it down hard, falling flat on his stomach as he did so.

He felt the air being sucked from his lungs, then the blast blew out every window and door in the bank, shattering the peaceful calm of the village.

At first Joe couldn't hear anything. He lifted himself up on one elbow and banged the side of his head, fearing he'd gone deaf. Then he heard a dog barking fiercely outside. He got up, covered in white ceiling plaster, and tried to dust some of it off. Then he remembered the safe.

He ran from behind the counter, across and into the manager's office. He peered through the white haze of dust at the corner.

The safe had gone. So had the corner. Through a gaping hole he could see the main street of the village and the dog yapping excitedly at something lying in the middle of the road. Joe moved forward cautiously, peering through the dust.

It was the safe. The explosive had blown it out into the street beyond. Joe stepped through the jagged hole in the wall and inspected the massive, inert object.

It lay on its side like a stranded whale, the back a slightly lighter colour than the rest, protected over the years by the wall it had rested against.

It appeared to be totally undamaged. Hopefully Joe tugged at the handle. The door remained firmly shut. Joe gazed at it in stunned admiration. 'Shit!' he said inadequately.

At that moment he saw a BSA army motorbike leaning against the side of the bank and heard the sound of the Harley-Davidson spurting into life. The red machine came hurtling out from behind the bank and whipped around to halt in a cloud of dust thirty feet from him. Joe recognized the rider instantly. It was the Yank he'd taken it from during the ambush. He raised the submachine-gun and levelled it at the American.

Hillier pushed his goggles up over his forehead and stood up straddling the bike with his legs. The engine was idling powerfully. 'This is mine, you bastard,' he yelled, 'and I'm taking it back.'

From the corner of his eye Joe could see some people emerging from their homes. They stopped and stared silently at the two men and the huge safe lying incongruously in the middle of the road. Even the dog had stopped its yapping. It stood watching the red motorbike warily, its fur ruffling up along its spine.

Joe could have killed the American then, but he didn't. He waited.

Hillier gripped the throttle of the bike and revved the engine. Whirling the machine around in an arc and quickly accelerating, he sped out of the village.

Joe stared after the diminishing figure, then turned abruptly and shouted to the people in the vicinity, indicating the safe. 'Take it. Open the bloody thing if you can. It's yours.'

He slung the Thompson over his shoulder and leapt on to the other bike, kickstarting it first time. He shot out, hotly pursued by the dog who seemed to have woken from its trance.

The American grinned to himself and pushed the throttle of his machine up a few more notches. There was no way that any bike was going to match the performance he could coax out of the Harley. But he relished the chance to demonstrate its power, and he was entitled to some fun with this guy.

The sun was warm now, still low on the horizon and directly in their eyes. The narrow country road, bounded by hedgerows, threw back the sound of the engines as though they were in a tunnel. Hillier never fully opened up the Harley-Davidson, allowing Porter to stay sufficiently close to be in the chase but always tantalizingly out of reach.

The hedgerows began to thin, and they emerged from the low hills into flat, crop-growing country. The corn was high, gently ruffling in the breeze, and Hillier was getting tired. He waited until he saw a gap, then roared through it into the field beyond, cutting a giant swathe through the growing wheat ahead.

Porter didn't hesitate. He followed blindly, determined not to be shaken off. He knew how fast the Harley-Davidson could go. And he knew that, for some reason, the Yank was allowing him to tag along behind. It didn't worry him. If the American liked games, he'd give him one. He just needed a single mistake and Joe'd be on to him. Meanwhile Joe hung on grimly, staying in close as he could to the red machine.

Hillier could ride, Joe could see that. He had an expertise with his machine that was almost uncanny. Off the road it was even more apparent. Somehow he always seemed to know where the gap or the crossing into the next field would be. All Joe had to do was to stay with him.

They came to some grazing land, and as Joe plunged through the hole in the half broken fence after him, he saw Hillier come to a stop in the middle of the field and turn to face him.

Joe slowed down, freewheeling the bike towards him. Hillier laughed and pulled his goggles over his nose, then began to race around Joe, dipping and weaving, mocking him as the Englishman tried pointlessly to keep up with him.

It was hopeless and Joe knew it. He stopped, feet planted on either side of his bike, and waited like a baited bull in a ring while Hillier ran circles round him, taunting him, ridiculing his attempts to catch him.

Joe didn't move or make any attempt to unsling the Thompson from his shoulders. He knew that was what the Yank wanted and that he would be away and out of range before Porter could even level the weapon. But Joe wanted this man alive. Suddenly Hillier peeled off and shot away towards a small, circular copse surrounding a low hill in the middle of a near-by cornfield. Joe started after him. Hillier's red machine flailed through the wheat, flattening it, leaving a path for Joe to follow.

The sun glanced off the ripening sea of corn and something flickered briefly across his eyeline from the small hilltop in the trees. Porter yelled a warning to the American, but the sound was swallowed up by the roar of the bike's engine. Joe grabbed the Thompson from his shoulder and fired a short burst into the air.

Hillier turned and stared back at him. Joe waved, pointing towards the low hill, but before the American registered the danger, the raw clatter of a Spandau machine-gun ripped into the corn around Hillier, and the bike skidded on to its side as Hillier rolled away into cover.

Joe leapt from his machine, the high corn breaking his fall as the bike zig-zagged madly by itself for a moment before crashing on to its side, the engine still threshing the rear wheel around in the wheat. He crawled silently towards the spot where the American had disappeared, cradling the Thompson in his arms, using his elbow and knees to push himself forward.

The first Hillier knew of his presence was when he felt the hard, round barrel of the Thompson on the side of his neck.

He froze and turned slowly. Joe's eyes were empty, devoid of expression.

'Hello, Yank,' he whispered. 'Enjoying yourself?' He smiled, exposing his teeth, but there was no humour in the expression. 'You really shouldn't play games. Not in this part of the country. You might get yourself killed.' He prodded his prey gently with the Thompson. 'Racing around on a bike like that in the middle of a cornfield, you could draw fire from anybody. German, British . . . anybody.'

Joe let it hang there for a moment while the American absorbed the implication. He smiled mirthlessly again. He was enjoying this.

'What's your name?'

The American rolled over carefully on to his back, making sure the Luger he held did not threaten Porter. 'Hillier,' he said shortly, keeping the anger from his voice.

Joe's eyes fastened on the hand gun. 'Give that to me, butt first.'

Hillier transferred the gun to his other hand, holding it by the barrel, and gave it to the Englishman. Porter took it and examined it briefly.

'Nice one. Where did you buy it?'

Hillier stared at him. 'I didn't. I got it from a German in that ambush while you were stealing my machine.'

For a moment he thought he'd pushed his luck too far. Porter went very still, his eyes opaque. Then suddenly he smiled and threw the Thompson into Hillier's arms.

'OK, Yank, we've got work to do. You give them an occasional burst with that, then move fast before they've got your position. I'll take this and circle behind them.'

Hillier was too startled to protest. He watched Porter's legs begin to disappear into the corn, then Joe turned and shouted back to him.

'Yank?'

'Yeah.'

'Be sure to be here when I get back.'

Hillier stared at him quizzically. 'Just get back, that's all. We've got things to talk about.'

Porter vanished. Hillier hardly saw him go and heard nothing. He stared at the Thompson and wondered how the hell Porter was going to tackle a machine-gun with a Luger. But somehow he never doubted, not for an instant, that the Englishman would do it. There was an implacable, chilling efficiency about him that made everything possible. Porter was right: he'd been stupid to play games, and if that Spandau had been accurate, he'd have paid for it.

He grasped the Thompson, stuck it up above his head and loosed off a quick burst of fire in the general direction of the hill. Then he swiftly rolled away from the spot he'd occupied, crawling as fast as he could without revealing his progress.

The Spandau coughed its ugly sound in reply, the lead ripping through the wheat, close to where he'd been a moment before.

Hillier smiled to himself. If he was going to keep this up, changing his position from one to another, his future would depend on out-guessing that Spandau up in the hill.

He raised the Thompson up above his head again, loosed off about twenty rounds, then moved backwards fast. Bit like chess, he thought, only if he made the wrong move in this game, he could be dead.

Joe had reached the edge of the copse undetected. The hill rose above the level of the small trees and undergrowth, and the position was dug in on the top. It gave them a fine view of the surrounding countryside, but they were vulnerable.

He crawled silently through the undergrowth, pausing every few feet to listen and judge their position. As he drew closer to the foot of the low hill, he occasionally heard voices. There were two of them and, judging by their tone, they were very nervous.

An argument began to develop in between the frequent bursts of fire, and it was clear they had no real idea of where Hillier was firing from or if he was part of a larger group.

Joe was within striking distance now, about eighteen feet below their position. He carefully detached the two grenades from his belt, then looked up, assessing the length and weight of his throw.

He waited for Hillier's next burst of fire, then as the Spandau opened up he jerked out the pin and threw the first grenade into the German emplacement in a gentle arc. A moment later he threw the second.

He heard one of the soldiers scream a warning and heard their frantic scrambles to find the first grenade before it exploded. Then both grenades detonated, one immediately after the other.

Joe lay in the undergrowth while earth sprayed down around him. Then silence – not a sound. He ran fast, crouching, to the top of the hill and leapt into the small trench, holding the Luger. He didn't need it. He'd seen the grotesque positions of death often enough to recognize them.

He pulled himself out of the trench and yelled at the American to come up, then jumped back down between the twisted bodies.

When Hillier reached the top of the rise Porter was going through the pockets of the Germans. Joe glanced up at him and saw the look in his eyes.

'I need their pay books and insignia. It's all useful information for intelligence – they get to know where Jerry is.'

Hillier didn't believe him. 'Is that why you've taken that watch in your haul as well?'

Porter ignored him and searched the bodies until he was satisfied. Then he climbed out beside the American. He stared at him. 'I take what I can. I'm entitled. They're mine.'

Hillier didn't contest the claim. 'How did you get this close?'

Joe glanced down at the two dead bodies. 'It wasn't hard. They're young and raw. It was a bad position. They could see a long way but couldn't keep anyone out of range. The corn was perfect cover for me, and their trench was too close to the edge of the undergrowth. They were stupid.'

Hillier turned away from the hill and started back towards the bikes.

Joe called out. 'I'll take the Thompson now.'

Hillier stopped and looked hard at Joe. He held the submachine-gun loosely in his hand. 'That's my machine down there, Porter. You don't get that.'

Joe shrugged. 'I don't want it any more. You can use it better.' He held out his hand. 'The gun. Give me the gun.'

Hillier weighed it carefully in his hand, then made up his mind and tossed it to him. Porter caught it expertly and pulled the Luger from his belt, giving it to Hillier. He smiled.

'That makes us quits.'

Silently they walked back through the cornfield, parting the grain. Hillier glanced at him quizzically.

'What the hell were you doing with that safe anyway?'

Joe slung the Thompson over his shoulder. 'Trying to open the bloody thing. It must have weighed a ton.'

Hillier grinned. 'You didn't have to blow down the fuckin' bank. I could have sprung that in five minutes.'

Joe stopped and gazed at him incredulously. 'Are you serious?'

Hillier nodded. 'No problem. I opened a few cans down the West Side and they were a great deal younger than that baby.'

Delight gleamed in Joe's eyes. He slapped Hillier on the shoulder. 'You know something? I think we're in business.'

CHAPTER
SEVEN

The small apartment was silent. Only the occasional blare of a car horn and the hum of the evening traffic drifted up through the open windows as Manfred prepared some coffee.

He enjoyed this place. It had an atmosphere of its own. Unmistakably feminine. The bright curtains billowing slightly in the cool summer breeze, the faint smell of perfume and the small pieces of bric-à-brac cluttered around the place all betrayed Lissette's touch and taste.

He whistled soundlessly to himself as the delicious smell of fresh coffee percolated through the apartment. Lissette would be delighted. It was one of the small favours he could obtain for her – and he wanted to please her, especially tonight.

He wouldn't tell her. There was no need as yet. But he had been warned to have his flak unit ready for departure if the need arose. The Allies had broken clear in Normandy. Caen had fallen after an intense and bloody siege, and now the British and Canadians were spreading eastwards towards Belgium and Holland, while the Americans, led by Patton, pushed to the Ardennes.

Antwerp was a vital strategic link, and Manfred knew that they would defend it bitterly if the Allied armies got this far. He hoped they wouldn't, but the fact that they had cut through the German defences in Normandy was ominous. The sea walls had been regarded as impregnable. Manfred feared the worst.

His thoughts were interrupted by the rattle of Lissette's key in the lock, and he walked into the small vestibule to greet her. He wrapped his arms around her in a huge bear hug and buried his face in her hair.

Lissette held him close for a moment, then she smelt the aroma and pushed him back a little. Her eyes shone.

'Coffee?'

He nodded deliberately.

'Fresh coffee?'

'Yes,' he said, enjoying the pleasure of her surprise. 'Extracted from the cook at enormous expense.'

She was suddenly serious, her practical streak dampening her enthusiasm.

'How much?'

He led her into the small kitchen sucking in his breath portentously. 'A lot.'

She suddenly saw through his pretence. 'Don't play with me. How much?'

He wrapped his arms around her again, kissing her neck lasciviously. 'Why not? I like playing with you.'

She half-heartedly tried to push him away. 'Listen, I won't drink my coffee until I know what you paid for it.'

'An invitation to our wedding,' he said grandly. Then, seeing her face, he added, 'Two tickets to your cinema next Friday.'

She laughed and kissed him passionately. 'God, you are a menace, Manfred.'

She felt him responding to her proximity and turned away. 'No,' she said firmly. 'I want my coffee first.'

He grumbled but accepted the promise and poured out the cups, handing one to her. She sipped it delicately, and nodded her approval.

'It's good.'

He grinned. 'I know, let's go to bed.'

'I've only just come in,' she protested.

He cupped her breasts in his hands. 'That's the best time.'

She groaned and pushed her body against him, feeling his erection hard against her stomach. Her hand slid down, holding him. Then the doorbell rang, and she leapt back from Manfred, startled.

He smiled. 'No need to feel guilty, Lissette. This is your apartment.'

She smoothed her clothes down and titivated her hair. 'Nevertheless, you are not supposed to be here. You'd better go into the bedroom.' She glanced at him over her shoulders. 'I'll join you in a minute.'

Manfred grinned and sauntered into the bedroom. As soon as he was out of sight, Lissette opened the door.

It was Henri Duparc. She could see he was frightened and instinctively she knew what was wrong. He pushed the door shut behind him and leant back against it, closing his eyes as if to banish the fear. He was out of breath, as though he had been running, and Lissette waited for him to gather himself together.

He lifted his head and looked at her.

'You must help me.' His voice was toneless, drained of emotion.

She took his arm. 'Come and sit down. I'll make you some coffee.'

She led him into the kitchen and he slumped into a chair. Lissette poured out another coffee from the pot Manfred had made and put a little milk in. She knew he liked that.

Henri was about fifty. A recent liaison of her mother's. She knew he had been living at her house for at least a year and a half.

He gulped down the coffee and thanked her. 'I haven't tasted fresh coffee for years.'

He didn't ask her where she had got it. He could guess. He knew she ran the cinema for the Germans and that gave her a somewhat privileged position. Now his life depended on it.

Lissette sat down across the table from him and clasped her hands together.

'What is it? What's wrong?'

He examined the frayed cuff of his shirt, trying to find the best way of broaching the subject. 'You know I have been staying with your mother?'

She nodded. 'You mean living with her, Mr Duparc. There is no need to be delicate with me. My mother has had many . . .' she paused fractionally, '"friends" over the years.'

His lips tightened. He was embarrassed by her frankness.

'Yes, of course, I understand.' He hurried on. 'Well, someone must have informed on me. Somehow they have found out. Luckily I was not in and your mother managed to get a message to me.' He turned his head away and tried not to show his fear.

Lissette didn't like him very much, but she felt compassion for his terror and she knew the reasons. 'You mean because you are a Jew?'

He nodded again. 'You think maybe . . .' He stopped, staring at her. 'How did you know?'

She paused a moment before telling him.

'When you began to . . . work for my mother – arranging her, shall we say, appointments – I made sure I knew everything about you. I checked up on your story in Paris. It was not difficult for me. I have to make long distance phone calls all the time.' She glanced at him. 'Maybe someone else has been doing some checking also.'

She waited for him to say something, but he gazed morosely at the table.

'Did Sophie know you were a Jew?'

He shook his head. 'No.'

Lissette almost smiled. It must have been a shock for her mother.

He looked at her. 'She told me never to come back.'

Lissette nodded. 'She would.' She saw his look. 'Nothing my mother does, Henri, surprises me a great deal. She has few secrets from me as far as her men are concerned.'

He stared at her, realizing for the first time something of her bitterness and the nature of her relationship with her mother.

'Will you help me?'

Lissette gazed past him, looking at the bedroom door, wondering how much Manfred had overheard. She turned her attention to Duparc. 'Wait here. I shall only be a moment.'

He watched her intently as she walked from the small kitchen and across the vestibule into the bedroom. He heard the murmur of voices and realized she had a man in the apartment. He gripped the top of the table, torn between his terror of what lay outside and fear of betrayal by Lissette. He crouched in the kitchen in an agony of suspense.

Lissette walked over to the window and stared down at the cobbled street outside, waiting for Manfred's reaction. She had spared him nothing, loving him as she did. Her own desperate emotional insecurity had forced her to be blunter than she need have been. She knew what she was doing, even as she did it, but she could not stop herself – Manfred was being put to the test. She waited, hating herself for being so stupid, so unfair. She didn't deserve a decent man like him.

She heard him move and stood taut and frightened, waiting to hear the door close behind him. She was about to turn when she felt his arms surround her, holding her close. She twisted round, burying her head on his chest as he cuddled her in his arms, stroking her hair.

'It's all right, Lissette, it's all right. He will be safe with you. Whatever cruel games the S S play, they will hear nothing from me.'

She looked up at him. He could see she was very close to tears. Her voice was choked. 'I will do what I can. There may be someone who can help him.' She gripped his arm. 'But he will have to stay here tonight at least.'

He pushed her hair away from her eyes. 'Yes, I know. I will leave.'

She started to protest, but he stopped her.

'No, I must, Lissette. He is a very frightened man. When he sees me, it will be hard enough. When I have gone, you will be able to reassure him, only try to get something organized.' He paused, then held her close again. 'You are placing yourself in grave danger. You must try to get him out of the city as soon as possible. If there is anything I can do, let me know. We can always make contact at the Cinéac.' He kissed her hair. 'Now I must go.'

He put his tunic back on and Lissette watched him quietly. When he was ready she went to the door of the bedroom.

'What will you say to him?'

He shrugged his shoulders. 'I don't know, but I shall be brief. The longer I stay, the more likely he is to bolt.'

Lissette kissed him. 'I shall speak to you tomorrow.'

He squeezed her hand reassuringly. She opened the door and led the way into the vestibule.

Duparc was still sitting by the table in the kitchen, but when he saw the Luftwaffe uniform, he stood up terrified, his eyes darting round the kitchen looking for a way out.

There was none.

Lissette tried to calm him. 'Henri, this is my friend Manfred.'

Duparc instinctively backed away from the German.

Manfred smiled. 'It's all right. I'm just about to go.' He paused, seeing the frozen terror in Duparc's eyes. 'Try not to be afraid. I know Lissette well. You can trust her, and she will try to help you.'

There was no response. The two men stared at each other, the gulf between them too deep to be bridged by words. Manfred knew it was useless. He turned and made his way to the door of the apartment. He opened it, then paused for a moment, looking back at Duparc who was still standing in the kitchen, watching him.

'I don't know if you like music, Duparc, but before the war, back in Germany, I always used to listen to Mendelssohn. He was my favourite composer – he still is. Goodnight.'

The door closed behind him and Lissette locked it with the catch, then went into the kitchen. Duparc hadn't moved. She refilled his cup and put it down on the table before him.

'Would you like something to eat? I am about to make some dinner.'

Duparc was still staring at the locked door of the apartment. He sat down and reached for the cup, his thoughts chaotic. He turned to Lissette. His voice was querulous, but the fear had gone, replaced by a kind of stunned amazement.

'Did you hear what he said about Mendelssohn?'

Lissette nodded. 'Yes.'

He looked up at her, puzzled. 'Mendelssohn was a Jew.'

Lissette smiled. 'I know.'

Lissette walked casually, not hurrying, as though she were on her way home after a day out. Most women who lived in this area did not work. They did not need to.

The houses were high, terraced and elegant, built before the First World War by businessmen who had made their money from shipping. Antwerp was a busy, prosperous port then and crucially important now.

She scanned the tree-lined avenue, trying to see if anyone was observing her mother's house. There was no movement she could discern; there wasn't even an occupied car. She slipped down the narrow alleyway between two houses and made her way along to the high wooden door that led up to the small patio at the back of the house.

It was open as promised.

She shut it behind her and walked quickly to the back door. She knocked twice and waited. It did not take long. Her mother was expecting her.

She stood outlined in the doorway. Lissette could not see her face – it was in shadow – but the familiar expensive perfume was unmistakable. Sophie waved her sharply inside, then led Lissette to the downstairs living room, closing the door firmly behind her.

She gazed steadily at her daughter. 'Well, where is he?'

Lissette returned her mother's look. She had no intention of being intimidated. 'Do you mind if I take my coat off first?'

Sophie gestured impatiently. 'Do as you please.' She crossed the room to a small table and selected a cigarette from a silver box, lit it and drew on it hungrily, as Lissette removed her coat and draped it over a chair.

'Well?' Sophie repeated.

Lissette looked curiously at her mother. She never seemed to change. Her high cheekbones and flawless chin gave no indication of her true age. She was well into her fifties now, yet still retained the youthful looks Lissette remembered from her childhood. It was uncanny. They could almost have been sisters, except that her mother was beautiful, while she was, at best, merely passable. Lissette shuddered inwardly, aware of what it cost in time and effort for her mother to maintain her appearance.

'He is still with me,' she answered shortly.

Sophie stared at her aghast. 'Still in your apartment?'

Lissette had expected this. 'Yes, mother, still in the apartment.'

She heard the sharp intake of breath that presaged a tirade and hurried on before it could burst around her ears. 'The people at the "safe" house cannot take him until tomorrow. He had to stay. There was nowhere else for him to go.'

She paused, staring hard at her mother.

'You certainly would not have had him back.'

Sophie's cigarette glowed angrily as she drew upon it. 'It is impossible for him to come back here. I don't know when the S S intend to pick him up.' She stared icily at her daughter. 'It is fortunate that one of the junior officers comes here fairly regularly, and he saw Henri's name on the list. Apparently they have discovered, belatedly as always, that he is not only French but also a Jew.' The cigarette glared. 'The little sod never told me he was a Jew. He could have put my whole establishment in danger.' She looked hard at Lissette. 'Not that I suppose you care.'

Lissette could not resist a smile and Sophie saw it at once. She stared hard at her daughter, realizing the truth.

'You knew!'

Lissette had never been able to lie to her mother, and she made no attempt to now. 'Yes. I checked him out.'

Sophie went very still. Lissette could feel her venomous anger reaching across the room towards her.

'Why didn't you tell me?'

Lissette shrugged. 'Why should I? There did not appear to be any danger. Besides, he was doing such a good job for you. He was never less than welcoming to most of the officers who used him to arrange their appointments.'

Sophie's calmness was more terrifying than her normal histrionics. She advanced slowly towards Lissette.

'If I get caught because of this, neither you nor your beloved Manfred will survive.' She smiled without humour. 'That I promise you, Lissette.'

For a moment Lissette felt a real sense of panic. She knew that her mother's threat was no empty one. Then her mind began to function again and she realized that the solution was in her own hands. Henri had a safe house to go to, and Sophie would never betray her unless she was taken by the SS herself.

'You'll have to be more careful who represents you in future, mother.'

Sophie ignored the barb and walked over to the high mantelpiece. 'Where are you going to put him?'

'There is a farm about six miles out where I used to go riding.'

Sophie was genuinely surprised. 'The Peeters? I would hardly have thought they were the type to risk their lives for a little French Jew.'

Lissette was disgusted. 'Yes, mother, it's odd, isn't it? Those who turn out to really care are those who are merely expedient.'

Sophie's eyes glittered at her from across the room. Lissette remembered that look from her childhood, when the pistol had been held to her head. She flinched in spite of herself.

'Odd perhaps, Lissette. But what kind of expediency permits you still to run the Cinéac for the Germans and to keep another one in your bed?'

Lissette knew she'd asked for that, left herself wide open. Somehow in her mother's presence she was always at her most vulnerable. She could feel the tears stinging behind her eyes, but she was determined not to cry in front of her. She picked up her coat and walked to the door. She had been stupid to come.

She paused in the doorway and stared back at her mother, still standing by the tall mantelpiece, her face half in shadow.

'At least I don't get paid for it.' She closed the door, shutting off the terrible sight of her mother's blazing eyes.

CHAPTER
EIGHT

It was a dingy place. A battered door sandwiched between two shop fronts led down some creaky, well-worn stairs to a half lit basement area that passed for a club. The bar sold mostly canned American beer, bought from the PX at the usual price, and there was gin of sorts and Irish whiskey, which suited Eddie fine.

Hillier stuck to the beer and Porter drank the Irish. It wasn't bad, but it was ridiculously expensive. The real attraction for most of the men holding up the bar was just being able to get away from their units, away from the war, for a few hours. And, of course, to see Josie.

Josie was, by all accounts, something special. She would do amazing things with her anatomy. Her fame had spread to most of the units in the sector, and if they could get down here, they did.

Hillier took a swallow of the beer and grimaced. It was tepid. He took in the tiny stage crammed into one corner, the stained curtains and threadbare carpet. He glanced at Eddie.

'Christ, this beer is lousy. Who runs this place?'

Eddie shrugged. 'Don't know. One of the locals, I suppose.' He sipped his whiskey contentedly. 'But it's popular,' he added.

Hillier surveyed the crowded bar. It was full of servicemen. Mostly British because of the sector, but there was a scattering of Americans.

Porter was relaxed but as vigilant as ever. He indicated the can Hillier had set down on the table. 'What did you pay for that?'

'Too much.'

Porter held his glass up and examined the golden fluid. 'Me, too.'

He turned the glass, not looking at the American. 'Could be a lot of money behind that bar.'

The remark was uttered casually, quietly so that only Hillier and Eddie could hear it. The American leaned forward, staring hard at Porter.

'Yeah, I guess so.' He paused and looked round the basement. 'But we could get more and better if we ran a place like this ourselves.'

Joe absorbed that. 'But there would be problems.'

'Such as?'

'How could *we* run it? A place like this needs full-time control.' Hillier sipped his drink distastefully. 'That's what it would get.'

Porter glanced at Eddie, who was watching them both, riveted. Joe shifted his attention back to Hillier.

'How?'

'We go. We cut the connections. Work on what we want to do all the time.'

Joe allowed a flicker of amusement to cross his face, pleased by the thought. 'You mean desert?'

Hillier pulled his seat a little closer. 'Why not? Between us we know more, do more, connect more, than any of the guys with the braid.'

Joe was listening. Hillier began to expand.

'Look, why waste your talent picking up the odd bits of loot here and there, risking your life for peanuts?'

Joe gazed at the American expressionlessly. 'Because I enjoy it.'

Hillier sat back. 'O K, why not? You can continue to enjoy it but for some big bucks.' He waved his can at the crowded room. 'Notice anything about these guys?'

Eddie dragged his gaze from the two of them and glanced around. 'They're nearly all army.'

Hillier nodded. 'Yeah, but they're not all *still* army.'

Joe picked him up. 'You mean some are deserters?'

'That's right.' Hillier leaned forward again. 'In *Stars and Stripes* it said that there were nearly 5,000 U S Army deserters behind the lines already. Multiply that by the British, the Canadians and the Poles and you got an awful lot of material there.'

Joe was getting the picture, and it appealed to him. 'Yeah. It could work.'

Eddie stared at them, dumbfounded. 'What . . . what could work?' he demanded loudly, then looked round, alarmed by his volume.

Joe ignored him. He smiled at Hillier. 'I know just the place we could set up.'

Hillier grinned. 'And you've got the transport.'

Joe looked at Eddie. 'That's true, isn't it?'

Eddie was confused. 'What is?'

'We've got the transport.'

Eddie nodded, relieved to identify something he knew. 'You mean the lorries. Yes, that's right. We've got lots of transport.'

Hillier picked up his can of beer. 'I'll drink to that.'

Joe raised his glass. 'To the success of *our* transport.' And he swallowed the remains of his whiskey. Eddie, mystified, did the same.

Before they could order some more, the lights faded and a scratchy recording of 'I'm in the Mood for Love' began. The single row of footlights disguised the dowdy curtains, creating an illusion of theatre, and a spotlight manipulated from the far corner swung on to the centre of the small stage as the tabs parted.

Josie was stunning. She was dressed in a short, tight skirt and an equally tight cotton vest that allowed her ample breasts just enough room to move. And Josie knew exactly what kind of movement was required.

It could hardly be called dancing. In that confined space, dance would have been impossible anyway. But what she did do concentrated the attention of every man there wonderfully.

There was a sinuousness about her movement, an element of primitive challenge, as she ran her hands over her breasts and down between her legs with an overt suggestion of masturbation. It was clear she had nothing on beneath the short skirt, and she allowed the audience an occasional erotic glimpse of her dark pubic hair as she slid down on to the stage, wrapping her legs around a strategically placed smooth pillar.

What she did with that lightweight plaster phallic symbol left nothing to the imagination, and with the exception of one or two regular barmen, there was hardly a man in the room who was not stiff with desire for Josie. As the record came to its scratchy climax, Josie fell back on to the stage in mock exhaustion, and the place exploded with applause and excitement.

Josie rose to her feet and stood arrogantly, legs splayed wide, looking down at the wildly applauding soldiers. She held up her hand for silence, then as the noise gradually subsided, she spoke. Her voice was husky, attractive, with just the faintest of accents, and every man in the room felt certain she was talking only to him. Josie was an expert.

In another age, at a better time, she would have found fame with a wider audience. Like Josephine Baker in Paris, whom she envied and admired and from whom she had taken her name. She could have been more sophisticated, less crude. But none can choose the time and few of us the place. Josie did her best with what she had, and there was no demand from these lonely, scared men for subtlety or sophistication. They needed women, and Josie gave them as much as she could.

'Good,' she said. 'Did you enjoy that?' Raucous shouts of approval left little doubt. 'Now I'm going to come down and share your table.'

A lonely British corporal, older than most present, banged his enthusiastically. 'You can have this one any time, Josie.'

Josie smiled. 'Give me time, corporal, and I'll visit you as well.'

She had them in the palm of her hand, encouraging them and their bawdy sexual innuendo, feeding their desire, yet keeping them sufficiently good-humoured to maintain her distance.

She gestured them to be quiet. 'Now, if you want me to come to your table, gentlemen, this is what you must do.'

They listened intently.

'Reach deep into your pockets and feel for the silver in there.'

The corporal laughed, and Josie was on to him in a flash. 'I said feel for the silver, nothing else, corporal.'

The room exploded with laughter.

'Now, place the coins, one on top of the other, on the corner of your table, as high as you can.' She paused, eyeing them hungrily. 'Then I will come to you, and if I can take the silver coins from the table without using my hands, I keep them.'

Hillier looked at Josie, puzzled. The Englishman smiled. He'd heard of Josie's famous trick. It was what had enticed him down here in the first place.

He took every piece of silver but one from his pocket and piled them on the corner of the table in a neat stack about three inches high. He glanced at Hillier.

84

'You got any?'

Eddie and the American added a few more. All the other tables had arranged similar small collections.

When Josie was satisfied that everything was ready, she walked to the back of the stage. The lights dimmed again and the same record played its plaintive invitation to love. The spotlights stayed with Josie as she moved with a graceful, lithe action from the stage into the room, working her way to the nearest table.

She feigned to caress a young soldier sitting alone, ruffling his hair while her body moved rhythmically to the slow, dreamy music. She could almost feel the sexual tension straining through the crowded club. Then swiftly, without effort, Josie swung her left leg over the edge of the table. Raising her skirt to the top of her thighs, slowly, with heavy deliberation, she sat down, engulfing the small circular tower of coins.

Joe heard someone in the room groan with pent-up excitement. There was a nervous, uncontrolled snigger of amusement from the audience. Then silence as Josie raised herself from the table and moved away. The coins had gone.

Her hand slipped down erotically between her legs and came back holding the silver. Slowly, she dropped them one by one, in tempo with the music, into a black velvet pouch she took from between her breasts. As the last one disappeared, the applause thundered ecstatically.

Joe puffed quietly on his cigar until it glowed, and surreptitiously pulled one silver half crown from his pocket that he had deliberately retained.

Josie sidled over to their table, concentrating her attention on Eddie. He smiled uncomfortably as she slid her hands suggestively down his body, and crouched in front of him, taking his leg in her hands.

She pushed it between her thighs and sat on it, sliding slowly up it towards him.

Eddie didn't know how to respond, and one or two of the audience began to give him some ribald advice. Josie knew it had gone far enough. She moved to straddle herself over the coins, but Joe raised his hand, stopping her.

He held the half-crown between his thumb and forefinger, and it

85

glittered as he turned it slowly in the spotlight. Deliberately he set it down on the stack of silver, then sat back.

Josie smiled, accepting the challenge and she placed herself above the coins, her eyes locked on Joe's. Slowly she lowered herself until she was above them.

Joe watched her, a faint trace of amusement half hidden in his gaze.

Josie moved, then suddenly screamed, leaping from the table, scattering the coins and the drinks to the floor. Joe laughed, leaning back in his chair, drawing contentedly on the cigar. He picked up a coin and held it over the end, heating it, then tossed it to Josie, who was still holding herself in pain on the floor.

She gazed up at his grinning face, loathing him. Joe held her look. Hatred he could understand; faked, taunting sexuality he despised.

She leapt at him, clawing and spitting, but Porter was ready for her. He gripped her arm but could not prevent her free hand from scratching at his face. He felt the blood trickling down his cheek and he flung her brutally to the floor.

But Joe had ignored the mood of the men in the room. They liked Josie. They had been enjoying the simple pleasure she provided, and the corporal was the first to respond as Josie lay hurt on the floor.

He leapt on Joe, flinging him back against the wall, knocking the breath from his body with his weight, his fist sinking into Joe's stomach. Hillier and Eddie turned to pull them apart, but suddenly they were engulfed in a mass of fighting, struggling soldiers.

Joe, Hillier and Eddie had little chance against the combined fury of that cheated audience, and they would have been mercilessly beaten if the MPs, on permanent stand-by for just that kind of trouble, hadn't suddenly appeared blowing their whistles and flailing their truncheons at anyone within reach.

Joe took his hands from the corporal's windpipe and dragged him to his feet as they were suddenly faced with a common enemy.

'Come on,' he shouted savagely in the corporal's ear.

He grabbed Eddie by the collar of his tunic and bounced an empty bottle off a British soldier who was holding Hillier in a neck lock and punching him with his fist.

Josie was still cowering on the floor in danger of being trampled to death by the heavy, booted feet of the soldiers. Joe picked her up and flung her over his shoulder, pushing his way towards the stage through the bodies still milling furiously.

Once into the back stage area, they ran past a screaming middle-aged lady who was Josie's dresser. Porter lifted Josie off his shoulder and pushed her into the open arms of the woman.

'Look after her,' he yelled. 'She's bloody good.'

They ran towards the exit. It opened into an alleyway, then into the street beyond. The M Ps were nowhere in sight.

Joe kept running until he came to the jeep. He leapt on to the driving seat and started the engine as the others, including the corporal, piled in behind.

They moved off fast towards the outskirts of the town.

Once Hillier had got some of his breath back, he yelled at Joe through the slipstream of the open vehicle.

'You stupid asshole, what the hell did you want to do that for?'

Joe swung the jeep around a corner. 'I just wanted to see her jump. She's a terrific mover.'

Hillier stared at Porter through the darkness, trying to fathom him. He couldn't. But whatever had made Joe the man he was, it had left him equipped with a sadistic sense of humour.

Hillier filed the thought away. It needed to be remembered.

Manfred drove the car slowly up to the checkpoint on the bridge over the Rupel. Lissette sat beside him; Duparc was in the back seat.

The defence emplacements around the bridge were more than he had expected. Barbed wire festooned the approaches, and trenches had been dug to provide positions for machine-gun fire across the river to the south and along the approach road from Brussels.

A look-out post on the roof of the bridge house gave a clear view for more than a mile until the road disappeared over a railway viaduct.

He had deliberately chosen to wear his Luftwaffe uniform for the trip to the Peeters' farm near Wolverton, and his identification was given only a routine inspection. He was just another lucky bastard out with his girlfriend and a passenger. He passed through the barrier and headed south over the viaduct.

Duparc wiped his sweaty palms on the knees of his trousers and let out a slow sigh of relief. Lissette looked round.

'All right, Henri?'

He nodded, staring at the back of Manfred's head as he drove the car. 'Thank you, Herr Kepner. I am indebted to you.'

The German inclined his head slightly and explained.

'It is important, strategically. The defences there at Boom protect the main roads into Antwerp as well as the Albert Canal and railway. I knew they had just reinforced the bridge and, without papers for you, Duparc, Lissette by herself would have had very little chance.'

Lissette placed her hand on Manfred's knee and squeezed it. He glanced at her and smiled, then concentrated on driving as carefully as he could. It was not the time to attract any unwelcome attention. He'd been lucky at the bridge. His uniform had got them through without the usual formalities, and he had chosen the time and day well. Sunday morning. A weekend run with his girlfriend into the country. If they'd asked about Duparc in the back, he would have said he was giving him a lift to his church in Wolverton.

But he would make sure that when they had dropped Duparc off at the farm, he returned to Antwerp by a different route.

The countryside was flat but still beautiful in the heat of the late summer. The windows of the car were open and the scent of wild flowers was unpolluted by exhaust. There were very few vehicles on the road because of the severe gasoline restrictions, and once they turned westwards off the main Brussels road, he seemed to have the winding country lanes entirely to himself.

Lissette remembered her trips to the farm near the Scheldt, the sudden sense of freedom when she saw her mother leaving, sometimes for weeks at an end. She had loved the farm, and the horses especially. They seemed so big and gentle, their soft noses nuzzling her hand for sugar.

She knew the Peeters disapproved of her feeding the horses titbits, but she always managed to hide something from breakfast for them. It didn't matter to her that her holidays on the farm were simply an excuse for her mother to get her out of the way. She was glad to be free of her persistent cross-examinations and vigilant eye. And the constant chain of men who came to her mother's expensive house for 'visits'.

There were no children at the Peeters' farm to mock her mother's 'visitors', and it was a blessed relief to be able to relax by herself and give herself entirely to the lovely horses.

She wondered how the Peeters were now. They would be well into their sixties. They had not been able to have children, and for the first time Lissette realized how selfish had been her pleasure in their attention and love.

They had given her the affection that would have gone to their own child, if they had been able to have one. And now here they were again, helping someone in trouble, only this time the stakes were higher. They could lose their lives.

She glanced at Manfred. 'It's not far now. There is a turn off to the left that leads to the farm, but drive straight by and stop further along.'

Manfred nodded gravely. 'Yes, of course.'

She suddenly felt an overwhelming, aching sense of love for him. He was kind and reassuring, understanding her mood in a quiet, subtle way, without ostentation. She held his arm tightly for a moment, pressing her cheek against the sleeve of his tunic.

He grinned, pretending to have difficulty with steering the car.

'Hold on, otherwise you'll have us all in the ditch.'

She released his arm, then pointed to the turn-off ahead. 'It's there, on the left.'

He nodded. 'I'll pull in just past it.'

The car drew quietly to a halt in the lane and Lissette turned to Henri. 'Are you ready?'

'Of course.' He leaned forward towards Manfred. 'You'd better not wait here with the car. It might look suspicious.'

Manfred glanced at his watch. 'How long will you be?'

Duparc looked to Lissette for a lead. She shrugged.

'Not long. I just want to say hello and thank them. I haven't seen them for a long time.'

Manfred smiled reassuringly. 'It's all right. I can drive down by the river and be back any time you like.'

Lissette thought for a moment before replying. She didn't want to be too long. She had to get Manfred out of this situation as quickly as she could. The consequences for him as a member of the armed forces could not be exaggerated. Worse, if anyone associated with the resistance saw him here they would kill him rather than risk the exposure of a 'safe' house.

'Come back in half an hour. I'll be here.'

She kissed him and got out of the car. Duparc followed, then leaned inside the open window.

'Thank you again, *monsieur*.' He held out his hand. Manfred grasped it in his own and studied the Frenchman quietly.

'Good luck.'

There was just a moment when their eyes met, a brief, endless moment, when nothing was said but everything understood. Then their hands unclasped and Duparc stepped back.

Manfred slipped the car into gear and drove off. Duparc watched it disappear round the bend. He stood quite still, immersed in his thoughts, listening to the sound of the engine as it slowly faded.

Lissette waited for a second, then touched his arm. 'Come,' she said.

He turned, almost as if he were surprised to see her. He nodded in recognition of his slowness. 'Yes, of course.' He smiled. 'Thank you.'

For Duparc the Peeters' farm was about as far away from his habitual city haunts as he could get. At first he felt a curious mixture of relief from his terror of the SS and then gradual boredom with the slow rhythm of country life.

He liked to think of himself as a sophisticate, an urbane, intelligent man, and he felt no guilt in his association with Sophie. He had always lived off women, but in his eyes they needed him as much as he needed them. He performed a service – he arranged certain introductions, the *right* sort of introductions for Sophie. She was a special kind of woman, who appealed to a certain kind of clientele. It was a delicate matter, one that he exercised with considerable skill and subtlety and took pleasure in so doing.

But a farm?

Theo and Francine Peeters were, as he feared, always up early, and their clatter gradually began to wake him in the early hours of the morning. There was nothing to do during the long summer evenings except listen to the radio and read. Surprisingly, the Peeters had a fine collection of books, and Duparc began to enjoy reading again. But the early nights and clamour of activity after dawn forced him out of his bed long before his usual late-morning rise.

Amazingly, he began to get used to it, and at first he endeavoured to help Francine about the house; then, finding she was not pleased to have her routine disrupted by a man, he moved outside with Theo, who was glad of the company.

It was an odd combination, yet it began to work. Duparc discovered that Theo, far from being a man of limited imagination, had an appetite for information, not just about the war and the German occupation, but also about creative things. He seemed interested in painting. It was also one of Duparc's pleasures. He enjoyed browsing through an art gallery in the afternoon – when it was quiet and empty of noisy family outings. He missed that.

It was late one evening after dinner, and Duparc was in his room reading when Theo knocked on his door. He entered after Duparc had responded and stood in the doorway, slightly in shadow. Duparc glanced up. There was something unusual in his manner. He seemed hesitant, unsure of himself.

Duparc smiled. 'Come in, Theo.'

He still clung to the doorway. 'I don't want to disturb you.'

'It's all right. I'm just reading. What is it?'

Theo advanced slightly into the room and Duparc noticed for the first time that he was holding something beneath his arm.

Duparc indicated it. 'Is that a present for me?'

Theo was not overly blessed with a sense of humour and gazed at him blankly for a moment. 'What?' Then he pulled the frame from beneath his arm. 'Oh, this.'

The Frenchman could see it was a picture.

Theo looked embarrassed. 'Oh, no. No, I wanted you to see it, if you were not too busy.'

Duparc stood up and eyed him. 'No, there's not much call for my services out here, I'm afraid.' He smiled with just a hint of irony that passed completely over Theo's head and held out his hand.

'Let me see.'

Theo handed it to him and the Frenchman placed it on his chair where the light could reach it. He stepped back a pace and examined it. He recognized the landscape: the river and one of the meadows just ten minutes walk away. Duparc glanced quickly at Peeters.

'Did you do this?'

Theo nodded. He looked at the Frenchman anxiously. 'I've never shown it to anyone else except Francine. I . . .' He stopped for a moment. 'You spoke so eloquently about painting the other day. I . . . I thought you might like to see it.'

Duparc had been studying the painting while Theo spoke. He glanced at him.

'Do you want to know what I think of it?'

Theo looked horrified for a moment, as if he expected Duparc to be destructive. Then his face cleared. He said determinedly, 'Yes, yes, I do. I must know the truth. Francine likes it, but she is my wife and I fear she knows as little of real painting as I do.'

Duparc beckoned him closer. 'Look at the meadow, Theo.'

Intrigued, he peered at the painting, then looked at Duparc, puzzled. The Frenchman smiled.

'Look closer. What strikes you most about the meadow?'

Theo stared again at his painting. 'The field is in blossom.'

Duparc put his hand on Peeters' shoulder.

'Exactly. The field *is* in blossom. It is alive, Theo. I can see no people in your landscape, but still it is alive. There is life in the field, in the flowers and hedges, even in the river – see how it moves.'

The excitement in Duparc's voice communicated itself to Theo. He stared wonderingly at Duparc.

'You like it?' There was disbelief in his question, as if it were too much to hope that Duparc appreciated his work.

The Frenchman shook his head, composing himself. 'I am no expert, Theo. Plainly, the style is raw but, yes, I do like it. It has a simplicity, a reality, that comes from your work in the fields, and it is on the canvas. I like it very much, Theo.'

Peeters looked at him for a long time, trying to gauge the Frenchman's response. But he could see no deception in his eyes. Just a blunt appraisal, a kind of pleasure. He nodded quietly to himself and turned to pick up the picture.

Duparc restrained him.

'May I look at it for a while?'

Theo nodded. 'Of course. As long as you like.' He moved slowly to the door, then paused. 'I will leave the painting here tonight for you to see. It will be a change from my stuffy attic.'

He turned again to leave, then looked back at the Frenchman. 'Thank you, Duparc. I think I shall remember this evening.' He closed the door quietly behind him and Duparc turned his attention back to the painting.

It *was* good. And perhaps he could be of some service after all. Perhaps if he could get back to the city, he would be able to find a purchaser for Theo's work – for a small commission, of course. Maybe twenty-five per cent. Yes, twenty-five would be fair.

He looked once more at the glistening river. It seemed almost to move. He felt a sudden sense of excitement once more. Suppose Theo were *really* good. Then, almost at once the next thought. He must encourage him to do more. Perhaps he could help. Find the right locations. Do some of the tasks around the farm so that Theo could paint – but not *too* many tasks. Helping him with his painting was one thing. Becoming a farm hand was something else.

He climbed into his bed and stared at the painting on the chair for a long time before switching off his light. But he didn't find it easy to sleep. When he did doze off he dreamed of blazing meadows and a cool river flowing gently past the foot of his bed. When he awoke the nightmare had begun.

They wasted no time on the front door. It was ruthlessly battered down in seconds, and a black-uniformed officer of the SS led the German troops up the stairs to drag out Theo and Francine from their bed. A moment later they had their Jew. Duparc stood, dazed and terrified, between two German soldiers. He stared blankly at Theo, his eyes haunted, exposing the terror that was turning his stomach to water. Then they bundled him roughly down the stairs.

Theo did not protest. It would be useless. They had both lived with this possibility for a long time, and he knew they could expect no mercy. He put his arm around his wife's shoulders and politely asked if they could put on some clothes.

The officer stared at them for a moment, then nodded to one of the troopers.

'Stay with them.'

Theo thanked him and led Francine back into their bedroom, closely followed by the German soldier.

Theo dressed unhurriedly, watching Francine do the same. He'd always felt a small glow of desire when seeing her put on and take off her clothes. Even now, at the age of 63 and with a German soldier in her bedroom, there was a delicacy, a graceful femininity, about her movements that pleased him.

She buttoned up her dress and turned to him. 'Should I wear my cardigan, Theo?'

He studied her face with infinite longing and tenderness, stretching the moment endlessly. Then he smiled.

'Yes, you will need the cardigan. There is an early chill in the air.'

She looked deeply into her husband's eyes, seeing his love. She nodded understandingly.

'Of course, I'd forgotten how cold it can be this early in the morning.'

She turned to the soldier. 'I wonder if you'd be kind enough to pass me that cardigan on the chair behind you.'

The young man glanced at them both briefly, sensing their intensity. But he could see no danger in the request. He turned and picked up the red cardigan. As he did so both Theo and Francine took a small pill from the pockets of their clothing and placed it in their mouths.

They reached across the bed as the soldier turned back. Their fingers touched, their hands clasped and simultaneously they bit hard on the pills.

The cyanide killed them almost at once and they fell together on the bed where they had shared their lives and now their death.

Later a furious SS officer left the farm, clutching the picture from Duparc's room. He intended to have that at least.

He knew it was good.

CHAPTER TEN

The two machines droned along the drowsy country road like a couple of sedate bumblebees enjoying a lazy summer afternoon, Hillier on his red Harley-Davidson and Joe on the dull green BSA 720 with which Hillier had originally pursued him. Less powerful than the American's flashy machine, it was standard issue for the British Army, but it would run for ever.

Hillier was tense and alert. He wasn't sure of their position; he didn't know whether they were behind the advanced columns heading for the Seine crossing or ahead of them. He yelled across at Joe.

'You sure you know where we are?'

The Englishman waved a nonchalant arm. 'It's OK. I've been this way before. We'll be there in half an hour.'

Hillier cursed silently under his breath. He wished to God he'd never agreed to this trip. But he could hardly refuse to look at the proposed base for their operations, since he had suggested the setting up of it in the first place. He'd already made contact with at least thirty men who were willing to join them. The corporal Joe had nearly battered to death in the club had been a bonus. Gus Kenwright was about as close to the typical bull-necked NCO as you could get – except that he'd had a bellyful of the army and was keen to lick their planned enterprise into shape.

They passed over a crossroads and entered a one-street village that at first seemed empty of life. Then, faintly, they heard the sound of a brass band trying very hard to play 'In the Mood'.

They rounded a bend and found themselves faced by a village square jammed with a jostling crowd in fairly high spirits. In the centre, in full regalia, was the local brass band. But the crowd's attention was centred on something else that neither Joe nor Hillier could see through the throng.

Then suddenly someone saw them. In moments they were surrounded by an exuberant crowd delighted to see their uniforms. One of them pressed a bottle of wine into Joe's hand. He took a healthy swig and handed it back. Then he saw what had been attracting the crowd's attention.

Watching them with a glimmer of reborn hope in their eyes were about forty German prisoners under the guns of a few French resistance fighters.

One of the Maquis was older than the others – Joe estimated about fifty. His hair was close-cropped, steely grey. A thick-set man with a short neck and a shorter temper.

He approached Joe, eyeing him with disfavour, but his English was good. He nodded peremptorily and indicated the prisoners.

'I'm pleased to see you. We can hand these over to you now.'

Joe suddenly realized he had a problem. He glanced at Hillier, who was making the most of a friendly reception by a well endowed country girl. Hillier's hands were full.

Joe turned back to the Frenchman. He smiled deprecatingly and tapped the dispatch box on his machine. 'Can't do that. I, er, we have urgent signals to deliver to our units.' He smiled again and added. 'But the Armoured Brigade are not far behind. You hang on to them for now.'

The Frenchman was not convinced. He gazed at Joe, irritated by the delay.

'Hang on to them?'

Joe nodded, and signalled urgently to Hillier. 'That's right, for now, until tomorrow at the latest.'

Hillier managed to get his hands off the heaving bosoms of the girl and revved his way through the crowd, who continued to slap him on the back as he rode clear of them. Joe waved briefly to the Maquis leader and took off after him.

Once clear of the volatile crowd in the square, they accelerated up the main street and out of the village.

The brass band had now swung into Glenn Miller's 'Little Brown Jug'. It sounded no better than 'In the Mood', except that they were hitting more sharps than flats.

Hillier yelled at Joe above the noise of the engines. 'Jesus Christ, did you see her tits?'

Joe shook his head disgustedly. 'See them? You couldn't take your hands off them.'

Hillier threw back his head and laughed.

'They were beautiful, like works of art. They talked to me, Joe.'

Porter yelled across, 'Oh, yeah? What did they say?'

Hillier took his hands off the handlebars and cupped them in front of him. 'Don't leave,' he yelled back. 'Don't leave!'

Hillier was elated by the reception and the exultation of the crowd. As far as the French were concerned, the war was over. But the American was too sharp to be complacent. One thing still worried him. Joe had said the Armoured Division were *behind* them. He kept his head down and his eyes open.

Five minutes after leaving the village Joe waved him behind and pointed to a turning on the right.

It was the entrance to the *château*. They throttled down until their engines made as little noise as possible and rode slowly up the drive. There was no sign of life apart from two cows chewing silently on the cud, but as they drew closer to the front of the house, Joe could see that the sign he had nailed to the door was still in place.

They dismounted and kicked down the back stand supports for their bikes, facing the machines down the drive in case they had to make a quick getaway.

Joe took the Colt from beneath his camouflaged para smock and signalled Hillier to follow him. He began to work his way around to the back of the *château*. The stables were off to the left, clear of the house and the garden where Joe had buried the German soldier. From behind the stables they could hear the sound of voices, women's voices.

Hillier sighed with relief, but Joe didn't put the gun away – not yet. They walked quickly across the cobbled courtyard and between the stables. The sharp smell of manure wrinkled Hillier's nose, and as they came to the rear of the buildings the cause of the aroma became clear.

A small mountain of the stuff, some of it steaming freshly on the top, occupied the corner of a makeshift vegetable garden. There were rows of potatoes, onions and lettuces. The three women were working on the bean poles, picking the long green runners and placing them in a single basket.

The vegetable garden extended some hundred yards or so behind the stables, but as far as Joe could see, only the women occupied it.

He put the gun away and advanced from the corner of the stables. Annette saw him first. She thrust the beans in her hand into the pocket of her summer dress and rushed towards him, throwing her arms around his neck. She kissed him passionately, twice before Joe could disentangle himself. He pushed her gently away and indicated the American standing just behind him.

'This is Hillier.'

Maria had already dropped her sensuous eye upon his American uniform and come to a decision. Hillier too had got the message. Maria sauntered towards him, wiping her hands on her rough cotton skirt. The white blouse gaped open at the neck, emphasizing her brown, smooth skin.

She looked him up and down and Hillier smiled. He felt as if he had been undressed – not that he minded.

Joe glanced quickly from one to the other and decided it would be a shame to interrupt their interplay with an introduction. They were doing fine.

He looked past them at the old woman still standing among the bean poles. She stared at him impassively for a long moment, then resumed her work without a word.

Joe turned away and indicated the house to Hillier.

'Come on, I think you'll like this.'

The American grinned, looking hard at Maria. 'I like it already.'

But he followed Joe, glancing behind him to see if Maria was coming. The two girls linked arms and laughed, enjoying a confidence. Joe's and Hillier's short-term future had been decided.

Porter flicked on the light in the basement and crossed the stone floor, pulling back a heavy green tarpaulin to expose the press. He glanced back at Hillier.

'What do you think?'

The American walked slowly towards the machinery and examined it carefully. It was in perfect condition and well looked after. He turned triumphantly to Joe.

'Oh boy, this is really something. What's it doing *here*?'

Joe shrugged, then glanced behind him up the steep stairs. He could hear the girls in the kitchen.

'I'm not sure. But Jerry used this house a lot and not just for the company. Whatever it was, I don't think it matters. That thing's ours now.'

Hillier turned back to the printing press.

'We can do anything with this thing. Print forms, authorizations, passes – anything we need.'

Joe nodded, grimly. 'That's what I thought.'

Hillier started pacing around the basement agitatedly. 'Jesus, don't you see it, Joe?' He looked at the Englishman, his eyes glittering with excitement. 'The guys I've contacted, some of them on the run and others wanting out. We could set up here, turn it into a complete bona fide unit. Just like this was a transport section base, like the one you and Eddie work out of.'

Joe could see the possibilities but he didn't want Eddie going AWOL. Not yet.

'We'll keep Eddie in there. He can be our contact, give us the information when the convoys are moving up to the front and what they're carrying.'

Hillier shook his head. 'No, no, we don't want any of that. It's not the goods we need, it's the trucks. *Everyone* needs transportation, army or civilian. Be much easier and give us a lot less flak if we just hijack the odd truck here and there until we have what we need. That way no one is going to get on to us. We can still use Eddie for inside information. That corporal in the club, Kenwright. He can help us too.'

Joe smiled, pleased with the plan.

'Yeah, we can set up guard positions at the end of the drive. Fuel is no problem. As long as we stay in uniform we can use the dumps. No one asks any questions.'

A burst of laughter from the kitchen filtered into the basement. Hillier pointed up the stairs.

'What about them?'

'No trouble. The girls need us to protect them from the village.'

'And the old lady?'

Joe remembered the German in the wardrobe. 'She needs to be on the right side too.'

Hillier slapped him on the back.

'Let's fraternize a little with the ladies.' He grinned in anticipation. 'I think she likes me, Joe, and I intend to enjoy the fruits of war, pardner.'

He bounded up the stairs, and Joe followed more slowly, after he had covered up the press.

The grandmother was in the kitchen. Joe had an idea she had placed herself there deliberately to embarrass them or to postpone any intentions that he or Hillier or the girls might have. The old lady was already too late as far as he was concerned, and he realized that she must know that too. She stood by the range stirring something, probably out of sheer cussedness.

The atmosphere between Hillier and Maria was pretty electric, with or without her presence, and Maria was making no secret of her desire for the American. She glanced at Joe calculatingly, and he began to understand the game. It was partly for her sister's benefit, partly for his. She was getting her own back because he had preferred Annette.

Joe helped himself to the jug of red wine on the table and sat down. Annette promptly placed herself on his lap and smiled wickedly at Maria.

There was no warning.

The kitchen door burst open and two Wehrmacht soldiers, their uniforms encrusted with grime, covered them with Schmeissers. The front door crashed open at the same time and heavy boots thudded down the passage to the kitchen. Two more Schmeissers pointed at them from the doorway.

Joe sat very still. There was nothing he could do. With Annette on his lap he was immobilized – she had practically saved his life. He kept his hands on the table and sat perfectly still. He could feel Annette trembling.

He heard more footsteps from the passage and an officer came into the kitchen carrying a Luger. He paused in the doorway and took in the frozen tableau.

He smiled and said something in French and the two girls moved quickly away from Joe and Hillier, joining their grandmother by the range.

The officer turned his attention to Porter and spoke in English.

'Stand up, please – very slowly.'

Joe raised himself carefully, always keeping his hands in full view. He could see these men were not novices, and he suspected that the only reason they had not tossed a grenade in first and asked questions later was because they were trying to keep their presence in the area as quiet as possible. The situation was fluid.

The officer inspected Joe curiously.

'That is a paratrooper's smock. I've seen them before at Pegasus Bridge, but I don't think the rest of it is quite right.'

He indicated Joe's feet.

'Brown boots are not standard issue for British paras, unless you are an officer.' He drummed his fingers on the top of the table and the sound echoed strangely around the silent kitchen. 'Take off the smock, please, but don't let me lose sight of your hands otherwise I shall be forced to kill you.' He waved the Luger expressively.

Joe pulled the smock very slowly over his head, making absolutely no move to go for the Colt in his belt. This was not the time or the place. He dropped the smock by his side.

The officer smiled.

'As I thought, you are merely a private. Put the gun on the table, please. Hold it by the barrel.'

Joe did so, pushing it into the centre, away from his reach.

The officer looked at Hillier.

'Now, why are you here? There are no American troops in this section.'

Hillier grinned. 'I got lost.'

The German officer's face hardened and he spoke very quietly. 'Don't take me for a fool. You cannot entirely lose contact with the American forces when you have such a colourful machine outside.'

Mentally Hillier kicked himself. He'd forgotten the bike.

'Well, not entirely lost, but enough to find myself in the wrong section and behind the German lines.'

He shot Joe an evil look, then waited to see if the officer would take the bait. But he didn't respond with any information. He turned to one of the troopers and barked something in German. The soldier stepped forward and prodded Joe in the back with the Schmeisser.

Joe saw Annette's hand fly to her mouth in horror and he guessed what the order had been. These men were desperate. He knew they were cut off from the main German forces who had retreated from this section, and they would not be taking any prisoners.

He and Hillier were marched from the kitchen and along the passage to the front door. Joe realized he didn't have much time and he was ready to leap at whatever slim chance presented itself.

As he was pushed through the front door with Hillier he heard the sound of an armoured car coming up the drive to the *château*.

It was German.

He saw the machine-gun barrel twist towards them and was suddenly aware that stone and woodwork were splintering around him. He and Hillier dived to the ground as one of the German troopers behind him screamed in pain.

Joe didn't wait to find out what was happening or why. He grabbed Hillier's arm and ran, crouching, as fast as he could for the corner of the building. What saved them was the movement of the vehicle itself. It turned to give the gunner a better angle, causing him to lose accuracy for a moment. The lead ricocheted from the stone-work, but they made it to the corner and ran towards the stables.

The gap between the buildings echoed the sound of their booted feet, then they ran clear into the vegetable garden.

Both of them stopped. Hillier looked around him in dismay. He could hear the sound of pursuit closing up behind him and there was no cover at all. The garden ended in a flat ploughed field, and they'd be taken out before they made a hundred yards across it.

Joe grabbed his arm. 'Come on,' he screamed. He dragged the American past the rows of bean poles and pointed. 'In there!'

Hillier stared.

'In that?'

Joe grabbed his tunic front with one hand. In the other, as if by magic, was a wickedly gleaming knife.

'It's either that or this,' he snarled.

Hillier swallowed hard. 'OK, that.' He could hear feet clattering on the cobblestones, running to the gap between the stables.

They both dropped down on their bellies and pushed their way, feet first, into the loose, steaming mess of the manure.

Hillier felt the bile rising in his stomach, and he heaved. Joe heard him retch and knew that if the American threw up, they were as good as dead. He stuck the knife about a quarter of an inch into

Hillier's arm. The American was so shocked by the sight of his own blood that he forgot about the overpowering stench.

Joe whispered savagely in his ear, 'Breathe in, hold it and then cover your head with your arms.' He dragged the reluctant American into the small mountain of shit with him.

Hiller didn't know how long he stayed inside that soft, fetid mass. He held his head down between his hands and arms, creating a small space for him to breathe. The air, if it could be called that, burnt the back of his throat, and there was not a single moment of that experience when he did not think he was about to pass out. Dimly he could hear the shouts and yells as the Germans searched for them through the vegetable garden and in the stables. Then slowly the noise faded. He felt a sharp pain in his arm as Joe grabbed it and pulled him slowly out.

Hillier gazed at him in amazement. He was covered from head to foot in the brown, evil-smelling stuff. Only his eyes, nose and mouth were untouched.

For some unaccountable reason Hillier felt an incredible desire to laugh.

'Jesus Christ, Joe, you really are a shitty sod.'

He threw back his head to laugh, but suddenly the knife point was tickling the flesh under his chin.

'You make one tiny little sound, Hillier, and I'll carve you up a slice of throat.'

The laugh died, constricted in his mouth. Hillier's Adam's apple bobbed uncomfortably against the sharp blade. His throat was dry with fear.

'Where are they?'

Porter didn't bother to answer. He moved off towards the wall of the stables and flattened himself against it, peering through the gap into the cobblestone courtyard beyond. It was silent, empty. Nothing moved.

He signalled to Hillier who joined him. Before Porter could move off the American grabbed his arm.

'Listen, you asshole, what the hell's goin' on?'

Porter looked at him and Hillier felt his blood run cold. There was in his eyes a blankness, a frozen inhumanity, that melted his hot anger as though it had not existed.

Porter turned away, ignoring him. Holding the knife loosely by the blade, ready to throw it if he had to, he advanced slowly to the cobbled courtyard.

He heard a horse snort and move restlessly in one of the stables, picking up his sour, pervasive smell. He suddenly realized the horse could betray him unless he could keep downwind.

He wiped his finger on some grass, trying to remove the muck, then stuck it in his mouth, wetting it. The taste was foul, but by holding his finger up to the faint breeze he was able to work out its direction.

So far, so good. It was blowing away from the house.

He checked the courtyard again. It was empty. One by one he went meticulously through each stable box. Only one was occupied by a horse. That left just the house.

He went back to Hillier.

'Wait until I reach the back door, then get across as quickly as you can.'

Hillier didn't like the sound of it one bit. They were unarmed, apart from Porter's knife. He watched Joe zig-zag across the open space between the stables and the house, but the *château* remained silent. Now it was his turn. He took a deep breath and ran from the corner of the stable as fast and as straight as he could. He slammed into the wall beside Joe and stood there, gasping for breath but still in one piece.

Joe gave him the knife.

'Stay here. I'm going round the front. There's a Thompson on the bike. I'll go in through the main door. If anyone bolts out through this one, use that.'

He indicated the knife.

Hillier didn't argue. He just nodded his acceptance.

He felt nothing but a huge sense of relief. He didn't want to go into that house. It was too quiet, too still, and he feared what he might find there.

Joe slipped around the corner of the building until he came to the point where it bordered the long drive. The two cows still grazed peacefully, oblivious of the battles for life and death surrounding them. He stared balefully at them, covered from head to foot in their muck, yet aware that but for the heap of shit in the vegetable garden he'd probably be dead.

He poked his head round the front of the building for a second. Nothing.

The two bikes still stood where they had placed them. They seemed undamaged, but he couldn't be sure from this distance.

He crouched below the level of the windows and moved swiftly, staying close to the wall. He reached the stone steps leading up the double doors of the main entrance. They were open and splintered by the automatic fire from the armoured car. But he could see no sign of the German who had been hit.

He flattened himself to the ground and, using the steps for protection, crawled on his belly as close to the bikes as he could get.

Now he had no option. If there was someone inside covering the entrance, he would be seen. All he had on his side was speed and surprise. They wouldn't be expecting anyone moving from his position.

He tensed, sprang upwards to grab the Thompson from the clip on the handlebars, then rolled down sideways to the front wall of the house.

There had been no response at all, not even a shout.

Joe slid along until he was by the steps again. Quietly he climbed over the iron rail protecting each side of the steps as they fanned out into the drive. Now he was standing beside the open double doors. Joe didn't hesitate. He slipped smoothly into the cool shade of the entrance hall and crouched in the well of the staircase. It gave him a good view of the passage into the kitchen.

He could see a pool of blood gleaming darkly on the wood floor of the entrance hall. He started to slide, his back to the wall, down the passage. As he got closer he smelt something cooking and heard a faint bubbling sound.

It was soup, steaming gently on the range in a large black pot. No sign of the women.

Joe cleared the ground-floor area, then made his way upstairs. That too was clear. The house was empty. But Joe didn't relax. There was still the basement. He went to the back door and pushed it open, remaining just inside the entrance. He didn't want his throat cut by an over-zealous Yank. He called softly.

'Hillier – it's me.'

He heard a faint scraping noise as the American moved along the wall, then an anxious face appeared in front of him.

'What happened?'

Joe shrugged. 'I'm not sure. The house seems empty, but I haven't checked the basement yet.' He stared at the American. 'Have you got any weapons apart from my knife?'

Hillier nodded. 'Yeah, in the dispatch box on the bike.'

Joe's face betrayed his disgust. Hillier spread his hands.

'Well, it's difficult on a bike.'

He clumped past Joe and out through the entrance hall to the front of the house before Joe could stop him. He might be a whizzkid with the ideas, but he wouldn't last long in combat areas if he didn't learn fast. Joe waited impassively for him to come back.

He had a P38 hand-gun, which he waved impressively. Joe sighed. The way he was carrying the bloody thing, he wouldn't hit a barn door at three paces.

'Is it loaded?' he asked laconically.

Hillier snorted his impatience.

'Of course it's loaded.' He stared at Joe affronted.

Porter pointed at the weapon. 'The catch. Release the catch, otherwise it won't go off.'

Hillier swore. 'Shit, I never was any good with these goddam things.' He handed Joe his knife. 'You'd better take this too. I'll probably cut myself,' he said disgustedly.

Joe folded the hunting knife and slipped it inside his sock.

He turned towards the staircase. The door to the basement was locked. Joe glanced at the American. Hillier grimaced.

'If they're down there, they sure as hell know we're here.'

Joe grinned. 'Let's find out.'

He reached across and banged heavily on the door. The sound echoed harshly through the empty house.

'Anyone there?' he yelled.

At first there was silence, then he heard someone move near the bottom of the stairs in the basement.

'Joe?'

He recognized the voice. It was Annette.

'Yes,' he called out. 'Are you all right?'

He heard her walking up the stairs and the bolts being pushed back in the door. She threw herself into his arms and kissed him, then drew back in disgust, wiping the muck from her hands. She looked at them.

'You are covered in *merde*!'

Porter looked surprised. 'That's not mud. It's muck, fertilizer or manure if you prefer it.'

Hillier tapped him on the shoulder. '*Merde* is French for . . .' He spread his hands uncomfortably, glancing at Annette. 'Manure,' he finished lamely.

Maria and her grandmother emerged from the basement and reacted with distaste to the evil-smelling excrement that clung to their uniforms and hair.

The old lady immediately took charge, issuing a string of orders to the girls. Baths were organized and washing for the clothing. Joe and Hillier were stripped, bathed and clothed in dressing-gowns.

Only when they were all sitting round the kitchen table once more did Hillier get a chance to broach the question that had been bothering him ever since they had walked out of the front door into the hail of lead from the German armoured vehicle.

'Why did he open up, hitting one of their own guys? We were prisoners, for Chrissake. And then why did they disappear so quickly?'

Joe broke off a piece of bread and spread some farm butter on it.

'They didn't know we were prisoners. It was a different unit. The view through the slits in those things isn't very good. All they would have seen is our bikes sitting outside the front door and us coming through it, so they opened fire.

'They shifted out pronto because they've been left behind. They're separated from the main Panzer Corps, and they're getting back across the Seine as fast as they can. That's why the officer was taking us outside to be chopped. He wouldn't have used guns – they make too much noise – and he didn't want to attract any attention. Once their position was blown by the armour, they slipped out and didn't find us in the muck heap.'

Hillier grimaced. He didn't want to be reminded of that. His hand went automatically to the bandage that Maria had tied tenderly around his arm. Joe saw the movement and smiled sardonically at Hillier, while he slowly chewed some bread. Hillier knew he would never have ducked under that stinking muck if Joe hadn't stuck him with the knife – but he didn't feel grateful to the Englishman for saving his life.

He knew Joe had enjoyed sticking the knife in his arm.

By morning the uniforms were dry and Hillier was exhausted. He wondered how a nineteen-year-old like Maria knew so much about bedroom arts and sciences.

But he had learnt something else too. The *château* was the ideal place to set up their planned operations. If it could be handled properly, with Joe up front on the bike, doing what he did best, finding new openings, bringing back information, and Eddie Pearce staying within the transport unit structure, feeding them the data they needed. They could make a fortune.

With his own sharp eye for detail and organization, a bogus transport group could set up here to move whatever they wanted from A to B and to supply whatever needs would make the fastest buck.

Hillier smiled quietly to himself. That's what he really wanted – some big, fast bucks.

They quit the *château* around ten that morning, waving their goodbyes to Annette and Maria and promising to return soon. The girls didn't know how soon, or on what scale, but Hillier had made his plans and Maria was just a detail – a very pleasant detail. It was the set-up he wanted to fix, and he was impatient to get started.

They rode back towards the village they had come through before, and as they drew closer they heard the grinding roar of heavy diesel engines and tracked vehicles.

They were the Sherman tanks of the 11th Armoured Division, heading up fast to a very fluid German front line that was falling back, trying to set up new positions across the Seine.

Joe and Hillier pulled their bikes into the side of the main street, watching the heavy tanks roll by in a cloud of dust. The people waved enthusiastically and Hillier spotted the big-breasted girl whom he had rested his hands upon briefly thirty-six hours before. Somehow she had climbed up on to the turret of a slow-moving tank. And a surprised but delighted Hussar's officer was having the same trouble keeping his hands off her delightfully heaving bosom.

Joe heard a voice in his ear and turned. It was the steely-eyed leader of the Maquis who had tried to hand him the problem of the German prisoners. The Frenchman indicated the tanks.

'It's real now. At last they are here.'

Joe rubbed a piece of grit from his eye, hoping the Frenchman wasn't bearing a grudge. 'Did you hand the prisoners over OK?'

He stared at Joe, puzzled.

'No.'

It was Joe's turn to be surprised. 'Why not? What happened?'

The Frenchman shrugged. 'There was no need.'

Joe still hadn't connected. 'What do you mean?' The Maquis leader offered the Englishman a piece of chewing tobacco, which Porter declined. Joe asked again, 'Where are the prisoners?'

The Frenchman's eyes widened slightly in surprise. 'They are all dead, of course.'

'Dead!'

'That's right. You told us to hang on to them so we did. Now they are dead.'

Joe was staggered. He looked at Hillier in disbelief, then back at the Frenchman.

'I said hang on to them until the others got here.'

The Frenchman gazed at him in mock innocence. 'You said hang on to them, *monsieur*. We did. We hanged them all yesterday after you'd gone.'

Joe and Hillier stared at him. They suddenly realized the Frenchman wasn't joking. The American turned away in disgust and spat into the road as the last tank rumbled by.

'Come on, let's get out of here.'

As they rode out Joe understood that Maria and Annette had every reason to fear retribution from the resistance fighters in the village. The Frenchman had known exactly what he had been doing – there'd been no real misunderstanding. There would be no mercy if they got their hands on the women in the *château*.

They'd have to be careful.

CHAPTER
ELEVEN

Lissette was working in her office, involved in the usual bureaucratic paperwork that had become almost a way of life since the occupation. Just to get films at all was becoming increasingly difficult as the war effort monopolized more and more of the transport facilities.

She did not know how long he had been standing there, but somehow she became aware of his presence. Manfred was in the doorway, watching her, and as she glanced up she caught the look of pain in his eyes before he had a chance to mask it.

She knew immediately something was wrong and she froze inside, not daring to move or speak.

Manfred saw the fear on her face and took a pace towards her, closing the door quietly behind him. When he turned she had composed herself, but the tears still lurked behind her eyes.

He stood silently in the middle of the office, not knowing how to tell her. Lissette could see his confusion and she made it easy for him.

'What's happened?'

'It's Duparc. The Gestapo have him.'

She sat quite still, the words echoing in her head like a bad dream. She had dreaded this, half expected it but always pushed it from her mind, hoping it would go away. But now it was happening – she knew it was real. Manfred was real, standing mutely before her, his eyes full of love and concern for her.

She swallowed, trying desperately to hang on to her composure. 'Theo and Francine, are they . . .?' She tailed off, seeing the look on his face.

'They are dead,' he said quietly. 'They took their own lives before they could be escorted from the farm.'

She stared at him piteously, like a child, searching his face as though hoping to find it was not true, desperately hoping he could make it all go away.

Manfred had never felt so helpless in his life. Instinctively he did the best thing he could. He held out his arms as her face crumpled, her control shattered.

She ran for the comfort of his embrace, burying herself in his warmth, clinging to him as he wrapped his strength around her.

She sobbed out the pain deep within her, an emotional dam bursting as she remembered the Peeters, and her own brief moment of peace and joy when her mother had gone. And she had Theo and Francine and the farm and the horses to herself.

As though reading her thoughts, she heard Manfred say she must not go back there. That the Gestapo had the farm under surveillance. She looked up at him quickly, brushing the tears from her eyes, suddenly aware of the dangers for him if anyone made the connection.

'Do they know about us?'

He shook his head vigorously. 'No. I have been keeping my eyes open. I found out through a routine check. If they knew anything about us, they would either have arrested me at once or kept it from me.'

Even as he spoke, the next thoughts were racing through her head.

'My mother, they will know about her . . .'

Manfred had already considered that possibility.

'I don't know – maybe, maybe not. It depends how they got their information. It's possible they heard about the safe house from an informer and just happened to pick up Duparc when it was raided. They may not know of his liaison with your mother. They were not married, were they?'

Lissette absorbed that.

It was possible, though as far as she knew her mother had been married only once, to her father. And as soon as she was pregnant, she had made his life a misery, making no secret of her lovers. She had disgraced her mild, weak father and received a handsome settlement for releasing him.

Manfred took his handkerchief from his pocket and handed it to her. He watched silently as she dabbed the tears from her eyes. He wanted to get out of this office. He needed to walk, to think this thing through. And there was something else he hadn't yet told her, something she had to know. He indicated the desk and the pile of papers.

'Can you leave this? We could go to the park. It's nice today.'

She straightened her hair, mentally preparing herself for the world outside, knowing that no hint of her information could be displayed. Only she could know how Theo and Francine had died. Another secret, another burden she had to carry alone.

But that was not true, not any more. She looked at Manfred. She did have someone to share it with, someone who cared.

She sighed, shudderingly, feeling an enormous sense of relief, sensing the dead weight lift from inside her. She smiled at him and reached up, touching his face tenderly. 'I shall only be a moment. They mustn't see me looking like this, must they?'

Lissette went into the small ante-room and he watched her as she stood in front of the mirror, dabbing on some powder to disguise her grief.

He wondered how, on the worst day of all, he could tell her . . .

They came out of the gloom of the Cinéac into the bright, hot sunshine and turned left down Quelling Straat. Manfred squinted, trying to adjust his eyes. The glare was fierce after the comparative coolness and shade of the cinema, and the heat bounced back off the pavement. He wished he did not have to wear his heavy Luftwaffe tunic. When they reached the park he would take it off.

They did not speak. Lissette held on to his arm, trying to blot out the terrible picture that flashed through her mind when she considered the suicides of Theo and Francine. Manfred had not told her how they killed themselves and she was grateful. She did not want to know. At least they had died together.

It struck her immediately that she was trying to rationalize the horror of their collective decision to die rather than submit themselves to the torture of the Gestapo. But the rationalization gave her comfort. She was glad they had died together. In spite of Manfred's confidence, which she knew was his way of protecting her, it was possible that Duparc might crack and expose them. Manfred could be shot.

She looked up at him, her face revealing her sudden fear.

'Manfred . . .'

He stopped her, squeezing her hand.

'No, not here – wait until we are in the park.' He pointed to the Y-junction ahead, and they crossed the road, entering Stadspark and cutting off the murmur of traffic. They found a quiet spot close to one of the ponds.

Manfred took off his tunic and spread it on the grass, loosening the collar of his shirt. They sat down together. It seemed as if they had this place to themselves. Lissette stared down at the gleaming water and told him of her fear.

Manfred listened, watching a solitary butterfly flutter around a dazzling flower bed, as if uncertain on which bud it would alight first.

There was no room for uncertainty in his own mind. Too much depended upon taking the right precautions – there was no margin for error. He understood her fear, but there was still hope. He waited until she had finished and chewed thoughtfully on a piece of grass before responding. He looked at her.

'Lissette, there is something I haven't told you.' He paused for a moment, then plunged on. 'I've been ordered to prepare the unit for transportation to the front. They have very few anti-tank weapons left, and the Flakvierling on the roof of your cinema can be used for that purpose.'

Lissette felt like screaming. She didn't want him to go. She needed him here, especially now after what had happened to Theo and Francine. But she contained herself, battening down the panic she felt inside.

'When?' she asked simply.

'We move out tomorrow.'

Lissette could not bring herself to believe it. 'Tomorrow,' she repeated, automatically.

'Yes. We are going to set up positions somewhere to the south of the city.'

He could see she wasn't listening. Her face was blank, un-comprehending. He gripped her arm. She looked at him, and he could see the tears filling her eyes. There was no time for that. He had to get her out of here. He took her other arm and pulled her around to face him.

'Listen to me, Lissette. The Allies will soon be here. I know that. The fact that I have to take a Luftwaffe unit and use an anti-aircraft weapon against tanks is a last resort. When they get here, perhaps even before, you will be in danger, and I don't think it is from the Gestapo. They are too busy trying to save their own skins right now to be interested in us. The danger for you is from those who will be after blood, seeking revenge. They may decide that you are a collaborator.'

Lissette was appalled. She cut across him. 'But I only run the cinema. Someone has to do it.'

'I know that. But once there is a mob, reason plays no part in its actions.'

He put his hand to her cheek, touching it gently, looking deep into her eyes.

'You must go, Lissette. Get out of the city. It doesn't matter where, just so long as you are clear of those who might want to report you.' He smiled. 'They might even be watching us now, seeing you with me, knowing how much I love you.'

She pressed her hand on his. 'Oh, Manfred, I could never hide my feelings for you.'

His face hardened.

'You must – I shall be gone by tomorrow. If anyone ever asks about me, I was just the sergeant in charge of the flak unit.'

She stared at him, wondering if she could ever say that, knowing that he was right, that she might have to.

He looked past her across the park at the twin steeples of St Josef's church on the Loosplats. His eyes came back to her. He held her hand tightly.

'Do you love me, Lissette?'

She stared at him for a long moment. 'How can you ask?'

She fell into his arms and he held her, stroking her hair, caressing her tenderly with his big hands. Then he lifted her to her feet, picking up his tunic.

'Let's go,' he said quietly. 'I want you to come with me.'

Lissette did not question him. She was not even curious. She was simply content to spend the rest of this last day with him.

They walked arm in arm through the sunlit park until they came to the Loosplats exit. They crossed the junction and entered the white stone archway into St Josef.

Inside they paused for a while, allowing their eyes to adjust to the dim interior. The church was empty. The strange hush that always descends in a church, stilling the sounds from outside, reminded Lissette of how long it had been since she had entered a place of worship.

She did not know why Manfred had brought her here, but somehow it seemed appropriate, and she felt a sense of calmness quelling some of her fears.

She turned to one of the empty pews near the rear of the church, but Manfred shook his head and guided her down the aisle closer to the altar.

He stopped just in front of it. Lissette looked at him, wondering what his intentions were. He indicated one of the pews and followed Lissette, kneeling to face the altar. She knelt beside him, closing her eyes in prayer.

When she looked up, Manfred was watching her. Silently he took her hand. His voice was quiet, almost a whisper in the silent church. She listened, dazed at first, then with a growing awareness of how deeply she loved him.

'Lissette, ever since yesterday when I found out that I had to leave, I wanted somehow to show you . . .' He paused momentarily. 'No, that's not right. I think you know how much I love you – what I really wanted to do was to seal that love. I want you to marry me, Lissette. I want to do it now, here in this church. Just you and me, before God and in our own eyes. And I want you to promise me something.' He searched her face, waiting for her response.

Lissette swallowed, trying not to let her tears spoil this moment. Dumbly she nodded her acceptance.

Manfred lifted her hand and touched it with his lips. 'Will you promise that if anything should happen to me, you will find someone else who will take care of you?' He blinked. 'I could not bear it if I thought you would ever be left alone.'

Lissette took his face between her hands and kissed him softly.

'Manfred, there is no one else. I could never feel this way about another man.'

'Promise me,' he insisted gently.

She gazed at him silently for a long moment. She nodded her agreement, unable to say the words.

Manfred looked at her, recognizing her vulnerability, knowing that once he left she would be alone. He wanted to crush her in his arms to protect her from that world outside. Instead he took her hand in his and faced the altar of the church.

Together they quietly vowed their love. Their hushed voices echoing strangely in the empty church. Then they stood and walked slowly back up the aisle and out into the bright sunshine of this first Friday of September.

Next day Manfred left with his unit after saying his goodbyes to Lissette in the privacy of her apartment. They did not remove the Flakvierling anti-aircraft gun from the roof of the cinema. It would have taken too long and it did not carry enough punch to be effective against tanks. Instead they linked their Luftwaffe truck to an 88-millimetre, and moved westwards out of Antwerp towards Ghent.

The roads were already crowded with vehicles and heavy columns moving in the opposite direction. Some of them were well armed and it was clear that the Wehrmacht was in full retreat.

Karl Hausser, who was sharing the cab of the truck with Manfred, was beginning to show some concern. He pointed to a Tiger tank rumbling as quickly as it could back the way they had come.

'Sergeant, why are we going this way when everyone is retreating?'

Manfred could hear the panic lying just behind the question. Hausser was a good young gunner. He had manned the Flakvierling through some of the most intense bombing raids on Antwerp without flinching, but for the first time he was seeing an army in full flight, and Manfred was not surprised that it had undermined his resolve. He had been mentally questioning his orders for the last thirty miles. But before he could come to a decision the matter was taken from his control.

He watched in amazement as one half of a staff car pirouetted skyward on a rising column of flame some five hundred yards ahead. Automatically his foot slammed down on to the brake pedal, but before his vehicle could respond, a black shadow thundered just above the road, spitting fire from its wings, tearing men and machines apart, as it traced a pattern of lead directly down the centre of the scattering column towards him.

He knew he had no time to stop. He jerked the heavy steering wheel round, trying to run the truck off the road before the armour piercing cannon hit them. But the truck was going too fast. It skidded sideways violently, and the bullets thudded into the rear of the vehicle, killing and maiming the rest of his unit travelling there. Manfred heard their screams as he wrestled with the wheel. The tyres suddenly gripped the macadam as the back of the truck ignited. It plunged through some wooden fencing at the side of the road and careered down a short embankment. As it came to the bottom the front wheels dug into the soft earth, trying to lift the heavy front axle, but before they could do so the nose of the vehicle buried itself into the ground and flipped the burning lorry over. It was rolled on to its side, whipping the flak gun round in a huge arc before it broke free of the cartwheeling truck.

The machine came to a halt in a mass of twisted, burning wreckage. Then the petrol tank exploded and set off the boxes of ammunition.

Hausser lay, inert, in the soft ground where he had been flung from the cab, burying his head in his arms until the lethal fusillade of ammunition gradually subsided. He lifted his head tentatively, looking to see if anyone else had survived, then he felt a sharp pain in his arm. Blood had stained through his torn tunic and dripped from the fingers of his hand.

He stood up, trying to make his fingers work, but they were numb and refused to obey him. He looked back up at the main road. No one had taken the slightest notice of the carnage that had enveloped his truck and killed his comrades.

He yelled for help, but the columns marched stolidly by, ignoring him. Painfully he climbed back up on to the main road. Then he understood. All around him were burning vehicles and ugly, crumpled bodies, some barely recognizable as human. Hausser felt the gorge rising in his throat and he couldn't stop it. He threw up on the side of the road and stood there coughing, tears of fear and pain streaming down his face.

He was lucky. An ambulance, moving slowly through the wrecked machinery and men, pulled up beside him, and a medical orderly silently pulled him inside and began to tear off the sleeve of his tunic.

★

In her office Lissette began to put as much in order as she could before she left. She had decided that before she went back to her apartment tonight, after the last screening, she would indicate to the cashier that she wasn't feeling too well and that she might take Monday as well as Sunday off. That would give her some leeway if she had to come back.

She guessed that it might be difficult to get out of the city, and if it was impossible, she wanted her options open.

Remarkably, the Cinéac was continuing to function in spite of the growing sense of siege and excitement. How long it could continue was doubtful. They were working on a day-to-day basis, but incredibly, in spite of the situation in Antwerp as the Allies drew closer, people still wanted to come to the cinema.

Lissette suspected they were trying to hang on to as much normality as they could. Maybe the cinema gave them a sense of continuity as other services gradually broke down. The Cinéac was lucky – it had its own generator so was unaffected by the fickle electricity supply.

Later, Lissette was down by the box office as the last takings were being collated when she heard the sound of a heavy vehicle draw up outside the entrance. She didn't take much notice. It stopped only for a moment, then drew away again. Lissette had her back to the glass doors. She was glancing at the admission numbers for the day, but she felt rather than saw the cashier stop counting and gaze past her at the entrance. Lissette looked up. Then, seeing the cashier's expression, she turned.

At first she didn't recognize the young soldier. His face was streaked with dirt and his arm was in a sling. The empty sleeve of his tunic hung limp and bloodstained by his side.

He was looking at her in a peculiar manner. He seemed apprehensive and at the same time deeply troubled. Then she recognized him. It was Hausser.

He was one of Manfred's unit. She had seen him many times on the roof, and sometimes he had arrived with Manfred for the change-over. She didn't move. She couldn't. All her strength had drained from her body. She didn't want him to speak. Perhaps if he didn't say anything, it would go away. Everything would be the same. Manfred would be alive.

Even as the thought struck her, she knew. She could see it in the young man's face. His eyes were despairing. He took a few paces closer until he was facing her, then opened his mouth to speak. Lissette held up her hand for silence. She studied his face, reading the truth there.

Her voice, when she did speak, seemed to be coming from someone else. It sounded strange and remote. 'How did it happen?'

Hausser blinked, the memory of those awful moments as the truck went off the road making his insides turn to water.

'We were attacked from the air. The lorry crashed down an embankment off the road and caught fire.' He stopped, staring at Lissette, seeing the pain in her eyes.

'And Manfred — Sergeant Kepner, where is he?'

Young Hausser spread his hands hopelessly. He did not know how to tell her, how to ease her taut despair. 'He is dead,' he said simply. 'They are all dead. The truck caught fire.'

Lissette's hand whipped up to cover her mouth as she half cried out.

He stumbled on. 'The truck turned over. I was flung out. No one could have escaped.' He paused, wanting to reach out and touch her but instinctively realizing that if he showed tenderness at this moment, her control would break. He knew how much she had cared for the sergeant, and Manfred had been unable to hide his feelings for her.

Hausser knew a good deal more than he should about Manfred and the manageress of the Cinéac. That was why he had come. The sergeant would have done the same for him. He half turned, indicating the doors behind him.

'I must go now. I have to try to reach the airfield.'

Lissette had not heard what he said. Her mind was blank, refusing to think. But she had seen him look at the doors and she nodded dumbly.

Hausser paused awkwardly. There was something he wanted to say, but he could not find the words.

Lissette saw his struggle. She touched his arm. 'It's all right. I will find him. Where did it happen?'

Hausser mumbled, 'On the main road to Ghent, about thirty miles . . . But it is no use, Fraülein.'

Lissette squeezed his arm tightly, stopping him. 'I understand. Thank you for telling me, Hausser. It was kind of you.'

He stared at her, worried by the strange look in her eyes, the pretence of normality in her voice.

'I'm sorry, *Fräulein*,' he said again. 'Manfred Kepner was a good sergeant and I thought you ought to know.'

Lissette bit her lower lip, and nodded brightly.

'Yes, he was.'

Hausser turned away from her and she watched him walk slowly across the foyer and out of the cinema.

She stood there, unmoving, trying desperately to collect herself together. She heard a voice behind her. It was the cashier.

'Are you all right, *madame*?'

Lissette jerked around, not looking at her, fearing what she might see in her eyes. 'Yes, I'm fine.' She stopped, wondering what she should do. 'I'm going home now.' Then she remembered her plan. 'I don't feel too well. I may not come in on Monday, but I'll let you know.'

She turned and walked back to her office. It seemed to last an eternity, then at last she was able to shut the door behind her. She stood leaning against it, staring blankly at her desk. Something dropped from her face on to the carpet. She gazed at the damp stain, and saw another drop beside it. Her hand went up to her face and came away wet with her tears. She realized she was crying.

Next morning Lissette drove out of Antwerp through the tunnel under the river and was immediately engulfed by hundreds of vehicles as people fled from the city for the second time in four years. She only had one thought in her head. Throughout the empty, sleepless night it had never left her mind. She had to find Manfred. Whatever had happened to him, she could not leave him lying out there in the middle of a war by himself.

He might be wounded, in need of help. If she could find him, she could get him back to Antwerp. And if he were dead, then at least she would know, she would have seen him. That mattered to her.

She inched the car forward, a few paces at a time, hardly making five miles by midday. Then they came to a complete stop. Half an hour later the refugee column was moved off the main road before they had even passed through St Nicolas.

Lissette abandoned the car and tried to continue down the main road on foot, but German soldiers just pushed her towards the side of the road. She guessed that they were trying to keep it clear for the retreating German forces.

She went back to her car and studied a map. Maybe she could get through if she circled around on the subsidiary route, but the car was useless. She parked it at the side of the road and took out a light bag with some food and bandages in it, then set off, trudging along the hot country road, surrounded by a jostling mixture of horses and carts, prams and anything that could transport a few pathetic belongings.

Around three in the afternoon Lissette left the column and crossed a field to a grassy shallow hill where she could rest. Her feet ached, and she slipped off her brown shoes, wriggling her toes in the fresh grass. She stared sightlessly into the half distance, trying to draw some peace from the sunlit meadow, to calm the turmoil inside her. She watched the refugee column beyond the hedgerow moving slowly along. It was too far away for the sound of its progress to intrude into her small haven of peace.

She was glad to be away from the pitiful cries of the babies, thirsty in this heat. She didn't know how much longer she could continue . . . After a while she lay back on the bank and rested, shielding her eyes from the sun, blotting out the cruel world that had taken Manfred from her and left her alone again.

CHAPTER
TWELVE

Eddie Pearce brewed the tea carefully, making sure it was given the right amount of time in the pot to bring it the right colour and taste.

Sergeant Robinson liked his tea sweet and milky, not too weak and not too strong, and today Eddie intended that it should be absolutely as he wanted it. Today he would surprise him. He needed to have Rainy Day Robinson in a good mood. Eddie knocked politely on the solid oak door of the makeshift orderly room and carried in the steaming mug of tea. Robinson looked up from his desk morosely and eyed the Irishman.

'What do you want, Pearce? And if you've come to ask me about that bloody friend of yours, he's still missing.'

Eddie shook his head and placed the mug of tea down in front of the sergeant. 'No, I've given up on Joe. He's a soddin' menace. He's either dead or in bed with some French tart. Taste that.' He indicated the tea.

Robinson surveyed the mug suspiciously.

'What's wrong with it?'

'Sure, there's nothin' wrong with it, sergeant. I was makin' one for meself and I thought you might like one.'

Robinson took a sip, then the taste of the sugar hit him and his face lit up. 'There's sugar in it!'

Eddie smiled. 'Some came in this morning.' He glanced across at the corporal waiting to be charged by Major Matthews. 'Would you like one too?'

Robinson interrupted before the corporal could reply.

'He's about to go up in front of the boss.'

Eddie shrugged his shoulders. 'It's no problem, sergeant. I've already made the pot and it's not often we get sugar. Would you like a refill?'

Robinson accepted the offer with alacrity and swallowed the remains of his tea, handing the mug back to Eddie. 'I never say no to a cup of tea, Pearce.'

Eddie took it and nodded casually to the corporal. 'I'll only be a moment.'

He was back within minutes, carrying two mugs this time. He handed one to Robinson, then crossed the orderly room to the corporal and gave him the other. As he did so, Eddie managed to get his body between Robinson and the corporal and quickly palmed him a rolled-up note. Eddie stared at him warningly and covered the corporal's look of surprise as best he could.

'Drink that,' he said. 'You should like it.' He turned back to Robinson. 'I'll go and have mine now. If you hear anything about Porter, let me know, sarge.'

The sergeant took another swallow of the delicious tea and gazed impassively at the Irishman.

'That silly bugger's finally copped it. I don't suppose we will hear anything unless someone brings in his tags.'

Eddie crossed to the door and opened it, then glanced back at Robinson. 'No, I don't suppose you will, sarge.'

He closed the door and grinned. He waited. He didn't know if the corporal would accept his invitation or not. If he did decide to take the chance, Eddie would not be standing here long.

He heard a thud, and something clattered loudly to the floor, then the door burst open and the corporal came shooting through.

Eddie grabbed his arm and pulled him into the wall out of sight. 'Just follow me.'

The corporal asked no questions. He was committed now.

Eddie raced down the passage that separated the main building from the temporary cookhouse, then stopped at the end, making sure the lorry was where he had parked it, close to the high wall that surrounded the former monastery.

It was, and the yard, as he had expected, was empty this early in the morning. He pointed to the truck and the wall.

'We're going over that. It's the only way out. The front entrance will be expecting you by now.'

The corporal nodded. Eddie checked again that no one was about, then ran for the truck. He grabbed the rope he'd left in the back, climbed up on to the bonnet, then the canvas roof. From there it was easy to haul himself up on to the wall. He doubled the rope around one of the stanchions on the roof of the lorry and dropped it down to the narrow street on the other side of the wall.

The corporal clambered up beside him and Eddie pointed to the rope.

'Quickly! Wait for me down there.'

He watched the corporal slide down the rope, then glanced around the ex-monastery. As far as he could tell, they had not been spotted. Eddie slid down the doubled rope, then pulled one end, freeing it from the stanchion so it slipped to the ground.

Eddie picked it up and ran, coiling the rope around his elbow and hand. He rounded the corner, with the corporal close behind him, and flung the rope into the parked jeep.

They both leapt into the vehicle, and Eddie revved the engine into life before driving without undue haste through the back streets of the town. Not until they were clear of the last of the built-up areas did the corporal venture to speak.

'Whose idea was this?'

'Mine.'

The corporal was puzzled. 'How the hell did you manage to set everything up so quickly?'

Eddie grinned. 'I didn't. I always leave the jeep parked there and the lorry by the wall in case I need it in a hurry.'

The corporal thought about that. 'Where are we going?'

. 'You'll find out, Corporal Marsh.' Eddie smiled when he saw the surprised expression on his face. 'I saw your charge sheet yesterday when Robinson wasn't looking. What's your first name?'

'Norman. Now tell me what the bloody hell's going on.'

Eddie stuck out his free hand. 'I'm Eddie Pearce.'

Marsh gripped it briefly and waited.

'There was something else on the charge sheet,' Eddie said, glancing at the flash on Marsh's tunic. 'You're in the medical corps.'

'So what?' Marsh replied disgustedly. 'I got caught pushing penicillin on the black market. Fat lot of good that's going to do me now.'

'Don't be downhearted, corporal. As far as I'm concerned, it's an ideal combination. You can be our doctor.' Eddie suddenly remembered something. 'Incidentally, I hope you didn't kill Sergeant Robinson.'

Marsh shook his head. 'I don't think so. I hit him with the bench.'

Eddie shrugged. 'As long as you hit him on the head, he'll be fine.'

Marsh was not amused. 'Look, Pearce, I appreciate you getting me out of there, but unless you tell me what this is all about, I may be forced to strangle you.'

In spite of the casualness of the remark, there was a steely resolve edging his voice and Eddie decided he would take no chances. He pulled his hand from his pocket and rested the pistol on his lap where Marsh could see it.

'Now, I wouldn't be after doing that, corporal. You could be missing out on a quiet little number. Besides, this thing could go off and that would spoil everything.'

The corporal sighed. 'Shit! Why did I get myself into this?'

Eddie laughed. 'You should have thought of that before you began to work the black market. Now the experience you had could be very useful.'

Marsh looked mystified. During the rest of the journey Eddie began to give him some idea of the operation. It didn't worry Eddie too much if Corporal Marsh decided he didn't want in. Joe would deal with that, and the Irishman didn't like to think much beyond that point.

When they finally reached the end of the drive that led up to the *château*, they were halted by two armed sentries and asked for their identification. Eddie was delighted.

The sentry boxes and uniforms were absolutely authentic. There was only one problem. As yet Eddie hadn't been given any way of establishing his identity. He noted the hostility of the guard and considered the best approach.

'Look, get on the blower and tell Hillier that Eddie Pearce is here.'

The guard indicated Marsh. 'And him?'

'Just say I've got a doctor for the company.'

The guard was good. He didn't relax, not for one instant.

'A doctor?'

'That's right.'

The guard signalled to his colleague. 'Keep these two covered while I make the call.'

The other guard held the Thompson loosely but expertly, and neither Marsh nor Eddie was in any doubt that he would use it.

The field telephone hanging inside the sentry box whirred as the call was put through. Eddie couldn't hear what was being said, but from the guard's quick, assessing look at him, it was clear he was being asked for a description. The phone was slammed down. Eddie did not like the expression on the guard's face as he advanced towards the jeep. Then he leapt into the back, covering them both with the submachine-gun.

He called to his colleague. 'You stay here – I'll take these two up to HQ.'

Eddie heaved a sigh of relief. The guard prodded him in the back with his weapon.

'OK. Drive slowly. I want everyone to see us coming.'

Eddie slipped the jeep into gear and drove sedately up the winding drive until they emerged into the long line of poplar trees that lead up to the *château*.

A soldier was carefully whitewashing the bottom two or three feet of the trunks of the trees to help to ease the black-out after darkness. Eddie smiled. It was looking good.

Hillier stood on the steps, flanked by Corporal Kenwright, who had a sten gun hung over his shoulder. As the jeep drew closer Hillier relaxed. He turned to Kenwright.

'It's him all right.'

Kenwright grinned. 'Yeah, I couldn't forget his face. Did you see the look on it when that dancer in the club picked up the coins?'

Hillier continued to watch the jeep as it drove slowly up in front of them. 'I wasn't watching Pearce, corporal.'

Hillier waited as the Irishman moved as if to clamber out of the vehicle. The guard poked him sharply in the back.

'Stay where you are,' he ordered.

Hillier smiled at him. 'It's OK. This is Eddie Pearce, and I'll see that he has some identification before he leaves.'

Eddie turned to the guard. 'All right if I get out now?'

The guard stared at him, unperturbed by the sarcasm.

'Yes, but you'd better have a pass when you come out, otherwise you're gonna be here for ever.'

He eased himself down from the jeep, threw the strap of the

127

Thompson over his shoulder and strolled casually back down the drive towards his position at the entrance.

Eddie watched him go, then looked up at Hillier. 'Who's that, for Christ's sake?'

'His name's Hoggart and, apart from the fact that he was on the run from a charge of killing a corporal, one of ours. I know nothing else about him. But he seems to be a very good guard.'

Marsh had climbed out of the jeep and was standing beside Eddie. The Irishman glanced at him.

'Now this feller is really something, Yank. Not only did he knock off Rainy Day Robinson with a wooden bench, but he happens to be a doctor.'

Marsh held up his hand in protest at the exaggeration. 'A medical orderly, to be precise.'

Hillier stared at him fixedly for a moment. 'Can you fix wounds?'

'Of course.'

'Then as far as I am concerned, you are now this company's M O.'

Marsh gazed at him in disbelief. 'Medical officer?'

Hillier smiled. 'That's right.'

Pearce slapped Marsh enthusiastically on the shoulder. 'Now isn't that the quickest promotion you ever had?'

Hillier waved them inside.

'Come on. There's coffee inside or something stronger if you want it.'

He led the way to the kitchen, where the old lady presided impassively over the range.

Hillier picked up the blackened coffee pot and, ignoring her, poured himself out a cup. He glanced at the others.

'You want some?'

Kenwright declined. 'No, I'll go and check out the printing. You can fill them in on what's happening.'

Eddie watched him leave, then turned back to Hillier. 'I'll have some, thanks.'

Marsh accepted the invitation too, and they sat down around the heavy kitchen table.

Eddie tasted the coffee. 'Not bad.'

Hillier indicated the old woman. 'The French make the best coffee in the world.'

Corporal Marsh looked mildly surprised. 'Better than New York?'

'Almost.' Hillier grinned.

A comfortable silence settled between them, punctuated by the occasional clatter from the range.

Eddie watched the old lady curiously. There seemed to be something ambivalent about her manner that he found vaguely disconcerting. She must resent their presence in her house, he thought, but it was better than being head-shaved as a collaborator, and, from what he'd seen so far, the desire for revenge had not abated. Geneva Conventions did not mean much to the Maquis and local populations. And the army intervened only when it had to.

The women in this house were safe just as long as the men were present. He hoped they realized it.

Hillier swallowed the last of his coffee. 'Come on, I want you to see this.'

He led Pearce and Marsh back through the entrance hall and down the stairs to the basement. As they descended Eddie could hear the pounding of the press. Kenwright had already left. The temperature down here was too much for him.

The noise and the heat were intense, and the two men working the press were stripped to the waist. There were piles of sheets and forms stacked around the basement on tables. Hillier picked up a couple to show them.

He shouted above the din, 'We're covering as many areas as we can, new identities for all the men here, civilian ration cards. They're very useful. We can get a good price for those.'

He picked up another batch. 'These are petrol coupons.'

Eddie interrupted. 'Not for us?'

Hillier shook his head. 'No, we don't need them. As long as we stay in uniform, we can just drive the trucks into the fuel dumps and fill up, but we can sell these to civilians. The main thing is picking up as many trucks as we can. That's where you come in, Eddie. We need to know when and where they are going to meet up for the night. Then we take one or two at a time, no more. I don't want these convoys seeking protection in any way.

'With the trucks we can move anything and anyone from A to B.

That's what everybody needs, transportation – and they're willing to pay well for it.'

The noise was giving Eddie a headache. 'Can we go back up?'

Hillier nodded, and they re-emerged in the comparative calm of the entrance hall. Eddie walked to the open front door and stood looking down the drive. The others joined him. Hillier watched Eddie, waiting for a reaction.

'What do you think?'

'It's good. The printing press is a godsend. The paperwork back at headquarters is beginning to increase the more we get established – that's where it's going to score. But it's still fairly lax closer to the front line.'

He had a sudden thought.

'What have you done with the sisters?'

Hillier jerked his thumb behind him. 'They're out back, working in the garden.'

Eddie could see only one bike parked, the red Harley-Davidson that belonged to Hillier.

'Where's Joe?' he said.

Hillier pursed his lips. 'Out on the road, I guess. He's somewhere up near the front line.'

Eddie was concerned. 'What for, now that we've got all this going?'

The American shrugged. 'Have you ever tried to stop him? He reckons we have to have something going for us in Antwerp as soon as possible.' He paused. 'He's right. It's the only port we're gonna get and a main centre for everything – women, penicillin.' He glanced at Marsh. 'That's your department. If we can get in there, we can clean up.'

Corporal Marsh looked from one to the other. 'Who's Joe?' he asked.

CHAPTER THIRTEEN

For a long time after the sound of the plane had faded, Lissette continued to lie on the grassy slope of the little hill with her head buried in her arms. She didn't want to look at what was left of the refugee column. She thought about the children and their weary mothers, trying desperately to cope with thirst and tiredness. What had happened to them?

She sat up and shielded her eyes from the sun. There seemed to be little movement, as the hedgerow concealed the country road. She stood and began to walk across the meadow. She reached the ploughed field that separated her from the road and continued across that. As she drew nearer, she heard someone crying, then a man's voice shouted out in torment.

She stopped, not wanting to go any closer. She knew she could turn and run, cross the fields and join up with the road later. She didn't have to see them, to involve herself.

She stood in the middle of the neatly furrowed field and tried to control the panic inside her. Gradually her fear abated and she moved forward again.

This time she didn't hesitate, grimly setting down one foot in front of the other as the cries of the wounded grew louder. She could smell the sharp tang of cordite now and something else, sweet and sickly in the warm breeze. The smell of blood.

She pushed through a gap in the hedgerow and stumbled down the bank into the road.

She stared, horrified, at the carnage around her. Horses and people lay entangled in death. Dark patches of blood, slowly congealing, soaked into the dirty, broken tarmac of the road, torn apart by the armour-piercing cannon.

A woman sat on the bank at the side of the road crying, holding a child in her arms. Lissette crossed slowly towards her and looked down at the girl's face. She was about five. She was dead. The woman rocked her gently in her arms, sobbing her name. She didn't see Lissette. She was unaware of anything except her child.

Some people were moving about dazedly, picking up items of furniture that had spilled from a cart and putting them back, though the animal that had drawn it lay dead in its harness.

For some reason, Lissette began to help them. It made no sense, but it was something to do. There was a purpose in filling up the cart. It gave the body some occupation while the mind tried to recover from the horror of the strafing attack.

In the course of that curious activity she must have decided that she was going home. She never remembered making that decision, but she did find herself walking back down the refugee column towards the main road. And later she realized it must have been a very conscious decision because she had picked up an abandoned bicycle and wheeled it gently between the broken bodies and vehicles littering the narrow country road.

No one took any notice of her at all. There were a few blank stares, some incomprehension because she was moving back *towards* the city, no cry for help even. Then at last she was clear of the dreadful shambles. The road wound back down a hill, and in the distance she could see traffic on the main road. She mounted the bicycle and allowed the machine to freewheel away from the column behind her and down the gentle slope.

The dreadful sounds gradually diminished. Within moments it was almost as if nothing had happened. Birds sang in the trees. The hum of the tyres on the road was familiar and reassuring. She could have been out for a Sunday ride in the country. But what kind of country was this, she thought, where nightmare became reality in a few short moments and then, a few hundred yards away from the nightmare, birds sang and the sun blazed down on beautiful green fields?

She could not reconcile the two experiences – they made no sense to her. But she was grateful for this brief, peaceful, dream-like interlude. As soon as she rejoined the main road the apprehension and fear on the faces of the retreating German soldiers was real enough.

She found the place where she had left her car, but it was gone, confiscated by demoralized, tired troops. Lissette cycled on, maintaining a steady pace as she steered her way through the lines of men marching wearily back towards Antwerp, too tired even to whistle or call out as she rode by on the man's bike, her skirt up around her thighs. It was odd, she thought, how fear drove sex completely from their minds.

Throughout that day Lissette listened intently for the sudden racket of machine-gun fire or the high-pitched whine of a diving aircraft. She heard neither, and in the late afternoon she began to enter the suburbs again, riding through the tunnel under the river, hardly noticing the German engineers preparing to mine it. She cycled through the city and, finally, down the familiar street where she lived.

She stood at the door of her apartment with an unutterable sense of relief, then closed it slowly behind her. She walked into the bedroom and stripped off her clothes, letting them lie where they dropped. Then she fell on to the soft mattress, breathing in the faint smell of her own perfume. She didn't care what the dangers were for her in the city. She was glad to be back here in her own bedroom and alive. That was her last thought before she fell into a deep, dreamless sleep. It was the evening of Sunday, 3 September 1944.

Joe crossed the Seine on Friday, 1 September, two days after the 11th Armoured Division. He was able to filter through the convoys and support systems without too much trouble. He had packed his para smock into his dispatch box with some food and carried his Thompson slung over his arm in the normal way.

He appeared to be just another dispatch rider moving north with communications for the advancing columns up ahead. That night he reached Amiens, where the citizens were still celebrating their liberation in the narrow streets.

He holed up there with a generous lady whose husband was fighting in the resistance – of which she herself offered very little. Her main aim seemed to be to get Joe into her bed as quickly and for as long as possible. He emerged next morning bleary-eyed and more exhausted than when he had arrived.

He decided that the grateful citizens needed to be avoided if he was to make any progress towards Antwerp, so he headed eastwards from Amiens and away from the run of the 11th Armoured, hoping to find an easier, less crowded route through Tournai and Ath.

It was not to be. The population was out in force, flocking the streets, greeting any representative of the army as a saviour. Joe decided he was too tired to risk their attentions again, and he turned north on to one of the smaller roads, looking for somewhere to spend the rest of the day.

He found a barn. It was in the middle of a field used to store feed for the winter, but no animals grazed nearby. Perhaps the farmer had decided he couldn't risk leaving them in the open in the middle of a war zone. In any case, the barn suited Joe fine. There was hay and a loft that provided a good vantage point while he rested.

He hid the bike among some bales, took out some food and his maps from the dispatch box and climbed the ladder to the loft, pulling it up after him.

He chewed on some tinned corned beef and bread and poured a cup of hot, sweet tea from his flask. Then he checked his position.

Ath and Halle were on the main route through to Brussels, with Antwerp to the north. Although he wasn't aware of it, the maps he was using, which he had found with the printing press in the basement of the *château*, were far better than the small scale maps with which the advancing British columns had been issued and which were causing them some delay. The maps were going to be crucial to Joe's progress later.

He spread his para smock on some straw and placed the Thompson within easy reach. Then he lay down and was instantly asleep.

The loft was in shadow when he awoke. He lay quite still for a moment, alert, listening. Something had disturbed his sleeping pattern. Then he heard a faint thudding sound in the distance. Joe identified it at once; he'd heard it many times before. It signified bombs, exploding on impact but a long way away.

He reached out and picked up the Thompson, then moved carefully across to the window of the loft. Long evening shadows were stretching across the field from the trees bordering the country road. The crump of the exploding bombs was more discernible now.

The noise was to the south, some twenty miles away at Mons, where the German Seventh Army, fleeing from the British armoured columns, had run smack into the 7th Corps of the American First Army.

Neither had expected to see the other. By the time the engagement ended, the Germans had suffered heavy casualties and 30,000 men had been captured.

Later that night Joe heard heavy transportation moving down the road that bordered his field. It was time to move out.

He waited until it was just light enough to see, then pushed his bike back towards the line before kicking it into life. It was Sunday, 3 September.

He rejoined the main road and turned left, heading north towards Brussels. He couldn't avoid Ath.

The crowds were thicker than ever, gathering around his machine, throwing flowers, kissing him. What Joe found most disconcerting was that the men kissed him too. Twice. Once on each cheek Continental-fashion. It was something he had never experienced before, and although the exuberance and affection were spontaneous, he found it both confusing and difficult to handle.

One old lady pushed her way alongside him as he tried to keep going forward and, despite her age, she managed to stay with him for a moment. She took his hand and kissed it. '*Je vous remercie, Tommy. Je vous remercie.*' And she pressed three cigarettes into his palm. It was all she had to offer him after four years of deprivation.

Joe was too worried to feel much at the time. He desperately wanted to get moving as quickly as he could. But he did keep the old lady's three cigarettes. It was a moment he would remember.

At last he broke free of the smothering crowds in Ath and started to pick up some speed. The next major town before Brussels would be Halle.

If Joe had been able to speak anything other than English, he would have known from the questions shouted at him in Ath that he was now *ahead* of the forward armoured cars of the Household Cavalry, who had in turn reconnoitred in front of the Welsh Guards. In fact, he was far enough in front to close up with one of the last of the fleeing German trucks, loaded with whatever food and booty they had been able to remove from their barracks in Ath. He was about fifteen miles south of Halle when he first picked up a whiff of exhaust.

At first he thought it might be a British or American truck, so he fed some more fuel into the engine of the BSA and accelerated. After several twists and turns the road straightened out, and he could see the truck ahead of him. Gradually he closed on it, then with a shock he recognized the German markings.

The gunners in the truck were under no illusions about him. As soon as he came within range they opened up with a Schmeisser. Joe braked hard, skidding the machine to the side of the road as lead ricocheted from the surface.

The German truck continued to speed northwards, and Joe watched it recede into the distance before he set off in its wake, this time giving it plenty of clearance.

He was lucky twice over. First, they had missed him. Second, if they were the last of Jerry, all he had to do was stay within striking distance and he had an open road – unless, of course, they decided to stop and set up a sniping position. But he didn't think that was likely. They were on the run now and wouldn't stop until they reached the Ardennes. Then, as he approached the outskirts of a small village, he heard automatic fire and the explosion of a grenade. He coasted the bike to a halt after switching off the engine and pushed it under some trees slightly off the road. He unslung the Thompson from his shoulder and, staying close to the side of the road, he moved forward through the trees which broadened into a small wood.

The firing continued sporadically, gradually becoming louder as he approached. The truck was sprawled halfway across the road, its nose buried in a ditch in front of a stone wall.

He could see the driver slumped over the wheel and another body lying in the road. But at least two German soldiers had taken cover on his side of the road. Behind them the woods stretched out invitingly, but a wider open space separated them from the cover of the trees, and now Porter could see why they had not attempted to cross it. From behind the stone wall deadly accurate weapon fire sprayed across the ditch, keeping the Germans effectively pinned down.

It was clear that the truck had been ambushed as it started to go through the village, but whoever was behind the wall could not finish off the action unless they could get closer, and the road was too wide for grenades.

Joe checked his own, and moved closer through the trees. He knew that the German troopers could crawl along the ditch, either towards the village or back the way they had come. They would not take long to decide which route was best.

The trees were quite widely spaced, but silent approach was what he was good at, and they would not be expecting an attack from their side of the road. There remained the problem of the open clearing behind them.

Then he became aware that someone else was in the wood. He froze, pressing himself against the trunk of a tree, diffusing the outline of his body, standing absolutely still. Only his eyes moved.

He waited until the man had eased ahead of him, closer to the ditch where the Germans were sheltering. Then, making no sound, Porter slipped closer, moving quickly from tree to tree.

The man had no warning of his presence. He was concentrating entirely on the soldiers in the ditch.

His breath was expelled from his body like a collapsing balloon as an arm-lock clamped around his throat and he was jerked backwards, the weapon in his hand torn from his grasp. He heard a voice speaking in English. He could hardly believe his ears. The arm-lock lessened fractionally and he managed to gasp, 'Jesus Christ, don't kill me. We're on the same fuckin' side.'

The American accent was unmistakable. Joe dropped his arm from the man's throat and stared balefully at him.

'What the hell do you think you're doing here?' he whispered savagely, examining the civilian clothes and the Schmeisser he'd taken from the American.

Mark Reynolds swallowed hard, trying to get his throat back into working order.

'I baled out about six months ago. Been holed up in that house over the road ever since.' He grinned. 'I thought it was about time I came out.'

Joe had no reason to disbelieve him. He looked through the trees towards the road. 'Who's behind that wall?'

Reynolds smiled again. 'Mr and Mrs Timmerman and their son.'

Joe stared at him in surprise, then gazed at the wrecked truck.

'You mean they did that?'

Reynolds nodded. 'With a little help from me. I circled round here to get behind them.'

Joe nodded. 'OK, here's what you do. Get to the edge of these trees, as close as you can to the ditch. Give me time to back up the road a bit. The trees join it further along. Then open up with this.'

He handed back the Schmeisser. 'They won't be expecting to be hit from this side as well, and they'll start to crawl along that ditch. That's when they'll meet me.'

Reynolds stared at him, puzzled. 'How can you be sure they won't move the other way?'

Joe's green eyes were expressionless. 'Towards the village after this reception?'

The American felt distinctly uncomfortable. He should have realized that.

'OK, I'll handle this end. How long do you need?'

Joe looked back through the trees the way he had come. 'Three minutes. No more.'

He slipped away without further comment. Reynolds glanced back at the road, then turned to watch the Englishman's progress, but he'd gone. The wood seemed empty.

Reynolds shivered. It was weird, and if it hadn't been for the pain in his neck, he would have doubted that the encounter was real. He felt his throat gingerly. It hurt right enough. He began to move cautiously towards the edge of the clearing.

Joe reached the position he wanted and waited. Firing continued; then came the distinctive sound of the Schmeisser. He checked the Thompson, making sure the ammunition clips were secure. They'd be here soon.

He heard a faint sound as they crawled on hands and knees along the ditch, keeping their hands well down. They were good. If he hadn't been expecting them, he wouldn't have known they were there. He left it until the last possible moment, then he made his move.

The two veterans didn't know what hit them – they had no real chance. On all fours, they saw nothing but a glimpse of a figure as Joe leaped down into the ditch ahead of them and opened up at point-blank range with the Thompson. It was the last thing they heard. Porter fired two quick bursts. It was enough.

Then he began to make his customary search, removing pay books, insignias and any valuables he could find. He didn't really need the insignias and pay books any longer. It was just habit.

He was unstrapping a wrist watch when he suddenly became aware of someone behind him. He whirled round, crouching, bringing up the Thompson to fire. Then he stopped.

Reynolds was standing, frozen by his swift movement, a faint look of disgust in his eyes. Joe kept the automatic pointing menacingly at his stomach. He pocketed the watch, then slowly let his weapon drop.

'Never creep up on anybody, Reynolds, if you want to get back in one piece. If I hadn't known it might be you, I'd have fired first and asked questions later. I took a chance. I don't like taking chances. That's how you end up dead.'

The wood was silent after the harsh, explosive sounds of killing. But Reynolds could feel the tension between them. The wood seemed to be waiting, as if anticipating his own death. He could hear nothing, no natural backdrop of noise, no birds. There was just the smell of cordite slowly dissipating through the trees.

He dismissed these strange, oppressive thoughts. He was alive. He had survived six months of concealment from the German forces as they had thundered to and fro on the road outside the home that had become his haven.

He shrugged, grinning. 'Sorry. I'm not used to ground fighting. Better off up there.' He jerked a thumb up at the cloudless, blue sky above the circle of trees. 'C'mon,' he said, 'I'd like you to meet Mr and Mrs Timmerman.'

He led Joe back through the wood to the clearing and yelled a greeting across the road. A middle-aged couple and a boy about thirteen years old emerged, all of them carrying, somewhat incongruously, captured German weapons.

The boy waved delightedly at Reynolds and ran across the road. He stopped in front of Joe, breathing quickly with excitement and gazing at Joe's uniform. 'You Tommy?' he asked haltingly.

Mr and Mrs Timmerman waited by the roadside. They spoke a little English, and Reynolds started to introduce Joe enthusiastically. Then he stopped. 'I'm sorry,' he said, 'I don't know your name.'

'Private Porter,' Joe replied, then changed the subject fast. 'Have any British or American columns been through here yet?'

Mr Timmerman shook his head. 'No, you are the first.' He contemplated the wrecked truck. 'But lots of Germans, all retreating,' he added with some satisfaction.

Mrs Timmerman cut in. 'Can you stop for a while?'

Joe shook his head. He had to stay close to the German rear if he could. 'No, I must push on. It's important I continue.'

The boy had run to the back of the truck and climbed inside. He began to throw boxes of canned food from the truck, calling out excitedly.

His parents crossed the road to help him unload. Joe gazed at them. He knew that wherever he went he was going to be stopped by enthusiastic crowds. One look at his khaki uniform and, since he was now ahead of the columns, there would be no stopping them. Then his eyes focused on the dead driver in the truck.

He started to strip off his tunic. Reynolds stared at him in amazement. 'Look, I know it's hot, but this is ridiculous. You could get arrested as a spy.'

Joe smiled for the first time. 'Maybe that's the idea.' He pointed to the truck. 'Go and get the uniform off that driver.'

The American shook his head but did as he was asked. Whatever Private Porter had in mind, one thing was clear – he knew what he wanted and he understood this kind of warfare.

Joe got behind the truck while the Timmermans continued to unload it, moving the food and anything else they could find inside their house. After four years of privation Mrs Timmerman had decided that tonight they were going to celebrate with a feast.

Reynolds gave the German uniform to Porter. It didn't fit too badly. Joe took the helmet from the soldier still lying in the road and waited to see how the Timmermans would react when they came out of the house.

Then he heard the growl of an engine coming up the road from the direction of Ath. It was moving fast and he yelled a warning to Reynolds, who took the Schmeisser from his shoulder as he emerged from behind the wrecked truck.

The German armoured car came round the bend fast, then slowed as the driver observed that the road was partially blocked. The gunner saw Porter wearing the German's uniform and a young man in civilian clothes carrying an automatic and running for cover. He opened fire at once, the bullets tracing a wickedly violent path across the macadam of the road and catching Reynolds just as he was about to dive over the wall.

He fell across it like a rag doll, killed instantly by the blast.

Mrs Timmerman saved her own family by slamming the front door shut as her husband and son were about to dash outside. They fell to the floor as the German gunner shattered the window and splintered the front door of the house as a precautionary measure.

The armoured car stopped, and a sergeant pushed himself up from the turret and yelled something in German at Joe. Porter had remained rooted to the ground, caught in the open without a weapon. If he tried to answer, he knew he was dead.

He waved an arm at the dead body of Reynolds and walked as normally as he could towards the American. Every second he expected the hot blast of lead in his back, and he wondered if he would feel anything before he died.

But it didn't happen.

He reached the body, brutally tore the weapon from Reynold's dead grasp and grabbed one of the grenades from his belt. He turned and exhibited the Schmeisser to the sergeant, waving it in triumph as he walked back to the armoured car.

The sergeant smiled and said to Porter in German, 'Good. You might need that.'

Porter grinned mirthlessly, and the sergeant watched in frozen horror as the muzzle of the weapon pointed at him and flamed red. He slumped back inside the vehicle.

Joe had waited until he was too close to the armoured car for the gunner to be able to use his machine gun. He leapt swiftly on to the vehicle as the driver, realizing the danger, turned to accelerate away. But Joe reached the turret, holding on grimly, and pulled the pin on the grenade, hurling it into the interior of the car through the turret before leaping from the moving vehicle.

He rolled over into the ditch as the grenade exploded. In the confined space of the armoured car it was lethal. The car careered off the road and crashed into a tree, bursting into flames.

Joe stood up and watched it for a few seconds. Then he walked slowly back across the road to where Reynolds still lay across the stone garden wall.

He slung the Schmeisser round his shoulder, then very carefully picked up the body of the American and carried it into the house.

Mrs Timmerman opened the door for him and indicated a sofa in the corner. Gently Joe laid the body down. Mrs Timmerman pushed him to one side and placed a cushion beneath the young American's head. Then, kneeling beside the body, she folded her hands in front of her and began to say a prayer.

Joe heard the boy behind him begin to cry and he turned to look at Mr Timmerman, who had his arm around his son. He was holding him close, stroking his hair. He wasn't looking at Joe. His eyes were full of tears. The Englishman walked slowly from the room. There was nothing he could say.

They had hidden the American airman for six months. If they had been caught at any single moment during that time, they would have been shot. But they had survived until this day of liberation, when the young American had been snatched from them. He would not be going home after all. He would stay for ever in Belgium.

Joe picked up his own uniform, collected his Thompson from the side of the truck and walked back down the road to where he had left his machine. He crammed the clothes into one of the dispatch boxes and kicked the engine into life. He drove slowly past the house.

The boy came to the door and watched him go. Joe raised a hand, but the boy did not respond. Seeing the Englishman in a German uniform was too much for the youngster. He slammed the door shut, blotting Joe from his sight.

Joe made swift progress. No one bothered him in Halle. Those who were out waiting watched him sullenly as he rode fast through the town. And then by the middle of the afternoon he was into the southern outskirts of Brussels.

A tank and some German armour was preparing positions in one of the suburbs, but Joe was able to zig-zag his bike through the defences without trouble and no one attempted to stop him. It occurred to him that someone might recognize his British machine, but the Germans were grimly intent upon their last stand before the city, and they knew it was hopeless.

They hardly glanced up from their work as the dispatch rider rode through their midst. They envied him his escape and wondered if they would still be alive when that sunlit Sunday came to an end.

Joe rode on into the city. He could feel the tension, the suppressed excitement, of the people as they strolled, watching German lorries being loaded, hiding their Belgian and British flags beneath their clothing. The feeling was almost tangible. He continued to head northwards past the Port du Roi. Later the Germans would set fire to the brilliant copper cupola of the Palais de Justice.

He turned left on to the Avenue de la Reine, crossing the Willebroeke Canal and heading out north-west from the city towards

Wolverton. He realized that the British armoured columns would be held up for a while south of Brussels, dealing with the defences he'd passed through, but he was already in the clear. He needed to slow down. If he got too far ahead, he might find himself stranded. He stopped and studied his maps.

Some twenty miles ahead were the bridges at Boom. The detail on the map was good, and he could see that the main road into Antwerp crossed a railway line, a canal and the river Rupel. If they were going to make a stand anywhere, it would be at Boom.

Evening was beginning to draw in, and the air was warm and balmy.

He rode on for a few more miles, then, as the shadows lengthened, he turned off the main road and found a pathway that led up through some small, rounded hills. He hid the bike in some bushes. There was a stream and, close by, blackberries hung ripe and heavy.

He picked enough to complement his bread and cheese, then settled down for the night, covering himself with his own uniform to keep himself warm.

Tomorrow he would decide which one he should wear.

CHAPTER FIFTEEN

Her heels clicked noisily on the pavement, their echo bouncing back from the old walls of the city. The sound preceded her down the deserted street, announcing her presence. She hadn't thought. The gunfire had woken her so suddenly that she had sat bolt-upright in the bed, straining her ears, hearing nothing. She seemed to sit there for an age, the silence thundering in her ears, wondering if she had dreamt it. Then it had come again – a rattle of gunfire from the direction of the docks. Lissette had dressed swiftly, too swiftly, not thinking that her footsteps might betray her. Now she regretted her haste as the silent street mocked her progress, tapping out the message for anyone to hear.

The rounded cobblestones gleamed sweatily in the half light before dawn, and for some reason the familiar route to her cinema seemed alien and vaguely menacing. She tried to dismiss the thought as fanciful. Normally she would not walk this boulevard for at least another five hours. Her duties as manager did not require her to be in her office before ten in the morning. But was it just imagination that made her examine every shadowy doorway? The gunfire had been real, and the Allies were closing in. It would not be long before they reached Antwerp.

The trees hung lifeless and mute, a grey mist that had filtered up from the river wrapping itself around them. She shivered, feeling the chill.

She reached the front of the cinema and let herself in through one of the glass doors with her keys. Immediately she felt a sense of relief. The familiar smell of the cool foyer and a pleasant mixture of warm carpets and the fragrance of pine disinfectant and tobacco in the kiosk gave her a sense of security.

She went to the usherettes' small changing-room and picked up a torch. No point in switching on the lights and risking attention. She ascended the staircase to the circle, her feet making no sound on the thick carpet, the light from the torch bobbing ahead of her. She crossed to the door on the left marked 'Private' and pushed it open. The air was colder here; the iron steps led up through a concrete well to the flat roof. She climbed them as quietly as she could and was breathing heavily by the time she reached the door at the top.

She twisted the spring lock, leaving it in a fixed position so that it would not shut automatically when it swung back into place, then stepped out on to the roof. The sky was lightening quickly now in the east, and the outline of the 20 mm Flakvierling stood out starkly against it, the four muzzles pointing almost directly upwards.

Lissette walked across to the gun and placed her hand on the metal. It felt cold beneath her touch. She remembered the first time she had seen the weapon on the roof. The concrete had been warm beneath her feet from the sun, and Manfred and two other members of the flak crew had been stretched out on a blanket, stripped to the waist. She remembered his smile as he had greeted her, the amusement in his eyes at her slight embarrassment. She took her hand from the cold metal and pressed it to her forehead, trying to clear her mind. She had no time for this, not now. His death was too close.

The flash lit up the sky for a moment and she felt the roof vibrate beneath her before she heard the explosion. She clapped her hands to her ears as the wave of sound engulfed her, then the sky darkened again as the light extinguished. She took her hands from her ears. She could hear glass breaking as it fell into the street below – shop windows shattered by the blast.

She rushed to the parapet and gazed out over the city to the east. Down by the docks a huge plume of dark, oily smoke, livid with flames, was rising slowly into the sky. She saw that the oil refinery had been sabotaged, and suddenly the city seemed alive with sound. The mournful wail of an air-raid siren rose in pitch, mistakenly signalling a raid. From the high, flat roof of the cinema Lissette could hear the city waken, leaping from its wary silence.

Below her a German light personnel carrier nosed its way cautiously along the tree-lined boulevard, the two rows of dark steel helmets glinting dully in the damp early light, heads turning, alarmed, searching for their enemy, half hidden by the fog snaking between the buildings.

Something glinted brightly as it curved through the air, twisting over and round as it arced towards the troop carrier from an open upstairs window. It sped accurately, falling into the rear of the vehicle, bursting as it hit the steel surface and showering the German infantry with burning petrol.

Lissette turned sharply away, horrified. She ran back from the parapet towards the door. She could hear the men's screams, then these were drowned by a shattering burst of automatic gunfire that erupted from the street below. She realized for the first time the gauntlet she had run to reach the cinema. The White Brigade must have been lying in wait, ready for the ambush, watching her all the way into the cinema.

Her legs were trembling as she descended the dark iron stairs. She felt sick.

The windscreen of the personnel carrier starred, punctured neatly by three holes from automatic fire. The driver collapsed over the wheel and slid on to the officer's lap, the blood from his throat wound still pumping, staining his trousers red. The lieutenant grabbed the handle of the door and forced it open. He felt the searing heat of the petrol bomb whip along the side of the vehicle from the open compartment behind him. He leapt from his seat, unbuttoning his tunic to try to smother the flames. A hail of bullets struck the pavement and road around him, some of them mercifully ending the torment of the blazing soldier. The officer crouched, bewildered for a moment by the intensity of the fire as bullets ricocheted and whined like a cloud of demented bees. Then he ran towards the shattered glass doors of the cinema across the road, bullets tracing a pattern behind him. He dived head-first through the frame of the door and rolled on the carpet as he fell into the shadows behind the kiosk. Unbelievably, he wasn't even scratched.

He crouched in the darkness, hardly daring to move, the blood pounding in his ears. He heard somebody breathing heavily behind him, and he felt the hair rising on the nape of his neck. He turned sharply, gripping the Luger in his hand. He pointed it at the shadowy figure of a man.

'Is that you, *Herr Oberst*?'

The young voice was frightened, hoarse. The lieutenant lowered his pistol, recognizing the voice.

'Yes, Thysson, it's me. Are there any others?'

'I don't know, Herr Leutnant I've seen no one.'

The fusillade outside ended as suddenly as it had begun. The boulevard was silent, waiting, just the sound of the personnel carrier still alight and the awful stench of burnt flesh and rubber tyres. The light from the flames flickered strangely inside the foyer of the cinema, illuminating the lurid posters and the bulbous mock-Egyptian decor.

The two men knelt quietly behind the counter of the kiosk. The lieutenant understood now that the ambush of his patrol had been well planned and executed as part of a general rising of the Belgian resistance, which was clearly intent upon securing the docks and bridges for the Allies as they advanced inexorably on the city. The Belgian White Brigade was ruthless. It took no prisoners. Some of the members might even now be occupying the upper floors of the building. The petrol bomb had been flung from above; and much of the automatic-weapons fire had hit them from high positions.

He remained motionless, listening. Until he knew what lay around him there was no point in revealing his position. Nothing moved. The fire continued to crackle and burn in the road outside. Thyssen suddenly gripped his arm.

'The stairs,' he whispered.

The officer glanced quickly across the foyer. The pale light of a torch was bobbing its way down the staircase towards them. He raised his Luger, aiming it slightly below the glow from the torch.

Lissette could smell the burning and could see the glittering pieces of broken glass that littered the foyer, reflecting the flames from outside. Then the cinema lit up. Everything stood out starkly in the harsh flash of light as the petrol tank of the half-track ignited. In that brief moment of time she saw a German officer kneeling behind the sweet counter, pointing a gun at her. The crashing sound of the explosion hit her almost simultaneously, and her breath seemed to be sucked from her body by the rush of air. She screamed, dropped the torch, turned and fled back up the stairs.

The lieutenant muttered a brief command to Thyssen. 'Try to locate the others and guard the entrance.'

Then he moved swiftly away from the shadows of the foyer and followed the woman up the stairs, picking up the torch she had dropped. There was no sign of her on the circle landing. Two doors to his right led up into the circle; there were two opposite. He checked. One was an office; the other was marked 'Private'. He opened that cautiously and discovered the iron steps that led to the roof. No light filtered into the well. He felt certain she would not have ventured up without the torch.

He closed the door and made his way across the landing to the circle entrance, ascending half a dozen steps that led into the auditorium. He stopped at the top and stood still, listening. He could hear the woman crying. The lieutenant switched on the torch and slowly ran the beam of light along the rows of seats until he found her.

Lissette had seated herself at the end of a row and was holding her face in her hands. She felt the light upon her. She brushed the tears away with the back of her hand, trying to shield her eyes from the beam of the torch.

His voice sounded hollowly through the empty cinema. 'Who are you?'

She blinked, trying to focus on the shadowy figure behind the torch. 'I am the manageress. My name is Lissette van der Elst.'

He stood quietly for a moment, studying her.

'Is there anyone else here?'

'No,' she said, 'just me.'

He transferred the beam to the steps beside her. 'You'd better come down. I need information, *Fräulein*.'

Lissette stood up and slowly made her way down the aisle to where he was standing.

He indicated the steps leading to the circle landing. 'Down there,' he said.

She descended the steps ahead of him. The morning light was filtering up from the front of the cinema. She paused on the landing and turned to face him. He was young, no more than twenty-five.

His hair, wavy and dark, was stuck down on his forehead, damp with sweat. Then she saw the blood on his trousers. He caught her look, as the beam of the flashlight was still on her face.

'My driver – he was killed.'

Lissette said nothing. She could hear the tension in his voice, and the gun in his hand had not wavered from her. For an instant.

'What are you doing here at this time in the morning?'

Lissette held out her hands in explanation. 'I heard some firing – it woke me up. I thought I had better come and check that everything was all right. Then I heard you being attacked and I came back downstairs.'

'Where were you?'

'On the roof. It's flat. I thought that from there I could see what was going on.'

He gazed silently at her for a moment, his eyes expressionless. 'Give me your hand.'

Lissette looked at him, startled by the order.

'Come,' he said harshly, 'I have no time to waste.'

He held out his hand and she proffered hers. Keeping the Luger trained on her stomach, he took it and held it up to his face. She suddenly understood that he was trying to detect if there was any smell of petrol on her fingers. He released it and she silently held out her other hand. He took it and held the palm to his face, then let it drop limply to her side.

He stared at her balefully. 'You are lucky, *Fräulein*. If I thought you were responsible for what happened out there to my men, your blood would be spilling on to this carpet.'

Lissette shivered. 'I saw what happened.'

He gripped her arm tightly. 'Where – where did it come from?'

Lissette tried to release herself from his grasp, but he dug his fingers tightly into her upper arm.

'Quickly. Where was it thrown from?'

Lissette bit her lip, trying not to cry out with the pain. 'One of the windows lower down the street, after you had passed. Someone threw it from inside and it fell down into the . . .' She stopped, remembering the horror.

He continued to hold her in a painful grip, then he pushed her roughly towards the top of the stairs. 'Move.'

She almost stumbled as she reached the top and gripped the polished metal handrail tightly to prevent herself from falling. She stepped apprehensively down towards the foyer entrance, which was lighter now as sunlight began to strike the boulevard.

As they reached the foot of the staircase there was another shattering blast of gunfire. Lissette could see a German soldier crouched near the entrance, screaming encouragement to someone outside. He began to give covering fire with his own weapon, then a Wehrmacht soldier staggered in through the broken doors and collapsed on to the carpet. The lieutenant and the other soldier leapt across the open foyer, grabbed the badly wounded man and hauled him into the well of the staircase where Lissette was sheltering. The lieutenant knelt down beside him and felt for the pulse in his neck. There was none. He turned to Thyssen and gripped the front of his tunic.

'I told you to guard the entrance, not to give away our position.'

The Luger quivered in the officer's hand; its barrel was rammed into Thyssen's stomach. The lieutenant's knuckles were white, the grip on the weapon betraying his fear.

Thyssen shook his head, denying the accusation. 'No, they were outside, two of them, in a doorway. They were pinned down. There was hardly any cover. It was only a matter of time, *Herr Oberst* – they would have been killed. I tried to help them but it was no good.'

The lieutenant released his hold on Thyssen. He had done only what any other soldier would have attempted in similar circumstances, but the officer realized he may have sealed their fate.

'Is there anyone else out there?'

Thyssen shook his head. 'No, *Herr Leutnant*, just the dead.'

The young officer stood in the well of the staircase, breathing heavily. His head drooped like a wounded animal's. He needed somewhere safe. This building had too many entrances and exits – he felt exposed and vulnerable. Now that the resistance knew where they were, it would not be long before it tried to needle them out. He turned to Lissette.

'The roof – you said it was flat?'

'Yes. There is a gun on it.'

'A gun?'

'It was used by the anti-aircraft unit until they were transferred to the front.'

The lieutenant considered this for a moment. He pointed upstairs to the door in the circle. 'Is that the only way to the roof?'

'Yes, you have to use those steps.'

He knew that once they were on the roof, there would be no way out. It might just be possible to escape through one of the exits and get back through the side streets, but he doubted it. The resistance fighters would already be anticipating such a move.

These considerations were suddenly cut short. A round black object came hurling in through the gaping doors and smashed a piece of broken plate glass as it fell on to the floor of the foyer. It rolled towards them. Thyssen screamed a warning and before the officer could stop him he ran, crouching, scooped up the grenade and flung it back outside the cinema, falling flat as he did so.

The crunch of the explosion shook the stills display cabinet in the foyer and it creaked gently open. Two of the photographs fluttered to the carpet beside Thyssen. He picked one up and stuffed it into the front of his tunic, glancing at the picture of the actress. He grinned at the officer.

'I've always wanted one of her.'

He turned to crawl back towards them. At that moment two more grenades thudded on to the carpet and rolled across the floor to stop on either side of him. They were too far apart for him to gather both and pitch them outside before they exploded, and in that heartbeat, as he realized the truth, he looked at the lieutenant. There was a mute, almost dog-like appeal in his eyes, but there was nothing the officer could do. Lissette looked from one to the other, frozen with horror, knowing what was about to happen.

The officer tore his eyes from those of Thyssen and pushed Lissette angrily down into the stairwell. The two grenades exploded simultaneously, the blast wave almost deafening them in the enclosed space of the foyer.

He grabbed Lissette's arm and dragged her back up the staircase. She kept her eyes averted from the ghastly remains of Thyssen and stumbled back towards the circle. Automatic-weapons fire began to clatter into the front of the cinema, and the lieutenant leaned down, yelling above the uproar in her ear, 'The roof! Come on!'

Lissette tried to protest, but he tightened his grip, his face contorted with anger.

'Do as I tell you.'

He dragged her to the door and kicked it open, grabbing the torch from his pocket and beaming it upwards. He pushed her ahead of him. Lissette felt numb. Her ears were ringing from the explosions and her mind was almost blank. She climbed the iron stairs automatically. They seemed endless as they stretched upwards, undulating. She focused her eyes on each step in turn and found it was easier to concentrate. The iron railing was cold against the palm of her hand, but its solidity was strangely smooth and comforting.

She reached the door at the top and went to push it open, but the lieutenant pulled her back. The firing outside stopped. He flattened himself against the wall and gently pushed the door slightly ajar with his foot. Lissette stared at him without expression, too shocked to understand what he was doing. He seemed satisfied but still pushed her out on to the roof ahead of him. It was empty. In daylight she could see the flak gun was already beginning to rust around its barrels where the heat had caused the camouflage paint to flake from the steel. The lieutenant scanned the roof quickly. Apart from the Flakvierling anti-aircraft gun there was no cover. The door opened on to the roof in one of the corners; the superstructure of the entrance backed on to the parapet. But the woman had spoken the truth. They could not be spotted from below. The sun was already warm on the roof. He ordered her to sit in one of the seats of the Flakvierling, then removed his forage cap and crouched down beside the parapet overlooking the front of the cinema.

Slowly and carefully he raised himself a few inches until he could peer over the top into the street below. There was no sound. He searched each doorway and window. Still nothing. Then he saw an arm wave from a shop entrance and, as if by magic, men carrying rifles, pistols, automatic submachine-guns, every conceivable kind of weapon, began to emerge on to the pavement. They stayed close to the buildings and moved cautiously, approaching the entrance of the cinema. He could have nailed two or three of them quite easily, but that would have revealed his hiding place.

He lowered himself from the parapet, crouching low, keeping his head down. The cinema was on a corner. There was only one building alongside it, an office block. The two structures were separated by an alleyway. The lieutenant moved quietly to the parapet facing the alley, wondering if he could leap across the gap.

There was only one problem. The offices were about three feet higher than the flat roof of the cinema, and even if he managed to jump it and get a handhold, before he could haul himself up he would be seen by the men in the street below. They would just pick him off, swat him like a stranded fly on a wall. Worse, they were already moving into the alleyway. He could hear the sound of their heavy boots as they ran the length of it, completely surrounding the cinema.

He was trapped. There was no way out. The lieutenant shielded his eyes from the sun, checking its position. It was rising behind the cowling over the entrance to the roof. That might give him a few brief seconds, but he wasn't kidding himself. Once they knew where he was, he was finished. He had nowhere to go.

He moved silently back to the woman by the gun. He slumped down into a sitting position facing the door. Methodically he began to load the Luger.

Lissette felt cut off, stunned. She stared at a small, round piece of rust on one of the barrels of the anti-aircraft gun, trying to concentrate her attention on that, wondering vaguely how long it would take to double its size. Everything had happened so quickly. Last night she had come home to her apartment in the city, trying to find some normality in familiar surroundings, trying to cushion herself from the horror, clinging to her routine to blank out the memory of Manfred.

She stopped, jerking herself upright. She could not think about Manfred; she would not be able to continue if she did. She tried to wipe her mind clean – then, very faintly, she heard a thud. It was at the foot of the iron stairs leading from the circle. She stared, terrified, at the German officer.

The lieutenant stood up, motioning her to be silent. He crossed the roof to the door noiselessly, pressing the side of his head to it, listening. It was impossible to ascend the iron stairs without making some noise, and he could hear the squeal of the metal as it moved fractionally under the weight of someone. Was it more than one?

The lieutenant indicated to Lissette that she was not to move. There was nowhere to hide and she nodded dumbly. She watched him climb on to the parapet, then inch his way carefully up to the top of the cowling that surrounded the entrance to the roof. He was now directly above the door and invisible to anyone coming through it.

Lissette sat motionless in the metal seat, her eyes fastened on the handle to the door. It seemed like an age, a lifetime. She could hear nothing from her position in the centre of the roof, but she could see the lieutenant peering over the edge of the cowling, his eyes watching her.

Then the door moved fractionally. Just enough for someone to see out on to the roof. Lissette wondered, quite calmly, if he would just shoot her on sight. The door opened a shade more. Now she could see the barrel of a rifle poking from the dark interior of the staircase, and behind it she could discern the shadowy figure of a man.

He emerged partially through the door, though not enough for the lieutenant to see him, and he stared at Lissette curiously, his eyes scanning the rooftop behind her. He waved his rifle, indicating the empty quadrangle of concrete.

'You are alone?'

Lissette watched him fixedly. She found it impossible to reply but she nodded. The man took another pace on to the roof, still staring at her.

'What are you doing up here?'

Lissette cleared her throat, trying to speak. The man could see that she was badly frightened. He put it down to his own presence and the fighting outside the cinema. Lissette was aware that the German officer was rising up on the cowling to leap upon the Belgian, and she wondered why he didn't shoot the man. She was too terrified to calculate that a shot would reveal their presence to the others.

The Belgian took another quick look around the deserted roof and turned to tell others behind him that it was clear – then he saw the German.

The lieutenant realized instantly that he could not reach the resistance fighter before he himself was shot. The man's rifle was already jerking up towards him. He fired the Luger twice and Lissette saw two gaping red holes suddenly appear on the back of the man's rough, dark tunic. The Belgian died immediately, his rifle clattering on to the roof as he was propelled violently backwards by the force of the high-velocity bullets smashing through the wall of his chest. He fell almost at Lissette's feet as she opened her mouth to scream but could not. Her jaw worked convulsively, her eyes bulging with the effort to release her fear.

Two men burst through the doorway, rolling on their backs in opposite directions and firing automatic rifles from the hip as they fell. The lieutenant was now totally exposed on the roof of the cowling. The converging lines of fire almost ripped him in half. He fell backwards, his body striking the concrete parapet before disappearing over the edge.

Lissette had not moved. She was frozen to the metal seat when she heard the German officer's body thud horribly on to the pavement of the boulevard below. Suddenly she screamed, then screamed again and again. The two men rose silently to their feet and watched, unmoved, letting their weapons drop to their sides.

Lissette sat hunched in the corner of the lions' cage. It was empty now. All the other women had gone, and she had a privacy of sorts. Strange that she could consider an empty cage in Antwerp's zoo as in any way private.

The thought lingered only for a moment, then faded. Even the overpowering smell of animal urine that pervaded the area no longer troubled her.

She was cold and hungry. Her thin summer dress gave her little protection from early-morning chill. Earlier she had huddled with the other women, all trying to keep themselves warm, longing for the warmth of the sun, cut off by the walls that surrounded them.

One by one the men had taken the women from the cage, grinning, treating it like a huge joke. Perhaps some of them smiled to cover their dislike of what they were doing, but most were enjoying their revenge.

It was something they had anticipated for nearly five years. Collaborators and informers had betrayed them, had taken a heavy toll of their comrades during the occupation. Many had died horribly at the hands of the SS and the Gestapo. They had seen some Belgian women consort with German officers, accepting the gifts of the conquerors in return for their company and their beds.

Now it was their turn.

And it seemed to them not too harsh or cruel to exact of these women a punishment, a token of their shame; their hair. Most had submitted meekly. Some had even smiled in order not to provoke, probably fearing worse to come. Lissette had watched through the iron bars of the cage as they had been sat upon an upturned box and their hair brutally chopped from their heads by a skinny, balding little man wielding a pair of shears.

At first the men had cheered as each lock fell to the ground. But then the novelty wore off and they just watched grimly, occasionally making an obscene remark if they recognized the women.

Finally the last ugly, close-cropped head had been led away, and the men had gone too, leaving Lissette in the corner of the cage by herself. She did not know why. It may have been something to do with her former position or the circumstances in which she had been taken. Perhaps they needed to make a decision about her.

She waited, her back to the stone wall of the cage, staring sightlessly out through the bars at the grounds of the zoo beyond. She had never been here before, not even as a child. It held no happy memories for her. Now she knew she would never forget it. Perhaps it was just as well; perhaps this was her punishment. The nuns in the convent had told her often enough, but she had ignored them, made her own life, tried to construct something away from the restraints and fears of her mother. Perhaps she had sinned. Maybe that was why Manfred had been killed. The tears blinded her eyes and she screamed involuntarily, 'No!'

Her voice echoed, bouncing back from the stone walls of the cage, resounding in her ears. She clasped her hands to her head, trying to blot out the painful memory, the fear. It was not true – she had loved Manfred, there was no sin. And he had loved her, but now he was gone. She hugged herself and murmured his name, gently rocking back and forth, finding some comfort in this simple physical movement.

A key scraped in the lock of the cage and Lissette leapt to her feet. The skinny man who had wielded the scissors eyed her speculatively from outside the bars, while another man, younger, struggled with the cage door. He paused for a moment when he saw her face.

'There is no need to be afraid,' he said. 'We will not hurt you.'

Lissette walked slowly across the cage and stopped before them. The tears had gone and her face was set, hard.

'I'm not afraid, certainly not of you.' She stared contemptuously at the little man. 'Have you brought your scissors?'

He looked up at her slyly, eyeing her torn dress. He brought his hand from behind him and held the shears aloft, as if they were a sword. Then he snapped them together in a clipping motion.

The younger man finally turned the lock, then glanced at the barber who was still taunting Lissette with the scissors. He grabbed them from him angrily and turned to the woman.

'It must be done. You cannot be treated any differently from the others.'

Lissette did not move. The implacability of her stance worried the young man, and he hesitated. The skinny man spoke for the first time.

'I must cut your hair, *madame*. It's too long.'

There was an oily suggestiveness about his remark that made Lissette tremble inside, but she did not allow the fear to show on her face. She transferred her gaze to him and he shifted uncomfortably.

'Oh, you can come in and take my hair.' Her voice was dead, almost toneless, yet frightening in its intensity. 'But I,' she added quietly, 'will have your eyes.'

Lissette held up her hands in front of her, palm inwards, the fingers extended like claws. Her nails were long and unbroken. She had tended them well because Manfred had always praised them, though the red nail varnish had chipped away since she had last painted them in her apartment twenty-four hours before.

Yet it was not the threat that decided the young man but her demeanour. There was madness in her eyes, an unnatural tone in her voice. He'd seen it once before in the heat of the ambush, when one of his men had disregarded an order and tried to rush intense automatic fire. He'd been cut down before he'd moved three paces from the doorway.

He knew the woman meant what she said. She would have to be overpowered and tied before the sick little bastard beside him could cut off her hair. He had no stomach for it any more. Not today, not this morning. Perhaps after he had had his breakfast, he thought. He locked the door to the cage and motioned the scissor man away. The man's look of disappointment would have made him smile if he hadn't been so bloody tired.

Lissette watched them go. She felt no sense of victory, not even relief, just overwhelming depression. She slumped in a corner and pulled some of the disgusting straw around her legs to try to keep them warm. The sun was slowly burning off the grey haze, and in the distance she could vaguely hear explosions and the rattle of gunfire. A shell whirled noisily overhead, then crashed down somewhere in the old part of the city. Perhaps the Allies were here. She didn't really care.

CHAPTER
SIXTEEN

Joe was grateful for the warmth of an extra uniform. The night had been cold and uncomfortable but without incident. He hadn't heard a sound.

He splashed his face in the stream and cleaned his teeth with some salt and his finger. He felt better afterwards, but he could have done with some hot tea. The flask was now empty.

He knew that the columns would be pushing on to Antwerp as fast as they could – if they were not there already. They needed a port to be operational as quickly as possible now that the supply lines were so stretched. The further they advanced, the more crucial Antwerp became.

Joe studied the maps carefully. As far as he could see, he had negotiated all of the main centres of population between himself and the port. Only one more remained, and that would be heavily defended. He decided to put the German uniform away for now.

He stuffed it into a dispatch box and slipped into his own uniform covering it with the para smock. Then he wended his way back to the main Brussels–Antwerp road and turned right. He was about twenty-five miles south of Antwerp. But first he had to clear the defences at Boom . . .

He made good time. The road appeared to be deserted; the farm-houses he passed were still shuttered and asleep. A red sun glowed through the heavy mist on the horizon, spreading its light as it quickly dispersed the foggy tendrils that lay across the flat, open countryside.

Porter did not intend to take any unnecessary chances until he knew a little more. He nursed the machine as quietly as he could, keeping the engine note steady in top gear, stopping from time to time to scan the terrain ahead with his binoculars. Then, to his left, something flashed low in the rising sun.

He dismounted, trained his glasses and carefully quartered the area. He saw a patch of dust and, emerging from it, the aerials of a Sherman tank. The squadron was moving towards him, intent on reaching the main route into Antwerp as quickly as possible.

Joe smiled. He'd timed it well. He remounted and sped on northwards, keeping his eye on the slow column of tanks as it gradually drew closer.

They hit the main road behind him at Willebroek. He was only a few minutes ahead of the British Squadron when he approached the crossroads at Breendonk.

About half a mile further on he could see the road rising up on a viaduct over a railway line. There was a small café on the corner of the crossroads, and Joe wondered half-heartedly if he should get himself a hot drink or some food before he continued. Cafés might be open on a main road. He slowed down.

Robert Vekemans had been waiting at the crossroads since dawn. He studied the approaching dispatch rider carefully before making a move.

Joe saw the door to the café open. He swiftly grabbed the Thompson from the clip on the handlebars with his right hand and tucked it under his right arm to steady it, keeping the machine on course with his left. The man was in civilian clothes, wearing a raincoat, though the weather now was clear and dry. He appeared to be unarmed.

Joe coasted to a stop just in front of him. He was relaxed but ready to fire instantly if the man did anything stupid.

Vekemans was very much aware of the round hole in the muzzle of the Thompson levelled at his stomach. He kept his hands in the British soldier's sight. He had no wish to be gunned down at this stage of the war by a nervous trigger finger. He pointed towards the viaduct behind him.

'Is that the way you intend to go?'

Joe nodded. He was surprised by the quality of the man's English. 'Probably,' he said shortly.

Vekemans gazed at the Englishman. There was something odd about his uniform. The para smock was not standard issue for dispatch riders. Vekemans was a former lieutenant in the Belgian Army, repatriated by the Germans after being captured in 1940. He had helped to cover the evacuation of the British Expeditionary Force from the beaches at Dunkirk, so he was familiar with normal issue. Then there were the brown boots. And what was he doing *ahead* of the liberating forces?

Joe interrupted his thoughts, casually keeping the weapon pointing at Vekemans.

'Why do you want to know?'

The Belgian decided to come clean. The dispatch bike was British, as was the uniform, even if it were not standard, and the rider could have got separated from the main thrust of the liberating columns.

'About a mile further on from that viaduct are the bridges over the river at Boom.'

Joe made no comment, waiting for him to continue.

Vekemans pointed again. 'They are mined, ready to be detonated the minute they see you approach. There is a lookout on the roof of the bridge house, and as soon as you reach the top of that rise, they will spot you.' He paused. 'That's when the bridge goes.'

The green eyes continued to drill into Vekemans unblinkingly.

'So?'

The Belgian indicated the Thompson. 'Do you think you could point that thing somewhere else?'

Joe let it drop down on to the handlebars and rest there. But Vekemans was uncomfortably aware that the Englishman's finger was still on the trigger.

'There is another way,' he said.

Joe glanced slowly around him, his senses alert for any possible trap, but the crossroads appeared to be deserted. To his right a gasworks squatted heavily, and he caught a whiff of ammonia on the early-morning breeze, coming from a factory alongside. Both seemed empty of any life or movement. He focused his attention on the man in front of him.

'How?'

Vekemans pointed to the road off to Porter's right, past the gasworks. 'Down there is a canal that runs parallel with the viaduct. You can cross on to the far bank, then turn left up alongside it. That will bring you to another bridge, the Pont van Enschodt. It crosses the river east of the main access.' He paused, gathering his thoughts. 'You can't be seen from the lookout point because of the gasworks, but there's only one shot at this, and once you try to cross it, they'll be alerted and the bridge will go.'

Joe thought about that. 'Is this the only way into Antwerp?'

Vekemans shrugged. 'Everything else will be mined as well. This is the only one that really has a chance.' He smiled. 'I've had four years to think about it.'

Joe believed him. Even if he got through, no one else would. He glanced behind him. The column he'd seen earlier was on his tail. It would reach this point within the next few minutes. He made up his mind.

'OK. You wait here. There will be an armoured column along soon — it's right behind me. Tell them what you have told me.'

Vekemans was concerned. 'What will you do?'

'I'll wait by the canal down there, out of sight of Jerry. As soon as I see you and those tanks coming, I'll try and get through. But you make sure they're right up my arse.'

The Belgian nodded vehemently. 'I'll do my best.'

Porter smiled grimly. 'You'd better, 'cos I'm going through anyway, and if they're not behind me, they'll lose their chance.' He looked past Vekemans at the café. 'You got any tea in there?'

'No. How about some coffee?'

'Fine, but make it quick.'

Vekemans turned back into the café and re-emerged almost at once with a bowl of coffee. 'Take mine,' he said.

Joe gazed at it in some surprise. He'd never used a drinking bowl before.

The Belgian handed it to him with a smile. 'Drink it. It's good.'

Joe held it gingerly in both hands, having balanced the Thompson across the top of the petrol tank. 'Christ, there's enough here to sink a battleship!'

He took a sip. It *was* good, and he suddenly realized how thirsty he was. Vekemans watched him drink from the bowl until it was all gone, then he took it back from the Englishman. 'Good luck,' he said quietly.

Joe clipped the Thompson back into place and eased up the revs on the engine. 'You be quick. As soon as they're here, make sure they get right behind me, OK?'

He pushed the machine away from the kerb and, as silently as he could, he moved off down the road away from the viaduct, making sure the gasworks masked him from any lookout on the main bridge. Behind him he picked up the first faint sounds of the approaching column of tanks.

Corporal Karl Berghauser had been given the task of detonating the charges on the little Pont van Enschodt. It was a temporary wooden structure, built in 1940 after the original one had been blown up by the retreating British Army. The main bridge would stay intact until the Allies appeared on the viaduct. But the corporal was not a happy man.

The two guards had retired to a safe position as he prepared to light the fuses. The covered wicks that lit the fuse had proved un-reliable in the past, so he was not surprised when they refused to light properly. He tried again, but once more they fizzled and went out.

The corporal shrugged. There was little he could do, except return to the main bridge and his parked L K W to get new fuses. He sighed exasperatedly and trudged back along the road that skirted the river, leaving the bridge still in one piece – and, for the moment, un-guarded.

It is on such mundane matters as a faulty fuse that battles turn. Those few short minutes, and the courage and daring of Robert Vekemans, were the pivot upon which the liberation of Antwerp would be decided.

Vekemans moved out into the centre of the road and signalled to the first tank. The heavy barrel twisted menacingly his way, but the Sherman rumbled on towards the viaduct over the railway line. The second tank ignored his presence and followed the first. Vekemans desperately signalled to the third. He had to stop them before they ascended to the top of the rise and were spotted by the German lookout on the bridgehouse.

A hand emerged from the third tank and indicated the fourth. Vekemans ran alongside the Sherman as it gradually ground to a halt. A dusty face with a day's growth of stubble pushed its way up out of the turret and surveyed him.

Major John Dunlop was already concerned about the viaduct. It was clear that once up that rise they would be in an exposed position and could be seen for miles around. Then the jig might be up. The river crossings into Antwerp were bound to be mined and heavily defended. On top of that viaduct they were vulnerable.

When Vekemans told him of the alternative he immediately ordered the first three Sherman tanks to return to the crossroads. They were within yards of the crest of the rise when they finally stopped, then slowly turned and rumbled back.

Dunlop checked with his commanding officer and received permission for the sidestep around the viaduct. But something still worried him. He rubbed the dust from his eyes and gazed down at the Belgian on the pavement beneath him.

'The other bridge – will it take this weight?'

He slapped the cowling of the Sherman to give emphasis to his words. Vekemans smiled up at him confidently.

'I was in the Engineers, major. I've checked *everything*. It will carry your tanks across safely.'

Dunlop had to decide.

'Right, you get in the scout car with Sergeant Spiden and direct Captain Stubbs in the leading tank. We'll stay right behind you.'

While Vekemans climbed into the open-topped Humber, Dunlop radioed Stubbs, the commander of the leading troop of Shermans, and briefed him about the situation.

Stubbs too was relieved not to be out in the open, but the other bridge would be mined as well. Could they get to it before they were spotted and the bridge blown?

It was a gamble, but the odds were better under the cover of the gasworks. He didn't hesitate.

'OK, I'll lead off. Tell Sergeant Spiden to stay in close behind me with the scout car. I may need the Belgian.'

Dunlop confirmed the manoeuvre. 'Move it fast, Stubbs. Stay out of sight for as long as you can. Once you are in the open and they can see you, we won't have long.'

*

Joe had kept himself out of sight under a railway bridge. As soon as he heard the heavy metalled tracks rolling down the road towards him, he pulled down his goggles and gunned the bike out from his cover, turning right and left, before crossing a small bridge over the canal. Once on the other side, he turned sharply up the cinder track that ran northwards beside the waterway. Off to his left the viaduct rose high above the railway before the road reached the main bridge over the Rupel. The wide river was the last barrier between the Allied armies and the city of Antwerp.

Joe kept his head down and pushed the machine as hard as he could along the track, cinders spewing out from beneath the rear wheel as he accelerated. Ahead of him was a long, partially wooden bridge over the river, less than half a mile east of the main crossing.

If the bridge was going to be blown, now was the time to do it. He was in the open and he could see the outline of the main bridge beyond the viaduct. If he could see them, they could see him. Joe opened the throttle wide, straining the bike to its limits. Now it was just a question of who reacted first . . .

There was no going back. He was totally committed. He hit the bridge at about sixty miles per hour. He could see the firing leads for the detonation of the explosives along the guardrail. There was no time to consider his fate if those fuses were already lit.

The wooden trellis work of the bridge flashed by, creating its own strange gaps of sound as the engine noise bounced back in its wake. Then he was over, and he suddenly saw that the road ended in a T-junction immediately after the end of the bridge.

He decided to go left.

He slammed on the brakes, throttled the engine down, taking the corner as wide as he could. He stuck his left boot out, the metal studs flashing off the cobblestones of the dock road.

Then he was round the bend and in front of him were the rear of the German defences on the main bridge. He could see men ahead of him scattering as he bore down. He braked sharply right, swerving down a side street, and then he was back on the main road again.

He was clear of Boom.

Ahead lay Antwerp. Joe let out his breath slowly, grinning to himself. He'd done it, but now he had to get himself off the thoroughfare. Back streets were safer.

He took the first turning he could find and slowed the machine down, moving as sedately as he could through the empty streets.

Behind him in Boom Corporal Berghauser had just completed his short walk to the L K W containing his equipment, when he heard machine-gun fire. He turned to see the leading tank commanded by Stubbs appear among the German positions guarding the main bridge.

In the time it had taken him to walk that short distance, Porter had gunned his way through, Stubbs had crossed the bridge, while Vekemans had halted the scout car, much to Sergeant Spiden's disgust, in the centre of the bridge, leaving him completely exposed to enemy fire. Calmly Vekemans had disconnected the fuses.

Thus the bridges at Boom were captured intact. Nobody was killed; the only casualty was a horse.

But it had been close.

The suburban streets remained silent and empty, doors and windows closed, no children playing. Joe was grateful. He knew how quickly the word would spread about the arrival of the British at Boom. And it was uncanny how soon the civilian populations seemed to know.

He had an uncomfortable feeling that a thousand eyes were watching him from behind the shuttered windows. And, like the bow wave of a vessel, the news would be spreading out in his wake. In a way Joe had become used to it. Nevertheless, he kept a wary eye open, scanning the road ahead for a German tank or ambush.

He did not race. There was no need. He'd got here in one piece; the 11th Armoured Division was at Boom; and, whatever pickings there were in the city, he was now in the best position to take advantage.

The B S A hummed quietly through the outskirts of the city. Joe approached the centre through a maze of back streets and secondary roads. It was a tactic that had paid off before.

Gradually the housing gave way to business premises and warehouses. Faintly, in the distance, he could hear gunfire from the area near the docks. He'd kept well away from that, easing himself in the direction where he anticipated he would find the commercial heart of the city.

His sense of direction was phenomenal. He often boasted that if you put him down, blindfolded, in any part of the world, he'd find his way home like a pigeon – home being whatever temporary base he happened to be settled in. Joe had never been permitted the experience of what is loosely called home.

The buildings were higher now, more densely packed, and still Joe had seen no one, not a living soul or a moving vehicle. The deserted streets reminded him of the area around the City of London early on a Sunday morning. It was dead, uncannily so, and the bike's engine sounded hollowly down the street ahead of him.

It narrowed until it was almost an alleyway, but it presented no problem to the motorbike. Joe could see an old-fashioned iron stanchion barring the middle of the street where it ended in a T-junction. Beyond was the foliage of one of the trees that lined the intersecting boulevard.

He could just hear something above the revs of the BSA. At first he could not identify it, and he slowed the machine to a walking pace, preventing it from overbalancing by sticking out his legs on either side and poling it forward. As he neared the iron stanchion the sound grew louder, washing up the street like the distant murmur of the sea. He reached the end, and as he pushed the bike across the pavement into the boulevard, the sound burst around his ears.

He stopped the machine and stared down the tree-lined avenue. About a hundred yards away to his left he could see a stationary German half-track, surrounded by a hundred or more cheering, exuberant civilians. Some had climbed inside the vehicle, and one of them, who appeared to be the leader of the victorious resistance, was in imminent danger of being wrestled to the floor by a lusty young girl, whose arms were locked around his neck, her lips glued to his.

Belgian, British and American flags had appeared, and the half-track was engulfed by the noisy, emotional crowd. It was clear that the local resistance was already having some success, and the background noise of gunfire from the docks indicated that its presence was being felt.

Joe looked up the boulevard to his right. That was as empty as the rest of the city had seemed. The gutted remains of a vehicle blocked the centre of the road. Joe turned away from the crowds. As yet they had not spotted his British uniform or they would have descended on him too. Joe had more important business to attend to.

But one man had seen him.

He slipped his captured German automatic weapon over his shoulder and detached himself from the crowd, following Joe as he quietly rode the machine along the pavement, past the wrecked vehicle and the burnt corpse of a soldier. Joe didn't know if the body was German or not. It was impossible to tell.

Another twenty yards along the boulevard and he came to the entrance of a cinema. The posters and stills were in their racks, but the plate-glass doors were shattered. Jagged pieces of glass covered the devastated foyer. Joe dismounted from the B S A, switched off the engine and leant it against one of the trees. Slowly he walked into the cool interior.

Sweets littered the floor among the broken glass and two more German corpses, one just inside the entrance, the other near the foot of the staircase. They lay still upon the deep-red carpet, the blood turning black around the bodies, the flies buzzing disgustedly from one to the other. Joe ignored them. He'd seen too much in the short three months since D-Day to be affected by death or its aftermath. He climbed the stairs and turned right at the top, then up six more steps into the darkened circle. He pulled a metal flashlight from beneath his para smock and beamed it round the interior. The cinema was large and, as far as he could see, undamaged.

Joe made his way round to a door at the side of the circle that led down some marble stairs to the area backstage, behind the screen. It was surprisingly spacious and had been built so that it could be used as a stage as well. There were dressing-rooms and a pair of high double doors backing on to the street outside to give access for scenery.

More steps led down from the dressing-room well to a basement. Joe descended and found himself confronted by a steel fire door. He managed to push it open, and it squeaked hollowly in the blackness beyond. Joe felt around inside the door and found a switch.

The strip lighting revealed a huge area stretching back under the auditorium that had been converted into a shelter. There were wooden benches, tables and even bunks. Joe gazed at it thoughtfully and allowed himself a brief smile. There was enough space here to empty a warehouse . . . The basement would do.

Joe retraced his steps up to the circle lobby. He'd noticed a door in the lobby with a sign in French. He guessed it was the manager's office, and it looked official enough to arouse his curiosity. Inside was a large desk, some filing cabinets and a small ante-room. Joe picked up the perfume of a woman, and there were other indications that it was a lady who had run this place.

In the ante-room, close to the mirror, were some lipstick and a powder box and puff. He checked the drawers of the desk. There were documents and typewritten copies of business replies with a signature, Lissette van der Elst. Then he found a small card, the sort of thing that comes with a present or flowers. The handwriting was German, with the name Manfred at the bottom.

Joe straightened. The woman had been careless. If she had been fraternizing with Germans, she could already be in the hands of the resistance. And if the celebrations going on in the boulevard were anything to go by, it was more than likely.

That would be a pity. He needed her.

Joe slipped the Thompson from around his shoulder and padded softly over to the wall just behind the open door. The noise had been very faint, but stairs don't squeak unless somebody treads on them, and somebody was climbing the stairs outside as quietly as he could.

Joe waited.

He sensed the man's presence in the half open doorway, then he smelt the sour, pervasive odour of tension and fear. The door was pushed further back, and Joe pressed himself to the wall. The man looked round the office. It seemed empty, but the ante-room door was closed. He advanced slowly into the room.

The hard metal ring of a gun muzzle pressed into his back and he froze.

Joe took the Schmeisser from him, then stepped back. 'OK,' he said, 'you can turn around now.'

The man did so. Joe stared at him.

'Do you speak any English?'

The man nodded. 'A little.'

Joe smiled grimly. 'Good.' He paused, glancing round the office. Then he said, 'The woman who runs this cinema – where would I find her?'

CHAPTER
SEVENTEEN

The cell was small, but the bunk she was lying on would once have accommodated another person above her. Lissette assumed she had been transferred to the prison because her hair had not been shorn like the others. Perhaps they had a different fate in store for her.

Graffiti daubed the walls: names, dates and a few pathetic messages. She knew the prison had been used by the Gestapo for its unspeakable purposes, and she shuddered, her imagination visualizing a thousand horrors, none of them as terrible as the reality.

Lissette had been fortunate. She could have been killed by the resistance fighters on the flat roof of the cinema. Her presence with the German officer would have been enough to have her shot as a decoy. No one would have questioned it. In the heat of battle everyone is an enemy until they are dead or proved innocent.

She did not feel lucky. She did not feel anything. The bunk was hard, but she continued to lie still on her back, gazing at the base of the bunk above, seeing nothing but the pictures in her mind.

She felt suspended, cut off. She could disappear into this dark cell and never be seen again. Who would know? Her mother – would she care? Lissette had walked out of her apartment – was it only in the early hours of this morning? It seemed a lifetime ago – and she could vanish off the face of the earth. All that would remain of her would be the cinema she had managed during the occupation.

If she was to die because of that, then she knew her mother would ask no questions. There would be a fine show of grief, a display of tears that would fool everyone except those who knew her well. But her mother would feel nothing. There was no one who would question her passing. The only person she had ever given herself to was dead. Like herself, swallowed up by the war. Perhaps it was best.

The thought stopped there. Something inside her screamed its defiance. She suddenly realized how far she had gone. This passive acceptance of her death: she had played with it, enjoyed its drama, her own self-pity enhancing its attractiveness.

No, she would not die. That was too easy. All she had to do was let it happen and, as night follows day, it would. It was harder to live, but Lissette had faced an empty world before. She had found a job then, a position and some self-esteem. She would do so again. She owed it to herself. There was no one else.

How long she had lain there, unaware of the passage of time, she would never know. She must have slept at some point, but when she woke it was still light. She tried blinking, not sure if she was asleep or awake, but she didn't move.

A metal bucket in another cell crashed over, ringing in her ears. She sat bolt-upright, swinging her legs over the side of the bunk. She stared at a man's name scrawled on the stone wall opposite. She wondered if he was still alive.

She heard a key rattle distantly in a lock, then a door shut loudly and footsteps strode slowly but evenly down the passage outside her cell. The unchanging gait came closer, the metal studs on the boots crunching solidly into the hard, stone-flagged floor of the passage. The noise seemed to swell inside her head, rebounding from the walls of her cell. She put her hands to her ears. Then it stopped.

She sat very still, her eyes fastened on the door. A key turned in the lock and the heavy door was flung back against the wall. The shadowy figure of a uniformed man stood outlined in the doorway. He didn't move and Lissette could not see his face. She wanted to scream, run, escape, but she remained frozen on the edge of her bunk.

A voice emerged from the indistinct figure. 'Come,' he said. 'A man is here to see you.'

She heard him speak but could not distinguish all the words. Only two. A man. What man? Not dear, sweet Manfred. He was gone. Her man was dead.

The warden's office was spacious but clammy. Its damp, cold interior contrasted sharply with the warm, sunny day he could glimpse through the barred, grimy window behind the warden's desk.

Joe crossed one leg elegantly over the other, displaying his freshly shined, brown officer's boots. The warden eyed Joe uneasily from behind his impressive desk. He was worried, and it showed. How soon he would be removed from his position he had no idea. Even less could he be sure what the Allies would do to him once they were fully aware of how the prison had been used while the Germans had been in control. True, he had been but a figurehead, unable to exercise any real power over the activities of the Gestapo. Nevertheless, he had remained warden, nominally in charge while the atrocities to which he had turned a blind eye had been carried out.

He had been expecting the arrival of the British for the past twenty-four hours, but not quite in the form it had taken. This solitary British officer, in his paratrooper's smock, was not what he had visualized. Still less had he expected the request for the custody of the woman who had been handed over to him by the White Brigade. They had left him in no doubt that they would be back, and he was thankful that no revenge had been taken on him as yet. Thus he had greeted the British officer's arrival with some relief, but now it seemed as if his stay would be a short one and the warden was frightened. He knew he could expect no mercy from the resistance fighters once they had finished with the Germans.

Joe smiled. 'I expect you have been fairly busy these last forty-eight hours or so?'

The warden found this apparently innocuous question unnerving. He gazed at Joe. There was something vaguely worrying about his green, empty eyes. He sensed an ambivalence in the officer's attitude. He decided it was best to ignore it.

'Yes, these are hectic days for us all.' He stopped, not sure how far he wanted to take this line of thought.

'When did Jerry leave?'

Joe kept the question polite – just. He was deliberately trying to keep this man off balance, to prevent any suspicions about his own presence from surfacing.

'Er, yesterday, I think. I can't be sure. There was some sabotage at the docks by the terror' – he corrected himself swiftly – 'by the resistance, then later that day I heard shelling and it was clear the Allies were about to enter the city.' He glanced at Joe curiously. 'And when did your unit arrive?'

'Today. I'm attached to the 11th Armoured Division – Intelligence. As I told you, we want Miss van der Elst back in London as soon as possible. We'll be flying her out later. I trust she is in good health?'

The barbed remark sank in and Joe could see the alarm spread across the warden's face.

'Oh, yes. She has not been tortured. The Gestapo left before she was brought in . . .' His voice faltered. He realized he had revealed too much, exposed his own duplicity. 'She is probably very tired,' he continued weakly, 'but nothing else.'

'Good,' Joe said, without expression. 'I'm glad to hear it. Will she be long?'

The warden shook his head. He seemed visibly to have shrunk behind the huge desk.

Lissette followed the uniformed figure along the passage, deliberately keeping her eyes directed upon the back of his legs as he walked slowly in front of her. His trousers were shabby. The bottoms were worn and threadbare and the heels of his boots were run down. He was a little unsteady on his feet, and it crossed her mind that he might be quite old. She hadn't seen his face, nor did she raise her eyes to see if his hair was grey. She had withdrawn into herself, cutting off the outside world. She did not want to see these surroundings.

She followed the warder obediently through several iron doors that had to be unbolted and relocked behind her again and up a winding stone staircase, until he eventually stopped in front of a wooden door. He knocked twice, then entered, pushing Lissette quite gently in ahead of him. She heard him speak.

'This is the woman, sir.'

Then somebody else spoke her name softly. 'Lissette.'

She dragged her eyes from the floor and looked at him. He was in uniform, a British soldier's uniform, some kind of smock and a beret. He smiled at her encouragingly.

'It's me Lissette.'

She gazed at him blankly. She'd never seen him before in her life.

The warder looked at Joe. 'I think she's in a state of shock, sir.' He nodded apologetically at Lissette. Like the warden, he was unsure of his own position with the new authorities and anxious to please. 'She came in today, sir, with the other women, but she has been kept apart from them.' He smiled ingratiatingly. 'They had their hair cut off, you see, and she . . .' He stopped and looked anxiously at the man behind the desk, wondering if he had said too much.

Joe walked towards Lissette and placed his hands on her arms. 'It's me, Lissette. Joe. Don't you remember?'

She didn't answer. He was quite close to her and only she could see his face. Then, astonishingly, he winked. Lissette was too bemused to react. Joe had judged it correctly. The time had come to make his move. He turned to the warden.

'Thank God they didn't shear her hair.'

'Yes, indeed,' the warden said with obvious relief. 'Apparently they suspected her of being an informer.'

'Not Lissette – she worked for us. The cinema was a public place, anonymous. A lot of valuable information was passed through by her. I'm just glad I got here in time.'

He put his arm around the woman, who was shivering beneath her thin dress. 'Come,' he said, 'I'll take you home.'

'Wait!' The warden stood up suddenly.

Beneath the smock Joe's hand tightened on the Colt. If the silly sod tried to stop him now, he would have to use it. He turned and faced him.

'Yes?'

'The woman – you are taking her?'

'Of course.'

The warden pondered for a moment. He felt uneasy, exposed. Could he let her go without any prior consultation?

Joe watched him unblinkingly. 'Of course, if you prefer it, I can contact London and tell them you have had her imprisoned in a cell.'

'No!' The warden had made up his mind. What did one woman more or less matter when the whole city was in turmoil? 'That won't be necessary. I'd just like you to sign for her release.' He sat down again and scribbled something on a piece of paper, then handed it to Joe.

Joe Porter didn't even look at it. He signed his name with a flourish, then added, 'Special Security Section'. It was meaningless, but it looked good. He stepped back and snapped up a very Sandhurst salute. The warden, slightly confused, as he was not wearing a hat and could not return it, stood up smartly to attention. Joe used military protocol whenever it suited him. It covered a multitude of sins, as did the paratrooper's smock. It gave him an advantage that he enjoyed. And it was working now.

The old warder led them from the room, and Lissette followed Joe dazedly through a maze of echoing corridors and clanging metal doors until they finally emerged into the warmth of a late but sultry afternoon.

The setting sun was low on the horizon. Lissette shielded her eyes from the light, trying to adjust to the glare. She gazed from beneath the palm of her hand and watched Joe put his leg over the motorbike and kick the engine into life. It roared throatily and Joe patted the pillion behind him.

'It's all right,' he said. 'Hop on.'

He smiled, his eyes warm and friendly, and for some reason – she never did know why – she climbed unquestioningly on to the back, as he had asked.

He reached behind him and gently took her hands, putting them around his waist. 'Hold tight.'

Automatically Lissette did so. Joe throttled up the engine, and they roared off along the cobbled street, her long brown hair streaming out behind her. She rested her head on the stranger's back and cried with relief, her cries drowned by the noise of the engine. Lissette did not know why he had rescued her: it didn't matter. She could feel the sun warm on her back, the wind tugging at her dress and blowing through her hair. She was free.

For some reason the keys to her apartment were still in the pocket of her dress. She opened the door and went inside, stopping in the small entrance hall as the familiar smells and surroundings suddenly seemed to weaken her. She felt disorientated and stretched out a hand to steady herself. Joe shut the door quickly and moved to her side, holding her elbow.

'Are you all right?'

She stared at him, then shook her arm free. 'Yes, of course.' Instinctively she moved to the kitchen. 'Would you like some tea?' she asked automatically.

Joe watched her carefully, aware of the strain in her voice, the attempt at normality. He needed to retain that. If she broke down now, he would learn nothing.

'Yes,' he said, 'I'd love a cup, but let me do it. I make a nice brew and you Continentals haven't mastered it yet.' He smiled to take the edge off the remark. 'You sit down there' – he indicated a chair in the kitchen – 'and I'll do the tea.'

Lissette sat down with an immense sense of relief. She gazed at the pattern of the linoleum on the floor, not absorbing the sounds Joe made as he moved around the kitchen, not hearing his occasional remark. Her mind was blank. But gradually she did become aware of his presence, and there was comfort in having a man in her kitchen.

The thought surprised her, and she looked at Joe as he warmed the teapot with some water from the kettle and carefully measured out three spoonfuls of tea.

How odd, she thought. Only two days ago Manfred had said goodbye to her, here in this room. He had kissed her lovingly and left after warning her again to leave the city. And now here was another man, an Englishman, Manfred's enemy. Someone like this man had killed him. Yet, curiously, it didn't seem to matter – she was glad of the presence of this stranger. Lissette didn't try to analyse it. She was too tired and grateful for her release from the prison.

Joe stirred the cup vigorously and placed it on the table in front of her. 'You drink that,' he commanded. 'It'll make you feel better.'

Lissette picked up the mug, holding it between her hands. She took a sip. It was hot, milky and sweet, and very English. She smiled for the first time that day. 'Thank you,' she said.

Joe sat down opposite her and glanced around the kitchen. 'It's nice,' he said. 'Your apartment.' He paused, weighing his next remark. 'You should be all right here.'

Lissette looked at him curiously. 'Why did you get me out of that prison? Why did you lie? I've never worked for you.'

Joe sipped the tea. 'No, but you have worked for the Germans in the cinema.'

She stared at him. It didn't make any sense.

'So why did you get me out?'

He stood up and walked across to the door, then turned towards her. 'Because I want you to work for me.' There was a finality about

177

his remark that chilled her. His green eyes were suddenly hard and unsmiling. Lissette looked down at the table, twisting the mug round in her hands.

'This morning,' she said tonelessly, 'I was in the lions' cage in the zoo.' Her voice broke and she stopped for a moment, trying to control herself. She continued, 'They cut the women's hair. They were going to cut mine because they thought I was a collaborator.'

Joe stood silently in the doorway, listening. She looked up at him and there was defiance in her eyes.

'I told them I would use these on them' – she held up her hands, curling her fingers into claws – 'if they tried it on me.' She lowered her hands back to the table and waited for his response.

Joe was surprised. He hadn't expected a challenge but it was good. The woman had courage and he respected that.

'Did you collaborate?'

Lissette shook her head. 'No, I ran the cinema. I am the manageress there. It is my job.'

Joe studied her for a moment, then crossed the room and sat opposite her again.

'And Manfred – who was he?'

He was close enough to see the pain that filled her eyes. She swallowed, blinking, trying desperately to hang on to her composure.

'How do you know about . . .?' She paused. She couldn't bear to say his name to this stranger. 'About him?'

Joe sat quite still, gazing straight into her eyes. 'I know he was your lover.'

How did he know, she thought? How could he know about Manfred? That was another time, an age ago. Her lip trembled. She wanted to run away, hide herself in her bed, but she could not tear her eyes from him.

'He's dead,' she said quietly, amazed at how normal her voice seemed when inside she felt empty. Her fists were clenched and Joe placed his hands over them tenderly.

'Is that why they put you in the lions' cage?'

Lissette looked down at his hands on hers, and slowly she unclenched them. Some of the tension eased from her.

'I don't know,' she said. 'They found me on the roof with a

German officer who was hiding. He forced me up there. He thought he would be safe from the resistance. They killed him,' she added simply.

Joe held her hands in his. 'Listen to me, Lissette. You will be safe now. I want you to run that cinema for me. Tell me about it.'

She looked at him, surprised by the question. 'What?'

He reassured her. 'Is there storage space, a basement?'

She nodded. 'Yes. There is an air-raid shelter for the customers.'

'It must be big.'

Lissette nodded. 'It is. Sometimes the cinema was full, even during the air raids.'

Joe was relieved. She had told him the truth. Now he knew it could work.

'Good. As soon as things settle down, you will re-open the cinema in the normal way. I will provide papers, authorization.'

She stared at him, puzzled. 'I don't understand.'

'You will.' He stood up. 'Now I think it is time for you to get some rest.' He saw the look that crossed her face. 'I'll sleep on the sofa – is there a sofa?'

Lissette nodded. 'Yes, but –'

'No buts,' he said. 'I'll be fine. A sofa will be luxury after the field I slept in last night.'

Lissette lay on her bed as the long evening gradually darkened into night. She could still hear occasional bursts of gunfire across the city where the last pockets of hostility were being mopped up. But, oddly, she felt secure and safe. There was something about the Englishman that calmed her fears. Knowing he was in the other room, that he was armed, made her little apartment seem like a fortress.

She had a defender, a stranger who had appeared from nowhere. She didn't care what his motives were, why he had come for her in the prison. She was just glad he was there.

She fell asleep then, exhaustion protecting her from thinking about Manfred. That would come tomorrow.

In the weeks that followed the liberation of Antwerp and Brussels, it became increasingly clear that the ease with which both cities had been freed took both the Germans and the British by surprise. This may have accounted partially for the British forces' lack of effort on 4 September to try to secure the Scheldt estuary, which stretches more than forty miles from Antwerp to the sea.

If the bridges over the Alhort Canal to the east of the city had been secured on 4 September, then a push northwards to Bredon would have cut off the German forces on the islands of Walcheren and South Beveland. As it was, the bridges were blown up by the time an attempt to cross the canal was made on 6 September. The delay would cost the Allies heavily.

Not until the dyke at Westkapelle was hit by Bomber Command on 3 October and Walcheren was flooded by the sea could the powerful batteries, embedded in concrete, be isolated.

Heavy fighting continued on the Beveland peninsula and did not end until 8 November. Between 1 October and 8 November the Canadian 1st Army took 41,043 prisoners. They lost 703 officers and 12,170 men were killed, wounded or missing. But Holland remained largely occupied by German forces throughout the hard winter. The Dutch continued to wait. It would be early spring before they would know the joy of liberation.

And so the major part of the VI sites continued to seed the skies over London. But Antwerp and Brussels too were now targets for the deadly doodlebug, as it came to be known. As long as you could hear the curious drone of its engine, you were safe. When it cut, you would duck for cover. If you were lucky, you would survive. Many did not. In Antwerp even soldiers on leave from the front were to become its victims.

Mine-sweeping the Scheldt began on 4 November and continued until 26 November. Two days later the first heavy cargo ship, the Canadian-built Fort Cataraqui, docked in Antwerp.

The port was now free, and the flood of supplies began . . .

CHAPTER
EIGHTEEN

Joe stayed on in the apartment with Lissette. It was convenient, and she wanted him there.

He understood her fear. As long as he remained, she had some protection if the resistance decided to come back for her. Joe didn't think that was likely. If the warden at the prison was called upon to explain why he had released Lissette, then the local resistance leaders were unlikely to question his handing her over to the British. For the moment the British could do no wrong. The celebrations in the city continued for nearly a week, and Joe was able to return with Lissette to the cinema and help her clean it up.

One by one her staff drifted back. The damage to the entrance lobby was repaired and, at the same time, Joe had the huge basement area beneath the stalls cleaned and readied for use.

At no time during this period did he make any advances to Lissette. He respected the privacy of her apartment.

He wasn't sure why he didn't attempt to share her bed. In the circumstances it would have been quite normal. In Antwerp, in those few heady days after liberation, for most people the normal boundaries disappeared. Just to have survived and to be able to couple was a celebration of life itself. But Joe sensed that it would not have been right for Lissette. And he needed her trust.

Slowly her confidence grew as her life at the Cinéac returned to its normal routine. A week after liberation it re-opened with an American film, *The Picture of Dorian Gray*. The cinema was full and Lissette began to talk.

When they were alone in her apartment she told him about Manfred and how much she had loved him. And Joe listened. He was a good listener and he wanted to know as much as he could about this vulnerable, contradictory woman.

Once she began, the emotional floodgates opened and she held back nothing. She wondered sometimes just why she revealed so much to this Englishman.

He was a stranger. A week before, she had known nothing of his existence. There was a quietness about the way he would listen, a stillness in his bearing as he gazed into the fireplace. Only his eyes would move as he glanced at her.

She told him how she had been raped by her mother's lover when she was ten, how jealous her mother had been, how she had held a small pistol to her head in the garden, forcing her to face the wall and demanding to know if it were true. Even at ten Lissette had been wise enough to deny it. The jealous rage in her mother's eyes had terrified her into the lie.

She had not been able to continue after that, but it did not seem to matter. In Joe's silence she had sensed a deep understanding of the privation of her childhood.

He had stood up and quietly prepared one of his famous cups of tea while she composed herself. And she had laughed as he gave it to her.

'A cure for everything, Joe?' she said.

He smiled. 'Almost everything.'

It had come as a shock to discover that he was leaving.

'Why?' she asked.

'I have to. There are things I must do. But I'll be back, probably inside a week.'

It was funny, she thought. Not once had she asked him what he really did. It did not seem to matter. She knew he had a personal interest in the cinema, and if she had thought at all about that, she would have guessed that it was not part of the official war effort. But she had seen the war effort and its horrifying effects. In a curious way she welcomed this somewhat private enterprise.

'Will you be all right?' he asked.

Lissette nodded. 'I think so. Why not? The cinema is open again. I may go and see if my mother is safe.'

That slightly worried Joe. 'Say nothing about me.'

Lissette picked up the slight edge in his voice. 'How do I tell her I got out of the prison?'

'Just say they released you,' Joe said sharply.

'Lots of people have been picked up by mistake and released.'

He stared at her. Perhaps it was time she was reminded a little. 'There is no reason for anyone to know you were arrested by the resistance. Only I know the truth and I will tell no one. It's our secret, Lissette. Why say anything to your mother?'

She could see the sense in that, but there was something slightly chilling about his eyes. They were cold, calculating. She turned away to look out of the window and dismissed her fears as imaginary. Hadn't Joe saved her? Then she realized she knew nothing about him. He had never spoken about himself.

It made her feel slightly uncomfortable when she thought about it after he'd gone. But she did want him to come back. The apartment seemed strangely empty when she was by herself. She hadn't thought that would matter. Most of her life she had lived alone. But now it was different. Manfred and Joe were very much a part of her life.

She had changed.

Joe decided not to retrace his steps. He needed to have as much information about the terrain and the state of the roads as possible. He took the route out of Antwerp that Manfred, and later Lissette, had taken. He rode past the wrecked, burnt-out truck that Hausser had been thrown from. It lay, twisted and blackened, at the bottom of the embankment, but Joe gave it no more than a cursory glance. Wrecked vehicles of all kinds, caught in the open by air strikes, had been pushed to the sides of the road to allow quick access for the convoys bringing supplies and food to the advanced Allied armies.

Manfred's truck was just one of many. Joe passed through Ghent and crossed the Belgian frontier into France at Roubaix. He stayed well north of Paris and reached the small town of St-Pol by midday.

Although the roads were crowded with military columns moving up to the front line and empty convoys returning to their assembly points and bases close to the mulberry harbour in Normandy, he had still made good time; he had covered the hundred miles or so in under four hours.

He rested there for a while. He found a quiet spot in a churchyard, where he relaxed, enjoying the warm sunshine and the French bread and cheese Lissette had prepared for him.

He could still hear the faint rumble of heavy transport in the background, but it was peaceful and quiet in the churchyard as the sun dappled the heavy foliage of autumn, creating small pools of light where the insects darted and suspended themselves. He finished his bread and cheese and dozed quietly in the sun.

It was the boy who woke him up.

Joe was instantly alert, his eyes searching through the trees of the churchyard for some movement. He could still hear a strange, choking sound, and he moved silently through the shadows towards it. Then he stopped.

A young woman was standing by a freshly dug grave. Beside her a small boy, about five years old, clinging to his mother's skirt. He was sobbing, trying hard not to cry but unable to contain his distress. His mother put her arm around the boy, comforting him, speaking to him softly in French. He looked up at her, his face streaked with tears, and she picked him up. Even from a distance Joe could see the pain on her face. He understood that pain and, curiously, he envied the little boy held tightly in his mother's arms.

He remembered watching other children when he was at school, seeing them run into their mothers' embrace when school was over. It stabbed him deeply and he turned away, running quickly through the graveyard to where he had left his machine. Savagely he kicked it into life and rode as fast as he could away from St-Pol, away from his bitter memories.

He reached the *château* in the late afternoon and pulled up behind an army truck at the main entrance. He presented his bogus credentials to the guard in the sentry box, then allowed the heavy vehicle to go up the drive ahead of him. He followed it slowly and watched it disappear behind the *château* and park in the courtyard by the stables. He tooled in behind it and pulled his bike up on its rear stand, leaving it with the other vehicles. There must have been about twenty trucks out of view behind the main building.

Hillier and Eddie were doing well.

Annette was delighted to see him. She flung her arms around his neck, hugging him. But Maria stood back, her arm around Hillier's waist, declaring her new allegiance.

Nick grinned at Joe. 'Seems like you've been missed.'

The Englishman tried to disentangle himself from Annette's enthusiastic greeting. 'It's always nice to be welcomed,' he said with some difficulty as she glued herself to him. Eventually he managed to hold her at arm's length. 'Listen, I'm hungry. How about some food for the returning soldier?'

Annette stepped away from him. '*Mais oui* – of course. Come into the kitchen.' They followed her down the hall, the two men hanging back.

'How was it?' Nick said quietly.

Joe stared at him, weighing his response. 'There's a lot to talk about.'

Gus Kenwright was sat at the long table, drinking some soup. He waved genially when he saw Joe.

'The wanderer returns. Where have you been? Berlin?'

Joe sat down. 'Not yet.'

Kenwright turned to Annette who was by the range, ladling some soup into a bowl. He shouted at her, 'Come on! Hurry up with that!'

Joe felt a hot surge of anger at his arrogance. 'Don't yell. She's doing it.' His voice was pitched low, but it was deadly.

Kenwright eyed him, but didn't challenge.

Annette filled the nasty silence that followed by bustling round the table. She gave Joe soup and some bread. He began to eat, saying nothing. Annette stood beside him uncomfortably, not knowing quite what to do next.

They were all aware that in this mood Joe could be dangerous.

Hillier realized that Joe was tired and hungry. Kenwright's crassness hadn't helped, but there was something else too.

Joe wanted the women out of the room. If they were going to talk business, then the less the girls knew, the better. He turned to Maria. 'Take Annette upstairs. Find something nice to put on. Maybe we'll go out later tonight.'

Maria pouted. She didn't like it, but she understood the necessity. She didn't want to know too much about what they did anyway. It could be dangerous.

She signalled to her sister with a jerk of her head. 'Come on.' Then she glanced back at Hillier, her eyes flashing angrily. 'Don't be too long, otherwise I might not be there.' She pushed Annette through the door and slammed it shut behind her, just to add emphasis to her words.

Hillier grinned, then turned back to Joe. He probed gently. 'How far did you get?'

Joe took another mouthful of the onion soup. 'Antwerp.'

Kenwright pursed his lips, expelling his breath in surprise. It was much further than any of them had expected.

Hillier was pleased. 'Is the port open?'

Joe shook his head. 'No, Jerry's got the approaches covered on both banks, and he'll take some shifting. But once he goes, all this heavy stuff moving up the roads from the beaches will stop. Our trucks will stick out like a sore thumb.' He looked out of the window at the lorries parked in the courtyard. 'You've expanded since I left.'

Kenwright grinned, forgetting his earlier confrontation. 'We've even got a medical officer.'

Joe raised his eyebrows. 'An MO? How?'

Hillier explained. 'Eddie brought him in. He was up on a charge – selling penicillin on the black market – and the Irishman sprang him.'

Joe was curious. 'Where is everybody?'

Kenwright leaned forward in his chair, his eyes gleaming. 'They go down to the village most nights. You remember that dancer in the club?'

Joe smiled. 'Josie? The one with the coins?'

'Yeah. Well, she's doing a regular spot there now. Seems she got moved on by the red caps. For once they did us a favour.'

Joe thought about that. Josie could be useful in Antwerp too. He looked at Hillier. 'I found a place we can use for storage.' He told them about the basement below the cinema.

Hillier listened. 'The woman that runs it . . .?'

'Lissette.'

'Yeah. Can we trust her?'

Joe nodded. 'You can take my word for it.'

He didn't explain and Hillier accepted his assurance.

'OK, so we've got a base there. How soon can we make use of it?'

'Soon as we like. Once the port is opened, there'll be so much stuff coming in we can siphon off whatever we can use. All it takes is *that*.' He rubbed his finger and thumb together.

Kenwright poured some wine out of a large jug. 'Have some of this. It'll kill the dust in your throat.'

Joe accepted the invitation and gazed at Kenwright from below his eyebrows. He was a stocky man, older than either of them, probably in his forties, his hair greying. The man irritated him for some reason. He seemed to be trying too hard to please. It worried Joe.

'Are you a regular, Kenwright?'

'Yeah. Been in it since I was eighteen.'

Joe studied him carefully. 'What made you want to pack it in?'

Kenwright glanced from Joe to the American. He'd caught the drift, the slight edge on the question. 'I'd seen enough.' He paused and took a swallow of his wine. 'Too much.'

Joe didn't believe him. 'It doesn't make any sense. If you're a regular, you should be used to it.'

Hillier watched Joe carefully. He was wary. The Englishman had got something into his head about Kenwright and he didn't know what the questioning was leading to.

Kenwright looked at the hard lines around Joe's mouth. But not even two days' growth of beard and his exhaustion could disguise his youth.

'I suppose if I was twenty again, I'd think like that too. But it gets harder, son, not easier. You'll find that out.' He thought back, trying to find the point when he'd decided he'd had enough. Surprisingly, he realized it was a long time ago. He wondered if Joe would believe him. He knew that in that hard, young man there would be no compunction about getting rid of him if he thought he were an informer. Strangely, he didn't really care.

'I've been in Antwerp before. We did some training exercises on the Continent a few years ago. That's one thing about the army, you do travel and see things other people never see.

'I was in Hong Kong in '29. They needed us to patrol the beaches. There are lots of islands and the Chinese were always trying to get into our territory. They could make a living if they could get into Hong Kong, but on the mainland they were starving, thousands of them. Yet we still had to stop them.'

He poured himself another drink from the jug and offered it to Joe, who declined. Hillier took it. Neither of them spoke. They sat waiting for Kenwright to continue.

'I was patrolling a beach late one night and I heard women's voices, shouting to each other. They were in the sea, swimming ashore. I stood there, waiting for them with my rifle. When they staggered up the beach they were about done for.

'One was older than the other. She was the mother. The daughter was heavily pregnant. I don't know how she managed to swim at all.

'We had orders to make them swim back or imprison them. If we did that, they went back to China on a train. I don't know what the Chinese did to them. But most of them preferred to swim. Anyway, I shouted at them, pointing my rifle, telling them to go.'

Kenwright stopped, and took another swallow of his drink.

'Then the girl started to have the baby, right there on the beach. I didn't know what to do, but the mother didn't seem worried, so I walked a little way along the beach to give them some privacy. Tell you the truth, I was a bit out of my depth. I gave them about half an hour, hoping that they would have gone. I didn't care where they went. As far as I was concerned they'd had enough, and there was no way I was going to force them to swim back.

'They were still there. But the girl had had the baby. She was just lying on the beach, exhausted. I couldn't see the baby. I tried to ask where it was. She spoke some pidgin English, enough for me to understand.' Kenwright swallowed, staring down at the table. 'She told me that they had put the baby back in the sea as I had ordered. She asked if they could stay.'

He looked up from the table, staring at Joe.

'That's when I decided I'd had enough. I told them to piss off. I didn't give a shit where they went.'

He looked at Hillier, then at Joe, his eyes full of anger. He picked up his glass and threw it at the range, smashing it. Some of the wine splashed on to Joe's face. He didn't move as it dribbled slowly down through the stubble on his chin.

Kenwright continued, his voice shaking a little. 'I started to look for the poor little bastard. I'd heard that sometimes babies can stay alive in the water. Not this one. I dug a hole in the sand dunes and buried it.' He stopped. He seemed shrunken, exhausted by the memory.

Joe was the first to break the silence. 'Was it a boy or a girl?'

Kenwright looked at him, stunned by the question. 'A boy,' he said.

Joe wiped the wine from his face. 'Poor little sod,' he said, 'poor little sod.' He blinked, and Hillier stared at him, seeing the pain in his eyes.

Eddie opened his eyes and gazed at the ceiling. It was cracked as usual, the plaster criss-crossed with lines after the heavy pounding the temporary barracks had taken from army boots, both German and British, these last four years. But something was wrong.

The room was light, the morning sun slanting in through the half closed curtains. Eddie checked his watch. It was just before seven.

What was it?

At first he couldn't work it out. Everything seemed normal enough. But then he heard birds, *singing*. He'd never heard birds singing in this place before. The noise of departing trucks drowned out most natural background noise and frightened away the rest. That was it. It was so quiet.

Eddie leapt from his bed and rushed to the window, pulling back the curtains. All the lorries were still parked. Nothing had gone out. Why?

He dressed quickly and made his way downstairs to Sergeant Robinson's office. He paused outside the door and composed himself. He didn't want to show too much interest.

As he opened the door Rainy Day came out of Major Matthews's office. He paused, seeing Eddie.

'What do you want?' he asked sourly.

'I have to check one of the fuel dumps further up the line. I think it's running low.'

Robinson sat down behind his desk. 'You sure about that?'

Eddie shrugged. 'No, I'm not. I'm going to make sure. I can't afford to take any chances.'

There was something wrong, Eddie knew it now. Normally it was routine and Robinson just checked him out.

Robinson chewed it over. The fuel dumps had priority, but Matthews had told him nothing left the base today unless it was vital. He made up his mind.

'OK, but you'll need a special sticker.'

Eddie stared at him in surprise. 'What for?'

The sergeant reached irritably into a drawer and slapped one down on the desk in front of him. 'Because nothing goes on the 'roads today without one of these, otherwise you'll finish up in the glasshouse.'

Eddie was still staring at him.

Rainy Day slammed the drawer shut. 'Listen, you silly sod. Nothing's going out today. Not just here, but throughout the Command. Trucks have been going missing from here, right through to the front lines, and the Americans have been losing heavily too. So someone came up with the idea that we shouldn't go out at all today, but anyone who does has to have one of these.'

He banged his hand down on the sticker. Eddie got it.

'So any truck out there today without one of these' – he picked up the sticker – 'is a stolen vehicle?'

Rainy Day nodded emphatically. 'That's right, Pearce. The red caps are out in their droves, so I suggest you display that prominently.'

Eddie backed away from the sergeant's desk.

'Right, sarge. Thanks a lot. I'll do that.' He reached for the door, and then froze.

'Pearce!'

Eddie turned, slowly and looked at Rainy Day.

The sergeant stared grimly at the Irishman. 'I want to know the state of *all* the dumps as far as Amiens, is that understood?'

Eddie sighed with relief. 'Sure, sarge. I'll be back by evening.'

Joe was in the kitchen when he heard the jeep turning up the drive to the *château*. He grabbed the Thompson from the back of his chair and ran through the passage to the front door.

Eddie skidded the vehicle to a halt and raced up the steps to where Joe was standing.

'The trucks, have they gone out yet?'

Joe nodded. 'Yes. What's wrong?'

Eddie was slightly out of breath. He looked past Joe as Hillier came to the open door behind him.

'There's an op on. Nothing is being allowed on to the roads unless it carries identification.' He pointed to the sticker on the windscreen of his jeep. 'Without that the red caps take you in.'

Hillier and Joe exchanged a look. Both of them realized instantly that their operation was over. The red caps would have a field day with the stolen trucks already on the road. Now it was just a matter of time.

Joe slung the Thompson over his shoulder. 'How long have we got?'

Eddie shook his head. 'There's no telling. As soon as they're seen on the road or they try to pick up fuel at one of the dumps . . .' He shrugged his shoulders.

Hillier butted in. 'We've got to leave right away. Someone's bound to blow the gaff on us.'

Joe thought quickly. 'We need the press. Can we get it on to a truck?'

Hillier shook his head. 'We haven't the time.'

'We have to make time,' Joe said savagely. 'If we can get it to Antwerp, we can put it in the basement of the cinema.'

Hillier leaned forward. 'You're forgetting one thing – we don't have any ID.'

Joe pointed to the jeep. 'Use the one on that.'

Eddie was aghast. 'What about me?'

Joe ran down the steps and ripped off the sticker.

'If you stay on the back roads, you'll be OK. Come on, we need your help.'

Eddie didn't argue. He knew it was useless.

The press was heavy, but they were able to dismantle it so that the various parts could be slowly manoeuvred out of the basement.

The sentries were alerted on the gate and the last remaining truck driven round to the front of the *château*.

It was sweaty, tense work and Joe could smell the fear as they laboured in the basement and handed the press up the steps.

Annette and Maria watched fearfully, wondering what their fate would be. The old lady did not condescend to come down. She remained in her room to the end.

Hillier asked the two sisters what they wanted to do. Joe had already decided. He was pleased when they both said they wanted to come. There was no way he intended to leave them here. They knew too much, and in Antwerp two pretty girls would be an asset.

Hillier looked at Joe. 'What about the grandmother?'

'Leave her here. She knows nothing.' Porter stared hard at the American. 'We need the girls . . .'

Hillier picked up the guarded inference and told the two sisters to pack something quickly.

The last few pieces of the press were loaded on to the truck with the motor cycles. Joe grabbed Eddie's arm and steered him out of earshot of the others.

'Now, listen. Take it easy on the way back. Stay off the main roads. If you do get stopped, you lost the sticker. It blew off or something. All they've got to do is telephone Matthews and he will vouch for you.'

Eddie knew it made sense. 'Where will you be?'

Joe handed him a piece of paper. 'I've written down the name of the place. It's called the Cinéac. The woman who runs it is a Lissette van der Elst. Call her if you have to. You can trust her. Otherwise wait until you're there.

'As soon as they can get the port open, all the transportation will be moved up from here. The mulberries will be just back-up. Contact me when you arrive, O K?'

Eddie looked worried. 'Do you think you'll get through?'

Porter grinned. 'How can I fail? I've got your identification and important presses for HQ in Antwerp.'

Eddie liked it. 'Jesus Christ, Joe, you should be running this soddin' war. It would be over by now.'

Joe put his arm around the diminutive Irishman's shoulders and walked him back to the jeep. 'If I was running it, what part would you want?'

Eddie thought for a second. 'I'd have to be chancellor, in charge of finance!'

Joe laughed and bundled him into the jeep. 'Mind how you go.'

Eddie started the engine and began to back the vehicle round to face the drive. Joe held up his hand.

'If you see that dancer in the club . . .'

Eddie smiled. 'You mean Josie?'

'Yeah – bring her with you.'

The Irishman waved. 'I'll do my best.' The jeep disappeared down the drive, dust billowing up behind it.

Kenwright pushed the girls up into the back of the truck and threw their luggage in after them. He yelled at Joe. 'C'mon, let's get out of here!'

Hillier suddenly remembered Corporal Marsh. 'Where's our MO?'

Joe didn't know. He hadn't seen him all morning. He heard Kenwright swear.

'The silly sod got a lift into the village. He wanted something.' He stopped, staring at Joe, waiting for the verdict. He was worried.

Hillier shrugged his shoulders. 'We could try and find him . . .'

Joe shook his head. 'There's no time – we'd be risking everything. Marsh has had it.'

No one said anything. They knew he was right, but neither Hillier nor Kenwright could bring himself to admit it. Joe decided for them.

'Let's go.'

He strode around to the cab, climbing in behind the wheel. Hillier sat beside him, while Kenwright clambered up into the back with the girls. He banged the side of the vehicle.

'All clear.'

The truck moved off.

The old woman stood in the window upstairs and watched the lorry go down the drive through the trees, then disappear around the bend, the sound of its engine gradually fading.

The *château* was quiet now. She stood there a long time, listening to the silence, watching the dust slowly settle back on the drive.

Slowly she realized she was completely alone. She was glad.

CHAPTER NINETEEN

Lissette was listening to the radio when her doorbell rang. She remembered later that she was irritated by the interruption. She had tuned the waveband to the nine o'clock news from the BBC in London.

She had done so openly. No need any longer for secrecy, though the volume was turned down so that no one could hear. It was hard to adjust to the normality of being able to sit back, relaxed, and listen to a reasonable level of speech. It made her feel almost exultant, this simple freedom to listen to whatever she pleased, when she pleased. And the news was good. The last of the German forces had been cleared from the Beveland peninsula, and the first cargo vessel's arrival in Antwerp was imminent.

She turned the knob, switching the radio off, and went to the door of her apartment. It was her mother. Lissette was too surprised to speak. Her mother had never visited her before. She stood, dumbfounded, in the doorway until Sophie pushed her way past her into the apartment.

'I'm sorry I didn't warn you of my arrival, but I don't intend to stand out in the hall all evening.'

She ignored the kitchen and went into the living room, gazing round the apartment haughtily. 'Well, it's clean, and cosy. But it's so *small*. How do you manage?'

Lissette closed the door and followed her into the room. 'Because there's only me, mother.'

Sophie turned to face her, her eyes hard. 'For the moment, Lissette. Now that the German has gone.'

Lissette felt the hot rush of colour rise from her neck and blot her cheeks red. It made her angry, this ability her mother had to shatter her defences and make her feel inadequate. Sophie turned away and picked up a cushion from a chair, plumping it up.

'But let's not quarrel, Lissette. I came to see how you were. Are you well?'

She was tempted to tell her mother of her imprisonment, but she bit off the words. Her mother would find a way of using it against her. She always did.

'The Peeters at the farm – you remember them?'

Her mother adjusted her skirt. 'Of course.'

'They are dead,' Lissette said brutally.

Sophie stared at her, disbelief and shock in her eyes. She shook her head.

Lissette continued quietly. 'You know I took Duparc there. They had hidden people before.'

Sophie stood up and walked slowly to the mantelshelf over the fireplace. 'Henri . . . Did they . . .?'

'Yes, the Gestapo took him. The Peeters killed themselves. They . . . they must have planned it long before. They had pills.'

Sophie kept her back to Lissette, one hand resting on the mantelshelf. She didn't want her daughter to see her face, and she struggled to keep her voice calm. 'Do you know what happened to Henri?'

'No. He hasn't been seen since.' Lissette stared at her mother's back, conscious for the first time of a chink in her armour. She felt little sympathy for her display of emotion. 'Why did you force him to leave, mother? Don't you like Jews?'

'No, it wasn't that. I liked Henri. He had his little habits, shall we say. I didn't mind those.' Sophie straightened, and turned to face Lissette. 'But he lied to me and put us all in great danger by continuing to parade himself so openly. If I had known he was a Jew, I'd have made sure those risks were eliminated. When I found out the Gestapo were after him, it was too late. So I ordered him not to come back.'

Lissette was curious. 'And the officer who warned you – he was German?'

The question incensed Sophie. 'And if he was, who are you to be so smug? Like mother, like daughter perhaps?'

The words bit deeply into Lissette. She recoiled from the thought of being compared with her mother, whom she despised. All her life she had striven to cut herself off from her. There could be no truth in the accusation. She had *loved* Manfred. He was not just a client, a customer. But still she felt the pain. For the first time there was a niggling seed of doubt.

She turned away blindly and walked unsteadily into the kitchen. She rested both hands on the table, trying to compose herself. She heard her mother's voice from the doorway.

'Lissette, we must not quarrel like this.' She came closer. Lissette was surprised to hear a note of sympathy in her mother's voice. 'I do not want to fight you, but somehow we always seem to bring out the worst in each other. I know how hard it has been for you, and I know that you loved Manfred. I saw him once.'

Lissette turned and gazed at her disbelievingly. 'How?'

Sophie smiled. 'Well, I do go to the cinema occasionally, and I was curious about your German.' She saw Lissette's look and held out her hands. 'Why not? Why shouldn't I be curious about my daughter's first lover?'

She paused, thinking back. 'He came into the lobby on his way up to the roof.' She looked coquettishly at her daughter. 'He was tall and strong, very handsome, my dear.'

Lissette hated her. She never wanted her mother to see Manfred, to eye him in the way that she used on all her men.

'You have no idea what he was like, mother.' Her voice was low, vicious. 'No one has ever really loved *you*. Men have desired you perhaps, but they have never loved you. You don't know the meaning of the word.'

Her voice was breaking with emotion, and she hated herself for not being able to stop her tears.

'Manfred loved me. He respected me. Before he left he took me into St Josef's and married me. Has anyone ever really married you, mother? Am I an abortion that failed, a bastard? Where is my father? What happened to him?' She slumped down into the chair, sobbing uncontrollably.

Sophie stood beside her, her face composed, only her eyes revealing how deeply the words had struck. She put out her hand, tentatively, to touch her daughter. Then stopped. She knew what the reaction would be.

She gazed distractedly around the small kitchen, then back to her daughter slumped over the table. She wanted to hold her, to cradle her in her arms, but the empty years gaped between them. Such a simple thing, to put your arms around your daughter, but so absolutely impossible.

She turned away, picked up her handbag from the other room and left the apartment, closing the door quietly behind her.

The club was crowded with servicemen, mostly British and US soldiers, but there were a few men from the Royal Navy minesweepers that had been clearing the Scheldt Estuary for the past month.

Joe was pleased. Josie's fame had spread quickly and the club was making money – the kind of money he had never seen before.

Hillier's skill in spotting an opening and developing it was an asset that Joe had not anticipated. A lot had happened since their hasty departure from the *château* in France. They'd only just got out in time, and most of the drivers had been picked off one by one.

The trap set by the military had been a brilliantly simple one, and if Eddie had not managed to warn them, they would be cooling their heels inside, along with everybody else. But Joe realized it had worked for them in a sense, because it had forced them to Antwerp much quicker than he'd expected.

Nick and Joe had taken over a first-floor apartment block not far from the cinema. They paid a good rent for it and secured the loyalty of the owner with the threat of a requisition order for the premises if he did not co-operate. The requisition order, as always, came from the press.

It was already providing all kinds of phoney order forms, leave passes and authorizations. Gus Kenwright had mastered the workings of the machine and operated it from the basement of the cinema. The chaos and confusion in the wake of the retreating German armies was fertile ground for a quick mind like Hillier's and the daring of Joe Porter.

Joe had found the derelict club, and when Eddie's unit was transferred to Antwerp in the middle of November to deal with the reorganization of the supply routes from the port, Eddie had seen to it that Josie accompanied them.

The club had been given a quick paint job. Plenty of drink had been installed and Josie given the billing. The customers had gone away happy and slightly awed by Josie's inexhaustible capacity. Word of mouth had done the rest.

Nick emerged from the office close to the stage and joined Joe at the bar. He was wearing civilian clothes, which he preferred, but Joe stayed in uniform. He felt he was less conspicuous that way.

Nick sat down on the stool next to him and glanced around the smoke-filled room. 'What do you think?'

'It's good,' Joe said admiringly. 'Let's hope it stays that way.'

Nick attracted the attention of the barman and ordered a drink. 'I've been talking to Josie, and she's got a few more tricks up her sleeve when they tire of this.'

Joe looked around the crowded room. 'There's no sign of it.'

'No, but you've got to plan for the future.'

Joe absorbed that. 'I've got a couple more ideas myself.'

Nick took a swallow of his whisky. 'Let's have them.'

Joe stared at him thoughtfully.

'Taxis.'

'Explain.'

'Well, Antwerp and Brussels are already becoming leave centres, and the public transport systems are lousy. I know a place where I can lay my hands on a whole fleet of captured German staff cars. A coat of paint and they can be taxi cabs.'

Hillier chewed on that for a moment. 'How much?'

Joe shrugged. 'I don't know yet. I've got to get there and find out. But what do you think?'

Hillier reached into his top pocket. 'I like it. Have a cigar.' He pulled one out and stuck it in Joe's tunic pocket. 'Let me know when you find out.'

'How are we fixed?'

'For cash?'

'Yeah. Can we handle something like that?'

Hillier smiled. 'If we can't now, we soon will.' His eyes strayed behind Joe. 'Here's your friend.'

Joe turned. It was Eddie. He looked worried.

Joe stood up. 'What's wrong?'

Eddie indicated the office. 'Can we go in there?'

The three men moved carefully through the tables, crowded close together, and slipped through the door. Joe shut it behind them, cutting off the noisy buzz of the club.

'What is it?'

Eddie looked quickly from one to the other. 'I don't know how true it is, but I've heard that the new money we're using is going to be thrown out.'

Hillier spoke first. 'Why?'

'I don't know. The word is that only the old money will be of any real value. Some of the officers are buying Dutch guilders.' Eddie turned to Joe. 'We're going to have to get the money into something more valuable until I find out what the truth of it is.'

'Don't worry about it,' Joe said. 'As long as we use the money to buy things like this club, property, then we'll be all right. You did well to let us know.'

Eddie relaxed visibly. His confidence had been badly shaken.

Joe continued. 'How are things your end?'

Hillier poured a drink and gave it to Eddie. He swallowed it gratefully.

'Not bad. We're settling in now.' He remembered something. 'That was the other thing.'

'You mean there's more?' Hillier said ruefully.

Eddie grinned. 'No, this is good news. The first ship comes in next Tuesday, the 28th.'

Hillier and Joe exchanged a look.

'That's good, isn't it?' Eddie asked.

Hillier nodded. 'It is. It means we can start getting our sticky fingers on some of those supplies.'

Eddie held up his hand. 'Don't tell me about that. I don't want to know how you do it.'

Hillier filled his glass again. 'Of course not. Just as long as you can tell me where and when, and as early as possible.'

Joe interrupted. 'You don't have to worry about Eddie.'

Hillier picked up the slight edge in his voice. He smiled. 'I'm not worried. If Eddie hadn't been on the ball, we'd all be behind bars right now.'

Joe didn't respond, and Eddie was aware of an uncomfortable silence. He swallowed the rest of his drink.

'I think I'll catch Josie's act.' He rattled the coins in his pocket.

'I've got some loose change for her.' He grinned, breaking the mood.

Joe opened the door for him. 'I'll be out soon.'

Eddie left, and Hillier stared thoughtfully into his drink. 'Guilders,' he said, half to himself.

Joe took out one of the new notes from his pocket and examined them.

'Maybe,' he said, 'it's time to buy some German staff cars?' He looked inquisitively at the American.

Hillier grinned triumphantly, and raised his glass.

'What a good idea!'

Eddie was curious.

He'd heard a lot about the woman who ran the cinema, and although his connection with the 'Company' was unknown to her, there was a way he could make contact.

He'd always liked movies and he was glad to get out of the rain. It bounced pitilessly off the cobblestones, seeping into his army boots through the laceholes, and he was grateful for the warmth of the cinema. He stopped just inside the glass doors and banged his forage cap on his leg to get rid of some of the moisture.

A cleaner polishing the brasswork gazed at him disapprovingly as a small damp patch spread on the carpet round his feet.

'Not open,' she said. She pointed to a nonexistent watch on her wrist. 'Later,' she added forcefully.

Eddie, to her dismay, advanced further into the lobby, which smelt sweetly of that fine combination, disinfectant and perfume. It was very evocative, reminding Eddie of his one and only visit to the Gate Theatre in Dublin.

'No,' he said, speaking carefully. 'I want the manager.'

The cleaner looked puzzled.

'Lissette van der Elst,' he said very clearly.

The woman's face cleared, and she smiled in understanding. She turned and pointed up the stairs leading to the circle.

Eddie nodded gratefully. 'Thank you.'

The cleaner resumed her vigorous polishing, then looked irritably at the damp marks as Eddie crossed the lobby to the stairs. She muttered angrily to herself and polished even harder.

Lissette was writing when she heard a respectful tap on the half open door of her office. She looked up. He was small, neat, but the sharp lines of his battledress were somewhat crumpled by the rain. He carried his cap in his hand and his hair was fine and slightly sandy. But she liked his eyes. They danced with humour, clear and blue.

'Sorry to trouble you.'

She smiled. 'That's all right.'

Eddie was relieved. Her English was good.

'You are the manageress?'

She nodded. 'I am, but don't stand there dripping over the carpet. Come in.'

Eddie apologized, closing the door behind him. 'It's absolutely pouring out there. Worst I've seen it since just before D-Day.'

Lissette indicated a chair opposite. 'Yes, it is bad. Do sit down.' She watched him pull the chair up. 'Do you mind if I ask you something?'

Eddie shook his head. 'No, fire away.'

'That word, D-Day, what does it stand for?'

Eddie rubbed his chin reflectively. 'Do you know, I can't remember anyone telling us that. There was D-minus-this and D-plus-that but no explanation of D-Day itself.'

Lissette sighed. 'Well, it's of no matter. I was just curious, that's all. I heard it a lot on the wireless.'

'Yes, so did we. I'll tell you what, I'll find out and let you know.'

Lissette was suddenly embarrassed. She didn't even know what this soldier wanted. 'No, that's all right. Don't put yourself to any trouble.'

Eddie cut across her. 'It's no trouble,' he said enthusiastically.

Lissette shuffled some papers on her desk, trying to look busy. There was a small silence, then Eddie held out his hands apologetically.

'Look, I'm sorry. I haven't even told you why I'm here.' He grinned at her, his eyes twinkling, but Lissette kept a straight face.

'Yes. What can I do for you?'

'Well, it's to do with the films you show.'

Lissette raised her eyebrows. 'In what way?'

'Oh, sure, there's nothing wrong with your films. It's more to do with ours, you see.'

Lissette was finding it difficult to follow the Irishman's line of thought. 'What do you mean?'

Eddie laughed. 'I'm not explainin' myself very well.' He took a breath and continued. 'You see, we have – that is, the army has – these film shows. Now there's nothing wrong with the films, you understand. They're very good. We had that boxing picture the other day, *Gentleman Jim*.'

Lissette interrupted his flow. 'With Errol Flynn.'

'That's right. He's Irish, by the way.'

Lissette didn't see the relevance of the remark, but she nodded affably, and Eddie went on.

'The problem we have is *where* we show them. I can't tell you how nice it is to come into a place like this – a proper cinema. Sure, it would be lovely if you could put on some of the films here.'

Lissette still wasn't quite certain what he meant.

'You mean for your soldiers?'

'Not just for them. No, I mean if I were able to get hold of a film or two, would you be able to show it in the normal way?'

Lissette looked at him regretfully. 'I see what you mean. But it's not possible. We have shown British and American films, but there have to be subtitles, usually in French, so that our customers can understand. Not everyone speaks English.'

Eddie exclaimed, 'Of course. Stupid of me. You see, I've sometimes seen posters with American films on them, but the language problem didn't occur to me. I should have thought about it.'

Lissette smiled. 'Sometimes even my distributor forgets it.'

Eddie slumped in his chair. He was disappointed. Although he wanted to see this woman, he'd also been looking forward to sitting in a proper cinema to see a film and not a converted, draughty hall somewhere.

Lissette felt sorry for him. She suddenly thought of something.

'Look, if there is a film that you would particularly like to see, I could arrange to have it shown privately on a Sunday. We're closed on Sundays.'

Eddie's face lit up. 'Could you?' His enthusiasm was infectious.

'Yes. Not for an audience, you understand, but for you.'

Eddie thought for a moment. 'Look, if I could get something for this weekend, would you put it on?'

Lissette pretended to consider it, although she knew there was nothing but an empty Sunday facing her.

'Yes, that will be OK, if you can get a copy of something.'

Eddie stood up, delighted. 'I don't think there will be any problem. What time?'

Lissette came round from behind her desk.

'Oh, in the afternoon, I think. That should be all right.'

Eddie took her hand. 'Thank you very much. This is very kind of you. I'm really looking forward to it.' He let go of her hand. 'Perhaps you might like to see it too?'

Lissette shrugged. 'Maybe. Shall we say about three o'clock?'

Eddie nodded. 'Yes, that'll be fine.'

He backed away towards the door. 'I'll see you then.' He opened it and looked at her.

'Thanks again.' He smiled shyly and left, closing the door behind him.

Lissette stared at it for a moment, then suddenly remembered. She rushed to the door and ran out into the lobby. He was halfway down the stairs. She called after him, 'Excuse me!'

He stopped and looked back up at her. 'Yes?'

'I don't know who you are.'

He grinned. 'I'm Eddie, Eddie Pearce.' He looked at her for a second, then waved. 'See you on Sunday.'

He turned and walked down the stairs and out through the front entrance. The cleaner was just finishing off the last of the brass. She glanced up at the manageress curiously.

Lissette felt the woman's eyes staring at her. She walked slowly back to her office and closed the door.

CHAPTER TWENTY

It was early morning. The streets were barely light as Hillier entered the apartment block and walked up the two flights of steps to the first floor. There were four apartments, two on each side of a central passage. Joe shared one with Annette; Gus Kenwright had another; one was empty; and he had the other.

He unlocked the door and went inside, flinging his jacket down on to a chair. He made himself a cup of coffee and took it with him into the bedroom. Maria was still asleep.

He put the coffee down and leaned over her, kissing the side of her neck. She groaned and turned over, not waking.

Hillier smiled to himself and sat down on the edge of the bed, sipping the hot coffee. He eased off his shoes, finished off the coffee, then slipped quickly out of his clothes and into the warm bed.

That did wake her up.

She shivered and wrapped her arms around him. 'You're cold,' she grumbled.

He couldn't deny it, and he was grateful for her warmth. He gradually thawed out but found it difficult to sleep. He had too many things on his mind. The German staff car deal, for instance. Joe had taken every red cent they had. And something else was beginning to occupy his thoughts. He had an enormous erection.

Maria had gone back to sleep, but even comatose she seemed to sense his condition. Her hand slid down between his legs and held him. She groaned once more and wrapped her legs around him, slipping his hard penis inside her.

He wasn't quite sure what the position was called. It was extraordinary and had happened almost by accident. He'd have to try and remember it, he thought, then he began to concentrate on the matter in hand.

She was beautiful and half asleep, but her instincts never failed. She devoured him hungrily and by the time he had finally spent himself inside her, any worries about Joe had vanished.

They relaxed in each other's arms, she fully awake now and he totally exhausted.

'You are wonderful, Nick,' she said throatily.

'I know.' He grinned.

She punched him playfully in the stomach and he feigned discomfort.

'Don't hit me there, for Chrissake. A few inches lower and I'd be ruined for life.'

She cradled his balls tenderly in her hand. 'I'm sorry. They are too beautiful to hurt.' She squeezed them gently. 'But you'd better be nice to me.'

'I'm always nice to you,' he protested and kissed her breasts to prove it.

She turned away from him. 'No, you're not. You tell me nothing about yourself. You like to be the big mystery man. You say nothing, and treat me like I am a girl.'

He raised himself up on one elbow and looked down at her. 'But you are my girl.'

Her eyes flashed angrily. 'Don't call me that. I am not your girl. I am nobody's girl. I belong to me.' She gestured arrogantly with her hand.

'You tell me nothing about yourself, so I say nothing to you.'

He could see she was serious. 'What the hell brought this on?'

She pointed her finger at him. 'You brought it on.'

'What did I do?'

She stared at him, still angry. 'Are you married?'

He collapsed back on the bed. 'Oh, shit!'

Maria sat up. 'Are you?'

He looked at her steadily, knowing there was no way of avoiding this. 'Yes,' he said quietly.

He saw the hurt in her eyes, quickly masked. She held his gaze.

'What is her name?'

'Kay.' He continued before she could ask any more questions. 'I have a son. His name is Paul. Now does that make it any better?'

She pulled back the covers and sat on the edge of the bed. 'Yes. I needed to know.'

He wanted to put his arms around her, but he didn't think she was ready for that yet.

'It doesn't make any difference to us, Maria. I'm here with you . . .' He stopped, his voice trailing off as his body tensed, listening.

High above their heads, approaching from the north, he heard the unmistakable sound of a V1. Its strange, almost friendly buzz as it doodled across the city disguised its deadly intent.

Maria heard it too. She stiffened at the edge of the bed. They waited, in their own small world of terror, to discover if the engine would stop over their heads.

It got closer, louder, until it seemed to be directly overhead. Still they sat apart, tense, sweating. Then slowly the sound began to fade, until they could hear it no more.

Maria didn't look at him. 'Do you love me?' Her voice was almost inaudible.

He reached out and placed his hand on hers. 'Yes, I do, Maria.'

She turned to him, searching his face for deception. There was none. She flung herself into his arms and he pulled the covers over her, rocking her gently.

'I love you,' he said.

Joe stood proudly on the stern of the Rhine barge and watched the twelve German staff cars being driven slowly on to the vessel's deck.

This same barge had been one of the sixteen used by the escaping German forces that had been trapped on the West Scheldt.

In four days, between 4 and 8 September, while the British remained in Antwerp and Brussels, ten thousand German troops had been ferried at night across the Scheldt from Breskens to Flushing. The staff cars were among the vehicles that didn't make it.

Joe had got a good deal on the cars and had got rid of all the new money in the process. The deal had included transportation down the estuary to Antwerp and, once docked there, Joe could take care of the cars.

As the barge sailed down the Scheldt towards Antwerp he kept his fingers crossed that the minesweepers had done their work and that no stray mine would bob up and sink his newly acquired fleet of taxis.

There was only one other problem – he wasn't licensed. Gus was going to be busy.

Lissette waited just inside the lobby for Eddie, and when his jeep pulled up, she helped him unload the cans of film, and they carried them into the cinema. She led the way up to the projectionist's box. Eddie was surprised to find it empty.

'Can you do this?'

Lissette took the first reel and began to thread it expertly through the equipment. 'I've worked here for nearly ten years now and this is the most important part of it. If the film is not in focus or the sound is out of synchronization, the audience quickly give you a bad name.' She glanced at the label on the can. 'This should be fine.'

Eddie looked through the round observation window into the auditorium. 'Will you be able to watch it with me?'

Lissette smiled. 'As long as you don't mind me running up here every twenty minutes to change the reel.'

Eddie shook his head. 'No, not at all. Do you like Bing Crosby?'

She gestured with her hands. 'Sometimes. *Comme ci, comme ça*. But this one should be good.'

Eddie enthused. 'I hope so. It won an Oscar for best film this year. I was lucky to be able to get it. I'm seeing it before the officers.'

Lissette shut the compartment on the projector. 'Right. I'm ready now. Why don't you go into the circle and I'll join you as soon as I've got the film started?'

Eddie left the box and made his way down a flight of steps into the circle lobby, then into the circle itself. As soon as Lissette saw him sit down, she lowered the lights and switched on the projector. By the time she had got down to the circle the credits were coming to an end. The director of *Going My Way* was Leo McCarey.

Eddie sat back in the comfortable seat with a subdued, but definite feeling of anticipation. He smiled quietly to himself. He'd really been looking forward to this. He noticed Lissette watching him from the corner of her eye. She was pleased by his obvious sense of enjoyment. He smiled.

'Thank you,' he said quietly, then transferred his attention to the silver screen.

The fact that *Going My Way* had won an Oscar was a bonus.

Eddie would probably have enjoyed anything that afternoon. As it was, the beautifully played antagonism between the young priest, played by Crosby, and the older one played by Barry Fitzgerald at his cantankerous best caused him to roar with laughter more than once. It didn't matter that the cinema was empty and his laughter echoed hollowly through the building. That inhibited him not one bit. His enjoyment communicated itself to Lissette. She relaxed in his company.

She nipped away several times to change the reels, but Eddie was totally unaware of her departure. His eyes never left the screen.

Finally it ended. The lights came on and he looked around for Lissette, then remembered. She would be operating the lights. He glanced up at the projectionist's box and she waved to him from the window. Eddie grinned at her, made his way down the steps into the circle lobby and waited.

There were photographs of film stars dotted round the walls. Since the liberation Lissette had been able to restore the faces of many of the American and British stars. He studied a picture of Jimmy Cagney. He fancied, secretly, that he looked a bit like Cagney. He was about the right height, he thought ruefully. He felt a tap on his shoulder.

'Did you enjoy it?'

He turned, smiling broadly at Lissette. 'It was smashing. I haven't enjoyed a film so much for ages.'

She looked into his shining eyes and believed him.

'Now it's my turn,' he said. 'I want you to allow me to buy you tea.'

She was tempted, but she wasn't hungry. Nor was she ready for a relationship with a man. 'No, I've got work to do at home. I must get back.'

He tried not to let her see his disappointment. 'Then let me walk you home. It's the least I can do.'

It would have been ungracious to refuse, and she liked the Irishman. He made her smile. They loaded the film back into the jeep, then walked slowly up the main road together. It was quiet, the late November afternoon already getting dark. The shops were all closed on Sunday, and there were only a few people out.

She pulled her coat collar up around her ears. The wind was chilly whipping in off the Scheldt. It was very different from the last time she had walked along this pavement with a man. She jerked her thoughts away from Manfred and smiled brightly at the Irishman.

'I liked the film.'

'So did I. It was very kind of you to do that for me. I haven't been in a proper cinema since before we left England. Then it was some little fleapit up in Norfolk.'

She looked puzzled. 'Fleapit?'

Eddie smiled, shamefaced. 'It's just an expression we use for an old, run-down sort of place.'

Lissette looked at him inquiringly. 'Fleapit?'

He nodded. 'Yes, that's right. But I would never use such an expression about your cinema.'

'How would you describe it?' she asked smiling.

'Oh, sure, it's magnificent. All that lovely brass and the fine seats. It's more like a theatre.'

They came to her apartment block and ascended in the ancient elevator. It creaked its way slowly to the top as Eddie gazed a little apprehensively through the open bars at the increasing drop beneath them.

'It's all right,' she said reassuringly. 'It always makes this noise.'

Eddie was not convinced, but he smiled bravely.

The elevator heaved itself to a stop and Lissette rolled back the gates. Eddie was glad to be on the solid floor of the landing. Lissette indicated her door.

'This is where I live.' She opened it with her key and turned back to the Irishman. 'Thank you for seeing me home.' She held out her hand and Eddie took it.

'You'll be all right now?'

She nodded. 'Yes, I'm fine. It was nice of you to come all this way.'

He shrugged his shoulders. 'It was no trouble at all. I couldn't leave a fine lady like yourself to walk all that way on a cold afternoon alone.'

He stopped and swallowed shyly, trying to find the right words.

'I can't tell you how much this afternoon has meant to me, Lissette. It's been a long time since I've enjoyed myself so much.'

She was touched by his sincerity. 'I'm glad, Eddie.' It was the first time she had used his name, and it frightened her slightly. She backed through the door. 'Goodbye.'

'Goodbye, Lissette.' He made as if to turn away, then suddenly remembered. 'Will I see you again?'

Lissette held the door open a fraction. 'Perhaps. You know where I work.'

It was only a polite response, but Eddie was delighted. He rubbed his hands vigorously together.

'God, it's cold. You'd better get inside.'

He grinned at her and turned to face the elevator. It struck fear into his heart. He was not going down in that thing.

Lissette leaned against her door after she closed it and smiled as she heard him clatter his way down the endless stairs. His footsteps gradually faded.

Five minutes later they knocked on her door. She was peeling potatoes, making something for her supper, and at first she thought Eddie had come back. It flashed across her mind that the film might have been stolen from the jeep. She had warned him about that.

Lissette rubbed her hands on a cloth and went to the door. As soon as she turned the key two men came bursting in. They were in civilian clothes but carrying arms, and she realized with a sickening rush of fear that they were the White Brigade.

It was happening again.

One of them watched her carefully while the other ransacked her apartment systematically, sometimes breaking things. It seemed to her that his brutality was deliberate. She did not protest. She knew that would be useless. But the thorough search gave her a few minutes to pack a small bag with as much clothing as she could. If she'd had a chance, she would have liked to leave a note. But there was never an opportunity for that.

Lissette was given no explanation. They hardly spoke to her. It was a method they found effective, creating a limbo of fear that would help to trigger her tongue when the interrogation began. But Lissette had one small advantage: she had been in the prison before. She knew what to expect.

The cell was as bare and cold as it had been the last time, but she tried to keep calm. If she was to survive this at all, she had to think it through. There was no room for despair.

She wrapped herself in all the clothing she could find and laid down on the iron cot in the corner. There was one thin blanket. She concentrated her mind on the bright, warm summer, remembering her walk with Manfred in the park and the cool interior of St Josef.

She must have slept. Hours later she became aware of a grey, opaque oblong of light. There were black shadows down its centre. As it gradually grew brighter, she realized it was the barred window of her cell. Her eyes remained fixed upon its slowly changing colour as the dawn gradually spread its light into the tiny cell.

Another day had begun.

The warden's office hadn't changed. It was as cold and clammy as before. But the man sat behind the heavy desk was different.

His dark hair was streaked with grey and receding. It emphasized his high forehead and his deep-set, piercing eyes. His face was sallow, and there was a sharpness about his features that gave no hint of mercy. Not that Lissette expected any. They must know about Manfred and that would be enough.

She was pushed down roughly on a hard chair in front of him. She kept her eyes firmly on the window just behind his head. It was important not to show fear or guilt.

Leo Bruneel studied her quietly for a moment, then stood up and walked around the desk.

'You are Lissette van der Elst?'

It was a statement rather than a question, but she answered, 'Yes.'

'You run the Cinéac?'

'I manage it,' she corrected.

She waited to see if he would question that, but he didn't. Maybe they didn't know about Joe Porter and the set-up in the basement.

'Did you *manage*' – he stressed the word slightly – 'the Cinéac during the occupation?'

'Yes. I continued to do what I had always done.'

Bruneel sat down on the edge of the desk in front of her. 'Not quite the same, surely?'

Lissette looked him directly in the eye. 'I don't know what you mean.'

'Oh, come, *mademoiselle*. The films, the German propaganda that was shown – they were your responsibility?'

'No, they weren't. I merely ran the administration. I was not responsible for the selection of programmes. They were sent directly to us by the German distributors and we had to show them.'

He gazed at her silently for a moment. 'What about the Charles Laughton film. You were responsible for that, weren't you?'

Lissette returned his gaze steadily. 'I was always trying to put entertaining films on. *The Hunchback of Notre Dame* was one of my few successes.'

'So you admit you did have some control over what was shown?' She did not reply. The trap had been neatly sprung.

Bruneel stood up abruptly and walked back behind the desk, staring out of the grimy window. When he spoke his voice was so low she could hardly hear it. 'Do you know a family called Peeters?'

Her eyes glazed as she understood why she had been arrested.

He turned quickly to look at her. 'Do you?' he said sharply.

'Yes.' She could not keep a note of pain from her voice, but she tried to mask it by hurrying on. 'They used to look after me sometimes when I was a child. Why do you ask? Are they all right?'

He smiled without humour. 'Oh, come now, you know what happened to them, don't you?'

Lissette did not have to fake the fear and apprehension in her face. 'No.'

Bruneel watched her, examining her reaction minutely, trying to decide how much was real or affected.

'They're dead, Miss van der Elst. They killed themselves when the Gestapo raided their farm to arrest a man you had taken there.' He leaned forward until his face was only inches from hers. 'Who was that man?'

She was terrified, the adrenalin rushing through her veins. She forced herself to think, to evaluate the information instantly. The question was crucial. She wanted to tell him that she had taken Duparc there for protection because he was a Jew. But that would connect him with her mother, and she might tell them about Manfred. If they ever found out about him, they would automatically believe that she had betrayed the Peeters. Nothing would save her then.

He screamed at her, 'Who was it?'

She put her hands to her ears, flinching from his voice.

'There was no man. I took no one there. I haven't seen the Peeters for months. It has been impossible. I didn't know they were dead.'

She broke down and cried as much from her own denial of their death as from the fear inside her.

He looked down at the top of her head. Her reaction had been right, yet instinctively he sensed that she was holding something back. The Peeters *had* been betrayed, that much they knew. The Peeters farm had been a very well protected safe house. But not even their connections with the police had been able to warn them in time. He needed more information before he could be sure it was this woman who was responsible.

There was digging to do.

Bruneel nodded to the uniformed guard who had brought her in. He took Lissette's arm and steered her out of the office to start the long walk back to her cell.

Eddie made his way determinedly through the interior lobby of the Cinéac and up the stairs to Lissette's office. He glanced at his watch, it was just coming up to one o'clock – he'd timed it well. Come what may, he intended to take her out to lunch.

He tapped on the door of her office and went in. There was somebody else behind the desk. He stopped, surprised.

'I'm sorry. I thought the manageress would be here.'

The cashier spoke only a little English. 'She not 'ere. Come in.'

Eddie paused, wondering what was wrong. 'Is she sick?' he asked slowly.

The woman shrugged. 'I don't know.'

Eddie apologized and made his way back downstairs. He was puzzled. She'd been fine yesterday and it worried him slightly.

He paced up and down the lobby once or twice, then decided. He walked quickly back to his jeep and drove the short distance to her apartment block.

He didn't bother with the lift, heading straight up the stairs he'd come down the day before.

By the time he reached the top floor he was out of breath and moving slowly. He paused on the landing to get his breathing under control. Then he noticed the door to her apartment was not closed.

He approached it quietly, not sure what to expect. It was the silence that worried him. He reached the door and stopped, listening. He could hear nothing. He pushed it open and went inside. Immediately he felt the hackles rising in the back of his neck.

The place had been wrecked.

He stood in the small entrance hall. Then he heard a sound. It was a glass rolling across the floor. Eddie drew a handgun from under his tunic and advanced silently towards the living room. A woman was standing in the middle of the room, her back to Eddie.

The Irishman sighed with relief. She turned, hearing him, and he saw it wasn't Lissette. She said something to him in French. Eddie let her see the weapon in his hand.

'What's going on here?' he said, cutting across her.

'I'm sorry, who are you?' she said sharply.

'I'm Lance-Corporal Pearce and I'm looking for the lady who lives here.'

He waved the pistol nonchalantly. 'Now you'd better tell me: what's happened?'

'I don't know.'

She could see his disbelief.

'I came here to see my daughter. The door was not locked, so I came in. I've been here only a few minutes.' Her eyes regarded him coldly. 'I might ask you the same question.'

Eddie tucked the pistol away. 'Is your daughter Lissette van der Elst?'

Sophie nodded. 'She is.'

Eddie believed her. There were certain physical resemblances, though it was hard to believe this woman could have a daughter of Lissette's age. 'I'm sorry. She's a friend of mine.' He looked around the apartment. 'This is a mess.'

If Sophie was worried, she didn't show it. 'What shall we do?'

Eddie had been thinking about that. If anyone was on to the operation at the cinema, then they were all in trouble. And he was sure that Joe would want to know about this woman.

'Look, I know someone who might be able to help. Perhaps we ought to go and see him. If anyone can trace her, he can.'

Sophie considered this. 'Why not? Something has certainly happened here.'

Eddie indicated the door. 'I've got transportation outside. It's not far.'

Sophie preceded him out of the apartment and summoned the lift before he could stop her.

He sighed deeply and waited apprehensively beside her as the contraption shuddered its way to the top floor. There was nothing he could do. He was trapped. If she was going to go down in it, he would too. Thank God he hadn't joined the Air Force.

He drove her round to the apartment block that Joe, Hillier and Kenwright shared. More stairs, but only one flight this time, then he pressed the buzzer on Joe's door.

He heard someone approach the door. It was opened by Annette. She smiled and started to greet Eddie, then she saw the older woman.

'It's all right,' he said hastily. 'This lady is a friend of mine. Is Joe in?'

He stopped as Joe appeared behind Annette. He nodded briefly at Eddie but never took his eyes off the woman.

Eddie could feel his suppressed anger, and he rushed into the yawning silence. 'This is Lissette van der Elst's mother.' He suddenly realized he didn't know her Christian name, and he paused, turning to her.

'My name is Sophie,' she said, looking contemptuously at the Irishman. 'Mr Pearce said you might know where I could find my daughter.'

Joe looked at Eddie. He didn't need to say anything. His eyes were coldly inquisitive, asking all the questions.

'I went round there,' Eddie said quickly. 'The apartment had been wrecked. There was no sign of Lissette.' He glanced at Sophie. 'Mrs van der Elst was in the apartment —'

Sophie interrupted him. 'I'd gone there to see Lissette.' She stared at Porter. She sensed the steel in this man and wondered what the relationship between Lissette and him could be. 'I'm sorry, I don't know who you are.'

Joe's eyes flicked up and down the passage. He stepped back inside the door. 'You'd better come in.'

Annette busied herself in the kitchen while Sophie arranged herself decorously on a sofa after removing a shirt flung there the night before by Joe.

The two men exchanged a look.

'Now,' Sophie said imperiously, 'hadn't you better tell me what you've done with my daughter?'

The sheer effrontery of the remark made Eddie's jaw drop in surprise. Joe felt a surge of irritation, but then he caught the glint in her eye and realized that her attack was a ploy, an attempt to unsettle him. He remembered how Lissette had talked about her mother. She was indeed formidable, and he might have to cut her down to size, but he didn't want to reveal too much, not yet. First he had to be certain of her silence. There was a lot at stake.

'All right,' he said slowly. 'You don't know where she is?'

Sophie hitched up her skirt a little and crossed her legs. They were still beautiful. 'I've already told your friend that. He said *you* could help me find her.' The sarcasm was biting.

'Maybe I can.' Joe gazed at her thoughtfully. 'Your daughter worked for the Germans in the Cinéac during the occupation.'

He paused, but Sophie didn't bother to deny it.

'She was also caught by the resistance on the roof of the Cinéac with a German officer.'

Sophie raised her eyebrows. 'My, you have been doing your homework.'

Eddie was surprised. He hadn't known anything about the German. But the expressionless look in Joe's eyes warned him not to say anything for the moment.

'I always do my homework, Mrs van der Elst.' Joe smiled sardonically. 'And Lissette wasn't the only one with German connections, was she?'

Sophie tried to convey innocent surprise, but it wasn't easy. 'What on earth are you talking about?'

Joe struck. 'When your boyfriend was discovered to be a Jew by the Gestapo, you were tipped off by a German officer – another one of your friends.'

Sophie stood up and strode to the window. She needed time to think. How much did he know? This much he could have learnt from Lissette, but even she did not know everything. She turned to face him. 'So what? I'm not afraid to say that I gave shelter to a Jew.'

Joe almost smiled at the nerve of this woman.

'But,' she continued, 'not all Germans were Jew-baiters, and I was warned by an acquaintance. And I'm not ashamed of it.'

Joe decided to demolish her defence. 'Except that until you were told by your "acquaintance" that Duparc was a Jew, you had no knowledge of it. Once you did know, you told him never to come back. Effectively you threw him to the wolves.'

Sophie's face paled beneath her make-up, but she stood her ground without flinching. 'So what do you intend to do about it?'

Joe crossed to the other window and gazed down at the busy street. Antwerp was getting back to normal. The silence in the room deepened. Annette who had been listening in the kitchen, stood quietly in the doorway, waiting to hear what Joe would say.

He spoke slowly, keeping his back to Sophie. 'For the moment I will do nothing, but if I hear so much as a peep that you have reported Lissette's disappearance to the authorities, I will personally see that your connections during the occupation are known.' Then he turned to her. 'But I shall not tell the British authorities. That would be too easy.' His voice was devoid of emotion, and it struck a raw nerve of fear in the woman. 'I shall inform the White Brigade. They are interested in collaborators.'

Sophie didn't move.

'Do you understand?'

She nodded.

Joe turned to the Irishman. 'Perhaps you'd better see her home.'

Sophie stared at Joe disdainfully. 'There will be no need for that.' Her voice seemed to be coming from someone else, but she swallowed hard, and managed to carry on. 'I can find my own way home.'

She strode to the door and Annette moved aside to let her pass. Then she stopped and faced Joe. 'If you find my daughter, please let me know.' She held Joe's eyes for a moment, ignored Eddie, then turned and left the apartment.

The door slammed shut. Eddie didn't move. He was waiting to see if Joe was going to turn his attention on him. He'd brought the woman here, but Joe clearly saw her as a threat.

When Joe did speak, his voice was utterly normal, as if nothing had happened. 'The pick-up at Leopolddok is working fine, but I need to know, as much in advance as possible, what is being shipped in and when.'

Eddie accepted that. 'I'll do my best, but I'll have to be careful too. It's pretty chaotic at the moment, setting up the new channels and routes for the transportation to this point. What are you looking for particularly?'

'Almost anything except heavy arms. Food, medical supplies, especially penicillin, any luxury goods . . .'

Eddie cut across. 'There won't be many of those.'

Joe smiled. 'Don't you believe it. We're getting close to Christmas and the officers will be making sure there's plenty to celebrate with.'

'OK. I'll keep my eyes open.' He paused, wondering if he should broach the subject, then took the plunge. 'Have you got any idea about Lissette?'

Annette came in and handed them mugs of coffee.

Joe took a sip and put his down to cool. 'She's probably been picked up on some sort of collaboration charge. Who else would take her?'

'What are you going to do about it?'

Joe stooped and picked up his shirt from the floor where Sophie had dropped it. 'Nothing.'

Eddie stared at him in amazement. 'What do you mean, nothing?'

Joe flung the shirt to Annette. 'Give that a wash.' He glanced at Eddie. 'Exactly that.'

He studied the Irishman's baffled face. 'Look, if she has been picked up and we try to get her out, we bring attention to ourselves. Why would a couple of soldiers, Hillier or myself, want to get a collaborator out of prison? Besides,' he added, 'I've already got her out once.'

Eddie looked at Annette in disbelief then back at Joe.

'When? Why?'

'Like I said, she was caught on the roof of the cinema with a German officer when the resistance took over just before I got here. I don't think there's any significance to it. She told me he had been up there because he was trying to find a way out. They killed him and took her in for questioning. I liked the possibilities of the Cinéac, so I got her out, said she was an agent for us. The warden was shit-scared he was about to be chopped and he let me have her. But it would be different now.'

'So you're just going to leave her there. Don't we need her in the Cinéac?'

If Joe was irritated by the Irishman's persistence, he didn't show it. 'No, we don't need her, not any more. I'll get rid of the cashier too and put in Maria and Annette.'

Eddie was dumbfounded. 'But Lissette helped us. We can't just leave her.'

Joe explained as patiently as he could. 'Look, if they get wind of what we are up to in the Cinéac, the whole operation is blown. We couldn't risk it.'

The Irishman was getting angry. Quite why he felt so disturbed he didn't know. He thought it was because Joe seemed to be betraying Lissette, but there was more to it than that. He cared about her.

'What about Lissette? Won't she tell what she knows about us?'

Joe shook his head. 'I don't think so.'

'Why not – if we just leave her there?'

'First of all, we don't even know what has happened to her.'

'What else?'

Joe shrugged. 'She knows that if we are implicated in any way, they would then find out about her mother. God knows what she was up to.'

Eddie had finally got the picture. 'You mean you'd tell them?'

Joe stared at him, and for once Eddie was not afraid of his implacable green eyes. He was too mad himself.

'Well, they don't know anything about *me*. I'm not connected with the cinema, so I'm gonna try and find out where she is. And I'll tell you this, Joe, if I do find her, I'll be trying to get her out.' He turned and slammed out of the apartment.

Annette was frightened. She had never seen them angry with each other before. It worried her that their friendship appeared to be cracking. She went over to Joe and rested her head on his chest, trying to comfort him and indicate her support. Absently he put his arms around her, but he was hardly aware of her presence. That was the first time Eddie had ever turned against him, and he was vaguely surprised to discover how much it hurt.

People had never worried Joe before.

CHAPTER TWENTY-ONE

He stood outside the elegant house. The trees in the avenue were bare, like thin black skeletons reaching up to the grey December sky.

The chill was biting, but even in winter this road had character. He walked slowly up the steps to the front door and rang the bell. He knew she was at home. Her footsteps tip-tapped over the polished wooden floor of the entrance hall and she opened the front door.

The man took off his hat and smiled thinly. He had good teeth, Sophie thought.

'I'm sorry to trouble you, *madame*' – he flashed a card – 'but I would like to ask you a few questions. May I come in?'

Sophie stared at him. 'You are –?'

His eyes glittered at her tone, but he continued to smile. 'My name is Leo Bruneel. I am with security.'

Sophie stepped back into the hall. 'I'm sure that has some significance, Monsieur Bruneel. Do come in.'

He stepped past her while she closed the door. She took his overcoat and put it on the stand, and then he followed her into the living room.

He glanced quickly around. It was furnished with quality and taste, though he found it somewhat opulent and overpowering. Sophie indicated an armchair but he waited for her to sit before doing so himself.

'Well,' she said, smiling, 'what can I do for you?'

Bruneel made a pretence of examining his notebook. 'You have a daughter, Lissette van der Elst?'

'I do.' Sophie waited.

'She is the manageress of the Cinéac?'

'That's right. She has worked there for some time.'

Bruneel nodded. 'Since before the war, in fact.'

Sophie inclined her head slightly. 'Ungallant of you to indicate my age, Monsieur Bruneel. But that is correct. Lissette has worked there since before the war.'

He did not respond to her invitation to lighten the conversation. Sophie watched him guardedly, but maintained her pose of elegant relaxation.

'Do you know the Peeters family?'

She thought about that for a moment. 'Yes. They run a farm. Lissette used to go out there when she was young for the horse riding.'

Bruneel watched her closely. 'Have you seen them recently?'

Sophie shook her head. 'Heavens, no, not for years. Not since Lissette was about fifteen.'

She waited for him to speak, but he continued to sit silently in the armchair.

'Is anything wrong?'

'Yes,' he said, matter-of-factly. 'They are dead.'

An expression of shock crossed her face. 'I'm sorry,' she said. 'They were nice people. Lissette will be upset. She was quite close to them.'

Bruneel decided it was time to take the gloves off.

'They killed themselves when the Gestapo raided their farm to pick up a Jew who was sheltering there. We have arrested your daughter. We think she informed on the Peeters.'

Sophie stared at him in amazement, and she was not faking. Then she stood up, her eyes blazing with anger.

'That is nonsense. Lissette loved the Peeters. She would never do anything to hurt them. You are making a dreadful mistake, Monsieur Bruneel, if you think my daughter could have done that.'

Bruneel rose slowly, his manner unaltered. 'Lissette worked for the Germans in the Cinéac. It is possible that she may have made a mistake, left something lying around that incriminated the Peeters.' He waited to see if she would seize upon this.

'That is absurd. There was nothing secretive about my daughter's relationship with the Peeters. She has nothing to hide. You have made a mistake. Furthermore, I do not like some of your questions. I shall be speaking to my lawyer about Lissette.' She regarded him coldly. 'Where are you holding her?'

Bruneel didn't answer at once. He studied her thoughtfully, wondering how much of this was true, how much of it bluster. Of one thing he was sure – this woman would not crack easily, not unless he could bring pressure to bear.

He smiled without warmth, his eyes devoid of expression. 'She is in the prison, *madame*. I will bid you good day.' He turned and left the room, his feet echoing loudly on the hall floor as he collected his coat and left.

Sophie didn't move until she heard the front door close behind him. Then she sat down suddenly, fear draining her face. She had to help Lissette, but she would have to be careful.

Sergeant Robinson looked at her in some surprise. 'Who?' He could not keep the astonishment out of his voice.

Sophie smiled patiently. 'Corporal Eddie Pearce. I'd like to see him, if it's possible.'

Rainy Day Robinson stood up respectfully. He didn't know what she wanted with a character like Corporal Pearce, but he knew class when he saw it and this lady had it in buckets.

'If you'd like to sit down on this chair, ma'am.' He pulled a hard-backed seat from beneath the other desk in the office and offered it to her.

Sophie accepted it graciously. She understood the sort of man the sergeant was and knew how to play this role to perfection. It had worked equally well on the German military.

Robinson smiled deferentially. 'I'll be back in a moment. I think I know where he is.'

He found Eddie with his feet up, warming them on the huge, black, pot-bellied stove that dominated the former dormitory they had occupied.

'Pearce!' he yelled.

Eddie leapt to his feet. 'Sergeant?'

Robinson stared, with some incredulity, at the small Irishman. 'There's a lady to see you, Pearce, in the orderly room.' He jerked his thumb for Pearce to follow and strode back as fast as he could the way he had come. Eddie had to half run, half trot to keep up with him.

'Who would it be, Sergeant?'

Rainy Day gazed rigidly ahead. 'I wouldn't know who it is, Pearce, or what she wants with you, but you mind your manners, otherwise you'll have me to deal with.'

Eddie gazed up at his stony face and decided to say no more. It was a wise decision. Rainy Day was upset. A woman like that and a man like Eddie offended his sensibilities. It didn't feel right to him. The sergeant was a snob.

Sophie stood up as Eddie came into the room. She tried to cover his evident surprise at seeing her.

'Ah, you've found him, Sergeant,' she said brightly, beaming at Rainy Day. 'Thank you so much. It was extremely kind of you.'

Eddie choked on a suppressed laugh as Robinson almost fawned with pleasure.

'It was no problem, ma'am. Happy to oblige.'

Sophie inclined her head delicately and took Eddie's arm. 'Come, Corporal Pearce, there is much to discuss.' She led him from the orderly room before Rainy Day could muster an objection. She gripped the Irishman's arm tightly and didn't let go until they had crossed the quadrangle of the former boarding school, now crowded with military trucks.

Eddie was curious. 'How did you find me?'

'Not *that* difficult. I knew your name and I'd seen the unit number on the jeep you drove.'

He glanced at her admiringly. She was dressed elegantly in a long, black coat with a fur collar to keep out the winter chill.

'I know a café,' she said. 'Would you like some coffee?'

Eddie smiled, remembering the sergeant's warning. 'I never say no to a drink, especially with a lady.'

It was a smart place on a corner, with an awning out over the pavement that would be decorated with tables in the summer. Sophie led him into the warm interior and to a table that gave them some privacy.

Eddie decided to bide his time and let her make the running. It did not take long. Once the coffee had been delivered, she leaned forward and spoke quietly, but there was an urgency in her voice that was unmistakable. 'I know where Lissette is.'

Eddie gazed at her calculatingly. 'So do I.'

For once Sophie was speechless. She sat back, momentarily deflated.

Eddie continued, 'She's in the prison, charged with collaboration and under suspicion of betraying a safe house to the Gestapo.'

Sophie stared at him in some surprise. 'How did you find out?'

Eddie grinned. 'I knew her name,' he said, 'and we have connections with the local resistance leaders. It wasn't too difficult.'

Sophie was not without a sense of humour. She smiled ruefully *'Touché!'* Then her voice hardened. 'We have to get her out.'

Eddie raised an eyebrow. 'We?'

Sophie didn't hesitate, she had already decided what she intended to do. 'Listen to me, Eddie. Those charges are ridiculous. The people she is accused of betraying she absolutely adored. She always stayed with them during the summer holidays when she was a child. She could never betray them.'

Eddie nodded. 'I think you're right.'

Sophie sighed with relief. 'Good.' She paused for a moment, before continuing. 'I want you to help me get her out, Eddie. I'll make it worth your while. I have some money. And if you have to bribe anyone, I'll pay.'

Eddie gazed at her in disbelief. 'Make it worth my while? You mean bribe me as well?'

Sophie realized she had miscalculated. Suddenly, instinctively, she understood why Eddie already knew where Lissette was.

'I'm sorry,' she said. She twisted the coffee cup around in its saucer. 'You must understand, if you can, that living in an occupied country for four years changes people's attitudes. I'm afraid I have changed too. It seems I have come to believe that everything has to be bought.'

She waited for him to respond. It had been a nice speech, she thought, and she had recovered well.

Eddie almost believed her. But the turn-round had been just a mite too pat. 'Don't you worry about your daughter, Mrs van der Elst.'

Sophie tried not to wince at the 'Mrs'.

'I'll find a way of getting her out.'

Eddie remembered how Joe had reacted to Lissette's disappearance. As far as Joe was concerned, she was now expendable.

But not to him. Eddie cared much more deeply than he had at first realized. It was something Sophie now understood better than he.

'Thank you Eddie,' she said, and sipped her black coffee. Now she would leave it to him.

Eddie gazed at her contemplatively, trying to understand her complete change of tack. He knew he had to get Lissette out. He also knew there was no official ploy he could try. Joe had already made use of that once before. And whatever he did must not in any way throw the spotlight on to the cinema itself. That was Joe's excuse for doing nothing, though Eddie did have one advantage: no one knew of his connection with the operation at the cinema.

It had to be something else.

He examined his own reasons for wanting to get Lissette's release, and the solution he came up with was brilliant in its simplicity. It would make his request virtually impossible for any liberated Belgian to refuse.

CHAPTER TWENTY-TWO

'I don't want to go,' Maria shouted angrily.

Annette tried to placate her. 'But it will only be for a few hours each day, won't it?' She looked pleadingly at Hillier. The American shrugged. 'Until Lissette comes back.'

Hillier gazed exasperatedly at Maria. 'There's no need for all this. What's the big deal? All I want you and Annette to do is run the front of house for a while – we're short-staffed. It's better than sitting around here all day.'

Maria paced the room moodily. 'I wasn't going to stay here all day.'

Hillier cottoned on. 'You mean you have somewhere to go?'

'Yes.'

'Like where?'

She tossed her head angrily. 'That's my business.'

Hillier knew there was no point in arguing with her. She was in a rebellious mood, and until the mood changed he was wasting his time. He looked at Annette.

'Well, I'm going. How about you?'

Annette looked at her sister, but Maria turned her back.

'All right,' she said, 'I'll come.'

Hillier nodded. 'Thanks.' He glanced at Maria, but she kept her gaze averted. He picked up his coat and slipped it on, handing Annette hers from the hook on the door.

'Right,' he said shortly, 'let's go.'

He opened the door and held it for Annette. She glanced once more at Maria, hoping she would change her mind, but her sister gazed sulkily out of the window. Hillier shut the door and followed Annette down the passage to the stairs. Before they could reach them he heard the door open and slam shut behind them. He did not turn round.

Maria caught up with them on the stairs. 'You can drop me off at the café,' she said. Annette could not disguise her disappointment, but Hillier gazed stonily ahead, ignoring Maria.

They drove in angry silence in the jeep, Maria and Hillier each intent upon wounding the other as deeply as possible, waving their animosity like a banner in front of Annette, spreading their unhappiness.

And it did upset Annette.

She was too young to understand this lovers' quarrel. It seemed so serious, so hurtful. She did not understand why her sister was unwilling to help at the cinema.

But then she was not like Maria. It was not the cinema or even the tedium: Maria always did find something to quarrel about. It was her way of establishing herself, a cost factor that Hillier, or any other man, had to pay for her love. It was uncalculating and quite instinctive, and it made every lover wary, so that he could never take her for granted. You could say she was testing.

But it was a risk. Hillier would eventually either accept or reject this side of her character. The fact was, she loved him so much that unless she did this to him, she was too vulnerable.

Hillier drew up outside the café and Maria slipped out of the seat next to him on to the pavement. He turned and looked at her. If he had, at that moment, asked her to forget it and come with him to the cinema, she would have laughed and done so.

'Is this where you wanted?' he said coldly.

He saw the funny, half-hidden, sad look in her eyes and instantly regretted it. There were a hundred things he could have added to take the sting from the remark, if only he'd had time to think, but she tossed her head and froze him with her disdain.

'This will do fine.'

She wrapped her red coat around her like a cloak, swung round on her heels and marched into the restaurant.

Hillier gazed after her bleakly. Then, angry as hell, he jammed the vehicle into gear and shot off into the traffic, cursing an unfortunate cyclist who was foolish enough to be passing at that moment.

At first his anger and his aggressive driving through the morning traffic blotted out the sound. Then he saw people on the pavement gazing up apprehensively at the sky. They began to scatter and suddenly he was jerked from his own thoughts as he realized what was happening. He glanced quickly at Annette and saw the fear on her face.

He slammed on the brakes, skidding the jeep into the kerb. He glanced up at the grey sky overhead and immediately heard the trundling, haphazard note of a doodlebug approaching from the north.

As he grabbed Annette's arm, its engine died. There was no time to reach cover. He pulled her from her seat and thrust her down beside the jeep, crouching next to her.

They waited in a silent agony of terror for the bomb to strike. Hillier felt rather than heard the rush of air as it fell from the sky. Then the explosion shook the ground and the jeep almost bounced as the shock waves spread around them.

He looked up. The street was deserted. Vehicles were spread across the road; people like himself poked their heads out of cover to see what damage had been inflicted.

But the bomb had struck several hundred yards and three blocks away, just around the corner. Hillier could see the pall of dust rising from behind the buildings.

Then he felt the blood draining from his face as he realized where the bomb had landed.

Moments before he had watched Maria enter that building in her scarlet coat. Annette saw his face pale and the fear in his eyes. She looked back up the street and saw the rising cloud of dust. She screamed, leapt to her feet and before he could stop her she began to run. He was stunned by the speed of her reaction and her stricken cry of pain. He began to run after her.

She was calling out Maria's name, her voice sharp-edged with fear and apprehension. Her feet seemed to have wings and his own moved as if filled with lead, slowing him. He dreaded what he might find when he turned the corner.

But first he had to catch Annette. It was a strange, unreal experience, as if he were in a nightmare, his feet and legs sinking into cottonwool as he tried to catch up with her. He saw frightened faces peering at him from doorways, while the empty pavement echoed his pounding feet like a hammer in his brain, and all the time he could hear Annette's voice calling out in despair, 'Maria! Maria! Maria!'

Her body seemed to float above the ground in front of him, always tantalizingly just out of reach. He put out his hand, trying to stop her. He could see his fingers in front of him clawing at the air.

Then, suddenly, his hand was on her shoulder. He twisted her round and her face was before him. Her eyes were wide and frightened, tears streaming down her face.

He heard his own voice, hollow and empty, telling her to calm down, that everything would be all right.

They rounded the corner together and stopped. The flying bomb had struck the main part of the building behind the restaurant. At first he thought the café had escaped serious damage. But as he approached he saw that the pavement was littered with broken glass where the front windows had completely blown out. A shadow moved inside the restaurant and then staggered into the light. The man's face was so covered in blood that it was impossible to discern his features. His clothing was in tatters, his flesh blackened and burned.

He felt Annette shudder as he dragged her round, averting her eyes from the ghastly figure weaving inside the shambles of the restaurant.

A man appeared beside him, gazing in horror at the spectacle. Hillier thrust Annette into his arms. 'Hold on to her,' he said savagely. 'Don't let her follow me.'

The man stared at him.

'Do you understand?' Hillier gripped the stranger's arm brutally. Hillier saw him nod dumbly, then he turned and ran towards the entrance of the restaurant. He saw the misshapen figure stagger blindly into a wall, then sit down abruptly as though his legs had been jerked from beneath him.

Hillier stopped for a second just inside the entrance and looked at the bloodied man slumped against the wall. He knelt beside him and tried to lift him up, but the man gazed blankly past him, then Hillier saw that the back of his head was almost blown away. He toppled over lifelessly, his head lolling against Hillier's shoulder for one ghastly moment before he could jerk away.

Hillier stood up quickly, trying to control his nausea, swallowing down the bitter bile of horror in his throat. He gazed hopelessly into the shattered shambles that had once been a restaurant crowded with people.

All he could see in the choking, dust-filled gloom was debris and strange pieces of human flesh and limbs blown apart and scattered among the matchwood of the furnishings. One table, made of cast iron, was still recognizable. It stood upended against the far wall, its spindly legs sticking out drunkenly towards him. A hand lay upturned on the floor beside it, a flash of red overcoat disappearing behind the flat top of the iron table.

Hillier made his way across the wet, slippery floor, oblivious to the sweet, sickening smell of blood. He reached the table and tried to move it from the wall. It was heavy and seemed to be jammed. He kicked aside some of the debris and tried again. This time it slid a few inches. He pulled once more until there was enough room for him to squeeze himself behind the table.

She was lying on her back, her red overcoat covered in a fine, white, powdery dust. She did not appear to be injured. She had been protected from the awful effects of the devastating explosion by the iron table.

He knelt beside her and, lifting her head, gently brushed the white powder from her face with his hand. Her eyes were shut, her face composed, but she was dead, killed by the vast pressure wave of the bomb. He remembered the look on her face when he had asked 'Is this where you wanted?', the sad, hurt look in her eyes before she had walked away from him, out of his life and towards her own death. His head dropped, spilling his tears on to her face as he held her tightly to him, burying his head in her hair.

He wasn't sure how long he stayed with her in the café. It was something that he would never speak of as long as he lived. He remembered gathering her up in his arms and carrying her, very carefully, through the devastated wreckage of the restaurant. Then he emerged into the open, the grey morning blinding him with its light.

He saw Annette staring at him, and he walked slowly towards her.

CHAPTER TWENTY-THREE

Leo Bruneel studied the man before him curiously. It was an un-expected turn of events, but the demand could not have been more forthright.

Eddie was aware of his scrutiny and he kept his thoughts to himself. It was for Bruneel to respond.

'When did you meet this woman?'

The Irishman was irritated by the way the question was put. 'You mean Lissette van der Elst?'

Bruneel acquiesced. 'Yes.'

'Shortly after we were moved up to Antwerp in September.'

Bruneel thought about that. It was perfectly feasible that the British soldier could have met Lissette then.

'And when do you intend to marry her?'

Eddie smiled for the first time. 'As soon as you release her.'

'What makes you think I will release her?'

Eddie leaned forward across the desk. 'Because she is engaged to a British subject and, having liberated your city, we are not exactly unpopular right now.' He let the Belgian think about that for a moment, then continued, 'Besides, why would you want to hold on to Lissette? You say that she may have betrayed a family she knew when she was a child. But why would she do that? All you have against her is the fact that she ran the Cinéac while the city was occupied. Are you going to lock up everyone who traded in Antwerp while the Germans were here?'

Bruneel gazed at him expressionlessly but made no comment.

Eddie decided to play his ace. 'If you don't release her, I'll marry her here in the prison, and once we are married that will make her a British subject.' He thought it was best not to mention that in fact he was Irish – that would only complicate matters.

Bruneel was almost convinced but not quite. Maybe it was just as the soldier suggested. Maybe there was no connection between Lissette and the woman who had been seen arriving with the Jew, Duparc. So far he had been unable to establish any link between them. At any rate, if the soldier was serious about Lissette, and he did not doubt it, then he could not keep her here. He knew the British military authorities could make it very difficult for him if he tried to prevent the marriage. And he needed their co-operation if the White Brigade were to gain control. There were enough political factions among the resistance without weakening his own position any further. Besides, with the woman free he might be able to learn more.

He smiled suddenly. 'Why not? Who am I to stand between a British soldier and a Belgian girl?'

Eddie smiled right back, not allowing suspicion to cloud his face. 'Good. We'll drink to your health.' But he knew then that he'd also have to keep a wary eye on the Belgian. He didn't trust Bruneel, not for an instant.

Lissette sat beside Eddie in the jeep, gazing sightlessly ahead, unaware of the bustle of Christmas, the first to be celebrated in the city since its liberation. She didn't want to see the few street decorations that were on display or acknowledge her apparent freedom. She was too frightened to enjoy the thought, fearful that once again it might be snatched from her. Twice now she had been imprisoned and twice freed by a British soldier. She didn't know how Eddie had managed to secure her release; she didn't want to know. She just wanted to be back in her own apartment. Even then she would always fear the heart-stopping knock on the door, the grim, expressionless faces.

Eddie sensed this instinctively, and he had no wish to try to explain in the open vehicle. He too felt exposed. Bruneel worried him. As far as he could tell, no one was following them, but then he didn't have to. Bruneel knew where he was taking her and he could pick them up any time he wanted. And for Lissette's sake it was important to play this absolutely straight. Her future depended on it.

He pulled up the jeep outside her apartment block, and leapt out and round to her side. Lissette continued to sit slumped on the hard seat, seemingly unaware of their arrival.

Eddie gently took her arm. 'We're here.'

She turned and looked past him at the entrance, then allowed him to help her from the vehicle. There was a weary acceptance of his guidance, no elation, no spark of life. He led her through the entrance and pushed open the heavy metal doors of the lift.

It heaved and clanked its usual noisy way to the top, and Eddie opened the gates, helping her over the gap between the lift and floor. He had found her keys in the apartment, and he unlocked the door.

As it swung back, Lissette stood in the entrance and gazed inside. Eddie had spent a long time tidying it up, and he'd also found a few Christmas decorations to brighten the rooms. He'd even lit a fire, convinced that he would be able to bring her home.

She walked slowly inside and Eddie shut the door carefully, following her into the living room that faced on to the street below. She sat quietly in the chair by the fire, not taking off her coat. Eddie didn't say anything. He had one more surprise. He went to the kitchen and prepared the coffee. It was real, not *ersatz*, and he'd managed to acquire it only by some judicious string-pulling in the transport section.

It was the delicious aroma that finally pulled Lissette from her daze. She looked up at Eddie gratefully as he handed her the hot cup. She sipped it hesitantly, then as she caught the taste she smiled, looking at him. 'It's real.'

Eddie grinned. 'It had better be. It cost an arm and a leg to lay me hands on that.'

Lissette shivered. Her love had come back to haunt her. Manfred had stood where Eddie was now, pleased in the same way to obtain a small luxury for her, to make her happy. She gazed up at Eddie, at his uniform. A soldier, like Manfred. Only Eddie was real, not a sad, lovely memory.

She sipped the coffee, enjoying the warmth of the fire glowing in the grate. She began to feel alive again. There was comfort in Eddie's presence, and the small living room was a haven from the cold, grey day outside. He had sat down opposite and was staring into the fire, the flames reflected in his eyes.

'How did you get me out?'

Eddie had known she would ask that question, and the more he had thought about it, the less he knew what to say.

He sighed, shaking his head. 'Oh, you're never going to believe what I told them, Lissette.'

She looked at him, puzzled, then half smiled. 'I might,' she said. 'After all, I am here. You did get me out.'

Eddie gazed down at his feet a little self-consciously, wondering what to say. Then he looked at her directly, searching her face.

'You remember that Sunday you let me come in to see the film?'

She nodded. 'Bing Crosby,' she said.

'God, it was a good film.' He was distracted by the memory for a moment. 'Barry Fitzgerald is a funny man.'

Lissette sat quietly, too numbed to enjoy his enthusiasm. 'He is.'

A comfortable silence developed between them as they contemplated that afternoon. Then Eddie remembered what he had been talking about.

'I'm sorry, what was I saying?'

'You were about to tell me –'

He cut across her. 'Yes, I was. Well, something happened to me in the cinema.'

'I remember you laughed a lot.'

He shook his head. 'No, there was more to it . . .'

She stared at him, realizing how serious he was. 'What do you mean?' she asked gently.

Eddie was unable to articulate his feelings; it was impossible for him. 'I told the man there in the prison, Bruneel . . . I told him we were to be married.'

Lissette stared at him in total surprise.

He rushed on. 'Of course I know it is ridiculous, and maybe I shouldn't have done it. But I knew, you see, that they would never hold you if they thought you were going to marry a British soldier. Not unless they had something definite.' He swallowed nervously, waiting for her response.

Lissette nodded. 'I see.' She paused, thinking about what he'd said. 'So you made up this story just to get me out?'

'Yes,' Eddie blurted out, then, changing his mind, 'No. No, it's not exactly like that.' He gazed at her, his face a picture of frustration and indecision.

She tried to help him. 'What is it, Eddie? What are you trying to say?'

He cleared his throat. 'Lissette, they only let you out because they believe we are going to marry. If we do not, they could easily take you back again, and I don't want that to happen.'

She did not allow the dreadful feeling of horror to show in her face. Somehow she managed to speak calmly, though Eddie heard the quiver in her voice. 'Are you saying that you will marry me to stop me from being imprisoned again?'

This time she could not hide her fear. Eddie saw it in her eyes. He lifted himself from the armchair, and knelt in front of her, taking her hand in his.

'I'm saying that I want to marry you because I love you, Lissette.'

She looked down at him, disbelievingly, but there was no dishonesty in his face. She swallowed, trying to hold back the tears, but one rolled down her face, and she wiped it away angrily.

'Look what you've made me do.'

He touched her face with his hand, cupping her chin in the hollow of his palm. 'You'll be safe with me, Lissette. I will look after you and see no harm ever comes to you again.'

She took his hand and kissed it. 'Oh, Eddie,' she said. 'How was I ever lucky enough to find you?'

She put her arms around him and held him close. She knew she would have to tell him, but not now. She didn't want to spoil this moment. It could wait. She was entitled to this.

They were married quietly within the week. It was a civil service and only Hillier, Sophie and Kenwright came. Annette had left Antwerp. She had gone back to France to tell her grandmother about Maria.

Joe didn't come either.

That hurt Eddie more than he would have thought possible. Ever since they had been conscripted together in Gallowgate, Joe had protected him, had been his friend, his strong right arm against the prejudice and the bullying he'd had to endure because he was small and came from Southern Ireland. But when he had told Joe of his plans and of how he had rescued Lissette from the prison, there had been no friendliness in Joe's response.

Instinctively Eddie had sensed his hostility to the marriage and his veiled contempt. Suddenly there was a gap between them where before there had been an unspoken but implicit comradeship. Eddie knew Joe distrusted Lissette, but he didn't know why.

There was one uninvited guest. Bruneel watched them emerge from the large, squat municipal building. He kept himself out of sight. He knew who the older woman was, but he had never seen Hillier or Kenwright before.

He followed the small entourage of two jeeps in his own car and waited outside Lissette's apartment until Hillier and the other man emerged half an hour later. That led him as far as Hillier's building.

Bruneel was getting closer.

Lissette resumed her role as manageress at the Cinéac. She welcomed her normal duties like lost friends, glad to be back among her familiar working surroundings. Eddie lived with her in the apartment, and in the warmth of his quicksilver, gentle humour she gradually relaxed. The fears slowly receded, but they would never completely go away.

She had one additional task at the Cinéac now. The staff were not to be allowed to enter the huge basement beneath the auditorium. But that was not a real problem. The steel door beneath the backstage stairs was an effective block, and the area had hardly been used except as a proposed shelter. The patrons and staff had never been given access to it. And since the storage and printing operation only ever took place when the cinema was closed, at night and on Sundays, the system worked. Lissette never inquired about the basement or what might be going on. She did not want to know, and as far as Hillier and Joe were concerned, the less she knew the better.

She was in her office, dealing with some routine papers, and the matinée performance had just begun. She could hear in the background the muffled sound of the trailers for next week's films as they climaxed. It was something she enjoyed, a backdrop to her work that was reassuring and gave her a sense of continuity.

She felt, rather than saw, the presence of someone in the doorway, someone looking at her. She didn't know how long he had been there, but suddenly she was aware of something and she looked up.

At first she didn't recognize him. His clothes were scruffy, his face was stubbled and unshaven and his left arm was in a sling. It was his eyes that told her his identity. She felt her face grow cold, and her mouth went suddenly dry.

He took one step towards her and then she knew he was real, not just a figment of her imagination. She stood up and rushed around the desk, flinging her arms around his neck as his one good arm embraced her.

It was Manfred.

She held his rough face in her hands and kissed him passionately, pressing her body against his. Then she felt him stagger slightly and she stepped back, examining him, seeing his fatigue for the first time. She shut the door quickly, and led him to the other chair in her office.

'Come,' she said. 'Sit down, let me get you something.'

He forced a grateful smile. 'Thank you, Lissette.' His voice was gruff and tired.

She went into the back room and found a glass and a bottle of whisky, kept specially for distributors whom she wished to impress. She poured him a generous amount and gave it to him.

'Drink this,' she instructed.

He took the glass and sipped it. It bit the back of his throat and warmed him all the way down to his stomach. He swallowed the rest quickly.

'Some more?' she asked, concern edging her voice.

He shook his head, feeling the welcome glow inside him. 'No, I'd better not. I'm not used to it.' He glanced round the familiar office. 'I don't suppose you have anything to eat?'

She could have wept. She leant over him and kissed his matted hair, then went behind the desk and opened a drawer. She handed him the sandwiches Eddie had packed for her before he left the apartment early that morning. She gave them to Manfred.

'It's only cheese, but the bread is fresh.'

He undid the paper and chewed the bread hungrily. Lissette went back to the ante-room and made him some tea, boiling the water on a gas ring. She stood in the doorway watching him demolish the sandwiches and wondering where he had come from.

'Hausser told me that you were dead.'

Manfred looked up at her. 'He is all right?'

She nodded. 'He told me that the lorry crashed after an attack from the air. That you were inside when it . . .' She stopped, unable to continue. She struggled to complete the sentence. 'He said you were – killed.'

Manfred stood up suddenly and put his arm around her. 'I'm OK. I was thrown clear, knocked unconscious, and when I came to, I was on a British stretcher being taken to a field hospital.' He lifted the arm in a sling. 'This was broken. Otherwise I was unhurt. It's nearly better now.'

The kettle began to boil and she broke free to pour water into the teapot.

'How did you get here?'

Manfred shrugged. 'They kept me in a hospital. I think it was in Ghent. I knew that I could not get far without civilian clothes, and the security was good, but it was easier than being penned in a prisoner-of-war cage.'

Lissette recoiled inside, shrinking from the memory of the lions' cage, but he didn't see it.

'The arm took a while to heal. It mended wrong at first. But it gave me a chance to work in the hospital as a porter, and I managed to steal these clothes from a cupboard. They belonged to someone who had been rushed in after a car accident. I waited for the right moment, then I got out at night.' He smiled wearily. 'I've walked here.'

She put her arms around him again, hugging him tight, then poured out a cup ot tea and gave it to him. He sipped the hot drink gratefully and looked at her over the rim.

'What about you? How have you managed?'

She smiled. 'Not too badly,' she lied. 'As you can see, I'm still here in the cinema. The city is free, though things are still very bad. We still get bombed, only from the other side now.' She laughed, but the sound was brittle. 'It seems we are a target no matter who claims our city.'

For the first time she realized the danger he was in, and she thought desperately for a solution.

'What are you going to do?' she blurted out.

'Well, I don't want to go back to Germany, nor do I want to be a POW in England. If you could hide me for a while, maybe I'll be able to get some papers, then find a job.'

She could not tell him about Eddie. She knew it would destroy him. Yet she owed the Irishman her life. She sat down behind her desk, her legs suddenly bereft of strength.

Manfred gazed at her, concerned. 'What's wrong?'

'Nothing. I'm fine. I'm trying to think of what's best. I don't think my apartment is a good idea. I'm certain the authorities are keeping an eye on me because I ran this' – she indicated her surroundings – 'while we were occupied. But there is somewhere.' She thought about it for a second. 'Yes, I think it might work.' She looked at him across her desk. 'We will go there together once it's dark.'

She glanced at the door of her office. 'You are in danger here. I always leave the door open. People just walk in.'

He nodded. 'I know. That was how I first took advantage of you.' He smiled at the memory. 'Look, I will go and watch the film. I have a ticket. I waited in the circle until after it had started.' He glanced at the clock on the wall. 'It will be dark by five o'clock. What time does the film finish?'

'Just before.'

'OK. I can pretend I have not seen the whole programme and I'll stay in my seat. Come and look for me when you are ready.'

That fitted in with what she had in mind. 'I sometimes go out between programmes. After I come into the circle, you leave by the side exit. Wait in the alleyway beside the cinema and I will join you as soon as I can. That way, if anyone is watching for me, they will not see us together.'

He smiled, and reached across the desk, taking her hand. It was cold. He held it tightly, gazing into her eyes. 'I'll see you soon, after the film.' He grinned. 'Will I enjoy it?'

She nodded. 'I think so. It's an American film – only the second one we've had.' She didn't tell him that Eddie had managed to arrange it for her, with subtitles, nor did she repeat the title: *To Have and Have Not.*

Manfred waited silently in the dark alleyway beside the cinema. The black-out dimmed the headlights of the vehicles passing in the main road, but there was still enough light to see the silhouette of anyone stepping into the narrow, gloomy alley.

A cold wind gusted suddenly, causing a can to rattle unnaturally loudly in the alley as it banged into the wall and skidded along. It didn't concern Manfred. He was lucky and he knew it. He'd survived the crash and managed to escape successfully from the hospital. He'd also found Lissette. He was happy to freeze for a while.

He heard the exit door being opened behind him and her slight figure emerged. She gripped his hand. 'God, it's cold.'

He saw her teeth flash in the dark as she smiled.

'Come on,' she said, 'I'm taking you home to mother.'

She led him down the alley towards the back of the cinema, then through a number of side streets until they turned back on to the main road. They travelled across the city together in a tram. It clanked its way slowly into the wintry suburbs, commuters jammed together as the rush-hour traffic developed.

There were hundreds of cyclists. Manfred wondered how they managed to negotiate the darkened, cobbled streets and still avoid catching their narrow bicycle wheels in the tram lines.

Eventually they alighted near the top of the boulevard that led to Sophie's house. As they walked down it, her hand tucked under Manfred's arm, Lissette broached the subject that worried her most.

'You never met my mother, did you?'

'No.' He looked at her. 'You never talked about her much.'

'Didn't I?' She paused, thinking about that. It was odd in a way, considering she had told Joe everything.

'Well, let's just say that we have not been close, but recently she has tried to improve our relationship.' She remembered how pleased her mother had been at the wedding.

She gripped Manfred's arm tightly and he smiled at her.

'Don't worry,' Lissette said brightly. 'I talked about you on the phone this afternoon and she knows we are coming.'

He glanced quickly behind them. 'No sign of anyone.'

Lissette was relieved. 'Good. I think if anyone was keeping me under surveillance, we lost them at the cinema.'

She paused in front of the steps leading up to the house, then took him round the back.

Manfred laughed. 'Am I not good enough for the front entrance?'

She scolded him quietly. 'Don't be silly. I just don't want to take any chances.'

Lissette tapped on the glass window in the door. Sophie was waiting and let them in. She took them to the living room where a fire had been lit in the large, high room.

Lissette watched her mother closely. If she was taken aback at all by Manfred's rough appearance, she didn't show it.

Sophie held out her hand. 'I'm Lissette's mother, but you may call me Sophie.'

Gravely Manfred took her hand in his own. 'I am Manfred Kepner, and I am grateful for your hospitality. You show me great kindness.'

'Nonsense,' Sophie said curtly. 'You are a friend of my daughter and you have helped her in the past. These are strange times, *monsieur*. Now let me take your coat.'

He had difficulty in getting it off because of the sling, and Lissette quickly helped him. He glanced at the dirty overcoat.

'Forgive the state of my clothing, *madame*, but . . .'

Sophie brushed his apology aside and moved briskly to the door, taking the coat from her daughter.

'Enough of that, Manfred. You are cold – warm yourself by the fire.' She glanced at Lissette. 'Shall I take your coat too?'

Lissette shook her head. 'No, I must get back to the Cinéac before I am missed.'

Manfred was surprised. 'You are leaving me?'

'I must.'

'I'll see you to the door.'

Sophie stopped him. 'Say your goodbyes here, Manfred, while I hang up your coat. I don't want anyone to see you at the door.' She closed it diplomatically behind her, leaving them alone.

He took a pace towards Lissette. 'How soon before I see you?'

She thought quickly. 'Tomorrow, in the morning, before I go to the Cinéac. We'll have some time to talk then, as I don't have to be there before half past one.'

He put his one good arm around her. 'I shall miss you tonight.'

Lissette could not look into his eyes. She rested her head on his chest. 'And I shall be thinking of you.'

He gripped her hand. 'Come as early as you can tomorrow. I've got so much to tell you.' He searched her face. 'I love you, *mein Liebchen*. Take care.' He kissed her hard on the lips, holding her tightly, then buried his face in her hair, remembering her fragrance.

Lissette pulled away, touching his cheek with her hand. 'Until tomorrow.'

He nodded. 'Tomorrow.'

She gazed at him, imprinting his face on her memory. She had almost forgotten what he looked like. Then she turned and opened the door. Sophie had waited patiently in the hall.

Lissette glanced once more at Manfred. He smiled.

Lissette walked with her mother to the front door. Sophie opened it, then put her arm across in front of her daughter.

'Have you told him about Eddie?' Her voice was low, but hard-edged.

Lissette shook her head. 'I couldn't, not yet. It's too soon. I'm coming to see him in the morning. I'll tell him then.'

Sophie took her arm away. 'Make sure you do.'

Lissette nodded dutifully and stepped out into the cold night, away from the man she loved.

'Goodnight, mother.'

Sophie watched her go down the steps. 'Goodnight, Lissette.'

She closed the door, shutting out the chill blast of air, and walked back into the living room. Manfred was rubbing his hands together in front of the fire. He glanced around him.

'This is a lovely room, *madame*.'

Sophie inclined her head. 'Thank you, but I would prefer it if you called me Sophie.'

He nodded affably. 'Of course – Sophie.'

She smiled. 'That's better. Now would you like me to prepare a meal, or would you sooner have a bath first?'

'A bath!' he exclaimed. 'Sophie, you do not know how much I have longed for a hot bath.'

'Then you shall have one, and that will also give me time to prepare dinner. I will show you.'

She led him up the wide staircase to a sumptuously fitted bathroom that smelled deliciously of rose petals. She indicated the bath.

'There, enjoy yourself. I have put my husband's shaving gear on the shelf by the sink if you want to shave.'

In fact, the brush and razor were Duparc's, but she had no intention of telling him that. Manfred knew their ownership was a lie, but he respected her privacy and was delighted at the prospect of a bath *and* a shave.

'You seem to have thought of everything.'

Sophie smiled. 'I haven't finished. There is a dressing-gown and some pyjamas behind the door. Dinner will be completely informal, and it will give me a chance to decide what to do about your clothes.'

He nodded, slightly embarrassed. 'Thank you, Sophie.'

She turned in the doorway. 'Enjoy your bath.' Then she closed the door behind her.

Manfred looked at the bath. It was magnificent, long and deep. He took the plug on the chain and placed it in the hole. Then, tentatively, he turned on the hot tap.

The water gushed, steaming, into the bath and he could have cheered. Instead he turned and grinned at himself in the mirror. 'It works,' he said to no one in particular. As quickly as he could, he stripped off the clothes he had been wearing for three days and nights since he had escaped from the hospital. He hung the sling over the hook on the door and removed the protective bandage from around his arm.

It had almost completely healed. The sling was there to support it until his muscles developed properly again. The bath would do it good.

He flung the rest of his clothing into the corner. Then he turned on the cold tap until the bath was nicely filled.

It was still too hot to sit in. Back on came the cold and he stirred it around, using both of his hands until the temperature felt just right.

Slowly he lowered himself into the hot, soothing water. He slid down the bath, his head just poking above the surface, feeling the tension slipping from his body, the hot water smoothing away his aches and pains.

It was such luxury, one that he had not experienced since he was last in Lissette's apartment. He felt tremendous and, ducking his head beneath the water, rubbed soap vigorously into his hair until he'd got a fine soapy mass of foam on his head. He burst spontaneously into song.

Downstairs in the kitchen Sophie smiled. It was a long time since she'd heard a man sing in her bath. She enjoyed it. She hoped he was enjoying it too, because his pleasure would not last much longer.

Manfred felt completely relaxed as he sat in front of the fire in the living room, his legs stretched out, contemplating the glowing coals.

The meal had been excellent. Where she had got the chicken from he had no way of knowing, nor did he intend to inquire, but it would not have come cheap on the black market. And it had been an age since he'd had home-made ice-cream.

The fire was making him drowsy and his eyes almost closed. He jerked himself awake. It would have been impolite to fall asleep while Sophie was making the coffee. He reached over and seized the poker. The fire did not need raking but it gave him something to do.

Sophie brought in the coffee on a silver tray and placed it on a small table. He watched her delicate movements as she poured the coffee and handed him the cup.

'Thank you,' he said politely, smiling. 'I can see where Lissette gets her elegance.'

Sophie looked up, surprised and pleased by the compliment. 'That is good of you.' She indicated the coffee. 'I'm sorry, I have no sugar.'

Manfred shrugged. 'No matter. I like coffee without it.'

Sophie sat down in the armchair opposite, and a long silence developed between them. It was Sophie who spoke first.

'You care a good deal for Lissette?' Her tone was gentle, inquiring.

Manfred was slightly surprised by the question, but he answered seriously. 'Yes, I love her very much.'

Sophie considered carefully before she responded.

'How much has she told you about what has happened since you left?'

Manfred stared at her, puzzled. 'Not a lot. Just that she has been able to continue her job at the Cinéac.'

Sophie pursed her lips. 'I see.'

Manfred was concerned. 'What do you mean?'

Sophie sighed deeply. 'I'm afraid she has been less than honest with you, Manfred.' He looked at her questioningly and she continued. 'Lissette has been imprisoned twice.' She stopped and let the words hang there.

He was wide awake now. 'What happened?'

'The first time she was caught on the cinema roof with a German officer who was trying to escape from an ambush by the White Brigade –'

He interrupted. 'Was this before the British got here?'

She nodded. 'Yes, they put her in the lions' cage in the zoo. Later she was released.' She paused.

'And the second time?' he asked.

'The second time they arrested her in her apartment because they said she was a collaborator . . .' Sophie paused fractionally. 'And that she had betrayed the Peeters to the Gestapo.'

'That's nonsense,' Manfred said hotly. 'I drove her out there myself.'

Sophie shrugged. 'Precisely.'

Manfred stood up suddenly. He felt a surge of pain and guilt. He strode over to the curtained window, then turned and looked at Sophie. She could see the torment in his eyes.

'How did she get out?'

Sophie stood up, facing him. 'A soldier, a man who had met Lissette at the Cinéac, just as you did, went to the leader of the resistance and told him that they were engaged and that if she was not released, he would marry her in the prison.'

Now Manfred began to understand. 'A British soldier?'

'Yes.'

'And they released her?'

'Of course – the British control the city and the White Brigade is only one of the resistance factions seeking power. It could not afford to keep her locked up.'

Manfred absorbed that, then walked slowly across the room until he was standing in front of the fireplace. He rested his good arm on the mantelpiece and gazed into the flames. The silence extended, then he straightened and looked at her.

'Are they married?'

The fire spat behind him, as a minor impurity in the coal ignited.

'Yes,' Sophie said. 'They were married as soon as she was released.'

Manfred swallowed, feeling hollow inside. He sat down on the armchair, rubbing his forehead. Sophie could see the despair etched on his face. But she knew this was not the time for sympathy. She went and sat down opposite him.

'Look at me, Manfred.'

Her voice was determined, hard. He stared at her, surprised.

'As long as Lissette is married to this soldier, she is safe from the

White Brigade. But they are quite ruthless, Manfred. The things that have happened here since the Germans left have been desperate. Anyone working with the Germans is at risk. But it is worse than that for Lissette. They think she is responsible for Duparc's and the Peeters' deaths.' She took his hand in her own. 'Someone must have seen you arrive with her, Manfred.'

He gazed at her silently, his whole world crumbling inside him. Everything that he had hoped for with Lissette had turned to dust.

Gently he disengaged his hand from Sophie's. He stood up, not looking at her. 'What do you want me to do?'

Sophie chose her words carefully. 'You have to go, Manfred. Every minute you are here in Antwerp you increase the risk for her. As long as they don't find you – and as long as she remains a British soldier's wife – she is safe. But even that will not protect her if they discover you here.'

He considered it, but he knew he was simply wasting time. 'You are right, *madame*.'

This time she did not ask him for the informality of her name. She sensed that his instinctive acknowledgement of her status was correct. He turned and looked at her.

'When would you like me to leave?'

Sophie did not allow the satisfaction to show on her face. 'First you must have some sleep, and I will find you decent clothes. But you must go before Lissette comes in the morning, otherwise she will simply sacrifice herself for you. You know how much she loves you.'

A sad smile flickered briefly on his face. 'Yes, I do know. But I will leave before it is light. I will not see her.'

He thought for a moment.

'Would you object, *madame*, if I wrote her a letter?'

Sophie stood up. 'Of course not – but you must not tell her where you are going or she will follow you. Her whole future in this city depends upon how she behaves.'

Manfred understood completely.

'Yes, I know. You have nothing to fear. I will make that clear myself.'

Sophie nodded. 'Thank you, Manfred.'

He stared at her for a moment. He felt tired and empty, and he found it difficult to speak.

'I think I will go to bed now.'

Sophie touched his face gently. She felt pity for him, but it had been something she had had to do. Not only did Lissette's life depend upon her marriage but Sophie's own past in this house during the occupation might be thrust into the spotlight, and the thought of having her hair shaved off and being publicly humiliated made her shudder.

'You must sleep,' she said. 'You are tired. There is writing paper in the desk in your room. I will give the letter to Lissette myself.'

Manfred walked slowly to the door and opened it. He paused, then looked back at her. 'Will you wake me?'

She inclined her head slightly. 'I will.'

He stared at her across the room, the firelight glinting in her long auburn hair. She was still a beautiful woman, he thought.

'Goodnight, *madame*.'

'Goodnight, Manfred.'

He closed the door, leaving her alone by the fire. She turned and stared into the flames. She knew then that she would not give the letter to her daughter.

Lissette left the apartment early, as soon as Eddie had driven off to his unit. She was careful to leave the bedroom curtains drawn and made her way through a back entrance that was seldom used except by maintenance staff and tradesmen. Lissette was sure no one had seen her.

She had hardly slept at all. All night the same thoughts had tortured her endlessly. Just the presence of Eddie in her bed was a constant reminder of how much she owed him. And yet she had been ashamed to acknowledge that she resented his body lying next to her own. He was a good man, and in a sense she loved him for that, for the warm and lively man he was. But he could never take Manfred's place and, unbelievably, Manfred had come back. Tired and injured, he had escaped to return to her.

He was alive!

Even in her doubt and uncertainty she wanted to shout with the joy of his living, but the prosaic Belgians in the tram on their way to work daunted and silenced her. But they could not suppress her exultation. That was hers and Manfred's. Whatever the future might

247

hold, the fact that he was alive gave her life a new meaning. It gave her back the man she loved.

She went round the back of her mother's house as usual, hoping no one would see her ducking down the passage that led to it.

Sophie let her in without a word and walked back to the living room. Lissette knew immediately that something was wrong. She stopped in the doorway, gazing at her mother.

'What is it?'

Panic bells were jangling in her head. Her mother didn't answer at once. She stood with her back to Lissette.

'Where is he?'

Again, no reply.

Lissette's hand flew to her mouth. 'Oh, God, *no*!'

She turned and ran up the staircase screaming his name, but there was no answer, just her own cries echoing hollowly in her ears.

She found his bedroom, the sheets flung back where he had slept. She sank to her knees beside the bed and buried her head in the covers. His smell was still faintly detectable. She sobbed bitterly, pounding the mattress with her fists.

'Don't go!' Her voice was choked with bitterness and despair. 'Please don't go, Manfred. I need you!'

Sophie could hear her daughter's despair, but she remained in the living room. The tears had to come if the pain was to ease, and Sophie knew in her heart that Lissette would never forgive her for what she had done. But she did not regret it – there was no other way that gave either of them a chance.

Then she climbed the stairs and looked down at her daughter lying crumpled over the side of the bed. She lifted her gently to a sitting position and cuddled her in her arms, rocking her slightly as if she was a child again. It did bring Lissette some small physical comfort, and she held on to her mother as the tears slowly abated.

Then she began to think. It was a dark, intrusive thought, spreading bitterly through her. She pushed herself away from her mother.

'Why did he go?'

Sophie could see the look in her eyes. Now would come the reckoning.

'I told him about Eddie.'

Lissette closed her eyes, clenching them shut as if to cut out what was happening.

'Why, mother? Why, for God's sake?'

Sophie stood up, moving away from the bed. 'Because you owe Eddie your life, and I knew you would not stay with him if Manfred was here. He realized that too.'

Lissette stared disbelievingly at Sophie. 'Manfred?'

'Yes. If you left Eddie now, left his protection, they would have you. Worse still, they would have Manfred too. They would put one and one together and come up with four. If they knew you had loved a German here in Antwerp, in their eyes that would prove everything.'

Lissette sprang to her feet. 'But how would they know, mother, unless you told them?'

The accusation was bitter and hurt more because it was Sophie's deepest fear. She knew she could never take imprisonment and that had been the real reason for sending Manfred away. But she would not admit it, not even to herself.

She lifted her head in disdain. 'You may not believe that I have done this for you, but Manfred knows the truth.'

She turned and walked out of the bedroom, and started down the stairs.

Lissette ran after her and screamed at her from the landing, 'The truth! You don't know what the truth is. You never did. Manfred is the father of my child!'

Sophie stopped halfway down the stairs, frozen, unmoving.

'Don't you understand? I was going to tell him today. I would have gone with him. I loved him. He was mine – and now you've taken him from me again.' She slid slowly down beside the bannister and collapsed on to the landing.

Sophie heard the thump as Lissette's head hit the floor, and she ran back up the stairs and knelt beside her. Lissette was distraught, hysterical, her face twisted with despair and anguish. Sophie tried to calm her, but it only seemed to make her worse.

Her mother could see the hysteria in Lissette's eyes. She pulled back her arm and slapped her daughter hard round the face, stinging her cheek red with the force of the blow.

Lissette stopped at once. She stared tearfully at her mother.

Sophie lifted her up. 'Stop this. You must rest for a while,' she commanded. Lissette did not resist. She allowed her mother to lead her back into the bedroom and lay her down on the bed. Sophie took off her shoes, just as she had done sometimes when Lissette was a child. She tucked the cover up around her neck and then under the mattress to keep her warm.

'I'll go and make you a hot drink. You'll feel better then.'

She tried to brush Lissette's damp hair from her wet face, but she jerked her head away.

Sophie straightened up.

'I shall not be long. You must try to sleep, Lissette.' She looked down at her daughter, but her eyes were clenched shut. Sophie went to the door. 'I'll be back in a few minutes,' she said.

When she came back, Lissette had gone.

Sophie waited until she knew the Cinéac must have opened, then she telephoned. The cashier confirmed that Lissette was in her office and Sophie made an inquiry about film times, then hung up.

She was relieved that her daughter had not done anything stupid. Knowing Lissette, she had guessed that she would find greatest comfort in her work.

Then she telephoned Eddie's unit and charmed Rainy Day into allowing her to speak to the Irishman. They agreed to meet at Lissette's apartment at six.

Eddie was surprised by the call but did not ask why she wanted to see him. Robinson's ears were practically twitching and he had detected a slight warning tone in Sophie's voice.

At six promptly the apartment doorbell rang and he let Sophie in. She settled herself in her usual spot by the fire, which he had lit. The wind blowing off the Scheldt was icy.

Eddie didn't sit down. 'Is there anything I can get for you?'

Sophie smiled winningly. 'No, I had some tea before I left.'

She studied the Irishman, wondering how he would react.

'I'm going to ask you something, Eddie, that you may not understand or welcome, but trust me, please, because there is a good reason for the question.'

Eddie raised his eyebrows. 'What is it?'

250

'Were you ever intimate with Lissette before you were married?'

Eddie was more shocked than he cared to admit. His own Catholic background had not prepared him for the sophisticated morals of someone like Sophie. And although his experiences since he'd joined the army had opened his eyes to almost every sexual appetite, he had still managed to keep that knowledge separate from his regard for marriage.

He shook his head. 'No. Why?'

Sophie didn't hesitate. 'Because Lissette is pregnant.'

Eddie was dumbfounded. He grinned foolishly. 'But that's great!' Then he saw the expression on Sophie's face, and he remembered her question. 'What is it?'

She stood up and moved across to the window. 'I don't think it's your child, Eddie.' She had thought about this ever since Lissette had told her about her condition. If it was Manfred's child, and she had no reason to doubt it, then her daughter was nearly three months gone. There was no way she could have pretended it was Eddie's child, particularly in view of his reply to her question. She waited for him to respond.

'You mean she was pregnant when she married me?'

Sophie faced him. 'Yes, she must have been, but she didn't know until yesterday. She came to me this morning and told me.'

Eddie looked down at the floor. 'I see.'

There was a small silence. Only the tick of the clock intruded.

'I wonder if you do.'

Eddie lifted his head. 'What do you mean?'

'Did she ever tell you she was put in the lions' cage at the zoo because they thought she had collaborated?'

Eddie shook his head. 'No, *she* never told me. I knew she had been imprisoned when they caught her on the roof of the Cinéac with the German. But I do know about the cage – I found out.'

Sophie kept her eyes on him and nodded her agreement. 'Yes. I only realized because of something she let slip. I think that is when she became pregnant.'

'Are you sure?'

Sophie shrugged. 'No, not for certain. But I know my daughter and she has never been promiscuous. Besides, the time fits according to the doctor. I rang him myself.'

Eddie looked hard at Sophie, his eyes challenging her. 'What difference does it make?'

Sophie shook her head slightly. 'I don't know, Eddie. That depends on you. I know Lissette won't hold you to the marriage.'

Eddie stared at her incredulously. 'But I love her. The baby makes no difference. I'll raise the child. And we will have more.'

Sophie looked into his open face and knew she had guessed right. She took a step towards him and placed her hands on his shoulders. She leaned forward and kissed him. 'You are a good man, Eddie. My daughter is very lucky to have you. In some ways I envy her.' She smiled wistfully. There was more truth in that last remark than she cared to admit.

Eddie was embarrassed by her display of affection, but he needed to know more. 'Did you tell her you would be speaking to me?'

'No!' Sophie said vehemently. 'She knows nothing of my visit. I made sure of that. She is at the Cinéac.' She thought for a moment. 'Will you tell her you know?'

'I will have to.'

She could see that made sense. 'Then I will speak to her first.'

Eddie shook his head. 'No. I want to discuss this with her.'

Sophie could see the danger. Lissette might think that she had told him about Manfred.

'Eddie, listen to me. She feels bad enough about this already. If she thought I had deliberately betrayed her to you, she would never speak to me again. Please, let me explain first. I'll say nothing of your reaction, just that you know and want to talk to her.'

She waited. This was crucial. She could tell Lissette anyway, but the Irishman was astute enough to detect any lie attempted by her daughter. Deceit was not something Lissette was good at. It was a talent she had not inherited.

Eddie acquiesced. 'All right, but I shall be meeting her later when she finishes at the Cinéac.'

Sophie was relieved. There was something else, however, and now was the best time to broach the subject, while she had his compliance.

'How much do you know about the resistance factions here in Antwerp?'

'I know they are fighting to establish themselves politically.'

'Lissette is still in danger. So am I.'

'Why you?'

'Lissette was not the only one who had dealings with the Germans while they were here.'

She let the remark hang there for a while.

Eddie had heard what Joe had said about Duparc – how Sophie had forced him from her house once she discovered he was a Jew. He stared at her contemplatively. 'You mean they could drop on you and implicate Lissette?'

'That's right. I've already had one man nosing around, allegedly a connection with Lissette.'

'Leo Bruneel?'

'Yes.'

'That was the man I dealt with at the prison.'

'Then you can see the danger.'

Eddie could. 'We have to get her away somewhere.'

It was what Sophie had been waiting for. 'Send her back to Ireland.'

Eddie was nonplussed. He hadn't expected that.

'She's your wife,' Sophie urged. 'She can have the baby in peace there and be safe from harassment, no matter what happens.'

It all suddenly fell into place.

Eddie too had been worried about Lissette's connection with the operation at the cinema. Now the way was clear for him to send Lissette home. It would not be too difficult. Other British soldiers were fraternizing and marrying local girls.

'All right,' he said, 'leave this with me – but don't say anything to Lissette, not till I can arrange it.'

Sophie heaved a sigh of relief. She didn't know just what the Irishman was involved in. The hard-nosed Englishman he had taken her to had frightened her. He knew too much. His threat of exposure to the White Brigade was not a light one. He had meant every word, and Sophie knew enough about men not to underestimate him. But why hadn't he wanted to help Lissette? What was going on between him and Eddie? Then there was the American who had come to the wedding, Hillier. At least she knew his name. All she knew about the Englishman was that Eddie had called him Joe. Once Lissette was

253

safe in Ireland, she would find out more. That was something she was good at.

Eddie was still waiting for a response.

Sophie smiled. 'Don't worry, you can rely on me.'

She didn't say what for.

She noticed that the ceiling had cracked. It must have been the shock wave from the blast of the V1 that had destroyed the café three blocks away.

It was quite wide and meandered across the ceiling of her bedroom like a river looking for a way to the sea — like herself in a way.

'What do you think?' Eddie asked.

She continued to gaze at the ceiling. 'I'm not sure.'

Eddie turned to look at her as the darkened headlights of a car passing outside traced a pattern round the small bedroom. He saw her face in the reflected glow. She looked sad and vulnerable. He raised himself on one elbow, gazing down at the pale oval of her face.

'It'll be all right, Lissette, you'll see.'

'But what about you?' she said. 'When will I see you?'

'I'll be home for leave at Easter. Maybe before. Depends how long this lasts. But you'll be with my mother. She'll look after you. And you could not be having the baby in a better place. Both me sisters have had children and mother had four.' He leant down and kissed her cheek. 'You'll be safe there, Lissette. I don't feel happy about all these bombs flying in the way they do. You in that cinema every day working from lunch time until after ten o'clock — that's no good for you or the baby.'

She put her arms around him, feeling his hard-muscled body press close to her own. He was right, of course. How could she deny that it was safer for her and the baby to be in Ireland? But she could not tell him that she wanted to stay, that she longed for Manfred to come back and take her away, that she would give anything to have him lying next to her in this bed, where she had conceived their child.

Even as these thoughts flashed through her mind she despised herself for them. It was Eddie who had saved her, taken her out of the prison, given her a life again. And now, knowing the child was ot his, he wanted to raise it in safety and comfort in his own country.

She clasped him tightly to her, pressing her mouth to his ear. 'I love you, Eddie. Come to me quickly in Ireland.'

He held her tenderly. He could feel her desperation, and her tears were salty on his cheek. 'Don't worry, my darling girl, I'll look after you always and I'll be back to Ireland before you can even look round.'

They celebrated Christmas together, and six days into the new year of 1945 Lissette sailed from Antwerp on a coal boat bound for Dublin.

As she watched the Scheldt Estuary merge imperceptibly with the English Channel, she felt a great gulf of depression open up before her. Manfred had gone, and she was drawing further and further away from him. She might never see him again. It seemed so cruel that he should come back only to be jerked out of her life again.

But Eddie, she knew, would not fail her. He had risked everything to make her own future safe and her unborn child's life secure. She wondered if she could ever tell him whose child it was.

He did not seem to want to know.

Maybe it was best this way. When Eddie came back to Ireland, she would be a good wife to him. He loved her, and in a way she liked him more than any other man she knew.

That thought surprised her. But she knew it shouldn't. Eddie was kind and he made her laugh. There was hope for the future – for her, for her child and for Eddie.

She pushed the depression aside and went below to the warmth of her cabin. The voyage to Ireland would be long, with plenty of time to ponder the future. But one thought was never far from her mind. What would Ireland be like?

CHAPTER TWENTY-FOUR

Leo Bruneel studied the translation of the document for the third
time. It was clear, concise and quite chilling in its matter-of-factness.

It was a record of Duparc's arrest, torture and subsequent execution, all laid out bureaucratically on official paper, completed in
triplicate. Bruneel half smiled to himself. He wondered if any other
country would have kept such a complete and authoritative record
of its inhumanity. Perhaps, he thought, in some way they felt
absolved them from the horror by making it look official, part of
normal government procedure.

It was the way the information had been obtained that interested
him most. There it was, in black and white – the name of the
informant: van der Elst, Mrs *Sophie* van der Elst.

He had the connection at last but not the one he had been looking
for. He snapped the document shut. The rest should be routine.

Joe was uneasy.

He finished loading the boxes of cigarettes that had just been
delivered on to the shelves and wiped his brow. He was sweating
heavily and it was not just from the labour.

He glanced around the huge basement below the auditorium of
the cinema. The dim lighting created pools of darkness, and there
was always a damp chill to the place, no matter how much they used
the electric fires.

Hillier was at his desk, working on papers, keeping a record of all
the various transactions. He was thorough; it was necessary to know
exactly whom they supplied and how much had been received. The
goods they were able to siphon off from the ships arriving in the
port had to be limited and selective to avoid compromising Eddie

position in the MT section. As long as losses could be put down to petty thieving by dock workers, both in Antwerp and at the port of embarkation, no one was likely to be any the wiser.

The noise from the printing press operated by Gus was constant, but it did not seem to affect Hillier. He had grown used to it. Joe, however, had never really felt happy down here. It was too claustrophobic for him. He preferred the other side of their operation, the night club and the deliveries.

Soon they would be extending their enterprise with the newly painted German staff cars. Joe was proud of them. He'd picked one up today and it looked great painted yellow, the way he'd seen New York cabs in the cinema.

He called out to Hillier, 'I'm going upstairs. Be back in a minute.'

The American acknowledged his words with a brief nod and resumed his paperwork. Joe picked up a torch and made his way to the steel door, then climbed the stairs to the backstage area. Once the steel door was closed shut, the sound of the press cut out completely.

There was always a vaguely musty smell back here. It didn't matter how much they opened the high double doors to accept delivery of goods, it never really went away.

He worked his way through the darkened cinema up the stairs to the circle foyer, using the torch. They never switched on any lighting once the staff had gone home in case it attracted attention.

Joe could not pin down his nervous tension. It was a little like the feeling he got when he was out behind the enemy lines, but not quite the same. There was no fear for him in those circumstances, just a still kind of alertness. Then he identified it.

When he and Eddie had come in on the LST towards the beaches of Normandy, he'd felt just like this. It was that uncertainty, being unable to control, or be responsible for, his own safety that created the tension, mixed with a strange sense of excitement. Anticipation.

But anticipation of what?

He slipped through the door that led to the steps up to the roof. He trod softly on the iron steps. It was instinctive. He didn't know why he did it. He kept the torch down by his feet, moving quietly.

When he reached the door to the roof at the top he switched it off. The darkness closed around him. Carefully, making sure the door did not squeak, he pushed it open. Immediately he heard the faint background hum of the city, the occasional late-night vehicle passing in the main road below.

He closed the door softly behind him and stood absolutely still, listening. There was nothing else. His eyes had already adjusted to the dark and he could see the skeleton outline of the Flakvierling still pointing up at the night sky, slowly rusting away, unused on the roof.

Joe padded silently towards the parapet by the front of the building and looked below. It appeared to be normal.

The main road was wet, the cobblestones reflecting the shaded lights of a passing car. He stood there silently, unmoving. Every instinct was now warning him, making the hair on the back of his neck tingle in the night air.

Still nothing.

Then something scraped in the doorway of a shop opposite the entrance of the cinema. A boot, highly polished, moved back into the shadow of the doorway. Joe examined each doorway carefully. He could not be sure in the dark, but he sensed the presence of men in each one.

He heard the approach of a late-night tram clanking up from the river area and he waited. It came, drunkenly swaying around the bend in the street, the driver pushing the old machine as fast as he could, anxious to get home to a warm bed.

As it went by, the faint light from its interior lit up the doorways for an instant and Joe saw the shadowy armed figures, the pale waiting faces and the armbands of the White Brigade.

He waited no longer.

Like a wraith he flitted across the roof and down the iron steps to the circle, moving fast, using the torch only when he had to. The nervous tension had gone. He was calm and still inside. He knew what his enemy was, and he had identified it.

He reached the steel door and pushed it open. Hillier and Gus were still working, but the American felt the cool draught of air as the door closed behind Joe and he looked up.

He froze.

Joe moved swiftly, gathering up his Thompson submachine-gun and another from the arms cache. He tossed it to Hillier and called to Gus, 'C'mon, we've got to get out of here fast.'

Kenwright moved to turn off the press.

'No!' Joe shouted, 'Leave it on. They may think we're still here. Grab one of these.'

Kenwright armed himself, and Joe led the way to the steel door. He paused, flattening himself against the wall, then pushed the door slowly open.

Nothing.

He slipped up the stairs, followed by Hillier and Kenwright. It was as before, silent and empty.

Hillier gripped his arm. 'Do we make a break out the back way?'

Joe kept his eyes on the backstage door, by the empty porter's cubicle. 'No, they'll have the place surrounded. We'll never make it.'

Hillier felt a surge of fear and irritation. 'Then how, for Christ's sake?'

Joe looked at his tense face and smiled thinly. 'The roof.'

He didn't wait to explain, but moved off fast. After a moment's hesitation, Hillier followed, whispering savagely to Gus, 'Let's go.'

They reached the circle lobby, and then the silence was smashed by the sound of breaking glass as the windows and doors caved in. Joe heard feet crashing upstairs towards them from the foyer below. He fired off a burst from the Thompson and heard a body thump to the steps and roll slowly back down.

He pushed open the door to the roof. 'This way. Quick!' Hillier and Gus passed him. 'I'll cover until you make the top.'

They didn't hesitate, working smoothly together. Joe heard them clambering the steps, then turned his attention back to the cinema.

Sporadic fire broke out in the backstage area, then someone raked the lobby from the bottom of the stairs, the rounds splintering the woodwork panelling around him. Joe ducked, then let off another burst himself. He heard voices below, shouting orders in French, and let them have some more.

Hillier's voice echoed down the iron staircase. 'OK, Joe.'

He slammed the door shut and pushed the bolt across, then leapt for the steps, slinging the Thompson round his shoulders. He clattered up the steps, the sound reverberating in the confines of the narrow concrete stairwell. Silence didn't matter now, only speed.

He heard someone try to open the door below, then a short burst of fire through it shattered the bolt fastenings. He reached the final few steps as the door below crashed open.

Hillier gripped him and pulled him through on to the roof as automatic fire ricocheted off the iron steps, then the roof door was slammed shut by Kenwright.

He grinned at Joe. 'That was close.'

Joe did not respond, but there was a dark glitter of excitement in his eyes. He was in his element. Hillier stared at him.

'Christ,' he said, 'you're *enjoying* this!'

Joe glanced at him, and Hillier felt his flesh crawl. There was something almost alien about Joe's pleasure in this tight corner, but he was sure as hell glad to have him on his side.

Joe moved to the side of the cinema where it pressed close to the next building. The space of the alleyway separated them from the flat roof of the office block.

Unlike the German lieutenant before him, Joe had two advantages. One, it was dark. That made it possible to attempt the jump up and across without being spotted. And, two, there were others to give covering fire and pull them over the parapet – if the first one made it.

Gus stared down at the dark slit of the alleyway below. 'Jesus Christ, how do we get across? I can't jump that.'

Joe didn't argue with him. 'You are going to jump it, otherwise you stay here. There's no other way.' He paused, allowing his words to sink in. 'It can be done. I'll go first.' He handed his weapon to Hillier. 'Hold this.'

The American took it. He looked dubiously at the gap facing them. 'Can we do it?'

Joe grinned. 'It's easy.'

He placed himself carefully on the parapet surrounding the roof of the cinema. It was about twelve inches wide, giving him some space, but it would have to be a jump from a standing start.

He did not look down, gazing steadily at the parapet opposite. Now that he was standing on the wall surround of the cinema, his head and shoulders were above the level of the other one. The gap was about three feet – easy enough to jump normally, but without any run up and a drop of nearly a hundred feet if he made a mistake.

Joe tensed, then flung himself forward, propelling himself up. He

260

made no attempt to clear the parapet; his aim was to be certain of getting his arms across it.

He crashed into the wall, knocking the breath out of himself but easily holding on to the low parapet. He swung his legs over and stood up, signalling to Hillier for the Thompson.

Quickly the American tossed it over and then threw his own.

He didn't like heights. Nor did he have Joe's nerveless ability to ignore the danger of falling. But he steeled himself not to look down and eased himself slowly up on to the parapet. He didn't wait. He knew if he stopped to think about it all his strength would drain away.

He flung himself with all the power that the adrenalin surging through his veins gave him and crashed into the other side. Joe was waiting and grabbed him instantly, pulling him over.

Now there was only Gus.

He stood looking across the gap that seemed to grow wider with every second. He hesitated, fear rooting his feet to the spot.

Joe and Hillier positioned themselves on either side of the spot opposite and Joe held out his hand.

'The gun, throw the gun.'

Gus looked down stupidly at the weapon in his hands. He heard Joe's icy voice.

'Quickly, Gus.'

Automatically he followed orders, throwing the Thompson. Joe caught it and placed it down beside him. From the other side another sustained burst of automatic fire raked the stairwell from below. This time there was no answering burst. All the weapons were on Joe's side of the alleyway.

'Come on,' he called out hoarsely, 'it's no problem, Gus, we'll get you.'

Gus could hear the silence from the well of the staircase. He knew they were coming.

He felt his legs carry him to the parapet and he stood on it, not daring to look anywhere except at Joe's reassuring face.

Joe could see the almost trance-like fear gripping Gus. Somehow he had to shake him loose from its clutches. He screamed like a sergeant major, 'You are going to jump this, Kenwright, and God help you if you don't.'

Gus stared at him and then slowly he seemed to relax. He even smiled, recognizing the silliness of Joe's instruction.

'God'll have to help me if I don't.' He tensed and just as he was about to fling himself across he felt a hot, searing pain burst through his stomach and blood spilled hot and wet down his sides.

He staggered on the parapet as another burst of fire from the alleyway below ricocheted around him, missing him. But the strength was draining from his legs as he tried desperately to prevent himself from falling.

His feet sought the inside of the parapet and he toppled backwards on to the roof of the cinema. He lay there for a moment, stunned. From a distance he could hear Joe's voice calling to him.

He lifted himself up and gestured for the weapon.

'Sling me the gun, Joe, and piss off, for Christ's sake.'

Hillier stared at him. He could see how badly he was hit. 'I'm going back.' He made as if to climb on the parapet, but Joe pushed him savagely back.

'They're just waiting for you to do that.' He looked across at Gus, then back at the American. 'Besides Gus has had it.'

He picked up the Thompson and held it above his head.

'OK, Gus?'

Kenwright managed a weak smile. 'Quick, Joe.'

The gun arced over the alleyway and another burst splintered the masonry, whining around their heads. Joe cursed and loosed off some ammunition into the alley below, then looked over at Gus.

'How is it?'

Kenwright was surprised at how calm his voice sounded. It seemed to be coming from someone else. 'I'll hold them up for a while. Now fuck off, will you?'

Joe gazed at him, then turned to Hillier. 'Let's go.'

The American knew that he was right. He looked at Gus slumped against the parapet. 'Good luck,' he whispered, half to himself. Then he followed Joe.

Gus tried to crawl to the Flakvierling, but he nearly passed out. He didn't want to look at the hole in his stomach. He'd seen enough wounds to know his was mortal.

He pushed himself up against the parapet and wedged the Thompson on his knee, checking the magazine clip. It was full enough to cause some damage before they got him. He didn't have any more ammunition. He knew he wouldn't need it.

The door handle quivered, then flew open. Gus pulled the trigger, blasting a hail of lead into the dark space of the entrance on to the roof.

'Come on, you bastards!' he yelled, 'Come on!'

Hillier paused on the stairs, hearing the familiar rattle of the tommy-gun. He glanced behind him, gazing back the way they had come.

Joe stopped and looked at him. He could see the uncertainty on Nick's face, the desire to go back and help Gus. 'There's nothing we can do.' His voice was deliberately harsh, masking his own disgust at leaving Kenwright behind. 'As long as we can hear the Thompson, he's giving us some time. That's all he can give us, Nick.'

It was the truth and Hillier knew it. He turned his back on the gunfire and rushed past Joe down the stairs.

They emerged on to the ground floor of the office block. Joe led the way round the back. They moved as quickly as they could through the dark offices and down a passage which ended in an outside door.

They were lucky. It was only bolted. Softly Joe eased the bolts off, then stood with his back to the wall. Hillier was on the other side of the doorway.

Joe whispered softly, his voice strangely hollow in the darkness. 'I've got a car parked. Stay right with me, Hillier.'

Gently he pushed the door open a fraction, listening intently. From above came the staccato sound of combat as Gus fought to keep the roof clear. The night outside was paler than the Stygian black-out of the office block, and Joe pushed the door wider, slipping through it and flattening himself against the wall.

Faintly, from the other block, he could hear shouted instructions and running feet, then the quick rattle of the Thompson from the roof again. It was followed by a series of blasts from automatic weapons, culminating in a crescendo of sound. Then silence.

Joe glanced at Hillier and waved him out. They knew that Gus was dead. The Englishman pointed down the narrow street.

Bruneel stooped and peered at the blood-stained, bulky figure of

Kenwright. He recognized him as one of the men he'd seen at Lissette's wedding. They quickly searched the roof, but there was no sign of the others.

Then he got a belated report from the man stationed near the exit in the alleyway. Bruneel cursed and, followed by half a dozen men, he raced back down through the cinema and out to the back door of the office block.

It gaped open. They'd gone.

Bruneel knew they could not be far away. He split his forces into groups of three and ordered them into the back streets. They were to fan out in all directions.

If he could get to his quarries before they reached a vehicle, there was a chance. Bruneel led two men directly down the dark street opposite. It seemed the most likely route.

Joe set off, running swiftly, crouching low. Hillier ran behind him, keeping his pounding feet as silent as possible, his blood thumping like a sledge hammer in his ears.

Joe turned a corner ahead of him, disappearing from his sight. For one heart-stopping moment Hillier thought Joe would leave him in the dark if he didn't get there quickly enough. But as he turned the corner Joe's familiar shape in front of him filled him with relief.

The sounds of conflict had stopped completely. The silence behind them was heavy, menacing. Joe twisted round two more corners, Hillier close behind, then he came to a stop beside a freshly painted ex-German staff car. It was bright yellow.

Joe grinned. 'Like it?' he said proudly.

The American was too out of breath to reply. He nodded and Joe unlocked the door.

At that moment a vehicle swung silently round the corner, its shaded headlights catching them both fully in its glow, their weapons shining dully.

It was a British Military Police jeep, ordered to the area to investigate the gunfire. From behind Joe and Hillier three men led by Bruneel emerged at the other end of the street.

Bruneel dropped to one knee and immediately opened fire, raking the car outlined in the lights of the jeep. The jeep slewed across the road and stopped.

Joe and Hillier leaped into the staff car and the Englishman pressed the starter, shouting to Hillier to keep down.

The engine whined damply. Joe cursed, savagely jerking at the starter again as lead splattered through the windscreen close to his head.

This time the engine engaged. Joe didn't waste time trying to turn the car in the narrow street. He revved it forward as fast as he could, heading straight for the small group of men lined across the road firing at him. He could see the flicker of gunfire from the muzzles of their weapons in the dark, and he felt the bullets thudding into the body of the vehicle all around him. None hit him.

He jammed his foot on the accelerator, aiming the car at the three men.

They leapt for their lives as the car thundered down the street towards them. Two of them managed to avoid the oncoming vehicle, but one was not so lucky.

The heavy bonnet caught him in full flight. Joe felt the bone-crushing impact and heard the man scream as he was tossed like a broken doll on to the roof and smashed into the cobbled street behind them.

Bruneel whipped the automatic up to his shoulder and levelled it at the fast receding shadow, holding the weapon as steadily as he could. He fired one last burst and saw the sparks fly red and white from the back of the car. Then it screamed round the corner and disappeared.

Bruneel called to his colleague and ran up the street towards the MPs' jeep as it began to move in their direction. He stood in its path, holding up his automatic in the headlights so that they could see the White Brigade armband on his camouflage jacket.

He leapt in behind the startled MPs. 'Get your foot down, sergeant!'

The sergeant didn't hesitate. The hard metal barrel of the automatic was sticking in his side, and the other man was loosely covering his colleague.

He slammed the jeep into gear and skidded round the corner after the yellow German staff car.

Joe headed south through a maze of back streets, making for the

bridge at Boom. He wanted to get out of the city. He needed a
breathing space to think this thing through. Somehow the White
Brigade had discovered the existence and whereabouts of their operation. He had to know how.

He felt Hillier's weapon slide down by his leg and he turned his
attention from the dimly lit road. The American's face was white,
sweat shining damply on his upper lip. His eyes were open but
dark with pain, and a red patch was widening on the front of his
jacket.

Joe glanced into the driving mirror. He could see no sign of
pursuit. He waited until he saw a side road, then pulled into it,
parking the car close to the kerb and killing the lights.

Hillier protested feebly. 'Keep going, Joe.'

Porter ignored him and gently pulled open the jacket. Blood
pumped steadily from a gaping wound in his chest, and his shirt was
torn round the edges where a bullet fired during Bruneel's last salvo
had emerged after hitting the American in the back.

Joe took off his own jacket and ripped his shirt into strips. He
packed them into the wound to stem, as far as possible, the flow of
blood.

Hillier watched him quietly, his face calm as he tried to contain his
strength.

'How is it?'

Joe smiled at him. 'You'll live, but I have to get you to a doctor.'

He adjusted Hillier's position in the passenger seat, tenderly
propping him upright. Hillier winced.

'Don't lie, Joe.'

'I wasn't lying. I've seen worse.'

'I know you were lying – you smiled.' The American tried to
grin, but it turned to a grimace as his breath caught and he gagged,
blood spilling from the sides of his mouth.

He gasped, trying to regain control of his breathing. The blockage
subsided and he relaxed as his lungs filled with air again.

Joe heard a horrible bubbling sound from the wound in his chest,
and he knew that Hillier only had a few moments left.

'Is there anything I can do, Nick?' He paused. 'Anyone . . .?'

Hillier grasped his arm, his hand holding it ferociously as he tried
to hang on to consciousness. He could feel his body shivering with

cold. Joe's face, pale in the darkness, seemed to be closing in on him.
He swallowed some blood, trying to speak.

'Kay,' he said.

Joe leaned down close to him.

'If there's anything left, get it to Kay and my son.'

He stared up desperately at Joe, his mouth moving soundlessly.

'Maria . . .,' he said. Then his hand clutched convulsively at Joe's
sleeve and his body arched in pain. Joe put his arms around him
and held him tightly as Hillier cried out his name, panic edging
his voice.

'Joe!'

The Englishman felt his body tremble in his arms, then relax as his
breath exhaled in a long, juddering sigh.

He was dead.

For a long while Joe didn't let go of the American's body. He sat
quietly in his seat, staring sightlessly out through the splintered
windscreen. Then he heard a vehicle coming fast down the main
road and he waited. It shot past the end of the street where he was
parked, and the sound of the speeding jeep quickly faded.

Joe eased Hillier's body back into the passenger seat and wiped the
blood from his hands on the lining of his jacket.

His shirt was in shreds so he pulled the jacket on, turning up the
collar round his neck. Then he started the engine and eased the car
quietly back into the main road, heading south again. The road was
deserted, the few vehicles in the city that did have petrol safely
parked in the dead, early hours of the morning.

Rain began to splatter against the windscreen, and Joe turned on
the wipers. In spite of the bullet holes in the glass, they operated with
reasonable efficiency, though his view was restricted. He peered
through the gloom, keeping his eyes open for the jeep, but the road
remained empty, the cobbles shining wetly in the glow of his
headlamps.

He negotiated the bridge at Boom, heading out over the long
viaduct and down to the crossroads at Breendonk where he had been
welcomed by the Belgian, Vekemans.

He wondered what had happened to him. Probably a hero by
now, he thought. He glanced at Hillier. He almost seemed to be
sleeping, his face peaceful. Only the darkening stain on his jacket

betrayed his mortality. Joe turned right at the crossroads, into the rain-drenched countryside.

He thought about what Hillier might have been going to say about Maria. He'd never quite been able to understand how close the American had become to her. For Joe the relationship with Annette had been a casual one, and when she had left to go back to her grandmother after Maria's death, it had simply ended. But he knew Nick had been badly cut up when Maria was killed, although he'd tried not to let it show.

Then there was his wife Kay and his son Paul in New York. He would have to try and contact them. There was money. Eddie handled the banking. As the only front man, he could open accounts, and his identification could be checked. Officially neither Joe nor Nick had existed.

He would have to find out if Eddie was OK and warn him not to try to make contact. That would be his first task after he had buried Hillier.

The rain had abated, and the skies were clearing when he turned off the main road and the car bumped along a rocky path through some dense woods, then skirted a low hill.

He stopped. The hill would serve as identification. He had no intention of leaving Nick's body here for ever, and he needed to be able to find it when the time came.

He got out of the car, removing a pickaxe that was in the boot. It had been put there as a weapon, but it would be equally useful now. He walked to the top of the hill. The sky was just beginning to lighten in the east, and he was able to make out the contours of the land.

The hill rose about thirty feet from the track where he'd left the car. On one side were the woods he'd come through, and away to the west he could just discern the pale glint of the river Scheldt as it wound its way through the flat countryside to the sea.

This was as good a spot as any.

He carefully cut away an area of grass turf, using the sharp side of the pick, then rolled it back, piece by piece until he had cleared the earth. Then he began to dig.

He worked steadily for nearly forty-five minutes until he felt the hole was deep enough. Only then did he pause. By now the light was much stronger and he moved quickly down the hill to the car. He could not afford to be seen.

He carried Nick's body effortlessly back up the hill on his shoulder and laid him down gently by the side of the grave. He didn't waste any time. He had nothing to wrap the body in, so he rolled it into the hole and immediately began to push the soft earth in on top of it.

It did not take long. He pounded the soil down as firmly as he could, using up most of the earth that he had taken out. Then he carefully laid the turves of grass back as exactly as he could, sprinkling the remaining earth into the cracks and stamping it down.

It wasn't perfect, but no one would be likely to notice it once the rain had settled the grass again, and there was plenty of it about. The dark clouds were already beginning to thicken after the brief early-dawn respite.

Joe stood on top of the hill and looked around him, imprinting the exact location firmly in his mind. He stared down at the place where he had buried Hillier, then lifted his face to the sky as the first drops of rain rolled down his forehead, wiping away his sweat.

Joe closed his eyes. 'I'll be back Nick, soon as I can, to take you home. That's a promise.' He turned round, swung the pickaxe on to his shoulder and made his way down the side of the hill.

He turned the yellow car around so that it was facing back the way it had come, then glanced once more up the hill. Grey swathes of rain began to hammer on the roof of the car and to wash away all traces of his presence on the hill. Slowly he rolled up his window and wiped the moisture from his face.

He sat there for a moment thinking, then switched on the wipers, clearing the windscreen. There was nothing more to do here. Joe slipped the car into gear and drove slowly away into the gloom of the dripping trees.

CHAPTER TWENTY-FIVE

Eddie picked up the phone in the apartment and waited, hearing the coins drop into the box. A voice he recognized instantly came on the line.

'Eddie?'

'Yes.'

There was a silence for a moment.

'Is everything OK your end?'

'Yes, of course. What's wrong?'

'We were hit.'

'Jesus Christ. What happened?'

Porter could hear the consternation in his voice. 'The White Brigade raided the cinema late last night. Don't go near it. You got that?'

Eddie's breathing was harsh, close to the phone. 'Are you all right, Joe?'

'I'm fine.' He paused fractionally. 'Hillier and Gus are dead.'

Eddie controlled his voice. 'What about you? Where are you?'

'I'll let you know as soon as I can – we have to meet.'

'Of course.'

'Don't make a move until you hear from me. They may be watching you.'

'What makes you think that?'

Joe considered it before replying. 'Someone must have tipped them off. If that person knew about you, then they'll be watching, otherwise they'd have picked you up already.'

Eddie thought quickly. 'Have you got somewhere to go?'

'I think so. I'll give it a try, then make contact. You sit tight.'

Eddie gripped the phone. 'Don't worry about me. Ring me soon as you can.' He waited, but then the telephone clicked and went dead. Joe had gone.

Slowly Eddie replaced the receiver and sat down. He stared at the carpet, wondering where the hell Joe could go.

Joe slipped silently down the alleyway to the back entrance and knocked on the door. He waited and heard someone moving upstairs. Then the footsteps came closer and a light went on behind the black-out curtains of the kitchen.

A woman's voice called through the door, 'Who's there?'

'It's me. Eddie's friend.' He banged again on the door. 'Open up.'

There was a silence, and he was just about to smash the door down when he heard the locks slide back. It opened fractionally and Joe pushed it hard, throwing Sophie back against the kitchen table. He shut the door quickly behind him and faced her.

She gazed at him. His face was grey with fatigue beneath the growth of stubble, and his jacket clung heavily to him, soaked by rain. She could see he had no shirt on beneath it, but it was the submachine-gun in his grip that held her eyes.

He jerked it in the direction of the passage that led to the rest of the house. 'Anyone else here?'

She shook her head. 'No, I am alone.'

He stared at her grimly. 'You'd better be.'

He studied her silently and it made Sophie nervous. His green eyes were cold and unblinking.

'I need a place to hide,' he said finally.

She stared at him in astonishment. 'Do you, indeed? What makes you think I would shelter someone like you?'

Joe didn't rush his reply. He let her sweat on it for a few moments. 'Because I know a few things that might interest those who are looking for me.' She didn't answer, so he filled in the silence. 'Do you want me to list them for you?'

She shook her head. 'No, you bastard, you can stay.' She stared at him silently, not bothering to hide her dislike.

Joe was watching her reaction carefully and there was something about it that he didn't trust. Maybe it was her easy acceptance of his demand for hiding. He wasn't sure. But something was nagging away at the back of his mind. He waited.

'Who is after you anyway?' she asked.

'The White Brigade.'

He saw her jaw muscles clench convulsively. 'What do they want with you?' she asked.

There it was again. He sensed instinctively that the question was false, as though she already knew the answer. If she did, then she had *expected* the White Brigade to hit his operation.

He smiled for the first time, but it was entirely without humour. 'All right Mrs van der Elst, let's have a look round.' He indicated the passage.

Sophie knew it was useless to argue. She turned on her heel and led him on a search of each room in the house.

Joe didn't know what he was looking for, but if there was anything, he intended to find it. His method was deliberately brutal. He needed to shake this woman from her complacency.

He turned everything over. Drawers were pulled out, their contents scattered on the floor. Wardrobes were emptied. Sophie watched in horror as each room was systematically turned into an untidy mess, her well ordered surroundings devastated.

But Joe found nothing.

Not until he came to her bedroom. There was a writing bureau by the bay window. One drawer yielded a small nickel-plated pistol. He held it in his hand and looked at Sophie balefully.

'Have you ever used this on anybody except Lissette?' He saw the fear in her eyes. 'She told me how you held her against the wall in the garden with this to her head because you were jealous, because you thought one of your men had been paying too much attention to your daughter.'

He paused. The contempt in his eyes shrivelled her.

'What did she tell you, Sophie?'

She didn't answer, staring at him in frozen horror, sensing what was to come.

'She said nothing had happened, didn't she?'

Sophie nodded dumbly.

'Well, she lied. She was too frightened of you to tell you the truth. Your lover raped her, Sophie. He took your daughter and bedded her.'

He waited for some response, but there was none. Sophie felt herself crumbling inside. She wanted to fling herself on the bed and pound it in her despair. But she would not let *him* see it. No man would know her true self.

She stood silent in front of him, her eyes glazed. Joe felt no pity. She deserved this, and more, for what she had done to Duparc and her daughter.

'She was only ten, ten years old, and too frightened to tell you the truth.'

She didn't focus on him. Somehow she was trying to blot him out.

Joe threw the Thompson on the bed and gripped her arms, forcing her to look at him. 'It was you, wasn't it, who told the Gestapo where they could find Duparc?'

This time she did see him. There was a strange calmness in her gaze. She looked into his eyes. 'Yes, I told them. They came back here. They'd found out that he had lived with me. There was an evil little man who promised to spend his time changing my looks if I did not tell him where Duparc had gone. I had a choice. Either I could say nothing and be disfigured. *That* I knew I could not endure. Or I could tell them about Lissette or the Peeters. Duparc was there by then. The Peeters had telephoned me. They were worried about Lissette's work at the Cinéac. They knew of her contacts with the Germans and feared she might cave in under pressure. So I had a choice, a horrible choice. I could protect the Peeters or my daughter. I told the Gestapo about the farm. They picked him up there.'

Joe pushed her away from him. 'And let yourself off the hook.'

She smiled faintly, trying to regain her composure. 'Yes, I suppose so, but Lissette was alive too.'

Joe turned away in disgust and went back to the bureau, jerking out each drawer and throwing the contents on the writing surface. A letter spilled out, neatly folded, and he picked it up. He heard Sophie move towards him and turned, holding the letter away as she tried to snatch it from him.

'Give me that,' she snarled, her face distorted by anger. Joe pushed her roughly away. He opened it, and she watched him, her eyes glittering with rage. It was the letter from Manfred that Sophie had never shown to Lissette. Joe read it.

It was restrained. Manfred had realized that if he betrayed too much emotion, Lissette would never have been able to settle to the idea of living with Eddie Pearce, knowing how much he still loved her. Instead Manfred stressed how much it had taken for Eddie to go to the prison and claim that they were engaged, how hard it was going to be to try to re-establish himself in Germany when the war ended.

Joe wasn't interested in the detail, but it revealed that Manfred was still alive and that Lissette had seen him before she left for Ireland. He tucked it carefully into his pocket and buttoned up the flap.

Sophie chose that moment to make her move. She flung herself on to the bed grabbing at the Thompson, swinging it round to point at Joe. In one motion he ran forward and leapt on top of her, knocking the weapon from her grasp before she could pull the trigger. He pinned her arms back behind her head and straddled her body.

He leaned down over her, his face close to hers. 'Was I going to be another you could add to your collection?'

She spat in his face and spittle dribbled down over his mouth. He wiped it away and then brought his hand back and slapped her viciously. 'I'm not like Duparc. I don't go quietly.'

He pushed her arms back higher and she cried out in pain.

'Who did you tell about me, Sophie? Who was it?'

In her pain and humiliation she forgot any caution. She just wanted to hurt him as he was hurting her. 'They'll get you. You won't get away from them.'

'Who, Sophie?' His voice was soft, menacing.

Suddenly she realized her danger. 'Whoever is after you, the authorities, the resistance. You and Eddie must have been involved in something. That's why you're hiding here.'

She was good. Her hatred almost convinced him.

She saw a shadow of doubt cross his face, and then it was gone instantly. She pressed home her advantage. 'And what about Eddie? What's he doing? Have they picked him up as well?'

Joe rolled off her, grabbing the Thompson and slinging it round his shoulder. She stood up facing him, straightening her clothing. She had one last thrust of bile.

'That baby Lissette is having . . .'

He looked at her, surprised by the remark.

'It's not Eddie's, you know.'

He shrugged. 'So?'

'It's Manfred's. The German made her pregnant before he left Antwerp. Tell that to your Irish friend.'

She smiled malevolently. She didn't care any more. Lissette was safe in Ireland, and anything she could do to hurt and wound gave her some small satisfaction.

Joe slowly took the Thompson from his shoulder and levelled it at her. Sophie didn't flinch. For once she had found the courage to face up to whatever this cold-blooded Englishman could inflict, and she saw her death in his eyes.

But then he lowered the weapon. He knew he couldn't kill her. He needed this refuge until he could get out. He needed her.

'That's good, Sophie. Maybe I'll pass that on to Lissette, tell her how I found out. She'd be interested in this letter too, I imagine.'

He took it from his pocket and held it up in front of her, waving it gently, taunting her. She didn't try to snatch at it this time, but she wanted it. He could see her desperation.

'Lissette doesn't know about this letter, does she?'

She gazed at him in despair. He'd guessed correctly. He had what he needed.

'Right, now listen. I need to stay here until I can find a way out. This letter means nothing to me, and I don't care whose bloody baby it is. You turn me in and I'll see that Lissette knows everything about you – who betrayed the Peeters, the letter, everything.'

He paused, letting that sink in.

'But you keep your mouth shut and I'll say nothing. It's up to you.'

Sophie was beaten and she knew it. She had discovered that it did matter to her what happened to Lissette. She did want to see her baby and she knew also that the Englishman would never let her live if she told Bruneel where he was.

She smiled brightly, masking her thoughts. 'I'll make you some soup.'

He followed her downstairs into the kitchen and sat on one of the hard chairs, watching her prepare a meal. He suddenly realized how hungry he was; he hadn't eaten in over twenty-four hours. He was tired too.

Joe remembered the kitchen in the *château* in France and Maria's face as she pulled Nick close to her, showing him who she had decided upon. Then in his head he heard Nick's last cry as he died in the car, calling for him. He thrust the thought savagely from his mind and glared at Sophie. Maybe he could trust her now. He knew too much for her to risk anything.

'That soup's hot enough,' he said. 'Give it to me.'

The telephone rang harshly in the kitchen, jerking Eddie from his contemplation. He walked quickly through and picked it up.

'Hello.' He knew who it was before he heard the voice.

'Listen, Eddie, you're gonna have to get me out.'

Joe waited to see if there would be an objection, but the Irishman remained silent.

'I need a passage on a boat. Can you do that?'

Eddie didn't hesitate. 'Yes. I've already made some inquiries since you called.'

Joe was relieved. 'Good, but I need passage on an American boat – New York if you can fix it.'

'I'll do my best. Some of the convoys load in New York, but if I can't get one there, how about further up the coast?'

Joe didn't argue. It might prove academic anyway.

'That's fine, but I'll need documents. Did Gus give you those passports you wanted to make the last deal?'

'Yes, I've still got three I might be able to trade.'

'See what you can do.' Joe paused. 'There's something else.'

'Just name it, Joe.'

'The money – how much have we got?'

'Nearly twenty thousand.'

'Pounds?'

'Yes.'

'Keep five and the taxis. You should be able to dispose of them. Change the balance of fifteen into dollars and bring it to me when we meet.'

The Irishman's reaction was crucial.

His reply was immediate. 'I'll do it right away.'

'Be careful,' Joe warned. 'If they've made the connection between you and the cinema, they'll be keeping an eye on you.'

'Don't worry, Joe. I can handle it. How do I contact you when I'm ready.'

'You don't. I don't want anyone to know where I am.'

Eddie knew then that Joe didn't trust him. It might have been simply to protect him in case he was picked up. What he didn't know he couldn't divulge. But he understood Joe better than that. Instinctively he sensed the suspicion. He heard Joe's voice again.

'How long will it take you to organize things?'

'Depends if there are any Liberty boats going back, but the docks are choked with vessels bringing in supplies. It shouldn't take too long.'

'A couple of days?'

Eddie was dubious. He didn't know if he could arrange it that quickly, but he didn't want to have to hold things up either.

'Yes, maybe.'

'O K. Just to be on the safe side, I'll call you every day around this time. That way if anything comes up, we won't lose out.'

Eddie was satisfied. 'That's good.'

There was a silence.

'You still there, Joe?'

'Yes.'

'Is everything O K where you are?'

'It's fine, Eddie. I'll call you tomorrow.'

Eddie heard the line click and the dialling tone resume. He put down the receiver.

He had a lot of work to do, and he would have to be careful. More careful than even Joe realized.

CHAPTER TWENTY-SIX

Three days later a rendezvous was arranged. The vessel, a battered Liberty boat, veteran of a dozen convoys across the Atlantic, was leaving on the morning tide for New York. Joe would board soon after dawn.

Eddie had drawn the money from the bank in dollars and he approached the meeting fatalistically. He knew what he was going to do.

Joe could not carry the Thompson. It was impossible to conceal it. But he had a long-bladed folding knife inside his sock and a handgun in his pocket, as well as Sophie's nickel-plated pistol. Maybe at last it would get fired in anger.

She asked him for the letter before he left. Joe shook his head.

'No, this belongs to Lissette. Whether I give it to her or not is up to you. If I hear that Eddie has been picked up, I'll want to know why.'

She stared at him for a long moment, examining his face. 'You are such a bastard.'

He knew she meant it. 'Right first time, Sophie. I was found in a women's lavatory on Waterloo Station. That's why they called me Porter.' He smiled at her. 'She tried to drown me at birth,' he laughed mockingly. 'I'll bet you wish she'd succeeded.'

Sophie wondered if he was serious. She was puzzled. There was a funny look in his eyes that she couldn't identify, then she realized it was pain. For a second she felt a flash of sympathy.

'No. I wouldn't want that to happen to any child.'

Joe picked up the tone of pity in her voice and pounced on it immediately. 'Not even Lissette?'

Sophie turned away in disgust. 'Just go, will you?'

He grabbed her arms, turning her to face him. 'Don't you ever feel pity for me. Pity yourself for what you've done to her, to your daughter? I understand her.'

She didn't answer and that made him angrier.

'You listen to me, you bitch. I can handle anything you or any other woman can fling at me.'

He shook her, trying to make her understand, but she didn't react. 'I don't need you. I don't trust you.'

His words sounded empty and hollow in his ears, echoing futilely. He stopped and let her go, stepping back a pace, shaken by his outburst. It had come out of the blue, for no reason he could see. It worried him because he'd almost lost control.

Sophie broke the silence. She turned and picked up a small parcel from the table and gave it to him. 'I made you some sandwiches. God knows when you'll eat next.'

He looked at her uncomprehendingly, trying to understand her act of kindness. It didn't make any sense.

Sophie pushed them into his hands. 'Go on, take them, it's not a bloody bomb.'

He accepted them reluctantly and turned to the kitchen door, opening it. He stood there, his back to her, unable to decide what to do. He could not articulate his thanks, the words just stuck in his throat.

Sophie knew that. She said it for him.

'Goodbye, Joe.'

He pulled the door shut behind him and walked slowly down the short path to the gate. Sophie watched it close behind him. She knew she had learned more about Joe in that brief, bitter goodbye than anything that had gone before.

She thought at last she understood him, and that was what he found impossible to accept. She poured herself a cup of coffee and sat down in the kitchen. She wondered if he would get away.

Oddly, she wanted him to.

It was still dark when Joe reached the area near the dock gates. He stopped by the end of the cobbled street and examined the long, straight road thoroughly.

It was empty of traffic and, as far as he could see, utterly deserted. But looks can be deceptive . . .

He slipped along the pavement, keeping close to the buildings and checked the next road. That too was empty. There was no other cover within striking distance of the dock gates, so he approached them and passed through.

They were unguarded and nothing was parked inside. Down by the first warehouse, beneath the glow of arc lamps, he could see figures moving about as a vessel was unloaded. There was no other sign of life.

The sea air was cold, blowing in off the estuary, and faintly on the breeze he could smell diesel oil. He made his way back to the gates and stood in the shadow of the dock wall, waiting.

Half an hour later, just as light was beginning to permeate the narrow dock streets, he heard the buzz of a jeep's engine gradually drawing closer. It pulled up by the gates and Joe could see the familiar shape of Eddie tucked down into the bucket driving seat. He stepped from the shadows of the wall.

'Eddie!'

He saw him start in surprise, then peer in his direction. 'Joe?'

'Over here.'

Eddie got out of the jeep, and walked towards him. He was carrying a haversack over his shoulder. They faced each other. Joe could feel Eddie's tension.

'Everything all right?'

Eddie nodded vigorously. 'I think so. The vessel is further down. They are expecting you.'

Joe began to walk towards the huge stone warehouses, and Eddie fell in alongside him. Their footsteps echoed back from the long, unbroken wall, and in the river a ship's fog horn boomed mournfully across the water.

'What time does she sail?'

Eddie glanced at his watch. 'In about half an hour. I told them I'd bring you on board as late as possible.'

Joe didn't question it. It made sense. The longer he was on board *before* sailing, the greater the risk for them.

'How much did you pay?'

Eddie grimaced. 'A lot – three thousand dollars.'

Joe looked at him, his eyes narrowing.

Eddie shrugged. 'Well, I wanted to get you into New York, and this is the only vessel for ten days.'

Joe didn't comment.

They circled clear of the pool of activity around the vessel being unloaded. It was still low in the water and the wharf was crowded with huge packing cases full of spare parts.

Joe indicated the cargo. 'At least you won't be involved in that any more.'

They moved on, the arc lights fading as the morning light grew stronger. Joe could see the vessel now. She was broadside on to the dock, her superstructure rusting and what was left of her dull, grey paintwork peeling slowly away. She was a Liberty boat, built, like all of them, from pre-fabricated parts in American shipyards, where they were welded together. Rumour had it that they occasionally fell apart, but Joe didn't allow that to worry him too much.

The stern bore the name *Danny Boy*. Joe grinned and looked at Eddie. 'So that's why it cost us three thousand.'

The Irishman smiled too.

It was a brief flash of humour, reminiscent of their early days together when they had been conscripted. They stopped at the bottom of the gangway and looked up. There was a man in a cap with some gold braid waiting, and Joe moved to ascend.

Eddie stopped him. 'No, let me go first, I've got the papers.'

Joe followed him up the steeply rising gangplank, all his senses alert. He was committed now. If there was a trap, this was the best place to spring it, where he was locked in. Both ends could be sealed, and he'd be caught in the open with nowhere to go. He touched the pistol in his jacket. It felt good.

They reached the gunwale of the ship, and Eddie pulled a British passport from the haversack. He indicated Joe. 'This is the man I told you about.' He handed the passport over.

Joe kept his hand in his pocket, on the reassuring butt of the pistol. The officer examined the passport, then looked from the picture to Joe. They matched. He grunted and handed it back.

'It's in order,' he said. He glanced at Joe. 'There's a cabin for you. Shall I take you now?'

Joe shook his head.

'No, I'll wait here until we sail, then you can show me.'

The officer nodded curtly. 'Fine by me.'

He turned to Eddie. 'We'll be raising the gangplank in abou
fifteen minutes. You'll have to go ashore then.'

Eddie smiled tightly. 'Thanks.'

The officer clambered expertly up a companionway, leaving them
alone. Joe walked slowly round to the stern of the ship and bellied
up against the gunwale, looking down at the dockside. Eddie stood
beside him.

Joe waited. He had considered whether he would tell the Irishman
about the child, who the father really was. He knew how much i
would hurt Eddie if he knew it was Manfred, a German – Lissette'
lover.

A child born of love, not rape: it was a weapon he could wield i
he chose to do so. But first he wanted to see what the Irishman
would do. There was a price to pay.

The silence grew longer.

'It was me who betrayed you, Joe.' Eddie's voice was soft, barel
more than a whisper, but he knew Joe had heard him. Eddie paused
There was no reaction.

He didn't look at Joe. He gazed out over the roof of the warehouse
towards the city and tried to explain.

'They came for me. It was the man I'd seen in the prison when
got Lissette out. His name is Bruneel.'

Joe's eyes flicked to him, absorbing the name, storing it for future
reference.

Eddie pressed on. 'He's a hard man, Joe, as hard as any I've seen
He'd been tipped off about my involvement in the operation by
Sophie, Lissette's mother. She didn't know your name, Joe, or if we
were working together, though she must have suspected it. From
the way Bruneel questioned me, I think she was trying to give a
little as possible. Enough to save her neck, no more. Bruneel got on
to her through German records. She was the one who told them
about the farm where Lissette had taken the Jew.'

'I know.'

It was the first thing Joe had said. Eddie was not surprised by hi
knowledge. Nothing Joe did surprised him any more.

He continued, 'Well, Bruneel offered me the same deal he'd
offered Sophie. As long as I told him everything, I could go
free.'

282

Eddie stopped, waiting for Joe to say something, but he stood ently, gazing out over the ruffled surface of the estuary.

The Irishman plunged on. 'At first I didn't believe him. But he new I was involved in a black-market ring. That's what he was ally interested in. That was the only thing he wanted. To get his ands on the operation and break it up. It was political, Joe. It would ve him a better chance of gaining control if he could smash it. He ld me he'd have a job getting a conviction for me because I was a serv- g British soldier, so unless I coughed up, I wouldn't see the light of ay. He'd have had me killed, Joe. He meant it. I know he did.'

Eddie faced him, trying to convey his own certainty. Joe didn't ok round.

'So you turned me in.' His voice was calm, matter-of-fact and illing in its menace.

Eddie knew then that his fate was sealed, that Joe was unforgiving. e hadn't really expected anything else after Gus and Hillier had en killed. He sighed a long, juddering sigh, remembering how ose they had once been, right from that first day, how Joe had ought to protect him, the dangers they had survived together on the eaches of Normandy. Joe had been the only real friend he'd had, nd he'd been tormented by guilt ever since he'd told Bruneel in rder to save himself.

He knew what the consequences would be, and he accepted them. lready he felt a sense of relief, a lifting of his spirit, now that he had onfessed to Joe. He took the haversack from his shoulder and gave to him.

'Your papers are in there, and the money. I put in my five thousand r Nick's wife and son . . .'

His voice tailed off, and he looked up into Joe's face as he took the aversack. There was no sign, but Eddie knew. He knew what Joe ould do. In a strange way, he welcomed death at the hands of the nglishman. It would be a release. No more pain and despair eating ke a cancer into him every time he thought about how Gus and ick had died.

Deliberately Eddie turned away and looked at the preparations on he dock for the ship's departure, offering his back to Joe.

At first there was nothing, just the noises of the men on the quay elow, and the slap of the water under the stern. Then he heard the sharp click as the long knife sprang open. He tensed slightly. H couldn't help it. He waited for the steel armlock around his neck, th searing blade in his heart.

He was surprised to find that he wasn't praying, asking for salva tion. He looked up at the sky in the east as the sun tried to fight i way through the low morning cloud.

He closed his eyes, waiting, but the death blow didn't come. H heard the blade slip back into its groove as it was folded and he turne to face the Englishman.

Joe bent down and slid the knife back into his sock, never takin his eyes off Eddie. It was at that moment, seeing those pitiless eye that Eddie knew his fate.

He was not to have the satisfaction of a quick release, an end to h shame. He would have to live with his guilt, knowing that any da Joe might return and claim his vengeance.

That was the lowest moment in Eddie's life. He swallowed har holding back the tears of his self-contempt, his despair at the loss c their friendship. He turned and without a word walked back to th gangplank and down its steep slope to the dock below.

As soon as he was ashore the officer who had greeted the supervised the raising of the gangplank, clearing it away on to th deck.

Men scurried round the dock loosing off the heavy ropes bindin the ship to the shore. They were hauled, dripping, up on to th decks, and the ship bellowed once from its foghorn before the screw began to thrash the muddy water, easing the rusty old bucket awa from the quayside.

Eddie stood on the dock and watched the vessel draw itself slowl into the river. By the stern, unmoving, stood the solitary figure o Joe, getting smaller and smaller as the ship receded.

Then Eddie saw him raise his hand. At first he didn't react. H stared, not believing his own eyes. Then he raised both hands high not to wave but more as a signal of his own sense of joy, an unut terable feeling of exultation, an acknowledgement of their tru friendship. Both hands stayed up, held aloft, as the sun at last brok through the covering cloud and turned the rust on the old ship t gleaming red.

At that moment Joe lost sight of the Irishman on the quay as th

essel eased around the slow bend in the Scheldt. He became aware
f a deep sense of loss, and the feeling was new and strange to him.

Gradually, as the ship moved out into the estuary he began to
erceive how much he had changed. He was no longer an inde-
cructible destroyer of all that stood in his way. He felt vulnerable.
or the first time in his bitter struggle with life, he cared about
omeone.

He liked Eddie.

He liked him a lot.

You will find no record of Joe Porter in the annals of World War Two. But Joe did exist. Max remembered him well.

Max Murphy was someone I knew, a journalist who, years ago, wrote encouragingly about my work as an actor. Much later he contacted me again and asked me if I would be interested in writing about Joe Porter.

I was fascinated by the stories Max told me of how they had been conscripted into the Army together when they were eighteen and of their experience during D-Day and the months that followed.

It was clear from the way he spoke that he and Porter had been very close. There is a lot of Max in Eddie. Max asked me me if I would fulfil a promise he once made to Joe. This book is the result. I hope he would have approved.

Lissette occupied the same time and the same place as Joe. They never did meet but they shared childhoods that damaged them, set them apart. They are both survivors. The slings and arrows have bitten deep but have not destroyed them. Their experiences in that catastrophic war are dramatic and touching, harsh and cruel. Lissette lived to tell the tale, as did her Irishman until he died a few years ago. He overlaps with Eddie Pearce just as Max does. This book is a part of Lissette's life too.

The Engagement at Boom

Robert Vekemans, Major John Dunlop, Captain Gibson Stubbs, Sergeant Spiden and Corporal Karl Berghauser are different. Their contribution is a part of the recorded history of that war.

Robert Vekemans did make his way to the crossroads at Breendonk, after reconnoitring the bridges at Boom. On the evening of 3 September 1944 Vekemans had heard a BBC announcement that the Allies had crossed the border into Belgium and reached Tournai. He realized that the British were likely to come from the south next day. He knew that once they poked their heads above the crest of the viaduct south of Boom, both bridges would be destroyed.

They were mined, and the lookout was waiting. Vekemans was able to see that part of the route to the smaller bridge, Pont van Enschodt, was hidden from the German defenders by the gas works and the industrial landscape at Breendonk, just the other side of the viaduct. It was possible that if he could stop the British forces before the Germans saw them, he might be able to lead them, under cover, to the smaller bridge, so that they could cross it before it was blown up.

It was clearly a dangerous operation to attempt, and there was no guarantee of success. But Vekemans felt the risk was worthwhile. If the British armour could get across the river Rupel, Antwerp would be liberated more swiftly.

He spent the night of 3 September with his parents-in-law who lived locally. Then, at dawn, he stationed himself in the café at the crossroads of Breendonk and waited.

What happened next was much as I describe it in the book, *except* that there was no Joe Porter on a motorbike and he did *not* precede the tanks across the bridge into Boom. That is fiction.

The rest is fact. The first three tanks did begin to climb to the crest of the viaduct. Major John Dunlop listened to Vekemans and called them back on the radio in the nick of time. Captain Stubbs said he would lead the first tank across the mined bridge of Pont van Enschodt, and Vekemans climbed into the scout car driven by Sergeant Spiden.

As the first two tanks, followed by the scout car and the rest of the squadron, moved off on their new route, sidestepping the viaduct, Corporal Karl Berghauser was attempting to blow up the Pont van Enschodt bridge. The German defenders had not seen the British tanks. It was merely a precautionary measure, prior to the destruction of the main bridge, should British armour be spotted.

The German guards on the bridge had retired to a safe position, but the fuse refused to stay alight. It fizzled and went out. Corporal Berghauser tried again. Again it went out. Berghauser left the bridge and returned to his Opel LKW near the main bridge to get new fuses. In that moment the British tanks made the crossing.

Vekemans, in the unprotected, open scout car, asked Sergeant Spiden to stop, and in full view of the German forces he disconnected the fuses and made the bridge safe. Sergeant Spiden's comments are not recorded.

The sudden appearance of the Sherman tanks *behind* the German defences demoralized the surprised defenders, and resistance caved in. The bridges were intact and in British hands. As I relate in this book, there were no fatal casualties at all apart from one unfortunate horse.

The local resistance in Antwerp had risen up against the Germans the day before, causing massive disruption of their defences and, crucially, preventing the Germans from flooding the dock areas.

The swift advance of the British, made possible by Vekemans' brave action and Major Dunlop's quick thinking, brought relief to the hard-pressed resistance and, to the city of Antwerp, liberation after four years of occupation.

J.C., London, 1986

Memoirs
of a
Revolutionary

The son of exiled Russians, Victor Serge was born in 1889 in Brussels, where from the first he knew the horrors of poverty and hunger. As a young man he took an active part in the anarchist movement in Paris and was imprisoned for the first time in connection with the Bonnot scandal. At the outbreak of the Russian Revolution he was dividing his time between Petersburg, Moscow, and Berlin, where he directed a newspaper.

Victor Serge continued his revolutionary activities until 1933, when his close association with Trotsky brought about his deportation to Siberia. The protests which this action brought from his friends in France—Andre Gide among others—caused his release, and he left Russia forever. He worked in southern France for a while, and at the outbreak of Second World War he moved to Mexico where he died in 1947.

CONTENTS

INTRODUCTION

Victor Serge, who was born in 1890 and died in 1947, was an anarchist, a Bolshevik, a Trotskyist, a revisionist-Marxist, and, on his own confession, a 'personalist'. Belgian by place of birth and upbringing, French by adoption and in literary expression, Russian by parentage and later by citizenship, he eventually became stateless and was put down as a Spanish national for purposes of his funeral documents. He was a journalist, a poet, a pamphleteer, a historian, an agitator, and a novelist. Usually he was several of these things at once; there were few times in his life when he did not combine at least two or three nationalities, ideologies, and professional callings. Nevertheless, although there is no way of describing him in brief without an inventory of discordances, he was very much an integral man. To read his memoirs is to receive the impression of a strong and consistent personality, of an approach to life and to politics which is complex but unified, of a heart which, however it may be divided, is so because reality tears it asunder, not because its loyalties are confused. When we list the varying political trends that entered into Victor Serge's make-up, we are simply recording his continual sensitivity to certain perennial dilemmas of action. Serge hated violence, but he saw it, at times, as constituting the lesser evil. He believed that necessity in politics might sometimes be frightful, but was necessity no less; only he was not inclined to glorify it into a virtue. He mistrusted the State, but he recognized it as an inevitable form in the progress of society. So general a statement of political predicaments is doubtless banal, but it is in fact rather rare to find a public figure (let alone a revolutionary public figure) who plainly registers both extremes of a dilemma with equal sensitivity, even though his ultimate choice may incline very definitely towards one pole or the other.

An appreciation of the complexity of political choice probably does not conduce to effective Left-wing theory or leadership. The improvising politician, concerned above all to seek the key to social transformation, has almost of necessity to over-emphasize some features of social reality at the expense of others. But the revolutionary of mixed origins and impulsions may well make a very good *witness* to the great upheavals of his time. Standing at the confluence of several radical traditions, he will be able to judge the programmes, actions, and ideas of the competing parties with a certain detachment; and yet his detachment will not be of the uncomprehending, noncommittal kind which would make it impossible to describe the revolution at all, except perhaps as a sequence of despotic acts. Thus it is N. N. Sukhanov, an ex-Social Revolutionary, ex-Menshevik Bolshevik sympathizer, who is responsible for a brilliant and uniquely valuable history of the revolutionary year of 1917.[1] To the subsequent epoch of the Revolution, its opening and continuing phases of mass violence, terror, and degeneracy, Serge brings a mind already matured in the experience of heroism and its corruption. When he entered the service of the Revolution, at the age of twenty-eight, he had behind him several years of disgust with the commercialized Social-Democracy of Belgium, three years of mounting disillusionment with anarchist terrorism, and five years' unspeakable existence as a convict among convicts. Steeped in the 'individualist' psychology of his libertarian past, he retained an intense and wary consciousness of the many-sidedness of human motivation, of man's potential both for Titanic endeavour and for regression to the brute.

In the writings of Serge particular political tendencies stand displayed as the expression of moral and psychological resources within the individual. Not Marxism or reformism, Stalinism or liberalism are primary, but will, fear, sensitivity, dishonesty, courage, mental rigidity, psychic dynamism, and their opposites or absences. Serge tells you that a certain man is an obsessive, or that he leans too much upon favour, and this information is intended to mean quite as much as the facts about his party alignment; indeed, the political characterization is perhaps causally dependent on the more personal one. Serge often manages his evocation of the person by means of physiognomic detail: how this face was puffed (*bouffi*), that one solid-looking (*carré*), how certain eyes were gentle, or harsh, or firm. On his return to Western Europe, in 1936, Serge drew a long train of political conclusions (which stood the test of time considerably better than the more catastrophic expectations of his comrades) from one simple anatomic observation: that the Belgians

[1] N. N. Sukhanov, *The Russian Revolution, 1917: A Personal Record* (edited and abridged by Joel Carmichael), Oxford University Press, 1955.

were now *fat*.

Serge's fascination with the expressive externals of people is of particular use to ᴴᴵᴹ in the many thumbnail portraits of revolutionists, writers, and plain folk that fill the pages of the *Memoirs*. As Serge progresses on his various expeditions with the political and the literary vanguard, he leaves behind him a trail of single paragraphs or sparse sentences each bearing the vivid imprint of a summarized personality: Gramsci, Toller, Lukács, Yesenin, Balabanova, Gide, Trotsky, Vandervelde, Pilniak, Barbusse—the improbable list could be extended indefinitely, though there would be little point in trying to do so since much of Serge's appeal lies in the most obscure of his characters. While these portrayals are succinct and bold they are not, generally speaking, caricatures, for Serge maintains a scrupulous fairness towards his memories. He can summon up a trio of German Social-Democrats, a clique of Comintern functionaries or a collection of deadbeat *illégalistes*, and project their living presence into the odd paragraph or so with utter sympathy and at the same time with transparent fidelity to his own point of view. There is a passage in his novel *L'Affaire Toulaév* in which he shows us Stalin, at the height of the purges, not as a sadist or a villain but as a hopelessly solitary man, viewed in the white light of compassion. And yet Serge's concern for human beings is by no means the same type of concern that a non-political writer would display, confronted by the same personages. Although Serge's portraits of political characters are rounded, nuanced, and humane, he is all the time seeing and selecting their traits from a specifically revolutionary standpoint; basically he is asking himself, 'Is this man the kind of person who will help to make the revolution? Or will he perhaps help to make the wrong kind of revolution?' Towards the end of the *Memoirs*, and again in his diaries, Serge remarks that one of the greatest problems in politics is that of reconciling intransigence, which he thought indispensable to any worthwhile convictions, with the equally necessary principles of criticism towards ideas and respect towards men. 'Intransigence is steadfastness, is *living* . . . Nietzsche was quite right to consider "possession of the truth" as allied to the will to dominate.' It is Victor Serge's exceptional merit as a revolutionary witness, not only that he conceived of the problem at all, but also that he himself so often resolved it in a mode of perception that fused both intransigence and love.

The marked independence of Serge's vision can be detected very early in his Bolshevik career. Writing in May 1921 from Petrograd to a French anarchist comrade, he reflects that 'the prime error of the present Russian regime is to have created an entire bureaucratic mechanism to manage production instead of leaving it to the workers organized by industry (i.e. syndicalism). It has failed principally in attacking, through methods of centralized discipline and military repression, any individual initiative, opposition, or criticism (even a fraternal and revolutionary one), any aspiration towards liberty; in short, in being guided by a spirit contrary to that of anarchism'. Well before a fraction of the party leadership itself (around Trotsky, Zinoviev, and Kamenev) will rally an opposition to the regime's bureaucratization, Serge voices a libertarian and syndicalist protest, reviving his old allegiance to anarchy's black flag:

> To be precise, what we need is a new anarchism, equipped with a practical programme, enriched by all the experience of the proletarian revolution, capable of guiding the movement of the masses. Its basis, like that of the reorganisation of production itself, can lie only in syndicalism.

The propagation of any views such as this had in March 1921 been declared incompatible with Party membership at the C.P.S.U.'s Tenth Congress, and would, soon after Serge wrote, become anathematized as an international heresy at the Comintern's Third Congress—whose sessions he attended as a staff member. Small wonder that he asked his correspondent to 'destroy this letter or at any rate don't leave it lying around'.[1]

In his public writing Serge was more guarded but still went to the very limits of caution. In August 1921 a French Socialist publishing-house brought out his booklet, *Les Anarchistes et l'expérience de la révolution russe*; it had been written in the summer of 1920, before the banning of the party factions whose positions had corresponded most closely with his own. In it (as he himself hints on p. 114 of the *Memoirs*) we find, sometimes in rudimentary but often in quite developed form, all the basic concepts deployed by Serge in his later analyses of the Red dictatorship and its totalitarian leanings. Fundamental to his critique is a distinction between the avoidable and the unavoidable aspects of degeneration in revolutions. Unlike most

[1] Letter of 29 May 1921 to ' camarade Michel ' (otherwise unidentified), now in the Musée Social, Paris. I am indebted to Colette Chambelland for access to the Victor Serge papers held there.

other supporters of Bolshevism, he does not idealize the existing regimentation, or deny it for what it is. 'The proletarian dictatorship has, in Russia, had to introduce an increasingly authoritarian centralism. One may perhaps deplore it. Unfortunately I do not believe that it could have been avoided' (p. 29). However, the role of necessity must not be invoked as an unrestricted excuse licensing any conceivable measure of despotism: 'The rise of a Jacobin Party and its exclusive dictatorship do not then appear to be inevitable; and at this point everything depends on the ideas which inspire the party, on the men who carry out these ideas, and on the reality of control by the masses' (p. 31). What is more, 'Every revolutionary government is by its very nature conservative and therefore retrograde. Power exercises upon those who hold it a baleful influence which is often expressed in deplorable occupational perversions (*déformations professionnelles*)', (p. 34; *cf. Memoirs*, p. 99).

All the greater, therefore, was the responsibility of free-thinking revolutionaries: 'It will be the task of libertarian Communists to proclaim by their criticism and activity that the crystallization of the workers' State must be avoided at all costs' (p. 34). The solution to the problem of all-embracing State ownership must be 'production to the producers, that is to the trade unions' (p. 39), even though this policy holds the danger that the unions will themselves turn into a new State bureaucracy. Anarchism is vindicated in its proclamation of 'the terrible harm residing in authority, the harmfulness of Statism and authoritarian centralism' (*ibid.*). Indeed, in the very successes of the Revolution 'little credit is due to Authority. Many things have been achieved in spite of it' (p. 41); here Serge seems to prefigure his later emphasis on the economic disadvantages of Stalinism (*cf. Memoirs*, p. 378). All the same, anarchists must be 'with the Revolution, unhesitating and ubiquitous, or they will be nothing' (p. 43). They will be Communists, but 'in contradiction to numerous others they will strive to preserve the spirit of freedom, and so will be gifted with a more critical approach and a sharper awareness of ultimate ends. Within any Communist movement their lucidity will make them the most formidable enemies of the climbers, the budding politicians and commissars, the formalists, pundits and intriguers.'

It is this continuous record of fundamental unorthodoxy that makes Victor Serge's record so different from most other ex-Communist autobiographies. Through his personal tenacity and his intellectual pluralism Serge could mentally balance the various risks of political action, hedging, as it were, expectations which for others were staked upon a fanatic's throw of all or none, and so insuring himself against the chances both of blind commitment and of stark disillusion. Harking back to the turbulent and frightful years of his youth, he could remark simply *je ne regrette rien pour moi*, and there is the same absence of personal remorse when he recounts his Bolshevik career. The vividness and immediacy of Serge's recollections do not strike us as being artificially tinted by hindsight; and in fact the judgements he passes on Russian events are very often repeated identically in writings separated by decades, quoted back and forth with a touch of clairvoyant's vanity.

Over the last twenty-five years or so considerable controversy has waxed over the question: is Stalinism the logical, organic, and inevitable continuation of Bolshevism? Most Western observers have replied with a simple affirmative; and an equation of similar form, but with the signs of all quantities reversed from negative to positive, was propounded until quite recently by political algebraists within the Soviet sphere of influence. On the other hand, the Trotskyist school of Marxism has long insisted that Stalinism is the 'direct negation' of Bolshevism, while official Soviet theory after 1956 has increasingly tended to posit much the same kind of polar opposition between 'Leninist norms' and at least some of the 'excesses, abuses, and crimes' of Stalin's day. Victor Serge's answer to the problem was persistently double-sided. As against Trotsky and his followers he stresses the fatal rigidities and ambiguities of Leninist and Marxist doctrine, and the sources of degeneracy in such early Soviet institutions as the Cheka. As against the pairing of Bolshevism with Stalinism, he simply describes what, in his experience, Bolsheviks and Stalinists were like, and details the severe limitations set upon a free development of Soviet Socialism by the Civil War and its aftermath of havoc. Serge was suspicious of any notion tending to establish historical fatalism, and this set him both against the easy appeal to necessity which Leninists and Stalinists employed in their apologias of butchery, and against the common Western habit of regarding the degenerescence of revolutions into tyranny as virtually the only Iron Law which it is still permissible to detect within history. One locus in Serge's polemical writings is particularly worth citing

THE LINE GENERATED BY A
POINT OR THE SURFACE
GENERATED BY A LINE — MOVING
ACCORDING TO SPECIFIED
CONDITIONS

TO LAY DOWN/POSIT A
FACT OR PRINCIPLE

FROM POLEMUS (GR. — WAR)
POLEMIC: A CONTROVERSY OR CONTROVERSIAL
DISCUSSION
POLEMICAL: PERTAINING TO CONTROVERSY;
CONTROVERSIAL; DISPUTATIOUS

in this respect.[1] In 1938 and 1939 Trotskyist and libertarian circles were hotly involved in debating the nature of the Kronstadt rising of 1921, whose ruthless liquidation by the Bolsheviks lent itself to obvious comparison with the ongoing Great Purge. Serge entered into combat both with Trotsky, who had no qualms at all about the Bolshevik treatment of the mutineers, and with a Yugoslav ex-Trotskyist, Anton Ciliga, who saw the Kronstadt rising as a proletarian revolution against the bureaucracy, and its suppression as a proof of the linear descent of Stalin's Party from Lenin's. Trotsky had brusquely dismissed Serge's earlier reminiscences of the Kronstadt massacres: 'Whether there were any needless victims I do not know. On this score I trust Dzerzhinsky more than his belated critics. . . . Victor Serge's conclusions on this score—from third hand—have no value in my eyes.' Serge retorted that his information on Kronstadt came from anarchist eyewitnesses he had interviewed in prison immediately after the rising; whereas Dzerzhinsky's conclusions were 'from seventh or ninth hand', the head of the Cheka having been absent from Petrograd at the time. 'The single fact that a Trotsky did not know what all the rank and file Communists knew—that out of inhumanity a needless crime had been committed against the proletariat and peasantry—this fact, I repeat, is deeply significant. . . .'

On the other hand, Serge maintained against Ciliga that the socio-political composition of the non-Party masses at the time of Kronstadt was very far from progressive. 'In 1921, everybody who aspires to Socialism is inside the Party. . . . It is the non-party workers of this epoch, joining the party to the number of 2,000,000 in 1924, upon the death of Lenin, who assure the victory of its bureaucracy.' The conscious revolutionaries in the leadership of the mutiny 'constituted an undeniable élite and, duped by their own passion, they opened in spite of themselves the door to a frightful counter-revolution.' Serge's comment on the general issue in question could well be taken as a summing up of his lifelong attitude to the Revolution: 'It is often said that "the germ of all Stalinism was in Bolshevism at its beginning". Well, I have no objection. Only, Bolshevism also contained many other germs—a mass of other germs—and those who lived through the enthusiasm of the first years of the first victorious revolution ought not to forget it. To judge the

[1] *New International*, February 1939, pp. 53–4.

living man by the death germs which the autopsy reveals in a corpse
—and which he may have carried in him since his birth—is this very
sensible?'

In one sense the political career of Victor Serge terminated with
the demise of the European Left after the fall of France in 1940.[1] He
was never again able to participate in any social movement with a
recognizable influence upon public events. The last six or seven
years of his life passed in virtual political solitude; his refugee status
forbade any intervention by him in Mexican affairs, and he could
find no wider international audience to hear him out. None the less,
Serge never at any stage retired from his vocation as a revolutionary
writer. He went on writing his fine novel on the Purges during the
rout of France, in the fugitives' warren of Marseilles, and on the
troubled voyage that took him to his final asylum. Once in Mexico,
he wrote without respite: novels, essays, poems, articles, biography
and autobiography. Anxious to keep abreast of the major social and
cultural developments of the time, he devoured every significant
book, periodical or journal that he chanced on, in Russian, French,
Spanish, German, or English. He kept a voluminous diary, amassed
material on Mexican history and culture, and sent off long political
letters to his circle of friends abroad, as well as to any prominent
foreign publicists that he felt like criticizing. The lengthy studies he
undertook as *rapporteur* to a small Socialist exile group, destined for
the eyes of a mere handful, are composed with the same measure and
density as the works he intended for publication. All these millions of
words were typed by Serge in cramped single-spacing on reams of
the cheapest flimsy, with rarely an erasure or amendment. When one
manuscript was finished he went straight on to the next without
looking back. Reading over the text of the *Memoirs*, his friend Julián
Gorkín remarked that the book was 'condensed and excessively
laconic, through the adoption of this telegraphic style'; surely
material so rich should be developed and expanded? Serge gave a
sceptical smile, and answered, 'What would be the use? Who would
publish me? And besides, I am pressed for time. Other books are
waiting.' He worked on, sometimes with a haunting sense that his

[1] Except where otherwise stated, the material for the following outline of Serge's
last years is drawn from Julián Gorkín's invaluable appendix to the 1957 edition of
the *Memoirs*, from Serge's published notebooks, or from the issue of the review
Témoins containing his letters to Antoine Borie. Details of these are to be found in
the bibliography.

faculties might be weakening through the sheer vacuity that surrounded him. 'Terribly difficult,' he notes, 'to create in the void, lacking the least support, the least real environment.' He speaks of 'writing for the desk-drawer alone, past the age of fifty, unable to exclude the hypothesis that the tyrannies will outlast the remainder of my life . . .'; and 'I am beginning to wonder if my very name will not be an obstacle to the novel's publication.'

This oppressive sense of failure was not without its foundation in recent experience. As soon as Serge arrived in Mexico he paid the familiar penalty for his clairvoyance. His book on the Nazi aggression against Russia (*Hitler Contra Stalin*) proved to be too frank for the public taste, since it predicted disastrous Soviet reverses in the early stages of the war, with the peasants actually welcoming Hitler's invaders. As a result, the small firm that had published the book expired in ruin. Serge's dark forecasts turned out of course to be perfectly accurate. Public meetings addressed by Serge, Gorkín, and others from their circle were brutally assailed by Communist groups, on one occasion by an armed gang of 200 men. Several times he and his friends had to go into hiding. At his lodgings, which he seldom left if he could help it, he had a spy-hole cut into the front door so that he could identify callers before opening to them. The danger was not always so bluntly physical. A protracted barrage of slander was directed against Serge and his circle by the many organs of the Mexican Press influenced by the Communists and their powerful associates (such as the trade-union leader Lombardo Toledano). The strong German Stalinist emigration (*Freies Deutschland*), including such veteran propagandists as André Simone (Katz) and Paul Merker, added their quota of venom to the campaign.[1] Serge's friends were Socialist militants of long standing like Marceau Pivert, the leader of the pre-war French Socialist Left; Gustav Regler, lately a political commissar with the International Brigades in Spain; Julián Gorkín, the former international secretary of the independent Marxist party P.O.U.M.; and other Spanish comrades of that complexion. Nevertheless, they (and Serge and

[1] Some of the slanderers were subsequently themselves targets for the same type of treatment. In January 1953 Paul Merker was accused by the East German régime of having, during his Mexican exile, made *Freies Deutschland* into a 'propaganda journal for Zionist ideas'; he and his old collaborator Jungmann were arrested and imprisoned. This purge was conducted as part of 'the lessons of the Prague Trials' of November 1952, as a result of which Simone-Katz was hanged as a British Intelligence agent, allegedly recruited by Noël Coward in 1939.

Gorkín particularly) were incessantly denounced as Nazi agents, enemies of the United Nations, allies of the *sinarquistas* or local Fascists, founders of a new Trotskyist International, and fomenters of railway strikes. One by one, Mexican publications closed their columns to this obscure band of troublesome foreigners. The editor of one weekly which still admitted Gorkín as its foreign editor, and Serge as a contributor, was called in to see Miguel Alemán, the Minister of the Interior and future President of the Republic; there he was informed that the Soviet and British Ambassadors were pressing the Mexican Government to withdraw from Serge and Gorkín all public means of expression. Although the editor refused to accede, his journal afterwards acquired a new management enjoying the favour of the Soviet Embassy, and he, Gorkín, and Serge were all unceremoniously ousted. The boycott was now total, and Serge found it increasingly hard to keep body and soul together. Only one more book of his saw print during his life, a novel published in Canada and (in translation) in the United States. He tried in vain to get the *Memoirs* published in the U.S.A. 'In every publishing-house', he bitterly concluded, 'there is at least one conservative and two Stalinists; and nobody has the slightest understanding of the life of a European militant.' He died penniless, and his friends had to make a collection among themselves to pay the expenses of his burial.

The estrangements and dissensions typical of *émigré* political groups bore particularly heavily upon Serge. Within the independent Socialist colony he was the only member with a specifically Bolshevik background. His collaboration with Socialists from other traditions was warm and unstinted, but we can gain some inkling of a certain isolation that he felt, to judge from a note he entered in his diary in mid-January 1944. Here he records his pleasure at the resumption of friendly relations with Trotsky's widow Natalya, noting how they, 'the sole survivors of the Russian Revolution here and perhaps anywhere in the world, used to be separated so completely by sectarianism; and this was not like the human spirit of the real Bolsheviks . . .' He reflects that Natalya is going to be pained by certain anti-Trotskyist observations in a book which he had just brought out in co-authorship with his friends; 'she will perhaps not realize my solitude in these collaborations'. He concludes sadly, 'There is nobody left who knows what the Russian Revolution was

really like, what the Bolsheviks were really like—and men judge
without knowing, with bitterness and basic rigidity.'

Yet in other respects Serge was far too much of a revisionist for his
more traditional Marxist comrades, many of whom were nursing
hopes for their post-war return to the Old World on the crest of a
European Revolution. Serge had no such hopes. For him the Second
World War was a 'war of social transformation' (and not simply a
classical imperialist war as nearly all his comrades thought), usher-
ing in an era of controlled and planned economies that would,
under the conditions of post-war reconstruction, burst the fetters of
capitalist private property even in the absence of proletarian upheavals. 'European big capital, weakened and discredited by the
war it has brought on, will find itself in *opposition* to the growth of
production and the common good, *now in clear evidence*.'[1] Serge
believed that this inevitable collectivist transformation would have a
marked totalitarian bias, which could, however, be largely counteracted by class-struggle on the political level. Parliaments, munici-
palities, trade unions, and workers' councils offered a possible focus
for this countervailing influence by the masses. Serge maintained
this perspective well after the war: 'I wonder if some kind of
collectivism, quasi-totalitarian but *enlightened*, guaranteeing the
human rights that have been acquired over several centuries,
will not eventually establish itself for the reconstruction of the
old continent; such a system I would find acceptable if it were
directed by technicians and effectively controlled by the masses.'[2]

So pessimistic an outlook, based (despite its undoubted insights)
upon speculative impressionism rather than on any thorough
economic analysis, could not fail to irritate most of his comrades.
Their charges of 'technocratism' ('Just one more little "deviation"
in my life-history', as he remarked) irked him, and he in his turn
could not take seriously their pipe-dreams for an insurrectionary
post-war settlement in Europe. There was no basis for the growth of
mass revolutionary parties in the conditions of Occupied Europe,
and in any case nowadays 'a popular revolution which possesses no
aeroplanes will inevitably be beaten'. There could be no question
any longer of a specifically proletarian hegemony; the 'vanguard'
must be sought preponderantly within the growing social strata of

[1] Unpublished MS., *Economie Dirigée et Démocratie* (no date).
[2] Letter to Borie, 26 September 1947.

technicians and white-collar employees. 'The education of the working class has to be managed afresh. . . .'

Serge's reflections on the Western social order are suggestive but
often highly ambiguous. He was on surer ground as a commentator
upon Soviet perspectives, which he indeed saw as determining the
direction of all politics, and especially Socialist politics, in the rest of
Europe. He shared none of the current illusions that the Grand
Alliance of Churchill, Roosevelt, and Stalin would survive the end
of hostilities with Germany. As early as January 1944 we find him
noting that 'Stalinist hegemony over Europe would not be a liberation but a new nightmare' and that 'it would also mark the beginning of the Third World War'. Serge's last years were increasingly
clouded by this prospect of 'the permanent war' (as he terms it in a
diary entry for October 1944), anticipated by him at a time when
Western politicians often displayed the most grotesque naïvety over
Stalin's intentions. Rarely can his sense of 'the appalling powerlessness of accurate prediction' have afflicted him so acutely as when
he watched the unfolding of the promised nightmare: Stalinist sub-
jugation of Eastern Europe, extremist demands for preventive
nuclear war on the Western side. The letters and notebooks of this
period reflect the division of his fears between the threat of Stalinism
and the threat of war. It would be possible to excerpt fragments of
these sources in such a way as to present either a pro-Western
Victor Serge or a kind of 'New Left' archetype, repelling both
capitalism and Communism with a libertarian disgust. The
truth must be that within a man of Serge's loyalties the Cold War
engendered contradictions which he could only express, never
surmount.[1]

Serge was convinced that the sources of Soviet expansionism lay
in the extreme inner weakness of the social organism underneath the
totalitarian armour. In an unpublished essay written in English[2] he
observes: 'The training of a popular revolution who [which] has
survived against the worst odds has formed in the governmental
circles a mentality of offensive bluff and courageous risk, daily
expediency, belief only in force and fact. In the greatest danger the
régime will not think of retreat, evolution, compromise, but of an

[1] For a discussion of one particular crux in Serge's correspondence, see Appendix, *Victor Serge and Gaullism*, p. 383.
[2] Unpublished MS., *On the Russian Problem* (October 1945).

offensive struggle in which compromises are expediency, more apparent than real.' In Serge's view the post-war era might evolve along any of three possible directions. If the Soviet system yielded neither to internal nor external pressure, there would be war. Alternatively the régime might back down in the international field while refusing any concessions at home; 'war is then postponed, but not removed altogether'. Or again, 'under the combined pressure of the masses at home and of the international conflicts which will arise in various ways, the régime may try and evolve towards a democratization. Upon the slightest relaxation of terrorist totalitarianism, immense possibilities are opened out, which may cause the emergence in Russia of a Socialist-inclined or Socialist democracy, and permit a peaceful collaboration with the world outside. The nightmare of war is then removed.'[1]

It was in fact this last possibility that aroused Serge's closest interest. His papers and letters refer repeatedly to the idea of something quite odd and unforeseen happening in Russia, which would transform the situation most favourably for its people and for the world outside. Serge is deliberately vague as to what this change might consist of. It is certainly not an anti-Stalinist revolution of the kind advocated by Trotsky. He calls the prospect one of 'internal crisis',[2] 'change of régime in Russia',[3] or of a 'great Soviet reform'.[4] One illuminating episode of March 1944, recorded subsequently in his diary, indicates the strength of Serge's conviction on this score. He had met Trotsky's grandson, Siova Volkov, on a bus. Siova was about seventeen years old at this time, and was understandably bitter about things Russian. In the course of his childhood his mother had been driven to suicide in Berlin and his father had disappeared forever in Russia. Having taken refuge with his grandfather in Mexico, the boy had had to crouch beneath a bed, wounded in the foot, amidst a hail of machine-gun bullets directed throughout the house by the artist Siqueiros; he had lived in the same house in the time when Trotsky was murdered by an agent who had ingratiated himself with the whole family. Siova now told Serge that he had completely forgotten the Russian language. 'You'll have to learn it, then,' said Serge. 'What for?' Siova replied violently, 'Out of sentimental attachment? No, thank you!' And Serge answered,

---

[1] Unpublished MS., (no title, no date).   [2] Letter to Borie, 26 September 1947.
[3] Ibid., 16 April, 1947.   [4] *On the Russian Problem.*

'Russia will be changing a great deal, before very long. We must remain faithful to her, and keep up great hopes.'

This long-term optimism of Serge, which now seems uncannily prescient, arose from the same source as his dark immediate forebodings: from his certain belief, based on long personal experience in Russia, that the terrorist edifice of Stalinism was founded on unendurable social strains, which had been accentuated even further by the ruin of the Second World War. He probably, too, still believed that what he called 'the moral capital of the Socialist revolution' had still not been exhausted even by the long years of blood and lies. Serge had been one of the first people (before anybody else, he thought) to use the word 'totalitarian' of the Soviet State, but unlike some Western thinkers he did not mean it to imply a finished, impervious, and stable structure, governed omnipotently at the top by considerations of pure power. The detail of his prediction, where there was detail at all, might be fanciful; a few days before he died, he told his son Vlady, 'I won't live to see this but you probably will—monuments to Trotsky and to Stalin in the public squares of Russian cities.'[1] There is no reason to suppose that he would have regarded the present Russian régime as the 'Socialist-inclined or Socialist democracy' of his hopes. Nevertheless, in broad outline and to an astonishing degree, Serge's sense of Soviet reality, of its double-sidedness for the future as well as for the past, has been justified by the turn that events have in fact taken.

To say this much is not to elevate Serge into an expert oracle, a sort of Nostradamus of twentieth-century revolutionism. Because his background and experience were so intensively Russian, he is sometimes a much less valuable guide to certain areas of politics outside the frontiers of the Soviet Union itself. His references to colonial nationalist movements, in the *Memoirs* as elsewhere, are nearly always distant or disparaging. Later in life he tended to regard all non-Russian Communist Parties (of whom he had never held a very high opinion) as little more than extensions of the Kremlin and N.K.V.D. apparatus. When, in late 1944, he encountered the suggestion that Communist-led resistance movements might develop an autonomous character, free of Muscovite control, his response was wholeheartedly scornful: there were only 'totalitarian-Communist

[1] Information supplied by Vlady.

condottieri of the Mao-Tse Tung or Tito type, cynical and *convinced*,
who will be "revolutionary" or "counter-revolutionary"—or both
simultaneously—depending on the orders they receive, and capable
of an about-face from one day to the next'.[1] It would of course be
senseless to reproach Serge for not foreseeing the Yugoslav and
Chinese schisms of Communism; but enough has been said to
suggest that his clairvoyance was principally that of an exceptionally sensitive eyewitness and participant of the Bolshevik
movement.

About Victor Serge's death, as in his life, there was a retiring
quality. He had been in poor health over a number of years, with a
record of heart-attacks going back to his convict years in France.
The high altitude of Mexico City did not suit his condition, and
even his long, lyrical excursions into country parts could offer small
convalescence after the years of deprivation and persecution. In the
middle of 1947 he suffered two attacks of angina. He looked frightfully old and tired, but was optimistic and full of plans. There were
offers of publication (for *L'Affaire Toulaév*) from Canada, France,
and the U.S.A., of collaboration with Mexican reviews, even of a
possible visa for the United States. Early in the small hours of
Monday, 17 November, he read his wife a poem he had just written.
It was a meditation on a Renaissance terracotta of a pair of hands,
old and with knotted veins. Serge had tears in his eyes as he read the
poem out; the hands symbolized generations of human suffering and
resistance, and the knots on them were so like those of his own veins.
He went to bed after typing the poem, and had his breakfast around
ten the next morning, discussing anthropology with his wife, something about the mystical significance of gold. She had to go to work
then; there is no record of the rest of Serge's day until eight in
the evening, when he went out to see his son Vlady. He wanted to
have a talk about Vlady's paintings, but his son was not at home.
He met his friend Julián Gorkín in the street; they talked for a while,
and shook hands when they parted. This would be around 10 p.m.
Not long after that, doubtless feeling himself ill, Serge hailed a taxi,
sank back into the seat, and died without telling the driver where to
take him. His family found him stretched out on an old operating-
table in a dirty room inside a police-station. Gorkín recounts what

---

[1] *Carnets*, p. 172–3; cf. also Serge's letter on '*Stalinism and The Resistance*' in
Politics, February 1945.

he looked like: his upturned soles had holes in them, his suit was threadbare, his shirt coarse. Really he might have been some vagabond or other picked up from the streets. Victor Serge's face was stiffened in an expression of ironic protest and, by means of a bandage of cloth, the State had at last closed his mouth.

Liverpool, 1963 Leeds, 1977   Peter Sedgwick

EDITOR'S NOTE TO THE 1978 IMPRESSION

Since the first publication of the *Memoirs* in English, many titles have been added to the repertory of Serge's available works. The Bibliography has been updated, and the Appendix and Introduction revised in the light of newly available material.

It is fitting to note at this point the considerable indebtedness of English-speaking Serge readers to the efforts of Dr. Richard Greeman, whose work on the translation and promotion of the novels—a task of genuine scholarship as well as of devotion—deserved a better appreciation. The indefatigable labour and devotion of Jean Rière has re-established and republished many Serge texts—though the name of Victor Serge is still nowhere to be found in any directory or history of modern French literature. With the main body of Victor Serge's work now in print or on its way to publication, I will bow out as translator by adding a short unpublished poem of his (sent to me by his son Vlady), along with an English version, composed for the wedding of my comrades Jim and Ellen Edmondson:

> *O nuit pleine de toi, ô nuit pleine d'étoiles*
> *j'ai besoin, pour t'aimer, de comprendre le monde*
> *pour comprendre le monde, j'ai besoin de t'aimer.*

> A night filled with stars, a darkness filled with you:
> So that I could love you I had to understand the world
> And before I could understand the world, I had to love you.

ACKNOWLEDGEMENTS

The text of this translation is shorter, by about an eighth, than the French original. With the exception of the final chapter, which is intact, pruning has taken place throughout the length of the book. The paragraphing of the original is generally longer than here and Serge's frequent habit of dissolving the end of a sentence in three dots (. . .) has on the whole been abandoned in the translation. Purely mechanical errors on the part of Serge (e.g. in the translation of foreign names) have been corrected wherever they have been noted.

In the preparation of this edition I am greatly indebted to Victor Serge's son Vlady for the loan of material from his father's archives, and for a lively, moving, and deeply informative correspondence; both forms of assistance have been of considerable help to me in the Introduction. I am also grateful to Jean Rière, Julián Gorkín, J.-P. Samson, Enid Starkie, André Malraux, Paul Avrich, Richard Greeman, Michael Futrell, Gero Neugebauer, Jean Maitron, Pierre Naville, Paul Schmierer, Pierre Frank and Boris Björklund for their help with footnotes and editorial material. Many of the most awkward points in the text itself were resolved with the help of Pierre Marteau, Philip Burnett, and Gill Seidel. On a matter of history: it was George Orwell to whom Serge first transmitted the manuscript of Serge's *Memoirs* for publication in English; and Isaac Deutscher who supported my request to the Oxford University Press to be allowed to translate and edit the present edition.

1

WORLD WITHOUT ESCAPE
1906–1912

Even before I emerged from childhood, I seem to have experienced, deeply at heart, that paradoxical feeling which was to dominate me all through the first part of my life: that of living in a world without any possible escape, in which there was nothing for it but to fight for an impossible escape. I felt repugnance, mingled with wrath and indignation, towards people whom I saw settled comfortably in this world. How could they not be conscious of their captivity, of their unrighteousness? All this was a result, as I can see today, of my upbringing as the son of revolutionary exiles, tossed into the great cities of the West by the first political hurricanes blowing over Russia.

On 1 March 1881, nine years before my birth, on a day of shining snow, a fair-haired young woman, her face calm and determined, who was waiting near a St. Petersburg canal for the passing of a sledge escorted by Cossacks, suddenly waved a handkerchief. There was an echo of muffled, soft explosions, the sledge came to a sudden halt, and there on the snow, huddled against the canal wall, lay a man with greying side-whiskers, whose legs and belly had been blown to shreds: the Tsar Alexander II. The party called *People's Will* published his death-sentence on the following day. My father, a non-commissioned officer in the cavalry of the Imperial Guard, was at that time stationed in the capital; he sympathized with this underground party, which demanded 'bread and liberty' for the people of Russia, and had no more than about sixty members and two or three hundred sympathizers. Among those responsible for the assassination, Nikolai Kibalchich,[1] a chemist and distant relative of my father, was arrested and hanged, together with Zhelyabov, Ryssakov, Mikhailov, and Sofia Perovskaya, daughter of a former Governor of St. Petersburg. In court, four of the five condemned to death defended their libertarian demands with dignity and courage; on the scaffold, they embraced one another and died calmly.

My father had joined in the struggle, entering a revolutionary military group in the south of Russia which was soon completely broken; for several days he hid in the gardens of the oldest monastery in Russia, St. Lavra of Kiev; he crossed the Austrian frontier by swimming under the bullets of the police; and he went on to Geneva, in a land of sanctuary, to start a new life.

He intended to become a physician, but geology, chemistry, sociology, and philosophy also interested him passionately. I never knew him as anything but a man possessed with an insatiable thirst for knowledge and understanding which was to handicap him during all his remaining years in 'the struggle for life'. Along with the rest of his revolutionary generation, whose masters were Alexander Herzen, Belinsky, and Chernyshevsky (then a deportee in Yakutia), and also by reaction against his religious training, he became an agnostic, after Herbert Spencer, whom he heard speak in London.

My grandfather on my father's side, a Montenegrin by origin, was a priest in a small town in the Chernigov province; all I knew of him was a yellowing daguerreotype of a thin, bearded cleric with a high forehead and a kindly expression, in a garden full of bonny, bare-footed children. My mother, born of Polish gentry, had fled from the bourgeois life of St. Petersburg, and she too went to study at Geneva. I was born at Brussels, as it happened, in mid-journey across the world, because my parents, in quest of their daily bread and of good libraries, were commuting between London (the British Museum), Paris, Switzerland, and Belgium. On the walls of our humble and makeshift lodgings there were always the portraits of men who had been hanged. The conversations of grown-ups

[1] Nikolai Ivanovich Kibalchich (1854–81) was, as well as the manufacturer of the bombs that blew up the Tsar, a leading theoretician of the *Narodnaya Volya*. In his death-cell he prepared a design for a flying-machine propelled by rockets, which is claimed by present-day Soviet science as an antecedent to the Sputniks.

A LEVEL PLACE - ESP. A LEVEL WALK OR
DRIVE BY THE SEASIDE — HERE: A CLEAR
SPACE BETWEEN THE CITADEL & THE HOUSES
OF A FORTIFIED TOWN.

World without Escape: 1906–1912   3

dealt with trials, executions, escapes, and Siberian highways,
with great ideas incessantly argued over, and with the latest books
about these ideas. In my childhood's memory I accumulated images
of the world: Canterbury Cathedral, the esplanade of old Dover
Castle above the sea, the dismal red-brick street in Whitechapel, the
hills of Liége. I learned to read through cheap editions of Shakes-
peare and Chekhov, and, dozing off to sleep, I dreamt for hours of
blind King Lear leaning, in his journey over the cruel waste-land,
on the tender attentions of Cordelia. I also acquired bitter experience
of that unwritten commandment: 'Thou shalt be hungry.' I think
that if anyone had asked me at the age of twelve, 'What is life?'
(and I often asked it of myself), I would have replied, 'I do not know,
but I can see that it means "*Thou shalt think, thou shalt struggle, thou
shalt be hungry*".'

It must have been some time between the age of six and eight that
I became an evildoer. Through this episode I was to learn another
commandment: *Thou shalt fight back.* I was a well-loved child, being
the first-born; but for some years I became, inexplicably, a criminal
child. With a devilish cunning, the criminal child worked his
mischief as if he wanted to avenge himself against the universe and
even, what was most cruel, against those he loved. The precious
pages of my father's scientific notes were found torn up. The milk,
stored for supper in the cool of the window-ledge, was found dosed
with salt. My mother's clothes were mysteriously burnt with
matches or else slashed with scissors. Ink was surreptitiously spilt
on newly-ironed linen. Objects disappeared without trace. Nobody
could intercept the hands of the criminal child—my hands. I was
harangued at length, I was admonished, I often saw my mother's
eyes fill with tears; I was beaten too, and punished in a hundred
ways, because my petty crimes were mad, exasperating, incomprehensible. I drank the salted milk, I denied everything (naturally),
I melted into wretched promises, and then went to bed, in in-
consolable grief, thinking of King Lear leaning on Cordelia. I
became taciturn and introverted. Now and then the crimes would
stop, and life would become bright, until the coming of another dark
day which I had learnt to expect with a vigilant inner certainty.
Eventually a time came when I acquired a sure foreknowledge of
evil: I knew and felt, inwardly, that my mother's pinafore would
be dirtied or slit with scissors. I waited upon chastisement, and

lived amid rebuke—and yet I used to play and climb trees as if evil had never existed. I had entered an unfathomable mystery, I had become wise; I carried the problem inside my head and let its solution ripen. The end of this episode, which I am sure made a deep impression on my character, left me with the most exalting memory of tenderness that I have ever experienced. I was about to learn that two individuals could, with a deep gaze and an embrace, understand one another utterly and conquer the worst evil. We were living on the outskirts of Verviers, in Belgium, in a country house which had a big garden. Two days before, some gross misdeed, whose precise nature I no longer remember, had cast a shadow over the household. However, I spent that particular day in the garden with my little brother Raoul. As twilight appeared, my mother called us back into the big kitchen, where a delicious smell of warm bread hovered in the air. First she busied herself with my brother, washing him, feeding him and putting him to bed. Then she made the wicked child sit on a chair, knelt before him, and washed his feet. We were alone, lapped in an unforgettable sweetness. My mother looked straight up at me and suddenly, in a tone of reproach, asked, 'But why do you do all this, my poor little man?' and then the truth flashed out between us, because a strange power was bursting within me: 'But it isn't me,' I said, 'it's Sylvie! I know everything, everything!'

Sylvie was an older adolescent cousin adopted by my parents and living with us, a blonde and graceful girl, but cold-eyed. I had accumulated so many observations and proofs, and with such analytic power, that my headstrong, tearful exposition was irrefutable. The matter was closed, with a full and permanent recovery of trust. I had fought back steadfastly against evil, and had been delivered from it.

My first great experience of hunger dates from a little later, at the age of eleven. I used to recall how one day in England we fed on grains of wheat prised out of the ears which my father had picked up from the side of a field; but that was nothing. We spent a hard winter at Liége, in a mining district. Above our lodging a café proprietor used to work: *Mussels and Chips!* Exotic odours. . . . He gave us a little credit, but not enough, for my brother and I were never satisfied. His son would steal sugar to trade with us for bits of string, Russian postage stamps, and various oddments. I became accustomed to finding exquisite delicacy in the bread we soaked in black coffee (which was well-sugared, thanks to this commerce), and it was evidently good enough for me to survive on. My brother, two years my junior—eight and a half at that time—did not take to this diet, and grew thin, pale and depressed; I saw him wasting away. 'If you don't eat,' I told him, 'you're going to die'; but I had no idea what it was to die, and he even less, so it did not frighten us.

The fortunes of my father, who had been appointed to the Institute of Anatomy of the University of Brussels, took a sudden turn for the better. He summoned us to his side, and we ate sumptuously. Too late though for Raoul, who was confined to bed, sinking fast but fighting back for a few weeks. I put ice on his forehead, I told him stories, I tried to convince him that he would get better, I tried to convince myself; and I saw something incredible happening within him: his face became that of a little child again, his eyes glittered and grew dim at the same time, and all the while the doctors and my father came into the dark room on tiptoe. Alone together, my father and I took him to the cemetery at Uccle, on a summer's day. I discovered how alone we were in this seemingly happy town—and how alone I was myself. My father, believing only in science, had given me no religious instruction. Through books, I came across the word 'soul'; it was a revelation to me. That lifeless body that had been bundled away in a coffin could not be everything.

Some verses of Sully Prudhomme that I learned by heart gave me a kind of certainty which I dared not confide to anyone:

> *Blue eyes, dark eyes, loved and lovely,*
> *Exposed to endless dawn,*
> *From beyond the tomb still see*
> *Tight though their lids be drawn.*

In front of our lodging there was a house topped with a finely wrought gable, which I found a magnificent sight. Golden clouds used to rest over it every evening. I called it 'Raoul's House', and often dawdled to gaze at this house in the sky. I detested the lingering hunger of the poor children. In the eyes of those I met, I thought I saw Raoul's look. They were nearer to me than anybody else, they were my brothers, and I felt that they were condemned. These feelings were rooted deeply, and have remained with me. After

forty years, when I returned to Brussels, I went to see that gable
in the sky on the road to Charleroi; and throughout the rest of my
life it has been my fate always to find, in the undernourished urchins
of the squares of Paris, Berlin, and Moscow, the same condemned
faces of my tribe.

My first friendship dates from the following year. Wearing a
Russian smock in white and mauve check, which my mother had
just finished, I was going home along a country street in Ixelles
carrying a red cabbage; proud of my smock and feeling a little
ridiculous on account of the cabbage. An urchin of my own age,
thick-set and bespectacled, squinted at me sarcastically from across
the road. I deposited my cabbage in a doorway and walked up to
him, meaning to pick a quarrel with him by calling him bat-eyed.
'Glass-face! Goggles! Want me to push your face in?' We measured
each other up like the small gamecocks that we were, jostling one
another's shoulders a little. 'Just you dare!' 'Get started!'; all
without fighting, however, but forming from then on a friendship
which was, through all its enthusiasms and tragedies, never far from
conflict. And when he died on the scaffold at the age of 20, we were
still friends—and foes. It was he who, after the squabble, came and
asked me if I wanted to play with him, and thus established a
dependence on me against which, despite our affection, he ever
afterwards rebelled in his inmost heart. Raymond grew up as far
as he could in the street, anything to get away from the stifling back
room that was his home, behind a cobbler's stall where his father
patched the shoes of the district from morning till night. His father
was a spiritless drunk, an old Socialist disgusted with Socialism.
From the age of thirteen I lived alone, owing to the journeys and
estrangements of my parents; Raymond often came to seek refuge
with me. Together we learnt to forsake the tales of Fenimore Cooper
for Louis Blanc's great *History of the French Revolution*, whose illustra-
tions showed us streets, just like those that we haunted, overrun by
sansculottes armed with pikes. Our favourite pastime was to share two
sous' worth of chocolate between us, reading these gripping stories.
They moved me particularly because their legends of the past lent
substance to the ideals of men I had known of since the first awaken-
ings of my intelligence. Together, though much later, we were to
discover Zola's overwhelming novel *Paris* and, in an effort to relive
the despair and rage of Salvat, trapped in the Bois de Boulogne

after his essay in murder, we wandered for hours throu͟
de la Cambre in the autumn rain.

My father, a university teacher of small means, kept up hi͟
émigré existence. I saw him in close combat with the money-͟
His second wife, worn out with child-bearing and poverty, ͟nder-
went terrible crises of hysteria. From the 1st to the 10th of each
month, the household (which I seldom visited) ate reasonably well,
from the 10th to the 20th less well, and worst of all from the 20th
to the 30th. Certain memories, already old, remained embedded
in my soul like nails in flesh: for example (when we were living
somewhere in the new district behind the Cinquantenaire park), my
father going out one morning with a cheap little coffin of yellow
wood under his arm. His emotionless face: '*Thou shalt seek to obtain
thy bread on credit.*' On his return, he retired to the solitude of his
anatomy and geology atlases. I had never been to school, for my
father despised this 'stupid bourgeois instruction for the poor', and
could not pay for a college education. He worked with me himself,
not often and not well—but the passion for knowledge and ihe
radiance of a constantly armed intelligence, never allowing itself
to stagnate, never recoiling from an inquiry or a conclusion, shone
from him so powerfully that I was quite hypnotised by it, and went
the rounds of museums, libraries, and churches, filling up my notebooks and ransacking encyclopaedias. I learned to write without
ever knowing grammar; I was eventually to learn French grammar
by teaching it to Russian students. For me, learning was not
something separate from life, it was life itself. The mysterious
relationships between life and death became clear through the very
unmysterious importance of the fruits of the earth. The words
'bread', 'hunger', 'money', 'no money', 'credit', 'rent', 'landlord'
held, in my eyes, a crudely concrete meaning which was, I think, to
predispose me in favour of historical materialism. . . . Still, my
father wanted to make me take up higher education, despite his
professed contempt for certificates. He spoke of this often, hoping to
influence me in that direction. A pamphlet by Peter Kropotkin[1]
spoke to me at that time in a language of unprecedented clarity. I

[1] Peter Kropotkin (1842-1921): outstanding Anarchist writer; imprisoned for
agitation in Russia, he escaped from jail to England (1876) where he settled after
various wanderings in Europe. Returned to Russia after the February Revolution
of 1917.

have not turned back to it since, and at least thirty years have elapsed since then, but its message remains close to my heart. 'What do you want to be?' the anarchist asked young people in the middle of their studies. 'Lawyers, to invoke the law of the rich, which is unjust by definition? Doctors, to tend the rich, and prescribe good food, good air, and rest to the consumptives of the slums? Architects, to house the landlords in comfort? Look around you, and then examine your conscience. Do you not understand that your duty is quite different: to ally yourselves with the exploited, and to work for the destruction of an intolerable system?'

If I had been the son of a bourgeois university teacher, these arguments would have seemed a trifle abrupt, and over-harsh towards a system which, all the same. . . . The theory of a Progress that advanced ever so gently as the ages passed would probably have seduced me. . . . Personally, I found these arguments so luminous that those who did not agree with them seemed criminal. I informed my father of my decision not to become a student. It was a fitting time to tell him: the disastrous end of the month.

'What are you going to do then?'

'Work. I'll study without being a student.'

To tell the truth, I was too afraid of sounding pompous or of starting a great disputation of ideas, to dare to reply, 'I want to fight as you yourself have fought, as everyone must fight throughout life. I can see quite clearly that you have been beaten. I shall try to have more strength or better luck. There is nothing else for it.' That is pretty near what I was thinking.

I was just over fifteen. I became a photographer's apprentice, and after that an office-boy, a draughtsman and, almost, a central-heating technician. My day's work was now ten hours long. With the hour and a half allowed for lunch and an hour's journey, there and back, that made a day of twelve and a half hours. And juvenile labour was paid ridiculously low wages, if it was paid at all. Plenty of employers offered two years' apprenticeship without pay, in return for teaching a trade. My best early job brought in forty francs (eight dollars) a month, working for an old businessman who owned mines in Norway and Algeria. . . . If, in those days of my adolescence, I had not enjoyed friendship, what would have I enjoyed?

There was a group of us young people, closer than brothers. Raymond, the short-sighted little tough with a sarcastic bent, went back every evening to his drunken old father, whose neck and face were a mass of fantastically knotted muscles. His sister, young, pretty, and a great reader, passed her timid life in front of a window adorned with geraniums, amid the stench of dirty old shoes, still hoping that, some day, someone would pick her up. Jean, an orphan and a part-time printer, lived at Anderlecht, beyond the stinking waters of the Senne, with a grandmother who had been laundering for half a century without a break. The third of our group of four, Luce, a tall, pale, timorous boy, was blessed with 'a good job' in the *L'Innovation* stores. He was crushed by it all: discipline, swindling, and futility, futility, futility. Everyone around him in this vast, admirably organized bazaar seemed to be mad, and perhaps, from a certain point of view, he was right to think so. At the end of ten years' hard work, he could become salesman-in-charge, and die as the head of a department, having catalogued a hundred thousand little indignities like the story of the pretty shop-assistant who was sacked for rude behaviour because she refused to go to bed with a supervisor.

In short, life displayed itself to us in various aspects of a rather degrading captivity. Sundays were a happy release, but that was only once a week, and there was no money. Now and then we would wander along the lively streets of the town centre, gay and sardonic, our heads full of ideas, spurning all temptations with contempt. We were too prone to contempt. We were lean young wolves, full of pride and thought: dangerous types. We had a certain fear of becoming careerists, as we considered many of our elders to be who had made some show of being revolutionary, and afterwards. . . .

'What will become of us in twenty years' time?' we asked ourselves one evening. Thirty years have passed now. Raymond was guillotined: 'Anarchist Gangster' (so the newspapers). It was he who, walking towards the worthy Dr. Guillotin's disgusting machine, flung a last sarcasm at the reporters: 'Nice to see a man die, isn't it?' I came across Jean again in Brussels, a worker and trade-union organizer, still a fighter for liberty after ten years in gaol. Luce has died of tuberculosis, naturally. For my part, I have undergone a little over ten years of various forms of captivity, agitated in seven countries, and written twenty books. I own nothing. On several occasions a Press with a vast circulation has hurled filth at me because I spoke the truth. Behind us lies a victorious revolution gone astray, several abortive attempts at revolution, and massacres in so great number as to inspire a certain dizziness. And to think that it is not over yet. Let me be done with this digression; those were the only roads possible for us. I have more confidence in mankind and in the future than ever before.

We were Socialists: members of the *Jeunes-Gardes*.[1] Ideas were our salvation. There was no need to prove to us, textbook in hand, the existence of social conflict. Socialism gave a meaning to life, and that was: struggle. There were intoxicating demonstrations under heavy flags that were awkward to carry when you had not slept or eaten properly. And then we would see, ascending the balcony of the *Maison du Peuple*, the slightly satanic forelock, the domed forehead, the twisted mouth of Camille Huysmans.[2] There were the warlike headlines of *La Guerre Sociale*. Gustave Hervé, leader of the insurrectionist element of the French Socialist Party, organized a poll among his readers: 'Should he be killed?' (This was under a Clemenceau government). In the wake of the big anti-militarist trials, French deserters brought us the whiff of the aggressive trade unionism of Pataud, Pouget, Broutchoux, Yvetôt, Griffuelhes, Lagardelle.[3] (Of these men, most are now dead;

[1] *Jeunes-Gardes Socialistes:* Belgian federation of Socialist youth groups, founded in 1890 and still in active existence at the present day. Affiliated to the Belgian Socialist Party.

[2] Camille Huysmans (1871–1968): prominent Belgian Socialist, secretary of the Second International before the First World War; later an eminent Parliamentarian, being President of the Chamber 1936–9 and 1954–8, Minister of Education 1925–7 and 1947–9, and Prime Minister in 1946–7.

[3] Pouget, Yvetôt and Griffuelhes dominated the French trade union scene in this decade. Emile Pouget (1860–1932) was a brilliant journalist, editor of the explosive anarchist journal *Le Père Peinard*, then of the C.G.T. organ *Voix du Peuple*; organizer, pamphleteer and advocate of the eight-hour day. Georges Yvetôt (1868–1942) was secretary of the trade-union Labour Exchanges from 1901, an anti-militarist, and author of *L'A.B.C. Syndicaliste*. Victor Griffuelhes (1874–1923) was the untheoretical but highly effective secretary of the C.G.T. from 1902 to 1909. Emile Pataud was an electricians' leader, co-author (with Pouget) of a syndicalist Utopia. Benoît Broutchoux was a syndicalist miners' leader and journalist. Hubert Lagardelle (1874–1958) founded the review *Le Mouvement Socialiste* (1898); in 1904 he joined the Socialist Party and advocated a variety of Sorelian syndicalism; went to Italy after the rise of Fascism and became economic adviser and confidant to Mussolini; was Pétain's Minister of Labour (1942–3).

Lagardelle lived to become an adviser to Mussolini and Pétain.)
Men escaped from Russia told us of the Sveaborg mutiny, of the
dynamiting of an Odessa prison, of executions, of the 1905 general
strike, of the days of liberty. The first public discussion I ever
opened was on these topics, for the Ixelles branch of the *Jeunes-
Gardes*.

Our young contemporaries talked about bicycles or girls in a
most loathsome way. We were chaste, expecting better things both
from ourselves and from fortune. Without benefit of theory, adolescence opened up for us a new aspect of the problem. In a sordid
alley, at the end of a dark passage hung with gaudy washing, there
lived a family we knew: the mother gross and suspicious, nursing the
vestiges of her beauty; a lecherous daughter with bad teeth; and a
stunning younger girl, of pure Spanish beauty, her eyes all charm,
innocence, and softness, her lips like blossom. It was all she could
do, when she passed us chaperoned by her dam, to manage a
smiling 'Hello' to us. 'It's obvious', said Raymond, 'they're sending
her to dancing lessons and keeping her for some rich old bastard.'
We discussed problems like this. Bebel's *Woman and Socialism* was
on our reading-list.

Gradually we entered into battle, not with Socialism, but with all
the anti-Socialist interests that crawled around the working-class
movement: crawled around it and seeped into it and ruled over it
and smeared dirt on it. The halting-points on the routes of local
processions were arranged to suit certain tavernkeepers associated
with the workers' Leagues—impossible to suit them all! Electoral
politics revolted us most of all since it concerned the very essence of
Socialism. We were at once, it now seems to me, both very just and
very unjust, because of our ignorance of life, which is full of complications and compromises. The two per cent. dividend returned by
the co-operatives to their shareholders filled us with bitter laughter
because it was impossible for us to grasp the victories behind it.
'The presumption of youth!' they said: but in fact we were athirst
for the absolute. The Racket exists always and everywhere, for it is
impossible to escape from one's time and we are in the time of
money. I kept finding the Racket, flourishing and sometimes salutary,
in the age of trade and in the midst of revolution. We had
yearned for a passionate, pure Socialism. We had satisfied ourselves
with a Socialism of battle, and it was the great age of reformism.

At a special congress of the Belgian Workers' Party, Vandervelde,[1] young still, lean, dark, and full of fire, advocated the annexation of the Congo. We stood up in protest and left the hall, gesturing vehemently. Where could we go, what could become of us with this need for the absolute, this yearning for battle, this blind desire, against all obstacles, to escape from the city and the life from which there was no escape?

Socialism meant reformism, parliamentarism, and unrelieved Talmudism. Its intransigence was incarnated in Jules Guesde,[2] who made one think of a city of the future in which all the houses would be alike, with an all-powerful State, harsh towards heretics. Our way of correcting this doctrinal rigidity was to refuse to believe in it. We had to have an absolute, only one of liberty (without unnecessary metaphysics); a principle of life, only unselfish and ardent; a principle of action, only not to win a place in this stifling world (which is still a fashionable game), but to try, however desperately, to escape from it since it was impossible to destroy it.

That principle was offered us by an anarchist. He of whom I am thinking has been dead many years. His shadow lingers on, greater than the man himself. A miner from the Borinage, recently released from prison, Emile Chapelier had just founded a communist—or rather communitarian—colony in the forest of Soignes, at Stockel. At Aiglemont, in the Ardennes, Fortuné Henry, brother of the guillotined terrorist Emile Henry, was running a similar Arcady. 'To live in freedom and work in community, from this day on. . . .' We went along sunlit paths up to a hedge, and then to a gate. Buzzing of bees, golden summer, eighteen years old, and the doorway to Anarchy! There was an open-air table, loaded with tracts and pamphlets. The C.G.T. *Soldier's Handbook, The Immorality of Marriage, The New Society, Planned Procreation, The Crime of Obedience, Citizen Aristide Briand's Speech on the General Strike.* Those voices were alive. A saucer full of small change, and a notice, 'Take what you

---

[1] Emile Vandervelde (1866–1938): Belgian Socialist leader, prominent in the Second International; entered the Cabinet during the First World War. Foreign Minister 1925–7.

[2] Jules Guesde (1845–1922): Republican revolutionary under the Empire, jailed for opposition to the Franco-Prussian War. Exiled in Switzerland after the suppression of the Commune, he espoused Bakuninist ideas, before turning to State 'collectivism'. Joined the 'Cabinet of National Defence' at the outbreak of war.

want, leave what you can'. Breathtaking discovery! The whole city, the whole earth was counting its pennies, one was presented with money-boxes on special occasions: No Credit, Trust Nobody, Shut the Door Firmly, What's Mine is Mine, yes? Monsieur Th——, my employer, a colliery-owner, issued all postage-stamps himself; impossible to cheat this millionaire out of ten centimes! We were amazed at the pennies abandoned by Anarchy to the sky.

A little farther on, and we came to a small white house under the trees: *Do What You Will* over the door, which was open to all-comers. In the farmyard, a big black devil with a pirate's profile was haranguing a rapt audience. A real style to the man, his tone bantering, his repartee devastating. His theme: free love. But how could love not be free?

Printers, gardeners, a cobbler, a painter were working here in comradeship, together with their womenfolk. It would have been idyllic, if only. . . . They had started with nothing, like brothers; they still had to tighten their belts. Usually these colonies collapsed quite quickly, for lack of resources. Although jealousy was formally prohibited in them, quarrels over women, even though resolved by bursts of generosity, did them the greatest mischief. The libertarian colony of Stockel, transferred to Boitsfort, spun out for several years. There we learned to edit, set up, proof-read and print, all by ourselves, our paper *Communiste*, which consisted of four small pages. Some tramps, a short, prodigiously intelligent Swiss plasterer, a Tolstoyan-anarchist Russian officer, Leon Gerassimov, with a pale, noble face, who had escaped from a defeated insurrection and, the following year, was to die of hunger in the Fontainebleau woods; also a redoubtable chemist, from Odessa via Buenos Aires—all these helped us to investigate the solutions of many a great problem.

The individualist printer: 'Friend, there is only yourself in the world. You must try not to be a bastard or a ninny.'

The Tolstoyan: 'Let us be new men. Salvation is within us.'

The Swiss plasterer, a disciple of Luigi Bertoni:[1] 'All right, so long as you don't forget your hob-nailed boots: you'll find those in the factories.'

---

[1] Luigi Bertoni (1872–1947): Swiss printer and publisher of anarchist literature, firstly of the bilingual journal *Le Réveil* (*Il Risveglio*) from 1900 to 1940, then of various pamphlets; in opposition to both World Wars. Publisher of Kropotkin, Malatesta, and other anarchist writers.

The chemist, having listened long, said in his Russo-Spanish accent: 'All this is claptrap, comrades; in the social war we need good laboratories.' Sokolov was a cold-blooded man, moulded in Russia by inhuman struggles, apart from which he could no longer live. He came out of the storm, and the storm was within him. He fought, he killed, he died in prison.

The idea of 'good laboratories' was of Russian origin. From Russia, swarming through the whole world, came men and women who had been formed in ruthless battle, who had but one aim in life, who drew their breath from danger. The comfort, peace, and amiability of the West seemed stale to them, and angered them all the more since they had learned to see the naked operations of a social machinery which no one thought of in these privileged lands. In Switzerland, Tatiana Leontieva killed a gentleman she mistook for a minister of the Tsar. Rips fired on the *Gardes Républicains* from the top deck of a bus in the Place de la République. A revolutionary, in the confidence of the police, executed the head of the Okhrana's secret service in a hotel room at Belleville. In a mean quarter of London called Houndsditch (a name appropriate to such squalid dramas), Russian anarchists withstood a siege in the cellar of a jeweller's shop; the picture of Winston Churchill, then a young Cabinet Minister, directing the siege became a photographer's cliché. In Paris, Svoboda was blown up while trying out his bombs in the Bois de Boulogne. 'Alexander Sokolov' (whose real name was Vladimir Hartenstein) belonged to the same group as Svoboda. In his little room behind a shop in the Rue de la Musée, he had installed a complete laboratory, just a few yards from the Royal Library, where he spent part of his day writing to his friends in Russia and Argentina, in Greek characters but in Spanish.

It was a time of pot-bellied peace; the atmosphere was strangely electric, the calm before the storm of 1914. The first Clemenceau government had just drawn working-class blood at Draveil (in 1908), where police had entered a strike meeting only to shoot and kill several innocent people, and at the funeral demonstration for these victims, where troops opened fire. (This demonstration had been organized by the secretary of the Food Workers Union, Métivier, an extreme-Left militant and police spy who the previous day had received his personal instructions from the Minister of the Interior, Georges Clemenceau himself.) I remember our anger when

we learnt of these shootings. That same evening a hundred of us
youngsters showed the red flag in the neighbourhood of the Government buildings, willingly battling with the police. We felt ourselves
close to all the victims and rebels in the world; we would have fought
joyfully for the men executed in the prisons of Montjuich or Alcala
del Valle, whose sufferings we recalled each day. We felt the growth
within us of a wonderful and formidable collective awareness.

Sokolov laughed at our demonstration, mere child's play. He
himself was silently preparing the real reply to the workers' murderers. At the end of a sad train of events, his laboratory was discovered; he found himself hounded down, without means of escape.
Flight was impossible because of his face, notable for its intense eyes
and conspicuous in a crowd because the top part of his nose had been
crushed (apparently with a blow from an iron bar). He shut himself
up in a furnished room at Ghent, loaded his revolvers and waited;
and when the police came, he fired on them as he had fired on the
Tsar's police. The peaceful sergeants of Ghent paid for the Cossacks'
pogroms and Sokolov laid down his life, 'whether here or there
matters little, so long as one lays it down on the great day, for the
awakening of the oppressed'.

In the Rue de Ruysbroek, at the shop of a little grocer-cum-
bookseller who was suspected of being an informer, I had met
Edouard, a metal-turner; he was thick-set, with the physique of
some outlandish Hercules, and a heavy, muscular face lit up by his
timorous, shifty little eyes. He had come from the factories of Liége
and was fond of reading Haeckel's *Riddle of the Universe*. Of himself,
he said, 'I was well on the way to becoming a splendid ruffian!
I was lucky to begin to understand. . . .' And he told me how on the
barges of the Meuse he had lived a ruffian's life ('Just like the others,
only tougher, of course'), terrorizing the women a little, working
hard, with the odd bit of pilfering from the docks, 'Without knowing
what a man is or what life is.' He asked to be admitted into our
group. 'What ought I to read, do you think?'

'Elisée Reclus,' I answered.[1]

'It isn't too difficult?'

'No,' I replied, but already I was beginning to see just how

[1] Elisée Reclus (1830–1905): French geographer, one of five brothers outstanding in the subject; an associate of the First International. Banished to Belgium
after the suppression of the Commune.

tremendously difficult it was. We let him join, and he was a good comrade. Our times together were not clouded by the foreknowledge that he would die, by his own hand, close to me.

Paris called us, the Paris of Salvat, of the Commune, of the C.G.T., of little journals printed with burning zeal, the Paris of our favourite authors, Anatole France and Jehan Rictus; the Paris where Lenin from time to time edited *Iskra* and spoke at *émigré* meetings in little co-operative houses; the Paris where the Central Committee of the Russian Social-Revolutionary Party had its headquarters, where Burtsev lived, who had just unmasked, in the terrorist organization of this party, Evno Azev, engineer, executioner of Minister von Plehve and of Grand Duke Sergei, and police spy. I took my leave of Raymond with bitter irony. I noticed him on a street corner, unemployed, handing out advertisements for a tailor's shop. 'Hello there, Free Man!' I said, 'Why not Sandwich-Man?'

'Perhaps it will come to that,' he said, laughing, 'but no more towns for me. They are nothing but treadmills. I want to work or bust on the open road; I shall at least have fresh air and countryside. I've had a bellyful of all these deadpans. I'm only waiting to get enough to buy a pair of shoes.' He went off with his mate by the Ardennes roads, to Switzerland and the open spaces, helping with the harvest, raising limestone with masons, cutting timber with woodcutters, a floppy old felt hat over his eyes, a volume of Verhaeren in his pocket:

> *Drunk with the world and with ourselves, we bring*
> *Hearts of new men to the old universe.*

I have often thought since then that poetry was a substitute for prayer for us, so greatly did it uplift us and answer our constant need for exaltation. Verhaeren, the European poet nearest to Walt Whitman (whom we did not yet know), flashed us a gleam of keen, anguished, fertile thought on the modern town, its railway stations, its trade in women, its swirling crowds; and his cries of violence were like ours: '*Open or break your fists against the door!*' Fists were broken, and why not? Better that than stagnation. Jehan Rictus lamented the suffering of the penniless intellectual dragging out his nights on the benches of foreign boulevards, and no rhymes were richer than his: *songe-mensonge* (dream-lie), *espoir-désespoir* (hope-despair). In springtime '*the smell of crap and lilacs. . . .*'

One day I went off, all at random, taking ten francs, a spare shirt, some work-books, and some photos which I always kept with me. In front of the station I chanced to meet my father, and we talked of the recent discoveries on the structure of matter which had been popularized by Gustave Le Bon.

'Are you off?'

'Yes, to Lille for a fortnight.'

I believed it; I was never to come back, never to see him again, but the last letters I had from him in Brazil when I was in Russia, thirty years later, still spoke of the structure of the American continent and the history of civilizations.

Europe at that time knew no passports, and frontiers hardly existed. I stayed in a mining village at Fives in Lille; two and a half francs a week (fifty U.S. cents), payable in advance, for a clean garret. I wanted to go down the mine. Some cheery old miners laughed in my face: 'You'd be finished in two hours, friend.' On the third day, I had four francs left. I went to look for work, rationing myself; every day a pound of bread, two pounds of green pears, a glass of milk (bought on credit from my kind hostess), twenty-five centimes to spend. Annoyingly enough, the soles of my shoes began to let me down, and on the eighth day of this routine, attacks of giddiness forced me to seek the haven of benches in the public gardens. I was obsessed by a dream of bacon soup. My strength was ebbing, I was going to be good for nothing, not even for the worst possible existence. An iron footbridge over the railway-line in the station began to exert an absurd fascination over me, when I was saved by a providential meeting with a comrade who was supervising drain-digging in the street. Almost at once I found work with a photographer at Armentières, at four francs a day—a fortune. I was unwilling to leave the mining village, and went out at dawn in the sad morning mist with the workers in their leather helmets. I travelled to work amongst slag-heaps, then shut myself up all day in a poky laboratory where we worked alternately by green light and red. In the evening, before fatigue could prostrate me, I would spend a little while reading Jaurès' *L'Humanité*, with mingled admiration and annoyance. A couple lived behind the partition. They adored one another, and the man used to beat his wife savagely before taking her. I could hear her murmur through her sobs, 'Hit me again, again.' I found inadequate the studies of working-class women which I had hitherto read. Would it after all take centuries to transform this world and these human beings? Yet each one of us has only one life in front of him. What was to be done?

Anarchism swept us away completely because it both demanded everything of us and offered everything to us. There was no remotest corner of life that it failed to illumine, at least so it seemed to us. A man could be a Catholic, a Protestant, a Liberal, a Radical, a Socialist, even a syndicalist, without in any way changing his own life, and therefore life in general. It was enough for him, after all, to read the appropriate newspaper; or, if he was strict, to frequent the café associated with whatever tendency claimed his allegiance. Shot through with contradictions, fragmented into varieties and sub-varieties, anarchism demanded, before anything else, harmony between deeds and words (which, in truth, is demanded by all forms of idealism, but which they all forget as they become complacent). That is why we adopted what was (at that moment) the extremest variety, which by vigorous dialectic had succeeded, through the logic of its revolutionism, in discarding the necessity for revolution. To a certain extent we were impelled in that direction by our disgust with a certain type of rather mellow, academic anarchism, whose Pope was Jean Grave in *Temps Nouveaux*.[1] Individualism had just been affirmed by our hero Albert Libertad. No one knew his real name, or anything of him before he started preaching. Crippled in both legs, walking on crutches which he plied vigorously in fights (he was a great one for fighting, despite his handicap), he bore, on a powerful body, a bearded head whose face was finely proportioned. Destitute, having come as a tramp from the south, he began his preaching in Montmartre, among libertarian circles and the queues of poor devils waiting for their dole of soup not far from the site of Sacré Coeur. Violent, magnetically attractive, he became the heart and soul of a movement of such exceptional dynamism that it is not entirely dead even at this day. Libertad loved streets, crowds, fights, ideas, and women. On two occasions he set up house with a pair of sisters, the Mahés and then the Morands. He had children to whom he refused to give State registration. 'The State? Don't know it? The name? I

---

[1] Jean Grave (1854–1939): anarchist militant and author, founder of the journal *La Révolte*; novelist and essayist. Manufactured a bomb, but never threw it.

don't give a damn, they'll pick one that suits them. The law? To the devil with it.' He died in hospital in 1908 as the result of a fight, bequeathing his body ('That carrion of mine', he called it), for dissection in the cause of science.

His teaching, which we adopted almost wholesale, was: 'Don't wait for the revolution. Those who promise revolution are frauds just like the others. Make your own revolution, by being free men and living in comradeship.' Obviously I am simplifying, but the idea itself had a beautiful simplicity. Its absolute commandment and rule of life was: 'Let the old world go to blazes.' From this position there were naturally many deviations. Some inferred that one should 'live according to Reason and Science', and their impoverished worship of science, which invoked the mechanistic biology of Félix le Dantec,[1] led them on to all sorts of tomfoolery, such as a saltless, vegetarian diet and fruitarianism and also, in certain cases, to tragic ends. We saw young vegetarians involved in pointless struggles against the whole of society. Others decided, 'Let's be outsiders. The only place for us is the fringe of society.' They did not stop to think that society has no fringe, that no one is ever outside it, even in the depth of dungeons, and that their 'conscious egoism', sharing the life of the defeated, linked up from below with the most brutal bourgeois individualism.

Finally, others, including myself, sought to harness together personal transformation and revolutionary action, in accordance with the motto of Elisée Reclus: 'As long as social injustice lasts we shall remain in a state of permanent revolution.' (I am quoting this from memory.) Libertarian individualism gave us a hold over the most intense reality: ourselves. *Be yourself.* Only, it developed in another 'city without escape'—Paris, an immense jungle where all relationships were dominated by a primitive individualism, dangerous in a different way from ours, that of a positively Darwinian struggle for existence. Having bade farewell to the humiliations of poverty, we found ourselves once again up against them. To be yourself would have been a precious commandment and perhaps a lofty achievement, if only it had been possible; it would only have begun to be possible once the most pressing needs of man, those which identify him more closely with the brutes than with his

[1] Félix le Dantec (1869–1917): Lamarckian biologist, theorist of evolution and rationalist.

fellow humans, were satisfied. We had to win our food, lodging and clothing by main force; and after that, to find time to read and think. The problem of the penniless youngster, uprooted or (as we used to say) 'foaming at the bit' through irresistible idealism, confronted us in a form that was practically insoluble. Many comrades were soon to slide into what was called 'illegalism', a way of life not so much on the fringe of society as on the fringe of morality. 'We refuse to be either exploiters or exploited,' they declared, without perceiving that they were continuing to be both these and, what is more, becoming hunted men. When they knew that the game was up they chose to kill themselves rather than go to jail.

One of them, who never went out without his Browning revolver, told me, 'Prison isn't worth living for! Six bullets for the sleuthhounds and the seventh for me! You know, I'm lighthearted.' A light heart is a heavy burden. The principle of self-preservation that is in us all found its consequence, within the social jungle, in a battle of One against All.

A positive explosion of despair was building up in us unbeknown. Man is finished, lost. We are beaten in advance, whatever we do. A young anarchist midwife gave up her calling 'because it is a crime to inflict life on a human being'. Years later, awakened into hope by the Russian Revolution, I wanted to reach Petrograd, then in flames, and agreed to pass through a sector of the Champagne front, at the risk either of being left there in a common grave or of killing men better than myself in the opposite trench. I wrote: 'Life is not such a great benefit that it is wrong to lose it or criminal to take it.'

René Valet, my friend, was a lively, restless spirit. We had met in the *Quartier Latin*, we had discussed everything together, usually at night, around the St. Geneviève hill, in the little bars jostling on the Boulevard St. Michel: Barrès, Anatole France, Apollinaire, Louis Nazzi. Together we muttered scraps of Vildrac's *White Bird*, Jules Romains' *Ode to the Crowd*, Jehan Rictus' *The Ghost*. René was law-abiding and prosperous, he even had his own locksmith's workshop, not far from Denfert-Rochereau. I can see him there now, standing up like a young Siegfried, criticizing Anatole France's treatment of the destruction of this planet. Having had his say, René would sink slowly down on the asphalt of the boulevard, with a sly grin. 'What is certain is that we are all mugs. Yes, mugs!'

I remember his fine, square-set ginger head, his powerful chin, his green eyes, his strong hands, his athlete's bearing (an emancipated athlete, naturally). He liked to wear the navvy's wide corduroy trousers, with a waistband of blue flannel. Once, on an evening of riots, we wandered together around a guillotine, ridden by our gloom, sickened by our feebleness, mad with anger. 'We have a wall in front of us,' we told each other, 'and what a wall.' 'Oh, the bastards!' muttered my ginger-headed friend, and next day he confessed to me that all that night his hand had been closed upon the chill blackness of a Browning revolver. Fight, fight, what else was there to do? And if it meant death, no matter. René rushed into mortal danger out of his sense of solidarity with his defeated mates, out of his need for battle and, at the heart of it, out of despair. These 'conscious egoists' were going to get themselves slaughtered for friendship's sake.

I had arrived in Paris a little after the death of Libertad. The luxurious Paris of Passy and the Champs-Elysées, and even of the great boulevards of commerce, were for us like a foreign or enemy city. Our own Paris had three centres: the great working-class town that began somewhere in a grim zone of canals, cemeteries, waste plots, and factories, around Charonne, Pantin, and the Flandre bridge; it climbed the heights of Belleville and Ménilmontant, and there became a plebeian capital, lively, busy and egalitarian like an ant-heap; and then, on its frontiers with the town of railway stations and delights, became cluttered with shady districts. Small hotels for a 'short time', 'sleep-sellers' where for twenty sous one could gasp in a garret without ventilation, pubs frequented by procurers, swarms of women with coiled hair and coloured aprons soliciting on the pavements.

The rumbling trains of the *Métro* would suddenly plunge into a tunnel under the town, and I would linger in a circle of passers-by to hear and see Hercules and the Boneless Wonder with their fantastic patter, clowns with a waggish dignity who always needed just another fifteen sous before they would perform their best tricks, upon an old rug spread on the pavement. And inside another circle, as evening came on and the workshops emptied, the blind man, his stout female assistant and the soulful orphan-girl would sing the popular songs of the day: '*The riders of the moo-oon. . . .*'

and in the ballad there was also some mention of 'dusky night' and 'desperate love'.

Our Montmartre adjoined, but never met, the Montmartre of artists' taverns, bars haunted by women in feathered hats and hobble-skirts, the *Moulin Rouge*, etc. We acknowledged only old Frédé's *Lapin Agile*, where people sang old French songs, some perhaps going back to the days of François Villon, who was a wandering, despairing, merry young sprig, a poet, a rebel like us—and a gallows-bird. The old Rue des Rosiers, where the generals Lecomte and Clément Thomas were shot under the Commune, now renamed the Rue de la Chevalier de la Barre, had, since the time of the barricades, only changed its appearance at one point along its extent. There, at the top of the slope, the basilica of Sacré Coeur de Jésus was slothfully nearing completion, in a sort of fake-Hindu, monumentally bourgeois style. Hard by the stone-yards here, young radical thinkers had put up a statue of the young Chevalier de la Barre who had been burnt by the Inquisition.

The basilica and the white marble Chevalier looked down on the roofs of Paris: ocean of grey roofs, over which there arose at night only a few dim lights, and a great red glow from the tumultuous squares. We would pause there to take stock of our ideas. At the other end of the street, a lopsided square stretched at the crossing of two roads, one a steep incline, the other rising in flights of dull grey steps. In front of a tall and ancient shuttered house, the journal *Causeries Populaires* and the offices of *L'Anarchie*, both founded by Libertad, occupied a shabby building, filled with the noise of printing-presses, singing, and passionate discussion. There I met Rirette,[1] a short, slim, aggressive girl-militant with a Gothic profile, and Emile Armand[2] the theoretician, sickly and goateed, his pince-nez all askew, once a Salvation Army officer, lately a convict in solitary confinement, a stubborn, often subtle dialectician who used to argue purely on the basis of self. 'I only propose, never impose,' he would almost splutter; yet out of his spluttering emerged

---

[1] Rirette and Serge were in fact lovers, and later married during his imprisonment at Melun. She joined him in Spain, but had to return to France and thence lost contact with him, except by correspondence.

[2] Emile Armand—pseudonym of Ernest Jouin (1872–1962): after being influenced by anarchism during his period in the Salvation Army, founded a Christian-Tolstoyan-anarchist journal (*L'Ere Nouvelle*), then turned to individualist anarchism and edited *L'Anarchie* and subsequently *L'En-Dehors*.

the most disastrous theory possible: that of 'illegalism'. This transformed lovers of liberty, 'outsiders', enthusiasts for comradely living, into technicians of obscure and illicit crafts.

The most important subject of our discussions, some of which ended in shooting and blood-letting among comrades, was 'the importance of science'. Should scientific law regulate the whole life of the New Man, to the exclusion of irrational sentiment and of all idealism 'inherited from ancestral faiths'? Taine's and Renan's blind cult of science, here reduced to almost algebraic formulae by fanatical popularizers, became the catechism of individualist revolt: 'Myself alone against all', and 'Nothing means anything to me', as the Hegelian Max Stirner[1] once proclaimed. The doctrine of 'comradely living' slightly counteracted the unpardonable isolation of these rebels; but out of it was emerging a constricted coterie, equipped with a psychological jargon demanding a long initiation. I found this coterie at once fascinating and repellent. I was at some distance from those primitive conceptions; other influences were at work on me, and there were other values which I neither could nor would abandon: basically, the revolutionary idealism of the Russians.

I had happened to find work easily at Belleville, as a draughtsman in a machine-tool works, ten hours a day, twelve and a half including the journeys, starting at 6.30 a.m. In the evenings I went, by the funicular railway and the *Métro*, to the Left Bank, the Latin Quarter, our third Paris—the one I liked best, to tell the truth. I had an hour and a half at my disposal to read at the St. Geneviève Library, with eyes that stubbornly refused to stay open over political economy, and a tired intellect functioning now only at half-cock. I took to alcohol to help me to read, but I only forgot everything the following day.

I left the brutalizing atmosphere of my 'good job', the pallid fascination of the Chaumont hills in the morning and the fascination of evening, when the street was full of lights and the eyes of working-girls. I proceeded to settle myself in the garret of an inn, in the Place du Panthéon, trying to live by teaching French to Russian students and by doing jobs of routine brain-work. It was better to

[1] Max Stirner (1806–56): German anarchist philosopher, author of *The Ego and His Own*: 'Nothing means anything to me', is the opening of this work (*Ich hab' mein' Sach' auf Nichts gestellt*, a quotation from Goethe).

feel a faint pinch of hunger reading in the Luxembourg Gardens than to eat my fill by sketching crankshafts till I could no longer think.

From my window I could see the square, the Panthéon gate, and Rodin's 'Thinker'. I would have liked to know the exact spot on which Dr. Tony Moilin had been shot in 1871 for tending the Commune's wounded. The bronze Thinker seemed to me to be meditating on that crime, and waiting to be shot himself. After all, how insolent he was, doing nothing but thinking; and how dangerous if he ever came to a conclusion.

A Social-Revolutionary had introduced me to the members of his party among the Russian emigration. He was a large, hairless gentleman of Americanized manners, often sent off by the party on missions to the United States. The Russian Social-Revolutionary Party was passing through a serious crisis of morale, since several police agents had been unmasked in its Battle Organization; for example, Azev and Zhuchenko. The militant who had greeted me on my arrival, with whom I had often discussed Maeterlinck and the meaning of life all night long, was called Patrick. He led an exemplary life, kept faith amid the general demoralization, and cultivated a healthy optimism. When the Paris archives of the Okhrana's secret service were opened in 1917 we found that Patrick was also a police agent, but that was really no longer of any importance.

I led a many-sided life; I was attracted by the partisan warriors of Paris, that sub-proletariat of *déclassé*, 'emancipated' men, dreaming of freedom and dignity and constantly on the verge of imprisonment; and among the Russians I breathed a much purer air, distilled in sacrifice, energy and culture. I taught French to a stunning young woman who always wore red dresses, a Maximalist,[1] one of the rare survivors of the attempt at Aptekarsky Island, in St. Petersburg. There three Maximalists had presented themselves in uniform at a reception in the villa of the Prime Minister, Stolypin, and suffered themselves to be roasted in the hall, so as to make sure that the villa would be blown up to practically nothing. People around me spoke of them as if they had only just gone out of the

---

[1] The Maximalist party split from the Social-Revolutionaries in 1906, advocating the socialization of industry as well as of land, together with a wider application of terrorism (to include pillage and incendiarism of estates, as well as individual assassination). The movement's general position was in some ways close to that of the Anarchists. By 1908 the movement was virtually extinguished, though it did make a brief reappearance after 1917.

room; of Salomon Ryss, alias Medved, the Bear, who had joined the Okhrana to disrupt and disorganize it, had been caught and recently hanged; of Petrov, who had done the same at St. Petersburg, and had lately assassinated the head of the secret police; of Gershuni, who refused a pardon out of contempt for the Tsar—they dared not hang him all the same—then escaped, and died here, not far from us, of tuberculosis; of Yegor Sazanov who twice offered up his life, first when he threw a bomb under von Plehve's carriage, and again when he killed himself in jail, a few months before he was due for release, in protest against the maltreatment of his comrades.

Coming from these discussions, I would meet old Edouard Ferral, selling his copies of *L'Intransigeant* on the corner of the Boulevard St. Michel and the Rue Soufflot. *L'Intran, L'Intran!*: he proclaimed his wares in a soft, trembling voice. He sported an improbable pair of worn-out boots, and a complete, authentic tramp's outfit. A disgraceful yellow straw hat sat like a halo on his head. Bearded like Socrates, a lively glow in his eyes (which were the colour of Seine water), he lived, wanting even elementary necessities, among the lowest of the low. I never knew under what strains he had been brought so low, for certainly his was one of the finest intelligences of the libertarian movement, naturally heretical, loved and admired by the young. Deeply learned, reciting and translating Virgil with lyrical passion in down-at-heel pubs in the Place Maubert (where we willingly followed him), a disciple of Georges Sorel and himself a theoretician of syndicalism, he blended this theory with the ideas of Mécislas Golberg,[1] who practically died of hunger in the Latin Quarter affirming that the highest revolutionary vocation was the thief's.

It was Ferral who introduced me to the terrifying world of utmost poverty, spiritless degradation; the borderline of humanity under the rubble of the great city. There, a tradition of total, overwhelming defeat had been kept up—as it still is—for at least ten centuries. These wretches were the lineal descendants of the first beggars of Paris, perhaps of Roman Lutetia's meanest plebs. They were older than Notre Dame, and neither St. Geneviève nor the blessed

---

[1] Mécislas (Mieczyslaw) Golberg (1870–1907): Polish anarchist and Bohemian, resident in Paris after 1894; an associate of Apollinaire, Picasso and other literary-artistic figures of the time, Golberg edited a periodical for the unemployed, evolved a theoretical basis for Cubism (*La Morale des Lignes*, 1908), and acted as a lively influence in the thinking of his milieu.

Virgin had ever been able to do anything for them: proof, of course, that they were beyond redemption. I saw them in the pubs of *La Maub'*, drinking their draught wine, eating the pork-shop's refuse, repairing the dressings (sometimes spectacularly faked) on their sores; I heard them discuss the affairs of their guilds, the allotment of a particular begging-pitch that had become vacant through the passing of a certain member, lately found dead under a bridge. Others would be replenishing their trays with matches and shoe-laces, others again delousing themselves discreetly. I observed, terrified, what the city could do to man, the mangy, pestiferous, kennelled cur's existence to which it reduced him; and this helped me to understand Peter Lavrov's *Historical Letters*,[1] concerning social justice.

The *clochard* is a spent individual, squeezed dry of personal initiative, who has learnt to enjoy, feebly but stubbornly, the meagre vegetable existence which is all that he has. The rag-pickers were a world apart, adjacent but separate, centring on the Barrière d'Italie at St. Ouen; some of the less abandoned managed to accumulate a positive treasure by exploiting an abundant raw material: the town's refuse. The genuine human refuse could not even do that, having too little energy and too much sloth to pursue the systematic efforts of the dustbin brigade.

I translated Russian novels and poems—Artzybashev, Balmont, Merezhkovsky—for a charming Russian journalist under whose signature they appeared. Thanks to this employment I was enabled to buy onion soup for Ferral at the stroke of midnight by a brazier in Les Halles beneath the squat, massive silhouette of St. Eustache. One of the peculiar features of working-class Paris at this time was that it bordered extensively on the underworld, that is, on the vast world of irregulars, outcasts, paupers, and criminals. There were few essential differences between the young worker or artisan from the old central districts, and the ponce from the alleys by Les Halles. A chauffeur or mechanic with any wits about him would pilfer all he could from the boss as a matter of course, out of class conscious-ness ('It's all on the guv'nor!') and because he was 'free' of old-fashioned prejudice. Working-class attitudes, aggressive and anarchic, were pulled in opposite directions by two antagonistic

[1] Peter Lavrov (1823–1900): Russian Populist Socialist of the non-insurrectionary school.

movements, the revolutionary syndicalism of the C.G.T. which, with a fresh and powerful idealism, was winning the real proletariat to the struggle for positive demands, and the shapeless activity of the anarchist groups. Between and beneath these two currents, restless and disaffected masses were being borne along. Two extraordinary demonstrations of this time marked an epoch for me and for the whole of Paris; I think that no historian will be able to ignore their significance.

The first one took place on 13 October 1909. On that day we heard the news of an incredible event: the execution of Francisco Ferrer,[1] decreed by Maura and permitted by Alfonso XIII. The founder of the Modern School in Barcelona, condemned absurdly for a popular uprising of some days' duration, fell back into the ditch at Montjuich shouting to the firing-squad: 'I forgive you, children! Aim straight!' (Later on he was 'rehabilitated' by Spanish justice.)

I had written, even before his arrest, the first article in the great Press campaign conducted on his behalf. His transparent innocence, his educational activity, his courage as an independent thinker, and even his man-in-the-street appearance endeared him infinitely to the whole of a Europe that was, at the time, liberal by sentiment and in intense ferment. A true international consciousness was growing from year to year, step by step with the progress of capitalist civilization. Frontiers were crossed without formalities; some trade unions subsidized travel for their members; commercial and intellectual exchanges seemed to be unifying the world. Already in 1905 the anti-Semitic pogroms in Russia had roused a universal wave of condemnation. From one end of the Continent to the other (except in Russia and Turkey) the judicial murder of Ferrer had, within twenty-four hours, moved whole populations to incensed protest.

In Paris the movement was spontaneous. By hundreds of thousands, from every *faubourg*, workers and ordinary folk, impelled by a terrible indignation, flowed towards the city centre. The revolutionary groups followed rather than guided these masses. The editors of revolutionary journals, taken aback by their sudden influence, spread the call: 'To the Spanish Embassy!' The Embassy would

[1] Francisco Ferrer (1859–1909): pacifist, anarcho-syndicalist, and educational reformer. His *Escuela Moderna* in Barcelona taught rationalist and libertarian principles to its pupils. Much influenced by the French C.G.T., he translated and distributed French syndicalist material and founded the journal *Solidaridad Obrera*.

have been ransacked had not Lépine, the Police Commissioner, barricaded all entries to the Boulevard Malesherbes. Angry riots started in these prosperous thoroughfares, lined with banks and aristocratic residences.

The backwash of the crowds carried me among newspaper kiosks blazing on the pavéments and overturned omnibuses whose horses, painstakingly unharnessed, gazed stupidly at their empty contraptions. Police cyclists charged, weaving their machines to and fro at random. Lépine was shot at from ten yards by a revolver from somewhere in a group of journalists belonging to *La Guerre Sociale*, *Le Libertaire*, and *L'Anarchie*. Weariness and the onset of night calmed the outburst, which left the people of Paris with an exultant sensation of strength. The Government authorized a legal demonstration two days after, led by Jaurès; we marched along, 500,000 of us, surrounded by mounted *Gardes Républicains* who sat all subdued, taking the measure of this newly-risen power.

There was a natural transition from this demonstration to the second. Miguel Almereyda[1] had participated in the organization of the first, and was the moving force behind its successor. I had helped him hide in Brussels, where he had brusquely ridiculed my momentary Tolstoyan fancies. In short, we were friends. I told him, 'You're just an opportunist. Your people have started off quite wrong.' He answered 'As far as Paris is concerned you are an ignoramus, my friend. You can purify yourself with Russian novels, but here the revolution needs cash.'

He incarnated human achievement in a measure so far practically unknown to me. He had the physical beauty of the pure-bred Catalan—tall forehead, blazing eyes—allied with an extreme elegance. A brilliant journalist, a captivating orator, a capable libertarian politician, adroit in business, he was able to handle a crowd or fix a trial, to brave the bludgeons of the police, the revolvers of certain comrades or the spite of the Government, and to concoct fantastic intrigues. In the ministries, he had his connexions; in the slums, his devoted friends.

He was behind the disappearance from Clemenceau's drawer

[1] Miguel Almereyda (Bonaventure Vigo) (1883–1917): revolutionary militant and writer; organized the *Jeunesses Révolutionnaires* (1908), then founded the political-satirical review *Le Bonnet Rouge*, which led a 'defeatist' campaign in 1916–17 until it was suppressed. Almereyda was then accused of receiving German funds and arrested.

of a receipt for 500 francs signed by an *agent-provocateur* in the syndicalist movement. He then presented himself at the Assize Court and was acquitted with the jury's congratulations. He organized the circulation of *La Guerre Sociale*, whose guiding spirit he was, together with Gustave Hervé ('The General') and Eugène Merle, who was to become Paris's most powerful and Balzacian journalist. Almereyda had experienced a scarifying childhood, partly in a reformatory for a minor theft. It was he who, after the Ferrer demonstration, seized upon the Liabeuf affair. This was the prelude to a number of other dramas.

It was a battle of low life. Liabeuf, a young worker of twenty who had grown up on the Boulevard de Sébastopol, fell in love with a little street-walker. The vice-squad, those persecutors of girls, saw them together and had him condemned as a ponce. This he was not; on the contrary, his dream was to rescue this girl from 'the game'. The officially-provided defence counsel did not turn up at the trial, the accused man's protests were naturally of no avail, the petty sessions magistrate hurried through the proceedings in five seconds (as usual with these matters) and the police were, of course, on oath. Liabeuf felt branded with infamy. Once out of prison, he armed himself with a revolver, donned spiked armlets under his cloak, and went in quest of vengeance. To arrest him they had to nail him to the wall with a sabre blow. He had wounded four policemen, and was condemned to death. The left-wing Press indicted the vice-squad and demanded a pardon for Liabeuf. Commissioner Lépine, a short gentleman capable of a cold hysteria, whose goatee presided every year over the bludgeoning of the May Day demonstrators, demanded his execution. Almereyda wrote that if they dared to set up the guillotine, there would be more blood around it than beneath it. He appealed to the people of Paris to stop the execution by force. The Socialist Party lent its support to the movement.

On the night of the execution assorted crowds, from all the *faubourgs*, all the bounds haunted by crime and misery, converged upon that unique spot in Paris, always ghastly by day and sinister by night: the Boulevard Arago. On one side, bourgeois houses, insensitive to everything, with their windows neatly drawn on 'every man for himself' (and 'God for all', if you please), on the other, two lines of stout chestnut trees, beneath the wall—a wall of **great** cemented stones, dull greyish-brown, that most silent, most pitiless of walls, the prison wall: twenty feet high. I had come with Rirette, with René the Angry, with old Ferral who, positively fanatical in affliction, seemed to float along, unbelievably weak, inside his ragged suit. The militants from all the groups were there, forced back by walls of black-uniformed police executing bizarre manœuvres. Shouts and angry scuffles broke out when the guillotine wagon arrived, escorted by a squad of cavalry. For some hours there was a battle on the spot, the police charges forcing us ineffectively, because of the darkness, into side-streets from which sections of the crowd would disgorge once again the next minute. Jaurès was recognized at the head of one column and nearly brained. Almereyda manœuvred in vain to break through the human barrier. There was plenty of violence and a little bloodshed—one policeman killed. At dawn, exhaustion quietened the crowd, and at the instant when the blade fell upon a raging head still yelling its innocence, a baffled frenzy gripped the twenty or thirty thousand demonstrators, and found its outlet in a long-drawn cry: '*Murderers!*' The barriers of policemen now moved only lethargically. 'Do you see it?—The wall!' René shouted to me.

When in the morning I returned to that part of the boulevard, a huge policeman, standing on the square of fresh sand which had been thrown over the blood, was attentively treading a rose into it. A little farther off, leaning against the wall, Ferral was gently wringing his hands: 'Society is a filthy trick.'

From this day dates the revulsion and contempt that is aroused in me by the death-penalty, which replies to the crime of the primitive, the retarded, the deprived, the half-mad or the hopeless by nothing short of a collective crime, carried out coldly by men invested with authority, who believe that they are on that account innocent of the pitiful blood they shed. As for the endless torture of life imprisonment or of very lengthy sentences, I know of nothing more stupidly inhuman.

After the fight for Ferrer the philosopher, the battle for Liabeuf the desperado proved (although we did not see it) the seriousness of the deadlock in which the revolutionary movement of Paris was situated, no tendency being exempt. Energetic and powerful in 1906-7, the *Confédération Générale du Travail* began to decline, mellowed after a mere few years by the development of highly-paid

sections among the working class. The 'insurrectionism' of Gustave
Hervé and Miguel Almereyda revolved in a vacuum, expressing
nothing in the end but a craving for verbal and physical violence.
Bloated Europe, whose wealth and prosperity had grown to an
unprecedented degree in the thirty years since 1880, still based its
social system upon ancient injustices, and thereby created in its
great cities a limited but numerous social stratum to whom industrial
progress brought no real hope, and only that minimum of consciousness that sufficed to shed light upon its own misfortune. More:
through its excess of energy, as well as the incompatibility of its
historical structure with the new needs of society, the whole of this
Europe was drawn towards resolving its problems in violence. We
breathed the oppressive air of the prelude to war. Events heralded
the catastrophe clearly enough. The Agadir incident, the partition
of Morocco, the massacre at Casablanca; Italy's aggression against
Tripolitania began the dismemberment of the Ottoman Empire,
and the 'futurist' poet Marinetti detailed the splendour of bowels
steaming in the sun of a battlefield. The Austrian Empire annexed
Bosnia-Herzegovina. The Tsar continued to borrow money from the
French Republic and to hang and deport the best of the Russian
intelligentsia. From the two ends of the globe the Mexican and
Chinese revolutions flamed out to illumine our enthusiasm.

On the Left Bank, bordering the Latin Quarter, I had founded a
study-circle called 'Free Inquiry' (*La Libre Recherche*), which met
upstairs in a Socialist co-operative in the Rue Grégoire-de-Tours,
down dark corridors cluttered with barrels. The houses near by were
brothels, with red lamps, large numerals, brightly-lit doors and signs
in seventeenth-century script: *The Basket of Flowers*. The crowded
thoroughfare of the Rue de Buci, packed with stalls jutting on to the
pavement, unsavoury little bars, and costermongers, gave me the
sensation (or so I thought) of going back to the Paris of Louis XVI.
I was familiar with all the old doors along the street and on the
peeling façades above the advertisements for the hire of evening-
dress, I discerned the brand, invisible to others, of the Reign of
Terror.

In public meetings, I would dispute with *Le Sillon*'s Christian
Democrats,[1] who were fond of tough, strong-arm tactics, and with

[1] *Le Sillon:* journal of social Catholicism founded by Marc Sangnier in 1894;
condemned by Pius X in August 1910.

the Royalists, who were roused to white-hot frenzy by Léon Daudet.[1] When the tall Léon appeared on the platform with his plump profile, rather like that of a declining Bourbon or an Israelite financier (the similarity between these would be exact), we would form a battle-square in a corner of the hall we had picked beforehand, and as soon as his thunderous voice proclaimed 'The monarchy, traditional, federalist, anti-Parliamentarian!' etc., our jeering interruptions would chime in: 'A century behind the times! Coblenz![2] The guillotine!', and I would demand leave to speak, protected by a rampart of stalwart comrades. The *Camelots du Roi*[3] waited for this moment to charge our square, but we were not always defeated.

By contrast Georges Valois,[4] a former anarchist himself but recently converted to royalism, was very willing to discuss his syndicalist-royalist doctrine; he invoked Nietzsche, Georges Sorel, 'the social myth', the communal guilds of the Middle Ages, national sentiment. Meanwhile, certain comrades suggested that I should again take up the editing of *L'Anarchie*, now transferred from Montmartre to the Romainville Gardens, and threatened by splits among the different tendencies. I made it a condition that the previous editorial and printing staff, a collection of 'scientific individualists' whose leading light was Raymond, should get out and that I should be allowed to recruit my own colleagues. Nevertheless, for a month two staffs co-existed, the old one and mine.

For a while I caught up again with Raymond and Edouard. They were intoxicated with their algebraic formulae and in thrall to their dietary discipline (absolute vegetarianism, no wine or coffee, tea or infusions, and we who ate otherwise were 'insufficiently evolved'). They were already, or were becoming, outlaws, primarily through the influence of Octave Garnier, a handsome, swarthy, silent lad whose dark eyes were astoundingly hard and feverish. Small,

[1] Léon Daudet (1868–1942): son of Alphonse Daudet; co-founder of the monarchist and extreme Right *L'Action Française*. Novelist and anti-Semitic writer.

[2] Coblenz: the base of the Royalist *émigrés* during the French Revolution.

[3] *Camelots du Roi*: nickname given to the young toughs who sold *L'Action Française*.

[4] Georges Valois (Alfred Gressent) (1878–194?): first an anarchist and organizer of the first bookshop assistants' union (1903); subsequently a leader of *L'Action Française*, and founder of the first French fascist movement (*Les Faisceaux*) (1925–8); later reverted to a left-wing, anti-State position. A prolific writer through his various phases, Valois died in a Nazi concentration-camp.

working-class by origin, Octave had undergone a vicious beating on a building site in the course of a strike. He scorned all discussion with 'intellectuals'. 'Talk, talk!' he would remark softly, and off he would go on the arm of a blonde Rubensesque Flemish girl, to prepare some dangerous nocturnal task or other.

No other man that I have met in my whole life has ever so convinced me of the impotence and even the futility of the intellect when confronted with tough primitive creatures like this, rudely aroused to a form of intelligence that fits them purely technically for the life-struggle. He would have made an excellent seafarer for a Polar expedition, a fine soldier for the colonies; or, at another period, a Nazi storm-troop leader or an N.C.O. for Rommel. There was no doubt of it, all he could be was an outlaw. His was a restless, uncontrolled spirit, in quest of some impossible new dignity, how or what he did not know himself. Petty quarrels multiplied. Raymond, Edouard, and Octave departed soon enough, and I transferred our print-shop, in which we lived together as comrades, to the top of Belleville behind the Chaumont hills, in an old workingmen's house in the Rue Fessart. I set out to give a new emphasis to the paper, in the form of a turn from individualism to social action. I opened a polemic against Elie Faure the art historian who, citing Nietzsche, had just proclaimed the civilizing function of war. I noted, almost enthusiastically, the suicide of Paul and Laura Lafargue, the son-in-law and daughter of Karl Marx; Lafargue, having reached the age of sixty, an age at which, he decided, active creative life was over, administered poison to himself and his wife. I sought to affirm a 'doctrine of solidarity and revolt in the here and now', quoting Elisée Reclus: 'Man is Nature become conscious of itself.' Of Marx I knew practically nothing. We denounced syndicalism as a future Statism, as terrible as any other. The cult of 'the workers', a reaction against the politicians (who were primarily lawyers interested in their Parliamentary careers), struck us as being over-rigid and as carrying within itself the seeds of an anti-intellectual careerism.

The end of 1911 saw dramatic happenings. Joseph the Italian, a little militant with frizzled hair who dreamed of a free life in the bush of Argentina, as far away as possible from the towns, was found murdered on the Melun Road. From the grapevine we gathered that an Individualist from Lyons, Bonnot by name (I did not know the man), who had been travelling with him by car, had killed him, the Italian having first wounded himself through fumbling with a revolver. However it may have happened, one comrade had murdered or 'done' another. An informal investigation shed no light on the matter and only annoyed the 'scientific' Illegalists. Since I had expressed hostile opinions towards them, I had an unexpected visit from Raymond. 'If you don't want to disappear, be careful about condemning us.' He added, laughingly, 'Do whatever you like! If you get in my way I'll eliminate you!'

'You and your friends are absolutely cracked', I replied, 'and absolutely finished.' We faced each other exactly like small boys over a red cabbage. He was still squat and strapping, baby-faced and merry. 'Perhaps that's true,' he said, 'but it's the law of nature.'

A positive wave of violence and despair began to grow. The outlaw-anarchists shot at the police and blew out their own brains. Others, overpowered before they could fire the last bullet into their own heads, went off sneering to the guillotine. 'One against all!' 'Nothing means anything to me!' 'Damn the masters, damn the slaves, and damn me!' I recognized, in the various newspaper reports, faces I had met or known; I saw the whole of the movement founded by Libertad dragged into the scum of society by a kind of madness; and nobody could do anything about it, least of all myself. The theoreticians, terrified, headed for cover. It was like a collective suicide. The newspapers put out a special edition to announce a particularly daring outrage, committed by bandits in a car on the Rue Ordener in Montmartre, against a bank cashier carrying half a million francs. Reading the descriptions, I recognized Raymond and Octave Garnier, the lad with piercing black eyes who distrusted intellectuals. I guessed the logic of their struggle: in order to save Bonnot, now hunted and trapped, they had to find either money, money to get away from it all, or else a speedy death in this battle against the whole of society. Out of solidarity they rushed into this squalid, doomed struggle with their little revolvers and their petty, trigger-happy arguments. And now there were five of them, lost, and once again without money even to attempt flight, and against them Money was ranged—100,000 francs' reward for the first informer. They were wandering in the city-without-escape, ready to be killed somewhere, anywhere, in a tram or a café, content to feel utterly cornered, expendable, alone in defiance of a horrible world. Out of solidarity, only to share this bitter joy of trying to be killed, without any illusions about the struggle (as a good many told me when I met them in prison afterwards), others joined the first few, such as red-haired René (he too was a restless spirit) and poor little André Soudy. I had often met Soudy at public meetings in the Latin Quarter. He was a perfect example of the crushed childhood of the back-alleys. He grew up on the pavements: T.B. at thirteen, V.D. at eighteen, convicted at twenty (for stealing a bicycle). I had brought him books and oranges in the Ténon Hospital. Pale, sharp-featured, his accent common, his eyes a gentle grey, he would say, 'I'm an unlucky blighter, nothing I can do about it.' He earned his living in grocers' shops in the Rue Mouffetard, where the assistants rose at six, arranged the display at seven, and went upstairs to sleep in a garret after 9 p.m., dog-tired, having seen their bosses defrauding housewives all day by weighing the beans short, watering the milk, wine, and paraffin, and falsifying the labels. . . . He was sentimental; the laments of street-singers moved him to the verge of tears, he could not approach a woman without making a fool of himself, and half a day in the open air of the meadows gave him a lasting dose of intoxication. He experienced a new lease of life if he heard someone call him 'comrade' or explain that one could, one must, 'become a new man'. Back in his shop, he began to give double measures of beans to the housewives, who thought him a little mad. The bitterest joking helped him to live, convinced as he was that he was not long for this world, 'seeing the price of medicine'.

One morning, a group of enormous police officers burst into our lodgings at the press, revolvers in hand. A bare-footed little girl of seven had opened when the bell rang, and was terrified by this irruption of armed giants. Jouin, the deputy Director of the *Sûreté*, a thin gentleman with a long, gloomy face, polite and almost likeable, came in later, searched the building, and spoke to me amiably, of ideas, of Sébastien Faure[1] whom he admired, of the deplorable way in which the outlaws were discrediting a great ideal.

'Believe me', he sighed, 'the world won't change so quickly.' He seemed to me neither malicious nor hypocritical, only a deeply distressed man doing a job conscientiously. In the afternoon he

---

[1] Sébastien Faure (1858–1942): after a period of Guesdism, became an anarcho-communist writer and publicist; editor of *L'Encyclopédie Anarchiste*.

sent for me, called me into his office, leant on his elbows under the
green lampshade, and talked to me somewhat after this fashion:

'I know you pretty well; I should be most sorry to cause you any
trouble—which could be very serious. You know these circles,
these men, those who are far away from you and those who have a
gun in your back, more or less. They are all absolutely finished, I can
assure you. Stay here for an hour and we'll discuss them. Nobody
will ever know anything of it and I guarantee that there'll be no
trouble at all for you.'

I was ashamed, unbelievably ashamed, for him, for myself, for
everybody, so ashamed that I felt no shock of indignation, nor any
fear. I told him, 'I am sure that you must be embarrassed yourself,
talking to me like this.'

'But not at all!' All the same, he was doing the dirty job as if he
were overwhelmed by it.

In a cell of La Santé, behind a wall in the specially guarded
section reserved for men condemned to death, I began to study
seriously. The worst of it all was the constant hunger. From a legal
point of view I could easily have cleared myself, since the paper's
management and editorship was in the name of Rirette; but I was
determined to assume all responsibility.

The murders and collective suicide continued. Of these I picked
up only distant echoes. Meanwhile the reward of 100,000 francs
was burrowing into the brains of certain 'conscious egoists', and the
arrests began; Bonnot was besieged for a whole day at Choisy-le-
Roi, defending himself with a pistol and writing, in the intervals of
the firing, a letter which absolved his comrades of complicity; he lay
between two mattresses to protect himself against the final onslaught,
and was killed, or else killed himself, no one really knows which.
Octave Garnier and René Valet, caught up at Nogent-sur-Marne
in a villa where they were roughing it with their women, underwent
an even longer siege, taking on the civil police, the *gendarmerie* and
the Zouaves. They fired hundreds of bullets, viewing their attackers
as murderers (and themselves as victims) and, when the house was
dynamited, blew out their own brains. Rebellion's just another
dead-end, nothing we can do about it; we may as well hurry up and
re-load! At heart, they resembled the *dynamiteros* of Spain who stood
up in front of tanks shouting *Viva la Fai!*; bidding defiance to the
world. Raymond, betrayed by a woman for a considerable sum, was

surprised and arrested. André Soudy, betrayed by an anarchist writer, was arrested at Berck-Plage where he was nursing his tuberculosis. Edouard Carouy, who had no part in these events, was betrayed by the family hiding him, and arrested, although armed like the others, without any attempt at self-defence; this athletic young man was exceptional in being quite incapable of murder, though bent on suicide. The others too were all betrayed. Some of the anarchists shot at those informers, one of whom was killed. Nonetheless, the shrewdest one of them continued to edit a little Individualist review on the blue cover of which the New Man could be seen struggling up from the shadows.

My examination was short and pointless, since I was actually accused of no offence. The first magistrate who interrogated me for identification purposes, an ageing, refined personage, nearly threw a fit of temper as he meditated on my future. 'A revolutionary at twenty! Yes—and you will be a plutocrat at forty!' 'I do not think so,' I replied in all seriousness, and I am still thankful to him for that outburst of revealing anger. I endured the long, enriching experience of cell-life, allowed no visits or newspapers, with only the squalid statutory rations (which were picked at by all the thieves on the staff) and some good books. I understood, and ever since have always missed, the old Christian custom of retreats which men spent in monasteries, meditating face to face with themselves and with God, in other words with the vast living solitude of the universe. It will be good if that custom is revived, in the time when man can at last devote thought to himself. Some very simple rules will suffice for that end: physical and intellectual discipline, exercise (absolutely necessary for the man in a cell), walks for meditation (I did my six miles around the cell every day), intellectual work, and recourse to that exaltation, or slight spiritual tipsiness, which is furnished by great works of poetry. Altogether, I spent around fifteen months in solitary confinement, in various conditions, some of them hellish.

The trial of 1913 assembled on the benches of the Assize Court about twenty prisoners, of whom maybe half a dozen were innocent. In the course of a month, 300 contradictory witnesses paraded to the bar of the court. Against the half-dozen main culprits there was no worthwhile evidence since they denied everything. Six witnesses out of forty contradicted each other in their identifications of the most incriminated defendants; but sometimes, in this hotchpotch of confused testimony, a single word would hit the mark and convince the jury. Someone had recalled a word pronounced with a certain accent, a shout of Soudy's ('The man with the rifle') in the middle of a minor street-fight: 'Come on, fellows, let's blow!' And no further doubt was possible because of the tone, the accent, the slang. It was hardly a piece of scientific evidence, but it was human evidence all the same.

On some days, it became a trial of the police, who were pumping a star witness, an old half-blind, half-deaf peasant woman, to make her identify photographs. The head of the *Sûreté*, Xavier Guichard, a man of aesthetic pretensions, admitted having hit a woman, shouting at her: 'You're young. You can still become a tart! As for your kids, they can go to hell on the Public Assistance!'

Dr. Paul, an expert in forensic medicine, pomaded, elegant and somewhat fleshy, lectured on the corpses with visible relish. He had been conducting post-mortems on all the murder victims of Paris for the last forty years—after which he would go off to a good lunch, select a tie to wear for tea and, leaning against the mantelpiece of some drawing-room, recount his 10,000 anecdotes of crime. Beaming M. Bertillon, the inventor of anthropometry, modestly admitted that he could be mistaken over finger-prints: there was a probability of error of about one in a billion. The lawyer who, in an attempt to embarrass Bertillon, had elicited this bombshell from him, could not recover from his own confusion.

The principal defendants, Raymond Callemin, André Soudy, Monier, a gardener, and Eugène Dieudonné, a joiner, denied everything and, in theory, had a plausible case. In reality, irrefutable signs of guilt were killing them, apart from Dieudonné who was in fact innocent, not of all complicity but of the particular aspect in which he stood accused. His arrest had arisen from a resemblance between his dark eyes and another pair of eyes, still darker, which were in the graveyard. He alone shouted his innocence in frenzy, with no sign of apathy; which made a striking contrast with the real culprits, insolent and jeering, whose whole behaviour was a calm challenge: 'We dare you to prove it.' Since everyone knew the truth, proof was superfluous, as they themselves were aware, but they continued acting after their vocation as desperadoes; smiling, blustering, taking notes. Raymond 'denied the right of the court to judge', but weakened in the face of authority, directing little sallies,

like a peevish schoolboy, at the President of the court. Soudy,
cross-examined as to whether a rifle was his property, replied, 'Not
mine, but as you know, Proudhon said that property is theft.'

The prosecution had intended to unearth (for the benefit of the
public) an authentically novelettish conspiracy, assigning me to
the role of its 'theoretician', but had to abandon this project after the
second session. I had believed that I would manage to be acquitted,
but now understood that in such an atmosphere the acquittal of a
young Russian, and a militant at that, was impossible, despite the
entire clarity of the facts of the case; for no direct or indirect responsibility for these tragedies could be laid against me. I was there only
because of my categorical refusal to talk; that is, to become an
informer. I demolished the prosecution's case on various points of
detail (which was easy). I defended our principles—of uninhibited
analysis, solidarity and rebellion (which was much more difficult);
and I annoyed the 'innocent' culprits by demonstrating that society
manufactured crime, criminals, desperate ideas, suicides, and the
poison of money.

Bonds of genuine sympathy were formed between the defendants
and their counsel—except for Paul Reynaud, who defended some
accessory or other with reasonable skill, but still remained aloof.
Moro-Giafferi, leonine in appearance, a Napoleon in a neck-tie,
thundered on behalf of Dieudonné. His grand, arm-waving elo-
quence, invoking the crucified Christ, the French Revolution, the
grief of mothers, the nightmare fears of children, sickened me at first.
By the end of twenty minutes of it, I was hypnotized, just like the
jury and the gallery, by the power of his astounding dialectic. A
relationship almost of friendliness drew me towards Adad (who
committed suicide in Paris some years ago—and what better course
was there for an old, penniless lawyer?) and to César Campinchi, a
cool, brilliant debater who appealed only to reason, though with a
certain irony. I was to see him again much later, seriously wounded
in the First World War, and Minister of the Navy in the Second.
(One of those who favoured resistance to the death, he died under
house-arrest in Marseilles in 1941, just as I was embarking for
America.) I reflected that if these desperadoes had been able, before
their struggle, to meet men like this, understanding, cultured and
liberal-minded, both from inclination and by profession (perhaps
more apparently than really so, but even that would have been

enough), they would not have entered upon their paths of darkness. The most immediate cause of their revolt and ruin seemed to me to lie in their isolation from human contacts. They were living in no company but their own.

During the trial we were confined in the tiny cells of the Conciergerie, dark holes honeycombed in the ancient stonework of the same buildings where tourists still go to visit the prison of the Girondins and Marie-Antoinette's cell. Going to court, we would reassemble, escorted by *Gardes Républicains*, beneath old archways which gave us the feeling of being underground. We would walk up a corkscrew staircase inside one of the pointed towers which overlooked the Seine and, passing through a little side-door, enter the great court-room of the Assizes, which would be buzzing with the presence of a crowd. The last session took twenty hours and the verdict was announced at dawn. We waited for it, sitting together in two anterooms, in a strange atmosphere rather like our old meetings in Montmartre. The usual arguments started all over again. Our lawyers, pale-faced, came to fetch us. Then, the sweltering silent court-room, and twenty prisoners, tense, erect and hard-faced. Four death-sentences, several condemned to hard labour for life. The only acquittals were for the women, who were in any case innocent, but apart from this Parisian juries were reluctant to find women guilty. (They had acquitted Mme Steinheil, who was accused of murdering her husband; they acquitted Mme Joseph Caillaux, wife of the former Prime Minister, who had killed the editor of *Le Figaro*; later they acquitted the anarchist Germaine Berton, who had killed a Royalist leader.)

Dieudonné was condemned to death even though no one doubted his innocence (which was compromised by his faulty alibis); once more he shouted his guiltlessness and, alone among the accused, seemed on the verge of collapse. Raymond, who had demanded an acquittal, jumped up, his face crimson, and interjected violently: 'Dieudonné is innocent—it's me, me that did the shooting!' The President requested him to sit down, for the pleadings were over and confession no longer had any juridical value.

I myself received five years' solitary confinement, but I had managed to get Rirette acquitted; two revolvers discovered on the premises of the paper served to justify my conviction, which was provoked, no doubt, by my calm hostility during the hearings.

I found this justice nauseating; it was fundamentally more criminal than the worst criminals. This was incontestably obvious; it was just that I was an enemy, of a different sort from the guilty ones. As I pondered the judgement, its enormity did not surprise me. I only wondered if I would be able to live that long, for I was very weak—at any rate physically. I made up my mind to live it out, and was very ashamed to be thinking of myself like this, next to others who. . . .

We said our farewells to one another beneath the high vaults of the Terror. Through a frightful slip, while I was talking to Raymond I used an expression for which I have never forgiven myself. 'You live and learn,' I remarked, I cannot now say why, perhaps because I had just decided in favour of living. He stared, and then broke into laughter: 'Living is just the problem!'

'Forgive me,' I broke out.

He shrugged his shoulders. 'Of course, man! My mind's set.'

An hour later, in the pale light of morning, I was once again pacing around my suffocating cell. Somebody was sobbing incessantly in the next cell, and it got on my nerves. A little old warder, kindly and sad, came in, averting his face: 'Carouy (Edouard) is dying. Can you hear him?' I could indeed hear a queer panting noise, coming from beyond the sobs next door. 'That's him gasping away. . . . He took some poison which he'd got hidden in the soles of his shoes. . . . Well, well, what a life!' He had not been condemned to death.

The obviously innocent Dieudonné was reprieved, in other words given forced labour for life. For eighteen years he fought fantastically against his servitude, escaping several times and spending years in solitary confinement. After his final escape he reached Brazil. Through the good offices of Albert Londres,[1] he was able to return to France.

Raymond was so stolid in the death-cell that they did not keep the date of the execution from him. He spent the waiting period in reading. In front of the guillotine he noticed the group of reporters and shouted to them: 'A nice sight, isn't it?'

Soudy's last-minute request was for a cup of coffee with cream and some fancy rolls, his last pleasure on earth, appropriate enough for that grey morning when people were happily eating their

[1] i.e. through a Press campaign on his behalf.

breakfasts in the little *bistros*. It must have been too early, for they could only find him a little black coffee. 'Out of luck', he remarked, 'right to the end.' He was fainting with fright and nerves, and had to be supported while he was going down the stairs; but he controlled himself and, when he saw the clearness of the sky over the chestnut trees, hummed a sentimental street-song: 'Hail, O last morning of mine'. Monier, usually taciturn, was crazy with anxiety, but mastered himself and became calm. I learned these details only a long time afterwards.

So ended the second explosion of anarchism in France. The first, equally hopeless, was that of 1891–4, signalled by the outrages of Ravachol, Emile Henry, Vaillant, and Caserio.[1] The same psychological features and the same social factors were present in both phases; the same exacting idealism, in the breasts of uncomplicated men whose energy could find no outlet in achieving a higher dignity or sensibility, because any such outlet was physically denied to them. Conscious of their frustration, they battled like madmen and were beaten down. In those times the world was an integrated structure, so stable in appearance that no possibility of substantial change was visible within it. As it progressed up and up, and on and on, masses of people who lay in its path were all the while being crushed. The harsh condition of the workers improved only very slowly, and for the vast majority of the proletariat there was no way out. The declassed elements on the proletarian fringe found all roads barred to them except those which led to squalor and degradation. Above the heads of these masses, wealth accumulated, insolent and proud. The consequences of this situation arose inexorably: crime, class-struggles and their trail of bloody strikes, and frenzied battles of One against All. These struggles also testified to the failure of an ideology. Between the copious theorizing of Peter Kropotkin and Elisée Reclus, and the rage of Albert Libertad, the collapse of anarchism in the bourgeois jungle was now obvious. Kropótkin had grown up in a completely different Europe, one less stable, where the

[1] Ravachol exploded bombs in the homes of two officials connected with a recent anarchist trial; he was guillotined in 1892. Vaillant was executed for a bomb-explosion in the Chamber of Deputies in December 1893, which killed nobody. Emile Henry threw a bomb in the Café Terminus, which (much against his intentions) caused only minor injuries; executed in May 1894. Caserio, a young Italian anarchist, stabbed President Carnot to death in June of the same year.

ideal of liberty seemed to have some future and people believed in revolution and education. Reclus had fought for the Commune; the confidence inspired by the greatness of its thwarted vision had lasted him for the rest of his days; he believed in the saving power of science. On the eve of war in Europe, science was functioning solely to assist the progress of a traditionalist and barbaric social order. One felt the approach of an era of violence: inescapable.

In other lands, namely Poland and Russia, the revolutionary movement confronted régimes of a mongrel character, half-absolutist and half-capitalist: there the movement was able to concentrate these diffuse energies and channel them along ways of sacrifice, at the end of which lay victories that were not only possible but popularly desired.

The men, the situations and the conflicts were almost the same, only with a historical complexion different from that in France, the 'Rentier State' as Yves Guyot[1] put it. In Poland, Joseph Pilsudski's Socialist Party (P.P.S.) was raiding Treasury vans and tax-offices, attacking governors and policemen. In Russia, the Social-Revolutionary Party was conducting a similar campaign, and the combat groups of the Bolshevik fraction of Social-Democrats—including the extraordinary terrorist Kamo,[2] the intellectual and laboratory-maker Krassin, the skilful organizer Koba-Stalin, the man of action Tsintsadze and the courier Litvinov—were conducting the struggle for the Party's income on the highways, the public places of Tiflis and the ships of Baku, bomb and revolver in hand. In Italy, in *Pagine Libere* of 1 January 1911, a young Socialist agitator, Benito Mussolini, was chanting the praises of the anarchist desperadoes.

Of this hard childhood, this troubled adolescence, all those terrible years, I regret nothing as far as I am myself concerned. I am sorry for those who grow up in this world without ever experiencing the cruel side of it, without knowing utter frustration and the

[1] Yves Guyot (1843–1928): free-trade economist, Deputy, and Minister of Public Works from 1889 to 1892.

[2] 'Kamo': the Party name of S. A. Ter-Petrosian (1882–1922), Bolshevik revolutionary who committed numerous robberies, was four times sentenced to death, and feigned insanity for four years in Germany in order to prevent his extradition to Imperial Russia. 'Koté' Tsintsadze, Kamo's less sensational colleague, undertook similar activities in the pre-revolutionary period; later became a prominent Georgian Bolshevik, at odds with Stalin; was arrested in 1929, and died in captivity in 1931.

necessity of fighting, however blindly, for mankind. Any regret I have is only for the energies wasted in struggles which were bound to be fruitless. These struggles have taught me that, in any man, the best and the worst live side by side, and sometimes mingle—and that what is worst comes through the corruption of what is best.

2

LIVE TO PREVAIL

1912–1919

Of prison I shall say here only a little. It burdened me with an experience so heavy, so intolerable to endure, that long afterwards, when I resumed writing, my first book (a novel) amounted to an effort to free myself from this inward nightmare, as well as performing a duty towards all those who will never so free themselves (*Les Hommes dans la Prison*). It is reasonably well known in France and the Spanish-speaking countries. In the jail where I did the most time, there were three or four hundred of us in torment, mostly doing long sentences between eight years and life. Among these men I encountered the same proportions of weak spirits, human scum, average types, and exceptional men, gifted with some spark of divinity, as anywhere else. Generally speaking, with only a few exceptions, the warders, of whatever grade, were on a much lower level. They were criminals, respectably but obviously so, gifted with a guaranteed immunity from punishment and super-annuation at the end of their unspeakable lives. They included sadists, inflexible hypocrites, morons, racketeers, scroungers and thieves; and, incredible as it may seem, some who were good and almost intelligent.

The French prison itself, organized as it is according to ancient regulations, is nothing but an absurd machine for breaking those men who are thrown into it. Life there is a kind of mechanized madness; everything in it seems to have been conceived in a spirit of mean calculation how best to enfeeble, stupefy and numb the prisoner, and poison him with an inexpressible bitterness; his return to normal life must evidently be made quite impossible. This end is attained by an organization impregnated with the penal traditions of the pre-revolutionary order, with the religious idea of chastisement (an idea which now, lacking any basis in faith, is only a psychological justification for social sadism), and with the footling detail of our vast modern administrations. The hotchpotch mixing of malefactors, semi-lunatics, and victims of all descriptions; under-nourishment; the rule of complete and perpetual silence imposed at every moment upon all common activity; arbitrary punishments designed to humiliate, torture, and weaken; prohibition of any knowledge whatsoever concerning life outside, even if it be war, invasion, or national peril; the maximum possible deprivation of intellectual exercise, prohibition of study, even of reading more than one book a week, to be chosen from the idiotic novelettes of the prison library (fortunately it also contained Balzac). In the long run this treadmill turns out sexual inverts, cracked brains, worthless and depraved beings incapable of rehabilitation, dedicated in short to joining the ranks of tramps in *La Maub*'; or else parasitical toughs, hardened by suffering, who keep up their own special tradition. Cynics, but loyal to one another, such men preserve their 'emancipated' dignity with no illusions about either society or themselves. From this class professional criminals are recruited.

Truly wonderful was the struggle waged by some there, a pitiful minority, to preserve their capacity for living. I was very definitely one of these. For this purpose a considerable degree of a particular kind of will-power was necessary: passive to all appearance, yet artful and incorrigible. When we saw the 'new ones' arrive, we knew which of them, whether young or old, were not going to live. We were never wrong in these forecasts, but they had been wrong about me; I had appeared fated to die before long. A former budding lawyer of the Parisian bar, the victim of a shocking tragedy of middle-class life now serving a life sentence, had managed, with the aid of corruption, to found an efficiently concealed clandestine library of good scientific and philosophical works. His friendship and this precious food of the spirit was, I know, my salvation. In the poky, solitary cell in which each of us slept, whose window faced the sky, I was able to read only for a few moments in the morning, and for a few more in the evening. During my compulsory labour in the print-shop, I used to set up notes and comments in galley form for certain comrades to read. From the moment that thought and learning were possible for us, life was also possible, and worthwhile. The keen edge of this slow torture blunted itself against us, against myself especially. I was confident of beating the treadmill.

The outbreak of war was sudden, like an unexpected storm in a season of clear weather. We had not been able to observe its early symptoms, but knew of it through the unaccustomed panic which seized the warders (since many of them were liable to be called up). And this storm interpreted the world to us. For me, it heralded another, purifying tempest: the Russian Revolution. Revolutionaries knew quite well that the autocratic Empire, with its hangmen, its pogroms, its finery, its famines, its Siberian jails and ancient iniquity, could never survive the war. A gleam of light was at last visible: this would be the beginning of everything, the prodigious first day of Creation. An end to deadlock! This huge gateway would be open towards the future. No more problems now about the aims of the struggle or the rules of life, for the Russian Revolution was calling from the heart of the future.

For the time being, the sudden conversion to fratricidal patriotism of the German Social-Democrats and the French syndicalists, Socialists and anarchists, was incomprehensible to us. Did they then believe nothing of what they preached yesterday? Had we been right after all in refusing to trust them? Passionate singings of the 'Marseillaise', from crowds seeing troops off to the train, drifted across even to our jail. We could also hear shouts of '*To Berlin! To Berlin!*' This lunacy, which we could not explain, was the peak and climax of a permanent social crisis. At the risk of spending between sixty and eighty hours in the dungeons, with consequently almost certain death from tuberculosis, the half-dozen of us comrades who were scattered around the central prison carried on a feverish exchange of theses. Gustave Hervé, who a while before was proclaiming insurrection against war, was now demanding to be enlisted in the army; his *Guerre Sociale* changed its title to *La Victoire*. They were tricksters, nothing more: 'It's not the weathercock that's moving, it's the wind.' Fundamentally, the crowds were being swept along by an immense ignorance of the reality of modern war, whose existence had been forgotten since 1870. The infantrymen went off to the front line in their scarlet trousers, and the cadets of St. Cyr in their white gloves and plumed *képis*, just as though it were a parade. Over the whole of Europe, the masses were letting their suppressed energies run free. France forgot the disparity of forces whereby her 38,000,000 inhabitants, with a low birth-rate, engaged in mortal struggle against a fecund Germany of 60,000,000.

Our opposition to the war was essentially a matter of human feeling. The two coalitions had practically the same social organization: republics based on high finance, more or less monarchical but governed, with the sole exception of Russia, by bourgeois parliaments. On our side and on theirs, the same liberties equally stifled by exploitation, the same slow progress that crushed human beings. German militarism was a hideous peril, but we foresaw that an Allied victory would establish over the Continent a French militarism whose capacity for reactionary idiocy was revealed in the Dreyfus affair (not to mention General Galliffet, of bloody memory).[1] The invasion of Belgium was abominable, but the memory of the obliteration of the two little South African Republics by British arms was still fresh in our minds (1902). The recent conflicts over Tripolitania and Morocco showed that butchery was being unleashed over Europe in the cause of a redivision of colonies. The prospect of victory by either side appalled us. How was it that among so many victims, no men were to be found brave enough to rush across from either 'enemy' side and hail one another as brothers? In asking each other that question we experienced a new despair.

Without our knowing anything of it, the line of invasion rolled towards Paris. If we had been outside jail, I think that we would have followed the stream and felt immediately that, despite all theoretical considerations, a country under attack, unless it is at the height of a social crisis, must defend itself; primitive reflexes, infinitely stronger than principles, are at play; the sentiment of 'the nation in danger' prevails.

The prison is situated on an island in the Seine, twenty-five miles or so from the Marne. While the battle of the Marne was on, the population of Melun began to flee. No one believed in victory any longer, and Paris seemed lost. We learned that the prison would not be evacuated and that the fighting would probably reach the banks of the Seine. We would find ourselves cooped inside this cage,

---

[1] General Galliffet (1830–1909): noted for the pitiless severity with which he suppressed the Paris Commune. Later (1899) appointed for a time as Minister of War.

right in the middle of a battlefield. Warders and prisoners alike were sick with fear. I was not. On the contrary, I felt an ecstatic happiness at the thought that the cannonades would destroy this preposterous treadmill, even if we were entombed under the rubble as a result. The fighting moved away; everything went on exactly as before.

There were plenty of deaths in the jail. I saw young men gripped, three months before their release was due, with a kind of fever, losing their biological adaptation to the prison environment, awakening once more, eyes glittering, to some sort of life, and then suddenly dying in three days as though from an inner convulsion. I myself collapsed from undernourishment after six or eight months; I could no longer remain standing, and was admitted to the infirmary where broth and milk set me back on my feet within a fortnight. Then my sickness started again. On the first occasion I was afraid that I might be bound for the little reserved cemetery near by, thereby giving the convict in charge of grave-digging his little walk in the open air and his customary quart of wine (his rewarding position was a source of envy to us). Then I adapted myself, and made up my mind to survive. From beyond my conscious will I could feel another will, deeper and more powerful, asserting itself within me.

There came a certain winter dawn that arose over the Seine, over the tall poplars that I loved, over the sleeping, shabby little town where the only faces that passed by at this hour were humble, hardened and topped by helmets. I departed, alone, amazingly light-footed upon the ground, taking nothing with me, without any real joy, obsessed by the idea that, behind me, the treadmill was continuing endlessly to turn, crushing human beings. In the grey morning, I bought a cup of coffee in the station café. The proprietor came up to me with a kind of sympathy.

'Out of jail?'

'Yes.'

He wagged his head. Might he be interested in 'my crime', or my future? He leant over: 'You in a hurry? There's one hell of a brothel near here. . . .'

The first man I had met, in the mist of a gloomy bridge, had been a soldier with a mutilated face; this fat procurer was the second. Was it always to be the world-without-escape? What good

was the war doing? Had the dance of death taught nothing to anyone?

Paris was leading a double life. Walking along, spellbound, I
stopped in front of the lowly windows of the Belleville shops. The
colours of the darning-wools were a wonder, the mother-of-pearl
penknives enthralled me, and for several minutes I contemplated the
picture-postcards of soldiers and their fiancées sending each other
kisses through a messenger-dove, holding an envelope in its beak.
Men and women passing by—how astonishingly real! A cat, sitting
comfortably on the hot window-ledge of a bakery, with the smell
of warm bread escaping outside! I smiled at it drunkenly. Belleville
was the same, only sadder and poorer. 'Funerals in twenty-four
hours, moderate prices, payment by instalments. . . .' A marble-
cutter was displaying his enamel lockets; all of them represented
young soldiers. Housewives in shawls were coming from the town
hall, each bringing her sack of potatoes and her bucket of coal. The
grey façades of the Rue Julien Lacroix oozed out their ancient
misery in the cold.

People explained life to me: 'You know, it's almost a merry life.
Every house has several dead, but the men have been away for so
long that their wives are living with other men. There's no unemployment, there's a craze on for foreign labour, wages are
high. . . . There's heaps of soldiers from every country in the world;
some of them have money, the English and the Canadians, there's
never been so much love-making in all the odd corners. Pigalle,
Clichy, the Montmartre district, the fine boulevards, all those
parasites are amusing themselves: after us, the deluge! The war's
business, old chap. You'll see people are doing well out of it, nobody wants it to end any more. The troops are fed up, of course, but
the lads home on leave are showing off. "Nothing to do about it,
don't bother to try understanding it," that's what they say. Almereyda's running a daily paper in the smart end of town, he has two
cars and a big house . . . Jules Guesde and Marcel Sembat[1] are in
the Government; a Socialist is defending Jaurès' murderer—
Maître Zévaès, you know him. Chose, the Illegalist, has won
the Military Medal. Kropotkin has signed an appeal for the

---

[1] Marcel Sembat (1862–1922): revolutionary Socialist initially, then a leader of
the French Socialist Party and member of the 'Cabinet of national defence' after
1914.

war-effort, along with Jean Grave. Machin is in the munitions business. . . . What's that you say? The Russian Revolution? Poor old
chap, you're off the track. The Russians are solid, out there in the
Carpathians and, believe me, all that's nowhere near changing.
Only one thing to do: feather your own nest. It's a lot easier than
before the war.'

That was the sort of talk I heard. I watched the skinny Algerians
sluggishly sweeping the muck in the streets, and it never stopped, the
muck actually grew. Shivering Indo-Chinese, in helmet and sheepskin, guarded the Préfecture and La Santé. The *Métro* was carting
around its dense crowds, couple upon couple, convalescents lived
out their boredom at hospital windows, a disfigured soldier hugged
the waist of a working-girl under the bare trees of the Luxembourg
Gardens, and the cafés were crowded. The outskirts rotted in deep
darkness, but the centre of town, dotted with illuminations, throbbed
on well into the night. 'Nowadays, see, there are only two poles to
the world, love and money—and money comes first.'

I made inquiries about the Russians. The terrorist Savinkov[1]
was recruiting for the Foreign Legion. A number of Bolsheviks had
been killed at the front, as volunteers. Plekhanov was advocating the
defence of the Empire. Trotsky, escorted to the Spanish frontier by
two police inspectors, was about to be interned somewhere in
America. Almereyda, in his combined office, flat and private empire
in the smart boulevards, more elegant, more pushful than just lately,
told me that he had given up trapping police-spies in the working-
class movement, in case he did more harm than good: 'There are
too many of them!' The war was leading nowhere; he was working
for peace, whose supporters were growing and held the future in
their hands. 'Poincaré and Joffre are finished. . . . Soon everything's
going to change here.'

Certain people were harsh towards him: 'He's sold out to a
bankers' clique; he's got the Chief of Police in his pocket.' Maître
César Campinchi explained to me that France had been bled white,
but would win in a year or two, with the Americans on her side. I
went to see a performance of *The Bluebird*: in the theatre, couples,

---

[1] Boris V. Savinkov (1879–1925): Social-Revolutionary leader and terrorist,
assassin of Grand Duke Sergei and Minister von Plehve. Later War Minister
under Kerensky. Imprisoned for ten years in 1924 for conspiratorial work against
Soviet Government. Died in prison, reportedly by his own hand.

couples and uniforms. . . . Everything reinforced the mad sensation that we were falling into the abyss.

Farewell, Paris! I took the Barcelona express. The trains and railway stations unveiled another face of the war: the soldiers. They were toughness itself, rough-hewn, stiff, and uncomplicated as a mass of stone: ravaged. Beyond the Pyrenees, vistas of peace and abundance opened anew, with no wounded invalids, no soldiers on leave counting up the hours, no funeral black, no frenzy for life on the eve of death. In the little villages of Catalonia the squares, lined with tall trees and fringed by little cafés under arcades, breathed an air of nonchalance. Barcelona was making merry, with its Ramblas[1] illuminated at night and luxuriously sunlit by day, full of birds and women. Here too the cornucopia of the war was gushing away. Both for the Allies and for the Central Powers, the factories were working full blast and the companies were positively coining gold. Zest for life shining at you from faces and shop-windows, oozing at you from banking-houses, smacking you on the back. Everything was going mad.

I underwent a phase of intense wretchedness. The treadmill that crushed human beings still revolved inside me. I found no happiness in awakening to life, free and privileged alone among my conscript generation, in this contented city. I felt a vague compunction at it all. Why was I there, in these cafés, on these golden sands, while so many others were bleeding in the trenches of a whole continent? How was I worth more than they? Why was I excluded from the common fate? I came across deserters who were happy to be beyond the frontier, safe at last. I admitted their right to safety, but inwardly I was horrified at the idea that people could fight so fiercely for their own lives when what was at stake was the life of everyone; a limitless suffering to be endured commonly, shared and drunk to the last drop. This feeling was in sharp opposition to my reasoned thought, but much stronger than it. I can see now that this need for sharing in the common fate has always held me, and has been one of my deepest sources of action. I worked in print-shops, went to bull-fights, resumed my reading, clambered up mountains, dallied in cafés to watch Castilian, Sevillan, Andalusian, or Catalan girls at their dancing, and I felt that it would be impossible for me to live like this. All I could think of was the men at war, who kept calling to me.

[1] Boulevard thoroughfares of Barcelona.

It is certain that I would have finally enlisted in some army or other, if certain long-awaited events had not at last been simultaneously set in motion.

In *Tierra y Libertad* I wrote my first article under the name of 'Victor Serge', in defence of Friedrich Adler,[1] who had just been condemned to death in Vienna: a few months before he had assassinated Count Stürgkh, one of the politicians responsible for the war. My next article was on the fall of the Russian autocracy. Then, awaited so keenly that we eventually wondered whether we should still believe in it, the Revolution appeared, and the improbable became reality. Reading the dispatches from Russia, we were transfigured; for the images that they conveyed were simple, concrete. A minute clarity was shed over things; the world was no longer impelled along by helpless lunacy. Certain French Individualists mocked me with their store of cynical stock phrases: 'Revolutions are useless. They will not change human nature. Afterwards reaction sets in and everything starts all over again. I've only got my own skin; I'm not marching for wars or for revolutions, thank you.'

'In fact', I would answer them, 'you people are no longer good for anything. You're at the end of your tether: you won't march for anything any more—because you yourselves are not worth marching for. . . . Your kind are the products of the degeneration of everything: of the bourgeoisie, of bourgeois ideas, of the working-class movement, of anarchism. . . .'

My break with these 'comrades', who were no more than the shadows of comrades, became complete: it was useless to argue, and difficult to endure one another. The Spaniards, even the workers on the shop floor beside me, who were no militants, instinctively understood the Petrograd days, since their imagination transposed those events to Madrid and Barcelona. The monarchy of Alfonso XIII was no more popular or stable than that of Nicholas II. The revolutionary tradition of Spain, like that of Russia, went back to the time of Bakunin. Similar social causes were operating in both countries: agrarian problems, retarded industrialization, a political

[1] Friedrich Adler (1879–1960): Austro-Marxist, son of the founder of the Austrian Socialist Party, Victor Adler; his death-sentence was later commuted to imprisonment. Released at the end of the war, he became President of the Workers' and Soldiers' Councils. Subsequently, General Secretary for many years of the Second International.

régime at least a century and a half behind Western Europe. The wartime industrial and commercial boom strengthened the bourgeoisie, especially that of Catalonia, which was hostile to the old land-owning aristocracy and to the utterly hidebound royal administration; it also expanded the energies and appetites of a young proletariat which had had no time to form a working-class aristocracy, that is, to become bourgeoisified. Knowledge of the war aroused a disposition towards violence, and the low wages (I earned four pesetas a day, about eighty American cents) stimulated the workers to press their immediate demands.

From one week to another the horizon became visibly clearer. Within three months the mood of the Barcelona working class was transformed. Their fighting spirit mounted. The C.N.T. gathered strength. I belonged to a tiny trade union in the print-shop. Without any increase in the number of activists (there must have been about thirty of us) its influence advanced to such an extent that the whole body of workers seemed to have woken up. Three months after the news of the Russian Revolution, the Comitè Obrero began to prepare a revolutionary general strike, entered negotiations for a political alliance with the Catalan liberal bourgeoisie, and calmly planned the overthrow of the monarchy. The Comitè Obrero's programme of demands, drawn up in June 1917 and published in *Solidaridad Obrera*, was borrowed from the accumulated experience of the Russian Soviets. I was soon to discover that in France too, the same, intensely alive electric current was crossing from the trenches to the factories, the same violent hopes were coming to birth.

At the Café Espagnol, on the Paralelo, that crowded thoroughfare with its blazing lights of evening, near the horrible *barrio chino* whose mouldering alleys were full of half-naked girls lurking in doorways that gaped into hell-holes—it was here that I met militants arming for the approaching battle. They spoke enthusiastically of those who would fall in that fight, they dealt out Browning revolvers, and baited, as we all did, the anxious spies at the neighbouring table. In a revolutionary side-street, with a *Guardia Civil* barracks on one side and poor tenements on the other, I found Barcelona's hero of the hour, the quickening spirit, the uncrowned leader, the fearless man of politics who distrusted politicians: Salvador Seguí, affectionately nicknamed '*Noy del Sucre*'.[1] We used

[1] i.e. 'Sugar boy'; so called because of his fondness for sugar as a child.

to dine together in the faint flicker of a paraffin lamp. The meal, set on the table of smooth wood, would consist of tomatoes, onions, coarse red wine, and a country-style soup. The child's underclothes would be hanging on a line of string and Teresita would be nursing the baby. The balcony was open on the menacing darkness, on the barracks packed with killers, on the red, starry halo of the Rambla. There, we examined the various problems: the Russian Revolution, the coming general strike, alliance with the Catalan liberals, the trade unions, the ingrained anarchist hostility to any fresh forms of organization. As to the Russian Revolution, I was certain only on one point: that it would not stop half-way. The avalanche would carry on rolling right to the end. What end? 'The peasants will seize the land, and the workers the factories. After that, I don't know.'

I wrote: 'After that, struggles devoid of any greatness will begin once again, but on a rejuvenated soil. Mankind will have made a great leap forward.' The Comitè Obrero did not ask itself any fundamental questions. It entered the battle without knowing its ultimate perspective or assessing the consequences of its action; and, of course, it could hardly do otherwise. The Committee was the expression of an expanding power which could not remain inactive; nor, any longer, could it be simply beaten down, even if it fought badly. The notion of seizing Barcelona was straightforward: it was studied in detail. But Madrid? The other regions? Liaison with the rest of Spain was weak. Would it lead to the overthrow of the monarchy? Some of the Republicans who hoped for this, including Lerroux (still popular, though already discredited on the Left), wanted to throw libertarian Barcelona into the front line, with the way open for themselves to retreat if Barcelona was defeated. The Catalan Republicans associated with Marcelino Domingo were leaning on the power of the workers only to wrest a degree of independence from the monarchy; these kept tantalizing the Government with the threat of disorders. Together with Seguí, I followed the negotiations between the Catalan liberal bourgeoisie and the Comitè Obrero. It was a dubious alliance, in which the partners feared, justifiably mistrusted and subtly outmanœuvred one another.

Seguí summed up the position: 'They would like to use us and then do us down. For the moment, we are useful in their game of political blackmail. Without us they can do nothing: we have the streets, the shock-troops, the brave hearts among the people. We know this, but we need them. They stand for money, trade, possible legality (at the beginning, anyway), the Press, public opinion, etc.'

'But', I would reply, 'unless we have a brilliant victory, which I don't believe, they are ready to desert us at the first obstacle. We are betrayed in advance.'

Seguí could see the dangers, but he was still optimistic: 'If we are beaten, they will be beaten with us—too late then to betray us. If we win, we, not they, will be the masters of the situation.' It was Salvador Seguí who gave me the inspiration for the character of Dario in *Naissance de Notre Force*. A worker, and usually dressed like a worker coming home from the job, cloth cap squashed down on his skull, shirt-neck unbuttoned under his cheap tie; tall, strapping, round-headed, his features rough, his eyes big, shrewd and sly under heavy lids, of an ordinary degree of ugliness, but intensely charming to meet and with his whole self displaying an energy that was lithe and dogged, practical, shrewd, and without the slightest affectation. To the Spanish working-class movement he brought a new role: that of the superb organizer. He was no anarchist, but rather a libertarian, quick to scoff at resolutions on 'harmonious life under the sun of liberty', 'the blossoming of the self', or 'the future society'; he presented instead the immediate problems of wages, organization, rents, and revolutionary power. The anarchists would not hear any talk of the seizure of power. They refused to see that if the Comitè Obrero was victorious, it would be the Catalan government of tomorrow. Seguí saw this, but, afraid of starting a clash of ideas that would have isolated him, dared not talk of it. And so we went into battle, as it were in the dark.

Our enthusiasm and strength were gathering for the great day, and the preparations for it were almost ready. Towards the middle of July, squads of blue-overalled militants patrolled the town, hands on their revolvers. I went on these patrols, and we used to pass the *Guardia Civil* on horseback with their black cocked hats and their bearded faces. They knew that we were tomorrow's insurgents, but they had orders not to engage with us. The authorities had lost their wits, or else anticipated what was going to happen: the defection of the Catalan Parliamentary democrats. The building of La Calle de las Egypciacías, where I happened to be one day with Seguí, was surrounded by the black-hats; we helped Seguí to escape over the flat roofs on the house-tops. I was arrested, and spent three hateful hours in a tiny police cell painted in red ochre. I could hear the roar of the riots on the Rambla near by, a roar so loud that a kindly old police officer released me with his apologies. The plain-clothes men at our heels, distressingly courteous, assured us of their sympathy and apologized for pursuing so disgraceful a trade to earn their children's bread.

I doubted if we would win, but I would gladly have fought for the future's sake. Much later, in a meditation on the conquest of power, I wrote:

'Very likely, Dario, at the end of all this trouble we shall be shot. I have doubts about today and about ourselves. You would laugh, Dario, if I told you this aloud. You would say, spreading out your great, shaggy, brotherly, strong hands: "Me, I feel able to win all the way. All the way." That is how we all feel, immortal, right up to the moment when we feel nothing any more. And life goes on after our little drop of water has flowed back into the ocean. In this sense my confidence is one with yours. Tomorrow is great. We will not have prepared this conquest in vain. This city will be won, if not by our hands, at least by hands like ours, only stronger: perhaps stronger by being better toughened through our very weakness. If we are beaten, other men, infinitely different from us, infinitely like us, will come down this Rambla on an evening like this, in ten years, twenty years, it matters not, planning this same conquest; perhaps they will be thinking of the blood we have shed. Even now I think I can see them. I am thinking of their blood, which will also flow. But they will win the city.'

I was right. Those others did win the city, on 19 July 1936. They were called Ascaso, Durruti, Germinal Vidal,[1] the C.N.T., the F.A.I., the P.O.U.M. But on 19 July 1917 we were beaten almost without a fight, since the Catalan liberals took fright at the last minute and refused to join the struggle. We fought alone, in a day of sunshine and shouting, of impetuous crowds and chases in the streets, while the cautious black-hats charged lazily and pursued us without enthusiasm: they were afraid.

[1] Ascaso and Durruti were outstanding figures of the Spanish anarchist movement whose destinies were linked in imprisonment, exile, and then battle in the Civil War, in which each died a heroic death. Germinal Vidal was the Youth Secretary of the independent Marxist party P.O.U.M., who also died fighting on the Republican side. Serge's prophecy is from *Naissance de Notre Force*, written in 1929–30.

The Comitè Obrero sounded the retreat. Around noon I joined the multitude of comrades in the cramped Conde del Asalto hall. While we were awaiting instructions, the *Guardia Civil*, rifles raised, suddenly burst in from the Rambla and advanced on us, slowly herding us back. A small, sickly officer shouted that he would give the order to fire if we did not disperse. It was impossible for us to disperse, for behind us was another crowd—and we had no inclination to do so. A gap opened between us and this wall of men aiming at us with their rifles. Into it there suddenly leapt a young man in grey, his hand balancing a bomb wrapped in newspaper. He shouted, 'I am a free man! Sons of whores!' I rushed towards him and grabbed his wrists: 'Are you mad? You're going to start a useless slaughter.' We wrestled for a brief moment, while the police were motionless and hesitant; then some of the comrades surrounded us and dragged us away. . . . Isolated shots cracked out. In the opening of a door the young man, still shaking with exasperation, was wiping his forehead with his hand. 'You're the Russian, aren't you? Lucky I recognized you in time.'

In the evening, Seguí returned, worn out with fatigue. 'Cowards, cowards!' he kept whispering. I was never to see him again, for he went into hiding to organize the August rebellion. In 1921, when I was in Petrograd, I had a letter from him with the news that he was coming to Russia. He had become Barcelona's unchallenged tribune, and was returning from Minorca where he had been for some time under sentence of deportation. At the beginning of 1922 he was killed in the street, a few yards from the Rambla, by the *pistoleros* of the employers' agency *Sindicato Libre*.

The rebellion broke out in the August of 1917, resulted in a hundred-odd corpses on all sides, and was crushed, without, however, blocking the progress of the Barcelona working class. I was on my way to Russia. The defeat of 19 July had made up my mind for me: I had lost all hope of victory hereabouts, I was weary of discussions with militants who often seemed to me no more than great big children. The Russian Consul-General in Barcelona, a Prince K ——, received me at once when my name was sent in: 'How can I be of service to you?' This gentleman had just given his allegiance to the Provisional Government. I had previously been a little afraid of him, for any Russian revolutionaries of whose presence in the city he became aware were arrested by the Commandant at his instigation. Now all was sweetness. I asked him only for a recruiting form, so that I could go and do my military service in liberated Russia. 'But of course, with pleasure! At once!' We each understood what the other left half-said.

Paris. The Russian military headquarters in the Avenue Rapp was full of dapper officers, quite at home in the new situation: republicans within the week, and good republicans of course. Exceedingly polite, they enumerated all the difficulties to me and other callers. Communications with Russia were clogged with all kinds of obstacles. Why not, they suggested, serve our rediscovered country in the Russian formation fighting in France? That would be easy to arrange. However, I continued my efforts, only to learn at last that, as it appeared, the British Admiralty was refusing transit to the group of returning revolutionaries of which I was a member. We kept sending telegrams to the Petrograd Soviet and Kerensky, which made a deplorable impression, and it was not concealed from us that, what with one censorship and another, it was by no means certain that our telegrams arrived. Meanwhile, a Russian division, demanding repatriation, mutinied at the La Courtine camp; it was crushed by cannon-fire. I had the idea of journeying via the Foreign Legion, which was promising incorporation in the Russian army to its Russian volunteers; but then I found that most of the comrades who had tried this route had met a hero's death in the front line, while their representatives, who were mandated to put their demands, were shot somewhat farther behind the trenches.

In the ante-rooms of the military mission I made the acquaintance of a Russian soldier, about thirty, lately from Transjordania where he had fought in the British forces. Like me he was trying to return, though for different reasons, and he got his way before I did. He defined his position right from our first conversation: 'I am a traditionalist, monarchist, imperialist, and pan-Slavist. Mine is the true Russian nature, just as it was formed by Orthodox Christianity. You also have the true Russian nature, but at its opposite extreme, that of spontaneous anarchy, primitive violence, and unruly beliefs. I love all of Russia, even what I want to fight in it, even what you represent. . . .'

On these subjects we had excellent discussions, in our walks up and down the esplanade of Les Invalides. At least he was frank, daring in thought, tremendously in love with adventure and battle, and from time to time he would recite verses with magical effect. He was rather lean and singularly ugly: his face too long, heavy lips and nose, conical forehead, weird eyes, bluish-green and over-large, like a fish or Oriental idol—and indeed, he was very fond of the priestly statues of Assyria, which everyone came to think he resembled. This was one of the greatest Russian poets of our generation, already famous: Nikolai Stepanovich Gumilev. We were destined to meet several times in Russia, antagonists but friends. In 1921 I was to struggle vainly for several days, trying to stop the Cheka from shooting him. But of this approaching future we had no foreknowledge.

The Russian officers usually called themselves Social-Revolutionaries, and the fact is that the S-R Party was visibly inflated, like the frog in the fable, with no doubts at all that it would have the majority in the forthcoming Constituent Assembly. I knew only very little about Bolshevism, the very mention of which set the splendid officers foaming at the mouth. Its strength was being proved in the July troubles in Petrograd. The critical question that was put to everyone, including myself, was, all the time: 'For or against Bolshevism? For or against the Constituent Assembly?' To this I would reply as I was wont, rashly and frankly: the Russian Revolution cannot confine itself to changing the political order; it is, and must be, of a social character. In other words, the peasants are bound to seize the land, and will take it from the landlords, with or without uprisings, with or without the permission of a Constituent Assembly; the workers will insist on the nationalization or at the very least the control of large-scale industry and the banks. They did not kick out the Romanovs just to go back to their workshops as powerless as yesterday or to help the cannon-kings grow rich. This, for me, was a self-evident truth, but I saw very soon that although I confined myself to proclaiming it within the Russian military emigration, I ran a grave risk of getting into trouble with the French authorities. Trouble was indeed coming, in no uncertain manner. Without knowing it, I was 'on the line' advocated by Lenin.

The strangest feature of all this was the indignation of these newly-discovered Social-Revolutionaries when anyone reminded them that the cardinal point of their programme was the demand for the nationalization of land, immediate expropriation of the large estates, without compensation, and the liquidation of the landed aristocracy. 'But there's the war!' they exclaimed, 'Let's win first!' It was easy to reply to them that the autocracy had led the Empire to defeat and invasion; and that, since then, a conservative republic, without understanding of the people's needs, had been managing only to accumulate further catastrophes, until the day of some terrible social crisis when it would go down in unforeseeable ruin.

I was working in a print-shop on the Boulevard Port-Royal. Here and elsewhere, I had many contacts with the workers. They, too, were evidently annoyed at the unexpected direction taken by the Russian Revolution. At first they had greeted it with heart-felt pleasure; then they had been sold on the idea that disturbances and so-called 'maximalist' demands were weakening the Russian army. I was always being told (since people would say it for my benefit as soon as I disclosed my Russian nationality): 'The Bol-sheviks are rats, sold out to Germany', or 'The Russians are all yellow'. I was nearly brained in one *bistro* for opening a Russian newspaper. I kept telling myself that this people, already bled white, could not be expected to think calmly, still less to have a brotherly understanding of what another distant people, equally bled and overworked, was yearning for. I learnt that, through an outstanding coincidence of events, France had just passed through a submerged revolutionary crisis. March 1917: downfall of the Russian autocracy. April 1917: the mutinies in Champagne. These were actually more serious than has been made out since. A whole army practically disintegrated, and there was talk of its marching on Paris. Com-mander-in-Chief Nivelle, Joffre's successor, had in April tried to break through the German front at Craonne and Rheims, and paid so hard a price for a slight advance that he had to stop the offensive himself. At this point the mutinies broke out. They were quelled without excessive repression, which proved to be a most sensible move. Another supremely important psychological factor came to bear at just this moment to restore the army's morale; the entry of the United States into the war (6 April; the Nivelle offensive began on 9 April). Confidence was restored; from now on victory was possible; the Russian Revolution, which was complicating the situa-tion, became unpopular. A tiny working-class minority alone con-tinued to support it, together with the *Vie Ouvrière* group (Monatte

and Rosmer),[1] a few Socialists like Jean Longuet and Rappoport,[2] and anarchist elements which were more numerous but also
more muddled. Clemenceau came to power at apparently the most
critical hour; actually the worst moment of the crisis was over,
whichever way you looked at it. Psychological recovery had been
achieved, the American troops were landing, the Battle of the
Atlantic was turning in the Allies' favour (in April, the black month,
Britain had only three weeks' supply of food, because of the U-boat
campaign). He began by destroying the peace party from within; its
semi-official leader was Joseph Caillaux, Deputy for La Sarthe and
former Prime Minister, a cunning and reactionary financier whom
I had recently called '*Caillot de sang*' ('blood-clot') in a newspaper
headline.[3] The peace party was counting on the weariness of the
masses, on the fear of a European revolution, on the vacillations of
the Habsburgs and on the social crisis maturing in Germany, and it
was encouraged in various ways by German agents. Almereyda,
now editor of *Le Bonnet Rouge*, had become the factotum of this party;
if it had won, he would have made a popular minister able, honestly
but still treacherously, to exploit the feelings of the masses that were
sympathetic to Socialism and anarchism. Like nearly all the other
revolutionaries, I had stopped seeing him ever since he became
involved in what we ironically called 'high politics' behind the
scenes of high finance. Intoxicated with money and danger, he was

[1] Pierre Monatte (1881–1960): anarcho-syndicalist; strike-leader, union organizer, journalist; founder of the syndicalist weekly *La Vie Ouvrière*, important in
the years before the First World War, then of *La Révolution Prolétarienne*, which was
a platform for Serge over many years. Alfred Rosmer (1877–1964): internationalist in the First World War, delegate and Executive member of the Communist
International (1920–1), and prominent in the French Communist Party until his
expulsion as an oppositionist in 1924. Supporter of the Left Opposition abroad
and friend of Trotsky and Serge in exile. Author of books on working-class and
Communist history.

[2] Jean Longuet (1876–1938): lawyer, grandson of Karl Marx; editor of *L'Humanité* when it belonged to the Socialist Party, then a founder of *Le Populaire*. Deputy
and author. Charles Rappoport (1865–1941): former Russian citizen and member
of *Narodnaya Volya*; after settling in France (1887), active in the French Socialist
movement, founder-member of the French Communist Party (1920); resigned
from the C.P. after the show trials of Old Bolsheviks, many of whom he had
known personally.

[3] Joseph Caillaux (1863–1941): Radical-Socialist Deputy and Minister, was
arrested by Clemenceau's administration in December 1917, on a charge of
'dealings with the enemy', and found guilty in February 1920 of 'correspondence
with the enemy'. Sentenced to three years' imprisonment, after his release he re-
entered politics and became Finance Minister (1925–6) and a Senator.

dissipating his life, a morphine addict now, surrounded by theatricals, blackmailers, beautiful women and political touts of every description. The graph of his destiny had started from the Paris underworld, had mounted to a climax of revolutionary pugnacity, and was now tailing off in corruption, among the money-bags. When Clemenceau had him and his staff arrested,[1] I knew at once that it would be impossible to try him; he would have been too likely to put the war in the dock and thoroughly compromise the men behind him. He would probably have been shot: but not alone. A few days afterwards, he was found in his prison bunk, strangled with a shoe-lace. The business was never cleared up.

That summer Paris lived merrily, as much out of determined confidence as from recklessness. The American soldiers were bringing in plenty of money. The Germans had been at Noyon, 100 or so kilometres away, for so long that people had got used to them and felt no unusual anxiety. At night the approach of the Gotha bombers set off the reverberation of the warning sirens, everyone went down to the cellars, and a few bombs would fall. Suspicion, betrayal and fears were the rule everywhere; some poor wretches were arrested for a word spoken in the street. I was enjoying my precarious freedom by studying the history of art—what was there better to do while this respite lasted? One day I was arrested in the street by two terrified inspectors, who for some unknown reason were expecting me to resist to the death. They were visibly gratified when I told them that I had no arms and no intention of putting up a fight. Since there was strictly nothing that could be held against me, except perhaps 'dangerous thoughts', to use the happy expression of the Japanese legislator, I was conveyed by administrative decision to a concentration-camp at Précigné, in La Sarthe.

There I found a whole collection of revolutionaries, mainly Russians and Jews, like me labelled 'Bolsheviks' without, of course, being anything of the kind. At Précigné I quickly started a Russian revolutionary grouping, consisting of about fifteen militants and twenty or so sympathizers. It included only one Bolshevik, the chemical engineer Krauterkrafft, whose constant antagonist I was, since he advocated a merciless dictatorship, suppression of Press freedom, authoritarian revolution, and education on Marxist lines.

[1] Actually it was Ribot who had them arrested, before Clemenceau's second Cabinet came into being.

(Later on he refused to leave for Russia.) We desired a libertarian, democratic revolution, without the hypocrisy and flabbiness of the bourgeois democracies—egalitarian and tolerant towards ideas and people, which would employ terror if it was necessary but would abolish the death-penalty. From a theoretical point of view, we stated these problems very badly; certainly the Bolshevik put them better than we. From the human standpoint, we were infinitely nearer the truth than he was. We saw in the power of the Soviets the realization of our deepest hopes, as he did also. Our mutual understanding was based on deep misunderstanding, as well as on sheer necessity.

Guarded by weary Territorials, who never had an idea unless it was to re-sell us bottles of wine at a handsome profit, we would hold pro-Soviet meetings in the courtyard of this secularized monastery. Paul Fouchs, an impassioned old libertarian artlessly proud of his resemblance to Lafargue, used to take the platform with me. Belgians, Macedonians, and Alsatians, variegated 'suspects' (some of them genuinely, in fact horribly, suspect), would hear us out in silence, respectful but disapproving since we were 'in bad odour' with the authorities as well as throwing away any hope of release that we had; and then too, 'what has been will be, there's always been rich and poor, war is in man's blood, you won't change anything of that, you'd do better to get out of your own mess. . . .'

The Belgians and Alsatians were vaguely pro-German; the Macedonians, proud, destitute, and silent, were just Macedonians, ready to fight the whole world for their primitive mountain liberty. These lived as a community, all sharing the same misery, all lousy, hungry, and brotherly. Belgians and Alsatians were partitioned into the rich, the poor, and the corrupt middlemen, a miniature society, utterly self-contained and utterly divided, scorned by us and a little afraid of us.

The camp's regimen was reasonably fair and free. The only trouble was that we were hungry. Spanish influenza was rife and death was our perpetual companion. An infirmary improvised in a ground-floor room held the dying, with those of us who had volunteered as nurses sitting up by them. They were left to wheeze and go blue, or else spotty like a panther's skin, and then cold. . . . What could we do? For my part I spent the night in the open, near the doorway of this stinking mortuary, getting up now and then to give a drink to some dying man. Our group did not have a single death, although we had nearly all been infected; but our solidarity meant that we could eat better than the other poor devils. A quarter of the camp's population was carried off in a few weeks; however, not one rich prisoner died.

During the epidemic we continued to assemble and conduct our studies. During one of the meetings, which I was holding purposely on that particular evening to distract the guards' attention, one of our group tried to escape, under cover of a storm. He fell in the camp's perimeter, under the livid glare of searchlights: 'Twenty years old, and six bullets in his body,' it was remarked. On the following day we summoned the camp to revolt. The Starost, or Elder of the Macedonians, came and told us that they would support us. The Belgians and the Alsatians answered that this trifle was no business of theirs, that it would all come to grief, and as far as they were concerned, nothing doing. The local Prefect came, and promised us an inquiry. The commandant of the camp asked for a confidential interview with me. At it he disclosed that he knew of the plan of escape from a camp trader; that several internees were due to bolt (this was true) and that the guards had meant to kill another prisoner, a Rumanian scoundrel suspected of espionage, who was an informer into the bargain.

'On my word of honour, we did intend to let your comrade run off, and I am broken-hearted at what happened; a mistake, I assure you. . . .'

His information was correct, and the revolt subsided. We felt a physical revulsion for the spies. The reprieved informer continued to stroll up and down the yard, smoking his dirty-yellow cigarettes.

Civil war was breaking out in Russia. In consequence of the counter-revolutionary rising at Yaroslavl and Dora Kaplan's attempt against Lenin, the Cheka arrested Mr. Lockhart, the British Consul in Moscow, and the French military mission under General Lavergne. Negotiations were set in hand through the Danish Red Cross, with a view to an exchange of hostages. Chicherin, himself released from a British concentration-camp, demanded the liberation of Litvinov, who was imprisoned in London, and of the 'Bolsheviks' interned in France—us, that is. The negotiations were successful only after the general explosion of goodwill at the Armistice. The authorities offered us a choice between release, in the near future, or leaving now for Russia as hostages, with the safety of the French officers hanging over our heads. Five out of the fifteen or so in our group joined me in insisting on departure. We set off with our sacks over our shoulders, in the cold of the night, pursued by shouts of mirth from the whole camp. Several of the worst inmates had come to embrace us as we left, and we had no heart to push them away. The frozen snow echoed sharply under our feet, and the stars receded in front of us. The night was huge and buoyant.

We journeyed through bombarded towns, in countryside dotted with wooden crosses on the railway embankments, until we came into the territory of the 'Tommies'. One night, in a port whose houses were shattered by bombs, the sick man in our party, some police officers and I went into a tavern filled with British soldiers. They noticed our unusual appearance. 'Who are you lot? Where are you going?'

'Revolutionaries—we are going to Russia.' Thirty tanned faces surrounded us eagerly, there were hearty exclamations all round us, and we had to shake everybody's hand. Since the Armistice popular feeling had changed once again; the Russian Revolution was once more a distant beacon to men.

In the converted prison at Dunkirk another group of hostages was waiting for us, led from another camp by a Dr. N——ko. The exchange was being made man for man, and the Russians were tricked: out of forty hostages, hardly ten were genuine militants, and nearly twenty were children. Should we protest against this trickery? Dr. N——ko, very tall, white-haired and narrow-eyed, affirmed that 'a child at the breast is well worth any general'. Connected with the Russian seamen's union, he had organized a strike at Marseilles on ships loaded with munitions bound for the Whites. He and I were elected as delegates by the whole group.

'Are these hostages too, these kids less than ten years old?' I asked some of the officers, 'Do you think that is compatible with military honour?' They spread out their hands, mortified: 'We can do nothing about it.' Rather likeable men, they used to read Romain Rolland's *Above the Battle* in their cabins.[1] This conversation took place at sea, off the level shores of Denmark, on a milky sea from which the mast-ends of sunken ships could sometimes be seen

---

[1] Rolland's *Above the Battle* (*Au-dessus de la Mêlée*) was a collection of articles, originally published in the *Journal de Génève*, condemning the war.

emerging. Our remarks were apropos of a rumour then abroad that some French officers had perished in Russia; we were informed that we were in danger of reprisals.

It was a fine voyage, in first-class berths. A destroyer escorted our steamer, and now and then took long shots at floating mines. A dark gush would rise from the waves and the child-hostages applauded. From mist and sea there emerged the massive outline of Elsinore's grey stone castle, with its roofs of dull emerald. Weak Prince Hamlet, you faltered in that fog of crimes, but you put the question well. 'To be or not to be', for the men of our age, means free-will or servitude, and they have only to choose. We are leaving the void, and entering the kingdom of the will. This, perhaps, is the imaginary frontier. A land awaits us where life is beginning anew, where conscious will, intelligence, and an inexorable love of mankind are in action. Behind us, all Europe is ablaze, having choked almost to death in the fog of its own massacres. Barcelona's flame smoulders on. Germany is in the thick of revolution, Austro-Hungary is splitting into free nations. Italy is spread with red flags. . . . This is only the beginning. We are being born into violence; not only you and I, who are fairly unimportant, but all those to whom, unknown to themselves, we belong, down to this tin-hatted Senegalese, freezing under his fur on his dismal watch at the foot of the officers' gangway. Outbursts of idealism like this, if truth be known, kept getting mixed up with our heated discussions on points of doctrine. Then an amazing girl-child of twenty, whose big eyes held both smiles and a kind of suppressed fear, would come on deck to seek us out, telling us that tea was ready in the cabin, crammed with children, occupied by an old anarchist worker who was more enthusiastic even than we were. I called this girl-child 'Bluebird'; and it was she who brought me the news of the murder of Karl Liebknecht and Rosa Luxemburg.

From the Åland Isles onwards the Baltic was ice, studded with islands of white. A hundred yards ahead, a destroyer kept ramming the ice, and our steamer would advance slowly through the floe, by a narrow, gurgling channel. Enormous blocks of ice, torn away in some elemental struggle, floated round and round under our bows. We gazed at them till we were dizzy. There were moments of trance when I found this spectacle pregnant with meaning, and it was lovelier than all the enchantment of the countryside.

Finland received us as foes, for the White Terror was only just over. Hangö, a deserted port, under snow. We were caged in railway-carriages whose exits were guarded by silent blond giants, stony-eyed and cowled in white, with orders to shoot (as we were warned) at the first attempt to leave the train. I pressed my question: 'Please ask Monsieur the Finnish officer if this order applies to the child-hostages as well?'

Monsieur the officer was enraged: 'To everybody!'

'Please thank Monsieur the officer.'

The cold air was heavy with chilled violence. Without ever leaving the train, we crossed this huge land of sleepy woods, snow-covered lakes, tracts of whiteness, and pretty painted cottages lost in the wilderness. We went through towns so tidy and silent that they reminded us of children's toys. We had a moment of panic when, as evening fell, the train stopped in a clearing and soldiers lined up alongside the tracks: we were invited to get down. The women murmured, 'They're going to shoot us.' We refused to leave the train, but it was only to give us a breath of air while we waited for the carriages to be cleaned and the engine to be fuelled with wood. The sentries ignored their instructions and started to be pleasant to the children.

We crossed the Soviet frontier at dead of night, in the middle of a forest. Our progress was painful, blocked by the snow. The sharp cold bored through our thin Western clothing and our teeth chattered. The children, swaddled in bed-clothes, were crying. Men with lanterns, standing on a little white bridge in the misty moonlight, counted us as we passed. Choked with joy, we shouted 'Greetings, comrade!' to a Red sentry; he nodded, and then asked if we had any food. We had. Here, take it. The Revolution is hungry.

We gathered around a wood fire which lit us up with fantastic shadows. In the command-post of this dead sector of the front, a log hut unfurnished but equipped with telephones, we considered the strangeness of this first contact with our homeland, our Revolution. Two or three Red soldiers in worn greatcoats were busy at the telephones, without any sign of interest in us. Their faces were haggard and they did what they had to, rising above their prodigious fatigue. They livened up when we offered them some tinned food. 'What, aren't they hungry in France? Do they still have white bread over there?' We asked them for newspapers, but none were being delivered to them.

We never thought of sleep once we were in the goods-wagon. This was efficiently heated by an iron stove and pulled by an asthmatic locomotive that was taking us, through the pale, ideally pure dawn, to Petrograd. A wintry landscape, without trace of man. Brilliance of snow, borderland of emptiness. In a second forlorn little outpost, another soldier, indifferent to everything but hunger and food, found us a copy of *Severnaya Kommuna*, organ of the Petrograd Soviet. It was only a single, fairly large grey sheet, printed in pale ink. From it came our first shock. We had never thought that the idea of revolution could be separated from that of freedom. All we knew of the French Revolution, of the Paris Commune, of 1905 in Russia, showed us popular ferment, bubbling ideas, rivalry of clubs, parties, and publications—except during the Terror, under the 'Reign of the Supreme Being'; but the Terror of 1793 was simultaneously a climax and the beginning of a decline, the approach to Thermidor. In Petrograd we expected to breathe the air of a liberty that would doubtless be harsh and even cruel to its enemies, but was still generous and bracing. And in this paper we found a colourless article, signed 'G. Zinoviev', on 'The Monopoly of Power'. '*Our Party rules alone . . . it will not allow anyone. . . . The false democratic liberties demanded by the counter-revolution.*' I am quoting from memory, but such was certainly the sense of the piece. We tried to justify it by the state of siege and the mortal perils; however, such considerations could justify particular acts, acts of violence towards men and ideas, but not a theory based on the extinction of all freedom. I note the date of this article: January 1919. The desert of snow was still rolling on beneath our eyes. We were approaching Petrograd.

3

ANGUISH AND ENTHUSIASM
1919–1920

We were entering a world frozen to death. The Finland station, glittering with snow, was deserted. The square where Lenin had addressed a crowd from the top of an armoured car was no more than a white desert surrounded by dead houses. The broad, straight thoroughfares, the bridges astride the Neva, now a river of snowy ice, seemed to belong to an abandoned city; first a gaunt soldier in a grey greatcoat, then after a long time a woman freezing under her shawls, went past like phantoms in an oblivious silence.

Towards the city centre, gentle ghost-like hints of life began. Open sleds, pulled by starving horses, proceeded unhurriedly over the white expanse. There were practically no cars. The rare passers-by, eaten by cold and hunger, had faces of ghastly white. Squads of half-ragged soldiers, their rifles often hanging from their shoulders by a rope, tramped around under the red pennants of their units. Palaces drowsed at the end of spacious prospects, or in front of the frozen canals; others, more massive, lorded it over yesterday's parade-squares. The smart baroque façades of the Imperial family's residences were painted over in ox-blood red; the theatres, the military headquarters, the former ministries, all in Empire style, made a background of noble colonnades among huge stretches of emptiness. The high gilded dome of St. Isaac, upheld by mighty red granite pillars, hung over this wasting city like a symbol of past glories. We contemplated the low embrasures of the Peter-Paul Fortress and its golden spire, thinking of all the revolutionaries who, since Bakunin and Nechayev, had fought and now lay dead under those stones, that the world might belong to us.

It was the metropolis of Cold, of Hunger, of Hatred, and of Endurance. From about a million inhabitants its population had now fallen, in one year, to scarcely 700,000 souls.

At a reception centre we were issued with basic rations of black bread and dried fish. Never until now had any of us known such a horrid diet. Girls with red head-bands joined with young bespectacled agitators to give us a summary of the state of affairs: 'Famine, typhus and counter-revolution everywhere. But the world revolution is bound to save us.' They were surer of it than we were, and our doubts made them momentarily suspicious of us. All they asked us was whether Europe would soon be kindled: 'What is the French proletariat waiting for before it seizes power?'

The Bolshevik leaders that I saw spoke to me in more or less the same tones. Zinoviev's wife Lilina, People's Commissar for Social Planning in the Northern Commune, a small crop-haired, grey-eyed woman in a uniform jacket, sprightly and tough, asked me, 'Have you brought your families with you? I could put them up in palaces, which I know is very nice on some occasions, but it is impossible to heat them. You'd better go to Moscow. Here, we are besieged people in a besieged city. Hunger-riots may start, the Finns may swoop on us, the British may attack. Typhus has killed so many people that we can't manage to bury them; luckily they are frozen. If work is what you want, there's plenty of it!' And she told me passionately of the Soviet achievement: school-building, children's centres, relief for pensioners, free medical assistance, the theatres open to all. . . . 'We work on in spite of everything and we shall carry on working till our last hour!' Later I was to learn at first hand how hard she worked, never showing any sign of being worn down.

Shklovsky, People's Commissar for Foreign Affairs (in the Northern Commune), an intellectual with a black beard and a jaundiced complexion, met me in a room of what was lately the main military headquarters.

'What are they saying about us abroad?'

'They're saying that Bolshevism equals banditry.'

'There's something in that,' he replied calmly. 'You'll see for yourself, things are too much for us. In the Revolution the revolutionaries only amount to a very tiny percentage.' He outlined the situation to me, sparing nothing: a revolution dying, strangled by blockade, ready to collapse from inside into the chaos of counter-revolution. He was a man of bitterly clear vision. (He committed suicide around 1930.)

Zinoviev, the President of the Soviet, by contrast affected an extraordinary confidence. Clean-shaven, pale, his face a little puffy, he felt absolutely at home on the pinnacle of power, being the most long-standing of Lenin's collaborators in the Central Committee: all the same there was also an impression of flabbiness, almost of a lurking irresolution, emanating from his whole personality. Abroad, a frightful reputation for terror surrounded his name; I told him this.

'Of course', he answered, smiling, 'they don't like our plebeian methods of fighting.' And he alluded to the latest delegation from the Consular Corps, who were making representations to him in favour of the hostages taken from the bourgeoisie. He sent them about their business: 'If it was we who were being shot, these gentlemen would be quite happy, wouldn't they?'

Our conversation turned principally on the state of mass feeling in the Western countries. I kept saying that tremendous events were maturing, only the process was sluggish, halting, and blind; that in France, more particularly, no revolutionary upheaval was to be expected for a long time. Zinoviev smiled, with an air of kindly condescension. 'It is easy to tell that you are no Marxist. History cannot stop half-way.'

Maxim Gorky welcomed me affectionately. In the famished years of his youth, he had been acquainted with my mother's family at Nizhni-Novgorod. His apartment in the Kronversky Prospect, full of books and Chinese *objets d'art*, seemed as warm as a greenhouse. He himself was chilly even under his thick grey sweater, and coughed terribly, the result of his thirty years' struggle against tuberculosis. Tall, lean and bony, broad-shouldered and hollow-chested, he stooped a little as he walked. His frame, sturdily-built but anaemic, appeared essentially as a support for his head, an ordinary, Russian man-in-the-street's head, bony and pitted, really almost ugly with its jutting cheek-bones, great thin-lipped mouth and professional smeller's nose, broad and peaked. His complexion deathly, he was chewing away under his short, bristly moustache, full of dejection, or rather of anguish mingled with indignation. His bushy brows puckered readily, and his big, grey eyes held an extraordinary

wealth of expression. His whole being expressed hunger for knowledge and human understanding, determination to probe all inhuman doings to their depths, never stopping at mere appearances,
never tolerating any lies told to him, and never lying to himself. I saw him immediately as the supreme, the righteous, the
relentless witness of the Revolution, and it was as such that he talked
with me.

He spoke harshly about the Bolsheviks: they were 'drunk with
authority', 'cramping the violent, spontaneous anarchy of the
Russian people', and 'starting bloody despotism all over again'; all
the same they were 'facing chaos alone' with some incorruptible
men in their leadership. His observations always started from facts,
from chilling anecdotes upon which he would base his well-
considered generalizations.

The prostitutes were sending a delegation to him, demanding
the right to organize a trade union. The fate of the hostages in the
jails was nothing short of monstrous. Hunger was weakening the
masses, and distorting the cerebral processes of the whole country.
At present it was imperative to side with the revolutionary régime,
for fear of a rural counter-revolution which would be no less than an
outburst of savagery. Alexei Maximovich spoke to me of strange
tortures rediscovered for the benefit of 'Commissars' in remote
country districts; such as pulling out the intestines through an
incision in the abdomen and coiling them slowly around a tree.
He thought that the tradition of these tortures was kept up through
the reading of *The Golden Legend*.[1]

The non-Communist (i.e. anti-Bolshevik) intellectuals whom I
saw gave me more or less the same general picture. They thought
of Bolshevism as finished, consumed by famine and terror, opposed
by all the peasants of the countryside, all the intelligentsia, and the
great majority of the working class. The people who spoke thus to
me were Socialists who had been enthusiastic participants in the
March 1917 Revolution. The Jews among them were living in
terror of approaching pogroms. All of them expected chaos, replete
with massacres. The dissolution of the Constituent Assembly, and
certain crimes at the beginning of the Revolution, such as the execution (or murder) of the Hingleize brothers and the murder, in a hospital, of the Liberal deputies Shingarev and Kokoshkin, had left a

[1] *The Golden Legend*: a thirteenth-century 'Lives of the Saints'.

wake of enraged resentment. The violent acts of mob-agitators such as the Kronstadt sailors so offended the humane feelings of men of goodwill that they lost all their critical faculties. Against how many hangings, humiliations, ruthless repressions, threatened reprisals, did these excesses have to be set? If the other side won would it be any more merciful? Besides, what were the Whites doing in the areas where they ruled the roost? I moved among intellectuals who wept for their dream of an enlightened democracy, governed by a sagacious Parliament and inspired by an idealistic Press (their own, of course). Every conversation I had with them convinced me that, face to face with the ruthlessness of history, they were wrong. I saw that their cause of democracy had, at the end of the summer of 1917, stood between two fires, that is to say between two conspiracies, and it seemed obvious to me that, if the Bolshevik insurrection had not taken power at that point, the cabal of the old generals, supported by the officers' organizations, would have certainly done so instead. Russia would have avoided the Red Terror only to endure the White, and a proletarian dictatorship only to undergo a reactionary one. In consequence, the most outraged observations of the anti-Bolshevik intellectuals only revealed to me how necessary Bolshevism was.

Moscow, with its old Italian and Byzantine architecture, its innumerable churches, its snows, its human ant-heap, its great public Departments, its half-clandestine markets, wretched but colourful, taking up vast squares: Moscow seemed to live a little better than Petrograd. Here Committees were piled on top of Councils, and Managements on top of Commissions. Of this apparatus, which seemed to me to function largely in a void, wasting three-quarters of its time on unrealizable projects, I at once formed the worst possible impression. Already, in the midst of general misery, it was nurturing a multitude of bureaucrats who were responsible for more fuss than honest work. In the offices of Commissariats one came across elegant gentlemen, pretty and irreproachably powdered typists, chic uniforms weighed down with decorations; and everybody in this smart set, in such contrast with the famished populace in the streets, kept sending you back and forth from office to office for the slightest matter and without the slightest result. I witnessed members of Government circles driven to telephoning Lenin to obtain a railway ticket or a room in the hotel, i.e. the 'House of the Soviets'. The Central Committee's secretariat gave me some tickets for lodgings, but I got none, because initiation into the racket was more necessary than any ticket.

I met the Menshevik leaders, and certain anarchists. Both sets denounced Bolshevik intolerance, the stubborn refusal to revolutionary dissenters of any right to exist, and the excesses of the Terror. Neither group, however, had any substantial alternative to suggest. The Mensheviks were publishing a daily paper, which was widely read; they had recently announced their allegiance to the régime and recovered their legality. They demanded the abolition of the Cheka and sang the praises of a return to Soviet democracy. One anarchist group canvassed the idea of a federation of free communes; others saw no future except in fresh insurrections, although realizing that famine was blocking all possible progress in the Revolution. I learnt that, around the autumn of 1918, the anarchist Black Guards had felt powerful enough for their leaders to discuss whether or not they should seize Moscow. Novomirsky and Borovoy had won the majority over to the virtues of abstention. 'We would not know what to do about the famine,' they said. 'Let it exhaust the Bolsheviks and lead the dictatorship of the Commissars to its grave. Then our hour will come!'

The Mensheviks seemed to me to be admirably intelligent, honest and devoted to Socialism, but completely overtaken by events. They stood for a sound principle, that of working-class democracy, but in a situation fraught with such mortal danger that the stage of siege did not permit any functioning of democratic institutions. And their bitterness, arising out of their brutal defeat as the party of compromise, disfigured their thinking; since they waited on the coming of some catastrophe, their declaration of support for the régime was only lip-service.

Of the Bolshevik leaders, on this occasion in Moscow I saw only Aveli Yenukidze, Secretary of the Executive Committee of the All-Union Soviets—actually the key post in the Republic's government. He was a fair-headed Georgian, with a kind, sturdy face lit up by blue eyes. His bearing was corpulent and grand, that of a mountain-dweller born and bred. He was affable, humorous and realistic, striking the same note as the Bolsheviks in Petrograd.

'Our bureaucracy's a scandal, no doubt about it. I think Petrograd is healthier. I even advise you to settle down there unless you are too scared of Petrograd's peculiar dangers. Here, we combine all the vices of the old Russia with those of the new. Petrograd is an outpost, the front line.'

Gorky offered me employment with him in the publishing-house 'Universal Literature', but the only people I met there were ageing or embittered intellectuals trying to escape from the present by re-translating Boccaccio, Knut Hamsun, or Balzac. My mind was made up: I was neither against the Bolsheviks nor neutral; I was with them, albeit independently, without renouncing thought or critical sense. Certainly on several essential points they were mis-taken: in their intolerance, in their faith in statification, in their leaning towards centralism and administrative techniques. But, given that one had to counter them with freedom of the spirit and the spirit of freedom, it must be with them and among them. Possibly, after all, these evils had been impelled by civil war, blockade and famine, and if we managed to survive, the remedy would come of itself. I remember having written in one of my first letters from Russia that I was 'resolved to make no career out of the Revolution, and, once the mortal danger has passed, to join again with those who will fight the evils of the new régime. . . .'

I was on the staff of the *Severnaya Kommuna* (Northern Commune) the organ of the Petrograd Soviet, an instructor in the public education clubs, organizing inspector for schools in the Second District, lecturing assistant to the Petrograd militia, etc. People were in short supply, and I was overwhelmed with work. All this activity brought me the means of bare existence from one day to the next, in a chaos that was oddly organized. The militiamen to whom I gave evening classes in history and the first elements of 'political science' (or 'political grammar', as it was called) would offer me a cob of black bread and a herring if the lesson had been interesting. Happy to ask me endless questions, they would escort me after the lesson through the shadows of the city, right up to my lodgings, in case anyone should steal my precious little parcel; and we would all trip over the carcass of a horse, dead in the snow in front of the Opera House.

The Third International had just been founded in Moscow (it was now March 1919) and had appointed Zinoviev as President of its Executive (the proposal was actually Lenin's). The new Executive still possessed neither personnel nor offices. Although I was not a member of the Party, Zinoviev asked me to organize his administration. As my knowledge of Russian life was too limited, I was unwilling to assume such a responsibility by myself. After some days Zinoviev told me, 'I've found an excellent man, you'll get along with him really well. . . .'; and so it turned out. It was thus that I came to know Vladmir Ossipovich Mazin who, prompted by the same motives as myself, had just joined the Party.

Through its severely practical centralization of power, and its repugnance towards individualism and celebrity, the Russian Revolution has left in obscurity at least as many first-rate men as it has made famous. Of all these great but still practically unknown figures, Mazin seems to me to be one of the most remarkable. One day, in an enormous room in the Smolny Institute, furnished solely with a table and two chairs, we met face to face, both of us rigged out rather absurdly. I still wore a large sheepskin hat which had been a present from a Cossack and a short, shabby overcoat, the garb of the Western unemployed. Mazin wore an old blue uniform with worn-out elbows; he had a three days' growth of beard, his eyes were encircled by old-fashioned spectacles of white metal, his face was elongated, his brow lofty and his complexion pasty from starvation.

'Well,' he said to me, 'so we're the Executive of the new International. It's really ridiculous!' And upon that bare table we set about drawing rough sketches of seals, for a seal was required immediately for the President: the great seal of the World Revolution, no more, no less! We decided that the globe would be the emblem on it.

We were friends with the same points of concern, doubt, and confidence, spending any moments spared us from our grinding work in examining together the problems of authority, terror, centralization, Marxism, and heresy. We both had strong leanings towards heresy. I was beginning my initiation into Marxism. Mazin had arrived there through the path of personal experience in jail. With those convictions he combined an old-fashioned libertarian heart and an ascetic temperament.

As an adolescent in 1905 on the revolutionary day of 22 January, he had seen the St. Petersburg streets running with the blood of working-class petitioners, and at once decided, even while the Cossacks were clearing away the crowd with their stubby whips, to study the chemistry of explosives. He very soon became one of the chemists of the Maximalist group, who wanted a 'total' socialist revolution. He, Vladimir Ossipovich Lichtenstadt, son of a good liberal-bourgeois family, manufactured the bombs that went with three of his comrades who presented themselves, dressed as officers, on 12 August 1906, at a gala entertainment for the Prime Minister Stolypin, and who, in blowing up the house, blew themselves up too. Some time afterwards, the Maximalists attacked a Treasury van in the broad daylight of St. Petersburg. Lichtenstadt was condemned to death, then pardoned; he spent ten years in prison at Schlüssel-burg,[1] much of it in the same cell as the Georgian Bolshevik Sergo Ordzhonikidze, who was to become one of the organizers of Soviet industrialization. In confinement Lichtenstadt wrote a work of scientific meditation which was later published (*Goethe and the Philosophy of Nature*), and studied Marx.

After another prisoner, a friend whom he admired, was killed, Lichtenstadt adopted the dead man's name and called himself Mazin, to remain faithful to his example. As a Marxist, he was at first a Menshevik, because of his zeal for democracy, and then entered the Bolshevik Party to be on the side of those who were the most active, the most creative and the most imperilled. He had a consuming interest in great books, a scholar's soul, a childlike frankness in the face of evil, and few basic wants. For eleven years he had been wait-ing to see his wife again; she was at present separated from him by the Southern front. 'The faults in the Revolution', he would say to me over and over again, 'must be fought in the realm of action.'

We spent our lives among telephones, trailing around the huge, dead city in wheezy motor-cars, commandeering print-shops, selecting staff, correcting proofs even in the trams, bargaining with the Board of Trade for string and with the State Bank's printers for paper, running to the Cheka or to distant suburban prisons when-ever (which was every day) we were notified of some abomination, fatal mistake, or piece of cruelty, and conferring with Zinoviev in the evening. Since we were senior officials we lived in the Hotel Astoria, the foremost 'House of the Soviets', where the most respon-sible of the Party's militants resided under the protection of machine-guns posted on the ground floor. Through the black market I came

[1] Schlüsselburg: (also known as Petrokrepost or 'Peter's Fortress'); a redoubtable prison for political prisoners about forty miles up the River Neva from Petrograd.

into possession of a fur-lined riding-jacket which, cleared of its fleas, made me look wonderful. In the former Austro-Hungarian Embassy we found some Habsburg officers' clothes, in excellent condition, for some of the comrades on our new staff. We were enormously privileged, although the bourgeoisie, dispossessed and now addicted to every imaginable form of speculation, lived much better than we did. Every day at the table reserved for the Northern Commune Executive, we found greasy soup and often a ration of slightly high but still delicious horse-meat. The customary diners there were Zinoviev, Yevdokimov from the Central Committee, Zorin from the Petrograd Committee, Bakayev, President of the Cheka, sometimes Helena Stassova, Secretary of the Central Committee, and sometimes Stalin, who was practically unknown. Zinoviev occupied an apartment on the first floor of the Astoria. As an extraordinary privilege, this hotel of dictators was kept almost warm, and was lit brightly at nightfall since work there never stopped; it thus formed an enormous vessel of light above the dark public squares. Rumour endowed us with incredible comfort and even detailed our alleged orgies, with actresses from the *corps de ballet*, naturally. All this time, Bakayev of the Cheka was going round with holes in his boots. In spite of my special rations as a Government official, I would have died of hunger without the sordid manipulations of the black market, where we traded the petty possessions we had brought in from France. The eldest son of my friend Yonov, Zinoviev's brother-in-law, an Executive member of the Soviet and founder and director of the State Library, died of hunger before our very eyes. All this while we were looking after considerable stocks, and even riches, but on the State's behalf and under rigorous control. Our salaries were limited to the 'Communist maximum', equal to the average wage of a skilled worker. During this period the old Lettish Bolshevik, Peter Stuchka,[1] a great figure now forgotten, instituted a strictly egalitarian régime in his Sovietized Latvia, in which the Party Committee was also the Government; its members were forbidden to enjoy

[1] Peter Ivanovich Stuchka (1865–1932) was a founder of the Latvian Marxist movement and later a prominent Soviet jurist. A Bolshevik since 1903, he became People's Commissar for Justice (1917–18), Chairman of the Latvian Soviet Government (1918–19), Deputy People's Commissar for Justice of the R.S.F.S.R. (1921), and from 1923 till his death Chairman of the Supreme Court of the R.S.F.S.R. He wrote a number of works on Soviet legal theory.

any material privileges at all. Vodka was banned, though the comrades obtained it clandestinely from peasants, who through home distilling extracted a terrifying alcohol from corn, eighty degrees proof.

The telephone became my personal enemy; perhaps it is for that reason that I still feel a stubborn aversion from it. At every hour it brought me voices of panic-stricken women who spoke of arrests, imminent executions, and injustice, and begged me to intervene at once, for the love of God! Since the first massacres of Red prisoners by the Whites, the murders of Volodarsky and Uritsky[1] and the attempt against Lenin (in the summer of 1918), the custom of arresting and, often, executing hostages had become generalized and legal. Already the Cheka (the Extraordinary Commission for Repression against counter-revolution, speculation, and desertion), which made mass arrests of suspects, was tending to settle their fate independently, under formal control by the Party, but in reality without anybody's knowledge. It was becoming a State within the State, protected by military secrecy and proceedings *in camera*. The Party endeavoured to head it with incorruptible men like the former convict Dzerzhinsky, a sincere idealist, ruthless but chivalrous, with the emaciated profile of an Inquisitor: tall forehead, bony nose, untidy goatee, and an expression of weariness and austerity. But the Party had few men of this stamp and many Chekas: these gradually came to select their personnel by virtue of their psychological inclinations. The only temperaments that devoted themselves willingly and tenaciously to this task of 'internal defence' were those characterized by suspicion, embitterment, harshness, and sadism. Long-standing social inferiority-complexes and memories of humiliations and suffering in the Tsar's jails rendered them intractable, and since professional degeneration has rapid effects, the Chekas inevitably consisted of perverted men tending to see conspiracy everywhere and to live in the midst of perpetual conspiracy themselves.

I believe that the formation of the Chekas was one of the gravest

[1] V. Volodarsky (1891–1918): Bolshevik orator and Petrograd Commissar of Press, Propaganda, and Agitation. Assassinated by a Social-Revolutionary terrorist in June 1918. Moisei S. Uritsky (1873–1918): Bolshevik since 1917 and member of the Revolutionary Military Committee which directed the October rising; 'Left Communist' in 1918; Chairman of the Petrograd Cheka at the time of his murder by a Social-Revolutionary.

and most impermissible errors that the Bolshevik leaders committed in 1918, when plots, blockades, and interventions made them lose their heads. All evidence indicates that revolutionary tribunals, functioning in the light of day (without excluding secret sessions in particular cases) and admitting the right of defence, would have attained the same efficiency with far less abuse and depravity. Was it so necessary to revert to the procedures of the Inquisition? By the beginning of 1919, the Chekas had little or no resistance against this psychological perversion and corruption. I know for a fact that Dzerzhinsky judged them to be 'half-rotten', and saw no solution to the evil except in shooting the worst Chekists and abolishing the death-penalty as quickly as possible. . . . Meanwhile, the Terror went on, since the whole Party was living in the sure inner knowledge that they would be massacred in the event of defeat; and defeat remained possible from one week to the next.

In every prison there were quarters reserved for Chekists, judges, police of all sorts, informers and executioners. The executioners, who used Nagan revolvers, generally ended by being executed themselves. They began to drink and to wander around firing unexpectedly at anybody. I was acquainted with several cases of this sort. I was also closely acquainted with the terrible Chudin case. Still young, though a revolutionary of 1905 vintage, Chudin, a tall curly-headed lad whose roguish stare was softened by his pince-nez, had fallen in love with a girl he had met at a class. She became his mistress. A number of swindlers exploited his sincerity by prevailing on him to intercede for some genuine speculators, more than mere suspects, whose release they thus obtained. Dzerzhinsky had Chudin and his girl and the swindlers all shot. No one doubted Chudin's honesty; there was bitter dismay all round. Years later, comrades said to me, 'On that day we shot the best man among us.' They never forgave themselves.

Fortunately, the democratic manners of the Party were still strong enough to enable militants to intercede fairly easily with the Cheka against certain blunders. It was all the easier for me to do this since the leaders of the Cheka lived at the Astoria, including Ivan Bakayev, President of the 'Extraordinary Commission'. Bakayev was a handsome fellow of about thirty, with the careless appearance of a Russian village accordion-player; indeed, he liked to wear a smock with an embroidered collar and coloured border, just like such a player. In the performance of his frightful duty he exercised an impartial will and a scrupulous vigilance. I saved several people, although once I failed, in circumstances that were both cruel and ridiculous. This concerned an officer named (I think) Nesterenko, a Frenchwoman's husband, who was arrested at Kronstadt in connexion with the Lindquist conspiracy. Bakayev promised me that he would personally review the dossier. When I met him again he smiled: 'It isn't serious, I'll soon have him released.' I took pleasure in disclosing this good news to the suspect's wife and daughter.

A few days later I met Bakayev passing from room to room in the Smolny, joking as he loved to. When he saw me, his face grew pale: 'Too late, Victor Lvovich! While I was away they shot the poor devil.' He went past to his next business, spreading his hands wide in a gesture of powerlessness.[1]

Shocks of this kind did not happen often, but the Terror was too much for us. I arranged the release of a distant relative, a subaltern confined as a hostage in the Peter-Paul Fortress. He came to me to tell me that they had failed to give him back his papers on his discharge. 'Go and ask for them back,' I said. Off he went, only to return thunderstruck. 'An official whispered me an answer, "Don't press for it, you've been reported shot for the last ten days." ' He gave up bothering about the matter.

Often at the Cheka I would meet the man whom I came to dub mentally as the 'great interceder', Maxim Gorky. His efforts tormented Zinoviev and Lenin, but he nearly always got his way. In cases that were difficult I approached him, and he never refused to intervene. But, although he was working for the journal *Communist International*, not without violent arguments with Zinoviev over some wording in every article he wrote, he once greeted me with a kind of roaring fury. On that day I was coming from a discussion with Zinoviev. Gorky shouted out, 'Don't talk to me of that beast ever again—tell him that his torturers are a disgrace to the human image!' Their quarrel lasted until Petrograd underwent its new phase of mortal peril.

---

[1] After his period as Chairman of the Petrograd Cheka, Bakayev went on (1920) to fill a similar post in south-east Russia. Later a prominent member of the Zinoviev Opposition, he was sentenced to death and shot as a result of the 1936 'Trial of the Sixteen'.

The spring of 1919 opened with events at once expected and surprising. At the beginning of April Munich acquired a Soviet régime. On 22 March Hungary quietly became a Soviet Republic through the abdication of Count Karolyi's bourgeois government. Bela Kun, who had been sent to Budapest by Lenin and Zinoviev, came out of jail to take power. The bad news from the Civil War fronts lost their importance. Even the fall of Munich, captured by General Hoffmann on 1 May, seemed rather unimportant by comparison with the revolutionary victories now expected to follow in Central Europe, Bohemia, Italy, and Bulgaria. (However, the massacres at Munich did reinforce the terrorist state of mind, and the atrocities committed at Ufa by Admiral Kolchak's troops, who burned Red prisoners alive, had lately enabled the Chekists to prevail against those Party members who hoped for a greater degree of humanity.)

The Executive of the International was in session at Moscow, with Angelica Balabanova in charge of the secretariat; actually its political control was managed from Petrograd, by Zinoviev, with whom Karl Radek and Bukharin used to come and confer. The Executive held a session also at Petrograd; this was attended by Finns (e.g. Sirola), Bulgarians, the ambassador from Soviet Hungary, Rudniansky, and the Volga German Klinger. I was present at these meetings, although I had still not joined the Party. I remember that the anarchist William Shatov, for a short while the military governor of the old capital, was also invited. There the superiority of the Russians, compared with the foreign revolutionaries, amazed me: it was immediately obvious. I found Zinoviev's optimism terrifying. He seemed to have no doubts at all: the European Revolution was on the way, and nothing would stop it. I can see him now, at the end of the session, his finger-tips playing with the little tassels of silken cord which he wore instead of a tie, wreathed in smiles, and saying about some resolution or other, 'Always provided that new revolutions do not come and upset our plans for the forthcoming weeks!' He was setting the tone.

We had white nights, and superb weather. Towards one in the morning a faint bluish light lay over the canals, the Neva, the golden spires of the palaces and the empty squares with their equestrian statues of dead emperors. I went to bed in guard-houses, and did my turn of sentry-duty in outlying railway stations, reading Alexander

Herzen. Quite a few of us sentries took books with us. I searched people's homes: house by house we sifted apartments, looking for arms and White agents. I could have easily avoided this unpleasant work, but I went off to it with a will, knowing that wherever I went no brutality, thefts, or stupid arrests would take place. I remember a weird exchange of shots on the roofs of high buildings overlooking a sky-blue canal. Men fled before us, firing their revolvers at us from behind the chimney-pots. I kept slipping on the sheet-iron roof and my heavy rifle dragged on me frightfully. The men we were after escaped, but I treasured an unforgettable vision of the city, seen at 3 a.m. in all its magical paleness.

The city was saved mainly through Grigori Yevdokimov, an old seafarer, vigorous and grey-haired, with a *mujik's* roughness. Loud of voice, fond of the bottle, he never seemed to admit that a situation was hopeless. When it seemed impossible for the Moscow–Petrograd railway to operate, since there was not more than two days' supply even of dry wood, I heard him exclaim, 'Well, they can chop down wood on the way! The journey will be done in twenty hours, no more!' He was the organizer of the city's second line of defence, where the gun-batteries were lined up by young girls from the Communist Party.

The actual operations leading to the sailors' capture of the fort of Krasnaya Gorka were directed by Bill Shatov. I was present at a private meeting in his room at the Astoria, which concerned the best method of using the crews of the Fleet. Shatov explained that these merry youngsters were the best fed in the garrison, the best accommodated, and the most appreciated by pretty girls, to whom they could now and then slip a tin of food; consequently none of them was agreeable to fighting for more than a few hours, being concerned to get a comfortable sleep on board ship. Someone suggested that once they were disembarked, the ships should be sent away on some plausible pretext. They would then have to hold the front for twenty-four hours, having no further means of retreat!

How did Bill Shatov manage to keep his rotundity and good humour? He was the only fat man among us, with a remarkable face, like an American businessman's, clean-shaven and fleshy. Working-class, converted to anarchism by exiles in Canada, a lively and decisive organizer, he was the real leader of the Tenth Red Army. Every time he returned from the front, he loaded us with anecdotes, such as the tale of a certain small-town mayor who, mistaking the Reds for the Whites, and Shatov himself for a colonel, had come to him in the thick of the gunfire to present a complimentary address, specially written for the occasion. Bill knocked him down on the spot. 'Just imagine, the idiot had his big medallion from the Tsar hung around his neck!' Later, in 1929 or so, Shatov became one of the builders of the Turkestan–Siberia railway.

For several months we experienced a lull. The summer brought us inexpressible relief. Even the famine was a little diminished. I made frequent journeys to Moscow. Its circular, leafy boulevards were filled in the evening with a buzzing, amorous crowd, dressed in bright colours; there was very little illumination at nightfall, and the hum of the crowd could be heard from far away in the twilight and afterwards in the darkness. Soldiers from the Civil War, girls from the old bourgeoisie who packed the Soviet offices during the day, refugees from the massacres in the Ukraine, where nationalist bands were systematically slaughtering the Jewish population, men wanted by the Cheka, plotting in broad daylight two steps from the torture-cellars, Imagist poets and Futurist painters; all of them could be seen scurrying to live.

In Tverskaya Street there were several poets' cafés; it was the time when Sergei Yesenin was becoming famous, sometimes writing his splendid poetry in chalk on the walls of the now secularized Monastery of the Passion. I met him in a seedy café. Over-powdered, over-painted women, leaning on the marble slabs, cigarettes between their fingers, drank coffee made from roasted oats; men clad in black leather, frowning and tight-lipped, with heavy revolvers at their belts, had their arms around the women's waists. These fellows knew what it was to live rough, knew the taste of blood, the odd, painful impact of a bullet in the flesh, and it all made them appreciative of the poems, incanted and almost sung, whose violent images jostled each other as though in a fight.

When I saw Yesenin for the first time, I disliked him. Twenty-four years old, he mixed with the women, ruffians, and ragamuffins from the dark corners of Moscow. A drinker, his voice was hoarse, his eyes worn, his handsome young face puffed and polished, his golden-blond hair flowing in waves around his temples. He was surrounded by sheer glory: the old Symbolist poets recognized him as an equal, the intelligentsia acclaimed his slim volumes, and the folk of the street sang his poems! He deserved all of it. Dressed in a white silk smock, he would mount the stage and begin to declaim. The affectation, the calculated elegance, the alcoholic's voice, the puffy face, everything prejudiced me against him; and the atmosphere of a decomposing Bohemianism, entangling its homosexuals and exotics with our militants, all but disgusted me. Yet, like everyone else, I yielded in a single instant to the positive sorcery of that ruined voice, of a poetry which came from the inmost depths of the man and the age.

Coming from there, I used to stop in front of the glass cases, some of them with long cracks from last year's bullets, where Mayakovsky was sticking his agitational posters against the Entente, The Flea,[1] the White generals, Lloyd George, Clemenceau, and capitalism, this last being symbolized by a pot-bellied character in a top hat, smoking an enormous cigar. A small volume by Ehrenburg (now on the run) was in circulation: it was a *Prayer for Russia*, so ravished and crucified by the Revolution. Lunacharsky, People's Commissar for Public Education, had given the Futurist painters a free hand in the decoration of Moscow; they had transformed the stalls in one of the markets into gigantic flowers. The great lyric tradition, hitherto confined to literary circles, was seeking fresh outlets in the public squares. The poets were learning to declaim or chant their work before huge audiences from the streets; by this approach their personal tone was regenerated and their preciosity gave way to power and fervour.

As autumn approached we in Petrograd, the front-line city, sensed the return of danger, this time perhaps mortal. True enough, we were accustomed to it. In Tallinn (Reval), Estonia, a British general was setting up a provisional government for Russia, at whose head he placed a certain Mr. Liasoñov, a big oil-capitalist. That at any rate was not dangerous. In Helsinki, the exiles had a White Stock Exchange where they still quoted bank-notes bearing the Tsars' effigy. (This was pretty good, since we used to print them specially for the poor fools.) Here, too, they sold the real estate of Soviet towns and the shares of socialized enterprises; a ghost-capitalism was struggling to survive over there. That was not dangerous either. What was really dangerous was typhus and famine. The

[1] Mayakovsky's parody of Moussorgsky's famous song. In Mayakovsky's version the Flea is Denikin.

Red divisions on the Estonian front, exposed to lice and hunger, were demoralized. In the shattered trenches I saw emaciated, dejected soldiers, absolutely incapable of any further effort. The cold rains of autumn came, and the war went by dismally for those poor fellows, without hope, or victories, or boots, or provisions; for a number of them it was the sixth year of war, and they had made the Revolution to gain peace! They felt as though they were in one of the rings of Hell. Vainly the *ABC of Communism* explained that they would have land, justice, peace, and equality, when in the near future the world revolution was achieved. Our divisions were slowly melting away under the ghastly sun of misery.

A most mischievous movement had grown up inside the armies engaged in the Civil War, White, Red, and the rest: that of the Greens. These borrowed their title from the forests in which they took refuge, uniting deserters from all the armies that were now unwilling to fight for anyone, whether Generals or Commissars: these would fight now only for themselves, simply to stay out of the civil war. The movement existed over the whole of Russia. We knew that in the forests of the Pskov region, the Greens' effective forces were on the increase, numbering several tens of thousands. Well organized, complete with their own general staff, and supported by the peasants, they were eating the Red Army away. Cases of desertion to the enemy had also been multiplying ever since it became known that the generals were giving white bread to their troops. Fortunately, the caste-outlook of the officers of the old régime neutralized the trouble; they persisted in wearing epaulettes, demanding the military salute, and being compulsorily addressed as 'Your Honour', thus exhaling such a stench of the past that our deserters, once they had fed themselves, deserted again and came back to receive a pardon, if they did not join the Greens. On both sides of the front line numbers fluctuated constantly.

On 11 October the White army under General Yudenich captured Yamburg, on the Estonian border; in fact it encountered hardly any resistance. Our skeletons of soldiery (or, to be exact, all that was left of them) broke and fled. It was a nasty moment. General Denikin's National Army was now occupying the whole of the Ukraine and on the way to capturing Orel. Admiral Kolchak, the 'Supreme Head' of the counter-revolution, was in control of all Siberia and now threatened the Urals. The British occupied Archangel, where one of the oldest Russian revolutionaries, Chaikovsky, a former friend of my father, presided over a 'democratic' government which shot the Reds without quarter. The French and Rumanians had just been chased out of Odessa by a Black (anarchist) army, but a French fleet was in the Black Sea. Soviet Hungary had perished. In short, when we drew up the balance-sheet it seemed most probable that the Revolution was approaching its death-agony, that a White military dictatorship would soon prevail and that we should be all hanged or shot. This frank conviction, far from spreading discouragement, galvanized our spirit of resistance.

My friend Mazin (Lichtenstadt) went off to the front, after a talk we both had with Zinoviev. 'The front line is everywhere,' we told him. 'Out in the scrubland or the marshes you will die soon and without achieving anything. Men better fitted for war than you are needed for that, and there is no shortage of them.' But he insisted. He told me afterwards that since we were facing utter ruin, and were probably doomed, he saw no point in gaining a mere few month's reprieve for his own life, doing jobs of organization, publishing, etc., which were fruitless from now on; and that, at an hour when so many men were dying quite uselessly out in the wilds, he felt a horror of Smolny offices, committees, printed matter, and the Hotel Astoria. I imagined that the war-service of this myopic intellectual, absent-minded over the smallest things, was destined to last a fortnight at the most. Mazin-Lichtenstadt departed, and made war for a little longer than that. Zinoviev, doubtless wishing to save him, had him appointed political commissar to the Sixth Division, which was barring Yudenich's path. The Sixth Division broke under fire and was overwhelmed; its remnants fled in disarray over the sodden roads. Bill Shatov, scandalized, showed me a letter from Mazin which said: 'The Sixth Division no longer exists; there is only a fleeing mob over which I have no more control. The command no longer exists. I demand to be relieved of my political functions and given a private's rifle.'

'He is mad!' Shatov exclaimed, 'If all our commissars were so romantic, a fine state we should be in! I'm giving him a dressing-down by telegram and I won't mince my words, I assure you!'

Vladimir Ossipovich Mazin did as he had written: he renounced his command, picked up a rifle, collected a little band of Communists and tried to stop the rout and the enemy simultaneously. There were four of these determined comrades on the outskirts of a forest; one of the four was his orderly, who had refused to desert him. These four engaged in combat alone against the White cavalry, and were killed. Much later, some peasants pointed out to us the spot where the commissar had fired his last bullets before falling. They had buried him there. Four corpses, calcined by the earth, were taken back to Petrograd; one of them, a little soldier beaten to death with a rifle-butt, his skull battered in, was still making to protect his face with his stiffened arm. I identified Mazin by his fine finger-nails, a former prisoner from Schlüsselburg identified him by his teeth. We laid him in his grave in the Field of Mars. (This was after our victory, a victory in which I think none of us then believed.)

Naturally, like all the comrades, I performed a host of functions. I ran the Romance-language section and publications of the International, I met the foreign delegates who kept arriving by adventurous routes through the blockade's barbed-wire barrier. I carried out a Commissar's duties over the archives of the old Ministry of the Interior, i.e. the Okhrana; I was at the same time a trooper in the Communist battalion of the Second District, and a member of the Defence staff, where I was engaged in smuggling between Russia and Finland. From honest dealers in Helsinki we would buy excellent weapons, Mauser pistols in wooden cases which were delivered to us on a 'quiet sector' of the front (quiet because of this minor traffic) fifty or so kilometres from Leningrad. To pay for these useful commodities, we printed whole casefuls of beautiful 500 rouble notes, watery in appearance, with the image of Catherine the Great and the signature of a bank-director as dead as his bank, his social order and the Empress Catherine. Case for case, the exchange was made silently in a wood of sombre firs—it was really the maddest commercial transaction imaginable. Obviously the recipients of the Imperial bank-notes were taking out a mortgage on our deaths, at the same time furnishing us with the means for our defence.

The archives of the Okhrana, the late political police of the autocracy, presented a serious problem. In no event were they to be allowed to fall again into reactionary hands. They contained biographies and even excellent historical dissertations on the revolutionary parties; if we were to undergo a defeat, followed by White terror and illegal resistance (for which we were making preparation), the whole collection would provide precious weapons for tomorrow's hangmen and firing-squads. To add another relatively minor inconvenience, some scholarly and sympathetic archivists, who also anticipated our coming end, were surreptitiously pilfering these stirring old documents, out of an entirely admirable concern to see that they were not destroyed. There were no railway trucks to convey them to Moscow, and no time either, since Petrograd might fall any week now. While barricades were being raised at street-corners, I saw to the packing of those boxes considered the most interesting, so that I could try to get them out at the last moment; and I ordered arrangements to be made whereby, either in the Senate building or at the station itself, everything would be burnt and blown up by a squad of trusted comrades at the moment when any alternative course would cease to be possible. The archivists (from whom I concealed this plan) suspected that something was afoot and were sick with fear and vexation. Leonid Borisovich Krassin came on behalf of the Central Committee to inquire about the measures that were being taken to save or destroy the police-archives, in which he was a figure of perceptible importance. A perfect gentleman, dressed in bourgeois style with a genuine concern for correctness and elegance, he passed through our head-quarters, which were full of workers in cloth caps and overcoats with cartridge-belts. A handsome man, with a beard neatly trimmed to a broad point, an intellectual in the grand style, he was at the time of our snatched conversation so tired that I thought he was sometimes asleep on his feet.

On 7 October Yudenich captured Gatchina, about twenty-five miles from Petrograd. Two days later his advance forces entered Ligovo, on the city's outskirts, about nine miles away. Bill Shatov stormed away: 'The principles of military science, which my experts never stop reminding me of, require Divisional Head-quarters to be such-and-such many miles from the firing-line. Here we are, 200 yards away! I told them, "To hell with your scientific principles!" '

It seemed quite plainly to be our death-agony. There were no trains and no fuel for evacuation, and scarcely a few dozen cars. We had sent the children of known militants off to the Urals; they were travelling there now in the first snows, from one famished village to the next, not knowing where to halt. We arranged new identities for ourselves, trying to 'change our faces'. It was relatively easy for those with beards, who only had to shave, but as for the others. . . . An efficient girl-comrade, lively and affable as a child, was setting up secret arms-depots. I no longer slept at the Astoria, whose ground floor was lined with sandbags and machine-guns against a siege; I spent my nights with the Communist troops in the outer defences. My wife, who was pregnant, resorted to sleeping in an ambulance in the rear, with a case holding a little linen and our most precious possessions, so that we might be reunited during the battle and fight together in the retreat along the Neva.

The plan for the city's internal defence envisaged fighting along the canals dividing the town, a stubborn defence of the bridges, and a final retreat that was quite impracticable. The huge solemn spaces of Petrograd, in their pale autumn melancholy, fitted this atmosphere of inescapable defeat. So deserted was the city that riders could gallop at full speed along the central thoroughfares. The Smolny Institute (once an educational establishment for young ladies of the aristocracy) now the office of the Executive of the Soviet and the Party Committee, presented a stern picture with its show of cannon at the entrance. It is made up of two masses of buildings surrounded by gardens, standing between vast streets and the equally vast turbulence of the Neva, which is straddled not far from there by an iron bridge. There is a former convent, whose Baroque architecture is charmingly ornate, standing with its church, a rather lofty building with figured belfry-turrets; the whole is painted in a bright blue. Next to it is the Institute proper, with pediments and columns on all four sides, a two-floor barracks built by architects who knew of nothing but straight lines, rectangle upon rectangle. The convent housed the Workers' Guards. The great square office-rooms, whose windows overlooked the waste-lands of the dying city, were practically empty. A pale, puffy Zinoviev, round-shouldered and quiet-spoken, lived there amidst telephones, in constant communication with Lenin. He pleaded for resistance, but his voice was weakening. The most competent experts, engineers, and former pupils of the Military School (no less), considered resistance to be quite impossible and made constant reference to the massacres it would entail, just as though the city's surrender or abandonment were not bound to entail a massacre of a more demoralizing character.

The news from the other fronts was so bad that Lenin was reluctant to sacrifice the last available forces in the defence of a doomed city. Trotsky thought otherwise; the Politbureau entrusted him with the final initiative. He arrived at almost the last moment and his presence instantly changed the atmosphere at Smolny, as it did when he visited headquarters and the Peter-Paul Fortress.

Trotsky arrived with a train, that famous train which had been speeding to and fro along the different fronts since the day in the previous year when its engine-men, orderlies, typists and military experts had, together with Trotsky, Ivan Smirnov, and Rosengoltz, retrieved a hopeless situation by winning the battle of Sviazhsk. The train of the Revolutionary War Council's President contained excellent motor-cars, a liaison staff, a court of justice, a print-shop for propaganda, sanitary squads, and specialists in engineering, provisioning, street-fighting, and artillery, all of them men picked in battle, all self-confident, all bound together by friendship and trust, all kept to a strict, vigorous discipline by a leader they admired, all dressed in black leather, red stars on their peaked caps, all exhaling energy. It was a nucleus of resolute and efficiently serviced organizers, who hastened wherever danger demanded their presence.

They took everything in hand, meticulously and passionately. It was magical. Trotsky kept saying, 'It is impossible for a little army of 15,000 ex-officers to master a working-class capital of 700,000 inhabitants.' He had posters put up proclaiming that the city would 'defend itself on its own ground', that from now on this was the best strategic method, that the small White army would be lost in the labyrinth of fortified streets and there meet its grave. In contrast to this determination to win, a French Communist, René Marchand, who had just seen Lenin, told me of Vladimir Ilyich's remark, matter-of-fact and mischievous as usual: 'Oh well, we shall have to go underground all over again!' Or was this really so much of a contrast?

I caught only a glimpse of Trotsky in the street, then at a packed meeting of the Soviet, where he announced the arrival of a division of Bashkirian cavalry which we would launch relentlessly against Finland if Finland budged an inch! (It depended on Finland to deal us the death-blow.) This was an extremely skilful threat, which caused a chill of terror to pass over Helsinki. This session of the

Soviet took place beneath the lofty white columns of the Tauride Palace, in the amphitheatre of the old Imperial Duma. Trotsky was all tension and energy: he was, besides, an orator of unique quality, whose metallic voice projected a great distance, ejaculating its short sentences that were often sardonic and always infused with a truly spontaneous passion. The decision to fight to the death was taken enthusiastically, and the whole amphitheatre raised a song of immense power. I reflected that the psalms sung by Cromwell's Roundheads before their decisive battles must have sounded no different a tone.

Capable regiments of infantry, recalled from the Polish front, now marched through the city to take up their positions in the suburbs. The Bashkirian cavalry, mounted on small, long-haired horses from the steppes, rode in line along the streets. These horsemen, figures from a distant past, swarthy and wearing black sheepskin caps, sang their old songs in guttural voices to an accompaniment of shrill whistling. Sometimes a thin, bespectacled intellectual would ride at their head: he was destined to become the author Konstantin Fedin. They fought rarely and deplorably, but that was unimportant. Convoys of provisions, extorted God knows how from God knows where, were arriving too: this was the most efficient weapon. It was rumoured that the Whites had tanks. Trotsky had it proclaimed that the infantry was well able to knock tanks out. Certain mysterious but ingenious agitators spread the rumour, which may even have been true, that Yudenich's tanks were made of painted wood. The city was dotted with veritable fortresses; lines of cannon occupied the streets. Material from the underground drainage-system was used to build these fortifications, the big pipes from the sewers being particularly handy.

The anarchists were mobilized for the work of defence. Kolabushkin, once a prisoner at Schlüsselburg, was their leading light. The Party gave them arms, and they had a 'Black headquarters' in a devastated apartment belonging to a dentist who had fled. There, disorder and comradeship presided above all. There also presided the smile of a fair-haired and intensely charming girl, who came from the Ukraine with reports of frightful massacres and the latest news of Makhno. Tsvetkova was to die shortly of typhus. She brought a real beam of sunshine into that group of inflamed and embittered men. It was they who, on the night of the worst danger, occupied the printing-works of *Pravda*, the Bolshevik paper that they hated, ready to defend it to the death. They discovered two Whites in their midst, armed with hand-grenades and about to blow them up. What were they to do? They locked them in a room and looked at each other in embarrassment: 'We are jailers, just like the Cheka!' They despised the Cheka with all their hearts. A proposal to shoot these enemy spies was rejected with horror. 'What, us to be executioners!'

Finally, my friend Kolabushkin, the ex-convict, at the time one of the organizers of the Republic's fuel-supply, was charged with taking them to the Peter-Paul Fortress. This was a poor compromise, since there the Cheka would shoot them within the hour. Once in the Black Guard's motor-car, Kolabushkin, who in the past had made this very same journey himself between a couple of Tsarist gendarmes, saw their trapped faces and remembered the days of his youth. He stopped the car and impulsively told them, 'Hop it, you bastards!' Afterwards he came, relieved but vexed, to tell me about those unbearable moments. 'I was a fool, wasn't I?' he asked me. 'But you know, all the same, I'm glad of it.'

Petrograd was saved on 21 October at the battle of the Pulkovo heights, some ten miles south of the half-encircled city. Defeat was transformed into a victory so complete that Yudenich's troops rolled back in disorder towards the Estonian frontier. There the Estonians blocked their path. The White army that had failed to capture Petrograd perished miserably. About 300 workers who had hastened from Schlüsselburg had also blocked the Whites at one critical moment, before being mown down by a body of officers who marched into the fray as though on parade.

Mazin-Lichtenstadt's last message reached me after the battle. It was a letter that he asked me to send on to his wife. It said, 'He who sends men to their deaths must see that he himself gets killed.'

It was an extraordinary fact, and one that proves how deep-rooted in its causes, both social and psychological (they amount to the same), our resilience was: but the same apparent miracle was achieved simultaneously on all the fronts of the Civil War, although at the end of October and the beginning of November the situation seemed equally hopeless everywhere. During the battle near Pulkovo, the White army of General Denikin was beaten not far from Voronezh by the Red cavalry, hastily assembled by Trotsky and commanded by a former N.C.O. named Budyenny. On 14 November Admiral Kolchak, the 'Supreme Head', lost Omsk, his capital in western Siberia. Salvation had come.

The White disaster was the result of two cardinal errors: their failure to have the intelligence and courage to carry out agrarian reform in the territories they wrested from the Revolution, and their reinstatement everywhere of the ancient trinity of generals, high clergy, and landlords. A boundless confidence returned to us. I remembered what Mazin said, in the worst days of our famine when we saw old folk collapsing in the street, some holding out a little tin saucepan in their emaciated fingers. 'All the same' he told me, we are the greatest power in the world. Alone, we are bringing the world a new principle of justice and the rational organization of work. Alone, in all this war-sick Europe where nobody wants to fight any more, we are able to form new armies, and tomorrow we shall be able to wage wars that are truly just. Their house of cards must fall; the longer it lasts, the more misery and bloodshed it will cost.' By 'the house of cards' we meant the Versailles Treaty which, in June 1919, had just been signed.

Together with Maxim Gorky, P. E. Shchegolev, the historian, and Novorusky, the veteran of the *People's Will* Party, we founded the first Museum of the Revolution. Zinoviev had a large part of the Winter Palace allotted to us. Like most of the Party leaders, he really wanted to make it a museum for Bolshevik propaganda but, anxious to have the support of the revolutionary intellectuals, and at least the appearance of a scientific concern, he allowed us to make an honest beginning. I continued to investigate the Okhrana archives. The frightful mass of documents that I found there afforded a unique kind of psychological interest; but the practical bearing of my research was perhaps even greater. For the first time the entire mechanism of an authoritarian empire's police-repression had fallen into the hands of revolutionaries. Thorough study of this material could furnish the militants of other countries with useful clues. Despite our enthusiasm and our sense of right, we were not certain that one day reaction would not drive us back. We were, indeed, more or less convinced to the contrary: it was a generally accepted thesis, which Lenin stated several times, that Russia, agricultural and backward (from an industrial standpoint) as it was, could not create a lasting Socialist system for itself by its own efforts, and that consequently we should be overcome sooner or later unless the European revolution, or at the very least the Socialist revolution in Central Europe, assured Socialism of a broader and more viable base. Finally, we knew that former police-spies were at work among us, most of them ready to resume their services to the counter-revolution; this implied grave danger for us.

In the first days of the March 1917 Revolution, the Petrograd Palace of Justice had gone up in flames. We knew that the destruction of its archives, its anthropometric cards and collection of secrets had been the work both of the criminal underworld, which was interested in destroying these documents, and of police agents. At Kronstadt a 'revolutionary' who was also a police-spy had carried off the Security archives and burnt them. The Okhrana's secret collection contained between 30,000 and 40,000 records of *agents-provocateurs* active over the last twenty years. By devoting ourselves to a simple calculation of the probabilities of decease, and various other eliminations, and taking account of the 3,000 or so that had been unmasked through the patient work of the archivists, we estimated that several thousand former secret agents were still active in the Revolution; at least 5,000, according to the historian Shchegolev, who told me of the following incident which happened in a town on the Volga.

A commission, composed of known members of the different parties of the extreme Left and the Left in general, was interrogating the leading officials of the Imperial police on this question of provocation. The head of the political police apologized for not being able to name two of his ex-agents since they were members of this very commission; he would rather that these gentlemen obeyed the voice of their conscience and identified themselves! And two of the 'revolutionaries' stood up in confusion.

The old secret agents, all of them initiates into the political life, could pretend to be seasoned revolutionaries; since they were not at all troubled by scruples, they found it to their own advantage to rally to the ruling party, in which it was easy for them to obtain good positions. Consequently they played a certain role in the system: we guessed that some of them were under orders to select and follow the worst possible policies, engineering excesses and sowing discredit. It was extremely hard to unmask them. As a rule the records were classified under pseudonyms, and assiduous cross-checking was necessary before an identification could be established. For example, in 1912 there were in the revolutionary organizations of Moscow (which were by no means mass organizations) fifty-five police agents: seventeen Social-Revolutionaries, twenty Menshevik or Bolshevik Social-Democrats, three anarchists, eleven students, and several Liberals. In the same period the leader of the Bolshevik fraction in the Duma, and spokesman for Lenin, was a police-spy, Malinovsky. The head of the Social-Revolutionary Party's terrorist organization, a member of its Central Committee, was an Okhrana agent, Evno Azev; this from 1903 to 1908, at the time of the most sensational assassinations. Somewhere around 1930, to cut a long story short, several former police agents were finally unmasked among the Leningrad leadership! I found an extraordinary file, one in need of no deciphering, No. 378: Julia Orestovna Serova, wife of a Bolshevik deputy in the Second Imperial Duma; he was a fine militant who had been shot in 1918 at Chita. The catalogue of Serova's services, listed in a report to the Minister, revealed that she had betrayed caches of arms and literature, had Rykov, Kamenev and many others arrested, and spied for a great length of time on the Party committees. Having at last fallen under suspicion and been sent packing she wrote, in February 1917, a few weeks before the fall of the autocracy, to the head of the secret police asking to be re-employed 'in view of the great events that are drawing near'. She got married again, to a Bolshevik worker, and so was once again in a position to carry on her activities. The letters revealed a woman of practical intelligence, zealous, greedy for money, and perhaps hysterical. One evening, in a circle of friends having tea, we discussed this particular psychological case. An old woman-militant stood up flabbergasted: 'Serova? But I just met her in town! She's actually married again, to a comrade in the Vyborg district!' Serova was arrested and shot.

The psychology of the police-spy was usually double-natured. Gorky showed me a letter which one of them, still at large, had written to him. The gist of it ran: 'I hated myself, but I knew that my little betrayals would not stop the Revolution from marching on.' The Okhrana's instructions advised its minions to seek out those revolutionaries who were fainthearted, embittered or disappointed, to make use of personal rivalries, and to assist the advancement of skilful agents by eliminating the most talented militants. The old

barrister Kozlovsky, who had been the first People's Commissar for
Justice, told me his impressions of Malinovsky. The former Bolshevik leader in the Duma returned to Russia from Germany in
1918, even after his unmasking and, presenting himself at Smolny,
asked to be arrested. 'Malinovsky? Don't know the name!' replied
the commandant of the guard, 'Go and explain yourself to the Party
Committee!' Kozlovsky interrogated him; Malinovsky said that he
could not live outside the Revolution: 'I have been a double-dealer
despite my own best feelings. I want to be shot!' He maintained this
attitude in front of the revolutionary tribunal. Krylenko ruthlessly
demanded sentence ('The adventurer is playing his last card!'),
and Malinovsky was shot in the gardens of the Kremlin. Many
indications led me to believe that he was absolutely sincere and that
if he had been allowed to live, he would have served as faithfully as
the others. But what confidence could the others have in him?

Gorky tried to save the lives of the police-spies, who in his eyes
were the repositories of a unique social and psychological experience.
'These men are a sort of monster, worthy of preservation for research.' He used the same arguments to defend the lives of high
officials in the Tsarist political police. I remember a conversation on
these matters which wandered on to the question of the necessity for
applying the death-penalty to children. The Soviet leaders were
concerned at the scale of juvenile crime. Certain children, more or
less abandoned, formed actual gangs. These were put into children's
homes, where they still starved; then they would abscond and
resume a life of crime. Olga, a pretty little girl of fourteen, had
several child murders and several absconsions on her record. She
organized burglaries in apartments where a child had been left
alone by the parents. She would talk to it through the door, win its
confidence, and get it to open the door to her. . . . What could be
done with her? Gorky argued for the establishment of colonies for
child-criminals in the North, where life is rough and adventure
always at hand. I do not know what became of the idea.

The Civil War seemed about to end. General Denikin's National
Army was in flight across the Ukraine. In Siberia Admiral Kolchak's
forces, encircled by the Red partisans, were in retreat. The idea of
a normalization of life was exerting increasing pressure within the
Party. Riazanov tirelessly demanded the abolition of the death-
penalty. The Cheka was unpopular. In the middle of January 1920

Dzerzhinsky, with the approval of Lenin and Trotsky, recommended the abolition of the death-sentence throughout the country, except in districts where there were military operations.

On 17 January the decree was passed by the Government and signed by Lenin as President of the Council of People's Commissars. For several days the prisons, crammed with suspects, had been living in tense expectation. They knew immediately of the tremendous good news, the end of the Terror; the decree had still not appeared in the newspapers. On the 18th or the 19th some of the comrades at Smolny told me in hushed voices of the tragedy of the preceding night—no one mentioned it openly. While the newspapers were printing the decree, the Petrograd Chekas were liquidating their stock! Cartload after cartload of suspects had been driven outside the city during the night, and then shot, heap upon heap. How many? In Petrograd between 150 and 200; in Moscow, it was said, between 200 and 300. In the dawn of the days that followed, the families of the massacred victims came to search that ghastly, freshly-dug ground, looking for any relics, such as buttons or scraps of stocking, that could be gathered there.

The Chekists had presented the Government with a *fait accompli*. Much later I became personally acquainted with one of those responsible for the Petrograd massacre: I will call him Leonidov. 'We thought', he told me 'that if the People's Commissars were getting converted to humanitarianism, that was their business. Our business was to crush the counter-revolution for ever, and they could shoot us afterwards if they felt like it!' It was a frightful and tragic example of occupational psychosis. Leonidov, when I knew him, was in any case definitely half insane. In all likelihood the incorrigible counter-revolutionaries were only a very minute percentage of the victims. A few months later, during my wife's confinement, I had a conversation with a sick woman who had just given birth to a stillborn child. Her husband, the engineer Trotsky or Troytsky, had been shot during that abominable night. He was a former Social-Revolutionary who had taken part in the 1905 Revolution, and had been imprisoned for 'speculation', that is, for a single purchase of sugar on the black market.

Even at Smolny, this drama was shrouded in utter mystery. However, it redounded to the régime's profound discredit. It was becoming clear, to me and to others, that the suppression of the

Cheka and the reintroduction of regular tribunals and rights of defence were from now on pre-conditions for the Revolution's own safety. But we could do absolutely nothing. The Politbureau, then composed (if I am not mistaken) of Lenin, Trotsky, Zinoviev, Kamenev, Rykov, and Bukharin, deliberated the question without daring to answer it, being itself, I have no doubt, the victim of a certain psychosis born of fear and ruthless authority. Against the Party the anarchists were right when they inscribed on their black banners, 'There is no worse poison than power'—meaning absolute power. From now on the psychosis of absolute power was to captivate the great majority of the leadership, especially at the lower levels. I know the greatness of these men; but they, who belonged to the future, were in this respect the prisoners of the past.

The spring of 1920 opened with a victory—the capture of Archangel, now evacuated by the British—and then, all at once, changed its aspect. Again there was peril, immediate and mortal: the Polish invasion. In the files of the Okhrana I had photographs of Pilsudski, condemned years ago for plotting against the Tsar's life. I met a doctor who had attended Pilsudski in a St. Petersburg hospital where he had pretended to be mad, with a rare perfection, in order to get away. Himself a revolutionary and a terrorist, he was now hurling his legions against us. A wave of anger and enthusiasm rose against him. Brussilov and Polivanov, old Tsarist generals, volunteered for the fight in response to an appeal by Trotsky. I could see Gorky burst into tears on a balcony in the Nevsky Prospect, haranguing a battalion off to the front. 'When will we stop all this killing and bleeding?' he would mutter under his bristling moustache.

The death-penalty was reintroduced and, under the stimulus of defeat, the Chekas were given enlarged powers. The Poles were entering Kiev. Zinoviev kept saying, 'Our salvation lies in the International,' and Lenin agreed with him. At the height of the war the Second Congress of the Communist International was hastily summoned. I worked literally day and night to prepare for it since, thanks to my knowledge of languages and the Western world, I was practically the only person available to perform a whole host of duties. I met Lansbury[1] and John Reed on their arrival. I hid a

---

[1] George Lansbury did visit Russia in February 1920, but not for the Comintern Congress.

delegation of Hungarian Left Communists, who were in opposition to Bela Kun and in some kind of liaison with Rakovsky. We published the International's periodical in four languages. We sent innumerable secret messages abroad by various adventurous routes. I translated Lenin's messages, and also the book that Trotsky had just written in his military train, *Terrorism and Communism*, which emphasized the necessity for a long dictatorship 'in the period of transition to socialism', for several decades at least. Trotsky's rigid ideas, with their schematism and voluntarism, disturbed me a little. Everything was scarce: staff, paper, ink, even bread, as well as facilities for communication. All we received in the way of foreign newspapers were a few copies bought in Helsinki by smugglers who crossed the front lines specially for the purpose. I paid them 100 roubles per copy. On occasions when one of their number had been killed they came to ask for extra money, at which we did not demur. In Moscow, organizational activity was proceeding at an equally feverish pace under the supervision of Angelica Balabanova and Bukharin.

I met Lenin when he came to Petrograd for the first session of the Congress. We had tea together in a small entertainment-room in the Smolny; Yevdokimov and Angel Pestaña, the delegate from the Spanish C.N.T., were with me when Lenin came in. He beamed, shaking the hands that were outstretched to him, passing from one salutation to the next. Yevdokimov and he embraced one another gaily, gazing straight into each other's eyes, happy like over-grown children. Vladimir Ilyich was wearing one of his old jackets dating back to the emigration, perhaps brought back from Zurich; I saw it on him in all seasons. Practically bald, his cranium high and bulging, his forehead strong, he had commonplace features: an amazingly fresh and pink face, a little reddish beard, slightly jutting cheekbones, eyes horizontal but apparently slanted because of the laughter-lines, a grey-green gaze at people, and a surpassing air of geniality and cheerful malice.

In the Kremlin he still occupied a small apartment built for a palace servant. In the recent winter he, like everyone else, had had no heating. When he went to the barber's he took his turn, thinking it unseemly for anyone to give way to him. An old housekeeper looked after his rooms and did his mending. He knew that he was the Party's foremost brain and recently, in a grave situation, had used no threat worse than that of resigning from the Central Committee so as to appeal to the rank and file! He craved a tribune's popularity, stamped with the seal of the masses' approval, devoid of any show or ceremony. His manners and behaviour betrayed not the slightest inkling of any taste for authority; what showed through was only the urgency of the devoted technician who wants the work to be done, and done quickly and well. Also in evidence was his forthright resolve that the new institutions, weak though they might be to the point of a merely symbolic existence, must nevertheless be respected.

On that day, or perhaps the following one, he spoke for several hours at the first formal session of the Congress, under the white colonnade of the Tauride Palace. His report dealt with the historical situation consequent upon the Versailles Treaty. Quoting abundantly from Maynard Keynes, Lenin established the insolvency of a Europe carved up arbitrarily by victorious imperialisms, and the impossibility of any lengthy endurance by Germany of the burdens that had been so idiotically imposed upon her; he concluded that a new European revolution, which was destined also to involve the colonial peoples of Asia, must be inevitable.

He was neither a great orator nor a first-rate lecturer. He employed no rhetoric and sought no demagogical effects. His vocabulary was that of a newspaper-article, and his technique included diverse forms of repetition, all with the aim of a driving in ideas thoroughly, as one drives in a nail. He was never boring, on account of his mimic's liveliness and the reasoned conviction which drove him. His customary gestures consisted of raising his hand to underline the importance of what he had said, and then bending towards the audience, smiling and earnest, his palms spread out in an act of demonstration: 'It is obvious, isn't it?' Here was a man of a basic simplicity, talking to you honestly with the sole purpose of convincing you, appealing exclusively to your judgement, to facts and sheer necessity. 'Facts have hard heads,' he was fond of saying. He was the embodiment of plain common sense, so much so that he disappointed the French delegates, who were used to impressive Parliamentary joustings. 'When you see Lenin at close quarters, he loses much of his glamour,' I was told by one French deputy, an eloquent sceptic positively stuffed with witty epigrams.

The Comintern's Second Congress took up the rest of its work in Moscow. The Congress staff and the foreign delegates lived in the Hotel *Delovoy Dvor*, centrally situated at the end of a wide boulevard, one side of which was lined by the white embattled rampart of Kitay-Gorod. Medieval gateways topped by an ancient turret formed the approach to the nearby Varvarka, where the first of the Romanovs had lived. From there we came out into the Kremlin, a city within a city, every entrance guarded by sentries who checked our passes. There, in the palaces of the old autocracy, in the midst of ancient Byzantine churches, lay the headquarters of the Revolution's double arm, the Soviet Government and the International. The only city the foreign delegates never got to know (and their incuriosity in this respect disturbed me) was the real, living Moscow, with its starvation-rations, its arrests, its sordid prison-episodes, its backstage racketeering. Sumptuously fed amidst universal misery (although, it is true, too many rotten eggs turned up at meal-times), shepherded from museums to model nurseries, the representatives of international Socialism seemed to react like holiday-makers or tourists within our poor Republic, flayed and bleeding with the siege. I discovered a novel variety of insensitivity: Marxist insensitivity. Paul Levi, a leading figure in the German Communist Party, an athletic and self-confident figure, told me outright that 'for a Marxist, the internal contradictions of the Russian Revolution were nothing to be surprised at'; this was doubtless true, except that he was using this general truth as a screen to shut away the sight of immediate fact, which has an importance all of its own. Most of the Marxist Left, now Bolshevized, adopted this complacent attitude. The words 'dictatorship of the proletariat' functioned as a magical explanation for them, without it ever occurring to them to ask where this dictator of a proletariat was, what it thought, felt, and did.

The Social-Democrats, by contrast, were notable for their critical spirit and for their incomprehension. Among the best of them (I am thinking of the Germans Daümig, Crispien, and Dittmann), their peaceful, bourgeoisified socialist humanism was so offended by the Revolution's harsh climate that they were incapable of thinking straight.[1] The anarchist delegates, with whom I held many discussions, had a healthy revulsion from 'official truths' and the

[1] Arthur Crispien (1875–1946) and Wilhelm Dittmann (1874–1954) both opposed the '21 Conditions' for affiliation to the Communist International, and broke with it after this Congress; Ernst Daümig (1866–1922), an experienced shock-fighter and underground worker, who had led the Revolutionary Shop Stewards' movement in 1918, supported and joined the International at this juncture, but sided with Paul Levi after the latter's expulsion from the Comintern in 1921.

trappings of power, and a passionate interest in actual life; but, as
the adherents of an essentially emotional approach to theory, who
were ignorant of political economy and had never faced the problem of power, they found it practically impossible to achieve any
theoretical understanding of what was going on. They were
excellent comrades, more or less at the stage of the romantic arguments for the 'universal revolution' that the libertarian artisans
had managed to frame between 1848 and 1860, before the growth of
modern industry and its proletariat. Among them were: Angel
Pestaña of the Barcelona C.N.T., a watchmaker and a brave popular
leader, slender in build, with beautiful dark eyes and a small
moustache of the same hue; Armando Borghi, of the Italian *Unione
Sindicale*, with his fine face, bearded, young and Mazzini-like, and his
fervent but velvety voice; Augustin Souchy, red-haired and with an
old trooper's face, the delegate from the Swedish and German
syndicalists; Lepetit, a sturdy navvy from the French C.G.T. and
Le Libertaire, merry but mistrustful and questioning, who suddenly
swore that 'in France the revolution would be made quite differently!' Lenin was very anxious to have the support of 'the best of the
anarchists'.

To tell the truth, outside Russia and perhaps Bulgaria, there
were no real Communists anywhere in the world. The old schools of
revolution, and the younger generation that had emerged from the
war, were both at an infinite distance from the Bolshevik mentality.
The bulk of these men were symptomatic of obsolete movements
which had been quite outrun by events, combining an abundance of
good intentions with a scarcity of talent. The French Socialist Party
was represented by Marcel Cachin and L.-O. Frossard, both of them
highly Parliamentary in their approach. Cachin was, as usual,
sniffing out the direction of the prevailing wind. Ever mindful of his
personal popularity, he was shifting to the Left, after having been a
supporter of the 'Sacred Union' during the war and a backer, on
behalf of the French Government, of Mussolini's jingoist campaigns
in Italy: this was in 1916. The Paris Committee of the Third International had sent Alfred Rosmer; he of the Ibsenesque surname was
a syndicalist, a devoted internationalist, and an old personal friend
of Trotsky. Beneath his half-smile Rosmer incarnated the qualities
of vigilance, discretion, silence, and dedication. His colleague from
the same Committee was Raymond Lefebvre, a tall sharp-featured

young man who had carried stretchers at Verdun. A poet and novelist, he had just written his confession of faith as a man home from the trenches, in a luxuriantly poetic style. It was entitled *Revolution or Death!* He spoke for the survivors of a generation now lying buried in communal graves. We quickly became friends.

Of the Italians, I remember the veteran Lazzari, an upright old man whose feverish voice burned with an undying enthusiasm; Serrati's bearded, myopic, and professorial face; Terracini, a young theoretician with a tall, ascetic forehead, who was fated to spend the best years of his life in jail, after giving the world a few pages of his keen intellect; Bordiga, exuberant and energetic, features blunt, hair thick, black and bristly, a man quivering under his encumbrance of ideas, experiences, and dark forecasts.[1]

There was Angelica Balabanova, a slender woman whose delicate, already motherly face was framed in a double braid of black hair. An air of extreme gracefulness compassed her about. Perpetually active, she still hoped for an International that was unconfined, open-hearted, and rather romantic. Rosa Luxemburg's lawyer, Paul Levi, represented the German Communists; Daümig, Crispien, Dittmann, and another represented Germany's Independent Social-Democratic Party, four likeable, rather helpless middlemen, good beer-drinkers, one could be sure, and conscientious officials in stodgy, established working-class organizations. It was obvious at first glance that here were no insurgent souls. Of the British, I met only Gallacher, who looked like a stocky prize-fighter. From the United States came Fraina, later to fall under grave suspicion,[2] and

[1] Of these Italian delegates, Giacinto Serrati (1872–1926), a Socialist Party leader, hesitated for a time over the break with the 'reformists' demanded by the '21 Conditions', but later joined the Communist Party. Constantino Lazzari (1857–1927) was similarly inclined, but stayed with the Socialist Party. Umberto Terracini (1895–) became a leading Communist, was imprisoned by Mussolini from 1926 to 1943, and after the Liberation was President of the National Assembly (1947); now Chairman of the Communist group in the Senate, occupying an 'orthodox' position in the post-1956 internal debates on Stalinism. Amadeo Bordiga (1889–1970) was for a few years the main leader of Italian Communism, but was eventually displaced by the more pliant Togliatti, and went into the libertarian and sectarian wilderness.

[2] Louis Fraina (1894–1953) broke with the Comintern in late 1922; the 'grave suspicion' Serge mentions could refer either to a much-inflated story of embezzlement or to an earlier charge of being a police-spy, of which he was cleared at the time. After his break with Communism, Fraina made a reputation as an economist under the name of Lewis Corey, but still suffered for his past under McCarthy's witch-hunt.

John Reed, the eye-witness of the 1917 Bolshevik uprising, whose book on the Revolution was already considered authoritative. I had met Reed in Petrograd, whence we had organized his clandestine depature through Finland: the Finns had been sorely tempted to finish him off and had confined him for a while in a death-trap of a jail. He had just visited some small townships in the Moscow outskirts, and reported what he had seen: a ghost-country where only famine was real. He was amazed that Soviet production continued despite everything. Reed was tall, forceful, and matter-of-fact, with a cool idealism and a lively intelligence tinged by humour. Once again I saw Rakovsky, the head of the Soviet Government in a Ukraine that was now prey to hundreds of roving bands: White, Nationalist, Black (or anarchist), Green, and Red. Bearded and dressed in a soldier's worn uniform, he broke into perfect French while he was on the rostrum.

From Bulgaria Kolarov[1] arrived, huge and somewhat pot-bellied, whose noble and commanding face bore the stamp of assurance: he blurted out a promise to the Congress that he would take power at home as soon as the International asked him! From Holland there came Wijnkoop,[2] among others: dark-bearded and long-jawed, apparently aggressive, but destined as it turned out to a career of limitless servility. From India, by way of Mexico, we had the pockmarked Manabendra Nath Roy: very tall, very handsome, very dark, with very wavy hair, he was accompanied by a statuesque Anglo-Saxon woman who appeared to be naked beneath her flimsy dress. We did not know that in Mexico he had been the target of some unpleasant suspicions; he was fated to become the guiding spirit of the tiny Indian Communist Party, to spend several years in prison, to start activity again, to slander the Opposition with nonsensical insults, to be expelled himself, and then to return to grace—but this was all in the distant future.[3]

[1] Vasil Kolarov (1877–1950): became a leading Comintern emissary to West European parties, Secretary to the Comintern Executive (1922–4), and Prime Minister of Bulgaria after Dimitrov's death in 1949.

[2] David Wijnkoop (1876–1941): Dutch 'Tribunist' (one of the founders of the left-wing paper *De Tribune*, 1907), then Left Social-Democrat and Communist. Tried to set up an abortive semi-autonomous Communist centre in Amsterdam (1920); formed an opposition outside the party 1926–1931; then returned to orthodoxy.

[3] Serge is not altogether accurate on Roy's career. For example, Roy was expelled in 1929 as the result of his support for the Brandler group in Germany, and

The Russians led the dance, and their superiority was so obvious that this was quite legitimate. The only figure in Western Socialism that was capable of equalling them, or even perhaps of surpassing them so far as intelligence and the spirit of freedom were concerned, was Rosa Luxemburg, and she had been battered to death with a revolver-butt in January 1919 by German officers. Apart from Lenin, the Russians consisted of Zinoviev, Bukharin, Rakovsky (who, though Rumanian by origin, was as much Russified as he was Frenchified), and Karl Radek, recently released from a Berlin prison in which he had courted death and where Leo Jogiches[1] had been murdered at his side. Trotsky, if he indeed came to the Congress, must have made only rare appearances, for I do not remember having seen him there. He was principally occupied with the state of the fronts, and the Polish front was still ablaze.

The work of the Congress centred upon three issues, and also a fourth which, though even more important, was not touched upon in open session. Lenin was bending every effort to convince the 'Left Communists'—Dutch, German, or (like Bordiga) Italian—of the necessity for compromise and participation in electoral and Parliamentary politics; he warned of the danger of their becoming revolutionary sects. In his discussion of the 'national and colonial question', Lenin emphasized the possibility, and even necessity, of inspiring Soviet-type revolutions in the Asiatic colonial countries. The experience of Russian Turkestan seemed to lend support to his arguments. He was aiming primarily at India and China; he thought that the blow must be directed to these countries in order to weaken British imperialism, which then appeared as the inveterate foe of the Soviet Republic. The Russians had no further hopes for the traditional Socialist parties of Europe. They judged that the only possible course was to work for splits that would break with the old reformist and Parliamentary leaderships, thereby

never again achieved any prominence in the Indian Communist Party. He did, however, think highly of Stalin even in later years. Roy died in 1954, editor by then of his magazine *The Radical Humanist*. The 'unpleasant suspicions' mentioned by Serge probably arose from Roy's campaigning for Indian independence on German subsidies.

[1] Leo Jogiches (Tyszko) (1867–1919): founder of Polish Social-Democracy and later of German Communism; during the war organized the first *Spartakus* group along with Karl Liebknecht; after the assassination of Liebknecht and Rosa Luxemburg continued revolutionary activity and was murdered in prison in March 1919.

creating new parties, disciplined and controlled by the Executive in Moscow, which would proceed efficiently to the conquest of power.

Serrati raised serious objections to the Bolshevik tactic of support for the colonial nationalist movements, demonstrating the reactionary and disturbing elements in these movements which might emerge in the future. It was naturally out of the question to listen to him. Bordiga opposed Lenin on questions of organization and general perspective. Without daring to say so, he was afraid of the influence of the Soviet State on the Communist Parties, and the temptations of compromise, demagogy, and corruption. Above all, he did not believe that a peasant Russia was capable of guiding the international working-class movement. Beyond doubt, his was one of the most penetrating intellects at the Congress, but only a very tiny group supported him.

The Congress made ready for the splitting of the French Party (at Tours) and the Italian Party (at Leghorn) by laying down twenty-one stringent conditions for the affiliates of the International, or rather twenty-two: the twenty-second, which is not at all well known, excluded Freemasons. The fourth problem was not on the agenda and no trace of it will ever be found in the published accounts; but I saw it discussed with considerable heat by Lenin, in a gathering of foreign delegates in a small room just off the grand, gold-panelled hall of the Imperial Palace. A throne had been bundled away here, and next to this useless piece of furniture a map of the Polish front was displayed on the wall. The rattle of type-writers filled the air. Lenin, jacketed, briefcase under arm, delegates and typists all round him, was giving his views on the march of Tukhachevsky's army on Warsaw. He was in excellent spirits, and confident of victory. Karl Radek, thin, monkey-like, sardonic and droll, hitched up his oversize trousers (which were always slipping down over his hips), and added, 'We shall be ripping up the Versailles Treaty with our bayonets!'

A little later, we were to discover that Tukhachevsky was complaining about the exhaustion of his troops and the lengthening of his lines of communication; that Trotsky considered the offensive to be too rushed and risky in those circumstances; that Lenin had forced the attack to a certain extent by sending Rakovsky and Smilga as political commissars to accompany Tukhachevsky; and that it would, despite everything, probably have succeeded if Stalin and Budyenny had provided support instead of marching on Lvov to assure themselves of a personal victory.

Defeat came at Warsaw, quite suddenly, just at the moment when the fall of the Polish capital was actually being announced. Apart from some students and a very few workers, the peasantry and proletariat of Poland had not welcomed the Red Army. I remained convinced that the Russians had made a psychological error by including Dzerzhinsky, the man of the Terror, side by side with Marchlewski on the Revolutionary Committee that was to govern Poland. I declared that, far from firing the popular enthusiasm, the name of Dzerzhinsky would freeze it altogether. That is just what happened. Once more, the westward expansion of the revolution had failed. There was no alternative for the Bolsheviks but to turn east.

Hastily, the Congress of the Oppressed Nationalities of the East was convened at Baku. As soon as the Comintern Congress was over, Zinoviev, Radek, Rosmer, John Reed, and Bela Kun went off to Baku in a special train, whose defence (since they were to pass through perilous country) and command were entrusted to Yakov Blumkin, a friend of mine. I shall say more of Blumkin later, apropos of his frightful death. At Baku, Enver Pasha put in a sensational appearance.[1] A whole hall full of Orientals broke into shouts, with scimitars and yataghans brandished aloft: '*Death to imperialism!*' All the same, genuine understanding with the Islamic world, swept as it was by its own national and religious aspirations, was still difficult. Enver Pasha aimed at the creation of an Islamic state in Central Asia; he was to be killed in a battle against the Red cavalry two years later. Returning home from this remarkable trip, John Reed took a great bite out of a water-melon he had bought in a picturesque Daghestan market. As a result he died, from typhoid.

The Moscow Congress is associated for me with more than one such loss. Before I write of these deaths, I would like to say more of the circumstances of the time. My own experience was probably unique, since in this period I maintained a staunch openness in my approach, being in daily contact with official circles, ordinary folk and the Revolution's persecuted dissenters. Throughout the Petrograd celebrations, I was concerned with the fate of Voline, though some friends and myself had managed to save his life for the time

[1] Enver Pasha (1881–1922): Turkish Minister of War in 1913; opposed the Kemalist revolution and fled to Russia in 1918.

being. Voline, whose real name was Boris Eichenbaum, was a working-class intellectual who had been one of the founders of the 1905 St. Petersburg Soviet. He had returned from America in 1917 to lead the Russian anarchist movement. He had joined Makhno's 'Ukrainian Army of Insurgent Peasants', fought the Whites, resisted the Reds, and tried to organize a free peasants' federation in the region of Gulyai-Polye. After he had caught typhus, he was captured by the Red Army in the course of a Black retreat. We were afraid that he might be shot out of hand. We succeeded in preventing this extremity by dispatching a Petrograd comrade straight to the spot; he had the prisoner transferred to Moscow. Now I had no sure news of him: I was at the time, together with the Comintern delegates, watching the performance of an authentic Soviet mystery-play in the court inside the old Exchange. We saw the Paris Commune raise its red banners, then perish; we saw Jaurès assassinated, and the audience cried out in grief; we saw, at last, the joyful and victorious Revolution in triumph over the world.

In Moscow, I learned that Lenin and Kamenev had promised to see that Voline, now in a Cheka prison, would not die. Here we were with our discussions in the Imperial halls of the Kremlin, while this model revolutionary was in a cell awaiting an uncertain end.

After I left the Kremlin I would visit another dissident, this time a Marxist, whose honesty and brilliance were of the first order: Yuri Ossipovich Martov, co-founder, with Plekhanov and Lenin, of Russian Social-Democracy, and the leader of Menshevism. He was campaigning for working-class democracy, denouncing the excesses of the Cheka and the Lenin-Trotsky 'mania for authority'. He kept saying, 'Just as though Socialism could be instituted by decree, and by shooting people in cellars!' Lenin, who was fond of him, protected him against the Cheka, though he quailed before Martov's sharp criticism. When I saw Martov he was living on the brink of utter destitution in a little room. He struck me at the very first glance as being aware of his absolute incompatibility with the Bolsheviks, although like them he was a Marxist, highly cultured, uncompromising and exceedingly brave. Puny, ailing, and limping a little, he had a slightly asymmetrical face, a high forehead, a mild and subtle gaze behind his spectacles, a fine mouth, a straggly beard and an expression of gentle intelligence. Here was a man of scruple and scholarship, lacking the tough and robust revolutionary will that sweeps obstacles aside. His criticisms were apposite, but his general solutions verged on the Utopian. 'Unless it returns to democracy, the Revolution is lost': but how return to democracy and what sort of democracy? All the same I felt it to be quite unforgivable that a man of this calibre should be put into a position where it was impossible for him to give the Revolution the whole wealth available in his thinking. 'You'll see, you'll see,' he would tell me, 'Free co-operation with the Bolsheviks is never possible.'

Just after I had returned to Petrograd, along with Raymond Lefebvre, Lepetit, Vergeat (a French syndicalist), and Sasha Tubin, a frightful drama took place there, which confirmed Martov's worst fears. I will summarize what happened, though the affair was shrouded in obscurity. The recently founded Finnish Communist Party emerged resentful and divided from a bloody defeat in 1918. Of its leaders, I knew Sirola and Kuusinen, who did not seem particularly competent and had indeed acknowledged the commission of many errors. I had just published a little book by Kuusinen on the whole business; he was a timid little man, circumspect and industrious. An opposition had been formed within the Party, in revulsion from the old Parliamentary leadership which had been responsible for the defeat and which nowadays adhered to the Communist International. A Party Congress at Petrograd resulted in an oppositional majority against the Central Committee, which was supported by Zinoviev. The Comintern President had the Congress proceedings stopped. One evening a little later, some young Finnish students at a military school went along to a Central Committee meeting and shot the eight members present. The Press printed shameless lies blaming the assassination on the Whites. The accused openly justified their action, accusing the Central Committee of treason, and demanded to be sent to the front. A committee of three including Rosmer and the Bulgarian Shablin was set up by the International to examine the affair; I doubt if it ever met. The case was tried later in secret session by the Moscow revolutionary tribunal, Krylenko being the prosecutor. Its upshot was in some ways reasonable, in others monstrous. The guilty ones were formally condemned, but authorized to go off to the front (I do not know what actually happened to them). However, the leader of the Opposition, Voyto Eloranta, who was considered as 'politically responsible', was first condemned to a period of imprisonment, and then, in 1921, shot.

Travelling with Raymond Lefebvre, Lepetit, and Vergeat was a late friend of mine whom I had never actually met, Sasha Tubin. During my confinement in France he had given me patient assistance in keeping up my clandestine mail. Now while we were passing through Petrograd, I saw him, itching to go and obsessed by sombre forebodings. The four set off from Murmansk, on a difficult route over the Arctic Sea which was designed to break the naval blockade. Our International Relations Section had worked out this perilous itinerary: embark in a fishing-boat, sail well past the tip of the Finnish coast, and land at Vardoe in Norway, on ground that was free and safe. The four started on this route. In a hurry to attend a C.G.T. congress, they set out on a day of stormy weather, and disappeared at sea. Possibly they were engulfed in the storm, or perhaps a Finnish motor-boat intercepted them and mowed them down; I knew that in Petrograd spies had trailed our every step. Every day for a fortnight Zinoviev asked me, with mounting anxiety, 'Have you any news of the French comrades?' Around this disaster unworthy legends were to grow: they are all lies.[1] (This would be in August or September, 1920.)

I end this chapter in the aftermath of the Second Congress of the International, in the September and October of 1920. I have the feeling that this point marked a kind of boundary for us. The failure of the attack on Warsaw meant the defeat of the Russian Revolution in Central Europe, although no one saw it as such. At home, new dangers were waxing and we were on the road to catastrophes of which we had only a faint foreboding. (By 'we', I mean the shrewdest comrades; the majority of the Party was already blindly dependent on the schematism of official thinking.) From October onwards significant events, fated to pass unnoticed in the country at large, were to gather with the gentleness of a massing avalanche. I began to feel, acutely I am bound to say, this sense of a danger from inside, a danger within ourselves, in the very temper and character of victorious Bolshevism. I was continually racked by the contrast between the stated theory and the reality, by the growth of intolerance and servility among many officials and their drive towards

---

[1] i.e. as retailed in the bourgeois press, to the effect that the deaths were the deliberate result of Communist policy.

privilege. I remember a conversation I had with the People's Commissar for Food, Tsiuriupa, a man with a splendid white beard and candid eyes. I had brought some French and Spanish comrades to him so that he could explain for our benefit the Soviet system of rationing and supply. He showed us beautifully-drawn diagrams from which the ghastly famine and the immense black market had vanished without trace.

'What about the black market?' I asked him.

'It is of no importance at all,' the old man replied. No doubt he was sincere, but he was a prisoner of his scheme, a captive within offices whose occupants had obviously all primed him with lies. I was astounded. So this was how Zinoviev could believe in the imminence of proletarian revolution in Western Europe. Was this perhaps how Lenin could believe in the prospects of insurrection among the Eastern peoples? The wonderful lucidity of these great Marxists was beginning to be fuddled with a theoretical intoxication bordering on delusion; and they began to be enclosed within all the tricks and tomfooleries of servility. At meetings on the Petrograd front, I saw Zinoviev blush and bow his head in embarrassment at the imbecile flattery thrown in his face by young military careerists in their fresh shiny leather outfits. One of them kept shouting, 'We will win because we are under the command of our glorious leader, Comrade Zinoviev!' A comrade who was a former convict had a sumptuously coloured cover designed by one of the greatest Russian artists, which was intended to adorn one of Zinoviev's pamphlets. The artist and the ex-convict had combined to produce a masterpiece of obsequiousness, in which Zinoviev's Roman profile stood out like a proconsul in a cameo bordered by emblems. They brought it to the President of the International, who thanked them cordially and, as soon as they were gone, called me to his side.

'It is the height of bad taste', Zinoviev told me in embarrassment, 'but I didn't want to hurt their feelings. Have a very small number printed, and get a very simple cover designed instead.'

On another day he showed me a letter from Lenin which touched on the new bureaucracy, calling them 'all that Soviet riff-raff'. This atmosphere was often sharpened, because of the perpetuation of the Terror, by an element of intolerable inhumanity.

A notable saying of Lenin kept rising in my mind: 'It is a terrible misfortune that the honour of beginning the first Socialist revolution should have befallen the most backward people in Europe.' (I quote from memory; Lenin said it on several occasions.) Nevertheless, within the current situation of Europe, bloodstained, devastated, and in profound stupor, Bolshevism was, in my eyes, tremendously and visibly right. It marked a new point of departure in history.

World capitalism, after its first suicidal war, was now clearly incapable either of organizing a positive peace, or (what was equally evident) of deploying its fantastic technical progress to increase the prosperity, liberty, safety, and dignity of mankind. The Revolution was therefore right, as against capitalism; and we saw that the spectre of future war would raise a question-mark over the existence of civilization itself, unless the social system of Europe was speedily transformed. The fearful Jacobinism of the Russian Revolution seemed to me to be quite unavoidable; as was the institution of a new revolutionary State, now in the process of disowning all its early promises. In this I saw an immense danger: the State seemed to me to be properly a weapon of war, not a means of organizing production. Over all our achievements there hung a death-sentence; since for all of us, for our ideals, for the new justice that was proclaimed, for our new collective economy, still in its infancy, defeat would have brought a peremptory death and after that, who knows what? I thought of the Revolution as a tremendous sacrifice that was required for the future's sake; and nothing seemed to me more essential than to sustain, or rescue, the spirit of liberty within it.

In penning the above lines, I am no more than recapitulating my own writings of that period.

4

DANGER FROM WITHIN

1920—1921

The social system in these years was later called 'War Communism'. At the time it was called simply 'Communism', and any one who, like myself, went so far as to consider it purely temporary was looked upon with disdain. Trotsky had just written that this system would last over several decades if the transition to a genuine, unfettered Socialism was to be assured. Bukharin was writing his work on *The Economy In the Period of Transition*, whose schematic Marxism aroused Lenin's ire. He considered the present mode of organization to be final. And yet, all the time it was becoming simply impossible to live within it: impossible, not of course for the administrators, but for the mass of the population. In fact, in order to eat it was necessary to resort, daily and without interruption, to the black market; the Communists did it like everyone else. Bank-notes were no longer worth anything, and ingenious theoreticians spoke of the coming abolition of money. There was no paper or coloured ink to print stamps, so a decree was issued abolishing postal charges: 'a new step in the realization of Socialism'. Tram-fares were abolished, with disastrous effects, since the overloaded stock deteriorated day by day.

The rations issued by the State co-operatives were minute: black bread (or sometimes a few cupfuls of oats instead); a few herrings each month, a very small quantity of sugar for people in the 'first category' (workers and soldiers), and none at all for the third category (non-workers). The words of St. Paul that were posted up everywhere, '*He that doth not work, neither shall he eat!*' became ironical, because if you wanted any food you really had to resort to the black market instead of working. In the dead factories, the workers spent their time making pen-knives out of bits of machinery, or shoe-soles out of the conveyor-belts, to barter them on the underground market. The total of industrial production had fallen to less than 30 per cent. of the 1913 figure. If you wished to procure a little flour, butter, or meat from the peasants who brought these things illicitly into town, you had to have cloth or articles of some kind to exchange. Fortunately the town residences of the late bourgeoisie contained quite a lot in the way of carpets, tapestries, linen, and plate. From the leather upholstery of sofas one could make passable shoes; from the tapestries, clothing.

Winter was a torture (there is no other word for it) for the townspeople: no heating, no lighting, and the ravages of famine. Children and feeble old folk died in their thousands. Typhus was carried everywhere by lice, and took its frightful toll. All this I saw and lived through, for a great while indeed. Inside Petrograd's grand apartments, now abandoned, people were crowded in one room, living on top of one another around a little stove of brick or cast-iron which would be standing on the floor, its flue belching smoke through an opening in the window. Fuel for it would come from the floor-boards of rooms near by, from the last stick of furniture available, or else from books. Entire libraries disappeared in this way. I myself burned the collected *Laws of the Empire* as fuel for a neighbouring family, a task which gave me considerable satisfaction. People dined on a pittance of oatmeal or half-rotten horsemeat, a lump of sugar would be divided in tiny fragments among a family, and a single mouthful taken out of turn would start angry scenes. The local Commune did everything it could to keep the children fed, but what it managed was pitiful.

The co-operative provisioning system had to be maintained, since it catered primarily for the starved and battered proletariat, the army, the fleet and the Party activists. And so requisitioning detachments were sent out into the outlying countryside, only to be driven away, as likely as not, or sometimes even massacred by *mujiks* wielding pitchforks. Savage peasants would slit open a commissar's belly, pack it with grain and leave him by the roadside as a lesson for all. This was how one of my own comrades died, a printing worker. It took place not far from Dno, and I went there afterwards to explain to the desperate villagers that it was all the fault of the imperialist blockade. This was true, but all the same the peasants continued, not unreasonably, to demand both the abolition of requisitioning and the legalization of the market.

'War Communism' could be defined as follows: firstly, requisitioning in the countryside; secondly, strict rationing for the town population, who were classified into categories; thirdly, complete 'socialization' of production and labour; fourthly, an extremely complicated and chit-ridden system of distribution for the remaining stocks of manufactured goods; fifthly, a monopoly of power tending towards the single Party and the suppression of all dissent; sixthly, a state of siege, and the Cheka. This system had been approved by the Ninth Congress of the Communist Party in the March and April of 1920. No one dared to admit that it would not work, and the Party did not know that in February of that year Trotsky had asked the Central Committee to abolish requisitioning. Rozhkov, the Marxist historian, wrote to Lenin saying that we were heading for catastrophe; there must be an immediate change in economic relations with the countryside. The Central Committee ordered him off to Pskov, where he was obliged to live, and Lenin replied to him that he had no intention of entering on a policy of surrender before the rural counter-revolution.

The winter of 1920–1 was hideous. Searching for houses fit for our staff to occupy, I visited several buildings in the heart of Petrograd. In a mansion that had once belonged to the society beauty Morskaya, not far from our main military headquarters and the triumphal gateway that opens into the court of the Winter Palace, I found whole rooms plastered with frozen excrement. The w.c.'s would not flush and the soldiers billeted there had installed field latrines on the floor-boards. Many houses were in a similar condition; when spring came and the excrement began to run all over the floors, anything might happen to the city. Compulsory clearance-squads were organized hastily.

I remember what happened one day when I was tramping through the snow with one of the regional military commanders, Mikhail Lashevich, an old revolutionary for the last thirty-five years, one of the architects of the seizure of power and a fearless warrior. I talked to him of the changes that had to be made. Lashevich was a stocky, thick-set man whose face was fleshy and creased with wrinkles. The only solution he could envisage for any problem was a resort to force. Speculation? We'll put a stop to that! 'I shall have the covered markets pulled down and the crowds dispersed! There you are!' He did it too, which only made matters worse.

Political life was pursuing the same line of development; indeed, it could hardly do otherwise. The tendency to override economic difficulties by compulsion and violence led to the growth of general discontent; any free (i.e. critical) expression of opinion became dangerous and consequently had to be treated as enemy activity. I was exceptionally well placed to follow the progress of this evil: I belonged to the governing circles in Petrograd, and was on terms of confidence with various oppositional forces, anarchists, Mensheviks, Left Social-Revolutionaries, and even Communists—those of the 'Workers' Opposition', which was already castigating the growing bureaucracy of the régime and the wretched condition of the ordinary worker: wretched not only in material circumstance but (what was much worse) in point of law, since the administration denied him any possibility of speaking out.

Except for the 'Workers' Opposition' these dissenters, who were always falling out among themselves, had become politically bankrupt, in different ways. The Mensheviks were outright opponents of the seizure of power by the Soviets; in other words, they stood for the continuation of a bourgeois democracy that was quite unworkable and, in the case of some of their leaders, for the vigorous suppression of Bolshevism. The Left Social-Revolutionaries, led by Maria Spiridonova and Kamkov, had first boycotted the Bolshevik authorities, then collaborated with them, and then, in July 1918, raised an insurrection against them, proclaiming their intention to govern alone. The anarchists were chaotically subdivided into pro-Soviet, anti-Soviet, and intermediate tendencies. In 1919 the anti-Soviet anarchists had thrown a bomb into a plenary session of the Communist Party's Moscow Committee, with a total of fifteen victims.

However, these impassioned dissidents of the Revolution, crushed and persecuted as they might be, were still right on many points, above all in their demand, on their own behalf and that of the Russian people, for freedom of expression and the restoration of liberty in the Soviets. The Soviets indeed, which had been so lively in 1918, were now no more than auxiliary organs of the Party; they possessed no initiative, exercised no control and in practice represented nothing but the local Party Committees. But as long as the economic system remained intolerable for nine-tenths or so of the population, there could be no question of recognizing freedom of speech for any Tom, Dick, or Harry, whether in the Soviets or elsewhere. The state of siege had now entered the Party itself, which was increasingly run from the top, by the Secretaries. We were at a loss to find a remedy for this bureaucratization: we knew that the Party had been invaded by careerist, adventurist, and mercenary elements who came over in swarms to the side that had the power. Within the Party the sole remedy to this evil had to be, and in fact was, the discreet dictatorship of the old, honest, and incorruptible members, in other words the Old Guard.

It was with particular intimacy that I followed the unfolding drama of anarchism, which was to achieve historic significance with the Kronstadt uprising. During the Second Congress of the Communist International, I had observed the negotiations between Lenin and Benjamin Markovich Aleynnikov, an intelligent anarchist whose career had included exile, mathematics, and work as a 'Soviet businessman' in Holland. The discussion concerned co-operation with the anarchists. Lenin indicated his agreement with the idea. He had recently given a friendly reception to Nestor Makhno; Trotsky was, much later (in 1938, I think), to recount that Lenin and he had thought of recognizing an autonomous region for the anarchist peasants of the Ukraine, whose military leader Makhno was. That arrangement would have been both just and diplomatic, and perhaps an outlook as generous as this would have spared the Revolution from the tragedy towards which we were drifting. Two pro-Soviet anarchists, energetic and capable men, were working with Chicherin in the Commissariat of Foreign Affairs: Herman Sandomirsky, a young scholar who had once been condemned to death in Warsaw and had known the inside of a prison, and Alexander Shapiro, a man of critical and moderate temper.

Kamenev, the President of the Moscow Soviet, offered the anarchists the legalization of their movement, complete with its own press, clubs, and bookshops, on condition that they should draw up a register of themselves and conduct a purge of their favourite haunts, which were crawling with malcontents, uncontrollables, semi-lunatics, and a few ill-disguised genuine counter-revolutionaries. The majority of the anarchists gave a horrified refusal to this suggestion of organization and enrolment: 'What, are we to form a kind of Party—even us?' Rather than that they would disappear, and have their press and premises taken off them.

Of the anarchist leaders from that tempestuous year of 1918, one was now constructing a new universal language, entirely in mono-syllables, called 'Ao'. Another, Yarchuk, a notable figure among the Kronstadt sailors, was in the Butyrki prison, suffering the pains of scurvy. A third, Nikolai Rogdayev, was in charge of Soviet propa-ganda in Turkestan. A fourth, Novomirsky, a former terrorist and convict, had joined the Party and was now working with me in Zinoviev's service and displaying the bizarre passion of the newly initiated. A fifth, Grossman-Roschin, who in the old days of 1906 had been the theoretician of 'motiveless terror' (which was intended to strike the old régime anywhere, at any time), became a syndicalist and a friend of Lenin and Lunacharsky; he was developing a liber-tarian theory of the dictatorship of the proletariat. Finally, there was my old friend Appolon Karelin, a splendid old man I had known in Paris, studying co-operative problems in a little room on the Rue d'Ulm. He was now a member of the All-Russian Executive of Soviets, still living with his white-haired wife in a little room at the National Hotel (one of the Houses of the Soviets). There, broken by old age, his sight failing, his beard white and expansive, he would type, with one finger on an antique machine, his huge book, *Against the Death Penalty*, and expatiate upon the virtues of a federa-tion of free communes.

The group that was almost an ally of Communism, that of Askarov, was devising a 'universalist anarchism'. Another, the Kropotkinist formation under Atabekian, saw free co-operatives as the only remedy. Boris Voline, still in jail, refused to take up the post as director of education in the Ukraine which was offered him by the Bolshevik leaders. He replied, 'I will never treat with the autocracy of the commissars.' It was, altogether, a lamentable chaos of sectarian good intentions. Anarchism was basically a doctrine of far more emotive power than intellectual. When these men met together it was only to proclaim that '*We fight for the obliteration of all State frontiers and boundaries. We proclaim that the whole earth belongs to all peoples!*' (conference of the Moscow Anarchist Union, December 1919). Would it have endangered the Soviet régime if they had been granted freedom of thought and expression? It would be lunatic to think so. It was merely that the majority of Bolsheviks, true to the

Marxist tradition, regarded them as 'petty-bourgeois Utopians' whose existence was incompatible with the extension of 'scientific socialism'. Inside the brains of the Chekists and of certain bureaucrats who had fallen prey to the psychoses of authority, these 'petty-bourgeois' types were fast growing into a rabble of objective counter-revolutionaries who had to be put down once for all.

As Gorky often said, the character of the Russian people, moulded both by resistance to despotism and submission to it, engenders an 'anti-authoritarian complex', that is to say a potent element of spontaneous anarchism which has generated periodic explosions throughout history. Among the peasants of the Ukraine, their spirit of rebellion, their capacity for self-organization, their love for local autonomy, the necessity of relying on nobody but themselves as defence against the Whites, the Germans, the Yellow-and-Blue nationalists, and often against harsh and ignorant commissars from Moscow, heralds of endless requisitioning—all these factors gave rise to an extraordinarily vital and powerful movement: the 'Insurgent Peasant Armies' assembled in the regions of Gulyai-Polye by an anarchist schoolmaster and ex-convict, Nestor Makhno. Under the inspiration of Boris Voline and Aaron Baron, the anarchist *Nabat* (or 'Alarm') Federation provided this movement both with an ideology, that of the Third (libertarian) Revolution, and with a banner, the black flag. These peasants displayed a truly epic capacity for organization and battle. Nestor Makhno, boozing, swashbuckling, disorderly and idealistic, proved himself to be a born strategist of unsurpassed ability. The number of soldiers under his command ran at times into several tens of thousands. His arms he took from the enemy. Sometimes his insurgents marched into battle with one rifle for every two or three men: a rifle which, if any soldier fell, would pass at once from his still-dying hands into those of his alive and waiting neighbour.

Makhno invented a form of infantry mounted in carts, which gave him enormous mobility. He also invented the procedure of burying his weapons and disbanding his forces for a while. His men would pass, unarmed, through the front lines, unearth a new supply of machine-guns from another spot, and spring up again in an unexpected quarter. In September 1919, at Uman, he inflicted a defeat on General Denikin from which the latter was never to recover. Makhno was known as '*Batko*' (little father, or master).

When the railwaymen of Yekaterinoslav (later Dniepropetrovsk) asked him for money to pay their wages, he replied, 'Get organized and run the railway yourselves. I don't need them.' His popular reputation through the whole of Russia was very considerable, and remained so despite a number of atrocities committed by his bands; despite, also, the strenuous calumnies put out by the Communist Party, which went so far as to accuse him of signing pacts with the Whites at the very moment when he was engaged in a life-and-death struggle against them.

In October 1920, when Baron Wrangel still held the Crimea, a Treaty of Alliance was signed between the Black army and the Red Army. Bela Kun, Frunze and Gusev were the signatories for the Reds. This treaty was to be a preliminary to an all-Russian amnesty for the anarchists, the legalization of their movement and the convention of an anarchist Congress at Kharkhov. The Black cavalry broke through the White lines and penetrated into the Crimea; this victory, coinciding with that of Frunze and Blücher at Perekop, was the decisive blow against the White Crimean régime, which had recently received recognition from Britain and France.

In Petrograd and Moscow the anarchists were making ready for their Congress. But no sooner had this joint victory been won than they were suddenly (in November 1920) arrested *en masse* by the Cheka. The Black victors of the Crimea, Karetnik, Gavrilenko, and others, were betrayed, arrested and shot. Makhno, surrounded at Gulyai-Polye, resisted like a madman. He cut a way out for his troops and kept fighting right up to August 1921. (Later he was to be interned in Rumania, Poland, and Danzig, and end his days as a factory worker in Paris.)

This fantastic attitude of the Bolshevik authorities, who tore up the pledges they themselves had given to this endlessly daring revolutionary peasant minority, had a terribly demoralizing effect; in it I see one of the basic causes of the Kronstadt rising. The Civil War was winding to its close, and the peasantry, incensed by the constant requisitioning, was drawing the conclusion that it was impossible to come to any understanding with 'the commissars'.

Equally serious was the fact that many workers, including quite a few Communist workers, were pretty near the same opinion. The 'Workers' Opposition', led by Shliapnikov, Alexandra Kollontai, and Medvedev, believed that the revolution was doomed if the Party failed to introduce radical changes in the organization of work, restore genuine freedom and authority to the trade unions, and make an immediate turn towards establishing a true Soviet democracy. I had long discussions on this question with Shliapnikov. A former metalworker, one of the very few Bolsheviks who had taken part in the Petrograd revolution of February–March 1917, he kept about him, even when in power, the mentality, the prejudices, and even the old clothes he had possessed as a worker. He distrusted the officials ('that multitude of scavengers') and was sceptical about the Comintern, seeing too many parasites in it who were only hungry for money. Corpulent and unwieldy, with a large, round, moustach- ioed face, he was a very bitter man when I met him. The discussion on the trade unions, in which he was a passionate participant, yielded little result. Trotsky advocated the fusion of the trade unions with the State. Lenin stood for the principles of trade-union auto- nomy and the right to strike, but with the complete subordination of the unions to the Party. The Party steamroller was at work. I took part in the discussion in one of the districts of Petrograd, and was horrified to see the voting rigged for Lenin's and Zinoviev's 'majority'. That way would resolve nothing: every day in Smolny the only talk was of factory incidents, strikes, and booing at Party agitators. This was in November and December of 1920.

In February, old Kropotkin died at Dimitrovo, near Moscow. I had made no effort to see him, fearing that any conversation between us would be painful; he still believed that the Bolsheviks had received German money, etc. My friends and I had known that he was living in cold and darkness, working on his *Ethics* and playing the piano a little for recreation, and so we had sent him a luxurious parcel of wax candles. I knew the contents of his letters to Lenin about Bolshevik intolerance and the nationalization of the book trade. If they are ever published, the acuteness with which Kropot- kin denounced the perils of directed thought will be plainly evident. I went up to Moscow for his funeral. These were heartbreaking days: the great frost in the midst of the great hunger. I was the only member of the Party to be accepted as a comrade in anarchist circles. Around the corpse of the great old man, exposed to view in the Hall of Columns of the House of Trade Unions, untoward in- cidents multiplied despite all Kamenev's tact and good intentions.

The shadow of the Cheka fell everywhere, but a packed and passionate multitude thronged around the bier, making this funeral ceremony into a demonstration of unmistakable significance.

Kamenev had promised to release all the imprisoned anarchists for the day; so it was that Aaron Baron and Yarchuk stood on guard beside the dead man's remains. Frozen face, high, graceful forehead, narrow nose, beard like snow: Kropotkin lay there like a sleeping wizard, while around him angry voices were whispering that the Cheka was violating Kamenev's promise, that a hunger-strike had been voted in the jails: that so-and-so and so-and-so had just been arrested; that the shootings in the Ukraine were still going on. . . .

The lengthy negotiations to get permission for a black flag and a burial oration sent a wave of anger through the crowd. The long procession, surrounded by students making a chain of linked hands, set off to the cemetery of Novo-Devichy, accompanied by singing choirs who walked behind black flags bearing inscriptions in denunciation of all tyranny. At the cemetery, in the transparent sunlight of winter, a grave had been opened under a silvery birch. Mostovenko, the delegate from the Bolshevik Central Committee, and Alfred Rosmer, from the Executive of the International, spoke in conciliatory terms. Then Aaron Baron, arrested in the Ukraine, due to return that evening to a prison from which he would never again emerge, lifted his emaciated, bearded, gold-spectacled profile to cry relentless protests against the new despotism: the butchers at work in their cellars, the dishonour shed upon Socialism, the official violence that was trampling the Revolution underfoot. Fearless and impetuous, he seemed to be sowing the seeds of new tempests. The Government founded a Kropotkin Museum, endowed a number of schools with Kropotkin's name, and promised to publish his works . . . (10 February 1921).[1]

Eighteen days elapsed. On the night of 28–29 February I was awoken by the ringing of a telephone in a room at the Astoria next to my own. An agitated voice told me: 'Kronstadt is in the hands of the Whites. We are all under orders.'

The man who announced this frightful news to me (frightful, because it meant the fall of Petrograd at any minute) was Ilya Yonov,

[1] After the death of Kropotkin's widow in 1938, the Kropotkin Museum was suppressed and its contents dispersed.

Zinoviev's brother-in-law. 'What Whites? Where did they come from? It's incredible!'

'A General Kozlovsky.'

'But our sailors? The Soviet? The Cheka? The workers at the Arsenal?'

'That's all I know.'

Zinoviev was in conference with the Revolutionary Council of the Army. I ran to the premises of the Second District Committee, which I found full of gloomy faces. 'It's unbelievable, but it's true all the same.'

'Well', I said, 'everybody must be mobilized immediately!' I was given the evasive reply that this would be done, but that we were awaiting instructions from the Petrograd Committee.

I spent the rest of the night studying the map of the Gulf of Finland, along with some of the comrades. We gathered that a considerable number of small strikes were now spreading in the working-class suburbs: the Whites in front of us, famine and strikes at our backs! When I came away at dawn, I saw an old maid from the hotel staff, quietly making her way out with several parcels.

'Where are you off to like this, so early in the morning, grandmother?'

'There's a smell of trouble about the town. They're going to cut all your throats, my poor little ones, they're going to be looting everything, all over again. So, I'm taking my things away.'

Small posters stuck on the walls in the still empty streets proclaimed that the counter-revolutionary General Kozlovsky had seized Kronstadt through conspiracy and treason; the proletariat were summoned to arms. But even before I went to the District Committee I met comrades, rushing out with their revolvers, who told me that it was an atrocious lie: the sailors had mutinied, it was a naval revolt led by the Soviet. This was perhaps not less serious than the other story: quite the reverse. The worst of it all was that we were paralysed by the official falsehoods. It had never happened before that our Party should lie to us like this. 'It's necessary for the benefit of the public,' said some, who were none the less horror-stricken at it all. The strike was now practically general. No one knew whether the trams would run.

That same day I met my friends of the French-speaking Communist group (I remember that Marcel Body and Georges Hellfer

Party. And anyway, where would you go? You have to face it, there is no one but us.'

The anarchist mediating group met at the house of my father-in-law, Alexander Russakov. I was not present at this meeting since it had been decided that only the anarchists would undertake this initiative (in view of the influence they exerted within the Kronstadt Soviet) and that, as far as the Soviet Government was concerned, the American anarchists would take sole responsibility for the attempt. Emma Goldman and Alexander Berkman were received warmly by Zinoviev, since they were able to speak with authority, in the name of a still important section of the international working class. Their mediation was a complete failure. As a consolation, Zinoviev offered them every facility for touring the whole of Russia in a special train: 'Observe, and you will understand.' Most of the Russian 'mediators' were arrested, apart from myself. I owe this forbearance to the kindness of Zinoviev, Zorin, and others, as well as to my qualifications as a militant from the French working-class-movement.

After many hesitations, and with unutterable anguish, my Communist friends and I finally declared ourselves on the side of the Party. This is why. Kronstadt had right on its side. Kronstadt was the beginning of a fresh, liberating revolution for popular democracy: 'The Third Revolution!' it was called by certain anarchists whose heads were stuffed with infantile illusions. However, the country was absolutely exhausted, and production practically at a standstill; there were no reserves of any kind, not even reserves of stamina in the hearts of the masses. The working-class *élite* that had been moulded in the struggle against the old régime was literally decimated. The Party, swollen by the influx of power-seekers, inspired little confidence. Of the other parties, only minute nuclei existed, whose character was highly questionable. It seemed clear that these groupings could come back to life in a matter of weeks, but only by incorporating embittered, malcontent and inflammatory elements in their thousands, no longer, as in 1917, enthusiasts for the young revolution. Soviet democracy lacked leadership, institutions and inspiration; at its back there were only masses of starving and desperate men.

The popular counter-revolution translated the demand for freely-elected Soviets into one for 'Soviets without Communists'.

If the Bolshevik dictatorship fell, it was only a short step to chaos, and through chaos to a peasant rising, the massacre of the Communists, the return of the *émigrés*, and in the end, through the sheer force of events, another dictatorship, this time anti-proletarian. Dispatches from Stockholm and Tallinn testified that the *émigrés* had these very perspectives in mind; dispatches which, incidentally, strengthened the Bolshevik leaders' intention of subduing Kronstadt speedily and at whatever cost. We were not reasoning in the abstract. We knew that in European Russia alone there were at least fifty centres of peasant insurrection. To the south of Moscow, in the region of Tambov, Antonov, the Right Social-Revolutionary schoolteacher, who proclaimed the abolition of the Soviet system and the re-establishment of the Constituent Assembly, had under his command a superbly organized peasant army, numbering several tens of thousands. He had conducted negotiations with the Whites. (Tukhachevsky suppressed this *Vendée* around the middle of 1921.)

In these circumstances it was the Party's duty to make concessions, recognizing that the economic régime was intolerable, but not to abdicate from power. 'Despite its mistakes and abuses', I wrote, 'the Bolshevik Party is at present the supremely organized, intelligent and stable force which, despite everything, deserves our confidence. The Revolution has no other mainstay, and is no longer capable of any thoroughgoing regeneration.'

The Politbureau decided to negotiate with Kronstadt, then to present an ultimatum and in the last resort to order an attack on the fort and the battleships, which were now immobilized in the ice. In fact, no negotiations took place. An ultimatum was published, signed by Lenin and Trotsky and worded in disgusting terms: 'Surrender, or you will be shot down like rabbits.' Trotsky did not come to Petrograd, and acted only within the Politbureau.

At the end of the autumn or the beginning of winter, simultaneously with the outlawing of the anarchists on the morrow of the victory that had been won with their aid, the Cheka had outlawed the Menshevik Social-Democrats. In a quite frightening official document they charged the Mensheviks with 'conspiracy with the enemy, organization of railway-wrecking' and other enormities in equally odious terms. The Bolshevik leaders themselves blushed at it all. They shrugged their shoulders ('The Cheka is mad!') but did nothing to set matters right; the most they would do was to promise the Mensheviks that there would be no arrests and that everything would sort itself out. Theodore Dan and Abramovich,[1] the leaders of Menshevism, were arrested in Petrograd. The Cheka, which at the time, if my memory is not at fault, was run by Semionov, a red-headed little worker, rude and cruel, wanted to shoot them as the leaders of the strike, which was now almost of a general character. This was most probably untrue since the strike was three-quarters spontaneous. I had just had a row with Semionov on the subject of two students who had been kept in freezing cells and manhandled. I appealed to Gorky; at that very moment he was intervening with Lenin to save the lives of the Menshevik leaders. Once Lenin was alerted they were absolutely safe. But for several nights we trembled in our shoes for them.

At the beginning of March, the Red Army began its attack, over the ice, against Kronstadt and the fleet. The artillery from the ships and forts opened fire on the attackers. In several places the ice cracked open under the feet of the infantry as it advanced, wave after wave, clad in white sheets. Huge ice-floes rolled over, bearing their human cargo down into the black torrent. It was the beginning of a ghastly fratricide.

The Tenth Congress of the Party, which was meanwhile in session at Moscow, was now, on Lenin's proposal, abolishing the system of requisitions, or in other words 'War Communism', and proclaiming the 'New Economic Policy'; all the economic demands of Kronstadt were being satisfied! At the same time the Congress gave a rough time to the various oppositions. The Workers' Opposition was classified as 'an anarcho-syndicalist deviation incompatible with the Party', although it had absolutely nothing in common with anarchism and merely demanded the management of production by the unions (which would have been a great step towards democracy for the working class). The Congress mobilized all present, including many Oppositionists, for the battle against Kronstadt. Dybenko, a former Kronstadt sailor himself and an extreme Left Communist, and Bubnov, the writer, soldier and

[1] Theodore Dan (1871–1947): Right Menshevik; during the First World War a moderate internationalist; emigrated in 1922; published a review of rather pro-Soviet inclinations in New York, where he died. Rafail Abramovich (1880–1963): Bundist and then a Menshevik-Internationalist in the War; after leaving Russia became a leading figure in the Second International and editor of the journal *Sotsialistichesky Vestnik* from 1921 until his death.

leader of the 'Democratic Centralism' group, went out to join battle on the ice against rebels who they knew in their hearts were right. Tukhachevsky prepared the final assault. In these dark days, Lenin said in so many words to one of my friends: 'This is Thermidor. But we shan't let ourselves be guillotined. We shall make a Thermidor ourselves.'

The Oranienbaum incident, which has not been related by anyone, as far as I know, brought Kronstadt within an inch of a victory undesired by its revolutionary sailors, and Petrograd within an inch of ruin. A whole regiment was on the point of wheeling round in solidarity with Kronstadt and summoning the army to revolt. At that moment Zorin reinforced it with trusty men, doubled the strength of the outposts and sentries, and arrested the regimental commander. The latter, a former officer in the Imperial army, was brutally frank: 'I waited years for this moment. Murderers of Russia, I hate you. I have lost the game, and now life means nothing to me!' He was shot, along with a good many others. It was a regiment that had been recalled from the Polish front.

The business had to be got over before the thaw began. The final assault was unleashed by Tukhachevsky on 17 March, and culminated in a daring victory over the impediment of the ice. Lacking any qualified officers, the Kronstadt sailors did not know how to employ their artillery; there was, it is true, a former officer named Kozlovsky among them, but he did little and exercised no authority. Some of the rebels managed to reach Finland. Others put up a furious resistance, fort to fort and street to street; they stood and were shot crying 'Long live the world revolution!' There were some of them who died shouting, 'Long live the Communist International!' Hundreds of prisoners were taken away to Petrograd and handed to the Cheka; months later they were still being shot in small batches, a senseless and criminal agony. Those defeated sailors belonged body and soul to the Revolution; they had voiced the suffering and the will of the Russian people; the N.E.P. had proved that they were right; and, finally, they were prisoners of war, civil war, and the Government had for a long time promised an amnesty to its opponents on condition that they offered their support. This protracted massacre was either supervised or permitted by Dzerzhinsky.

The leaders of the Kronstadt rising were hitherto unknown men, thrown up from the ranks. One of them, Petrichenko, is perhaps still alive; he reached sanctuary quickly enough in Finland.[1] Another, Perepelkin, happened to be in jail with a friend of mine whom I used to visit, in the old House of Arrest on Shpalernaya Street, through which so many revolutionaries, including Lenin and Trotsky, had passed in the old days. From the depths of his cell Perepelkin gave us an account of what had happened. Then he disappeared for ever.

18 March was a sombre day. The morning papers had come out with flamboyant headlines commemorating a working-class anniversary, that of the Paris Commune. Meanwhile the muffled thunder of the guns over Kronstadt kept shaking the windows. A guilty unease settled over the offices in Smolny. People avoided talking except with their closest friends, and among close friends, what was said was full of bitterness. By a remarkable historical coincidence on this same day, 18 March, a Communist rising in Berlin collapsed; its failure marked a new turn in the tactics of the International, which was now to proceed from the offensive to the defensive.

Within the Party, Kronstadt opened a period of dismay and doubt. In Moscow Paniushkin, a Bolshevik with a distinguished record in the Civil War, resigned demonstratively from the Party to found a new political organization: I think it was called the 'Soviet Party'. He opened a club in a working-class street; he was tolerated for a brief while, then arrested. Some comrades came and asked me to intercede for his wife and child, who had been evicted from their apartment and were now living in a corridor. I could do nothing for them. Another old Bolshevik, a worker named Miasnikov, who had taken part in the 1905 Upper Volga rising and knew Lenin personally, demanded freedom of the Press 'for everybody from the anarchists to the monarchists'. He broke off relations with Lenin after a sharp exchange of correspondence, and was soon to be deported to Erivan in Armenia. From there he escaped to Turkey. (I was to meet him twenty or so years later, in Paris.) The 'Workers' Opposition' appeared to be heading towards a break with the Party.

The truth was that emergent totalitarianism had already gone half-way to crushing us. 'Totalitarianism' did not yet exist as a word;

[1] In Finland Petrichenko joined pro-Soviet *émigré* groups, and got into trouble with the authorities during the Second World War on account of these sympathies. He was repatriated to Russia in 1945 and immediately imprisoned there. He died in jail in 1946.

as an actuality it began to press hard on us, even without our being aware of it. I belonged to that pitifully small minority that realized what was going on. Most of the Party leadership and activists, in reviewing their ideas about War Communism, came to the conclusion that it was an economic expedient analogous to the centralized régimes set up during the war in Germany, France, and Britain, which they termed 'war capitalism'. They hoped that, once peace came, the state of siege would fall away spontaneously and some sort of Soviet democracy, of which nobody had any clear conception, would return. The great ideas of 1917, which had enabled the Bolshevik Party to win over the peasant masses, the army, the working class, and the Marxist intelligentsia, were quite clearly dead. Did not Lenin, in 1917, suggest a Soviet form of free Press, whereby any group with the support of 10,000 votes could publish its own organ at the public expense? He had written that within the Soviets power could be passed from one party to another without any necessity for bitter conflicts. His theory of the Soviet State promised a state structure totally different from that of the old bourgeois states, 'without officials or a police-force distinct from the people', in which the workers would exercise power directly through their elected Councils, and keep order themselves through a militia system.

What with the political monopoly, the Cheka and the Red Army, all that now existed of the 'Commune-State' of our dreams was a theoretical myth. The war, the internal measures against counter-revolution, and the famine (which had created a bureaucratic rationing-apparatus) had killed off Soviet democracy. How could it revive, and when? The Party lived in the certain knowledge that the slightest relaxation of its authority would give the day to reaction.

To these historical features, certain important psychological factors must be added. Capitalist industrial society tends to encompass the whole of the world, fashioning all aspects of life to its design. Consequently, ever since the beginning of the twentieth century, Marxism has aimed to renew and transform everything: the property system, the organization of work, the map of the world (through the abolition of frontiers), and even the inner life of man (through the extinction of the religious mode of thought). Aspiring to a total transformation, it has consequently been, in the etymological sense of the word, totalitarian. It presents the two faces of the ascendant society, simultaneously democratic and authoritarian. The greatest Marxist party, from 1880 to 1920, the Social-Democratic Party of Germany, is bureaucratically organized on the lines of a State, and functions as a means of achieving power within the State. Bolshevik thinking is grounded in the possession of the truth. The Party is the repository of truth, and any form of thinking which differs from it is a dangerous or reactionary error. Here lies the spiritual source of its intolerance. The absolute conviction of its lofty mission assures it of a moral energy quite astonishing in its intensity—and, at the same time, a clerical mentality which is quick to become Inquisitorial. Lenin's 'proletarian Jacobinism' with its detachment and discipline both in thought and action is eventually grafted upon the pre-existing temperament of activists moulded by the old régime, that is by the struggle against despotism; I am quite convinced that a sort of natural selection of authoritarian temperaments is the result.

For all these reasons, even the great popular leaders themselves flounder within inextricable contradictions which dialectics allows them to surmount verbally, sometimes even demagogically. Twenty or maybe a hundred times, Lenin sings the praises of democracy and stresses that the dictatorship of the proletariat is a dictatorship against 'the expropriated possessing classes', and at the same time, 'the broadest possible workers' democracy'. He believes and wants it to be so. He goes to give an account of himself before the factories; he asks for merciless criticism from the workers. He also writes, in 1918, that the dictatorship of the proletariat is not at all incompatible with personal power; thereby justifying, in advance, some variety of Bonapartism. He has Bogdanov, his old friend and comrade, jailed because this outstanding intellectual confronts him with embarrassing objections. He outlaws the Mensheviks because these 'petty-bourgeois' Socialists are guilty of errors which happen to be awkward. He welcomes the anarchist partisan Makhno with real affection, and tries to prove to him that Marxism is right; but he either permits or engineers the outlawing of anarchism. He promises peace to religious believers and orders that the churches are to be respected; but he keeps saying that 'religion is the opium of the people'. We are proceeding towards a classless society of free men; but the Party has posters stuck up nearly everywhere announcing that 'the rule of the workers will never cease'. Over whom then will they rule? And what is the meaning of this word *rule*? Totalitarianism is within us.

At the end of spring in 1921, Lenin wrote a long article defining what the N.E.P. would be: an end to requisitions and taxes in kind from the peasants; freedom of trade; freedom for production by craftsmen; concessions on attractive terms to foreign capital; freedom of enterprise (within certain limits, of course) for Soviet citizens themselves. It amounted to a partial restoration of capitalism: Lenin admitted this in so many words. At the same time he refused to grant the country any political freedom at all: 'The Mensheviks will stay in jail!' And he proclaimed a purge of the Party, aimed against those revolutionaries who had come in from other parties—i.e. those who were not saturated with the Bolshevik mentality. This meant the establishment within the Party of a dictatorship of the old Bolsheviks, and the direction of disciplinary measures, not against the unprincipled careerists and conformist late-comers, but against those sections with a critical outlook.

A little while afterwards, during the Third Congress of the International, I was present at an address which Bukharin gave to the foreign delegates. He justified N.E.P. in terms of 'the impossibility of breaking the rural petty-bourgeoisie (the peasants, with their attachment to small private property) by means of a single blood-letting—an impossibility which stems from the isolation of the Russian Revolution'. If the German Revolution, with Germany's industrial resources behind it, had come to our assistance, we would have persisted in travelling the path of total Communism, even if it had required bloodshed. I do not have the text of this speech before me, but I was responsible for printing it, and am sure that this is an accurate summary. It amazed me all the more since I had chanced to meet Bukharin several times at Zinoviev's, and genuinely admired him.

Lenin, Trotsky, Karl Radek, and Bukharin had, beyond any doubt, become the brains of the Revolution. They spoke the same Marxist language, and had the same background of experience with the Socialism of Europe and America. Consequently they understood one another so well, by the merest hints, that they seemed to think collectively. (And it is a fact that the Party drew its strength from collective thinking.) Compared with them, Lunacharsky, the People's Commissar for Education, seemed a dilettante: he was a playwright, a poet and a first-rate speaker, with a touch of vanity, who had translated Hölderlin and acted as the protector of Futurist painters. Beside them, Zinoviev was simply a demagogue, a popularizer of ideas worked out by Lenin; Chicherin, the foreign-affairs specialist, never emerged from his archives; Kalinin was no more than a wily figurehead, chosen for the post because of his splendid peasant face and his keen nose for the state of popular feeling. There were other outstanding figures, men of proven ability, but these were secondary characters, concerned purely with practical tasks: Krassin, Piatakov, Sokolnikov, Smilga, Rakovsky, Preobrazhensky, Joffe, Ordzhonikidze, Dzerzhinsky.

Nikolai Ivanovich Bukharin was thirty-three years old; for fifteen of those years he had been a militant. He had lived through a phase of exile in Onega, spent some time with Lenin in Cracow, and worked for the Party in Vienna, Switzerland, and New York. His devotion to theoretical economics was quite tireless. He had anticipated Lenin in elaborating a theory of the complete overthrow of the capitalist state. His mind was effervescent, always alert and active, but rigorously disciplined. The high forehead, balding at the temples, the thin hair, slightly turned-up nose, chestnut-brown moustache and small beard—all made him look just like the average Russian, and his careless manner of dress completed the picture. He dressed all anyhow, as if he had never found time to get a suit that fitted him properly. His usual expression was jovial; even when he was silent the look in his eye, sharpened by a humorous twinkle, was so lively that he always seemed to be just about to come out with some witticism or other. The manner in which he spoke of others savoured of a good-natured cynicism. He devoured books in several languages and had a playful touch in dealing with the most serious subjects. It was immediately obvious that what he most enjoyed was just thinking. He was habitually surrounded by crowds of smiling young listeners, who drank in all his incisive observations. He was bitingly contemptuous of the trade-union and Parliamentary politicians of the West.

Karl Bernardovich Radek (thirty-five years old) could, as we used to say, only speak his own language—the accent he used to express himself in all the others was so incredibly bad. A Galician Jew, he had grown up in the Socialist movements of Galicia, Poland, Germany, and Russia, all at the same time. He was a sparkling writer, with an equal flair for synthesis and for sarcasm. Thin, rather small, nervous, full of anecdotes which often had a savage side to them, realistic to the point of cruelty, he had a beard growing in a fringe around his clean-shaven face, just like an old-time pirate. His features were irregular, and thick tortoise-shell spectacles ringed his myopic eyes. His walk, staccato gestures, prominent lips, and screwed-up face, every part of which was continually expressive, all had something monkey-like and comical about them.

In 1918, when Lenin was thinking in terms of a mixed economy, Radek and Bukharin had been the first to demand the nationalization of large-scale industry. In the same year, during the Brest-Litovsk negotiations, they had accused Lenin, some fifteen years their senior, of opportunism, and advocated a romantic war of all-out resistance against the German Empire, even if it meant suicide for the Soviet Republic. In 1919 Radek had put his daring and common sense into an attempt to lead the German Spartakist movement, and was lucky to escape being murdered with his friends Rosa Luxemburg, Karl Liebknecht, and Leo Tyszko (Jogiches). I had seen him using his scornful dialectic to harry the German moderates. I can see him now, hitching up his trousers (which were always too big for him), as he stood on the rostrum and, demonstrating, after a grating '*Parteigenossen!*' that the collapse of the old order in Europe was shortly due. Although more of an extemporizer than a theoretician, he was also a scholar, and read every conceivable serious journal. He was now being called a Rightist because he did not mince his words about the German Communist Party, and believed that, for the time being, the period of insurrection and offensive in Central Europe was over.

The Third Congress of the Communist International met at Moscow, in an atmosphere much the same as that of the previous Congress, except that the attendance was larger and the proceedings were more relaxed. With the coming of the N.E.P., the famine was getting a little less severe, and people anxiously expected a policy of appeasement to follow. The foreign delegates showed no interest in the tragedy of Kronstadt and, except for a few, deliberately closed their minds to any understanding of it. They sat in commission to condemn the Workers' Opposition; this they did with enthusiasm, without giving it a hearing. They considered N.E.P., amenably enough, to be (as one of the French delegates put it to me) 'an inspired turn to the Right' that had saved the Revolution. It was hardly inspiration to yield to a famine after the situation had become quite insupportable. But the majesty of the Russian Revolution disarmed its supporters of all critical sense; they seemed to believe that approval of it entailed the abdication of the right to think.

At the Kremlin, in the great throne-room of the Imperial Palace, Lenin defended the New Economic Policy. As he spoke, he stood beneath tall, extravagantly gilded columns, under a canopy of scarlet velvet bearing the insignia of the Soviets. Dealing with international strategy, he argued for an armistice and a real effort to win over the masses. He was warm, friendly, genial, talking as simply as he could; it was as if he was determined to emphasize with every gesture that the head of the Soviet Government and the Russian Communist Party was still just another comrade—the leading one, of course, through his acknowledged intellectual and moral authority, but no more than this, and one who would never become just another statesman or just another dictator. He was obviously concerned to steer the International by persuasion. While some of the speeches were going on he would come down from the platform and sit on the steps, near the shorthand reporters, with his note-pad on his knee. From this position he would interrupt now and then with a little caustic comment that made everybody laugh, and a mischievous smile would light up his face. Or he would buttonhole foreign delegates, people who were almost unknown and practically insignificant, and take them into a corner of the hall to carry on, face to face, with the argument he had put forward. The Party must go to the masses! Yes, the masses! And not turn into a sect! And the N.E.P. was not nearly so dangerous as it looked from outside, because we still kept all the fullness of power.

Several times I saw him coming away from the Congress, wearing his cap and jacket, quite alone, walking along at a smart pace with the old cathedrals of the Kremlin on either side of him. I saw him batter Bela Kun with a speech of merciless invective, genial as ever, his face bursting with health and good spirits. This was at a meeting of the Executive Committee of the International, held during the Congress in a banqueting-room of a hotel on Theatre Square below the Kremlin, the *Continental*, I think. This speech marked a real turning-point in Communist policy.

I had some personal knowledge of Bela Kun, whom I found a

wholly unattractive personality. We had been most anxious on his behalf when, after the defeat of the Hungarian Soviets, he had been interned in a Vienna mental asylum, where the Austrian Social-Democrats actually lavished attention on him. A Socialist who in the course of military service had been taken prisoner in Russia, he had begun his revolutionary career in Siberia with the Tomsk Bolsheviks. At the time of the Left Social-Revolutionary uprising of 1918 in Moscow, he had won some distinction by his creation of an international brigade in support of the Party of Lenin and Trotsky. He was jailed at home and came out to become Chairman of the Council of People's Commissars of Hungary and leader of the Hungarian Communist Party. In these posts he had been responsible for a succession of faults and vacillations; he riddled his own Party with backstage repression and allowed a military conspiracy to gain control over practically the whole country. His personal role during the defeat of the Hungarian Soviets had been pathetic (though this was hardly ever mentioned, since a popular legend was being allowed to grow around his name). After some reverses the small Red Armies of Hungary regained the initiative. They beat the Rumanians and advanced into Czechoslovakia, where the popular movement gave them a sympathetic welcome. Clemenceau, alarmed by this recovery, sent a telegram to Bela Kun, asking him to call off the offensive and hinting that, if this were done, the Entente would negotiate with Red Hungary. Kun was taken in by this trick and halted the offensive; the Rumanians rallied their forces and counter-attacked. That was the end.

I cannot help thinking that for the rest of his life Bela Kun was dominated by his sense of failure, and never stopped trying to compensate for it. During his mission in Germany he had, on 18 March of the previous year (1921), instigated an uprising in Berlin which was both bloody and, given the undeniable weakness of the Communist Party, doomed to failure from the beginning. The Party emerged from the incident weakened, and divided by the expulsion of Paul Levi who strongly opposed such 'insurrectionary adventures'.[1] After his return from Germany in the disgrace of

[1] Paul Levi (1883–1930): Rosa Luxemburg's lawyer and a former leader of the Independent Social-Democrats; co-founder of the Spartakusbund and later a leader of the early German Communist Party; supported Serrati's objections to the '21 Conditions'; after 1921, founded a small independent group, then joined the Left wing of the Social Democrats; apparently committed suicide.

another failure, Bela Kun had gone off to win glory in the Crimea.

At a meeting of the Executive of the International Lenin made a lengthy analysis of the Berlin affair, this *putsch* initiated without mass support, serious political calculation, or any possible outcome but defeat. There were few present, because of the confidential nature of the discussion. Bela Kun kept his big, round, puffy face well lowered; his sickly smile gradually faded away. Lenin spoke in French, briskly and harshly. Ten or more times, he used the phrase '*les bêtises de Bela Kun*': little words that turned his listeners to stone. My wife took down the speech in shorthand, and afterwards we had to edit it somewhat: after all it was out of the question for the symbolic figure of the Hungarian Revolution to be called an imbecile ten times over in a written record!

Actually, Lenin's polemic marked the end of the International's tactics of outright offensive. The failure of this approach had to be clearly stated, and besides Russia was now entering a period of internal appeasement; of these two considerations, of unequal worth, I am not sure which was the more influential. In its official resolution the Congress still praised the fighting spirit of the German Communist Party, and Bela Kun was not removed from the Executive.

If the Revolution had not been in such a parlous condition at the time, Kun would have had to face questioning about two other crimes. He had been a signatory to the treaty of alliance with Makhno's Black army; he had also been one of those who tore it up as soon as the joint victory had been achieved. Then too, he had been a member of the Revolutionary Council of the Red Army, which in November 1920 had forced Baron Wrangel out of the Crimea. In this capacity Bela Kun had negotiated the surrender of the remnants of the White army. To this assortment of former Monarchist officers he promised an amnesty and the right to resume civilian work; later he ordered them to be massacred. Thousands of war prisoners were thus treacherously exterminated, in the name of 'purging the country'.

Trotsky came to the Congress many times. No one ever wore a great destiny with more style. He was forty-one and at the apex of power, popularity and fame—leader of the Petrograd masses in two revolutions; creator of the Red Army, which (as Lenin had said to Gorky) he had literally 'conjured out of nothing'; personally the

victor of several decisive battles, at Sviazhsk, Kazan, and Pulkovo;
the acknowledged organizer of victory in the Civil War—'Our
Carnot!' as Radek called him. He outshone Lenin through his great
oratorical talent, through his organizing ability, first with the army,
then on the railways, and by his brilliant gifts as a theoretician.
As against all this Lenin possessed only the pre-eminence, which was
truly quite immense, of having, even from before the Revolution,
been the uncontested head of the tiny Bolshevik Party which constituted the real backbone of the State, and whose sectarian temper
mistrusted the over-rich, over-fluid mind of the Chairman of the
Supreme War Council. For a short time there was some talk, in
various small groups at the Congress, of elevating Trotsky to the
chairmanship of the International. Zinoviev must have been outraged by these pressure-groups, and doubtless Lenin preferred to
keep his own spokesman at the top of the 'World Party'. Trotsky
himself intended to give his attention to the Soviet economy.

He made his appearance dressed in some kind of white uniform,
bare of any insignia, with a broad, flat military cap, also in white,
for headgear; his bearing was superbly martial, with his powerful
chest, jet-black beard and hair, and flashing eye-glasses. His
attitude was less homely than Lenin's, with something authoritarian
about it. That, maybe, is how my friends and I saw him, we critical
Communists; we had much admiration for him, but no real love.
His sternness, his insistence on punctuality in work and battle, the
inflexible correctness of his demeanour in a period of general
slackness, all imparted a certain demagogic malice to the insidious
attacks that were made against him. I was hardly influenced by these
considerations, but the political solutions prescribed by him for
current difficulties struck me as proceeding from a character that
was basically dictatorial. Had he not proposed the fusion of the
trade unions with the State—while Lenin quite rightly wanted the
unions to keep some of their independence? We did not grasp that
the trade-union influence might have actually worked upon the
structure of the State, modifying it more effectively in a working-
class direction. Had he not set up labour armies? And suggested the
militarization of industry as a remedy for its incredible state of
chaos? We did not know that earlier, in the Central Committee, he
had unsuccessfully proposed an end to the requisitioning system.
Labour armies were a good enough expedient in the phase of

demobilization. Had he not put his signature to a repulsively threatening manifesto against Kronstadt? The fact was that he had been in the thick of everything, acting with a self-confident energy which tried out directly opposite solutions by turns.

During one session, he came down straight from the platform and stood in the middle of our French group to give a translation of his own speech. He spoke passionately, in slightly incorrect but fluent French. He replied sharply when he was heckled—about the Terror, about violence, about Party discipline. Our little group appeared to irritate him. Vaillant-Couturier, André Morizet, André Julien, Fernand Loriot, Jacques and Clara Mesnil, and Boris Souvarine were all there. Trotsky was easy and cordial, but imperious in argument. On another occasion he flew at the Spanish delegate, Orlandis, who was attacking the persecution of the anarchists. Trotsky seized him violently by the coat-lapels and almost shouted, 'I should certainly like to see that happening to you, petty-bourgeois that you people are!'

During this summer of 1921 I formed, among the comrades from abroad, a number of lasting and even life-long friendships. I resorted to those who came to Moscow with more concern for truth than orthodoxy, more anxiety for the future of the Revolution than admiration for the proletarian dictatorship. Our relationships were always initiated by conversations of an absolute frankness in which I set myself the responsibility of disclosing all the evils, dangers, difficulties, and uncertain prospects. In an era of fanatical conformism this was, as I still believe, a meritorious thing to do, demanding some courage. I gravitated towards people of a free spirit, those who were fired by a desire to serve the Revolution without closing their eyes. Already an 'official truth' was growing up, which seemed to me the most disastrous thing imaginable. I became acquainted with Henriette Roland-Holst, a Dutch Marxist and a notable poet. Lank, scrawny and grey-haired, her neck disfigured by a goitre, she had a delicately sculptured face with an expression of gentleness and intellectual austerity.[1] The questions she raised with me were symptomatic of a most scrupulous anxiety.

[1] Henriette Roland-Holst (1869-1952): Dutch 'Tribunist' and then Communist; founded a short-lived Independent Communist Party in 1924; later became a Christian Socialist, pacifist, and opponent of colonialism; *doyenne* of Dutch literature over many years.

Two young men from the Spanish delegation gave us pledges for the future which they were destined to fulfil at tremendous cost: Joaquín Maurín and Andreu Nin. I have always believed that human qualities find their physical expression in a man's personal appearance. A single glance was enough to tell the calibre of Maurín, the teacher from Lérida, and Nin, the teacher from Barcelona. Maurín had the bearing of a young Cavalier from a pre-Raphaelite painting; Nin, behind his gold-rimmed spectacles, wore an expression of concentration which was softened by his evident enjoyment of life. Both of them gave their lives to the cause: Maurín destined to an unending succession of jails; Nin to a horrible death during the Spanish Revolution. At this time the overwhelming impression they conveyed was one of idealism and the thirst for understanding.

The French, more sophisticated and more sceptical characters, were generally of a different stuff. André Morizet, the mayor of Boulogne, paraded his admirably sound and practical face and his drinking-songs for the benefit of us all. (Even now, at Suresnes, in occupied France, he is still fighting to keep his office as Labour mayor; he has returned, after a long interval, to traditional Socialism.) André Julien was piling up countless annotations for a work so compendious that he was never to write it. (In 1936 and 1937, he was to be one of the Socialist stalwarts of the Popular Front.)

Paul Vaillant-Couturier, a tank officer during the war, a poet, popular orator and ex-servicemen's leader, was a tall, chubby young man of extraordinary talents, but fated to become a great disappointment to me. He understood everything that was going on; but in the future he was to acquiesce in his own corruption, to become increasingly entangled with all the villainies of Bolshevism's degeneration, and to die, in working-class Paris, enviably popular.

Boris Souvarine, a Russian Jew by origin but a naturalized Frenchman, had no Socialist background; he came to us, at the age of twenty-five, from the world of left-wing journalism rather than from the working-class movement, with an amazing zest for knowledge and action. Slight and short, his eyes masked by lenses of unusual thickness, speech lisping slightly, manner aggressive and often quick both to offend and to take offence, he had a habit of coming out suddenly with awkward questions; he would deliver mercilessly realistic verdicts on French personalities and events, and amuse himself by deflating swollen heads by smart pinpricks of his own devising. His stock was then very high, even though his first request on arrival was for a tour of the prisons. All the time he showed a magnificent facility for analysis, a lively grasp of realities, and an aptitude for polemic that was designed to leave a trail of indignation wherever he went. He became one of the leaders of the International and a member of its Executive Committee. Souvarine, despite his expulsion from the Comintern in 1924, was for some ten years to be one of the most trenchant and perceptive brains of European Communism.

I was on very close terms with both the French Communist groups in Russia, and was more or less the leader of the one in Petrograd. These groups formed striking instances of the law whereby mass-movements transform individuals, impel them into unpredictable courses of development, and mould their convictions. They also illustrated the law that the ebb-tide of events carries men away just as surely as the flood-tide brings them in. Although their ranks included several former French Socialists (whose inclinations had been quite alien to Bolshevism), these zealous Communists, who for the most part were perfectly sincere, came from all points of the political horizon only to make a speedy departure once again in equally variegated directions. The Moscow group was a little nest of vipers, although it was led by Pierre Pascal, a man of exemplary character. The quarrels, grudges, denunciations, and counter-denunciations of its two leading figures at the time, Henri Guilbeaux and Jacques Sadoul, completely demoralized it and finally earned the attentions of the Cheka. Guilbeaux's whole life was a perfect example of the failure who, despite all his efforts, skirts the edge of success without ever managing to achieve it. He wrote cacophonous poetry, kept a card-index full of gossip about his comrades, and plagued the Cheka with confidential notes. He wore green shirts and pea-green ties with greenish suits; everything about him, including his crooked face and his eyes, seemed to have a touch of mould. (He died in Paris, about 1938, by then an anti-Semite, having published two books proving Mussolini to be the only true successor of Lenin.)

Jacques Sadoul was quite different: a Paris lawyer, an army captain, an information-officer in Russia on behalf of Albert

Thomas,[1] a member of the Comintern Executive, a flatterer of
Lenin and Trotsky, a great charmer, a splendid raconteur, a
sybarite, and a cool careerist to boot. However, he had produced a
volume of *Letters* on the Revolution which is still a document of the
first importance. He had been condemned to death in France for
crossing over to the Bolshevik side, but was one day to return home,
times having changed, with an acquittal. After that he trailed
alongside the full course of Stalinism, both as a lawyer acting for
Soviet interests and as an agent in Parliamentary circles, though at
heart he did not entertain the slightest illusion about Russia. The
bread of bitterness tasted by revolutionaries held no temptations
for him.

René Marchand, once the Petrograd correspondent for the
Catholic-reactionary *Figaro*, was a fresh convert troubled by perpetual crises of conscience. He was soon to go off to Turkey, there to
renounce Bolshevism and become an apologist, doubtless a sincere
one, for Kemal Ataturk.

The outstanding figure in the Moscow French Communist group
was Pierre Pascal, probably a distant descendant of Blaise Pascal,
of whom he reminded me. I had met him in Moscow in 1919. There,
his head shaven Russian-style, sporting a big Cossack moustache
and smiling perpetually with his bright eyes, he would walk through
the city barefoot and clad in a peasant tunic to the Commissariat of
Foreign Affairs, where he used to draft messages for Chicherin. A
loyal and circumspect Catholic, he used St. Thomas's *Summa* to
justify his adherence to Bolshevism and even his approval of the
Terror. (The texts of the learned saint lent themselves admirably to
this task.) Pascal led an ascetic life, sympathizing with the Workers'
Opposition and hobnobbing with the anarchists. He had been a
lieutenant with the French Military Mission, in charge of coding;
he had crossed over to the Revolution in the middle of the intervention, to dedicate himself to it body and soul. He discussed its
mystical significance with Berdyaev and translated Blok's poems.
He was to suffer terribly as the birth of totalitarianism progressed.
I met him again in Paris in 1936. He was now a professor at the
Sorbonne, the author of a solid biography of the Archpriest

---

[1] Albert Thomas (1878-1932) was Minister of Munitions in the First World War
and visited Russia after the February Revolution of 1917 in an attempt to arouse
enthusiasm for the Allies.

Avvakum, and more or less a Conservative. We, who had almost been brothers, could not talk together about the battle of Madrid. . . .

The Executive had decided, on Russian initiative of course, to set up a trade-union International affiliated to the Comintern. Salomon Abramovich Lozovsky[1] (or Dridzo), an ex-Menshevik of recent vintage and an inexhaustible orator, was in charge of the new organization. He had the air of a slightly fastidious schoolmaster amidst his world-wide assortment of trade-union militants whose political horizons did not extend very far beyond their own working-class districts at home. Not far from him, a one-eyed giant would pass through the crowd, downcast and solitary, but now and then distributing vigorous thumps on the shoulders of his mates. This was Bill Haywood, a former timberman, organizer of the I.W.W.,[2] who had come to end his days in the stuffy rooms of the Lux Hotel, among Marxists not one of whom tried to understand him and whom he scarcely understood himself. Still, he got a big thrill out of the red flags in the public squares.

Here too I met a Russian militant who had been in a British prison and was now home from Latin America: Dr. Alexandrov, I think. He was thirty-five, with a swarthy commonplace face, dark hair, and black moustache; very well-informed on all the happenings in the great world outside. He was later to become Comrade Borodin, the Russian political adviser to the Kuomintang at Canton.[3]

On the whole, the foreign delegates were a rather disappointing crowd, charmed at enjoying appreciable privileges in a starving country, quick to adulate and reluctant to think. Few workers could be seen among them, but plenty of politicians. 'How pleased they are', Jacques Mesnil remarked to me, 'to be able to watch parades, at long last, from the official platform!' The influence of the International was expanded only at the expense of quality. We began to ask ourselves whether it had not been a grave error to split the Socialist movement to form new little parties, incapable of

[1] Lozovsky afterwards became Deputy Commissar for Foreign Affairs and then head of the Soviet Information Office; he was shot in 1952 at the age of 74.

[2] I.W.W.: Industrial Workers of the World. United States working-class movement of militant syndicalist complexion, founded in 1905 and achieving its prime between 1910 and 1920.

[3] Later still Borodin edited the *Moscow News*, an English-language newspaper produced, at first, largely for foreign technicians working in the Soviet Union. In 1949 he was arrested with most of his staff, and deported to Siberia, where he died early in 1953. Chinese intervention is said to have saved him from execution.

effective action, fed with ideas and money by the Executive's emissaries, and fated to become propaganda factories for the Soviet Government. We were already putting these problems to ourselves, but were reassured by the instability of Western Europe and the wave of enthusiasm which still held us. All the same, I did conclude that, in the International as well, the danger lay in ourselves.

The New Economic Policy was, in the space of a few months, already giving marvellous results. From one week to the next, the famine and the speculation were diminishing perceptibly. Restaurants were opening again and, wonder of wonders, pastries which were actually edible were on sale at a rouble apiece. The public was beginning to recover its breath, and people were apt to talk about the return of capitalism, which was synonymous with prosperity. On the other hand, the confusion among the Party rank-and-file was staggering. For what did we fight, spill so much blood, agree to so many sacrifices? asked the Civil War veterans bitterly. Usually these men lacked all the necessities: clothes, decent homes, money; and now everything was turning back into market-value. They felt that money, the vanquished foe, would soon come into its kingdom once again.

I personally was less pessimistic. I was glad that the change had taken place, though its reactionary side—the outright obliteration of every trace of democracy—worried and even distressed me. Would any other resolution of the drama of War Communism have been possible? This was by now a problem of only theoretical interest, but one worthy of some reflection. On this I developed some ideas, which I remember expounding on one occasion particularly, at a confidential meeting I had at the Lux Hotel with two Spanish Socialists. Fernando de los Ríos was one of them.[1] They ran as follows:

Through its intolerance and its arrogation of an absolute monopoly of power and initiative in all fields, the Bolshevik régime was floundering in its own toils. The big concessions to the peasantry were unavoidable, but small-scale manufacture, medium-scale trading, and certain industries could have been revived merely by

[1] Fernando de los Ríos (1879–1949): Professor of Ethics at Granada University, Minister of Justice and of Education in the first Spanish Republican Government, and Ambassador to Washington during the Civil War.

appealing to the initiative of groups of producers and consumers. By freeing the State-strangled co-operatives, and inviting various associations to take over the management of different branches of economic activity, an enormous degree of recovery could have been achieved straight away. The country was short of both shoes and leather; but the rural areas had leather, and shoe-makers' co-operatives would have easily got hold of it and, once left to themselves, would have sprung into action at once. Of necessity they would have charged relatively high prices, but the State could, in the process of assisting their operations, have exercised a downward pressure upon their prices, which in any case would have been lower than those demanded by the black market. In Petrograd I could see what was happening to the book trade; the stocks of the bookshops, which had been confiscated, were rotting away in cellars which as often as not became flooded with water in the spring. We were most thankful to the thieves who salvaged a goodly number of books and put them back, clandestinely, into circulation. The book trade could, if it had been turned over to associations of book-lovers, have speedily recovered its health. In a word, I was arguing for a 'Communism of associations'—in contrast to Communism of the State variety. The competition inherent in such a system and the disorder inevitable in all beginnings would have caused less inconvenience than did our stringently bureaucratic centralization, with its muddle and paralysis. I thought of the total plan not as something to be dictated by the State from on high, but rather as resulting from the harmonizing, by congresses and specialized assemblies, of initiatives from below. However, since the Bolshevik mind had already ordained other solutions, it was a vision confined to the realms of pure theory.

Ever since Kronstadt some of my friends and I had been asking ourselves what jobs we were going to do. We had not the slightest desire to enter the ruling bureaucracy and become heads of offices or secretaries of institutions. I was offered entry into a diplomatic career, in the Orient at first. I was attracted by the prospect of the Orient, but not by diplomacy. We thought we had found a way out. We would found an agricultural colony in the heart of the Russian countryside; while the N.E.P. reinstated bourgeois habits in the towns and furnished the new rulers with sinecures and easy careers, we would live close to the earth, in the wilds. The earth of Russia, with its sad and calm expanses, is endlessly fascinating. Without much ado we found a large, abandoned estate north of Petrograd, not far from Lake Ladoga, comprising some hundreds of acres of woodland and waste field, thirty head of cattle, and a landlord's residence. There, together with French Communists, Hungarian prisoners-of-war, a Tolstoyan doctor and my father-in-law Russakov, we founded 'the French Commune of Novaya-Ladoga'.

We made a valiant beginning to this experiment, which turned out to be very hard going. The estate had been abandoned because the peasants would not agree to exploit it collectively; they demanded that it be shared out among them. Two chairmen of short-lived communes there had been murdered in the space of eighteen months. The village nearby boycotted us, although the children came at all hours to stare at the extraordinary creatures that we were. At the same time they spied everywhere, and if you forgot a shovel it disappeared at once. One night our entire stock of corn, which was to last for both food and seed until harvest-time, was stolen from us. It was a real state of famine and siege. Every night we waited up in case anyone tried to set the house on fire. We knew who was hiding our corn, but we did not, as they expected, go out with our revolvers to search for it, which only increased the suspicion and hatred surrounding us. The peasants had all the necessities, but refused to sell anything to the 'Jews' and 'Anti-Christs' that we were.

We decided to break this blockade; I went off to the village with Dr. N——, an old believer and Tolstoyan whose musical voice and benign solemnity would, we hoped, have some effect. A peasant woman curtly refused us everything we asked for. The doctor opened the neck of his blouse and brought out the little golden cross that he wore over his breast. 'We are Christians too, little sister!' Their faces lit up and we were given eggs! And little girls made so bold as to come to see us in the evenings, when we would all sing French songs together. . . . However, it could not last; in three months hunger and weariness forced us to abandon the project.

Since Kronstadt there had been a revival of the Terror in Petrograd. The Cheka had just 'liquidated' the Tagantsev conspiracy by executing some thirty people. I had known Professor Tagantsev a little: a skinny little old man with white side-whiskers, a jurist and one of the longest-established university teachers in the former capital. With him they shot a lawyer named Bak to whom I used to send translation jobs and who had never concealed his counter-revolutionary opinions from me.[1] At the same time they executed the splendid poet Nikolai Stepanovich Gumilev, my comrade and adversary back in Paris. I called on his home at the Moyka Art House, where he had a room with his very young wife, a tall girl with a slender neck and the eyes of a terrified gazelle. It was a huge room, with murals showing swans and lotuses—it had once been the bathroom of a merchant who had a taste for poetry with this sort of imagery. Gumilev's young wife said to me in a low voice, 'Haven't you heard? They took him away three days ago.'

The comrades at the Soviet Executive gave me news which was both reassuring and disturbing: Gumilev was being very well treated at the Cheka, he had spent some nights there reciting his poems—poems overflowing with stately energy—to the Chekists there; but he had admitted to having drafted certain political documents for the counter-revolutionary group. All this seemed likely enough. Gumilev had never concealed his ideas. During the Kronstadt revolt the circle at the university must have believed that the régime was about to fall, and had thought to assist in its liquidation. The 'conspiracy' could have gone no further than that. The Cheka made ready to shoot all of them: 'This isn't the time to go soft!' One comrade travelled to Moscow to ask Dzerzhinsky a question: 'Were we entitled to shoot one of Russia's two or three poets of the first order?' Dzerzhinsky answered, 'Are we entitled to make an exception of a poet and still shoot the others?' It was dawn, at the edge of a forest, when Gumilev fell, his cap pulled down over his eyes, a cigarette hanging from his lips, showing the same calm he had expressed in one of the poems he brought back from Ethiopia: '*And fearless I shall appear before the Lord God.*' That, at least, is the tale as it was told to me. Over and over again, with mingled admiration and horror, I read the verses which he had entitled 'The Worker', where he describes a gentle, grey-eyed man who, before going to bed, finishes making '*the bullet that is going to kill me. . . .*'

[1] 'Monsieur Bak, a former businessman and journalist for an Iron and Steel Board in the days of the Empire, a small, smooth-faced gentleman, appallingly refined and nice, was agreeable to translating articles on theory, but not revolutionary appeals. "Pardon me, citizen," he would remark, "my conscience. . . ." Naturally, I respected his conscience. . . .' Serge, *Deux Rencontres*.

The faces of Nikolai and Olga Gumilev were to haunt me for years afterwards.

At the same time another of our greatest poets was dying of debility, which was the same thing as starvation: Alexander Blok, at the age of forty-one. I knew him only slightly, but admired him boundlessly. Together with Andrei Bely and Sergei Yesenin he had inspired the mystical vision of the Revolution: 'the Christ crowned with roses' who, 'invisible and silent', walks in the snow-storm before the Twelve Red Guards, soldiers in peak-caps whose rifles are aimed at the city's shadows. He had told me of his rebellions against the Revolution's new absolutism, and I had heard him reading his last great work. His two poems, 'The Twelve', and 'The Scythians', were being translated into many languages, and they remain spiritual monuments of that era. The first proclaimed the Messianic character of the Revolution; the second revealed its ancient, Asiatic face. Contradictory, but so was reality. Blok was a gentlemanly Westerner, rather like an Englishman, blue-eyed and with a long, serious face that hardly ever smiled. He was restrained in his gestures, with a fine dignity about him. Ever since the rise of Symbolism, fifteen years ago, he had been the foremost Russian poet. I followed his corpse to the Vassili-Ostrov cemetery at the moment when the Cheka was passing sentence on Gumilev.

I belonged to the last surviving free-thought society; in all probability I was the only Communist member. This was the Free Philosophic Society, or *Volfila*, whose real guiding spirit was another brilliant poet, Andrei Bely. We organized big public debates, in which one of the speakers was often a shabby, squinting little man, wretchedly dressed, whose face was scored with perpendicular wrinkles. He was Ivanov-Razumnik, the historian and philosopher, still one of the finest representatives of the old revolutionary intelligentsia of Russia. Sometimes the discussion would dissolve into grand lyrical effusions on the problems of existence, consciousness, and the Cosmos. Like Blok, both Bely and Ivanov-Razumnik were somewhat attracted, by reason of their revolutionary romanticism, to the persecuted and silenced Left Social-Revolutionary Party. On account of this sympathy, and because the philosophical flights of the two poets trespassed beyond the bounds of Marxism, the Cheka and the Party had their eye on the *Volfila*. Its organizers wondered every day whether they were going to be arrested. We held our private meetings at Andrei Bely's. At the time he was living in a huge room of the old military headquarters opposite the Winter Palace, just above the offices of the police-militia. There we would ask one another how we could preserve liberty of thought as a principle, and prove that it was not a counter-revolutionary principle. Bely suggested convening a World Congress of Free Thought in Moscow, and inviting to it Romain Rolland, Henri Barbusse, and Gandhi. A chorus of voices cried back: 'It'll never be allowed!' I told them that if they appealed to intellectuals abroad, who were certainly incapable of any real understanding of revolutionary Russia, the Russian intellectuals ran a risk of discrediting the Revolution, which was already the object of indiscriminate attacks by the *émigrés*.

Andrei Bely, a daring stylist, a splendid writer of poetry and prose, and a theosophist (or anthroposophist, as he himself termed it) was just over forty. He was embarrassed at being bald, and so always wore a black skull-cap beneath which his great seer's eyes, of a stony greenish-blue, gave out a continual glitter. The vitality and variety of his mind was prodigious. His whole behaviour reflected spiritual idealism, with sometimes the postures of a visionary, sometimes the frank outbursts of a child. In the aftermath of the 1905 Revolution, he had won fame through a psychological novel about the period, a mystical, revolutionary work impregnated with German and Latin culture. Now he was beginning to feel that his great energies were bankrupt.

'What can I do now in this life?' he asked me despondently one evening. 'I cannot live outside this Russia of ours and I cannot breathe within it!'

I answered that the state of siege was sure to end, and that Western Socialism would open out vast prospects for Russia. 'Do you think so?' he said thoughtfully. However, at the beginning of the autumn of 1921, as the carnage of the Terror was filling us with horror, we saw even the *Volfila* disintegrate.

I am well aware that terror has been necessary up till now in all great revolutions, which do not happen according to the taste of well-intentioned men, but spontaneously, with the violence of tempests; and that it is our duty to employ the only weapons that history affords us if we are not to be overwhelmed through our own folly. But at the same time I saw that the perpetuation of terror, after the end of the Civil War and the transition to a period of economic freedom, was an immense and demoralizing blunder. I was and still am convinced that the new régime would have felt a hundred times more secure if it had henceforth proclaimed its reverence, as a Socialist government, for human life and the rights of all individuals without exception.

The tragedies continued. From Odessa we had monstrous news: the Cheka had just shot Fanny Baron (the wife of Aaron Baron) and Lev Chorny, one of the theoreticians of Russian anarchism. Lev Chorny had been well known to me in Paris twelve years earlier. A figure straight out of a Byzantine icon, with a waxy complexion and eyes that flashed from hollow sockets, he lived in the Latin Quarter, cleaning restaurant windows and then going off to write his *Sociometry* beneath the trees of the Luxembourg Gardens. His death incensed Emma Goldman and Alexander Berkman. During the Third Congress of the International Emma Goldman had thought of making a scene, after the manner of the English suffragettes, by chaining herself to a bench on one of the public balconies and shouting out her protest to the Congress. The Russian anarchists had persuaded her to change her mind. In the country of the Scythians such demonstrations had little value; far better to keep on nagging at Lenin and Zinoviev.

Meanwhile, our persistent campaign for the release of the victimized prisoners had met with some success: ten anarchist prisoners, including the syndicalist Maximov and Boris Voline, were authorized to leave Russia, and others were freed. Kamenev promised that Aaron Baron would be banished; a promise that was not fulfilled, since the Cheka was to oppose it.[1] Certain Mensheviks, notably Martov, also obtained passports to travel abroad.

What with Kronstadt, these tragedies, and the influence of Emma Goldman and Alexander Berkman on the working-class movement in the Old World and the New, an unbridgeable gap was now to open between Marxists and libertarians. Later in history, this division would play a fatal part: it was one of the causes of the intellectual confusion and final defeat of the Spanish Revolution. In this respect, my worst forebodings were fulfilled.

The American background of Emma Goldman and Alexander

[1] Aaron Baron was later deported to the north; but he was arrested during the purges of 1937 and never heard of again.

Berkman estranged them from the Russians, and turned them into representatives of an idealistic generation that had completely vanished in Russia. (I have no doubt that they were just as disconcerted and indignant over a good deal of what happened in Makhno's movement.) They embodied the humanistic rebellion of the turn of the century: Emma Goldman with her organizing flair and practical disposition, her narrow but generous prejudices, and her self-importance, typical of American women devoted to social work; Berkman with the inward tension that sprang from his idealism in years long past. His eighteen years in an American prison had frozen him in the attitudes of his youth when, as an act of solidarity with a strike, he had offered up his life by shooting at one of the steel barons. When his tension relaxed he became dejected, and I could not help thinking that he was often troubled by ideas of suicide. In fact, it was only much later that he was to end his life, in 1936, on the Côte d'Azur.

The winds of an immeasurable calamity swept upon us from the parched plains of the Volga. The Civil War had crossed these regions, and now drought had destroyed them. Millions, starved of all necessities, fled from the famine. I saw them coming up even as far as Petrograd, on foot or in carts. Not everyone had the strength or the means to flee; these were all to die in millions on the spot. This scourge, which struck at both the Ukraine and the Crimea, devastated areas populated by 23,000,000 inhabitants. The blow was so severe that authority tottered. Could the Bolshevik dictatorship overcome the ghastly spectre of death? I met Maxim Gorky, bony, grey, and frowning as never before; he told me of the formation of a committee of leading intellectuals and non-Communist technicians, which was to appeal to all the latent energies of the country, and might well be the germ of tomorrow's democratic government. (The Government at first recognized this committee, which was headed by the Marxist-revisionist economist Prokopovich and the Liberal publicist, Ekaterina Kusskova; then it had these two arrested and expelled from the country.)[1]

[1] S. N. Prokopovich (1871–1955) and his wife Ekaterina Kusskova (1869–1958) were prominent on the Liberal (and subsequently the 'revisionist') wing of the Russian Labour and co-operative movement. Prokopovich served as a Minister under Kerensky and wrote in exile important works on the Soviet economy. Kusskova was a leading figure in the group of *émigrés* who believed in the eventual liberalization of the Soviet régime.

I did not share Gorky's opinion; the revolutionary régime seemed to me already encased in so impenetrable an armour that the skeleton hand of famine could not manage to dislodge it from power. And, despite everything, I was very definitely committed to the régime's survival; I had faith in its future and I knew that for some years Russia would be incapable of any fresh thrust forward from her present condition.

The two groups of friends whose company I kept, the French and the Russian, both suffered from a similar distress. Most of my comrades decided to abandon either political life or the Party. Novomirsky, a high official in the International, an ex-terrorist from 1905, an ex-convict and former anarchist who had been won for Bolshevism by Lenin's goodwill, now sent his membership card back to the Central Committee on account of his fundamental disagreements. He devoted himself to scientific work, and nobody thought of bearing him any grudge. (All the same, he was to be remembered in 1937 when he disappeared, along with his wife, into the concentration-camps.) Marcel Body, a Socialist worker, arranged to be sent to the Soviet Embassy in Oslo. Another got sent to Turkey. Another went to manage a sawmill in the heart of the Far East. Pierre Pascal quietly withdrew from the Party and earned his living as a translator, at the same time working on his history of the schism of the Russian Church. I was tougher inside, and enjoyed (as I think) a broader vision of the Revolution, as well as having less individualistic sentiment in my make-up. I did not feel disheartened or disoriented. I was disgusted at certain things, psychologically exhausted by the Terror and tormented by the mass of wrongs that I could see growing, which I was powerless to counteract. My conclusions were that the Russian Revolution, left to itself, would probably, in one way or another, collapse (I did not see how: would it be through war or domestic reaction?); that the Russians, who had made superhuman efforts to build a new society, were more or less at the end of their strength; and that relief and salvation must come from the West. From now on it was necessary to work to build a Western working-class movement capable of supporting the Russians and, one day, superseding them. I decided to leave for Central Europe, which seemed to be the focus of events to come. (The condition of my wife, who was now on the verge of tuberculosis as a result of all the privations, was another factor that encouraged me in this direction.) Zinoviev and the comrades on the Executive offered me a post in Berlin, working in illegality. If danger was within us, salvation must lie within us no less.

5

EUROPE AT THE DARK CROSSROADS

1922—1926

The train crossed a dismal no-man's-land furrowed with abandoned trenches, bristling with barbed wire. Soldiers in grey greatcoats, wearing the red star on their cloth helmets, watched us sadly as we went by. They were gaunt and grey as the earth. Farewell, comrades!

From Narva onwards, Narva the first town in Estonia, with its ancient gabled houses in the old German style, one suddenly breathed an air that was both less heavy and less bracing. We were coming from a huge entrenched camp governed by the harsh laws of congealed idealism, and entering instead a small, neat, comfortable bourgeois province whose modest shops we viewed as opulent and whose elaborate uniforms appeared loathsome and grotesque. With its puny million of inhabitants, without an economic hinterland, Estonia made a serious pretence at being a modern State, complete with Parliament, generals, and foreign diplomacy. Three parts Russified, it was now unlearning the language of Tolstoy, dismissing the Russian teachers from the University of Dorpat (now Tartu), and conjuring up a national intelligentsia lacking any idiom in common with the rest of the world. How long would it last, and at what price?

At Tallinn (lately Reval), I stopped, overwhelmed with emotion, in front of some houses that were being built. I had seen so much destruction that the simple work of bricklayers moved me deeply. From its hill the old castle dominated the empty streets, which were paved with the little pointed cobbles of medieval days. A horse-drawn omnibus went along a street lined with shops and cafés that sold pastries. At the sight of any one of these shops, our children of Russia would have shouted for joy. In the Volga territories the children of Russia were turning into living skeletons, hundreds of thousands of them. Better than through any theory, I now understood the meaning of the politics of 'self-determination of nationalities', raised as it was to perfection by the blockade of the Revolution.

Myself, my wife Liuba, and my son Vladimir, who was not yet a year old, were travelling illegally; it was, however, an easy form of illegality. From Petrograd as far as Stettin and several other Western cities, there were no obstacles in our path. There were a dozen of us, delegates and agents of the International, discreetly (or sometimes openly) accompanied by a diplomatic courier named Slivkin, a strapping, jovial young man who was entrusted with every imaginable variety of smuggling, and had bought over all the police, customs, and frontier officials along our itinerary. At the last moment we had discovered that the O.M.S. office (*Otdiel Mezhdunarodnoi Sviazy*, or International Relations Section of the Comintern Executive) had, in entering the details on our Belgian passports, forgotten to mention our child. . . .

'That's nothing serious,' Slivkin told me. 'During the frontier examinations I'll make a show of playing with him.' At Stettin he put himself to more trouble in getting an 'invalid' through: a tall, thin young man with dark, piercing eyes and an ashen face, sought by every policeman in the Reich as one of the organizers (Bela Kun was another) of the March 1921 insurrection. This was Guralski, whose real name was Heifitz, once a militant in the Jewish Bund, and now one of the hardest-working agents of the International.

Without any difficulty, I bought from the Berlin *Polizeipräsidium*, at the price of ten dollars and a few cigars, a genuine residence permit which, moreover, transformed me from a Belgian into a Pole. Soon I had to change my nationality again, this time into a Lithuanian, since the cafés in Berlin were plastered with notices saying: 'No Poles served here.' It was the time when Poland had just annexed several mining districts in Upper Silesia, although a plebiscite had yielded a result which in fact favoured the Reich. Germany was visibly gripped by a cold fury.

Inside post-Versailles Germany, governed as it was by the

Social-Democratic President Ebert, and by the most democratic of republican constitutions, one breathed in the atmosphere of a collapsing world. Everything was just in its place: people were unassuming, kindly, industrious, bankrupt, wretched, debauched and resentful. Right in the middle of town, beyond the dark Spree and the Friedrichstrasse, a huge railway station was being built. Bemedalled cripples from the Great War sold matches outside night-clubs in which girls, who had a price just like everything else, danced naked among the flower-decked tables of the diners. Capitalism was running riot, apparently under the inspiration of Hugo Stinnes,[1] and accumulating immense fortunes in the midst of insolvency. Everything was for sale: the daughters of the bourgeoisie in the bars, the daughters of the people in the streets, officials, import and export licences, State papers, businesses in whose prospects nobody believed. The fat dollar and the puny, puffed-up coin of the victors ruled the roost, buying up everything, even human souls if they could. The Allied military missions, burdened with the impossible task of controlling disarmament, walked around in their smart uniforms, surrounded by a polite but no less obvious hatred.

Permanent conspiracies of various sorts went on in limitless ramifications: the conspiracy of Rhineland separatists, financed from abroad, the conspiracy of reactionary military leagues, and the conspiracy of revolutionaries: our own. In philosophic language, Oswald Spengler proclaimed the Decline of the West: come, look at the corpse of Egypt, ponder on the end of Rome. The revolutionary poets were publishing 'Dämmerung der Menschen' (*The Twilight of Mankind*). The portraits of Oskar Kokoschka palpitated in all their lines, colours, and volumes with a cosmic neurosis; the metallic touch of George Grosz traced the silhouettes of piggy bourgeois and robot jailers, with ghastly prisoners and workers living like grubs beneath them. Barlach made statues of peasants stupefied in fear.

I myself wrote:

> *Life is like a sickness:*
> *Red-hot iron the only cure*
> *But instead they are using poisons.*

[1] Hugo Stinnes (1870–1924): a German industrialist who put his enormous fortune at the service of Nationalist interests; a power behind the Press, most of which was controlled by him, and in the general economy.

The little pointed red-brick churches slumbered on the edges of squares which were carved up into allotments. The Reichswehr's choicest old sweats, in heavy helmets, guarded a War Office whose windows were adorned with flowers. Raphael's Madonna, from within her brilliantly-lit room in the Dresden gallery, gazed deeply, darkly and goldenly at all comers. Organization had been so perfected that even in the utter solitude of the Saxony or Harz forests, I found waste-paper baskets and signboards saying '*Schönes Blick*'—Recommended or (as it were) Starred Landscape. At night the towns were magnificently lit up. After the comparison of our Russian penury, affluence had a lasting shock-effect.

Germany was bled white. Nobody there had any real confidence in the future, and practically nobody had any idea of the public good. The capitalists lived in terror of the revolution. The impoverished petty-bourgeoisie saw the old manners and hopes of yesterday vanishing beneath their eyes. Only the Social-Democrats believed in the future of capitalism, in the stabilization of German democracy and even in the intelligence and benevolence of the victors of Versailles! They had the enlightened, optimistic attitudes of the liberal bourgeoisie of 1848. The youth, which was nationalistic and Socialist-inclined, would have nothing to do with them. My impression was that young people hoped for a revolution, and for an alliance with Russia to wage a revolutionary war. Energy, when it was divorced from reason, took refuge in the military leagues; where it was coloured by dogmatic reasoning, it gathered around the Communist Party. Charles Rappoport, pulling a wry smile on his bearded, cynical face, said to me, 'There will be no German revolution for the same reason that there will be no counter-revolution in Russia: people are too tired and too hungry.'

Seen from here, the Russian Revolution appeared as a superb exploit. It preserved almost all its halo of newly-arisen justice and organization, as well as of unprecedented democracy. This was the case both with us and with the general public, and even with many reactionaries. The Social-Democrats were the only people who saw nothing but the cost of the Revolution, its despotic character, the famine and the long wars. Our Soviet poverty, our improvised egalitarianism (with its very modest privileges for the rulers), our blazing creative will and revolutionists' dedication contrasted with the brutal self-seeking of speculation, the arrogant, imbecile luxury of the rich, and the shameful destitution of the masses; and so we could easily forgive the Revolution her unbending harshness, her errors and Spartan ways. In this decomposing bourgeois world we recovered our confidence.

I was on the editorial staff of *Inprekorr*, the Press agency of the Comintern Executive, which published copious material, intended for the Labour Press of the whole world, in three languages, German, English, and French. At my office at the *Rote Fahne*, I was successively Siegfried and Gottlieb; in town I was Dr. Albert, on my papers Viktor Klein and, in my journeys to Russia, Alexei Berlovsky, a former Russian prisoner-of-war in Germany. Victor Serge datelined his articles (which were reprinted as far away as China) from Kiev, a city to which, as it happened, I had never been. I appeared only very seldom at the Soviet Legation in the Unter den Linden where, all the same, I managed to meet Krestinsky and Yakubovich. If I chanced to pass Radek on the Kurfürstendamm, we would exchange a knowing glance, but never greet one another, in case one of us was being followed.

At Grunewald I used to visit a friendly house, occupied by a celebrated French Communist, living (naturally) under a false name; in the next-door garden we could see a stout gentleman taking a stroll among his rose-bushes: Captain Eckhart, one of the leaders of the 'Black' (i.e. secret) Reichswehr and the military conspiracy. At Zehlendorff, in a rose-pink, solid-looking villa shaded by tall pines (this belonged to Eduard Fuchs, who was an active militant), we outlaws and emissaries of the International would meet from time to time, to talk Socialism or hear a little music. The guests there included Radek, the Vuyovich brothers, Otto Pohl (the Austrian Ambassador), L.-O. Frossard, and various Russians. Fuchs, a social historian, was a collector of works by Daumier and Slevogt, Chinese and Japanese *objets d'art*, and obscure facts about the dark corners of the German Revolution. A man on the fringe of the Communist movement, he was still rendering it services which were by no means devoid of risk.

Several times I just missed being arrested in the most idiotic way. When I was on the point of entering the doorway to the *Rote Fahne* office, my wife held me back by the arm: 'Let's walk on quickly, come on!' The vestibule was full of green *Schutzpolizei* uniforms. All the same it was a good idea to post them so openly.

I took a small, separate office away in town as a commercial broker
—what brand of commerce, I never discovered.

The editorial staff of *Inprekorr*, the intellectual and political mentor
of the world Communist movement, was of an outstanding mediocrity. In charge was Gyula Alpári, once a high official in the
Hungarian Soviet régime, a bloated, artful and well-informed
individual, whose sole conception of his role was already that of a
functionary discreetly heading, even through illegality, for an undisturbed career. He never committed himself on any issue, but
rode along passively and gently in a spirit of revolutionary conformism awaiting its due reward. He would explain to me, grinning
fatly: 'When a pretty girl says No, it means Yes; when a diplomat
says Yes, it means No; when I say Yes or No, it means neither Yes nor
No. . . .'

The German section was run by two deputies of the Prussian
Landtag, Bartz, the cartoonists' image of the petty official behind his
little window, and Franz Dahlem, a young man with hard features,
a prominent nose and expressionless eyes: Dahlem, the toiler
without personality, the militant without doubts, the fact-gatherer
without thoughts, who never asked himself a question of the slightest
vital interest but only carried out, all punctiliously, every instruction and directive he received. This was the Communist N.C.O.
type, neither a blockhead nor a thinker: obedient only. Bartz has
died, a faithful working-class Deputy; Alpári continued his career
as Comintern agent right up to the fall of Paris; Franz Dahlem,
after Thaelmann's arrest, became the leader of the German Communist Party, was interned in France, and then handed over to the
Gestapo by the Vichy Government, in all likelihood to his death.[1]
He had conscientiously performed all the infamous routines of
totalitarian Communism; he will die (if he has not already died)
like a good N.C.O., courageously. Already around 1922, the
International was unintentionally modelling factotum officials, who
were prepared to give passive obedience.

The march on Rome and the rise of Mussolini were understood
by no one in the International except a few isolated militants, who
included myself since I had followed the progress of Fascism from

[1] Dahlem survived, becoming a Politburo member and head of the cadres section
of the E. German S.E.D.; in 1953, dismissed from all posts for 'political blindness
towards imperialist agents'; in 1956–7 reinstated in some posts (Central Committee, Ministry for Higher Education in the G.D.R.); now (1977) writing his
memoirs.

fairly close quarters. The opinion of the leadership was that this was a piece of reactionary buffoonery which would soon die away and open the path to revolution. I opposed this view, saying that this new variety of counter-revolution had taken the Russian Revolution as its schoolmaster in matters of repression and mass-manipulation through propaganda; further, it had succeeded in recruiting a host of disillusioned, power-hungry ex-revolutionaries; consequently, its rule would last for years.

The International and the Soviet Government were proceeding along two parallel dimensions, and with two distinct objectives: first, to form disciplined parties over the whole of Europe with a view to events to come; secondly, to achieve toleration from the capitalist world and thence credits for the reconstruction of Russia. If such credits had been forthcoming, the Soviet system would probably have evolved in a liberal direction. I know that, at the time of the Genoa Conference, in May 1922, Lenin and Kamenev were considering the revival of some degree of Press freedom; there was talk of allowing a non-Party daily to be published in Moscow. A certain religious toleration was also envisaged, although the poverty of the State necessitated the seizure of precious metals from the churches, a measure which led to innumerable clashes and subsequent executions. Genoa was a setback for Russia, despite the flexibility displayed by Chicherin and Rakovsky. Chicherin made up for his losses at Rapallo, where he signed a treaty of friendship with Germany, thus ranging the Soviet Union decisively on the side of the losers of Versailles.

The Conference of the Three Internationals assembled the fraternal enemies for the first time around the same table (in one of the study-rooms in the Reichstag): leaders of the Socialist International, leaders of the Two-and-a-Half International (as we mockingly called the little groups conglomerated midway between the reformists and the Bolsheviks), leaders of the Third International. I attended the conference in my capacity as a journalist. These men presented a striking physical contrast. The Socialists, Abramovich, Vandervelde, and Friedrich Adler had the fine profiles of Western intellectuals and the behaviour of competent lawyers; their whole comportment expressed moderation. Facing them was Clara Zetkin's solid, powerful old face, the mobile, sardonic features of Radek, and Bukharin's impervious geniality. The Socialists insisted—and with good reason—that political persecution in Russia must be ended. Bukharin told me, 'That's only an excuse. Those people are determined never to fight for Socialism'; and he added, as though by way of a directive, 'Our Press must attack them mercilessly.'

The trial of the Central Committee of the Russian Social-Revolutionary Party actually ruined any chance of co-operation. The S.-R.s had taken part in the Civil War, against us. In 1918, Semionov, one of their terrorists, had organized the assassination in Petrograd of the Bolshevik orator Volodarsky; Dora Kaplan had shot Lenin. Semionov embraced Bolshevism and made a remarkably full confession. . . . The background to the attempts against Lenin was closely investigated—the authors of the first attempt, in Petrograd, had meanwhile joined the Communist Party—and the trial ended with a suspended death-sentence on the twelve principal defendants, who included Gotz, Timofeyev, and Gerstein.

From Berlin, I observed the proceedings with great distress. Now that the Civil War was over, were we going to shed the blood of a defeated party which, in the old days, had furnished the Revolution with so many of its heroes? The Politbureau hesitated. I heard it said: 'We are moving towards an inevitable collision with the peasantry. This peasant party has certain prospects; consequently it must be beheaded.'

I conspired with several friends to try and prevent this calamity. Clara Zetkin, Jacques Sadoul and Souvarine exerted pressure towards the same end; Maxim Gorky sent Lenin a letter breaking off all relations. . . . No blood was spilt. Thirteen years later, I was to see the aged Gerstein die in almost complete destitution, deported to Orenburg. He was an unyielding, conscience-racked idealist who until his last breath remained loyal to his democratic beliefs. Gotz was deported for a second time in 1936 to a town on the Volga.[1]

Shortly afterwards, at the end of 1922, I paid a short visit to Moscow. Russia was returning to life; Petrograd was bandaging its wounds and emerging from dilapidation. Night-time, with the pitiful state of illumination, exuded a terrible depression, but people

---

[1] Abraham R. Gotz (1882–1937), a former Social-Revolutionary terrorist, and later a strong supporter of Kerensky, was released in 1927. He then worked for many years for the State Bank. It is believed that Stalin had him shot in 1937.

were no longer hungry and a brisk pace of living was in evidence everywhere. The Terror had ceased, without being formally abolished, and everyone tried hard to forget the nightmare of arrests and executions. A new literature was bursting out in the 'Serapion Brothers' circle and among the writers, yesterday unknown, who overnight were now counted among the great: Boris Pilniak, Vsevolod Ivanov, Konstantin Fedin.[1] Their works were intense and impetuous, saturated with virile humanism and a critical spirit. They were rebuked because they were not at all Communistic, indeed very far from being so; but they were published, they were loved. The great tradition of Russian literature, interrupted during the stormy years, was being born again in the second year of peace! It was miraculous.

Small traders were springing up everywhere, crowds swarmed over the markets, the taverns exhaled their music, barefoot youngsters ran in the streets at dawn, following the cabs to offer flowers to lovers. There were plenty of beggars, but they were not dying of hunger. In official circles they were beginning to talk of the Reconstruction Plan advocated by Trotsky. It was a nation in convalescence, a nation on the march.

At the Kremlin I found the familiar atmosphere still there. An enlarged session of the Comintern Executive was studying certain problems whose nature escapes my memory. At it I met Amadeo Bordiga, gloomier, sturdier, and more quarrelsome than ever before, this time picking a quarrel over revolutionary morality. Zinoviev listened to him with a smile.

---

[1] Boris Pilniak (1894–?): novelist, not a Communist Party member; author of *The Story of An Unextinguished Moon* (1926), dealing with the touchy theme of Frunze's death after an operation (ordered by Stalin); *Red Wood* (1929); *The Volga Flows Into The Caspian Sea* (1930), a novel on the Five-Year Plan. Disappeared in 1937. Vsevolod Ivanov (1895–1963): led a varied life as sailor, actor, circus juggler, typesetter, comedian, and wrestler; joined the Red Army in 1917; early stories on the Civil War (*Partisans, Armoured Train No. 1469*); *Adventures Of A Fakir* (1934–5); memoirs of Maxim Gorky (1953); novels on the Second World War. Konstantin Fedin (1892–1963): early works inspired by his experiences as a soldier and prisoner-of-war in 1914–18; Red Army journalist and volunteer (1918); pessimistic at first regarding the future of the intelligentsia, but later adapted himself. Later novels *Early Joys, No Ordinary Summer*; now head of the Soviet Writers' Union, and generally held to be a liberalizing influence. Serge retained a very high opinion of Fedin's record and integrity as a writer (see the excerpt from Serge's *Diaries* in the *New International*, July–August 1950).

Corruption, servility, intrigue, backstage tale-bearing, and the official mentality began to assume an increasing role in the functioning of the International. The worst of it was that anybody who wanted to preserve any influence or political office had to kowtow persistently to the Russians and their emissaries. Besides, they had control of the cash, and the other parties presented the appearance of poor relations. Led by politicians accustomed to bourgeois living, these displayed no capacity for propaganda or action. The International would employ two or three methods to breathe some life into them: it would put 'grey eminences' in charge of them, who were mostly Russian (and therefore strangers to the Western mind), as well as being devotees of Zinoviev; it sent them sizeable funds; or it would remove the old time-honoured politicians and replace them with young militants who were sometimes no more than young careerists. The Parties went from one crisis to another.

At the crossroads of Berlin, I encountered many delegates and emissaries. They included a young engineer from Saint-Denis named Jacques Doriot, who was in high esteem as a 'real force'.[1] Frossard assured me of his intention to serve the Russian Revolution without falling back into the ways of the old Parliamentary Socialism of the Third Republic. Pierre Sémard, secretary of the railwaymen's union, a tall, poised man with a face typical of the Paris worker, spoke of the proletarianizing of the Party. Louis Sellier went into ecstasies over financial reform in Soviet Russia, a subject of which I immediately saw that he knew nothing.

Frossard broke with the International a few months later.[2] Sémard was to remain loyal to the Party till his death, despite many humiliations, despite even the atrocious allegation that he had been a police agent, a charge with which he was hypocritically smeared when he was to be removed from the leadership. (The Nazis shot him in Paris on 15 April 1942.)

[1] Jacques Doriot (1898–1945): subsequently built up a strong following in the working-class Paris suburb of St. Denis; he opposed the 'Social-Fascist' line of the Comintern, and broke with the French Communist Party in 1934, advocating a 'Popular Front' with Socialists and bourgeois-liberals. After being unseated in St. Denis, founded the *Parti Populaire Français*, which speedily became a blatant fascist organization. During the Occupation a virulent French Nazi; fought on the Russian front; killed by an Allied plane while travelling in a car.

[2] Frossard rejoined the Socialist Party in 1924, and became a 'moderate'; he left the Socialist Party in 1935 to become Minister of Labour in a succession of bourgeois Cabinets.

Marcel Cachin would relate how he had exhorted Lenin not to march on Warsaw; oh, if only people had listened to him! Cachin was likeable and open-hearted. He had the greying hair and moustachioed face of an old sailor or miner, a passionate voice, and a relentlessly perfect French diction, appropriate for the Parliamentary orator that he was. His thinking was purely that of a platform speaker; he worshipped the Party and lived exclusively on his popularity. To keep his reputation going he would strive always to follow the strongest current of opinion, which he was quick to smell out. A rather intelligent man, who could see practically everything that was going on, he—for a long time I am sure—experienced considerable anguish; but he never rebelled. Where would he have been without his Party, his Parliament, etc?

The crisis over the reparations imposed on Germany by the Versailles Treaty grew worse from day to day. When Vorovsky, the old Marxist humanist and then Soviet Ambassador to Italy, died in Lausanne, riddled with bullets by a young White Russian *émigré*, the atmosphere in Germany was so acute that an order from Moscow came insisting on a great Communist and pro-Soviet demonstration while the corpse was in transit across our territory. The funeral van arrived at the Silesia station on a foggy evening; the gloomy building was surrounded by a dense crowd, complete with red banners. Radek spoke from a lorry laden with flowers and bristling with flags. Torches flamed all around him. His strident voice was carried away in the electric night-air, but his short, austere silhouette could be clearly distinguished. Krestinsky,[1] the Ambassador, followed the procession on foot, protected only by a group of German Y.C.L.ers.

Krestinsky was a man of outstanding intelligence, discretion and courage. His whole life was dedicated to the Party of the Revolution but he was there as a sort of exile, having been dismissed from the General Secretaryship because of his democratic inclinations. He was still young, and astoundingly myopic, so that his shrewd eyes, hidden behind lenses a quarter of an inch thick, seemed to have a timid expression. With his tall, bare skull and his wisp of dark beard,

[1] Nikolai N. Krestinsky (1883–1938): a Bolshevik since 1907, repeatedly arrested; People's Commissar for Finance after 1917, later Deputy Commissar for Foreign Affairs; Secretary of the Central Committee 1919–21; defendant in the 1938 Bukharin–Rykov trial; repudiated his confession on the first day and repudiated the repudiation on the next; sentenced to be shot.

he made one think of a scholar; actually he was a great practical technician of Socialism. He was against taking unnecessary risks, but was not afraid of them; indeed he was quite ready, if it came to it, to defend his Embassy at pistol-point, along with his secretaries and office staff. On that evening he refused to take precautions for his own safety, saying that it was proper that Soviet Russia's Ambassador to Berlin should expose himself to a little danger. The torchlight demonstration around Vorovsky's coffin marked the opening of the period of revolutionary mobilization.

The Cuno Government announced that Germany was incapable of paying any more reparations. In this way the *Schwerindustrie* which backed the Government held over the head of Europe the threat of the Reich's bankruptcy and even of a revolution. Poincaré had the Ruhr occupied by French troops, who shot a nationalist agitator named Schlageter. French agents were at work creating a separatist movement in the Rhineland. Events, which I followed hourly, were hurrying onward at a dizzying pace. There was catastrophic inflation, speculation in currency; the rate of exchange of the dollar changed as often as twice a day and, in between telephone-calls heralding the latest rise, the holders of the precious greenbacks issued by the Federal banks of America stripped the shops of all their goods. . . . The central thoroughfares of the big towns could always be seen packed with people running along holding parcels. The Germans, of all people, actually rioted outside bakeries and grocers' shops; there was no rationing to inhibit them. Mobs loitered in the streets. How many trillions did it cost to stamp a letter? At the pay-desk of a Wertheim store I saw an old lady, with a black lace neckband, taking out of her handbag some hundred-mark notes dating from the previous year, the age of Walter Rathenau.

'But they are not worth anything now, *gnädige Frau* (honoured lady).'

'What do you mean? I don't understand. . . .' People guffawed at her. Walter Rathenau lay in his grave, his body hacked all over: this notable Jew had dreamed of a new, intelligently organized German capitalism; and he had held discussions on the subject with Radek.

Not far from the Alexanderplatz and the *Polizeipräsidium*, a little shop was being looted, in the most orderly manner. Nobody is to take more than three tins of food, see! Proletarian discipline. In another place I saw a shoe-business being looted. Two volunteers kept watch outside while people rapidly tried shoe after shoe for size; some, who had not found shoes to fit, came out scrupulously empty-handed. . . .

The working-class women of Wedding, Neukolln, and Moabit had the grey complexions that I had first seen on convicts in the central jails, and subsequently among the inhabitants of the famished towns of the Russian Revolution. Few lights at the windows, dim groups in the streets. Each day brought its windfall of strikes, and every night the sinister silence echoed with revolver-shots. The voice of the agitator would deliver a commentary in the street, surrounded by faces. The safe Social-Democrat, angry in a safe sort of way, the eager Communists, the patriotic member of the clandestine Leagues were all practically agreed: Versailles is a noose around the German nation's neck; woe unto France, woe unto Poland, woe unto capitalism! The Communists had an attractive scheme: industrial Germany and agricultural Russia could unite to save the world. Radek pushed through his 'Schlageter tactic' of conciliation with the Nationalists. It's playing with fire—all right, let's play with fire! Where shall we begin? Our agitators told us, with a word that snapped out of their mouths: *Loschlagen!*—Strike out! The decision was taken: we strike. After careful and thorough preparations, we have only to choose the moment. Trotsky's talks to the Moscow Military School are published in several languages; their subject—'*Can one lay down the date of a revolution in advance?*' Red Saxony and Thuringia, ruled by working-class governments (Communist and Social-Democrat) recruit two Red divisions. Arms arrive from Czechoslovakia; more are sold by the Reichswehr, and the dollars to pay for them come from Russia. (The consequence is that the Reichswehr deliver a wagonload of carbines one nightfall and, once they have their hands on the brand-new dollars, inform the *Schutzpolizei*, who come at dawn to seize the truck. . . .) The young militants have their orders to establish secret links with the troops; the railway workers, to shunt away and camouflage the ammunitions-wagons; the comrades in charge of transport, to look sharp, for God's sake! At night, outside the barred gates of the barracks, girls whose plaits are drawn into a topknot flirt with helmeted young men. 'You'll bring out some grenades, won't you, dear?' *Liebeslied* and sweet romance. . . .

Will the masses follow us? The Party makes up its mind only after the first big strikes in the Rhineland; it has held back the movement so as not to dissipate its forces. Are our forces gathering or weakening? Hunger has a habit of unnerving men. When the International has decided everything, what will be going on in the heads of the average Social-Democrat (who distrusts Communists) and the man in the street? From Moscow, where the Executive is in session, Boris Souvarine writes to me, 'We are trying to put ourselves into Lenin's shoes. . . .'

The Executive fixes the date of the uprising as 25 October, the anniversary of the seizure of power in Petrograd in 1917. At this moment the difference in dates between the Julian and Gregorian calendars is of small importance! I reply to Souvarine, and write to other contacts in Moscow, to the effect that unless the Party's initiative joins with the spontaneous movement of the masses, it is doomed beforehand. Every day I learn of stocks of arms being seized. The tense expectation in the working-class districts seems to be slackening strangely. The unemployed are passing, by swift stages, from an insurgent enthusiasm into weary resignation.

Voya Vuyovich arrives from Moscow: indented forehead, and grey eyes lighting up his young face. I knew of his history as a militant which had begun during the retreat from Serbia. Voya became a Socialist through the fact that among this beaten rabble there were men who could still think calmly. Then came imprisonment in France, little committees, the International, illegal journeys, secret messages, and factional intrigue inside the old Socialist parties. Voya was one of the hidden architects of the split in the Italian Socialist Party at its Leghorn Congress.

He tells me: 'Our propaganda among occupation-troops in the Ruhr has brought useful results. A police-spy has been disposed of in Cologne. . . .' Voya believes that, on the day, we shall win. 'Everything is going to be much better than in Russia. . . .' I hope you are right, Voya.

Other comrades are forming 'mopping-up' squads with a view to the aftermath of the rising: these are to liquidate the leading staff of the counter-revolution. Our top activists are full of zest, but they are the only ones to be so. A few days before the uprising a militant from the military section of the *Kommunistische Partei Deutschlands* gazed into my eyes when I put the question to him, and replied:

'We shall make a good showing when we get defeated, but we shall be defeated all the same.' We all feel like this: but meanwhile the Central Committee of the K.P.D. is allotting the portfolios of a commissars' Cabinet to its members, and Koenen, with his ginger goatee and his schoolmaster's specs, explains to us on behalf of the Central Committee's Information Department that everything is going along wonderfully. Even on the day after our main stocks of arms in Berlin have been seized, he is still proving it. Chance is my principal informer, an excellent one too. I learn that a Party official has been arrested coming out of Willi Münzenberg's house;[1] his briefcase actually contained our arms-accounts, intended for the eyes of the Comintern Executive. Thus the Party has been more or less disarmed in the capital. I also learn that the Government has decided in principle to dissolve it. I warn the members of the Central Committee of these facts, indirectly since it is now impossible for me to see them personally. They send a reply to the effect that this is indeed a current rumour in the streets, but that they know what's what; no one will dare to interfere! 'Of course, we may lose, in which case. . . .' They have already lost, but they still have no inkling that this is so.

Everything is set for the seizure of power on 25 October 1923! Red Saxony and Thuringia are to lead. In accordance with Comintern directives, Brandler, Heckert and Böttcher have entered the Dresden Cabinet under the Social-Democrat Zeigner. The Communists see this Government as the forerunner of insurrection; the Social-Democrats probably only as one more crisis-Cabinet: everything will calm down, just like all the other times. On the 21st, a conference of Factory Committees meets at Chemnitz; this foreshadows the Congress of Workers' Councils which will proclaim the dictatorship of the proletariat. The Workers' Hundreds stand guard outside it: young lads, proud to carry the five-pointed star on their sports shirts, or old Spartakists who have lived through November 1918, the rising of January 1919, the murder, in public, in broad daylight, of Karl and Rosa, the dictatorship of the man of blood, Gustav

[1] Willi Münzenberg (1889–1940): German Communist leader; Secretary of the International Socialist Youth League 1914–21, and then of the Young Communist International; later an outstanding behind-the-scenes organizer of many 'front' movements; broke with the Party in 1937 after the Moscow Trials; found hanged in France in 1940 after escaping from an internment-camp. His death is variously ascribed to the Gestapo and the N.K.V.D.

Noske, the worthy Social-Democrat. These men are ready to do anything that they may be asked. I live with them, they ask me timid questions about Russia, the tall youngsters are studying the technique of street-fighting.

While the Chemnitz conference is on, and Eberlein is seeing to secret preparations in Berlin, the Russian military experts review the strategic situation. They include Yuri Piatakov, who has experience of civil war in the Ukraine, and (I think) Lozovsky. This supply of arms would scarcely be enough even for fighting the campaigns around Kiev! There is nothing for it but to call the rising off. The lads return from Chemnitz, with long faces. Couriers leave with counter-orders for every *Bezirk* (or region) in the country. Will we have the chance to recover our breath and make up our armaments? It would be mad to think so. There are few of us who realize the full extent of the defeat in the first moments that follow.

The counter-order has not reached Hamburg; there 300 Communists start the revolution. The town is frozen in silence and tense expectation; they go off, filled with a terrible enthusiasm, methodically organized. The police outposts fall one after the other, and sharpshooters take up their positions in the top windows over the main thoroughfares. Hamburg is taken, taken by the 300! The whole of Germany has not moved an inch, and neither for that matter has Hamburg itself. The housewives go out shopping, while the police venture out again, having regained their confidence, and start firing against invisible rebels who melt away as they approach. The workers, at home, await the outcome with impatience.

'Another *putsch*,' say the Social-Democrats, 'will you never learn anything after all?' We answer back, 'And you—what have you learnt?' The Left of the Party denounces the leadership, who are Rightists: Thalheimer the dialectician and Brandler the humpbacked bricklayer with malice in his eyes. The Left wonders if the Comintern Executive is at last going to recognize that 'we are the real ones', the only revolutionaries, the only possible leadership for a German revolution. Ruth Fischer, Arkadi Maslow, Heinz Neumann, and Arthur Rosenberg believe that their hour has come. I have met Rosenberg on a number of occasions at the *Rote Fahne*. This brilliant intellectual gives me a slight jolt by asking 'Do you really think that the Russians want a German revolution?' He doubts if they do. Heinz Neumann, a pale, mocking young man, plays at conspiracy with the gusto of a romantic actor, but there is no acting in his courage. He carries false whiskers in his pocket; he has just escaped from a police station in the Rhineland; a house he is in is surrounded, and he gets away at the last minute; he purloins letters addressed to the comrades who are lodging him, members of the opposing tendency in the Party; he conducts, simultaneously, three or four different spheres of activity: one for the Party, one for the Left's Party-within-the-Party, and yet others more dangerous in nature—not forgetting the ladies. . . . Twenty-five years old, he is a young rogue who argues like a cynic. He has an infant prodigy's capacity for absorbing knowledge, a sense of history, merciless views on his elders, and a love for a theoretical working class besides which the actual working class is only highly imperfect human material.

'There are no more real Bolsheviks in Germany. They are all putrid with moderation, wisdom, detachable collars and respect for the *Polizeipräsident*—Do not Break the Glass in the Street Lamps, and all that. The proletariat is respectability itself. We shall have to pass through Fascism before they get cured of all that clap.' Heinz came several times, at dead of night, to air these opinions to me: he, with all the police of Germany after him, coming to see me, a man under observation, living just opposite the Lichterfelde barracks.[1]

The Social-Democratic President, Ebert, deals with the tail-end of the disturbances by granting full powers to General von Seeckt, whose ascetic face suddenly looms out from the newspapers. General Müller enters Dresden with a regiment and dismisses the Zeigner Government; there is no resistance. Every morning von Seeckt goes for a morning ride in the Tiergarten, followed by an *aide-de-camp*. On his route Heinz Neumann stations two workers, good marksmen and armed with revolvers. Twice these workers lose their nerve, and von Seeckt passes on. . . .

On 9 November Adolf Hitler, the puny agitator from a tiny party that is stirring up trouble in Bavaria, opens his absurd *coup* in Munich. The result: one revolver-shot in the ceiling above the beer-mugs, fourteen dead in the street, and the Führer-to-be out on the rocks with an empty belly and a very comfortable prison

[1] Neumann later organized the Canton Communist uprising in 1927. After the rise to power of Nazism, he took refuge in the Soviet Union and perished in the purges of 1937; his widow was handed over to the Gestapo after the Nazi-Soviet Pact.

waiting for him. See now, the Left and the Right are both absolutely useless!

The Weimar Republic only survives the crisis of October to November 1923 through the weight of the masses' inertia. Its opponents, whether revolutionary or counter-revolutionary, have neither guts nor following. The bulk of the population is uninvolved, since it has no confidence in either of them. It will take years of deception before the unemployed will be seen either selling themselves for a crust to the Nazi Party or, like others, hopelessly following a confused ideal. Nothing could be done without the Social-Democratic masses; and these were divided into officials with a stake in the foundering social system and canny workers ridden by fear of the revolution: as for revolution, the Russian one, the only one that had succeeded, had suffered too much famine, waged too much terror, and strangled too much freedom in its early years. Trotsky is to explain the German defeat in terms of 'the crisis of revolutionary leadership', but that crisis is itself an expression of two other crises: that of popular consciousness, and that of an already bureaucratized International.

There had been some talk of summoning Trotsky to Germany in the decisive hours; a suggestion which annoyed Zinoviev intensely: why not he himself, for that matter? The Politbureau had decided in principle to go as far as military intervention, if necessary, in support of the German rising; and divisions of troops were making ready. But now the E.C.C.I., solicitous above all for its own prestige, condemns the 'opportunism' and inefficiency of the two leaders of the K.P.D., Brandler and Thalheimer, who have been so incompetent in managing the German Revolution. But they did not dare move a finger without referring the matter to the Executive! But Brandler only learnt in the train that he had been made a Minister in Saxony! What's that you're saying? So you're trying to discredit the Executive, are you? Which comes first: the Communist International's reputation? Or your version of the truth, and the moral interests of individuals?

Scapegoats had to be found. Out of defeat came the lying, the suppression, the demoralizing discipline that ruins consciences. Nobody talked about the basic fault. The whole Party lived on the involuntary bluff of functionaries whose first concern was not to contradict their superiors. Misinformation was generated at the base through the personal interest of the poor wretch who, simply to keep his job, assured the *Bezirk* or Central Committee organizer that, yes, he had his fifty men available and that the fifty Mausers had been bought—when in fact he had ten men and was searching in vain to find Mausers for sale. Misinformation ascended stage by stage, through the whole hierarchy of secretaries, so that, at the end of it all, the delegate from the Central Committee of the K.P.D., could tell the President of the International, 'We are prepared', when nothing was prepared and everybody in the Party knew it was so, except those who drew up the confidential reports.

On the very morning of the proclamation of von Seeckt's dictatorship, I took the express for Prague, with my wife and four-year-old son. We had lived through critical days, working practically without money, without an identity to fall back on, and packed off in indecent haste at the last minute by the Soviet Embassy, which had no intention of compromising itself by assisting illegal workers. In the carriage some travellers asked my son, whose only fluent language was German, what he was going to do when he grew up, and he answered in a flash: '*Krieg gegen die Franzosen!*' ('War against the French!')

Prague was an oasis of urbane prosperity. Under its sober President Masaryk, it was enjoying affluence and liberty, the fruits of victory. Vienna was recovering painfully from its inflationary crisis: Austria, in the knowledge that it could not live behind its meagre frontiers, was playing for time, building workers' flats and enjoying sweet music in every café down to the smallest. I arrived with a diplomatic passport, which restored my identity with, however, some embarrassment to me, since I was not officially listed.

Andreu Nin, the secretary of the Red International of Labour Unions, who was passing through Vienna with Lozovsky, told me that Lenin was dying. Lenin still seemed to be completely conscious, but had no power to express himself or do any work. He would manage to stutter out a few words with difficulty; the heading of *Pravda* was spelt out to him letter by letter. Sometimes his eyes were heavy with a voiceless tribulation. Once, when he had felt better, he had wished to see the Kremlin again, and his work-table and telephones; he was taken to them.

'You can see him, leaning on Nadezhda Konstantinovna [Krupskaya] and Nikolai Ivanovich [Bukharin], dragging his feet weakly across his study, gazing, terrified in case he will no longer understand it, at the map on the wall, taking pencils between his fingers to make a rough signature, all like a dreamer, like a despairing old man in his second childhood. Bukharin often visits him in his country house out in the Gorky district; Bukharin makes merry in his company, and then hides behind a bush looking at him with tear-dimmed eyes. . . . It's definitely the end, my friend.'

'And afterwards?'

'Afterwards, there's going to be a riot. The unity of the Party nowadays depends upon that shadow of a man, no more than that.'

I remembered what Lenin had said to Dr. Goldenberg, an old Bolshevik who lived in Berlin and was summoned urgently by Lenin for a consultation at the beginning of his illness: 'We have demolished quite a lot! For that, certainly, we have been competent enough!'

I was travelling on a January day in 1924. The train bumped out of tunnels into vast landscapes on a mountain glittering with snow, where sombre armies of firs made a sudden descent. In this compartment full of fat, stodgy men, someone opened a newspaper and I saw: *Death of Lenin*. Then these men talked about the death, showing that they felt someone unique and very great had passed. I looked at their faces, folk from another world, Austrian petty-bourgeois closed to all new ideas, lamenting the death of a revolutionary; and Lenin was there, too, before my eyes, his hands open in the familiar gesture of demonstration, hunching a little towards the audience, marshalling the historical evidence, with his great firm forehead and the smile of a man who was sure of the truth, sure of himself. Together with a few others, this man had endowed an immense movement of faltering masses with a political consciousness that was supremely clear and resolute. Even when favourable social conditions are granted, such a human achievement is rare, unique, irreplaceable at the moment of its happening. Without it, the minds of those who marched would have been several degrees dimmer, the chances of chaos, and of defeat amid chaos, immeasurably greater; for a degree of consciousness, once lost, can never be measured.

Events continued to overwhelm us. Even where they took place at a distance I find it hard to separate them from my personal memories. All we lived for was activity integrated into history; we were interchangeable; we could immediately see the repercussions of affairs in Russia upon affairs in Germany and the Balkans; we felt linked with our comrades who, in pursuit of the same ends as we, perished or else scored some success at the other end of Europe. None of us had, in the bourgeois sense of the word, any personal existence: we changed our names, our posting and our work at the Party's need; we had just enough to live on without real material discomfort, and we were not interested in making money, or following a career, or producing a literary heritage, or leaving a name behind us; we were interested solely in the difficult business of reaching Socialism.

At 5.15 a.m. on 1 December 1924, 227 Estonian Communists, following the orders of the E.C.C.I., attacked the public buildings of Tallinn with the objective of seizing power. By 9 a.m., they were being slaughtered in all corners of the small capital. By noon, nothing was left of their ardour but splashes of blood on the little round cobbles. Yan Tomp was shot.

How could Zinoviev have initiated this imbecile adventure? The man terrified us. He refused to acknowledge the German defeat. In his eyes the rising had been only delayed and the K.P.D. was still marching to power. The riots in Cracow were enough for him to announce revolution in Poland. I felt that he was obsessed by the error in his otherwise sensible judgement which had led him in 1917 to oppose the incipient Bolshevik revolution; in consequence, he had now swung into an authoritarian and exaggerated revolutionary optimism. 'Zinoviev', we used to say, 'is Lenin's biggest mistake.'

In September of 1924 we learnt that a rebellion had just been crushed in Soviet Georgia. The comrades who came from Russia spoke of it, in their confidential discussions, with extreme bitterness. 'Collapse of our agrarian policy. . . . The whole Georgian Party, with Mdivani at their head, is in opposition to the Central Committee, and the whole country is in opposition to the Party. . . .'

Later we heard of the massacre, supervised by Sergo Ordzhonikidze, a former inmate of Schlüsselburg, an honest and scrupulous man tormented by recurrent crises of conscience. I learnt of the background to the tragedy; a people in ferment, their national pride outraged, provocation organized by the Cheka to unmask rebellious tendencies and then liquidate them; the imprisoned members of the Menshevik Central Committee of Georgia, receiving information of the preparation for the revolt, beg to be released for a few days so that they can avert irreparable disaster, even offering to take poison before they set out; they are kept inside, powerless, and later shot. . . . The political problem of the Caucasus was this: could Red Russia, as a great Power, agree that two little countries like Georgia and Azerbaijan, prone to hostile influences and bound to become a hunting-ground for foreign powers, should keep their petroleum, manganese and strategic roads all to themselves?

In Vienna we breathe the turbulent air of the Balkans. Of events there we catch only fragmentary glimpses, but these take in several vistas: propaganda, activity, whether openly acknowledged or disavowed, and secret intrigue. Bulgaria is still pregnant with revolution, despite all its previous miscarriages. In a public meeting at the Kremlin, I had heard Kolarov, an impressive deputy, and the thin Kabakchiev,[1] bearded up to his very eyes, speaking proudly of their Party, the only Socialist Party in Europe that was, like the Bolsheviks, intransigently loyal to principle. They called themselves *Tesnyaki*, The Narrows, by contrast with the broad, flabby opportunists of whatever country. They remarked that they would have already seized power if the Executive had not been dubious about the international complications; it was necessary to wait and allow Stambulisky's Peasant Party to exhaust itself and lose its credit with the rural masses, who would then turn to us. . . . While they were waiting, Professor Tsankov, supported by a military conspiracy, carried out his *coup*, in June 1923. Stambulisky, the huge frizzy-haired giant, was surprised at his country house, and straddled like a beast by brutes who murdered him with all the cruelty of primitive imagination. The powerful Communist Party, under Kolarov, Kabakchiev, and Dimitrov observed a neutrality which they justified in terms of the most strait-laced doctrinal intransigence: 'It is not for a working-class party to support the rural petty-bourgeoisie against the reactionary big bourgeoisie. . . .' When the Party was

[1] Hristo Kabakchiev (1878–1940): Comintern emissary in the early twenties; arrested and imprisoned in Bulgaria in 1923; released in 1926, joining Dimitrov and Kolarov in Russia; a member of the Soviet Communist Party in his last years.

persecuted immediately afterwards, its leaders acknowledged their mistake in Moscow and promised to set it right. It was too late. In September, the Communists took to arms, with poor support from an enfeebled and helpless peasantry. They fought, and were scattered; the noise of these relatively minor fusillades was lost in the great avalanche-roar of the advancing German Revolution. . . .

I was in Vienna when, at the beginning of April 1925, Tsar Boris, whom we dubbed 'the Butcher of the Bulgars', narrowly missed assassination; on 15 April General Kosta Georgiev fell to the bullets of a terrorist. On the 17th, the Government was assembled together for his funeral at the Cathedral of the Seven Saints in Sofia, when an explosive device shattered one of the domes. Twenty-five dead were unearthed from the rubble, including three deputies, thirteen generals, eight colonels, and eight high officials. By a singular chance the Government and the Royal Family were unscathed. The explosion had been organized by officers from the military section of the Communist Party, who were acting perhaps on their own behalf—for the Party was ravaged by dissension—or else in accordance with secret instructions; it surprised the Communists themselves, who were at once assaulted, fired on, tortured, and murdered by the troops and police. Shablin, a handsome, smiling man whom I had known in Russia, was (it seems) burnt alive in a furnace. The two men responsible for the explosion, Yankov and Minkov, were killed resisting arrest. In May, in front of 50,000 inhabitants of Sofia, three Communists were hanged, one of whom, Marko Fridman, had defended the ideas and record of the Party every inch of the way before his judges.[1] A French Communist, Eugène Léger, tried and condemned with these men, was subsequently released in obscure circumstances and took refuge in Moscow, where he disappeared. I was to discover later that he had spent a long period in the secret Isolator at Yaroslavl, whence he was transferred, now insane, to an asylum.

I became interested in the movement for Balkan Federation. The conception was noble: no other remedy was appropriate to the division of the small kindred peoples of the peninsula into feeble states, destined to be destroyed sooner or later through their mutual

[1] This is not strictly accurate. Before the end of the trial Fridman broke down and gave evidence on the internal organization of the Communist Party and its military section.

laceration. The Doctor, a big white-haired Bulgarian, scholarly and Parisified, would arrange appointments with me in discreet little local cafés. A taxi, and then the tram; we would head out to the vineyards, between Floridsdorf and Mödling. There we would meet a young stranger in an outsize overcoat, whom I immediately classified as a bodyguard; I thought I could see the enormous Browning revolver, the favourite weapon of Macedonians (who do not trust small bullets), bulging through his coat pocket. The overcoat-man, all smiles, hurried me along urgently: the tram again, and then we came to a village full of charming taverns, and after that to a villa, adorned with flowers like its neighbours, in which lived the last surviving leader of the Communist-influenced *La Fédération Balkanique*,[1] a former Member of the Ottoman Parliament. What, has there been an Ottoman Parliament? Oh yes, convened by Abdul Hamid, and on the day of its opening, bombs explode. . . . V——[2] rarely goes out now. Murder lies in wait for him at every street-corner, and at night trusted men stand on watch in the garden of his villa. In this very city his predecessor, Todor Panitza, was recently killed while watching a performance in a theatre. A short while before that, Panitza's predecessor, Peter Chaulev, had discovered that he was being trailed in these streets and took the train to Milan. In Milan he was murdered. A short while before that, the old leader of I.M.R.O. (*Internal Macedonian Revolutionary Organization*),[3] Todor Aleksandrov, had been killed at the end of a conference in the mountains, in which he had advocated co-operation with the Communists. I had drafted the three obituaries for the Press.

Around the great conception of Balkan Federation there swarmed hordes of secret agents, impresarios of irredentism, pedlars of the influential word, night-walking politicians engaged in six intrigues at a time; and all these smart gentlemen, with their over-gaudy

[1] *La Fédération Balkanique:* a multi-lingual review published in Vienna from 1924, and after 1931 in Frankfurt, with Communist backing but a wider appeal. It advocated a Balkan Federation including a united and independent Macedonia.

[2] V—— is Dimitar Vlahov, a leading Macedonian Communist and Comintern delegate. After 1935 he took refuge in the Soviet Union; in 1943 emerged as a partisan leader with Tito, with special responsibility for Yugoslav Macedonia, and died in 1951 as Vice-President of Yugoslavia.

[3] I.M.R.O. was a Macedonian nationalist and terrorist organization founded in 1893, and financed by a levy on all Macedonians; it was based on local activist bodies called *comitajis* which elected delegates to a national convention.

neckties, sought to harness the unbridled energy of the *Comitajis* and sell it to and fro to any buyer. There was the Italian wing, the Bulgarian wing, the Yugoslav wing, two Greek tendencies, one monarchist and one republican, ideologies, personal cliques, and vendettas. We knew the cafés in which the revolvers of any given group lay in wait, watched from the café opposite by those of another. *La Fédération Balkanique* was a focus for certain revolutionary romantics who were the survivors of other tragedies. Among them I met the Young Serbs of recent memory, friends and disciples of Vladimir Gaćinović, the Bakuninist and nationalist, who died of tuberculosis at the age of thirty after founding the group which was, on 28 June 1914, to carry out the assassination at Sarajevo. They cherished the memory of Gavrilo Princip and of the teacher Ilić. They declared that their leader, Colonel Dragutin Dimitrijević[1]— alias 'Apis', in underground circles—had, before initiating the action, been assured of support from Russia; this had been formally promised by Artamonov, the Russian Imperial military attaché in Belgrade, who had been informed of the project. I published these allegations in *Clarté* (in Paris), and heard them confirmed by a former colleague of Dimitrijević, Colonel Božin Simić, and also, more reticently, by a former Serbian Ambassador, M. Bogićević. As a consequence of this revelation, some Yugoslav friends advised me not to go too near the Yugoslav border in the course of my trips to the Wörthersee, and on no account to enter Yugoslavia; there were, they told me, certain highly confidential instructions of which I was the subject. These survivors of the Serb conspiracies against the Habsburg monarchy were shortly to join the Communist Party. In 1938 I found their names in a Communist newspaper which published the news of their expulsion. They disappeared in Russia.

Despite all these setbacks and the general atmosphere, the Russians still kept their plain integrity and abundant optimism. Men whose usefulness had been exhausted habitually ended by living in Soviet missions abroad, there to observe the decay of the bourgeois world. They were given these sinecures to keep them quiet. They included seasoned veterans of the persecution in the old

[1]Dimitrijević was the chief of Serbian Intelligence and a leading figure in the secret society called 'The Black Hand'; executed after a highly suspect trial in June 1917. Danilo Ilić was executed for his part in the assassination in February 1915; Princip, who actually shot the Archduke, was spared the death-penalty on account of his age and died in jail of tuberculosis in April 1918.

days, former Marxist exiles, and the ex-managers of those first Soviet institutions which had succeeded against everyone's expectation. Some of them were now only chatterers, nursing strained hearts and content to smoke good cigars and be driven out to the Cobenzl Restaurant. An obsequious riff-raff fussed about them, and observing their eccentricities, remarked complacently to themselves: 'That's what they are, these great revolutionaries, when you see them close up.' Of some of these men I will say nothing. But I wish to set down at this point a few character-sketches of worthy men, to whom my memory returns with affection. They typify a vanished generation.

I again met Adolf Abramovich Joffe, a little aged since I last saw him in Petrograd in the desperate days of resistance. He now reminded one of a wise physician, almost affluent in his appearance and almost comical in his gravity, who had been summoned to the bedside of a dying patient. He was now back from China and Japan, having won Sun Yat-sen for the cause of Soviet friendship. A sick man, and in disgrace because of the boldness of his views, he was accredited by the Soviet Union to the Austrian Republic, in other words to the Chancellor-Cardinal Seipel.[1] He was opposed to all adventures. He told me that a Yugoslav officers' league had made him an offer to instal, forcibly, a left-wing government in Belgrade. Stjepan Radić's Croat Peasant Party would give it support. . . . (We often talked of Stjepan Radić, who was worth far more than any Balkan politician; he was to be murdered not long afterwards in front of the whole Yugoslav Parliament.) Joffe, with his bearded Assyrian face, powerful lips, and eyes that disconcerted the newcomer, so severe was their squint, gave a vivid pout of disdain:

'They imagine that revolutions are made like that. No, thank you!' They were all for sale, *coups d'état*, dictatorships, republican leanings, pro-Soviet sympathies, shady dealings, what you like. A man like Joffe knew, better than anyone, the colossal frontier that separates revolutionary action from dubious adventurism. Others preferred not to know: these sponsored the establishment in Albania of a pro-Soviet Left Government under Monsignor Fan Noli.

[1] Mgr. Ignaz Seipel (1876–1932), Minister of Social Administration in the last Habsburg Cabinet, led the Christian-Social Party from 1922 to 1924 and was Chancellor from 1926 to 1929. While in office, encouraged the right-wing paramilitary *Heimwehr* and intrigued against the democratic constitution.

Ahmet Zogu's *putsch* followed it, and Albania passed into the Italian sphere of influence.[1]

This dark frontier-land was often skirted, as a matter of duty, by Dr. Goldstein, the Embassy Secretary. A specialist in Balkan affairs, Goldstein was tall, thin, and artful; a man of great modesty, he was quite straightforwardly a Socialist of the old breed, who carried out the worst possible directives in such a way as to do the least possible damage. Killer-squads from Sofia lay in wait for him all around the Schwartzenbergplatz. Fortunately their assignment was complicated by the fact that they had been told to liquidate him without causing any scandal. He showed me some photographs which had been taken, without my knowledge, of the contents of my drawer: 'I advise you to sack your maidservant. Some of the back-room chaps from the Whites have been paying visits to your papers; however, we have a man planted among them. . . .'

Old Kozlovsky, whose sympathetic face befitted his past as a St. Petersburg lawyer, had been our first People's Commissar of Justice. His function then was to combat excesses. He related to me how the Cheka had drawn up a document defining who was a suspect: '*Social origins:* aristocratic or bourgeois, *Education:* University. . . .' Kozlovsky took the sheet and went to knock on Lenin's door: 'Tell me, Vladimir Ilyich, surely this is a little matter for us two, isn't it?' 'The appalling imbeciles!' said Lenin. A provincial Cheka proposed in 1918 to bring back torture to make foreign spies talk. Kamenev and Kozlovsky were enraged at the idea, which received short shrift.

Yuri Kotziubinsky was a man with whom I could speak frankly of everything. His nimble life had survived only by some chance or miracle. He had been waiting in a Kiev cellar for his turn to go against the wall, when the Reds captured the town, so quickly that the Whites had no time to dispatch the last prisoners. He escaped from encircled townships, joining Piatakov and the last fighters for the Soviets who also functioned as the Government of the Ukraine. The country was subdued village by village; what was captured in the morning was often lost by nightfall. In those parts the names of the heroes of 1918 were Evgenia Bosch, Yuri Kotziubinsky, and Yuri Piatakov. He was a tall, handsome man with a

[1] The *coup* was in June 1924. Zogu soon afterwards assumed the royal title of King Zog.

thin line of beard round his jowl, an aquiline profile, and a head in the harmonious proportions of the young humanists of long ago, except that it was much more solidly stocked inside. Kótziubinsky was too popular among the working class of Kharkov, and so was exiled to the world.of diplomacy. He sympathized with the most radical Oppositional group, that of the 'Democratic Centralists': Sapronov, Vladimir Smirnov in the Ukraine, and Drobnis (the one shot in 1937). We would clamber up the steep slopes of the Leopoldsberg and there gaze out on the blue band of the Danube and discuss the problems of the Party. I see him now, laughing into the wind, his silk blouse, with a cord for its belt, billowing away. (From Vienna he went on to be Consul-General at Warsaw; he was shot without trial in 1937.)

Like Yuri Kotziubinsky, N—— usually wore only a Russian blouse under his jacket; but N—— only possessed one old grey suit, and had no idea that it was possible to wear anything else. Young, or rather ageless, without any official job in the Legation, without money (which he despised), known history or personal life, very Jewish, and childlike in his gaze, N—— was a courageous conspirator. His corner of the Embassy was confined to strictly secret duties; it was full of phials, chemical reactives and inks, photographic apparatus, and codes. I wondered if he had forgotten his real name as a result of changing his nationality and identity so many times (but then, what is one's 'real' name?). We talked passionately of our sick Party: sick, but what else on earth is there?

(Years went by. I had just come out of a Soviet prison when N—— called on me in Leningrad. 'Where have you come from, you old ghost?' 'From Shanghai.' Shanghai in 1928 was no sinecure. N—— had reorganized the trade unions there after the 1927 massacre. There he had met men more stoical, more cunning, more nameless than himself. 'The anarchists, too,' he remarked to me, 'they're wonderful—but what an ideology! Fit for twelve-year-old kids!' He had just learned, on his arrival back in Moscow, of the execution of Yakov Blumkin; he had sought out the comrades in the firing squad to discover how our mutual friend had passed his last moments. He came to me with the news.)

Angelica Balabanova, the first Secretary of the Comintern Executive, whose moral objections had often annoyed Lenin and Zinoviev, had just been expelled from the Third International. She lived now

sometimes in Vienna, sometimes in its outskirts, carting her possessions, those of the eternal poor student, from one furnished room to
another: the spirit-stove for tea, the small pan for omelettes, and
three cups for her guests; together with the huge picture of Felippo
Turati, the manly, glowing portrait of Matteotti,[1] files of *Avanti!*,
the correspondence of the Italian Maximalist Party, and notebooks
full of poems. Small, dark, and beginning to age, Angelica still led
her eager militant's life which, with its romantic fire, was about
three-quarters of a century too late. She should have had Mazzin-
ians and *Carbonari* around her, burning with zeal to fight for the
Universal Republic! After a life spent in the company of politicians
like Lazzari and Serrati, in whom a little of this fire still lingered,
decently displayed in their Parliamentary tactics, Angelica had
rushed to the service of the Russian Revolution (suffering in the
process a severe battering from a reactionary mob in Switzerland),
and lived in close contact with that world government of Marxism
which went by the name of the Executive of the Communist International.

It was no longer the atmosphere of Zimmerwald! Seats in the
different Commissions were adroitly packed, and couriers carrying
diamonds were sent to the fraternal Parties abroad (couriers and
diamonds both disappearing); other emissaries were sent to arrange
the expulsion of men who were still being called 'dear comrade'.
Revolutionary politics, when conducted with foresight and courage,
requires at certain decisive times the qualities of a good surgeon,
for there is no character in this world more humane and honest than
that of the good surgeon, even though he works on living flesh, amid
pain and blood. Angelica rebelled both against the political surgery
which led to the unceremonious removal of the reformist leaders
who were inclined to torpedo any offensive tactic, and against
Zinoviev's sordid little tricks of political bone-setting. She was quick
to detect the first symptoms of that moral sickness which after the
passing of some fifteen years was to bring on the death of Bolshevism.
Georg Lukács, the author of *Geschichte und Klassenbewusstsein*, once

[1] Felippo Turati (1857–1932): founder and leader of Italian reformist Socialism;
opposed Italian involvement in the First World War; extremely anti-Communist;
after 1926 an exile in Corsica and then France. Giacomo Matteotti (1885–1924):
Italian Socialist and anti-Fascist; peasant leader and Deputy: opposed any 'United
Front' with the Communists; fearlessly outspoken against Mussolini's violence;
murdered on Fascist instructions to silence him.

remarked to me: 'Marxists know that dirty little tricks can be performed with impunity when great deeds are being achieved; the
error of some comrades is to suppose that one can produce great
results simply through the performance of dirty little tricks. . . .'

Angelica gave me coffee on her window-sill and sent me her
friendly criticisms for the benefit of our official publications. I
recalled the days of the famine in Petrograd, when, as a present
for the birth of our son, she had sent us an orange and a bar of
chocolate, delicacies from another world, imported through the
diplomatic bag. In her hands lay great kindness, and in her eyes a
fortifying passion. I reflected that several times she had narrowly
missed the death of a Rosa Luxemburg.[1]

Antonio Gramsci was living in Vienna, an industrious and
Bohemian exile, late to bed and late to rise, working with the illegal
Committee of the Italian Communist Party. His head was heavy, his
brow high and broad, his lips thin; the whole was carried on a puny,
square-shouldered, weak-chested, hump-backed body. There was
grace in the movement of his fine, lanky hands. Gramsci fitted
awkwardly into the humdrum of day-to-day existence, losing his way
at night in familiar streets, taking the wrong train, indifferent to the
comfort of his lodgings and the quality of his meals; but, intellect-
ually, he was absolutely alive. Trained intuitively in the dialectic,
quick to uncover falsehood and transfix it with the sting of irony,
he viewed the world with an exceptional clarity. Once, we consulted together about the quarter-million workers who had been
admitted at one stroke into the Russian Communist Party, on the
day after Lenin's death. How much were these proletarians worth,
if they had had to wait for the death of Vladimir Ilyich before
coming to the Party?

After the example of Matteotti, like him a Deputy, like him living
among menaces, a frail invalid held in both detestation and respect
by Mussolini, Gramsci had remained in Rome to carry on the
struggle. He was fond of telling stories about his wretched childhood;
how he had failed his entry to the priesthood, for which his family
had marked him out; with his short bursts of sardonic laughter he
exposed certain leading figures of Fascism with whom he was closely
acquainted. When the crisis in Russia began to worsen, Gramsci did

[1] After the Second World War, Balabanova helped to found the P.S.D.I., the
pre-Western Social-Democratic party led by G. Saragat. She died in 1965.

not want to be broken in the process, so he had himself sent back to Italy by his Party: he, who was identifiable at the first glance because of his deformity and his great forehead. He was imprisoned in June 1928, together with Umberto Terracini and some others, and a fascist jail kept him outside the operation of those factional struggles whose consequence nearly everywhere was the elimination of the militants of his generation. Our years of darkness were his years of stubborn resistance. (Twelve years later, when I emerged from my period of deportation in Russia and arrived in Paris, in 1937, I was following a Popular Front demonstration when someone pushed a Communist pamphlet into my hand: it contained a picture of Antonio Gramsci, who had died on 27 April of that year in an Italian prison hospital, after eight years of captivity.)

The Hungarian emigration was deeply split. To the opposition within his Party, Bela Kun was a remarkably odious figure. He was the incarnation of intellectual inadequacy, uncertainty of will, and authoritarian corruption. Several of his opponents were starving to death in Vienna. Of these, I held Georg Lukács in greatest esteem; indeed, I owe him a great deal. A former university teacher in Budapest, and then commissar to a Red division in the front line, Lukács was a philosopher steeped in the works of Hegel, Marx, and Freud, and possessing a free-ranging and rigorous mind. He was engaged in writing a number of outstanding books which were never to see the light of day. In him I saw a first-class brain which could have endowed Communism with a true intellectual greatness if it had developed as a social movement instead of degenerating into a movement in solidarity with an authoritarian Power. Lukács' thinking led him to a totalitarian vision of Marxism within which he united all aspects of human life; his theory of the Party could be taken as either superb or disastrous, depending on the circumstances. For example, he considered that since history could not be divorced from politics, it should be written by historians in the service of the Central Committee.

One day we were discussing the problems of whether or not revolutionaries who had been condemned to death should commit suicide; this arose from the execution in 1919 at Budapest of Otto Korwin, who had been in charge of the Hungarian Cheka, and whose hanging afforded a choice spectacle for 'society' folk. 'I thought of suicide', said Lukács, 'in the hours when I was expecting to be

arrested and hanged with him. I came to the conclusion that I had
no right to it: a member of the Central Committee must set the
example.' (I was to meet Georg Lukács and his wife later, in 1928
or 1929, in a Moscow street. He was then working at the Marx-
Engels Institute; his books were being suppressed, and he lived
bravely in the general fear. Although he was fairly well-disposed
towards me, he did not care to shake my hand in a public place,
since I was expelled and a known Oppositionist. He enjoyed a
physical survival, and wrote short, spiritless articles in Comintern
journals.)

I was present, in my non-existent capacity as a representative of
the Soviet Press, at a Rumanian-Soviet peace conference. The head of
the Soviet delegation was Leonid Serebriakov, a former metal-worker
and inhabitant of Imperial prisons, a soldier for the Revolution
in Siberia and all over Russia, organizer of the Soviet Railwaymen's Union, reorganizer of our railways. A prominent figure in the
democratic Opposition in the Party, he was, at the age of thirty-four,
marked out by virtue of his moral authority, talents, and past as one
of the future leaders of the Soviet State. He was sent shortly afterwards to the United States where he made a reputation as a great
Socialist administrator in the world of business. Plump, vigorous in
manner, fair-haired, with a full, round face and an aggressive little
moustache, he kept dealing out good-humoured impudence to an
elderly Rumanian diplomat of the very oldest school. The negotiations failed completely, thank God. (Leonid Serebriakov was to be
shot in 1937.)

We had only very little contact with the Austrian Social-
Democrats. The tiny Communist Party, which was divided into two
warring factions (Tomann versus Frey), each numbering about 100
militants, plastered the walls of Vienna periodically with posters
demanding the arming of the workers and the dictatorship of the
proletariat. But meanwhile, Austrian Social-Democracy continued
in its great career, apparently without any suspicion that it was
living out its last years. (Actually it did suspect this, but was cutting
a fine figure of bravery, and even nonchalance, in the face of un-
favourable odds.) Austro-Marxism organized and influenced
over a million proletarians, it was master of Vienna, where it
was evolving a municipal Socialism rich in achievement, it could
mobilize, in a few hours, 50,000 *Schutzbundler* on the Ring, uniformed

in sports-tunics and (as everyone knew) tolerably well armed, it was led by the most able theoreticians in the working-class world; and yet, two or three times in ten years, through its sobriety, prudence, and bourgeois moderation, it failed its destiny.

If only. . . . If only a Red Austria had joined with the Hungarian Soviets, would not troubled Bohemia, and then Germany, have followed their example? Revolution was maturing in Italy during this same period. But perhaps it was already too late. If only, after 1918. . . . If only the commission on the nationalization of the main industries, established by the Socialist Government, had not been such a farce! If only the Social-Democrats of Austria had had a little of the impassioned energy of the Bolsheviks of Russia! All they ever did was to sip sweet white wine in the operetta-land of the Blue Danube, while the Bolsheviks were tramping in chains along Siberian highways. Its opportunities lost, its hours of daring past, little Austria found herself jammed in the middle of the expanding counter-revolutions of Hungary, Italy, and Germany; at home, Socialist Vienna found itself menaced by the countryside and the Catholic bourgeoisie. Prince Starhemberg was recruiting his peasant bands against it. I attended meetings of Social-Democratic Party activists: they were middle-aged men, few of them at all fit, who drank their beer as they listened to the speakers. The *Schutzbund* would march past the Town Hall with 30,000 bicycles garlanded with flowers! Otto Bauer, who was greeted on all sides by affectionate glances, watched the parade of this working-class force, so self-confident, so deserving of a glorious future. If only it had been a matter of just deserving! (Fourteen years later, in Paris, I was unable to recognize Otto Bauer, so cruelly had defeat shrivelled his solid, regular features, stamped not so long ago with a noble certainty. He was to die suddenly, from a heart-attack, but actually from the defeat of working-class Austria. On his death-bed his face recovered a wonderful expression of serenity.)

In the Mariahilferstrasse at night, I saw quite different groups of men, wearing uniforms and berets, marching in step by small detachments to the outlying hills, there to practise the use of weapons. Officers' associations, ex-servicemen, Starhemberg formations, crosses, swastikas . . . the politicians still denied that there was any fascist danger in Austria. I was probably the first to denounce the danger, in 1925, in Paris through the *Vie Ouvrière*, in Russia in an ineffectual pamphlet. This danger quite clearly arose from the fact that a working-class democracy, powerful in numbers, education and achievement, but hemmed in on three sides, was consequently harried by the alternatives of either hopeless resistance or total impotence. So long as the Weimar Republic survived in Germany, working-class Austria could still hope. Once German Socialism collapsed, she was doomed. If only France and Czechoslovakia had not opposed the German-Austrian *Anschluss* when Germany and Austria were both democracies, the united strength of the two working classes could probably have blocked the way to fascism; certainly they would have realized a number of impressive Socialist reforms. *If only. . . .*

Blood and despair hovered in the giddy air of Vienna. One evening, at the time of the New Year, we were walking in a silken snow-fall, surrounded by paper decorations and the *um-pa-pa, um-pa-pa* of Strauss waltzes, when an explosion rang out beneath the arcades of the Opera House: an unemployed man was blowing out his brains with a dynamite cartridge. Another fired on the Cardinal-Chancellor Seipel. Hugo Bettauer, a charming journalist who frequented nude dances, was propagating a sentimental Freudian eroticism in certain weekly journals with very special classified advertisements. A young fanatic drilled six bullets into the body of this 'Jewish corrupter of Austria's youth'.

I studied Marx and Freud and ran international Press campaigns against the terror waged by employers and police in Spain, where all my old comrades were dying, one after the other, under the bullets of the *Sindicato Libre*. I inveighed against the White terror in 'Bulgaria ruled by the knife'. I stood with the Opposition in the Russian Party, which in 1923–4 was led by Preobrazhensky and largely inspired by Trotsky. In Russia a struggle was beginning whose gravity was still gauged accurately by no one. At the time when the date of the German Revolution was being fixed, forty-six old militants warned the Central Committee of two sorts of danger: the weakness of an industry unable to satisfy the needs of the countryside, and the stifling dictatorship of bureaucracy. In the spiritual impoverishment of recent years there had been only two flashes of daylight: two close-written little books by Trotsky, the demands in *The New Course* and the analysis in *Lessons of October*—both works vilified by our official Press. We would meet discreetly in some outer district to read and discuss these pulsating pages. Then, bound by discipline, prisoners to our daily bread, we went on endlessly printing our news-sheets, with the same insipid, nauseating condemnations of everything that we knew to be true. Was it really worth while being revolutionaries if we had to ply this trade?

I refused to carry out a dishonest directive from Bela Kun, dealing with the French Party. A letter which had been sent to me from Moscow was mysteriously intercepted. A comrade who held high office in the International, and was about as sincere as a genuine bad penny, tried to make me see reason. After this vile conversation I put in a categorical request for my return to Russia. The atmosphere of the International's departments was becoming impossible for me to breathe. Men like Monatte, Rosmer, and Souvarine were being hounded out of the French Party merely for having shown some evidence of political courage in demanding to see things Russian in their proper light. The Parties were changing their faces and even their language: a conventional jargon was settling upon our publications—we called it 'Agitprop Pidgin'. Everything now was only a matter of 'one hundred-per-cent. approval of the correct line of the Executive,' of 'Bolshevik monolithism', of 'the speedy Bolshevization of fraternal Parties'. Such were the latest ingenuities of Zinoviev and Bela Kun. Why not 300 per cent. approval? The Central Committees of all the Parties, who send appropriate telegrams at the first wink, have not, as yet, thought of that one. The system appears to have been perfected. A crony of mine jokes: 'At the Fortieth Congress in Moscow a ninety-year old Zinoviev will be seen propped up by nurses and waving his Presidential bell. . . .' 'Schools of Bolshevism' are being established, like the French one at Bobigny under Paul Marion (the same who was to become a Minister of Pétain and Laval in 1941), and Jacques Doriot. The International still presents an imposing façade, and has thousands of working-class supporters who trust in it with all their heart; but I am watching it go rotten within. And I see that it can be saved only in Russia, by a regeneration of the Party. I have to go back.

'Above all', 'Yuri' Lukács told me, as we roamed in the evening beneath the grey spires of the Votive Church, 'don't be silly and get yourself deported for nothing, just for the pleasure of voting defiantly. Believe me, insults are not very important to us. Marxist revolutionaries need patience and courage; they do not need pride. The times are bad, and we are at a dark cross-roads. Let us reserve our strength: history will summon us in its time.'

I answered that if I found the Party atmosphere in Leningrad and Moscow too oppressive, I would ask for an assignment somewhere in Siberia and there, in the midst of the snows, far from the tortuosities of politics, I would write the books now maturing in my head, and wait for better days. In an effort to break definitively with an old nightmare which still haunted me from time to time, I had, on the shores of a Carinthian lake, begun to write *Les Hommes dans la Prison.*

6

DEADLOCK OF THE REVOLUTION
1926–1928

It is raining; the jetties are black. Two rows of dotted lamplight extend far back into the night. Between them, the black waters of the Neva. On both sides, cut into two, the dark city: inhospitable. It has not cast its misery aside. Four days ago, I was looking at the great glow outspread in the night sky over Berlin: Berlin that only recently knew an inflation more incredible even than ours. We never paid more than a million for a lemon: in Berlin postage-stamps were charged in trillions. Why does this prostration still weigh down on our Russian land? As we come out of the Customs, we are met by a run-down cab advancing over the puddles of mud; a ghost-horse and a rattling carriage, straight from some wretched town in Gogol's time. It has always been the same. A return to Russian soil rends the heart. '*Earth of Russia,*' wrote the poet Tyutchev, '*no corner of you is untouched by Christ the slave.*' The Marxist explains it in the same terms: 'The production of commodities was never sufficient, the means of communication were always short. . . .' And because of that the poor (and there have been some Christs among them), slaves to necessity, have had to take to the roads, barefoot, knapsacks on back, trailing from one steppe to the next, endlessly fleeing, endlessly seeking. . . .

The atmosphere I find is calm, gloomy, oppressive. Lutovinov has committed suicide.[1] The metalworkers' organizer used to wander at night in Berlin, with Radek. The cocktails of the Kurfürstendamm scorched his throat: 'When all's said and done, the bourgeoisie certainly invents some muck to get themselves drunk on! What am

[1] Yuri Lutovinov had caused offence through his leading part in the Workers' Opposition. His suicide occurred in May 1924.

I going to do if I go back? I have told the Central Committee over and over again: we must take another look at the wages question. Our engineers are starving. After that, the Health Commission of the Party sent me abroad for a cure. . . .'

Glazman has committed suicide. The background to this tragedy is hardly known; it all took place within the circle of Trotsky, President of the Supreme War Council. It is mentioned only in hushed tones. Glazman is not the only one.[1]

Certain young people, expelled from the Party for demanding 'the New Course', have turned revolvers on themselves. Young women, as every one knows, prefer veronal. What use is it to live if our Party refuses us the right of serving it? This newborn world is calling us, we belong to it and it alone—and look! In its name someone spits in our faces. 'You are disqualified. . . .' Disqualified because we are the Revolution's racked flesh, its outraged reason? It is better to die. . . . The graph of suicides is mounting. The Central Control Commission meets in extraordinary session.

Evgenia Bogdanovna Bosch has committed suicide. Nothing has been published abroad about the death of one of Bolshevism's greatest personalities. The Civil War, the Ukraine (where, together with Piatakov, she headed the First Soviet Government), the troubles in Astrakhan, which she dealt with severely, the peasant counter-revolution of Perm, armies under her command: through it all she slept with a revolver under her pillow. The Party debate of 1923, the juggling with workers' democracy in equivocal Central Committee resolutions, the purge of the universities and the dictatorship of the secretaries all combined to depress her, and her strong, plain fighter's face, with its piercing eyes, grew hollow with sickness. Once Lenin died, her mind was made up. What was there left to do, with the Party deceived and divided, with Ilyich gone, what was there left to wait for, since she could no longer do anything herself? She went to bed and shot herself in the temple with a revolver. The Committees deliberated the question of her funeral rites. The more rigorous comrades argued that suicide, however justified it might be by incurable illness, remained an act of indiscipline. Besides, in this particular case suicide was a proof of Oppositional leanings. There was no national funeral, only a local one; no urn in the Kremlin

[1] Glazman was Trotsky's young secretary, often at his side in the Civil War.

wall, only a place befitting her rank in the plot reserved for Communists in the Novo-Devichy cemetery. Forty lines of obituary in *Pravda*. Preobrazhensky exposed the underhand trickery of it all. When she had been handling the Germans, the Ukrainian Nationalists, the Whites, and the rural *Vendée*, what joker would have inquired into her official rank in the Party hierarchy? These very ideas did not exist then: Preobrazhensky was requested to hold his tongue. The spectre of Lenin's flesh, robbed of all substance and spirit, lies under the Mausoleum while the hierarchy is only too alive, voracious even—it has not finished showing us yet.

Sergei Yesenin, our matchless poet, has committed suicide. The telephone rings: 'Come quickly, Yesenin has killed himself.' I run out in the snow, I enter his room in the Hotel International, and I can hardly recognize him; he no longer looks himself. The night before he had been drinking, of course, and then had said good night to his friends. 'I want to be alone. . . .' In the morning he awoke depressed, and felt the urge to write something. No pencil or fountain-pen was at hand, and there was no ink in the hotel inkwell: only a razor blade, with which he slashed his wrist. And so, with a rusty pen dipped in his own blood, Yesenin wrote his last lines:

> *Au revoir, friend, au revoir. . . .*
> *. . . There is nothing new about dying in this life*
> *But there is surely nothing new about living either.*

He asked the hotel to keep everyone out. They found him hanging with a suitcase-strap round his neck, his forehead bruised by falling, as he died, against a heating-pipe. Lying there washed and combed on his death-bed, his face was less soft than in life, his hair brown rather than golden; he had an expression of cold, distant harshness. I observed at the time: 'One would think him a young soldier dying alone after some bitter defeat.' Thirty years old, at his peak of glory, eight times married. . . . He was our greatest lyrical poet, the poet of the Russian campaigns, of the Moscow taverns, of the Revolution's singing Bohemians. He proclaimed the victory of the steel horses over the red-maned colts in the 'fields without a glimmer'. He spawned lines full of dazzling images, yet simple as the language of the villages. He plumbed his own descent into the abyss: '*Where have you led me, you, my reckless head?*' and '*I have been loathsome, I have been wicked—and all so that I could blaze more brilliantly.. . .*'

He had tried to be in tune with the times, and with our official literature. '*I am a stranger in my own land. . . .*'; '*My poems are no longer needed now, and I myself am unwanted. . . .*'; '*Blossom, O young folk, in your healthy bodies. . . . Your life is alien, your songs are alien. . . .*'; '*I am not a new man, I have one foot in the past, and yet I wish, I the stumbler, I the cripple, to join the cohorts of steel once more. . . .*'

> *We have it: unrelenting harshness*
> *Which is the tale of man's suffering!*
> *The sickle cuts the heavy stalks*
> *As one cuts the throats of swans.*

Vladimir Mayakovsky, the most popular of our poets after Yesenin, addressed a reproachful farewell to him:

> *So you have gone off*
> *As the saying is:*
> *To the next world. . . .*
> *The void. . . .*
> *You circle in it,*
> *Hustling the stars.*

Mayakovsky, an athlete poised from top to toe in a bantering style of violence, hammered out his farewell before audiences for whom this death was turning into a symbol:

> *This planet's not well equipped for happiness;*
> *Happiness will only be won at a future date!*

And Mayakovsky is soon to kill himself too, with a bullet in the heart; but that is another story. Through the night, through the snow we carry the corpse of Sergei Yesenin. This is no age for dreaming and lyricism. Farewell, poet.

Lenka Panteleyev, one of the Kronstadt sailors of 1917, who stove in the gates of the Winter Palace with their rifle-butts, has just ended his life's course in Leningrad. A legend has grown up about him in the underworld (for we have an underworld again). When money came back, Lenka felt that his end must be near. He was not a theoretician, but a straight egalitarian. He turned bandit to rob the first jeweller's shops to be opened by the first neo-capitalists of N.E.P. The other night, the militiamen who told me the story—admirers of Lenka—cornered him in his *malina* or hide-out; betrayed, naturally—it was a tale of women and drink. He came, threw off his leather jerkin, downed a glass of vodka and took up his guitar. What should he sing? '*Roll under the axe, O head of Stenka Razin. . . .*' They felled him in the middle of his song. The dangerous guitar was stopped. The militiamen, on pay of forty roubles a month, wear on their caps the red star which the Pantaleyevs had been the first to sport.

There is I——; I had known him in the days when, skinny as a yogi, he had got our ghosts of factories working, without fuel or raw materials. One evening, in that year of ice, 1919—six years ago now—when we were returning from the front at Ligovo, thirty minutes away from the city, he had told me, 'We must throw all our last remaining forces into the firing-line, even the anaemic little seventeen-year-olds, everything except the brains of us. A few thinking heads at the rear, well guarded by machine-guns, and everything else into the firing-line: that's what I say!'

Nowadays even my friend I—— has stopped thinking. We have an evening reunion at his house, where we play cards. An atmosphere of mild affluence reigns in this flat: fine books, miniatures, heraldic tableware, dark mahogany furniture dating back to the Emperor Paul. This is what remains of the spoils of many an expropriation, such as is to be found in the houses of a number of Party stalwarts. I knew fair-haired Lisa I—— in the days when, emaciated and crazy-eyed, she saw her first child die of starvation. Now they have another child, who is far better fed than the children of our unemployed workers. Lisa is now a plump blonde who wears a necklace of heavy gems from the Urals. There is still a slight hint of madness in her eyes, which makes me long to come out with some sharp questions: '*Quite a smash-up in those days, wasn't it? Do you remember Mazin's body under the fir-trees? And the corpse of that little sculptor Bloch who got shot, we never knew why? And his wife's corpse, so childlike she was? Tell me, do you remember?*' But I say nothing of the sort; it would not be nice, the world has changed. Grisha Yevdokimov comes to make up a card-game with us. He is home from Germany, where the Central Committee had sent him for an alcoholics' cure. We talk about the Pushkov affair: and so life goes on. (We do not talk politics, because I am a disgraced Oppositionist and they know it, and because they are anxious for the future and I know it: within the Politbureau an odd coolness has sprung up between Zinoviev, with whom they are friendly, and Stalin.)

Pushkov I met in the old days, when he was running the *Petrokom-muna*, or Central Co-operative of the Petrograd Commune. The reason why he has just been cast into the darkness (which is what expulsion from the Party amounts to) was as follows. The Control Commission's resolution speaks of 'irregular conduct in management (to be referred to the courts) and demoralization'. Pushkov was a married man. At his place, too, people played cards on Sunday evening, with glasses of tea standing by. He loved his wife with a passion whose intensity ill fitted his character as a materialist administrator. When death suddenly took her from him, he forgot that matter is perishable, and that the cult of the dead is symptomatic of those ancestral ideologies which have been formally condemned by Party teaching. He had her remains embalmed, and a vault made for her in a cemetery where she could sleep under a canopy of glass. If Lenin could repose in a mausoleum, the better to survive in the memory of mankind, why should not she be likewise preserved for one man's remembrance? Pushkov is honest, but a glass coffin is expensive: he meddled with the funds of the collective. No one will mention him again. I do not know why, but what I find saddest of all in the whole affair is the thought of a dead woman consigned once again to oblivion.

The sordid taint of money is visible on everything again. The grocers have sumptuous displays, packed with Crimean fruits and Georgian wines, but a postman earns about fifty roubles a month. There are 150,000 without jobs in Leningrad alone: their dole varies between twenty and twenty-seven roubles a month. Agricultural day-workers and female servants get fifteen, with their board added, it is true. Party officials receive from 180 to 225 roubles a month, the same as skilled workers. Hordes of beggars and abandoned children; hordes of prostitutes. We have three large gaming-houses in town, where baccarat, roulette and chemin-de-fer are played, sinister dives with crime always hovering around the corner. The hotels laid on for foreigners and Party officials have bars which are complete with tables covered in soiled white linen, dusty palm-trees and alert waiters who know secrets beyond the Revolution's ken. What would you like—a dose of 'snow'? At the Europa bar thirty girls show off their paint and cheap rings to men in fur-lined coats and caps who are drinking glasses brimming with alcohol: of these a third are thieves, a third embezzlers, and another third workers and comrades deep in a black mood which, around 3 a.m., breaks out into fights and drawn knives. And then, the other night, I heard someone shouting, with a strange pride: '*I've* been a member of the Party since 1917!' The year when the whole world shook. Here, on snowy nights before dawn, sledges are halted, drawn by proud thoroughbreds, their drivers bearded just like those who served the playboys of Tsarist days. And the manager of a nationalized factory, the wholesaler in textiles from the Lenin Factory, the assassin hunted by informers who are drinking with him—all drive off smartly with some daughter of the Volga or Riazan squeezed up close on the narrow seat, some daughter of famine and chaos with nothing to sell but her youth, and too much thirst for life to join the list of suicides that it is my task as an editor to check. Leningrad lives at the cost of ten to fifteen suicides a day, mainly among the under-thirties.

You could take the lift to the roof of the Hotel Europa, and there find another bar, like any in Paris or Berlin, full of lights, dancing and jazz, and even more depressing than the one on the ground floor. Two of us writers were there in the deserted hall, just starting a drab night out, when Mayakovsky walked in with his usual athletic tread. He came and leant on the bar near us.

'How goes it?'

'All right. Hell!'

'Fed up?'

'No. But one day I'll blow my brains out. Everybody's a bastard!' It was several years before his suicide. Mayakovsky was earning a great deal of money publishing official poetry, which could sometimes be very powerful.

Our aim is still to be a party of poor men, and little by little money becomes master, money corrupts everything—even as it makes life blossom everywhere. In less than five years, freedom of trade has worked miracles. There is no more famine, and an intoxicating zest for life rises about us, sweeping us away, giving us the unfortunate sensation of slipping downhill very fast. Our country is a vast convalescent body, but on this body, whose flesh is ours, we see the pustules multiplying.

When I was Chairman of a co-operative tenement, I had a long struggle to get a girl student given a maid's room in our thoroughly bourgeoisified piece of property; the accounts, presented to me by an engineer, were absolutely crooked, and I had to sign them just the same. One of our fellow lodgers was quite openly enriching himself by re-selling, at high prices, textiles which had been sold him by a nationalized factory at the special cheap rate for the poorly paid. How was it possible? Because the demand for manufactured goods outran supply to the tune of 400,000,000 roubles' worth. The workers went to the taverns to escape their wretched family lives; the housewives in the area of the Red Putilov Works pleaded with the Party Committees to find a way of deducting some part of their drunken husbands' wages to hand over to them. On pay-day some workers could be seen sprawled blind drunk on the pavements, and others greeted all and sundry with cat-calls. They regarded me with particular venom as a bespectacled intellectual. A Committee for Child Relief ran the Vladimirsky Club, a disreputable gambling-den. There I saw a woman hit in the face and thrown down the steps with her clothes half torn off. The manager came over to talk to me and told me quite coolly, 'What are you so shocked about? She's nothing but a whore! Just put yourself in my shoes!' He is a Communist, this manager: we belong to the same Party.

Business livens up society, after a fashion, but it is the most corrupt kind of business imaginable. Retail trade, i.e. the distribution of manufactured articles, has passed into the hands of private enterprise, which has triumphed over the co-operative and State trading systems. Where does this capital, non-existent five years ago, all come from? From robbery, fraudulent speculation, and superbly skilful racketeering. Twisters start up a fake co-operative; they bribe officials to give them credits, raw materials, and orders. Yesterday they had nothing; the Socialist State has given them everything, on burdensome terms it is true, for contracts, agreements and orders are all fixed by corruption. Once launched, they carry on, determined to become the universal middlemen between socialized industry and the consumer. They double the price of everything. Soviet trade, as a consequence of our industrial weakness, has become the hunting-ground for a flock of vultures in whom the shape of tomorrow's toughest and smartest capitalists can be clearly discerned. In this respect, N.E.P. is an unquestionable set-back. The prosecutors, from Krylenko downwards, spend their days in useless trials for speculation. One shabby little character named Plyatsky, carroty and talkative, is at the hub of all corruption and speculation in Leningrad. This Balzacian man of affairs has floated companies by the dozen, bribed officials in every single department —and he is not shot, because basically he is indispensable: he keeps everything going. N.E.P. has become one big confidence-trick. The same holds good, although in a different form, in the countryside. A single year's sheep-raising in the south has produced Soviet millionaires of a most curious brand: former Red partisans, whose daughters live in the finest hotels in the Crimea, whose sons play for high stakes in the casinos.

In an entirely different sphere, the gigantic scale of certain royalties encourages the gradual growth of an official literature. The dramatists Shchegolev (the historian) and Alexei Tolstoy are reaping hundreds of thousands of roubles for their slick plays about Rasputin and the Empress, and many of our young writers dream only of imitating them. It is only a matter of writing in a style which fits popular taste and the directives of the Central Committee's Cultural Section. Not that this is so very easy. It is becoming obvious that, despite the sterling resistance of most of the young Soviet writers, we have on our hands a literature that is conformist and corrupt. Things are coming back to life: but everywhere we can see symptoms of a process that eludes us, threatens us, and portends our doom.

It was Konstantinov who gave the solution to the equation. We knew each other, though we had never met. I loathed him, but was beginning to understand him. Somebody told me, 'He is a literary man: he collects original manuscripts. He has some of Tolstoy, Andreyev, Chekhov, and Rozanov. A materialist, but he has begun to join the company of mystics. A bit cracked, but intelligent. Used to be in the Cheka—says he's very fond of you.'

In a tenement on the Right Bank I found a few people in a room lit by a chandelier. An old man spoke to us of Rozanov, in whom there had been something of Nietzsche, Tolstoy, and Freud, all subsumed in a carnal Christianity which was perpetually at war with itself. A saintly obsessive, who had delved very deep into the moral problem and the sex problem. He thought of himself as a moral reptile; not that he wanted to be, but he told himself that everyone is like that at heart anyway; and so, ever so slightly, he really became one. Author of *Fallen Leaves*: meditations on life, death, hypocrisy, fleshly impurity, and the Saviour, a book written on sheets of lavatory paper in the w.c. He had died at the same time as Lenin, and the memories he left among the Russian intelligentsia ran deep. They spoke of him as though he had just gone out of the room.

The company included some young women, and a thin, tall man with a little white moustache. I recognized him at once: Ott, head of the Cheka's administrative section in 1919 and 1920. An Estonian or Lett, gifted with a bloodless imperturbability, he attended to all the form-filling, with the executions going on all round him. Konstantinov had thinning hair, a bony nose, swarthy, lips and spectacles; I did not recognize him, although he treated me as an old acquaintance. It was only later on that he drew me aside and said, 'You know me well, all the same: I was the examining magistrate in the Bayrach case. . . .'

Indeed, how could I have forgotten him? This was the Cheka man against whom, in 1920, a French Communist and I had waged a long struggle for the lives of some indubitably innocent men, whom he wanted shot at all costs. I will not recount this trivial case. There was the incident of the blood-stained shirt that was brought to me out of jail; the incident of the girl with the face of an *odalisque* before whom this sadistic magistrate had dangled fantastic traps, and promises with degrading conditions attached to them. There were indeed many incidents, and finally we did save the accused men, by going to the leading circles of the Cheka, Xenofontov, I believe. At the Petrograd Cheka the comrades had talked of the examining magistrate in ambiguous terms: a hard man, incorruptible (he only pretended to be willing to sell his clemency), a sadist perhaps, 'but you must understand—it's all psychology!' I avoided meeting him, believing him to be a dangerous character, a professional maniac. And, seven years later, here he was offering me tea, treating me as a friend.

'Your protégés went off to Constantinople where, no doubt, they have become big racketeers. You were quite wrong to take so much trouble to stop me liquidating them. I knew of course that, from a formal point of view, they were innocent, but we had plenty on file against them. That's unimportant now. In other cases, I was never prevented from doing my revolutionary duty, even by much more powerful people than you. It was I who. . . .'

He had been one of those Chekists who, in January 1920, just as

Lenin and Dzerzhinsky were issuing the decree to abolish the death-penalty, had arranged an execution at night, involving the massacre of several hundred suspects at the very last minute, when presses were already rolling out the new decree.

'So it was you. And what now?'

Now, he was on the fringe of the Party, not positively expelled, but pensioned off and tolerated. From time to time he would take the train to Moscow and go to the Central Committee, where he would be received by a senior secretary. Konstantinov would bring out his file of secrets, bulging with fresh titbits and supplemented by that irrefutable source of accusation, his memory. He would utter proofs, accusations, and the names of high personages, but still did not dare to tell everything. They would kill him.

He proposed to tell me nearly everything. Whence came this confidence in me? 'You are an Oppositionist? You are missing the real question altogether. You don't suspect anything. . . .' At first he talked in hints, and we discussed what was going on; what Lenin had foreseen when he said, 'You think you are driving the machine, and yet it's driving you, and suddenly other hands than yours are on the wheel.'

Unemployment statistics, wage-scales; the home market ruled by private enterprise, itself born out of the plunder of the State; rural misery, and rise of a peasant bourgeoisie; Comintern incompetence and Rapallo policies; privation in the towns and arrogant *nouveaux riches*—do these results strike you as being quite natural? 'And have we done all that we have done, only to come to this?'

Konstantinov lays his cards on the table, unveils his secret to me. The secret is that everything has been betrayed. From the years when Lenin was alive, treason has wormed its way into the Central Committee. He knows the names, he has the proofs. He cannot tell me everything, it's too dangerous: they know that he knows. If anyone guessed that I have heard it from him I would be a doomed man. It is all tremendous and appalling. The exposure of this plot demands infinite clairvoyance, a genius for inquisition, and absolute discretion. At the peril of his life, he is submitting his analysis of the gigantic crime, studied over years, to the Central Committee. He whispers the names of foreigners, of the most powerful capitalists, and of yet others which have an occult significance for him. He specifies a city across the Atlantic. I follow his chain of reasoning with the secret uneasiness that one feels in the presence of some lunatic logician. And I observe that he has the inspired face of a madman. But in all that he says, he is driven by one basic idea which is not the idea of a madman: 'We did not create the Revolution to come to this.'

We leave each other bound by a mutual confidence. It is a white night, and the trams have stopped running. I walk away with Ott. Crossing a bridge which lies between dull sky and fog-coloured water, I notice that my companion has not changed in six years. He still wears his long cavalry-coat without badges of rank, he has the same stolid bearing, the same half-smile under his pale little moustache, as if he were still on his way out of Cheka headquarters on a winter night in 1920. He is entirely in agreement with Konstantinov. His argument is crystal-clear, isn't it? We hold the threads of the plot, this plot of blackest treachery and infinite ramifications, the world-wide plot against the first Socialist republic . . . everything can still be saved, if only . . . there are still a few men in the Central Committee. But who?

The pale city of two in the morning opened its great, depopulated vistas to us. It seemed preoccupied: a cold stone model, full of memories. We had passed by the blue cupola of the Mosque. On the little hill towards our right the five heroes of the masonic Decembrist conspiracy had been hanged in 1825. On our left, in the small mansion that had once belonged to a favourite of Nicholas II, the Bolshevik conspiracy of 1917 had been organized. The gilt spire of the Peter-Paul Fortress poked up above its casemates and the river. There in his chains Nechayev had dreamed his prodigious plot to overthrow the Empire. There too the conspirators of *Narodnaya Volya* had died: left to die of starvation, in the years 1881 to 1883. Many of their younger comrades are still alive: the link they forged continues down to ourselves. We were approaching the tombstones in the Field of Mars, walled around by red granite ramparts: our own tombstones. Just opposite, in the Engineers' Castle, Paul I was done to death by his own officers. 'Just one plot after another, isn't it?' said Ott, with his smile. 'All that was just child's play. Today. . . .'

I felt an urge to reply (but it would have been useless with a paranoiac like this): 'Today things are not nearly so easy as that.

It's all quite different. And, my poor Ott, these plots that you are inventing are quite redundant. . . .'

If I have sketched these portraits and recorded these conversations of the year 1926, it is because they reveal a certain atmosphere even then, the obscure early stages of a psychosis. Much later the whole of Soviet Russia was to experience years of tragedy when it would live ever more intensely in the grip of this psychosis, which must be a psychological phenomenon unique in history. (Konstantinov disappeared in the early thirties, after being deported to Central Siberia.)

The calm of the workers' city of Leningrad was suddenly broken by the dramatic incident of Chubarov Alley, which shed a sinister light on the conditions under which our youth lived. About fifteen young workers from the San-Galli works had raped an unfortunate girl, the same age as they, on a piece of waste ground near the October railway station. This took place in the Ligovka quarter, a district where the underworld and the working class met, full of scabby tenements. The Party's Control Commission, now overloaded with nasty little morals-cases, had a sort of epidemic of collective rapes to investigate. Doubtless sexuality, so long repressed, first by revolutionary asceticism and then by poverty and famine, was beginning to recover its drive in a society that had been abruptly cut off from any spiritual nourishment. Promiscuity fed upon the misery of the environment. Books like those by Alexandra Kollontai[1] propagated an oversimplified theory of free love: an infantile variety of materialism reduced 'sexual need' to its strictly animal connotation. 'You make love just as you drink a glass of water, to relieve yourself.' The most sophisticated section of youth, the university students, was discussing Enchmen's theory (contested by Bukharin) on the disappearance of morals in the future Communist society.[2]

The fifteen defendants from Chubarov Alley were given a show-trial in a workers' club-room, with the portrait of Lenin overlooking

[1] Alexandra Kollontai (1872–1952): Menshevik for a while, then a prominent Bolshevik. Commissar of Social Welfare in the first Soviet Government; 'Left Communist' and then leader of the Workers' Opposition; diplomatic activity in Mexico, Norway, and Sweden; sympathized with the Trotskyist Opposition but subsequently conformed.

[2] Emmanuel S. Enchmen, biologist and 'mechanistic' materialist. He did not admit of the existence of 'other minds'.

all. Rafail, the editor of the Leningrad *Pravda*, presided; he was a
tame, crafty-looking, bald official. At no moment did he give the
slighest indication of understanding the tangled complexity of
human baseness and poverty-induced corruption that it was his task
to unravel in the name of working-class justice. A hall full of men
and women workers followed the cross-examination in an atmosphere of suspenseful boredom. The accused fifteen had the typical
faces of Ligovka gutter-kids, fusing the peasant and proletarian
types with primitive brutality as their salient feature. They offered
confessions and denounced one another with no inhibitions about
giving details. If ever the case diverged from the strictly factual they
could not follow it, and found it all a great fuss to be made over
things that often just pass by without any bother. What was more
natural than sex on waste sites? And what if she didn't mind
mating with four, five, or six? She would have got just as pregnant
or diseased if it had only been one. And if she did mind, perhaps it's
because she had 'prejudices'.

Certain parts of the cross-examination are still clear in my
memory. The lack of any insight on the part of the accused was
so primitive in its quality that the magistrate Rafail, good com-
mitteeman that he was, was continually put out by it. He had
just been so foolish as to talk of 'new culture' and 'our wonderful
Soviet morals'. A short, fair-haired lad with a flat nose answered
him:

'Never heard of 'em.'

Rafail went on, 'Of course, you'd prefer foreign bourgeois morals,
wouldn't you?'

It was ridiculous, it was horrible. The boy replied, 'I don't
know nothing about them. Me, I've never been abroad.'

'You could have got to know about them through reading foreign
newspapers.'

'I never even see Soviet newspapers. The Ligovka streets, that's
the only culture I know.'

Five of the accused were condemned to death. In order to be able
to carry out the sentence, the authorities had to twist the law and
accuse them of 'banditry'. On the evening of the verdict, the sky
above the city glowed purple. I walked towards the glow: the whole
of the San-Galli works was in flames. The five condemned youths
were executed on the following day. There was a rumour that the

workers who had started the fire had been executed secretly, but this was impossible to confirm.

I was taken by a sudden yearning to know this social inferno of ours, whose great flames cried out into the night. I burrowed into our Soviet doss-houses. I was there when they rounded up the girls they kept sending, by administrative decree, to the concentration-camps of the Far North. I can honestly say that Dostoevsky did not see everything; in any case, I discovered that since Dostoevsky's day nothing, in certain dark corners of our world, has changed for the better. O my fellow-tramps of Paris, how difficult is social transformation!

It was at this time that Vassily Nikiforovich Chadayev waylaid me in the Leningrad Press Institute on the Fontanka Embankment, where the Countess Panina used to reside.

'*Taras has told me about you.* . . .' Taras was a password name that had been given me in Piatakov's circle in Moscow so that I could contact the clandestine Opposition in Leningrad. The 'Trotskyists' as a group had withdrawn from political activity, and since 1923 had been playing a waiting game. This was the Centre which guided the Left Opposition in the area, and I was invited to join it. We used to meet in a room at the Astoria, usually that of N. I. Karpov, a professor of agricultural science who had been an army commissar. Those who went there consisted of two or three students of working-class origin; two old Bolshevik workers who had been in every revolution in Petrograd for the last twenty years; X——, an un-assuming man, formerly the organizer of a Party print-shop, who had been dropped from various sinecures because of his excessive integrity and who, ten years after the seizure of power, was living as poorly as he always had, pale and scraggy under his faded cloth cap; Feodorov, a huge red-haired fellow, splendidly strapping, with an open face fit for a barbarian warrior, a factory-worker who was soon to leave our group, ultimately to meet his death as a member of the Zinoviev tendency. We also included two Marxist theoretic-ians of genuine worth, Yakovin and Dingelstedt. Grigori Yakov-levich Yakovin, aged thirty, had returned from Germany, on which country he had just written an excellent book. A sporting enthusiast with a constantly alert intelligence, good looks, and a spontaneous charm, he was to spend some years in ingenious daring and dangerous illegality, and then to do the rounds of the jails for an undetermined period, there to disappear in 1937.

Feodor Dingelstedt had been, at the age of twenty, one of the Bolshevik agitators (together with Ensign Roshal, Ilyin Genevsky, and Raskolnikov) who had been behind the mutiny of the Baltic fleet in 1917. He was in charge of the Institute of Forestry and was having a book published on 'The Agrarian Question in India'. Among us he represented an extreme-Left tendency similar to Sapronov's group, who considered that the degeneration of the régime was now complete. Dingelstedt's face, with its harsh, inspired ugliness, was a picture of invincible obstinacy. 'They will never break *him*.' I used to reflect. I was not mistaken: he was to follow the same path as Yakovin without ever giving in.

'Babushka', or 'Grandmother', usually took the chair at our meetings. Plump, her hair white over her kindly face, Alexandra Lvovna Bronstein was the last word in commonsense and honesty. She had some thirty-five years of militancy behind her, including exile in Siberia; she had been Trotsky's wife in his first years of struggle, and had borne him two daughters, Nina and Zina (who were both to perish . . .). The only work allowed her was elementary instruction in sociology to children of under fifteen, and that was not to last long. I have known few Marxists as free in their basic outlook as Alexandra Lvovna.

Nikolai Pavlovich Baskakov, a small, powerful man with a tall, indented forehead and blue eyes, thought it was now questionable whether the system could be reformed. He went into the jails, where I do not know what became of him. Together with Chadayev and myself, who specialized in international questions, this was the roll-call of the Centre. I insist on one historical point: there was never any other Centre of the Left Opposition in Leningrad.

Chadayev became my friend. He was to be the first of our number who was killed. Long before the Party leadership, he raised the question of the collectivization of agriculture, in a remarkable set of theses. He was the only one of us to put the question of a second party—in private—and the only one to foresee the great trials of deception. A fighter from 1917, an editor on the evening paper *Krassnaya Gazeta*, he was led through his knowledge of the condition of the working class to a realistic appraisal of political problems. He watched the disorders at the Labour Exchange, which was in the end wrecked by the unemployed.

'In that riot', he said, 'I saw a fantastic woman who reminded me of the best days of 1917. She gave purpose, and almost order, to the tumult. Her appearance was insignificant, but I could see that she was cut out to be a leader. And it is working-class women like her that have to come out against us!' Together we watched the disgusting trial of the Labour Exchange officials, who would not send a woman to a factory job unless she were reasonably good-looking and, what was more, obliging. He left behind him several precious booklets filled with observations which, like so many others, probably went to be pulped.

The Party was in a state of slumber. Meetings were hardly noticed by the apathetic public. Since the purge of the universities, the youth had turned in upon itself. All the same, we were, for the time being fairly optimistic, for Trotsky was publishing a series of articles proving that we were on the way 'to Socialism, not capitalism', and supporting the preservation of a marginal private sector (which would take the force of all crises) around the nationalized factories. I discussed these ideas in the Paris journal *Vie Ouvrière*. Victor Eltsin brought me a directive from the Old Man (Trotsky): 'For the moment we must not act at all: no showing ourselves in public but keep our contacts, preserve our cadres of 1923, and wait for Zinoviev to exhaust himself. . . .' Writing good books and publishing Leon Davidovich's *Collected Works* was to be our means of keeping up morale. Victor Eltsin had the cool temperament of a tactician. He also told me that in Moscow the Left Opposition could muster more than 500 comrades. Sermuks was a fair-haired, gentlemanly type, refined and circumspect, Poznansky a tall Jew with untidy hair. These were the three secretaries of Trotsky, all of them aged about thirty to thirty-five; towards the Old Man they would keep faith unshakeably, until Heaven knows what terrible death.[1]

The storm broke quite out of the blue. Even we were not awaiting its coming. Certain remarks of Zinoviev, whom I had seen weary and dull-eyed, should have warned me. . . . Passing through Moscow in the spring of 1925, I learnt that Zinoviev and Kamenev, who were

[1] Poznansky and Sermuks tried to join Trotsky in exile at Alma Ata. They were arrested, and disappeared. At the end of the voyage in which Trotsky was deported to Constantinople, a G.P.U. official accompanying him promised that Poznansky and Sermuks would be released and allowed to join him abroad. Nothing more was heard of this promise. (Serge, *Vie et Mort de Trotsky*.)

to all appearances still all-powerful as the two foremost figures in the Politbureau since Lenin's death, were about to be overthrown at the forthcoming Fourteenth Party Congress, and that Stalin was offering the Department of Industry to Trotsky. . . . The 1923 Opposition asked itself who its allies should be. Mrachkovsky, the hero of the Urals battles, declared, 'We will not ally ourselves with any one. Zinoviev would end by deserting us and Stalin would trick us.' The militants of the old Workers' Opposition proved to be non-committal, since they believed us to be too weak and, as they said, distrusted Trotsky's authoritarian temper. My own opinion was that it was impossible for the bureaucratic régime stemming from Zinoviev to get any harsher; nothing could be worse than it. Any change must offer some opportunity for purification. I was very much mistaken, as is now obvious.

Grossman-Roschin, a leader of the syndicalist group *Golos Truda* (*Voice of Labour*), who was also the only member of the group still at liberty, came to tell me how disturbed he was: 'Stalin is grumbling about the clowns and stooges in the Comintern, and is getting ready to cut off their rations once he has sacked Zinoviev. Aren't you afraid of some damage happening to the Communist International through this?' I answered, 'Nothing could be better for the International than to have all its rations cut off. The commercial characters will go elsewhere, the artificial Parties will die away, and the working-class movement will be able to recover its health.'

As a matter of fact, the Fourteenth Congress, of December 1925, was a well-rehearsed play, acted just as its producer had planned over several years. All the regional secretaries, who were appointed by the General Secretary, had sent Congress delegates who were loyal to his service. The easy victory of the Stalin-Rykov-Bukharin coalition was an office-victory over Zinoviev's group, which only controlled offices in Leningrad. The Leningrad delegation, led by Zinoviev, Yevdokimov, and Bakayev and supported by Kamenev —all doomed to the firing-squad in 1936—found itself isolated when it came to the vote. Zinoviev and Kamenev were paying for years of responsibility devoid of any glory or success: two defeated revolutions, in Germany and Bulgaria, the bloody and imbecilic episode of Estonia; at home the revival of class-distinctions, about 2,000,000 unemployed, scarcity of goods, conflict simmering between the peasantry and the dictatorship, the extinction of all democracy; in the Party, purges, repression (still mild, but shocking because it was new), the multiplication of slanders against the organizer of victory, Trotsky. Certainly Stalin had a share in the responsibility for all these doings, but he wriggled out of it by turning on his colleagues in the triumvirate. Zinoviev and Kamenev were quite literally falling under the weight of their own errors, and yet we could see that at this particular hour they were more or less right. They opposed the makeshift doctrine of 'Socialism in a single country', in the name of the whole tradition of International Socialism. Kamenev used the expression 'State capitalism' in speaking of the wretched condition of the workers, and advocated that the wage-earners should share in their factories' profits. Zinoviev's crime was that he demanded the right to take the platform at Congress to present his own report. The whole Central Committee Press chose to see in this an attack on the unity of the Party. Bukharin was sick of the reign of mediocrity; he hoped to become the 'brain' behind Stalin. Rykov, President of the Council of People's Commissars; Tomsky, the head of the trade unions; Voroshilov, the head of the army; and Kalinin, the President of the Central Executive, were all carefully watching the state of peasant discontent and uttering condemnations of international adventure. The mass of Party officials wanted nothing more than to live a quiet life.

Zinoviev, whose demagogy was quite sincere, believed every word he said about the warm support of Leningrad's working-class masses for his own clique. 'Our fortress is impregnable', I heard him say. He took the opinions which his subordinates cooked up in the Leningrad *Pravda* as being representative of real public opinion. He came back to make his appeal to the Party and the masses at a time when the Party was no more than a phantom in the imagination of bureaucrats and the masses were apathetic and dormant. The resistance of Leningrad, which I had seen for myself, was crushed in a fortnight, even though on certain nights workers loyal to Zinoviev came to mount guard over the newspaper's print-shop in anticipation of a forcible *putsch*. The proletarian district of Vyborg, which had been famous ever since the days of March 1917, was the first to give in. The same men were no longer there, neither was the same spirit. In every local committee there were shrewd folk who knew that a declaration in favour of the Central Committee was the first step in a career. The better members were disarmed by their respect, or rather fetishism, towards the Central Committee. The Central Committee sent Gusev and Stetsky along to us to instal new committees. Stetsky, a man of 35, was a disciple of Bukharin: his pose was that of the 'Soviet American'—neatly dressed, clean-shaven, genial, round head, and round glasses, very friendly to the intellectuals, joining them in investigating 'the problems'. (Later he was to betray Bukharin, temporarily replacing him as a theoretician in Stalin's circle, and then to develop a blatant theory of the totalitarian State, before disappearing into jail around 1938.)

I heard Gusev speaking to big Party meetings. Large, slightly bald and well-built, he got at his audience through the degrading hypnotism which is associated with systematic violence. In order to argue in this particularly foul manner one must, first, be sure of having force at one's elbow, and, secondly, make up one's mind to stop at nothing. It is, at bottom, a fear-making technique. Not a single word of his won conviction, but the losers had got themselves into hot water, there was nothing for it but to vote for the Central Committee. . . . We of the Opposition walked out before the vote was taken, silence all round us. The very low level of education of some of the listeners, and the material dependence of all of them on the approval of Party committees, guaranteed the success of the operation. Under Gusev's hammer-blows the formal majority that Zinoviev had enjoyed in Leningrad since 1918 crumbled away in a week.

Our own 'Leading Centre of the Left Opposition' had abstained in this battle. We were taken aback by the news that Trotsky had concluded an agreement with the 'Leningrad Opposition'. How could we sit at the same table with the bureaucrats who had hunted and slandered us—who had murdered the principles and ideas of the Party?

The old leaders of the Leningrad Party, nearly all of whom I had known since 1919, Yevdokimov, Bakayev, Lashevich, Zorin, Yonov, Makhimson, and Gertik, seemed to have undergone a change of heart overnight; I could not help thinking that they must have felt enormously relieved to escape from the stifling fog of lies and shake us by the hand. They spoke admiringly of Trotsky, the same man that they had covered with odious abuse a couple of days ago. They described, in considerable detail, the first talks he had held with Zinoviev and Kamenev. Their relationship was 'better than ever—just like in 1918'. This was the time when Zinoviev and Kamenev presented Trotsky with letters testifying how, in conference with Stalin, Bukharin, and Rykov, they had decided to fabricate a doctrine of 'Trotskyism' against which they could unloose smear campaigns. They made even more serious revelations with which I will deal later. They signed a declaration recognizing that on the question of the Party's internal régime the 1923 Opposition (Preobrazhensky, Trotsky, Rakovsky, and Antonov-Ovseyenko) had been right as against themselves.

Twenty or so sympathizers were gathered around our Leningrad Centre. The Zinoviev tendency declared that it could count on a clandestine membership of between five and six hundred. We had our doubts about this figure, but decided to open a recruiting campaign aimed at creating an organization of similar size, in preparation for the time when the forces of both tendencies would be brought face to face. The Zinoviev group, knowing our weakness, demanded the immediate fusion of the two organizations. We hesitated to hand over the list of our leading members to them. What would they be up to tomorrow? A number of us suggested that we conceal certain names from our newly-found allies—a proposition we rejected as being disloyal. Our agitators set to work. We held semi-clandestine meetings from district to district. Chadayev, the organizer of the central area, would come to see me at night, eyes blazing out of his wrinkled face, and announce the day's results: 'I tell you that we shall have 400 comrades organized on the day of the merger!' We were actually to surpass this total, but out of suspicion we kept putting off the merger.

Nechayev and Chadayev went to Moscow to inform Trotsky of our fears. I followed them for the purpose of briefing Leon Davidovich and presenting our objections to him. On that day Leon Davidovich was shivering with fever; his lips were violet-coloured, but his shoulders were still set firmly and the cast of his face displayed intelligence and will. He justified the amalgamation on the grounds of the necessity to unite the political forces of both the two working-class capitals, Leningrad and Moscow. 'It is a battle which will be difficult to win,' he said calmly, 'but we have excellent chances, and the salvation of the Revolution depends on it.' Someone brought coded telegrams in to him. In the large waiting-room at the Concessions Commission two bearded peasants in sheepskins and clogs of plaited bark were parleying with Sermuks for an interview with Trotsky, to whom they were anxious to submit an interminable legal dispute they had been having with the local authorities of a distant country district. 'Now that Lenin is dead', they kept repeating stubbornly, 'there is only Comrade Trotsky to give us justice.' .

'He will certainly see you,' Sermuks would answer patiently, all dapper and smiling, 'but he can do nothing now; he is no longer in the Government.' The *mujiks* shook their heads, visibly annoyed that someone was trying to make them believe that 'Trotsky can do nothing now'.

'Pretend to be blowing your nose when you go out,' one of the secretaries told me. 'The G.P.U. has put men with cameras in the house opposite. Apart from that, some of the "comrades". . . .'

Preobrazhensky and Smilga were sent to us by the Moscow Centre to unify the leadership of the two Leningrad oppositions. Preobrazhensky had the broad features and short auburn beard that befitted a man of the people. He had driven himself so hard that during the meetings it seemed that he might at any moment drop off to sleep; but his brain was still fresh, and crammed with statistics on the agrarian problem.

Smilga, an economist and former army leader who in 1917 had been Lenin's confidential agent in the Baltic fleet, was a fair-haired intellectual in his forties with spectacles, a chin-beard, and thinning front hair, ordinary to look at and distinctly the armchair sort. He spoke for a whole evening in a little room to about fifty workers who could not move at all, so closely were they squeezed together. A Latvian giant with gingerish hair and an impassive face scrutinized all who came in. Smilga, sitting on a stool in the middle of the room, spoke, in an expert's tone and without one agitational phrase, of production, unemployment, grain and budgetary figures, and of the Plan that we were hotly advocating. Not since the first days of the Revolution had the Party's leadership been seen in an atmosphere of poverty and simplicity like this, face to face with the militants of the rank and file.

Together with Chadayev, I was a member of the Party cell at the *Krassnaya Gazeta*, the big evening newspaper. (I had, of course, been removed from all committees and 'responsible' positions after my return from Central Europe.) There were about 400 of us: printers, typographers, linotype operators, clerks, editorial staff, and political activists attached to the paper. Three Old Bolsheviks, lost in this multitude, occupied managerial posts. Ten or so comrades had been in the Civil War. The other 387 (or thereabouts) were from the 'Lenin enrolment': workers who had joined the Party only at the death of Lenin, after the consolidation of power and at the height of N.E.P. We Oppositionists numbered five, one of whom was shaky; we were all of the Civil War generation. It was a miniature of the situation in the Party as a whole; many things are explained thereby.

The battle of ideas was joined on three issues, on which the maximum possible silence was maintained: agricultural system, Party democracy, Chinese Revolution. Chiang Kai-shek, with Blücher (Galen) and my comrade Olgin (lately one of the victors at Bokhara) as his counsellors, was beginning his triumphal march from Canton to Shanghai and winning startling victories on the way; the Chinese Revolution was in its ascendancy. From the very beginning the discussion in the whole Party was falsified, on orders from the bureaucracy. The cell committee, in obedience to the district committee, called an aggregate meeting every fortnight. Attendance was compulsory and all names were checked off at the door. A hack orator took two hours to prove the possibility of constructing Socialism in a single country and denounce the Opposition's 'lack of faith'. All he did was to spin out the statements published by the Central Committee's Agitation Department. The next to speak were those termed the 'activists', always the same ones, long-winded old workers who were favourites of the committee or eager young careerists who were actually offering themselves as eligible candidates for a minor position. I can still hear a young soldier expounding painfully from the platform how Marx and Engels doubtless did not conceive of one of the 'little Western countries', like France, Britain, or Germany, being able to build Socialism out of its own resources; but the U.S.S.R. constituted a sixth of the world. . . .

The Bureau, which consisted of workers loyal to the management, was always keen to have a long list of speakers, both to limit the time available for Oppositionists to speak and to give statistical proof of the participation of the masses in the life of the Party. Of the Oppositionists, three were lying low; Chadayev and myself were the only ones to go to the platform, and we were allowed five minutes. It was essential not to lose a second of the time, and accordingly we had invented a special style. We spoke in detached sentences which were all either declarations, statements of fact, or questions. Each one of them had to register, even if the shouting of the 'activists' drowned what came before. As soon as we opened our mouths to speak, interruptions and shouts, mingled with insults, would burst out at once: '*Traitors! Mensheviks! Tools of the bourgeoisie!*' One had to stay calm, remark to the chairman that half a minute had been lost by interruptions and start the mangled sentence over again. Somebody, a member of the Bureau, would be taking down hurried notes for the benefit of the city committee and the Central Committee. The body of the hall watched this duel in absolute silence. Twenty of the onlookers filled the place with their shouts; we only had them to face, and were troubled by the silence of the others.

The Chinese Revolution galvanized us all. I have the impression of a positive wave of enthusiasm heaving up the whole Soviet world —or at least the thinking part of it. The country felt, however confusedly, that a Red China could be the salvation of the U.S.S.R. Then came the Shanghai fiasco. I was expecting it; I had stated beforehand that it would happen. In Moscow I took part in the International Commission set up by the Oppositional Centre, together with Zinoviev's spokesman Kharitonov, Fritz Wolf (who soon capitulated, which did not stop him being shot in 1937), Andrés Nin, the Bulgarian Lebedev (or Stepanov, a clandestine Oppositionist who betrayed us and later worked as a Comintern agent during the revolution in Spain) and two or three other militants whose names I have forgotten. I was well briefed, by comrades who had come back from China and by material from Radek (then Rector of the Chinese University in Moscow), Zinoviev and Trotsky. Incredibly enough, the only non-Communist French newspaper that came into the U.S.S.R., *Le Temps*, a Conservative organ but reputable (money having no smell, as they say), provided me with valuable points of confirmation.

When he arrived before Shanghai, Chiang Kai-shek had found the town in the hands of the trade unions, whose rebellion had been superlatively organized with the assistance of the Russian agents. Day by day we followed the preparation of the military *coup*, whose only possible outcome was the massacre of the Shanghai proletariat. Zinoviev, Trotsky, and Radek demanded an immediate change of line from the Central Committee. It would have been enough to send the Shanghai Committee a telegram: 'Defend yourselves if you have to!' and the Chinese Revolution would not have been beheaded. One divisional commander put his troops at the disposal of the Communist Party to resist the disarmament of the workers. But the Politbureau insisted on the subordination of the Communist Party to the Kuomintang. The Chinese Party, led by an honest man, Ch'en Tu-Hsiu, had disavowed the peasant uprisings in Hopei and left the insurgent farmers of Chan-Sha to be slaughtered in their thousands.

On the very day before the Shanghai incident Stalin came to the Bolshoi Theatre to explain his policy to the assembled activists of Moscow. The whole Party noted one of his winged remarks: 'We are told that Chiang Kai-shek is making ready to turn against us again. I know that he is playing a cunning game with us, but it is he that will be crushed. We shall squeeze him like a lemon and then be rid of him.'

This speech was in the press at *Pravda* when we heard the terrible news. Troops were wiping out the working-class quarters of Shanghai with sabre and machine-gun. (Malraux was later to describe this tragedy in *Man's Estate.*)

Despair was in us all when we met. The arguments within the Central Committee were repeated with equal violence in every Party cell where there were Oppositionists. When I began to speak in my own branch, just after Chadayev, I felt that a paroxysm of hatred was building up and that we would be lynched on the way out. I ended my five minutes by flinging out a sentence that brought an icy silence: 'The prestige of the General Secretary is infinitely more precious to him than the blood of the Chinese proletariat!' The hysterical section of the audience exploded: 'Enemies of the Party!'

A few days later our first arrest took place: they arrested Nechayev, a new member of our Centre, a thoughtful worker who had once been an army commissar, with a rough, weary face and gold spectacles, about forty years of age. We spoke of the arrest at a meeting. The Bureau did not dare to accept any responsibility for it. We had prepared two angry interventions: Chadayev made his from the platform, but I spoke from the floor, the better to defy the fanatics in the front rows. I shouted 'You have arrested Nechayev. To-morrow you will have to arrest us in thousands. Know then that in the service of the working class we will accept prison, deportation, the Solovky Isles. Nothing will silence us. The counter-revolution is rising behind you, stranglers of the Party!' The activists kept up bursts of rhythmic chanting '*Slanderers! Traitors!*' These arguments were conducted in a hall where we suddenly felt, members of the same Party as we were, that the enemy was in front of us and prison was a step away; it had a shattering effect upon me.

On one other occasion we scored a point—but what a dismal point it was! I asked the audience to stand in homage to the memory of Adolf Abramovich Joffe; I had just kept watch by him as he lay on his death-bed in Moscow, dead for the Revolution's sake. The cell Secretary, who was always briefed by a confidential circular, gazed at us in fury, but yielded. We rendered homage, since the circular did not expressly forbid that. . . .

'And now, tell us why he died, and how!'

'The district committee has given me no information on those points,' answered the Secretary, adding that nobody had the right to speak on those points before the Central Committee did so. In the memoranda that passed from committee to committee, a death like this could disappear without trace. On this sacrifice the newspapers were silent; it was being squeezed into nothing under half a ton of paper.

We began to tire of this sterile battling in a low-level organization. Once, as Chadayev and I were walking along there in the rainy street, we looked at each other, each with the same thought in his eyes: 'What if we kept quiet this evening?' I forget now what was being discussed. After the activists had finished haranguing us, the Chairman announced, in a puzzled voice, that the list of speakers had no more names. Then, for the first time, the apathetic audience stirred. There was a flurrying all around us: 'Hey, what about you chaps?' Chadayev rose smiling and I saw him, looking very tall, and putting up his hand to ask to speak.

And this time, when it came to the vote on the final motion, when we were always the only ones to vote against—against 250 others—a third hand was raised at the same time as ours. A young printer was exclaiming: 'They're right! I am with them!'

He joined us in the street. We learnt that about forty workers, all bound by mutual confidence, were prepared to support us, but would only do so discreetly, for fear of losing their jobs. An equal number of sympathizers were around them. We went home in the darkness, tense but happy. The ice was beginning to break. From other sources we discovered that the same situation held in the Party as a whole.

'I think', Chadayev said to me, 'that they'll crush us to pulp before the big thaw ever happens.'

Now that Zinoviev had been dismissed from the Chairmanship of the Leningrad Soviet, he had not been in the city for months. He came along there with Trotsky for a session of the Central Soviet Executive, which of course was a purely formal gathering. Grey drizzle was falling over the stands decked in red calico, and on the demonstration marching past near the Tauride Palace. The leaders of the Opposition were standing on the platform well away from the official group. The crowd had eyes only for them. After delivering hurrahs to order before Komarov, the new Chairman of the Soviet, the procession found itself level with these legendary men who no longer meant anything in the State. At this point the demonstrators made a silent gesture by lingering on the spot, and thousands of hands were outstretched, waving handkerchiefs or caps. It was a dumb acclamation, futile but still overwhelming.

Zinoviev and Trotsky received the greeting in a spirit of happy determination, imagining that they were witnessing a show of force. 'The masses are with us!' they kept saying that night. Yet what possibilities were there in masses who were so submissive that they contained their emotions like this? As a matter of fact everybody in that crowd knew that the slightest gesture endangered his own and his family's livelihood.

Together with the two leaders we conducted a campaign of agitation, a legal one that is: the Party rules did not forbid members of the Central Committee to talk to militants. Fifty people packed a small room, sitting around a pale, plump Zinoviev, him of the curls and the low voice. At the other end of the table sat Trotsky, now obviously ageing, almost hoary but well-set, his features boldly chiselled, ever ready with a shrewd answer. A woman worker, sitting cross-legged on the floor, asked: 'What if we are expelled?' Trotsky explained that 'nothing can really cut us off from our Party'. It was a simple, reassuring sight: the men of the proletarian dictatorship, who had yesterday been the greatest in the land,

coming back like this to the districts of the poor, there to seek
support from man to man.

I was with Trotsky as he left one of these meetings in some
ramshackle apartment scarred by poverty. In the street Leon
Davidovich put up his overcoat collar and lowered the peak of his
cap so as not to be recognized. He looked like an old intellectual in the
underground of long ago, true as ever after twenty years of grind
and a few dazzling victories. We approached a cabman and I
bargained for the fare, for we had little money. The cabman, a
bearded peasant straight out of old Russia, leaned down and said,
'For you, the fare is nothing. Get inside, comrade. You are Trotsky,
surely?' The cap was not enough of a disguise for the man of the
Revolution. The Old Man had a slight smile of amusement:
'Don't tell any one that this happened. Everybody knows that
cabmen belong to the petty-bourgeoisie, whose favour can only
discredit us. . . .'

Using assumed names, I spoke in outlying districts. One of my
groups, consisting of half a dozen working men and women, held its
meetings in the shade of low fir-trees in an abandoned cemetery.
I would stand on the graves and discuss the confidential reports of
the Central Committee, the news from China, and Mao Tse-tung's
articles. (The future military leader of Soviet China was very close
to us in his ideas; but he stayed within the Party line to keep his
supplies of weapons and munitions.)

I had no confidence that we would win: I was even sure in my own
heart that we would be defeated. I remember saying this to Trotsky,
in his big office at the Concessions Commission. In the old capital we
could count on only a few hundred militants, and the mass of the
workers was indifferent to our case. Leon Davidovich spread his
hands wide: 'There is always some risk to be run. Sometimes you
finish like Liebknecht and sometimes like Lenin.' As far as I was
concerned everything was summed up in one conviction: even if
there were only one chance in a hundred for the regeneracy of the
Revolution and its workers' democracy, that chance had to be taken
at all costs. I was unable to confess these sentiments openly to any
one. To the comrades who, under the firs in the cemetery, or on a
waste plot near a hospital, or in poverty-stricken houses, demanded
some promise of victory from me, I would answer that the struggle
would be prolonged and harsh. So long as I confined this way of

talking to personal conversations with a few people, it worked, it made their faces harden; but if it was used against a more numerous audience, it cast a chill. 'You behave too much like an intellectual,' I was told by one of my friends in our Centre. Other agitators were lavish with promises of victory and I think that they themselves lived on such hopes.

We decided to use surprise tactics to occupy a hall in the Palace of Labour, where we would hold a big meeting with Zinoviev. (Kamenev had done this at Moscow, speaking by the glow of a few candles since the Central Committee had had the electricity cut off.) At the last minute Zinoviev cried off, afraid of being called to account, and Radek refused to speak by himself. So the hundred-odd of us went off to demonstrate at an engineers' conference at the Mariinsky Theatre. One of us was badly beaten.

Our Centre held a meeting at my lodgings with Radek, around the tea-table. Karl Bernardovich munched his pipe between his thick lips; his eyes were very tired. As usual he gave an impression of extreme intelligence, which was, at first encounter, disagreeable because of a certain flippancy; but beneath the sarcastic retailer of anecdotes, the man of principle shone through. Somebody had recalled the Workers' Opposition, which in 1920–1 had analysed the bureaucratization of the Party and the condition of the working class in terms which we scarcely dared repeat aloud seven years later. At the idea that this bygone Opposition had been right against Lenin, Radek was nettled. 'A dangerous idea. If you take it up, you will be finished as far as we are concerned. In 1920 there was no Thermidor in sight, Lenin was alive, and the revolution was simmering in Europe. . . .'

I questioned him about Dzerzhinsky, who had just died, on the couch where he had collapsed with a heart-attack on the way out of a stormy session of the Central Committee. Nobody doubted Dzerzhinsky's absolute incorruptibility. The petty deceit that had become current among our leadership must have made him ill. . . .

Radek remarked, 'Felix died just in time. He was a dogmatist. He would not have shrunk from reddening his hands in our blood.' At midnight the telephone rang: 'Scatter, look sharp! You're all going to get locked up, the orders have been given by Messing!'[1]

[1] S. A. Messing: a leading Soviet official of the Cheka and later of the G.P.U., himself to be arrested after the fall of Yagoda. He died in 1946.

Everyone dispersed unhurriedly. Radek lit his pipe again. 'Plenty of things are going to start happening again. The main job is not to do anything silly.'

The Central Committee authorized the 'activists' to break up 'illegal meetings' by force. Squads of husky fellows, ready to beat up anyone on behalf of the Central Committee, were formed in the various districts of the city, and provided with lorries. Concerned for its dignity, the Opposition recoiled from the prospect of fist-fighting; meetings were stopped or else held in absolute secrecy.

For some years now the country had been living on political formulae many of which were obsolete and some downright deceitful. The Opposition decided to give itself a programme, thereby proclaiming that the ruling party now had either no programme, or else one which no longer had anything to do with the Revolution. Zinoviev undertook to work out the chapters on agriculture and the International in collaboration with Kamenev; the chapter on industrialization was assigned to Trotsky; Smilga and Piatakov, helped by some young comrades, also worked on the draft, which was submitted, as each section came out, to our meetings and, wherever possible, to groups of workers. For the last time (but we had no suspicion that this was so) the Party returned to its tradition of collective thinking, with its concern to consult the man in the workshop. Typewriters clattered throughout entire nights in apartments where the Kremlin was still unable to intrude. The daughter of Vorovsky, the Ambassador who had been assassinated in Switzerland, wore herself out in this work (she was soon to die of the combined effects of tuberculosis, work, and privation). Some of the comrades got three or four typewriters together in a little room in Moscow. Agents of the G.P.U. besieged these premises quite openly. One of the Red Army leaders, Okhotnikov, came complete with the tabs on his collar and ordered this surveillance to be called off; we were able to save some of our stocks. The next day the newspapers announced the discovery of a 'clandestine printing-press'! A further crime: a former White officer was implicated in the plot—and this was partly true, except that the ex-officer was now a member of the G.P.U. For the first time a squalid police-intrigue was interfering with the life of the Party.

This odious legend was automatically publicized by the Communist Press abroad. Vaillant-Couturier put his name to the official statement. A few days later I met him in Moscow at an international writers' conference. I pushed away the hand he offered me. 'You know perfectly well that you have given your signature to a slander!' His large chubby face grew pale and he stammered, 'Come along this evening and I'll explain to you. I received the official reports. How could I check if they were true?' That night I knocked on his door, in vain. I will never forget his face, helpless with shame. For the first time I witnessed the self-debasement of a man who wanted to be a sincere revolutionary— who was, moreover, talented, eloquent, sensitive and (physically at least) courageous. They got him in a corner: 'You must write that, Vaillant; the Executive demands it!' Refusal meant breaking with the all-powerful Comintern that could make and break reputations, meant joining a minority without a press or resources. . . . He would more willingly have risked his neck on the barricades, than his Parliamentary career in this particular way. Besides, shame makes its impact only the first time.

All legal means of expression were now closed to us. From 1926 onward, when the last tiny sheets put out by anarchists, syndicalists and Maximalists had disappeared, the Central Committee had enjoyed an absolute monopoly of printed matter. Fishelev, an old companion of Trotsky in Canada and now the manager of a print-shop in Leningrad, published our *Platform* clandestinely; it was signed by seventeen members of the Central Committee (Trotsky, Zinoviev, Kamenev, Smilga, Yevdokimov, Rakovsky, Piatakov, Bakayev, etc.). Fishelev was convicted of misappropriating paper and plant, and sent to a concentration-camp in the Solovietsky Islands. Meanwhile we collected signatures to the *Platform*. 'If we get 30,000 of them', said Zinoviev, 'they won't be able to stop us speaking at the Fifteenth Congress. . . .' We managed, with considerable difficulty, to gather five or six thousand. Since the situation was taking a rapid turn for the worse, only a few hundred, the names of the men of the Bolshevik Old Guard, were sent to the Central Committee. Events were speeding to a conclusion which would make all this petitioning appear in its true light: as mere child's play.

The 100 pages of the *Platform* attacked the anti-Socialist forces that were growing under the N.E.P. system, embodied in the *Kulak* or rich peasant, the trader and the bureaucrat. Increase in indirect taxation, bearing heavily on the masses; real wages held static at an excessively low level, barely that of 1913; 2,000,000 unemployed; trade unions fast becoming executive organs of the employer-State (we demanded the preservation of the right to strike); 30–40 per cent. of the peasantry poor and without horses or implements, and a rich 6 per cent. cornering 53 per cent. of the corn reserves; we advocated tax-exemption for poor peasants, the development of collective cultivation (*kolkhozes*) and a progressive tax-system. We also advocated a powerful drive for technological renewal and the creation of new industries, and mercilessly criticized what was the first, pitifully weak version of the Five-Year Plan. On the other hand, we demanded the abolition of the State alcohol trade, which brought in a considerable revenue. We quoted Lenin's saying: 'We will sell everything, except ikons and vodka.'

On the political level, it was essential to restore life to the Soviets, to apply the principle of self-determination of nationalities 'in sincerity', and above all to revitalize the Party and the trade unions. The 'Party of the proletariat' was only one-third working class (no more than that) in its composition: 430,000 workers compared with 465,000 officials; 303,000 peasants (over half of whom were rural officials), and 15,000 agricultural day-labourers. We disclosed that two tendencies existed within the Central Committee. One of these, the moderate one, envisaged the formation of a rich peasant petty-bourgeoisie; this Right tendency was quite capable of precipitating an involuntary slide towards capitalism. It comprised Rykov (Chairman of the Council of Trade Unions), Kalinin (President of the Executive of the U.S.S.R.), Chubar (Chairman of the Ukrainian Council of People's Commissars), Petrovsky (Chairman of the Ukrainian Soviet Executive), and Melnichansky and Dogadov, of the Council of Trade Unions. (With the exception of Kalinin, and Voroshilov, all these men were to perish in 1937–8.)

'Centrist' was our designation of the Stalin tendency (Molotov, Kaganovich, Mikoyan, Kirov, Uglanov), because its only apparent motive was the preservation of power, to which end it would resort by turns to the policies of the Right and of the Opposition. Bukharin was unstable and drifted between the two. (In fact he belonged to the Right.) The Central Committee replied to this 'foul slander' by stating that 'never, even while Lenin was alive, had it been so perfectly unanimous' (I quote verbatim). In conclusion, the Opposition openly demanded a Congress for the reform of the

Party, and the implementation of the excellent resolutions on internal democracy that had been adopted in 1921 and 1923. The *Platform*, of course, fiercely criticized the policies of the Comintern, which in China were resulting in an uninterrupted series of bloody disasters.

By a significant coincidence of dates, the Soviet Thermidor was realized in November 1927, the anniversary of the seizure of power. In ten years the exhausted Revolution had turned full circle against itself. On 7 November 1917 Trotsky, Chairman of the Petrograd Soviet, organized the victorious insurrection. On the second day of November 1927 *Pravda* published the report of his latest speech, delivered in October to the Central Committee beneath a hail of shouting. While he was speaking from the rostrum, protected on all sides by a human rampart, he was constantly overwhelmed by gross insults, duly recorded by the shorthand-writers, from Skrypnik, Chubar, Unschlicht, Goloschekin, Lomov, and several others who, well-fleshed as they might be, had no suspicion that they were really no more than the restless ghosts of future suicides and firing-squad victims: 'Menshevik! Traitor! Scoundrel! Liberal! Liar! Scum! Despicable phrasemonger! Renegade! Villain!' Yaroslavsky threw a heavy book at his head. Yevdokimov rolled up his sleeves like the old worker he was, ready to take on a fight. Trotsky's voice, intolerable, sarcastic, beat on: 'Your books are unreadable nowadays, but they are still useful for knocking people down. . . .'

Pravda reported: '*The speaker*: Behind the bureaucrats stand the renascent bourgeoisie . . . (*Commotion. Cries of* Enough!) *Voroshilov*: Enough! Shame! (*Whistling. Uproar. The speaker can no longer be heard. The Chairman rattles his bell. Whistles. Shouts*: Get off the platform! *Comrade Trotsky continues to read, but not a single word can be distinguished. The members of the Central Committee begin to leave.*)'

Zinoviev left the rostrum overwhelmed by boos after saying: 'Either you will reconcile yourselves to letting us speak to the Party or you will have to imprison us all . . . (*laughter*).' Did these revilers believe what they were shouting? They were mostly sincere men, narrow-minded and zealous. These uncultured upstarts of the Revolution's victory justified their sharp practices and privileges by reference to their service to Socialism. Outraged by the Opposition, they saw it as treason against them; which in a sense it was, since the Opposition itself belonged to the ruling bureaucracy.

We decided to take part in the November demonstrations under our own slogans. In Leningrad, adroit marshals allowed the Oppositionists to march past the official dais under the windows of the Winter Palace, before cramming them away between the caryatid statues of the Hermitage Museum and the Archives building. I ran foul of several barriers, and was unable to join the procession. I stopped for a moment to survey the multitude of poor folk carrying their red flags. From time to time an organizer turned back to his group and raised a hurrah which found a half-hearted chorus in echo. I went a few paces nearer the procession and shouted likewise—alone, with a woman and child a few steps behind me. I had flung out the names of Trotsky and Zinoviev; they were received by an astonished silence. From the procession an organizer, roused from his sluggishness, answered in a spiteful tone: '—to the dust-bin!' No one echoed him, but all at once I had the very distinct impression that I was about to be cut to ribbons. Burly characters sprang up from nowhere and eyed me up and down, a little hesitant because after all I might be some high functionary. A student walked across the clear space that had arisen all around me and came to whisper in my ear, 'Let's be off, it might take a turn for the worse. I'll go with you so that you won't be hit from behind.' I knew that all that was needed was a proclamation, in the public square of a civilized town, that a man could be struck with impunity, and instantaneously all the suppressed violence would converge on his head. I tried to rejoin my comrades by means of a detour.

On the bridge at Khalturin Street (once the Millionaya) mounted militiamen were holding back groups of onlookers. A disturbance, stationary and curiously unmalicious, was flaring up at the feet of the grey granite statues that supported the Hermitage portico. Several hundred Oppositionists were there engaged in fraternal battle against the militia. The horses' breasts were constantly pushing back the crowd, but the same human wave returned to meet them, led by a tall, beardless, open-faced soldier, Bakayev, the former head of our Cheka. I also saw Lashevich, big and thick-set, who had commanded armies, throwing himself, together with several workers, on a militiaman, dragging him from the saddle, knocking him down, and then helping him to his feet while addressing him in his commander's voice: 'How is it that you are not ashamed to charge at the workers of Leningrad?' Around him billowed his soldier's cloak, bare of insignia. His rough face, like that of some drinker painted by Franz Hals, was crimson red. The brawl went on for a long time. Around the tumultuous group, of which I was part, a stupefied silence reigned.

That evening we held a meeting attended by Bakayev and Lashe-vich, whose uniforms were torn. Excited voices exclaimed, 'Oh, you've been fighting!' 'Who against?' others asked heatedly, 'Against our own people?' At home my son, seven years old, hearing all the talk of fights, charges and arrests, was most disturbed: 'What's happening, Daddy? Have the capitalists and fascists come here?' For he already knew that Communists never got charged in the street except by capitalists or fascist police. How could I explain to him? The newspapers accused us of fomenting an insurrection.

On 16 November the expulsion of Trotsky and Zinoviev from the Central Committee was published: this ensured that they would be unable to speak at the forthcoming Congress. Zinoviev, in his small apartment in the Kremlin, feigned a supreme tranquillity. At his side, covered by glass, lay a death-mask: Lenin's head lying aban-doned on a cushion. Why, I asked, had not copies of so poignant a mask been generally distributed? Because its expression held too much in the way of grief and mortality; considerations of propa-ganda compelled a preference for bronzes with uplifted hands. Zinoviev told me that he was about to be evicted, since only Central Committee members had the right to live in the Kremlin. He left the place, taking with him the death-mask of old Ilyich.

Trotsky had slipped past the watchers on his tail, and moved house discreetly; for a whole day the G.P.U. and the Politbureau, seized by a comical fright, had asked each other what plots he was up to. He was at Beloborodov's, in the House of the Soviets on Cheremetievsky Street. I found Radek, too, in the Kremlin but being ordered out of it, in the process of sorting and destroying his papers, which were scattered in the middle of a deluge of old books heaped in confusion over the carpets. 'I'm selling all this for buttons,' he told me, 'and then I'm clearing out. We've been absolute idiots! We haven't a halfpenny, when we could have kept back some pretty spoils of war for ourselves! Today we are being killed off through lack of money. We with our celebrated revolu-tionary honesty, we've just been over-scrupulous sods of intellec-tuals.' Then, without a pause, as though it were about the most commonplace matter: 'Joffe killed himself tonight. He left a political testament addressed to Leon Davidovich, which the G.P.U. of course stole in a flash. But I got there in time, and I've fixed a nice scandal for them abroad if they don't give it back.' (Officialdom maintained that all the papers of any top-rank militant belonged, once he was dead, to the Central Committee.) Radek deplored the fact that we had broken, on Trotsky's advice, with the Group of Fifteen (Sapronov and Vladimir Smirnov), which believed that the dictatorship of the proletariat had been replaced by a bureaucratic police régime. 'They exaggerate a bit; they're not as wrong as all that, maybe, don't you agree?' 'Quite,' I said. Kamenev and Sokolnikov dropped in. This was the last time that I met Kamenev, and I was surprised to see that his beard had become all white: a handsome old man with unclouded eyes. 'Would you like some books?' Radek asked me. 'Take away whatever you like. It's all being cleared out.' As a souvenir of that day, I took away a volume of Goethe bound in red leather: *The West-Eastern Divan.*

Joffe lay outstretched on a large table in the office where he had worked in Leontievsky Street. A portrait of Lenin, larger than life-size and with an enormous forehead, dominated the room, hanging just above the bureau at which the old revolutionary had written the last pages—wonderful pages—expressing his convictions. He slept, his hands placed together, his forehead bare, his greying beard neatly combed. His eyelids were tinged with blue, his lips dark. In the small black-edged hole in his temple, someone had stuffed a plug of cotton wool. Forty-seven years—prisons, the revolt of the fleet in 1905, Siberia, escapes, exile, Congresses, Brest-Litovsk, the German Revolution, the Chinese Revolution, embassies, Tokyo, Vienna. . . . Near by, in a little room full of children's toys, Maria Mikhailovna Joffe, her face dry and burning, talked to some of the comrades in a low voice. Since the correspondent of the *Berliner Tageblatt,* Paul Scheffer, had revealed the existence of Joffe's political testament, the Central Committee consented to release a copy to its intended recipient, Trotsky.

Joffe had, now that his mind was made up, written at great length. First he affirmed his right to commit suicide: 'All my life I have been of the opinion that the political man has the duty to depart at the right time . . . having most assuredly the right to abandon life at that moment when he is aware that he can no longer be useful to the cause which he has served. . . . Thirty years ago, I adopted the philosophy that human life has no meaning except in so far as it exists in the service of something infinite—which for us is humanity; since anything else is limited, to work for the sake of anything else is devoid of meaning. . . .' The man who wrote these lines, prepared to seal them with his own blood, here touched on heights of faith where neither reason nor unreason counts any longer; there has been no better expression of the revolutionary's communion with all mankind in all ages.

'My death is a gesture of protest against those who have reduced the Party to such a condition that it is totally incapable of reacting against this disgrace' (the expulsion of Trotsky and Zinoviev from the Central Committee). 'Perhaps these two events, the great one and the little' (Joffe's own suicide) 'in occurring together, will re-awaken the Party and halt it on the path that leads to Thermidor. . . . I should be happy to think so, for then I would know that my death was not in vain. But, though I have the conviction that the hour of awakening will sound one day for the Party, I cánnot believe that it has already sounded. In the meantime, I have no doubt that today my death is more useful than the prolongation of my life.'

Joffe addressed certain friendly criticisms to Trotsky, exhorted him to intransigence against orthodox Leninism, authorized him to make changes in the text of the letter before publishing it, and entrusted him with the care of his widow and child. 'I embrace you firmly. Farewell. Moscow, 16 November 1927. Yours, A. A. Joffe.'

The letter signed, the envelope closed and placed in full view on the writing-table. Brief meditation: wife, child, city; the huge eternal universe, and myself about to go. The men of the French Revolution used to say: Death is an everlasting sleep. . . . Now to do quickly and well what has been irrevocably decided: press the automatic comfortably against the temple, there will be a shock and no pain at all. Shock: then nothing.

The path of agitation was closed to Joffe because of his sickness. For the last time at his funeral we breathed in the salty air of times long past. The Central Committee had arranged two o'clock as the time for the departure of the procession which would accompany the body from the Commissariat for Foreign Affairs to the Novo-Devichy Cemetery; working people would not be able to come as early as that. The comrades delayed the removal of the body for as long as they could. At about four o'clock a crowd, singing and slowly tramping through the snow, and bearing a few red flags, went down towards the Bolshoi Theatre. It already numbered several thousand people. We went along Kropotkin Street, the old Ostozhenka. Long ago, on this very road, I had seen Kropotkin off to the self-same cemetery, accompanied by quite different victims of persecution; now our own persecution was beginning, and I could not but see a secret justice in this. At the approaches to the cemetery, incidents began. Sapronov, his aged, emaciated face surrounded by a mane of bristling white (at the age of forty), passed along the ranks: 'Keep calm, comrades, we mustn't let ourselves be provoked. . . . We'll break through the barrier.' A man who had organized the Moscow rising of 1917 was now organizing this painful struggle at the cemetery. We marked time for a moment in front of the high embattled gateway; the Central Committee had issued an order that only twenty or so persons should be allowed to enter.

'Very well,' replied Trotsky and Sapronov, 'the coffin will go no further and the speeches will be delivered on the pavement.' For a moment it looked as though violence would break out. The representatives of the Central Committee intervened, and we all went in. For one last instant the coffin floated above men's heads in the cold silence, then it was lowered into the pit. Some functionary, whose name I forget, presented official condolences from the Central Committee. Murmurs were heard: 'That's enough! Why doesn't he clear off?' It was so ponderous. Rakovsky towered over the crowd, stout and smooth-shaven; his words snapped out, carrying a great distance; '*This flag—we will follow it—like you—right to the end—on your tomb—we swear it!*'

The country at large did not hear Joffe's pistol-shot, and his last message remained secret. The country knew nothing of our *Platform*, an illegal document. We had copies of these texts circulated, and the G.P.U. came at night to search our quarters for them. The reading of either of them became an offence punished by imprisonment—in contravention of all legal procedure, be it noted. Official Russia was organizing the tenth anniversary of the October Revolution: congresses, banquets, etc. Foreign delegates, hand-picked by the Communist Party, the Friends of the U.S.S.R. and the secret service, poured into Moscow. Among them were two young Frenchmen, ex-surrealists, singularly upright in character and unflinchingly acute in intelligence, Pierre Naville and Gérard Rosenthal.[1] They had come with me to keep watch over Joffe's body. I took them to see Zinoviev and Trotsky. The interview with Zinoviev took place in the little apartment of Sachs-Gladnev, an old Marxist scholar who was a timid, fastidious man, myopic and bearded up to his eyes. Storks in white silk were visible in flight upon a Chinese tapestry. On his bookshelves, the twenty-five volumes of Lenin. The two French comrades questioned Zinoviev on the prospects for the Opposition in the International. Zinoviev said, more or less, 'We are starting the Zimmerwald movement all over again. Think of Europe at war and that handful of internationalists gathered in a Swiss village; we are already stronger than they were. We have cadres practically everywhere. In our time, history moves faster. . . .'

As we went out, Naville, Rosenthal, and myself exchanged glances, all somewhat horrified by this crude approach. Did Zinoviev believe what he told us? I think so, more or less. But he had besides a second and a third set of possibilities kept in reserve, and these he did not disclose. Poor Sachs-Gladnev, our host for that day, disappeared in 1937, classified as a 'terrorist'.

There was not a single Oppositionist among the 1,600 delegates of the Fifteenth Party Congress; Stalin, Rykov, Bukharin, and Ordzhonikidze waxed large on the theme of uninterrupted success in all fields. Bukharin denounced the crime of Trotskyism, which was preparing the establishment of a second party; behind this second party all those who hated the régime would rally; and so the split would lead to the undermining of the dictatorship of the proletariat, and the Opposition would be no more than the spearhead of that hidden 'third force', reaction. The Opposition greatly feared this mode of reasoning, whose accuracy it admitted, and sent the Congress yet another message expressing its loyalty in spite of all. The idea that the 'third force' was already organized in the heart of the ruling bureaucracy had occurred only to an unknown young comrade named Ossovsky, who was disowned by everybody.

[1] Pierre Naville (1903–): edited the review *La Révolution Surréaliste* (1924–5); then a Trotskyist; a prolific author in politics, psychology, and Marxist sociology. Gérard Rosenthal (1903–): lawyer and writer. Active first in the surrealist movement, and then in French Trotskyism, the Maquis, and in Sartre's *Rassemblement Démocratique et Révolutionnaire*; author of *Avocat de Trotsky* (1975).

The Central Committee knew what was going on inside the Opposition. The Leningrad tendency, Zinoviev, Kamenev, Yevdokimov, and Bakayev, favoured capitulation. 'They want to hound us from the Party; we have to stay in it at all costs. Expulsion means political death, deportation, the impossibility of intervening when the coming crisis of the régime begins. . . . Nothing can be done outside the Party. Humiliations are of small account to us.' Kamenev and Zinoviev, themselves builders of the system, realized the power of the bureaucratic machine outside which nothing could live; but they failed to see the nature of the transformation that had been accomplished within this machine, which was henceforth destined to crush all vital initiative not only outside but also within the ruling Party.

The Oppositional Centre sat in ceaseless debate throughout the Congress. Our Leningrad allies finally proposed: 'Let us throw ourselves on their mercy and drink the cup of humiliation.' The following exchange of replies took place between Zinoviev and Trotsky, on slips of paper passed from hand to hand. Zinoviev: 'Leon Davidovich, the hour has come when we should have the courage to capitulate. . . .' Trotsky: 'If that kind of courage were enough, the revolution would have been won all over the world by now. . . .'

The Fifteenth Congress decreed the expulsion of the Opposition, which it termed a Menshevik or a Social-Democratic deviation. Kamenev, who had just asked from the rostrum, in crushed tones, 'Is it to be demanded that we forswear our convictions overnight?' now spoke again to say, 'We submit unreservedly to the decisions of the Congress, painful as they may be for us.' They had got rid of Trotsky: what a relief! Bukharin, inexhaustibly sprightly and mocking, used an impressive phrase: 'The iron curtain of History was falling, and you got out of its way in the nick of time. . . .'

Iron curtain indeed, and even guillotine, but so much was not yet obvious. Rykov announced that the Party would be pitiless in the use of repressive measures against those who were expelled. Thus, in a single word, Soviet legality was liquidated and freedom of opinion received its death-blow. We saw the capitulation of Zinoviev and Kamenev as political suicide, doubly so because of their wretched recantation. Rakovsky, Radek, and Muralov for the last time affirmed the unshakeable loyalty of the expellees to their Party. And in this ecstasy of loyalty the split achieved its consummation.

Expulsion from the Party, as we had repeated often enough, amounted to our 'political death'. How could living people, full of faith, ideas and devotion, be turned into political corpses? There are no two ways of doing it. The general mood was still not set for harsh forms of repression. The Central Committee entered into negotiations with the most prominent of those expelled, and the local committees did the same with the less prominent. Since they declared themselves to be loyal despite everything, they were offered posts in Bashkiria, Kazakhstan, the Far East, or the Arctic. Trotsky was supposed to go off in this way, 'of his own free will', to Alma-Ata, on the frontier of Chinese Turkestan. He would have nothing to do with the hypocrisy of friendly deportation, and was given an administrative sentence by the G.P.U. under Article 58 of the Penal Code, which dealt with counter-revolutionary plotting. In order to make the business known at least to some extent in Moscow and the country as a whole, he decided to put up a resistance.

He was lodging with Beloborodov, the Bolshevik from the Urals who in 1918 had had the task of deciding the lot of the Romanov dynasty and had even lately been People's Commissar of the Interior; this was in the House of the Soviets in Granovsky (formerly Cheremetievsky) Street. It was there that I went to take leave of him, a few days before he was forcibly taken off and deported. Comrades kept watch night and day in the street and in the building itself, themselves watched by G.P.U. agents. Motor-cyclists took note of the comings and goings of any cars. I went up by a service staircase; on one floor, a doorway with guards outside: 'Here it is.' In the kitchen my comrade Yakovin was supervising the defence arrangements and at the same time drafting a document. The Old Man received me in a little room facing the yard, in which there was only a camp-bed and a table loaded with maps of all the countries of the world. He had on an indoor jacket that had seen much wear. Vigilant, majestic, his hair standing nearly white on his head, his complexion sickly, he exhaled a fierce, caged energy. In the next room the messages he had just dictated were being copied out; the dining-room was used to receive the comrades who kept arriving from all corners of the country, with whom he held hasty conversations between calls to the telephone. At any moment it was possible that we would all be arrested. After arrest, what then? We did not know, but we hurried to make the best of these last hours, for they assuredly were the last.

My own conversation with Trotsky turned chiefly on the Opposition abroad, whose activity had at all costs to be expanded and articulated. The Old Man had just received from Paris the first numbers of *Contre le Courant*, published by my friends Magdeleine and Maurice Paz, with my co-operation. He was pleased with the tone and tendency of this publication, and advised me to leave, illegally if necessary, for France, in order to work on the spot. For a moment we examined the possibilities. 'We have begun a fight to the finish', he said, 'which may last for years and require many sacrifices. I am leaving for Central Asia: you try and leave for Europe. Good luck!' We embraced one another. The lengthening shadows helped me to throw off the spies in the street. On the next day, if it was not the one after, the crowd blocked the Old Man's departure by occupying a station. The G.P.U. made a surprise call to take him away. To make sure that there could be no lies put out about the manner of his departure, the Old Man let the political police break down the door; he refused to walk, and let himself be carried out to the car which left for a small, deserted station. I reflected that he had reached the peak of his exalted destiny. If, as we all feared, he were mysteriously assassinated, he would still be the symbol of the murdered Revolution. Alive, he would continue his struggle and his work as long as a pen remained between his fingers, a single breath in his lungs, be it in the depth of dungeons. . . .

He had gone, vanished. *Izvestia*, in minute print, announced his deportation for 'insurrectionary plotting', a fantastic accusation. Eighteen months previously, a *coup* against the Politbureau of Zinoviev, Kamenev, and Stalin would have been possible, and in our Oppositional circles we had weighed this possibility. The army and even the G.P.U. would have plumped for Trotsky if he had wished; he was always being told this. I do not know if there were any formal deliberations on this subject among the leaders of the Left Opposition, but I do know that the question was discussed (end of 1925, beginning of 1926) and it was then that Trotsky deliberately refused power, out of respect for an unwritten law that forbade any recourse to military mutiny within a Socialist régime; for it was all too likely that power won in this way, even with the noblest intentions, would eventually finish in a military and police dictatorship, which was anti-Socialist by definition. Trotsky wrote later (in 1935):

'No doubt a military *coup* against the Zinoviev-Kamenev-Stalin faction would have presented no difficulty and even caused no bloodshed; but its consequence would have been a speedier triumph for the very bureaucracy and Bonapartism against which the Left Opposition took its stand.'

Rarely has it been made more sharply obvious that the end, far from justifying the means, commands its own means, and that for the establishment of a Socialist democracy the old means of armed violence are inappropriate.

Rakovsky was sent off to Astrakhan, Preobrazhensky to the Urals, Smilga to Minussinsk in Central Siberia, Radek to North Siberia, Muralov to the Tara forests, Serebriakov, Ivan Smirnov, Sapronov, Vladimir Smirnov, Sosnovsky, and Voya Vuyovich elsewhere; where we did not know, since everything was done in secret. I had just seen Christian Rakovsky, back from the Embassy in Paris, lodging at the *Sophiiskaya Naberezhnia*, the hotel reserved for diplomats. In the corridors there one might run into Krestinsky with his forehead of fine ivory, grave and wary even in the way he walked; and Karakhan,[1] splendidly elegant however carelessly he dressed, on account of the extraordinary nobility of his features and bearing.

Rakovsky had come back from Paris penniless; without illusions and in good humour, at the age of fifty-four, he contemplated the long struggle yet to be endured. His massive, regular face expressed a composure which almost smiled. His wife was more nervous— on his account. He said that Europe was entering a period of un-resolved instability, on which it was necessary to wait. To someone who invited him to capitulate to the Central Committee, he replied gently: 'I am getting old. Why should I blot my biography?'

Now and then I saw Ivan Nikitich Smirnov, People's Commissar for Posts and Telegraphs, in his little office on the Varvarka. A little over fifty, he was tall, upright, and gaunt, with timorous but resolute eyes, an introverted manner, and a good deal of youthfulness

[1] Lev N. Karakhan (1889–1937): former Menshevik, then a Bolshevik and participant in the October Revolution; negotiator for the Soviet side at the Brest-Litovsk Treaty (1918); Ambassador to China (1923). Shot at the end of 1937 without public trial.

reflected in the grey-green gaze behind his pince-nez. When I asked him one day whether all correspondence addressed abroad was opened (postal censorship did not exist officially), he answered briskly, 'All of it is. Don't trust anything to it. There's a positive factory run by the G.P.U. in my place dealing just with that and I haven't the right to go in there.' When his Ministerial portfolio was withdrawn he was quite content. 'It does us all good to go back to the ranks for a time.' Not having a farthing, he went to sign on at the Labour Exchange register of unemployed, in his old occupation of precision engineer. He hoped naïvely that he would soon be taken on in an factory. Some snooty little official saw this tall, greying, bright-eyed innocent bending in front of his window, and writing on the form he had to fill in, under the heading *Last Employment*: 'People's Commissar for Posts and Telegraphs'. The Labour Exchange contacted the Central Committee, and the G.P.U. deported Ivan Nikitich to the Caucasian Riviera; repulsive as it was, repression was beginning mildly.

At the battle of Sviazhk in 1918, along with Trotsky and Rosengoltz, typists and engineers from the Army's special train, cooks and telegraph-operators, Ivan Smirnov had swiftly halted the routing of the Reds and the victorious offensive of the Whites under Kappel and Savinkov. On that day the newly-born Republic was saved by this handful of men. Later, in 1920–1, it was Smirnov that Lenin commissioned to restore order in the chaos of Siberia and to bring Russian Asia under Soviet control. For the young generation, he was the incarnation of the idealism of the Party, devoid of gestures or fine phrases.

Deportations were very quick to follow, and in hundreds. The revolutionaries of October 1917 had been not at all demoralized, it seemed, by their ten years of power, the last years of which had passed smoothly for the most well-known, in legations, ministries, administrative councils and posts of command. What had seemed the bourgeoisification of smartly-dressed folk was revealed as so superficial that it was with positive gaiety that they went off to rough it in the desert wastes of Central Asia and Siberia, all for the salvation of the Revolution. I felt inexpressibly reassured at the sight of their various departures. A certain number of Communists had attached themselves to the Opposition out of design, believing that in it they saw the next government; experience showed that they were very few. We lost them forever and for good riddance at the first dark turning, after a few months. In their different ways, all the Oppositionists of 1927, whether they chose endless humiliation through loyalty to the Party, or endless resistance through loyalty to Socialism, followed the same terrible road right to its end.

What a striking contrast it was between these men and the foreigners, whether noted writers, Communist delegates or distinguished liberal guests, who were in Moscow at that time to celebrate the tenth anniversary of the Revolution. And they actually offered us lessons in wisdom! Jacques Sadoul gave me a friendly lecture. We had been friends, and had in common some pleasant and stirring memories of Russia and Germany. I loved his lively, mocking intelligence, his epicurean nonchalance, his political adroitness. The French Communist Party would not let him undertake any activity, although he could have made a first-rate Parliamentary leader. His mind and temperament were those of a moderate Socialist, but his need for good living bound him to the service of the Soviet State. Old Kalinin had just decorated him with the Order of the Red Flag, and he told me how Vaillant-Couturier, wishing to play down the importance of this honour, had proposed the simultaneous decoration of certain old Communards, some of whom, for all any one really knew, might be old hoaxers.

'The leaders of the Opposition', he said, 'will be shut up in comfortable villas on the Crimea and allowed to write tomes which nobody will read. But you others, Serge—you're going to catch it!' We were having dinner at the table for foreign visitors; young Indian girls draped in dark-coloured silks, who were sitting near us, caused our conversation to wander a moment. Jacques insisted, 'You're going to get yourselves persecuted still, and life is so beautiful! Look at those figures, how charming they are, think how. . . .' And so, affectionately, we parted. Jacques, bemedalled and equipped with sinecures, returned to Paris; I made ready to start all over again: prisons, hard living, etc.[1]

Sadoul at least did not pretend to be a saint. At that time Barbusse was writing his mystical books, *Jesus* and *The Judases of Jesus*; now he was in Moscow, the guest of other Judases. I admired his *Under Fire*, and the lyricism of some pages in *Jesus* impressed me as

[1] After Serge's return to France in 1936, Sadoul vigorously defended the Moscow Trials and tried to discredit Serge's testimony.

ringing true. I found Barbusse, with whom I had had some correspondence, at the Hotel Metropole, guarded by a male interpreter-secretary (G.P.U.) and accompanied by a very pretty female doll-secretary. I had just come from the overcrowded rooms of the outer city, from which comrades disappeared every night; I saw their wives with eyes too reddened, too racked with anxiety for me to incline to any indulgence towards the great official consciences from abroad now visiting our country; moreover, I knew who had been chased out of the hotel so that the great writer could stay there.

Barbusse had a large, thin, pliant body, topped by a small, wax-like and concave head, with the thin lips of a man who has known suffering. Right from the first I saw him as a quite different kind of person; concerned above all not to be involved, not to see anything that could involve him against his will, concerned above all to disguise opinions he could no longer express openly, sliding past any direct questioning, scurrying off along all conceivable tangents, his eyes vague, his slender hands circumscribing curves in the air around obscure words like 'immensity', 'profundities', 'exaltation' —and all with the real aim of making himself the accomplice of the winning side! Since it was not yet known whether the struggle had been definitively settled, he had just dedicated a book, at great length, to Trotsky, whom he did not dare to visit for fear of compromising himself. When I told him about the persecution, he pretended to have a headache, or not to hear, or to be rising to stupendous heights: 'Tragic destiny of revolutions, immensities, profundities, yes . . . yes. . . . Ah, my friend!' My jaws shuddered as I realized that I was face to face with hypocrisy itself. Some days later I learnt that International Class-war Prisoners' Aid,[1] then run by Helena Stassova, was devoting a considerable sum to the foundation of a 'cultural' weekly in France, under the control of Barbusse. This was *Monde*. And Barbusse enrolled me in the list of co-sponsors.

In the course of our struggles I had deployed my activity in two directions: in the Centre at Leningrad, and in Moscow and abroad (mainly in France) through my writings. I belonged to the editorial board of *Clarté* in Paris. In this review I published my articles—under

[1] International Class-war Prisoners' Aid: officially a relief and defence organization, founded around 1923, 'to accord assistance to all victims of the revolutionary struggle'.

my own name—on the Platform of the Opposition and the Chinese Revolution. For some months these articles forecast events with an accuracy that overwhelmed even myself. The last one had been signed by a comrade on my behalf, but its contents are still transparent. During the Party Congress, on 11 and 12 December 1927, the lightning success of the Canton Commune had supervened in a manner peculiarly suited to refute the Opposition, which considered that the Chinese Revolution had been defeated for a long time to come. The Press was in raptures. *Pravda* published decrees, strikingly similar to those of the Russian Revolution, which had been promulgated by the Communist dictators of the Chinese city—behind whom, on the very spot, stood the envoys of the General Secretary of the C.P.S.U., Lominadze and my late comrade Heinz Neumann; these were under pressure to supply the Fifteenth Congress with triumphal telegrams. Twenty-four hours later, the torch of Canton was doused in a sea of blood; the coolies who had thought they were fighting for the cause of social justice died in thousands for the cause of an official dispatch; and the staff of the Soviet consulate, both men and women, perished by impalement. I met Preobrazhensky, who asked,

'Have you written about Canton?'

'Yes, and sent it off.'

'But you must be mad! That could cost you several years in jail. Stop it from being published. . . .'

I changed the name under which it was signed. I was expecting to be deported anyway.

At last I was summoned before the Control Commission of the Leningrad Central District, and so appeared before the Party tribunal. A dejected old worker, Karol, was the Chairman; there were a woman worker, a young man with spectacles, and two or three others, sitting around a red tablecloth (the Party committee was housed in the old baroque palace that had belonged to the Grand Duke Sergei). Karol did not seem particularly keen to expel me, and offered me several ways out of the mess. But he had to ask the treacherous and decisive question: 'What is your attitude to the decision of the Congress pronouncing the expulsion of the Opposition?'

I answered, 'In accordance with discipline, I comply with all decisions of the Party, but I regard this decision as a grave error whose consequences will be fatal if it is not speedily mended. . . .'

The woman worker in a red head-scarf stood up, and said in a stupefied voice, 'Comrade, did you really say an *error*? Do you think then that the Party Congress can be mistaken, and commit errors?'

I cited the example of German Social-Democracy voting for the war on 2 August 1914, with only Karl Liebknecht and Otto Rühle voting against. This blasphemous comparison horrified the Commission. I was expelled forthwith. Vassili Nikiforovich Chadayev was called in. He likewise was expelled after a few minutes. We went out. 'Here we are, political corpses. . . .' 'That's because there's nobody but us left alive.'

A few days passed. My bell rang at about midnight. I opened the door, and understood at once (which was not difficult): a young soldier, and a young Jew in a leather outfit. They conducted a search, and made a bee-line for some translations of Lenin. 'You're seizing those too?' I asked ironically. 'Don't joke,' replied one of the pair, 'we are Leninists too, you know.' Perfect: we were all Leninists together.

Dawn hovered over Leningrad, in a blue like the depths of the sea, when I left the house between those two comrades, who apologized for not having a car at their disposal. 'We have so much to do every night. . . .' 'I understand,' I said. My son of seven wept when I embraced him before I left, but explained to me: 'Daddy, I'm not crying because I'm afraid, it's because I'm angry.' I was taken to the old House of Arrest.

The fire-blackened brick shell of the old Palace of Justice vividly recalled the great days of liberation. But inside the squat masonry, little had changed over half a century. A warder explained to me that he had served there for twenty years: 'I took Trotsky out for his walks after the 1905 Revolution. . . .' There was still an arrogant air about him; he was ready to get back to the same job. In a corridor, during one of those waiting periods which precede incarceration, I sat next to a fine-looking young lad who recognized me and whispered in my ear: 'Arnold, the Oppositionist from the Vyborg district, and B—— and C—— have been arrested.' Good enough. What else could we have expected? Through the half-gloom, I clambered up iron stairways linking the different floors of the prison. At long intervals from each other, lamps were burning in corners on the tables of the block supervisors. A door was opened for me in the dark, thick stonework, on the fifth or sixth floor. The dingy cell was already occupied by two men; a former officer, a municipal engineer accused of having sold ice from the Neva for his own profit instead of supplying it to the Soviet; and a creature of filth, babbling madness and futile suffering, a kind of lunatic tramp who had been arrested for vagrancy near the Catholic cemetery—he had been selling little metal crosses there. Since he was of Polish origin, he was charged with espionage. This creature with a shrunken old face never washed, and never spoke, except that he was perpetually mumbling prayers. Several times a day he knelt down to pray, banging his forehead against the side of the bed. At night a rather frightening babble would wake me, and I would see him on his knees, hands pressed together. Later a little book-keeper came in, accused of having served in Admiral Kolchak's White army. The examining magistrate declared that he recognized him as a White officer. It was all inhumanly grotesque.

I discovered that the prison was packed with victims, all targets for the hatred of functionaries who were obsessives, maniacs, and torturers by profession. In the never-ending twilight I read Dostoevsky once again; it had been kindly passed on to me by some harmless sectarian convicts who ran the library. The servant-lads gleefully brought us soup ('bum-wash' they called it) twice a day, uneatable at first but awaited impatiently from the fourth day on. One of these lads, a strapping, fair-haired boy with a pale smile, did not appear one morning, and the others had sullen faces. We knew that the absentee had been shot during the night. He had not expected it so late; the sentence had been on him for months and he had assumed he was pardoned. They came to fetch him a little before dawn. 'Say good-bye to your mates, and let's have no trouble, eh!' He was a boy from the frontier-zone, charged with crossing illegally to Poland and back again. His death did not even serve as an example since it was kept secret.

A shirtmaker from the Sadovaya, accused of tax evasion, was next door to us; he skipped over the parapet in the corridor, jumped into space and found his eternal rest. Someone else near us tried to hang himself, and another to open his veins. . . . We heard only faint echoes of these tragedies. Our days went by peacefully, without any particular anxiety or peevishness, since there were two of us, out of the three in the cell, to keep some sense of balance; we discussed Socialism. In my screeds to the Procurator I invoked the Constitution and Soviet law: a pretty joke.

My arrest had caused some commotion in Paris, and so was considered awkward in high circles. I had made up my mind not to agree to any recantation; they were content with an undertaking from me not to engage in any 'anti-Soviet activity'. It was a revolting distortion of language, for we had nothing whatever to do with anything anti-Soviet.

I shall never forget the wonderful sweetness of the young greenery along the Fontanka embankments, in the white night when I returned home after seven or eight weeks' absence. The porter of the house had explained my arrest very plausibly. 'The same under the old régime,' he said. 'The intellectuals were always arrested like this, just before the first of May. . . .' In Paris, Vaillant-Couturier reported in *L'Humanité* that I had been treated with the greatest possible consideration while in prison. Barbusse sent me embarrassed letters apologizing for the fact that, on learning of my arrest, he had deleted my name from the list of sponsors of *Monde*.

Chadayev, in whom Paris showed no interest, remained in jail for six months; then a personal friend who was a member of the Government got him out. Since he did not recant, his presence in Leningrad was deemed undesirable. The *Krassnaya Gazeta* sent him on an assignment to investigate the *kolkhozes* of the Kuban. His life was to end just when he believed that it was starting anew, in the enthusiasm of a fresh departure. We spent several hours rowing on the lake at Dietskoe Selo, among the scenery of the Imperial Park. Vassili Nikiforovich sang me the praises of prison, that benevolent retreat where a man takes stock of himself. He had his doubts about the regeneration of the Party, which many people believed to be now going on.

In the Kuban he pounced, with his writing-pads, his inquisitive eyes and his precise questions, upon all kinds of highly dubious rackets. Racket in building the harbour at Tuapse, racket in the layout of the beaches, racket in the repairing of roads, racket in the collectivization of agriculture!

'Banditry' on the dark roads intervened to dispose of these indiscreet interrogators. On 26 August 1928, on a summer evening filled with the cicadas' song, the local authorities vigorously pressed Chadayev to go off in a carriage with a number of other passengers to the neighbouring market-town. It was a night journey across the steppe and the fields of maize. A militiaman accompanied the caravan; he was the first to make himself scarce when rough voices came from out of the night: '*Stoy!* Halt!' Chadayev's carriage was the only one held back by the roadside. The coachman heard my poor Vassili arguing with the bandits: 'What's the matter with you? We're all human beings. What is it?' All I ever saw of him again were some dreadful photographs: the dumdum bullets, fired from sawn-off rifles, had harrowed his face and chest monstrously. We wanted to give him a funeral in the town that he loved. Was he not a fighter of the Year Seventeen? The Leningrad Committee opposed this: was he not expelled? His murderers remained unknown, naturally. A stone with an inscription, erected on the spot where he died, was broken into fragments.

THE YEARS OF RESISTANCE
1928–1933

These constituted five years of resistance waged by a solitary man—surrounded by his family, that is to say by weak creatures—against the relentless, overwhelming pressure of a totalitarian system. For his daily bread, his ration-card, his lodging, his fuel in the harsh Russian winter, the individual is dependent on the Party-State, against which he is totally defenceless. And he who, in the name of freedom of opinion, stands out against the Party-State, bears the brand of 'suspect' wherever he goes. The small amount of liberty that he still has left, and even his own courage (which seems quite mad), stand for him as a source of astonishment, mingled with anxiety.

The leaders of the now vanquished Opposition hoped to set up a clandestine organization strong enough to achieve rehabilitation in the Party at some future date with freedom of speech and propaganda. I did not share this illusion. I said that illegal methods would fail for two reasons: the unlimited power of the secret police would crush everything—and our own ideological and sentimental loyalty to the Party made us vulnerable both to political manœuvrings and, even more, to police provocation. I declared that, rather than allow ourselves to be bundled away into illegality, we should defend, absolutely openly, our right to exist, think, and write; we should form, also quite openly, an opposition which was strictly loyal (as being without any organization) but also strictly intransigent. It was a purely academic discussion, since both alternatives were equally impossible.

At the beginning of 1928, Alexandra Bronstein and myself were the only known Oppositionists in Leningrad still at liberty; in Moscow, Andreu Nin was free, but he had 'resigned' from the

Secretaryship of the Red International of Labour Unions, and was kept under close watch in the Lux Hotel. His status as a foreigner saved him from imprisonment. Of the Russians, Boris Mikhailovich Eltsin, a Bolshevik since 1903 and founder-member of the Party, former Chairman of the Soviet in Ekaterinberg (Sverdlovsk) in 1917, was also free because the G.P.U. needed his presence in the capital for a while. In an effort to maintain the connexions and inner life of the tiny circles of militants, old Eltsin, a sick man, confided in a young, vigorous—and invulnerable—fellow-activist, one Mikhail Tverskoy, who was an agent of the G.P.U. Tverskoy drew up idiotic leaflets, shortly to be classed as 'anti-Soviet' documents—the very purpose for which they were written. After having had the last Oppositional sympathizers in the Moscow factories arrested, he came to us in Leningrad in order, he said, to 'help us re-organize'. Alexandra Bronstein and myself refused to receive him. Without our being able to stop him he speedily set up a shadow-organization consisting of fifty or so workers, only to have it rally noisily to the 'general line' within two months, while those who resisted were thrown into jail. This police manœuvre was repeated in all the working-class centres. It was made easier by the moral confusion of the Communists. Oppositionists and officials outbid each other in loyalty to the Party, the Oppositionists being by far the most sincere.

Nobody was willing to see evil in the proportions it had reached. As for the idea that the bureaucratic counter-revolution had attained power, and that a new despotic State had emerged from our own hands to crush us, and reduce the country to absolute silence—nobody, nobody in our ranks was willing to admit it. From the depths of his exile in Alma-Ata Trotsky affirmed that this system was still ours, still proletarian, still Socialist, even though sick; the Party that was excommunicating, imprisoning, and beginning to murder us, remained our Party, and we still owed everything to it: we must live only for it, since only through it could we serve the Revolution. We were defeated by Party patriotism: it both provoked us to rebel and turned us against ourselves.

Three months after our expulsion, the grain crisis that we had forecast broke out, endangering supplies to the towns and the army. The peasants, having paid off their taxes, now refused to deliver their grain to the State because they were not being paid enough for it. The Central Committee decreed requisitions, applying, quite improperly, Article 107 of the Penal Code on concealment of stocks. Detachments of young Communists scoured the countryside, stripping the fields of their grain, flax, tobacco, or cotton, depending on the district. Just as in the years of the Civil War, Communists were found at the roadsides with their skulls split open. The stacks of confiscated grain were set on fire. There was no fodder at all; the countryfolk besieged the bakeries in the towns so that they could feed their livestock with black bread bought at the regulation price.

The requisitioning was no more than an expedient. The real policy had been outlined by Molotov at the Fifteenth Party Congress: the development of collective agricultural cultivation (*kolkhozes*) or of State grain-factories (*sovkhozes*). A slow development was envisaged, spread over many years, since collective agriculture could only replace piecemeal cultivation stage by stage as the State supplied the farms with the equipment that was indispensable to mechanized cultivation. But, as it was, war had been declared on the peasantry through the requisitioning. If the State confiscates the grain, what is the use of sowing? In the following spring, statistics will show that the area under wheat has shrunk: a peasants' strike. There is only one way of forcing them: compulsory co-operatives, administered by the Communists. Will persuasion succeed? The independent farmer who has resisted the agitation, or rather coercion, turns out to be freer and better fed than his fellows. The Government draws the conclusion that collectivization must be total and abrupt. However, the folk of the soil are putting up a bitter defence. How can their resistance be broken? By expropriation and mass deportation of the rich peasants or *kulaks* and of any that may be classified as *kulaks*. This is what is called 'the liquidation of the *kulaks* as a class'.

Will it ever be known how terrible was the disorganization of agriculture that resulted? Rather than hand over their livestock to the *kolkhoz*, the peasants slaughter the beasts, sell the meat and make boots out of the leather. Through the destruction of its livestock the country passes from poverty to famine. Bread-cards in the cities, black market, a slump in the rouble and in real wages. Internal passports have to be issued, to keep the skilled manpower in the factories against its will. Since total collectivization is heading towards disaster, its completion is declared when it has reached 68 per cent., and even then too late, in March 1930, when famine and terror are at their height.

The women came to deliver the cattle confiscated by the *kolkhoz*, but made a rampart of their own bodies around the beasts: 'Go on, bandits, shoot!' And why should these rebels not be shot at? In a Kuban market-town whose entire population was deported, the women undressed in their houses, thinking that no one would dare make them go out naked; they were driven out as they were to the cattle-trucks, beaten with rifle-butts. Sheboldayev of the Central Committee was in charge of the mass deportation in this region, never suspecting that, for his very enthusiasm, he would be shot in 1937. Terror reigned in the smallest hamlets. There were more than 300 centres of peasant insurrection going on simultaneously in Soviet Eurasia.

Trainloads of deported peasants left for the icy North, the forests, the steppes, the deserts. These were whole populations, denuded of everything; the old folk starved to death in mid-journey, new-born babies were buried on the banks of the roadside, and each wilderness had its crop of little crosses of boughs or white wood. Other populations, dragging all their mean possessions on wagons, rushed towards the frontiers of Poland, Rumania, and China and crossed them—by no means intact, to be sure—in spite of the machine-guns. And in a long message to the Government, couched in a noble style, the population of Abkhazia pleaded for permission to emigrate to Turkey.

A Russian scholar, Prokopovich, made the following calculation from official Soviet statistics—at a time, be it noted, when the statisticians were being imprisoned and shot. Up to 1929 the number of peasants households grew uninterruptedly:

> 1928: 24,500,000 households
> 1929: 25,800,000 households

When collectivization ended in 1936, there were no more than 20,600,000 households. In seven years over 5,000,000 families disappeared.

The transport system was worn down, and all plans for industrialization were turned inside-out to cope with the new demands. It was, to quote Boris Souvarine's expression, 'the anarchy of the plan'. Agricultural technicians and experts were brave in denouncing the blunders and excesses; they were arrested in thousands and made to appear in huge sabotage-trials so that responsibility might be unloaded on somebody. The rouble was in the process of disappearing; hoarders of silver coin were shot (1930). Crisis in the coal industry, Shakhty sabotage-trial, fifty-three technicians in court, executions. Naturally there is a meat shortage: execution of Professor Karatygin and his forty-seven co-defendants for sabotage of the meat supply—an execution without trial. On the day of the massacre of these forty-eight men, Moscow received Rabindranath Tagore; there were speeches about abundance and the new humanism, and a splendid official reception. In November 1930 there was the trial of the 'Industrial Party': Ramzin, the engineer and *agent provocateur*, who was pardoned, confessed to being its leader and to plotting military intervention against the Soviet Union in London, Paris, and Warsaw. It was raving madness, and five were shot.

At the same period a 'Peasant Party' including Professors Makarov and Kondratiev, who were opposed to total collectivization, was liquidated off-stage. There was the lunatic trial of the old Socialists (of Menshevik inclinations) in the Planning Commission: Groman, Ginsberg, the historian Sukhanov, Rubin, and Sher. There was the secret trial of the officials of the Finance Commissariat, Yurovsky and others. There was the secret trial of bacteriologists, several of whom died in prison. There was the execution of the thirty-five leading figures in the Commissariat of Agriculture; among them, several noted Old Communists (Konar, Wolfe, the People's Vice-Commissar, and Kovarsky). There was the secret trial of physicists and the deportation of Academician Lazarev. There was the secret trial of the historians Tarle, Platonov, and Kareyev. . . .

The accusation of sabotage which was directed at thousands, or rather tens of thousands of technicians, was in general a monstrous slander, justified solely by the need to find culprits for an economic situation that was now insupportable. Close examination of a whole number of cases proves this irrefutably, apart from the fact that the patriotism of the technicians was constantly appealed to in the course of wringing confessions out of them. The whole business of industrialization proceeded in the midst of such chaos, and under an authoritarian system of such rigidity, that it was possible to find 'sabotage' in any place, at any moment. I may add that in my experience the whole mentality of the technician is quite antagonistic to sabotage, dominated as it is by love of technique and a job well done. Even in these hellish conditions Soviet technical experts were full of enthusiasm for their tasks and, all things considered, worked wonders. The 'Industrial Party', just like the 'Peasant Party' of the leading agronomists—was no more than a police invention sanctioned by the Politbureau. All that there was in fact was a fairly widespread 'technocratic mentality'. Technicians saw themselves as indispensable and as distinctly superior to the men in the Government.

Many of them were punished for having actually foreseen the disastrous consequences of certain Government decisions. The old Socialist Groman was arrested after having had a sharp quarrel at the Planning Commission with Miliutin. Groman, at the end of his tether, shouted that the country was being led to the abyss.[1]

Although foreign espionage did exist, the technicians' plotting with the governments of London, Paris and Warsaw, and with the Socialist International, was ascribable purely and simply to conspiracy-psychosis and political deception. In the so-called 'Menshevik Centre' trial, the accused (who of course confessed) allowed themselves to be caught in a flagrant lie by inventing, all to order, a journey to the Soviet Union by the old Menshevik leader Abramovich. Later, the historian Sukhanov, when incarcerated in the Isolator of Verkhne-Uralsk, had documents passed around among the political prisoners relating how the text of confessions had been laid down for him and his fellow-defendants by the G.P.U. instructors, how an appeal to their patriotism had been combined with threats of death, and what kind of pledges their inquisitors had given them. (Sukhanov undertook lengthy hunger-strikes to obtain the liberty he had been promised; he disappeared in 1934.) During the 'Menshevik Centre' trial, I met people every day who were connected with the accused, and I was in a position to trace, line by line, the progression of the lie in their evidence.

The Politbureau knew the truth perfectly well. The trials served one purpose only: to manipulate public opinion at home and abroad. The sentences were prescribed by the Politbureau itself. The G.P.U. organized Labour Departments for the condemned

[1] Valentin G. Groman (1873–?): former Menshevik; a statistician and economist, he was one of the chief inspirers of a planned economy and occupied a number of important planning posts with Gosplan under the Soviet régime.

technicians, which continued working for industrialization. Some of the technicians were promptly rehabilitated. Once I had dinner with an outstanding expert in energetics who, in the space of twenty months, had been condemned to death, pardoned, sent to a concentration-camp (a Labour Department), rehabilitated, and decorated. The physicist Lazarev was similarly rehabilitated. The historian and Academician Tarle, the only non-Marxist Soviet historian of repute, spent long months in prison and was deported to Alma-Ata; today (1942) he is the most official of all historians in the Soviet Union. The engineer Ramzin, an accomplice (if it is to be believed) of Poincaré and Winston Churchill in the 'preparation of war against the U.S.S.R.' and condemned to the supreme penalty, was pardoned, continued his scientific work in mild captivity and was rehabilitated at the beginning of 1936, with his principal co-defendants, for distinguished services to industrialization.

On the other hand the old Socialists of the pretended 'Menshevik Centre' disappeared.

I was on very close terms with several of the scientific staff at the Marx-Engels Institute, headed by David Borisovich Riazanov, who had created there a scientific establishment of noteworthy quality. Riazanov, one of the founders of the Russian working-class movement, was, in his sixtieth year, at the peak of a career whose success might appear exceptional in times so cruel. He had devoted a great part of his life to a severely scrupulous inquiry into the biography and works of Marx—and the Revolution heaped honour on him: in the Party his independence of outlook was respected. Alone, he had never ceased to cry out against the death-penalty, even during the Terror, never ceased to demand the strict limitation of the rights of the Cheka and its successor, the G.P.U. Heretics of all kinds, Menshevik Socialists or Oppositionists of Right or Left, found peace and work in his Institute, provided only that they had a love of knowledge. He was still the man who had told a Conference to its face: 'I am not one of those Old Bolsheviks who for twenty years were described by Lenin as old fools. . . .'

I had met him a number of times; stout, strong-featured, beard and moustache thick and white, attentive eyes, Olympian forehead, stormy temperament, ironic utterance. . . . Of course his heretical colleagues were often arrested, and he defended them, with all due discretion. He had access to all quarters and the leaders were a little afraid of his frank way of talking. His reputation had just been officially recognized in a celebration of his sixtieth birthday and his life's work when the arrest of the Menshevik sympathizer Sher, a neurotic intellectual who promptly made all the confessions that any one pleased to dictate to him, put Riazanov beside himself with rage. Having learnt that a trial of old Socialists was being set in hand, with monstrously ridiculous confessions foisted on them, Riazanov flared up and told member after member of the Polit-bureau that it was a dishonour to the régime, that all this organized frenzy simply did not stand up and that Sher was half mad anyway.

During the trial of the so-called 'Menshevik Centre', the defendant Rubin, one of Riazanov's protégés, suddenly brought his name into the case, accusing him of having hidden in the Institute documents of the Socialist International concerned with war against the Soviet Union! Everything that was told to the audience was engineered in advance, so this sensational revelation was inserted to order. Summoned on that very night before the Politbureau, Riazanov had a violent exchange with Stalin. 'Where are the documents?' shouted the General Secretary. Riazanov replied vehemently, 'You won't find them anywhere unless you've put them there yourself!' He was arrested, jailed and deported to a group of little towns on the Volga, doomed to penury and physical collapse; librarians received the order to purge his writings and his editions of Marx from their stocks. To anybody who knew the policy of the Socialist International and the character of its leaders, Fritz Adler, Vandervelde, Abramovich, Otto Bauer, and Bracke,[1] the fabricated charge was utterly and grotesquely implausible. If it had to be admitted as true, Riazanov deserved to die as a traitor; but they merely exiled him. As I write this book I learn that he died a couple of years ago (in 1940?) alone and captive, nobody knows where.

Was there then no basis of truth at all in the trial of the 'Menshevik Centre'? Nikolai Nikolayevich Sukhanov (Himmer), a Menshevik won over to the Party, a member of the Petrograd Soviet from its inception in 1917, who had written ten volumes of valuable notes on the beginnings of the Revolution and worked in the

---

[1] Otto Bauer (1881–1938): Austrian Socialist, friend and colleague of Fritz Adler; Foreign Minister 1918–19; exiled after the destruction of the Austrian Left in 1934. Alexandre Bracke (Desrousseaux) (1861–1956): French Socialist and Deputy; editor of *Le Populaire* in 1936; a considerable classical scholar.

Planning Commissions with his fellow-defendants Groman, Ginsberg, and Rubin, did have a kind of *salon*, in which talk between intimates was very free and the situation in the country as of 1930 was judged to be utterly catastrophic, as it undeniably was. In this circle, escape from the crisis was envisaged in terms of a new Soviet Government, combining the best brains of the Party's Right (Rykov, Tomsky, and Bukharin, perhaps), certain veterans of the Russian revolutionary movement and the legendary army chief Blücher. It must be emphasized that for practically three years between 1930 and 1934, the new totalitarian régime maintained itself by sheer terror, against all rational expectations and with every appearance, all the time, of imminent collapse.

From 1928-9 onwards, the Politbureau turned to its own use the great fundamental ideas of the now expelled Opposition (excepting, of course, that of working-class democracy!) and implemented them with ruthless violence. We had proposed a tax on the rich peasants—they were actually liquidated! We had proposed limitations and reforms of N.E.P.—it was actually abolished! We had proposed industrialization—it was done, on a colossal scale which we, 'super-industrializers' as we were dubbed, had never dared to dream of, which moreover inflicted immense suffering on the country. At the height of the world economic crisis foodstuffs were exported at the lowest possible price to build up gold reserves, and the whole of Russia starved.

Beginning in those years, a good many Oppositionists rallied to the 'general line' and renounced their errors since, as they put it, 'After all, it is our programme that is being applied'; also because the Republic was in danger, and finally because it was better to capitulate and build factories than to defend lofty principles in the enforced indolence of captivity. Piatakov had been a pessimist for years. He kept saying that the European and Russian working class was going through a long period of depression, and that nothing could be expected from it for a long time; more, that he had only engaged in battle for the Opposition from a sense of principle and out of his personal attachment to Trotsky. He capitulated, to be put in charge of banking and industrialization. Ivan Nikitich Smirnov told one of my friends something like this: 'I can't stand inactivity. I want to build! In its own barbaric and sometimes stupid way, the Central Committee is building for the future. Our ideological differences are of small importance before the construction of great new industries.' He capitulated. So did Smilga. The movement of surrender to the Central Committee in 1928–9 carried off the greater part of the 5,000 Oppositionists under arrest (there had been five to eight thousand arrested).

Six months after the expulsion of the Party's left wing—us, that is—the Politbureau and the Central Committee was torn by savage quarrels: the right-wing Opposition, Rykov, Tomsky, and Bukharin, ranged itself against Stalin, against his policy of forced collectivization, against the dangers of premature industrialization (with no material basis and with famine as its price), against the ways of totalitarianism. The head of the G.P.U., Henry Grigorievich Yagoda, was another sympathizer of the Right. From personal motives whose nature is still obscure Kalinin and Voroshilov, despite their right-wing beliefs, gave a majority to Stalin and Molotov.

The Right Opposition was more of a state of mind than an organization; at certain junctures it included the great majority of officials, and enjoyed the sympathy of the whole nation. However, inspired as it was by men of moderate temperament, who on several occasions were insufficiently decisive, it suffered itself to be constantly outmanœuvred, slandered and finally annihilated. At the end of 1928, Trotsky wrote to us from his exile at Alma-Ata to the effect that, since the Right represented the danger of a slide towards capitalism, we had to support the 'Centre'—Stalin—against it. Stalin sounded the leaders of the Left Opposition even while they were in prison: 'Will you support me against them if I have you rehabilitated in the Party?' We discussed the question with some uncertainty. In the Isolator, that is the prison, at Suzdal, Boris Mikhailovich Eltsin demanded that a conference of expelled Oppositionists be summoned as a precondition, and raised the issue of Trotsky's return. The negotiations got no further than this.

In 1929, the hard core of our Opposition is reduced to the following: Trotsky; Muralov, in exile on the Irtysh, in the Tara forests; Rakovsky, now a petty planning official in Barnaul, Central Siberia; Fedor Dingelstedt in a market-town in Central Siberia; Maria Mikhailovna Joffe in Central Asia; a fine team of youngsters in prison, including Eleazar Solntsev, Vassili Pankratov, Grigory Yakovin. In Moscow Andreu Nin is at liberty, in Leningrad Alexandra Bronstein and myself. Leon Sosnovsky is in jail. Inside the prisons a few hundred comrades keep up hunger-strikes and struggles that are sometimes bloody; in deportation a few hundred others wait for prison to come their way. Our intellectual activity is prodigious, our political action nil. Altogether there must be less than a thousand of us. Between us and the 'capitulators' there is no contact, only a sharp and growing hostility.

As for the two irreconcileables, Timofey Vladimirovich Sapronov and Vladimir Mikhailovich Smirnov, the first has been deported to the Crimea, ill as he is, and the second to an Isolator where he is slowly dying.

Panaït Istrati[1] and myself paid a visit to Mikhail Ivanovich Kalinin, the President of the Central Soviet Executive. We were going to see him about certain criminal measures that were in hand against my relatives. Kalinin worked in a small, brightly-lit office, very soberly furnished, in an unpretentious house next to the Kremlin. His skin was weathered, his eyes lively, his goatee lank and groomed—an old slyboots of a peasant intellectual. We talked with a fair amount of freedom. I asked him the reason for these arrests of Oppositionists, which were contrary to the Constitution. He gazed calmly straight into our faces, putting on his most sympathetic air, and said, 'That's quite untrue . . . there are so many tales being put about! We have arrested only those involved in anti-Soviet conspiracy, no more than a few dozen people. . . .' Were we to call the Head of State a liar? But could he have said anything else to us? Outside in the street Panaït remarked, 'Pity, because he has a fine face on him, that old slyboots. . . .'

In these days there died in a Moscow jail, after a hunger-strike lasting either fifty-four or thirty days according to different reports, Georgi Valentinovich Butov, one of Trotsky's former secretaries; they had tried to extort confessions from him which might be used to implicate the Old Man. Let us pass this by in silence, please! Above all, let us not be embittered by the misfortunes of individuals! Only politics counts. In the October and November of 1929, I made

[1] Panaït Istrati (1884–1935): Rumanian novelist; led a vagabond existence for much of life life and won a reputation as 'a Balkan Gorky'. Conducted revolutionary work with Christian Rakovsky; disillusioned with Soviet Russia after a sixteen-months' stay in 1927–8; returned to Rumania and, destitute, offered all his rights as an author to King Carol's Government in return for a pension. It is not clear whether the bargain was accepted; in any case, Istrati died of tuberculosis in great privation.

some effort to shed light on another tragedy, this time in Leningrad, but with no success. On 21 October Albert Heinrichsohn had been arrested, one of our ordinary working-class comrades from the Red Triangle factory, a militant of 1905 and a Civil War Communist. Ten days later his wife was called to the House of Arrest, where all she found of him was a mutilated corpse, its mouth torn. The superintendent explained to the widow that the prisoner had committed suicide, and handed her a 100 rouble note. . . . The Party committees promised an inquiry, which they hushed up. We made our own inquiry, which took me to a tenement of old St. Petersburg: six floors of overpopulated apartments. The dead man's small son told us how he had been taken off there, to rooms which he described in detail, to attend a meeting of 'Daddy's friends'; these 'comrades' had interrogated him at length about the activities and statements of his father. G.P.U.? Or hysteria? We solved nothing.

A few months passed and there was the mysterious case of Blumkin. I had known and loved Yakov Grigorievich Blumkin since 1919. Tall, bony, his powerful face encircled by a thick black beard, his eyes dark and resolute, Blumkin then lived next to Chicherin in a freezing room at the Metropole. Recovering from an illness, he was making ready to conduct certain confidential assignments in the East. In the year before, even while the Foreign Ministry officials were assuring the Germans that he had been shot, the Central Committee was placing him in command of perilous operations in the Ukraine.

On 6 June 1918 Blumkin—then nineteen years old—had, on the orders of the Left Social-Revolutionary Party, killed the German Ambassador in Moscow, Count Mirbach. He and his comrade Andreyev had been sent along by the Cheka to look into the case of a German officer; the Ambassador received them in a small drawing-room. 'I was talking to him, looking into his eyes, and saying to myself: I must kill this man. . . . My briefcase contained a revolver among all the documents. "Wait," I said, "here are the papers," and I fired point-blank. Mirbach, wounded, fled across the big drawing-room, and his secretary flopped down behind the armchairs. In the drawing-room Mirbach fell, and then I threw my grenade hard on the marble floor. . . .'

It was the day of the Left Social-Revolutionary rising against the Bolsheviks and the Brest-Litovsk peace; the insurgents hoped to resume the revolutionary war, fighting side by side with the Allies. They lost. Blumkin also told me, 'We knew that Germany, as disintegrated as she was, could not start a new war against Russia. We wanted to give her a stinging reverse. We were banking on the effect of this action in Germany itself.' Again: 'We were negotiating with German revolutionaries who asked us to help them organize an attempt on the Kaiser's life. The attempt fell through because we insisted that the principal actor should be a German. They didn't find anyone.'

A little later, in the Ukraine, towards the time his comrade Bonskoy would be assassinating Field-Marshal Eichhorn, Blumkin rallied to the Bolshevik Party. His late party was now outlawed. His late comrades fired several bullets into him and came to throw a grenade into the hospital ward where he was; he threw it back out of the window. In 1920–1 he was sent to Persia to start a revolution, together with Kuchik Khan, in Gilan on the Caspian coast.[1] And I met him again in Moscow, in the uniform of the Staff Academy, more poised and virile than ever, his face solid and smooth-shaven, the haughty profile of an Israelite warrior. He declaimed lines from Firdousi[2] and published articles on Foch in *Pravda*. 'My "Persian tale"? There were a few hundred of us ragged Russians down there. One day we had a telegram from the Central Committee: *Cut your losses, revolution in Iran now off*. . . . But for that we would have got to Teheran.' I saw him later on his return from Ulan Bator, where he had just organized the army of the People's Republic of Mongolia. The Red Army's Secret Service entrusted him with missions in India and Egypt. He stayed in a small apartment in the Arbat quarter, bare except for a rug and a splendid stool, a gift from some Mongol prince; and crooked sabres hung over his bottles of excellent wine.

Blumkin belonged to the Opposition, without having any occasion to make his sympathies very public. Trilisser, the head of the G.P.U.'s secret service abroad, Yagoda, and Menzhinsky were well acquainted with his views. All the same, they sent him to

[1] Gilan is the northernmost province of Persia. In May 1920 an independent Soviet Republic was established there under Kuchik Khan, with Soviet recognition and military assistance. A march on Teheran was initiated, but repudiated by the Soviet Government which withdrew its troops. In October 1921 Persian troops entered Gilan and hanged Kuchik as a rebel.

[2] Firdousi: Persian national epic poet (tenth century A.D.).

Constantinople to spy on Trotsky—perhaps also to arrange some plot against the Old Man. Did Blumkin turn the tables by becoming Trotsky's bodyguard? At all events he met the Old Man in Constantinople and undertook to bring us a message from him, which was actually quite harmless. In Moscow he became suddenly aware of being watched at every turn: this surveillance was so minute that he knew he was lost. There is good ground for supposing that a woman G.P.U. agent called Rosenzweig, who had become a confidante of his, betrayed him. When he was on the point of being arrested, knowing that the code of the Secret Service left him without a chance, he went to see Radek. Radek advised him to go at once to the Chairman of the Central Control Commission, Ordzhonikidze, a harsh but scrupulous character who was now the only man who could save his life. Radek arranged the meeting—too late. Blumkin was arrested in the street. He betrayed nobody. After being condemned to death by the G.P.U.'s secret Collegium, I know that he requested and obtained a fortnight's reprieve to write his memoirs; they made a first-rate book. . . . When they came to take him to the execution-cellar, he asked if the newspapers would publish the news of his decease; they promised him this—a promise which, of course, was never kept. The news of Blumkin's execution was published only in Germany. Leon Sedov spoke to me later of Blumkin's secretary, an enthusiastic young French Communist of bourgeois origin who was shot at Odessa. Sedov's recollection of this young man was full of warmth; but my overburdened memory has let his name slip.

I can see us now, the few survivors that we were, in the gardens of the Marx-Engels Institute, gathered around a charming girl-comrade, assembling the different hints and scraps we had on the last days and death of Blumkin. Should we now, we asked one another, publish the letters of Zinoviev and Kamenev which told how in 1924 the General Secretary had suggested that they get rid of Trotsky 'by a Florentine technique'? Would we not cast discredit on the régime by publishing this abroad? I was of the opinion that, whatever else, the information about 'Florentine techniques' should be sent to our comrades in the West. I do not know if this was done.

Duplicity began its rule over the Party: a natural consequence of the stifling of free opinion by tyranny. The 'capitulator' comrades

kept their ideas, of course, and met together; as they were absolutely forbidden to participate in political life, they amounted to
no more than a circle viewed with suspicion by the Politbureau. I
came across Smilga, who gave me an admirable account of the way
these men were thinking. (This was in 1929.) He was sore at the
pin-pricks that Trotsky had dealt him in *My Life*, and shocked by
the apotheosis of Stalin; but he said:

'The Opposition is all astray with its sterile bitterness. One's
duty is to work with and in the Party. Think of what is at stake in
these struggles: the agony of a nation of 160,000,000 souls. See how
the Socialist revolution is already advancing over its predecessor,
the bourgeois revolution: with Danton, Hébert, Robespierre, and
Barras, all discussion ended on the guillotine. I am back from
Minussinsk. What do our petty deportations amount to? Oughtn't
we all to be walking around by now with our heads tucked underneath our arms?' Again: 'If only we can bring off this victory'
(collectivization) 'over the antiquated peasantry, without exhausting
the working-class, it will be quite splendid. . . .' He had his doubts
about it, to tell the truth. (He disappeared into jail in 1932, where he
died, doubtless after torture, in 1937.) The programme that we
hard-core Oppositionists have drawn up will not change now till
1937: the reform of the Soviet State by a return to working-class
democracy. The few of us that there are in the hard core are the
only ones to be saved from double-dealing by our intransigence;
but we too are just 'political corpses'.

Within the Party, the Right resists expulsion, and the Zinoviev
tendency, reinstated but humbled, keeps its forces intact. One of
the last actions of our Moscow 'Centre' had been the publication,
in 1928, of pamphlets which told of the confidential discussions
between Bukharin and Kamenev. Bukharin, who was still a member
of the Politbureau and the Party's official theoretician, said, 'What
can one do before an adversary of this type: a Genghis Khan, a
debased product of the Central Committee? If the country perishes,
we all perish [i.e. the Party]. If the country manages to recover,
he twists around in time and we still perish.' Bukharin also told
Kamenev, 'Nobody must know of this conversation. Don't phone me,
the line is tapped. I'm being shadowed and you are being watched.'
Our 'Centre' (B. M. Eltsin) may very well have much to answer for
in publishing these documents. From that moment onward, the

Right of Bukharin, Rykov, and Tomsky is *de facto* ousted from power.

In these critical years plot will succeed plot, in a Party where anyone who allows himself to think in terms of the national interest has to have two faces, one for official use and one for other purposes. I shall merely enumerate. At the end of 1930 the President of the Council of People's Commissars of the R.S.F.S.R., Sergei Ivanovich Syrtsov, disappears with a whole group of leaders accused of opposition (and his successor, Danil Yegorovich Sulimov, will later suffer the same fate). Together with Syrtsov go Lominadze, Shatskin, and Yan Sten, alias the 'Young Stalinist Left'. (Lominadze will kill himself around 1935; Yan Sten, classed as a 'terrorist', will be shot around 1937.)

At the end of 1932 the 'Riutin group' is imprisoned. Riutin, once the Secretary of the Moscow Committee, who had organized gangs of thugs against us, is close to several intellectuals of the Bukharin tendency, such as Slepkov, Maretsky, Astrov, and Eichenwald (all 'Red professors') and also with the old Bolshevik worker Kayurov. They have drawn up a programme of reform for nation and Party, had it distributed in some Moscow factories, and communicated its contents to Zinoviev, Kamenev, and several of us. It is a merciless indictment of the policies of the General Secretary, and concludes by calling for a fresh departure, with the implication that all expelled members, including Trotsky, should be reinstated. The situation of the régime is painted in such bold terms that the following speculation comes at the end: 'One might wonder whether these are not the fruits of an immense and quite conscious provocation. . . .' The General Secretary is compared to the police-spy Azev of olden times. Riutin, condemned to death by the secret Collegium, is pardoned for a short while. . . . For having read this document without informing on its authors, Zinoviev, himself betrayed by Yan Sten, is once more expelled from the Party: when Yaroslavsky tells him the verdict, he clutches at his throat, chokes and whispers 'I'll never live through it!' before falling into a faint.

At the end of 1932 two Old Bolsheviks in the Commissariat of Agriculture, freshly back from the Caucasus, denounce the results of collectivization in a circle of intimates, are arrested and disappear: this is the case of Eismont and Tolmachev. 1933 sees the beginning of the 'nationalist deviation' cases in the federated republics: imprisonment of Shumsky and Maximov in the Ukraine, the suicide of Skrypnik, who was one of Stalin's most determined partisans, purges in the governments of Central Asia. An engineer, back from deportation in distant Siberia, tells me, 'My prison train had three kinds of carriage: one kind lice-ridden and freezing, out of which corpses were cleared—this was for common criminals and abandoned children (*besprizornyi*); another kind, fairly tolerable, for technicians and "hoarders of currency"—the old Liberal Nikolai Vissarionovich Nekrassov, a former minister of Kerensky, died in one of them; and a privileged carriage for the People's Commissars of Central Asia. . . .'

Our communications with Trotsky were almost completely cut off. Communication among ourselves was so difficult that for months we thought Rakovsky was dead; he was in fact only sick. I had managed, in 1929 I think, to send Trotsky a voluminous correspondence passed out from the Verkhne-Uralsk prison, written in microscopic characters on thin strips of paper; it was the last he ever received from his persecuted comrades. The *Bulletin of the Opposition* that Trotsky published reached us only occasionally and in fragments, and ceased to reach us altogether at around this time. I was astonished at the thoroughness with which it was possible, in a country so large, to seal off hermetically the frontiers of the intellect, at all events in so far as these could be subject to police control. We knew of the line of Trotsky's thought only through officials imprisoned after returning from abroad, who discussed it all in the prison-yards, now the last resorts of free Socialist inquiry in the U.S.S.R. We were upset at the discovery that on several serious issues Trotsky, under the unfortunate influence of his Party patriotism, was grossly mistaken. At the time of Blumkin's execution, a normal G.P.U. crime, he still defended this Inquisition on principle. Later, he accepted as true the tales of sabotage and 'conspiracy' by technicians and Mensheviks, being unable to imagine the state of inhumanity, cynicism, and mania that our police-apparatus had sunk to. We had no means of informing him, though the views expressed on these monstrous impostures by the Socialist Press of the period were very sensible.

Together with Trotsky, we were against reckless industrialization, against forcible collectivization, against the inflated Plans, against the sacrifices and the infinitely dangerous strain inflicted on the country by bureaucratic totalitarianism. At the same time we recognized, through all the disasters, the successes achieved by this same industrialization. This we ascribed to the enormous moral capital of the Socialist revolution. The storehouse of intelligent, resolute popular energy which it had built up was now revealed as inexhaustible. The superiority of planning, clumsy and tyrannical as it was, in comparison with its absence, was also visibly manifest to us. But we could not, like so many foreign tourists and bourgeois journalists with a naïve propensity to the worship of force, fail to note that the cost of industrialization was a hundred times multiplied by tyranny. We remained convinced that the achievements of a system of Socialist democracy would have been better, infinitely better and greater, with less cost, no famine, no terror, and no suppression of thought.

A few days after my release from prison in 1928, I was laid out by an unendurable abdominal pain; for twenty-four hours I was face to face with death. I was saved by chance, in the shape of a doctor friend who came in at once, and another friend, a Menshevik, who would not leave my side in the Mariinsky Hospital till I was out of danger. It was an intestinal occlusion. I can still see the dim night illumination of that hospital ward in which quite suddenly, seized by a great fit of shivers, I emerged from semi-delirium to recover a rich and tranquil inner lucidity.

'I think that I am going to die,' I told the nurse, 'fetch the house-doctor.' And I reflected that I had laboured, striven and schooled myself titanically, without producing anything valuable or lasting. I told myself, 'If I chance to survive, I must be quick and finish the books I have begun; I must write, write. . . .' I thought of what I would write, and mentally sketched the plan of a series of documentary novels about these unforgettable times. A Russian nurse's pretty, broad-cheeked face was leaning over me, a doctor was giving an injection; I felt utterly detached from myself, and it occurred to me that my son was, at eight years, already old enough not to forget me. Then I saw the doctor making weird passes with his hand above my face. I managed to sit up, and saw that he was flicking away some great, bloated lice. 'Do you think that I shall live?' I asked him. 'I think so,' he replied seriously. 'Thank you for that.' On the following morning he told me that I was safe. I had taken my decision: that is how I became a writer.

I had renounced writing when I entered the Russian Revolution. Literature seemed quite a secondary matter—so far as I personally was concerned—in an age like this. My duty was dictated by history itself. Besides, whenever I did any writing, there was such a striking discrepancy between my sensibility and my opinions that I could actually write nothing of any value. Now that nearly ten years had rolled by, I felt sufficiently in tune with myself to write. I reflected that our own reactionary phase might be lengthy; the West, too, might be stabilized for years to come; and since I was refused the right to join the work of industrialization, except at the price of my freedom of opinion, I could (while remaining uncompromising as an Oppositionist forced into inactivity) provide a serviceable testimony on these times. Because of my love of history I had accumulated a pile of notes and documents about the Revolution. I set myself to writing *L'An Un de la Révolution Russe* and to gathering material for *L'An Deux*. I finished *Les Hommes dans la Prison*.

Historical work did not satisfy me entirely; apart from the fact that it demands both resources and undisturbed leisure of an order that I shall probably never enjoy, it does not allow enough scope for showing men as they really live, dismantling their inner workings and penetrating deep into their souls. A certain degree of light can only be cast on history, I am convinced, by literary creation which is free and disinterested, which is to say devoid of any market preoccupations. I had, and still have, an immense respect for literary activity—and an equally great contempt for 'Literature'. Many authors write for pleasure (especially the rich ones) and may do it well; many others practise a conscious profession for the sake of earning a living and winning a name. Those who have a message within them express it in the process, and their contribution has human value. The others are simply suppliers to the book trade. My conception of writing was and is that it needs a mightier justification: as a means of expressing to men what most of them live inwardly without being able to express, as a means of communion, a testimony to the vast flow of life through us, whose essential aspects we must try to fix for the benefit of those who will come after us. In this respect, I belonged to the tradition of Russian writing.

I knew that I would never have time to polish my works properly. They would be worthwhile without that. Others, less engaged in combat, would perfect a style; but what I had to tell, *they* could not tell. To each his own task. I had to struggle bitterly for my family's daily bread, in a society where all doors were closed to me, and where people were often afraid to shake my hand in the street. I asked myself every day, without any special emotion, but engrossed by the problem of rent, my wife's health, my son's education, whether I would not be arrested in the night. For my books I adopted an appropriate form: I had to construct them in detached fragments which could each be separately completed and sent abroad post-haste; which could, if absolutely necessary, be published as they were, incomplete; and it would have been difficult for me to compose in any other form.

Individual existences were of no interest to me—particularly my own—except by virtue of the great ensemble of life whose particles, more or less endowed with consciousness, are all that we ever are. And so the form of the classical novel seemed to me impoverished and outmoded, centring as it does upon a few beings artificially detached from the world. The commonplace French novel, with its drama of love and self-interest focussed, at best, upon a single family, was an example I was determined to avoid at all costs. My first novel had no central character; its subject was not myself, nor this or that person, but simply men and prison. I next wrote *Naissance de Notre Force*, sketching the surge of revolutionary idealism across the devastated Europe of 1917–18. After that *Ville Conquise*, a stern documentary on Petrograd in 1919. If anyone influenced me it was John Dos Passos, though I was not attracted by his literary impressionism. I had the strong conviction of charting a new road for the novel. Among Russian writers Boris Pilniak was venturing on a similar path.

Between 1928 and 1933 I thus completed one historical book and three novels, which were published in France and Spain. From Paris I received encouragement from Jacques Mesnil, Magdeleine Paz, the brilliant poet Marcel Martinet, Georges Duhamel, Léon Werth, and the review *Europe*.[1] I needed it to some small degree, since I was

[1] Jacques Mesnil (1872–1940): Socialist writer and journalist; supporter of Romain Rolland's anti-militarism during the First World War; later a companion of Serge in the early days of the Comintern in Russia. Magdeleine Paz: novelist and essayist; friend and supporter of Serge in both his periods of confinement in

working almost entirely alone, persecuted, and 'more than half beaten', as I wrote to my distant friends. In Paris itself, my books met hostility from two quarters. Bourgeois criticism viewed them as revolutionary works which were best passed over in silence (besides the author was the devil of a long way off, wasn't he?); left-wing critics, dominated, influenced or paid by the Soviet Union, boycotted me even more thoroughly. Despite it all, my books lived out their lives tenaciously; but they earned me very little.

In Russia my situation was critical. My old friend Ilya Yonov, the head of the literary publishing-house of the State Press, a former convict and once a Zinovievite Oppositionist, stopped the printing of my first novel when it was already translated, proof-read and made up in pages. I went to see him. 'Is it true what they tell me?' 'It's true. You can produce a masterpiece every year, but so long as you are not back in the line of the Party, not a line of yours will see the light!'

I turned my back on him and walked out.

At the time when my second novel was published in Paris, I raised the issue with Comrade Leopold Averbach, the General Secretary of the Association of Proletarian Authors. Our acquaintance was of long standing. He was a young Soviet careerist possessed of an extraordinary talent for the bureaucratic callings. Less than thirty, he had the hairless head of the young senior official, the verbal fluency of a Congress demagogue, and the dominating, false-sincere eyes of the manipulator of meetings.

'I will see to it, Victor Lvovich! I know about your attitude, but as for boycotting you let's just see! We've not got as bad as that!' While this was going on, the Leningrad Writers' Publishing Co-operative, which was about to sign a contract with me, ran foul of the categorical veto of the Regional Party Committee's Cultural Section. The hazards of politics did, it is true, give me my revenge on Averbach and his uniformed *literati*. I published in Paris a small book entitled *Literature and Revolution*, which inveighed against the conformism of so-called 'proletarian literature'.

the Soviet Union. Marcel Martinet (1887–1944): revolutionary poet; friend of Trotsky from the First World War until the latter's murder; resigned as literary editor of *L'Humanité* after the rise of Stalinism; campaigner on behalf of Serge. Georges Duhamel (1884–1966): the noted author of the sequence of 'Pasquier Chronicles'. Léon Werth (1879–1955): anti-colonialist French novelist; friend of Serge during the late thirties.

Scarcely had this volume left the press when Leopold Averbach learnt from the Soviet newspapers that the Association of Proletarian Authors had been dissolved by the Central Committee and that he was no longer the General Secretary of anything at all! He was still the nephew of Yagoda, the head of Security, and a good bureaucrat to boot. He delivered a number of speeches condemning his own 'cultural politics' of yesterday. People asked each other, smiling, 'Have you read Averbach's diatribe against Averbach?' And the Central Committee gave him the task of managing a Communist organization in Magnitogorsk. There Leopold Averbach initiated a sabotage-trial, acted himself as prosecutor against the technicians concerned, had them condemned to death according to the rite—and disappeared from my view. (He was, in 1937, after the fall of Yagoda, denounced in the Soviet Press for a traitor, saboteur, terrorist, and Trotskyist, and thence shot.) Although my little book on *Literature and Revolution* had anticipated the Central Committee's decision, it was banned in the U.S.S.R.

At this point I should have dealt at length with the Soviet writers whose life I shared; with their resistance, timid and stubborn at once, to the smothering of their creative freedom; with their humiliations and their suicides. I should have outlined portraits of remarkable men. I have no space to do so; and of these men, some are still alive. In speaking of them I might put them in danger. What I must tell here briefly is the tragedy of a literature of mighty spiritual sources, strangled by the totalitarian system—and also the diverse reactions evoked by this tragedy in men supremely gifted for creative work, whether poets or novelists.

Poets and novelists are not political beings because they are not essentially rational. Political intelligence, based though it is in the revolutionary's case upon a deep idealism, demands a scientific and pragmatic armour, and subordinates itself to the pursuit of strictly defined social ends. The artist, on the contrary, is always delving for his raw material in the subconscious, in the pre-conscious, in intuition, in a lyrical inner life which is rather hard to define; he does not know with any certainty either where he is going or what he is creating. If the novelist's characters are truly alive, they function by themselves, to a point at which they eventually take their author by surprise; and sometimes he is quite perplexed if he is called upon to classify them in terms of morality or social utility. Dostoevsky,

Gorky, and Balzac brought to life, all lovingly, criminals whom the Political Man would shoot most unlovingly. The new totalitarian states, constraining their writers by directives of strict ideology and absolute conformism, succeeded only in killing the creative faculty within them. Between 1921 and 1928 Soviet literature had its glorious season of full flower. From 1928 onwards it declines and dies out. Printing, no doubt of it, goes on; but – what gets printed?

Max Eastman found the right expression for it: 'Writers in uniform'. The conscription and uniforming of Russia's writers took several years to complete; creative freedom disappeared side by side with freedom of opinion, with which it is inseparably bound. In 1928 or 1929 the Leningrad writers were on the point of protesting openly against the censorship, the Press campaigns of slander and threatening, and the administrative pressure. Nothing was done, apart from interviews with high officials (who offered reassurances) and routine acts of petty cowardice. When the Press denounced Zamyatin and Pilniak as public enemies, the first for a biting satire on totalitarianism, the other for a fine realist novel, my author friends voted everything that was expected of them against their two comrades; this done, they were free to go and ask their pardon privately. When, at the time of the technicians' trial, the Party organized demonstrations in favour of the execution of the culprits, and universal votes for the death-penalty, the writers voted and demonstrated like everybody else; this although they numbered men who knew what was going on and were troubled by it, such as Konstantin Fedin, Boris Pilniak, Alexei Tolstoy, Vsevolod Ivanov, and Boris Pasternak.

During the Ramzin trial the Leningrad Writers' Union summoned me to an important meeting. Knowing that it was to concern itself with demanding executions, I did not go to it. A member of the Bureau came to see me:

'Doubtless you were ill, Victor Lvovich?'

'Not at all. I am on principle opposed to the death-penalty in our country at this present time. I think that the revolver has been abused in such excess that the only way of restoring any value to human life in the U.S.S.R. would be to proclaim the abolition of the death-penalty in accordance with the 1917 Programme. I request you to take note of this statement.'

'Certainly, certainly. In that case, will you kindly take note of our resolution, unanimously carried, on the trial of the Industrial Party, and give us your approval with your reservation about the death-penalty?'

'No. I think that trials are the affair of the courts, not of the unions.'

And yet . . . nothing happened to me. Two schoolmistresses who adopted the same attitude (I did not know them) were forthwith expelled from their union, hounded from their jobs, arrested as counter-revolutionaries and deported. The worst of it all was that after having gone to so much trouble to obtain an outcry for bloodshed, the Central Committee reprieved the condemned men.

Every time this sort of voting took place, the writers felt a little more domesticated. Our social tea-gatherings were divided into two parts. From eight to ten at night conversation was conventional and directly inspired by the newspaper editorials: official admiration, official enthusiasm, etc. Between ten and midnight, after a few glasses of vodka had been drunk, a kind of hysteria came out, and conversations—now diametrically at odds—were sometimes punctuated by fits of anger or weeping. Face to face with his neighbour, each one dropped the official style, and displayed instead an alert critical intelligence, a tragic gloom, a Soviet patriotism proceeding from living souls completely exposed.

Andrei Sobol, a notable novelist and a good revolutionary (once a convict), had killed himself at the same time as Sergei Yesenin, in 1926. There were several suicides of young folk; I remember that of Victor Dmitriev and his wife. On 14 April 1930, Vladimir Mayakovsky fired a bullet into his heart. I wrote of this (in Paris, anonymously): 'He was a wonderful "fellow-traveller"; he wasted his best talents in a weary quest for God knows what ideological line, demanded of him by petty pedants who made a living out of it. Having become the most-requested rhymester of hack journalism, he allowed his personality to be sacrificed to this daily drudgery. He felt that he was going to the dogs. He never stopped justifying himself and pleading that it was a surrender to superior force. . . .' Mayakovsky had just joined Leopold Averbach's Association of Proletarian Authors. In his last poem, 'At the Top of my Voice!' he wrote of '*the petrified crap of the present. . . .*'

I know that he had spent the previous evening drinking, in bitter self-justification, before his friends who kept telling him harshly, 'You're finished; all you ever do is piss out copy for the hacks.' I had only held one conversation of any significance with him. He was annoyed at a long article I had devoted to him in *Clarté* at a time when he was unknown in the West. 'Why do you say that my Futurism is no more than Past-ism?'

'Because your hyperboles and shouts, and even your boldest images, are all saturated with the past in its most wearisome aspects. And you write

> *In men's souls*
> *Vapour and electricity. . . .*

Do you really think that's good enough? Surely this is materialism of a peculiarly antiquated variety?'

He knew how to declaim before crowds; but not how to argue. 'Yes, I'm a materialist! Futurism *is* materialist!'

We parted cordially, but he became so official that I never met him again and most of the friends of his youth dropped him.

I no longer saw anything of Gorky, who had come back to the U.S.S.R. terribly changed. My near relatives, who had known him since he was a youth, had stopped seeing him since the day he refused to intervene on behalf of the five condemned to death in the Shakhty trial. He wrote vile articles, merciless and full of sophistry, justifying the worst trials on grounds of Soviet humanism! What was going on inside him? We knew that he still grumbled, that he was uneasy, that his harshness had an obverse of protest and grief. We told each other: 'One of these days he'll explode!' And indeed he did, a short while before his death, finally breaking with Stalin. But all his collaborators on the *Novaya Zhizn (New Life)* of 1917 were disappearing into jail and he said nothing. Literature was dying and he said nothing.

I happened to catch a glimpse of him in the street. Leaning back alone, in the rear seat of a big Lincoln car, he seemed remote from the street, remote from the life of Moscow, reduced to an algebraic cipher of himself. He had not aged, but rather thinned and dried out, his head bony and cropped inside a Turkish skull-cap, his nose and cheekbones jutting, his eye-sockets hollow like a skeleton's. Here was an ascetic, emaciated figure, with nothing alive in it except the will to exist and think. Could it, I wondered, be some kind of inner drying, stiffening, and shrinking peculiar to old age, which had begun in him at the age of sixty? I was so struck with this idea that, years later in Paris, at the very time when Romain Rolland, then sixty-five, was following exactly the same spiritual path as old Gorky, I was inexpressibly reassured by the humanity and clear-sightedness of André Gide, and I thought gratefully of John Dewey's honest perspicacity.

After this encounter I tried to see Alexei Maximovich, but was barred at the door by his secretary (G.P.U.), a robust character with pince-nez, generally despised and singularly well-named since he was called Kriuchkov, i.e. Hook.[1]

Boris Andreyevich Pilniak was writing *The Volga Flows Into the Caspian Sea*. On his work-table I saw manuscripts under revision. It had been suggested to him that, to avoid banishment from Soviet literature, he should remodel *Forest of the Isles*, that 'counter-revolutionary' tale of his, into a novel agreeable to the Central Committee. This body's Cultural Section had assigned him a co-author who, page by page, would ask him to suppress this and add that. The helpmate's name was Yezhov, and a high career awaited him, followed by a violent death: this was the successor to Yagoda as head of the G.P.U., shot like Yagoda in 1938 or 1939.

Pilniak would twist his great mouth: 'He has given me a list of fifty passages to change outright!' 'Ah!' he would exclaim, 'if only I could write freely! What would I not do!' At other times I found him in the throes of depression. 'They'll end up by throwing me in jail. . . . Don't you think so?' I gave him new heart by explaining that his fame in Europe and America safeguarded him; I was right, for a while. 'There isn't a single thinking adult in this country', he said, 'who has not thought that he might be shot. . . .' And he related to me details of killings which he had picked up drinking with tipsy executioners. He wrote a wretched article for *Pravda* on some technicians' trial, received a passport for travel abroad on Stalin's personal recommendation, visited Paris, New York, and Tokyo, and came back to us dressed in English tweed, with a little car to himself, dazzled by America. 'You people are finished!' he told me, 'Revolutionary romanticism is out! We are entering an era of Soviet Americanism: technique and practical soundness!' He was childishly pleased with his fame and material comforts.

[1] Kriuchkov was shot in 1938, after the Moscow Trial of that year, in which he 'confessed' to having caused the death of Gorky under Yagoda's instructions.

A little before my arrest, we took a long car trip together, to enjoy vistas of sunshine and unsullied snow. Suddenly he unbent and turned to face me, his eyes saddened: 'I do believe, Victor Lvovich, that one day I too will send a bullet into my head. Perhaps it would have been better if I had done that. I cannot emigrate like Zamyatin: I could not live apart from Russia. And I have the feeling that as I come and go, there is a gun in my back, with a pack of blackguards on the trigger. . . .'

When I was arrested he had the courage to go and protest to the G.P.U. (He disappeared without trial in 1937, quite mysteriously: one of the two or three real creators of Soviet literature, a great writer translated into ten languages, disappeared without anyone in the Old World or the New—except myself, and my voice was stifled—inquiring after his fortune or his end!) One critic has said that the works he had written with Yezhov 'shout the lie and whisper the truth'.

The star of Count Alexei Nikolayevich Tolstoy was climbing gently to its zenith. I had met him in Berlin in 1922, an authentic counter-revolutionary *émigré*, negotiating his return to Russia and his future royalties. Highly esteemed by the educated classes under Tsarism, a discreet liberal and honest patriot, he had fled with the White forces from the Revolution. He was a decent stylist and now and then a good psychologist, skilful enough to adapt to the public taste, to turn out a successful play or a novel of contemporary interest. In character, manner, and morals he was really a high Russian lord of olden days, loving beautiful things, good living, polite literature, cautiously liberal opinions, the odour of power—and, what is more, the Russian people: 'our eternal little *mujik*'.

He invited me out to his villa at Dietskoe Selo, where his furniture came from the Imperial palaces, to hear the first chapter of his *Peter the Great*. At this time he was not particularly well regarded, and was deeply distressed by the sight of the devastated countryside; he conceived of his great historical novel as a defence of the peasant folk against tyranny as well as an explanation of the present tyranny in terms of one of the past. A little later, the analogy he drew between Peter the Great and the General Secretary turned out to be strangely satisfying to the latter. Alexei Tolstoy, too, now began to protest aloud, when he was in his cups, that it was almost impossible to write in such an oppressive atmosphere. He told the General

Secretary himself as much, in the course of a writers' reception, and the General Secretary drove him home in his car, reassured him, lavished him with pledges of friendship. . . . On the following day, the Press stopped attacking the novelist; Alexei Tolstoy was revising his manuscripts. Today he is the official 'great writer' of Soviet Russia. But has he ever inquired after the fate of Boris Pilniak—or of so many others who were his friends? The quality of his writings has sunk quite incredibly, and falsifications of history can be found in them on a scale that is simply monstrous. (I am thinking of a novel of his about the Civil War.)

Three men far removed from this rising official celebrity used to meet in an old cottage in Dietskoe, and through them I made contact with a different set of values. These were representatives of the Russian intelligentsia of the great period from 1905 to 1917. The ancient, shabby interior of the place seemed pervaded through and through with silence. Andrei Bely and Feodor Sologub would be playing chess. Sologub, the author of the novel *The Petty Demon*, was in his last (the sixty-fourth) year of his life: a small man of an astounding pallor, his oval face well-proportioned, his forehead high, bright-eyed, timid and introverted. Since the death of his wife he had been delving into mathematics for some proof of an abstract form of immortality. His work had been concentrated variously on the mystical world, the sensual world, and the Revolution. His utterances displayed a childish ingenuity, and it was said of him that all he lived on now was 'his big secret'.

In the visionary eyes and passionate voice of Andrei Bely an inextinguishable flame still burned. He was fighting for his imprisoned wife and writing his autobiography, *At the Frontier of Two Epochs*; he lived even now in a state of intellectual fever. Ivanov-Razumnik, now failing, his face cadaverous and his suit threadbare, would from time to time emit some mordant observation; he was allowed to deal only with subjects of literary scholarship, writing his study of Schedrin—until he disappeared.

Censorship, in many forms, mutilated or murdered books. Before sending a manuscript to the publisher, an author would assemble his friends, read his work to them and discuss together whether such-and-such pages would 'pass'. The head of the publishing enterprise would then consult the *Glavlit* or 'Literature Office', which censored manuscripts and proofs. Once the book was published, official critics would issue their opinion, on which depended the sales of the book to libraries, whether it would be tolerated, or whether it would be withdrawn from circulation. I saw the entire edition of the first volume of an *Encyclopaedic Dictionary*, which had cost the intellectuals of Leningrad years of toil, sent to be pulped. Success was manufactured wholly by the Party offices. The chosen book, recommended to all the libraries in the land, was printed in tens of thousands of copies; the Foreign Languages Publishing House translated it into several languages, and the author, loaded with money and praise, became a 'great writer' in the space of a season, which of course deceived nobody. Such was the case with Maria Shaginyan and her novel *Hydrocentral*. In the same period, censorship and 'criticism' achieved the silencing of a masterly Communist writer who had risen from the people, Artem Vesioly. But then—the title he had given his outstanding novel was *Russia Washed in Blood*!

What I cannot reproduce is the atmosphere of overpowering, sickening absurdity that surrounded some of the meetings of writers who were compelled to fanatical obedience. One day in a small, dark meeting-room in Herzen House, we heard a report from Averbach on the spirit of the proletariat, the collective farm, and Bolshevism in literature. Lunacharsky, frozen in a stance of weary boredom, kept passing me ironical little notes—but he spoke nothing but a few quasi-official remarks, in terms more intelligent than the official speaker had used. Between the two of us Ernst Toller was seated, lately released from a Bavarian prison. Bit by bit the whole deadening speech was translated for him, and in his great dark eyes, in his face of strength and gentleness, a kind of confusion could be seen. Surely in his years of imprisonment as an insurgent poet, he had pictured the literature of the Soviets as altogether different from this. I remember a meeting of our Leningrad writers' union in which some young men of letters, who were none the less practically unlettered, suggested the formation of 'mopping-up' squads, to go to the second-hand bookshops and remove from them historical works which the Leader had just attacked. An uneasy silence fell across the room.

I certainly had no place in this literature of sacred cows; and my very relationships with its writers were not at all easy. My non-conformist attitude was a reproach to them, and my presence compromised them. The friendships I had left were brave ones; I have no right to speak of them here. How and on what could I live? For some time after my expulsion from the Party I was allowed to carry on with my translations of Lenin for the Lenin Institute, though my name was kept out of the published volumes and I was checked, line by line, by experts charged with the task of uncovering possible sabotage in the disposition of semicolons. I knew that Nadezhda Konstantinovna Krupskaya was working in similar conditions on her memoirs of Lenin; a committee was reviewing her every line. Gorky was altering his own memoirs on the demand of the Central Committee. Kreps, the head of International Social Publishing, a little red-eyed Tatar, greeted me rubbing his hands: 'I've just started up a bookshop in the Philippines!' He put on a friendly voice to let me know that, because of my correspondence abroad, I was in grave danger of being indicted for treason (a capital charge). This said, he invited me to reflect, hinting at a glorious future for me if I returned to the Party: 'One day you will run the Lenin Institute of Paris!' (Poor Kreps disappeared himself in 1937.)

Then came the years of rationing, famine, and black-marketeering. Authors with the right ideas received fantastic secret rations from the G.P.U. co-operatives, including even butter, cheese and chocolate! 'Do have a little taste', a friend asked me, 'of this highly confidential Gruyère. . . .' Doubtful writers, that is any who were lyrical, mystical, or unpolitical, got mediocre official rations. I got nothing except for an occasional bit of fish; and some of the comrades came to tell me that they had had to battle hard in committee to stop my name from being deleted from the list.

I lived with my wife and son in a small apartment in the centre of Leningrad, 19 Zhelyabova Street, in a 'communal flat' of a dozen rooms, occupied by, on average, a good thirty people. In several cases a whole family lived in one room. A young G.P.U. officer, plus his wife, child, and grandmother, lived in a small room overlooking the courtyard; I knew that he had been put there, in the room vacated by a jailed technician, so as to have 'someone' near me. In addition, a Bessarabian student was spying on me, watching my comings and goings and listening to my conversations on the telephone (which was situated in the corridor). A little G.P.U. secret agent lived in a hidey-hole next to the bathroom; he assured me of his friendship, without concealing the fact that he was always being interrogated about me; he was the amiable type of informer. Thus, even at home, I was under constant watch from three agents. A sham Oppositionist, who was visibly annoyed at the role he had to assume, visited me once or twice a week for confidential political discussions—and I knew that our conversation was filed away verbatim the next day in my dossier. A young relative on my wife's side came one night to knock on my door. He was a delicate youth, recently married, who lived poorly: 'Listen, I've just left the G.P.U. They want me to make detailed reports on the people who visit you —I'll lose my job if I refuse. What can I do, God, what can I do?'

'Don't fret,' I replied. 'We'll draw up your reports together. . . .'

Another time, also at night, an oldish intellectual, bespectacled, asthmatic and terrified by his own audacity, came in and sat for a long time recovering his breath in an armchair. Then, gathering all his courage together:

'Victor Lvovich, you do not know me, but I know you, and have a high opinion of you. . . . I am a censor in the Secret Service. Be discreet, discreet: they're always paying attention to you.'

'I have nothing to hide. I think what I think. I am what I am.'

He repeated, 'I know, I know, but it's very dangerous. . . .'

In my frequent sojourning in Moscow, I felt more and more that I was a hunted man. Stay at a hotel? Impossible, the hotels are reserved for officials. My relatives, who usually put me up, found my visits too compromising and begged me to go elsewhere. Most often I spent the night in houses that had just been emptied out by the G.P.U.; there, people had no fear of compromising themselves any further by being my hosts. Acquaintances avoided me in the street. Bukharin, whom I ran into just outside the Lux Hotel, slipped by with a furtive 'How's things?'—eyes right, eyes left, then off sharp. Pierre Pascal's small room, in a converted hotel on Leontievsky Street, was another spot that was devilishly spied on, but one breathed a free air there. The Italian Rossi (Angelo Tasca), who was still on the Comintern Executive, came there to stretch out on the couch. He had the broad, indented brow of a dreamer—and he still hoped to bring the International back to health! He was planning to join with Ercoli (Togliatti), in winning over a majority of the Central Committee of the Italian Party, and then offer support to Bukharin. (Ercoli betrayed him and Rossi was expelled.) He told me, 'I can assure you, Serge, that every time there are three of you together, one of you is an *agent provocateur*.' 'There are only two of us,' I answered, alluding to Andrés Nin, with whom, never out of temper, his long hair tossing in the wind, I used to stroll through Moscow, shadowed at each step.

Luck was on my side. One night I was going back through twenty degrees of frost to the house of some comrades to sleep in the bed of a friend who had been arrested. A frightened little girl half-opened the door to me: 'Get away quickly. They are turning the flat inside out. . . .' I did not know where to go, but I went. Another time I was asked to a private party, but missed the telephone-call inviting me; that evening all the guests were arrested. Perhaps my presence there had been anticipated? Still another time, I escaped from Maria Mikhailovna Joffe's house while the police were surrounding it. One of them, naturally, clung behind my heels; without turning round I hurriedly skirted the white façade of the Comintern building, turned the corner and made an acrobatic leap to grab a tram going along at full speed. How long could it be kept up? (The young widow of our great comrade Joffe disappeared for ever, deported to Central Asia with her son—who died there—and then imprisoned several times; her life ended in captivity in 1936, no one knows exactly where or how. I had known her as a fair-haired young girl, proud and coquettish; when I met her again she was a woman, charming in the way of Russian peasant women, earnest and yet playful; her moral stamina formed a salutary in-fluence in the Oppositionist deportee-colonies of Turkestan. She struggled for eight years without weakening.)

Later on, they uncovered a whole series of conspiracies. How could anyone conspire in these conditions—when it was scarcely possible to breathe, when we lived in houses of glass, our least gestures and remarks spied upon?

Our crime as Oppositionists lay simply in existing, in not dis-owning ourselves, in keeping our friendships and talking freely in each other's company. In the two capitals, the total extent of those relationships of mine which were based on free thinking was no more than twenty individuals, all differing in their ideas and characters. Spare, tough, dressed as the true proletarian that he in fact was, the Italian syndicalist Francisco Ghezzi, of the *Unione Sindicale*, emerged from imprisonment at Suzdal to tell us ardently of the victories of industrialization. His hollow face was lit up by his feverish eyes.

And he came back from the factory with a troubled brow. 'I have seen workers falling asleep under their machines. Do you know that real wages have sunk to one-twentieth during my two years in the Isolator?' (Ghezzi disappeared in 1937.)

Gaston Bouley, as full of whimsy as a seasoned Paris street-urchin, now working in the Commissariat of Foreign Affairs, was making plans to return to France, but did not dare ask for a passport: 'They'd lock me up straight away!' (He was deported to Kamchatka in 1937.) That much-mellowed anarchist Herman Sandomirsky, also on the staff of the Foreign Affairs Commissariat, was publishing his powerful studies of Italian Fascism, and acting as our middleman with the G.P.U.; he was putting up a quiet fight for the Kropotkin Museum. (He disappeared in 1937, deported to Yenisseisk and probably shot.) Zinaida Lvovna Bronstein, Trotsky's youngest daughter, was ill: she managed to go abroad, where she too soon committed suicide. Her character was, point for point, like that of her father, with a lively intelligence and a fine spiritual toughness. Her husband, Volkov, was in prison, never to be released. Andreu Nin sent parcels to the victimized comrades, gathered material on Marx, and translated Pilniak into Catalan. In order to get permission to leave for Spain, then in the midst of revolution, he sent the Central Committee a positive ultimatum, framed in dauntless language. He was allowed to leave—and I shall speak later of his dreadful end. Occasionally we would indulge in a few fantasies. I remember saying: 'If a madman were to shoot some satrap or other, there is a grave risk that we would all be shot before the week was out.' I did not know how truly I spoke.

The persecution went on for years inescapably, tormenting men and driving them crazy. Every week the system devoured a new class of victim. In this atmosphere my wife lost her reason. I found her one evening lying in bed with a medical dictionary in her hand, calm but ravaged. 'I have just read the article on *Madness*. I know that I am going mad. Wouldn't I be better off dead?' Her first crisis had come during a visit to Boris Pilniak's; they were discussing the technicians' trial, and she pushed back the cup of tea offered her, with revulsion—'It's poison, don't drink it!' I took her to psychiatrists, who were generally excellent men, and she settled down in the clinics. However, the clinics were full of G.P.U. people who won over the patients' confidence while curing their nervous difficulties.

She came home again a little better, for a while, and then the old story began again: bread-cards refused, denunciations, arrests, death-sentences demanded over all the loudspeakers placed at the street corners. . . .

She had suffered much from the disgusting persecution which was visited upon my in-laws—simply because they were my in-laws, and libertarians to boot. And always, at the root of it, was the 'struggle for life' in destitution. My father-in-law, Russakov, had fought in the 1905 revolution at Rostov, acted as Secretary to the Russian Seamen's Union in Marseilles, and was expelled from France in 1918 for organizing a strike on ships loaded with munitions for the Whites. Now he was a cloth-capped worker, living with his family in a princely couple of rooms in the same communal apartment as ourselves; from the moment that he became defenceless there were plans afoot to take them off him. People from the Party and the G.P.U. came to insult him in his own home and hit my wife in the face; they denounced him as a counter-revolutionary, ex-capitalist, anti-Semitic, and terrorist! He was hounded that same day from his job and his union, and indicted. To a signal from the agitators, whole factories demanded the passing of the death-penalty upon him—and they were on the way to obtaining it. This took place at a time when I was in Moscow, and the informers who kept watch on me at home thought I was under arrest, since they had lost sight of me. Actually I was staying with Panaït Istrati in a little villa lost in the depths of the Bykovo woods. Having learnt the news from the papers, Istrati, Dr. N——, and I took the train and, once in Leningrad, ran to the editorial office of the local *Pravda*. 'What is this senseless crime you are committing?' we asked angrily of the editor, Rafail, a hardened, spiritless official with a shaven head. 'We can prove a hundred times over that all this stuff is lies and that at the most there has been a half-hearted scuffle in a corridor, in which a young woman has been attacked and an old worker insulted!'

'I personally respect working-class democracy,' replied this perfect functionary, 'and I have here ten resolutions from factories demanding the death-penalty! However, out of consideration for you, I will suspend this campaign pending the investigation!'

The Party leaders, by contrast, proved to be understanding and moderate. Naturally the inquiry fizzled out. A public trial ended in the acquittal of my wife and her parents, to applause from the spectators. On the same day, the Communist cells ran meetings to demand the quashing of 'this scandalous judgement' and the District Attorney, yielding, as he told me, to 'the voice of the masses', obliged. A second trial took place, before a suitable magistrate. When Russakov was relating his life-history, complete with documentation, and was telling of his trips to New York (twenty years ago, as a dish-washer) and Buenos Aires (in the bilge with the other emigrants), this magistrate replied sarcastically, 'You pretend to be a proletarian, but I see you have made trips abroad!'

However, since all that was behind the case was a provocation on the part of a G.P.U. woman informer, the second trial resulted only in a verdict of censure, passed, it is true, upon the victims of the crime. This sordid affair lasted a whole year, during every month of which the Russakovs were refused bread-cards, on the grounds that they were 'ex-capitalists'; Russakov himself could find no work. The Workers' and Peasants' Inspectorate held its own trial and had him reinstated in the union, without managing to find him a job. . . . The investigator for the Inspectorate was a tall, thin young man with untidy hair and grey eyes, who displayed a singular honesty. His name was Nikołayev—and subsequently I wondered if this was the same Nikolayev, a former G.P.U. and Inspectorate officer, who shot Kirov in 1934.

Istrati went back to France, heartbroken by these experiences. It is with deep emotion that I recall his memory. He was still young, with the leanness of the Balkan highlander, rather ugly with his large, salient nose, but despite his tuberculosis so alive, so enthusiastic for living! Whether as a sponge-fisherman, a sailor, a smuggler, a tramp or a bricklayer's mate, he had passed through every port on the Mediterranean; then he began to write, and cut his throat to end it all. Romain Rolland rescued him; literary fame and the sweet money of royalties came to him out of the blue, with the publication of his Haiduk tales. He wrote without any idea of grammar or style, as a born poet madly in love with simple things like adventure, friendship, rebellion, flesh and blood. He was incapable of theoretical reasoning, and so could not fall into the trap of convenient sophistry. People told him, in my hearing: 'Panaït, one can't make an omelette without breaking eggs. Our revolution . . .' et cetera. He exclaimed, 'All right, I can see the broken eggs. Where's this omelette of yours?'

We came out of the model penal colony of Bolshevo, where hardened criminals worked in freedom under their own supervision. Istrati's only comment was, 'A pity that you can't have all this comfort and such a wonderful system of work unless you've murdered at least three people!' Of the editors of reviews who paid him 100 roubles per article he would ask sharply, 'Is it true that a postman here earns fifty roubles a month?' At every turn he would burst into fits of violent indignation. It took Istrati's inborn mulishness to enable him to resist the corrupt approaches that were made to him, and leave the Soviet Union saying, 'I shall write a book, full of enthusiasm and pain, in which I shall tell the whole truth.' The Communist Press immediately accused him of being an agent of the Rumanian *Siguranţa*. . . . He died, poor, forsaken, and utterly confused, in Rumania. It is partly owing to him that I am still alive.

Shortly afterwards I found great consolation in doing a little work alongside another great, indeed exemplary, character: Vera Nikolayevna Figner. I was translating her memoirs, and she overwhelmed me with corrections framed in her fastidious tones. She was, at 77 years of age, a tiny old woman, wrapped in a shawl against the cold, her features still regular and preserving the impression of a classical beauty, a perfect intellectual clarity and a flawless nobility of soul. Doubtless she looked upon herself proudly as the living symbol of the revolutionary generations of the past, generations of purity and sacrifice. As a member of the Central Committee of the *Narodnaya Volya* (People's Will Party) from 1879 to 1883, Vera Figner was responsible, together with her comrades, for the decision to take to terrorism as a last resort; she took part in organizing ten or so attempts against Tsar Alexander II, arranged the last and successful attack of 1 March 1881, and kept the Party's activity going for nearly two years after the arrest and hanging of the other leaders. After this she spent twenty years in the prison-fortress of Schlüsselburg, and six years in Siberia. From all these struggles she emerged frail, hard and upright, as exacting towards herself as she was to others. In 1931, her great age and quite exceptional moral standing saved her from imprisonment, although she did not conceal her outbursts of rebellion. She died at liberty, though under surveillance, not long ago (1942).

From week to week from 1928 onwards, the ring closes in relentlessly. The value of human life continuously declines, the lie in the heart of all social relationships becomes ever fouler, and oppression ever heavier; this will last up to the economic relaxation of 1935 and the subsequent explosions of terror. I asked for a passport for abroad, and wrote the General Secretary a resolute and forthright letter to this effect. I know that it reached him, but I never had a reply. All I got out of it was military demotion, though on friendly terms. I was the Deputy Commander of the Front Intelligence Service, corresponding to a rank of colonel or general. I expressed my astonishment at keeping this post at a time when the whole Opposition was being imprisoned, and the Commandant of Staff Selection told me with a smile. 'We know perfectly well that in the event of war the Opposition will do its duty. Here we are practical men first and foremost.' I was amazed by this display of sense. So that I might be free to obtain a passport the military authorities reduced me to the ranks and discharged me, on the grounds that I had passed the age limit for military service.

At the end of 1932, the economic and political situation suddenly grew even worse. An actual famine was raging through three-quarters of the countryside; news was whispered of an epidemic of plague in the Stavropol region in the northern Caucasus. On 8 November Stalin's young wife, Nadedzha Alliluyeva, committed suicide in the Kremlin, with a revolver-shot in the breast. A student, she had seen the portraits of her husband in the streets, covering whole buildings; she had lived not only at the summit of power, surrounded by the official lie and the tragedies of conscience, but also in the simple reality of Moscow. Kamenev's daughter-in-law, a young woman doctor who had given first aid to Alliluyeva, was held in custody for some days, and a legend ascribing the death to appendicitis was spread abroad.

Mysterious arrests began among the former Oppositionists who had rallied round the 'general line'. At long intervals, and with minute precautions, I would go and visit Alexandra Bronstein in Leningrad, on the other side of the Neva, in the great, red-brick workers' city of the Vyborg district. Her face calm beneath her white hair, she gave me first-hand news of the Old Man, then in exile at Prinkipo, on the Golden Horn. She corresponded with him openly, and was to pay for this bravery with her life (disappearing in 1936). She told me of the suicide of Zinaida Lvovna Bronstein in Berlin, and showed me a letter from Trotsky, which said that he was surrounded by so many dangers that he never went out, and took the fresh air only very discreetly in his garden. A few days later, the villa he occupied caught fire, perhaps by accident. . . .

I learnt of the arrests of Smilga, Ter-Vaganian, Ivan Smirnov and Mrachkovsky. Mrachkovsky, an unrepentant Oppositionist who had submitted to the Central Committee, was building a strategic railway-line to the north of Lake Baikal, and Stalin had a short while ago received him in a friendly fashion. The leader had complained of having only idiots around him: 'A pyramid of idiots! We need men like you. . . .' I saw Evgeny Alexeyevich Preobraz-hensky, and we opened our hearts for a moment in a dark little yard beneath leafless trees. 'I do not know where we are going,' he said. 'They are stopping me from breathing, I expect anything to happen. . . .' Symptoms of moral treason were being uncovered in his economic works on the world crisis. Hands in his pockets, melancholy and hunched against the cold night air, he was, as I inexplicably sensed, a doomed man.[1]

My own surveillance had grown so close that arrest was percept-ibly in the offing. It seemed to me that, in my communal apartment, the old mother and the wife of the G.P.U. officer and even this young officer himself, so punctilious and pleasant, were looking at me in a peculiar way. The old lady sought me out timidly and said, 'How terrible his job is! Every time my son goes out at night, I pray for him. . . .' She gave me a meaning look and added: 'And I also pray for *the others*. . . .'

I judged that I had a 70 per cent. probability of disappearing in the very near future. As a unique opportunity came my way to get a message to some friends in Paris, I drew up a letter, or testa-ment, addressed to Magdeleine and Maurice Paz, Jacques Mesnil and Marcel Martinet, asking them to publish the essentials of it if I disappeared. In this way the last years I had spent in resistance would not have been completely wasted.

I am sure that, in this document, I was the first person to define the Soviet State as a totalitarian State. 'For many, many years', I wrote, 'the Revolution has been in a phase of reaction. . . . One must not conceal the fact that Socialism carries seeds of reaction within itself. Cast on the soil of Russia these seeds have brought forth

[1] Preobrazhensky subsequently disappeared, it seems around 1937. He was never given a public trial or reported as having made a 'confession'.

a thriving blossom. . . . This régime is in contradiction with every-thing that was stated, proclaimed, intended and thought during the Revolution itself.'

I wrote:

'On three essential points, which take precedence before all tactical considerations, I remain and shall remain, though it may cost me dear, an open and dedicated intransigent, who will have to be coerced to keep quiet:

'I.—*Defence of man. Respect for man.* Man must be given his rights, his security, his value. Without these, there is no Socialism. Without these, all is false, bankrupt and spoiled. I mean: man whoever he is, be he the meanest of men—"class-enemy", son or grandson of a bourgeois, I do not care. It must never be forgotten that a human being is a human being. Every day, everywhere, before my very eyes this is being forgotten, and it is the most revolting and anti-Socialist thing that could happen.

'And on this point, without wishing to erase a single line of what I have written on the necessity of terror in revolutions threatened by death, I must state that I hold as an abomination unspeakable, reactionary, sickening, and corrupting, the continued use of the death-penalty as a secret and administrative measure (in time of peace! in a State more powerful than any other!).

'My viewpoint is that of Dzerzhinsky at the beginning of 1920 when, as the end of the Civil War appeared, he moved—and Lenin willingly ratified—the abolition of capital punishment for political offences. It is also that of those Communists who for several years have advocated a reduction in the inquisitorial powers of the Extraordinary Commissions (Cheka and G.P.U.). So low has the value of human life fallen, and so tragic is the result, that all capital punishment in the present régime must be condemned.

'Equally abominable, and unjustifiable, is the suppression, by exile, deportation, and imprisonment more or less for life, of all dissent in the working-class movement.

'II.—*Defence of the truth.* Man and the masses have a right to the truth. I will not consent either to the systematic falsification of history or to the suppression of all serious news from the Press (which is confined to a purely agitational role). I hold truth to be a precondition of intellectual and moral health. To speak of truth is to speak of honesty. Both are the right of men.

'III.—*Defence of thought*. No real intellectual inquiry is permitted in any sphere. Everything is reduced to a casuistry nourished on quotations. . . . Fear of heresy, based on self-interest, leads to dogmatism and bigotry of a peculiarly paralysing kind. I hold that Socialism cannot develop in the intellectual sense except by the rivalry, scrutiny and struggle of ideas; that we should fear not error, which is mended in time by life itself, but rather stagnation and reaction; that respect for man implies his right to know everything and his freedom to think. It is not against freedom of thought and against man that Socialism can triumph, but on the contrary, through freedom of thought, and by improving man's condition.' Dated: 'Moscow, February 1st, 1933.' I had no time to read it over. The friends who could see this message to its destination were on their way—and they fully expected to be arrested at the last minute.

On the day that this letter reached Paris my forebodings were proved true. Nobody knew what had become of me, and I did not know myself what would become of me next.

8

THE YEARS OF CAPTIVITY
1933–1936

My poor invalid has that look of absolute agony in her face. . . .
I go out in the cold morning to find her some sedatives and telephone
the psychiatric clinic. I also want to see the newspapers posted up
by the Kazan Cathedral, because somebody has just told me that
Thaelmann has been arrested in Berlin.[1] I am aware of being
followed, which is quite natural. Except that this time, 'they'
are trailing so close behind me that I begin to be worried. As I
come out of the chemist's they stop me. This on the pavement of
October 25th Prospect, with everybody bustling past all round me.

'Criminal Investigation. Kindly follow us, citizen, for purposes of
identification.'

Speaking low, they take out their red cards and station themselves on either side of me. I shrug my shoulders.

'I have quite certainly nothing to do with criminal investigations.
Here is my card from the Soviet Writers' Union. Here are some drugs
for a sick woman who cannot wait. Here is the house where I live; let
us go and see the caretaker; he will make my identity clear to you.'

No, it is absolutely necessary for me to come with them for ten
minutes, the misunderstanding will obviously be cleared up immediately. . . . All right. They have a consultation: which car? They
look carefully at the cars parked near by, pick the most comfortable
one, and open its door for me. 'Kindly take a seat, citizen.'

They have a curt exchange with the dumbfounded driver. 'To
the G.P.U., fast, come on!'

[1] Ernst Thaelmann (1866–1944): leader of the German Communist Party after
its Stalinization; 1924–33, leader of the Communist Party's Reichstag fraction;
arrested in 1933 and murdered at the end of the war in a concentration-camp.

'But I can't! The Director of the Trust will be coming out, I have to . . .' 'No discussions. You'll be given a chit. Move off!' And off we moved, straight to the new G.P.U. building, the handsomest in the new Soviet Leningrad, fifteen storeys high with façades of clean granite, at the angle made by the Neva and the former Liteynaya Prospect. A side-door, a spy-hole. 'Here's the criminal.' (The criminal is myself.) 'Kindly enter, citizen.' I only just find myself in a huge waiting-room when a friendly young soldier comes up to me and shakes my hand: 'Good day, Victor Lvovich! Did everything go off properly?'

Yes, more or less. . . .

'So,' I said, 'there is no doubt of my identity?'

He gave a knowing smile.

The building is spacious, stern and magnificent. A bronze Lenin welcomes me as it does everybody else. Five minutes later I am in the vast office of the investigating magistrate responsible for Party cases, Karpovich. He is a large, ginger-haired man, coldly cordial, sly and guarded.

'We are going to have some long talks together, Victor Lvovich. . . .'

'I have no doubt of that. But we shall have none at all unless first you grant some requests I have. I must ask you to arrange to have my wife transferred, no later than today, to the Red Army's psychiatric clinic; after that I want to talk over the telephone to my son—he is twelve years old—as soon as he comes home from school.'

'Certainly.'

Before my eyes Comrade Karpovich telephones the instructions to the clinic. He takes kindness so far as to offer to telephone my home while my sick wife is being collected. Then:

'Victor Lvovich, what is your opinion on the general line of the Party?'

'What? You don't know? Is it just to ask me this that you have caused all this trouble?'

Karpovich answers: 'Must I remind you that we two here are Party comrades?'

'In that case let me ask you the first questions. Is it true that Thaelmann has been arrested in Berlin?'

Karpovich thinks that the report must be treated with caution but that in Berlin 'things are going badly'. My second question bothers him:

'Has Christian Rakovsky died in deportation?'

The ginger-haired figure hesitates, looks into my eyes, says 'I can't tell you anything,' and indicates *No* by a motion of his head.

The interview which we are beginning is to last from midday to past midnight, interrupted by the meal I am given and by rests during which, when I feel the need to relax, I go for a walk along the big corridor outside. We are on the fourth or fifth floor, and through the huge window-panes I stare at the bustle of the town, I see twilight and then night falling over the teeming view, and I wonder when I shall again see this city that I love above all—if indeed I ever see it again? We talk of everything, point by point: agrarian question, industrialization, Comintern, inner-Party régime, etc. I have objections to the general line on all points; they are Marxist objections. I see them bring in all the papers that have been seized at my home, several trunkfuls. We shall not be short of subject-matter for theoretical discussion! We have tea. Midnight. 'Victor Lvovich, it is with great regret that I must have you transferred to the House of Arrest; however, I am giving orders that you are to be well treated there.'

'Thank you.' It is quite near by. A young plain-clothes policeman, clean-shaven and open-faced, goes with me and, since I ask it, we lean for a while on the embankment overlooking the dark waters of the Neva. The air from the open sea is bracing. I always find this river so charged with turbulent power that I am stirred by it as though by some Russian song.

The old House of Arrest has not changed since 1928—nor, doubtless, over the last fifty years. Are prisons then so durable as to prevail over revolutions and the fall of empires? Formalities of entry, a registration-office, and a series of partitions through which a man passes like a grain on its way into some intricate milling mechanism. In passing I meet a tall, elegant old man with a noble head of white hair; he tells me that he is from the Academy of Sciences, and that they have just taken his spectacles off him, which is the worst nuisance of all. . . . Iron staircases, ascended in dusk, then a door opens for me in the thick stonework, opens and then shuts. A poky cell, lit feebly by one pitiful bulb, just like an underground passage. Somebody rises from one of the two bunks, hails me and then introduces himself. He is a sorry kind of figure and I find it hard at first to follow him:

'Petrovsky, Writers' Union, Poets' Section. . . .'

'I'm a prose-writer myself,' I say.

I am shivering with nervous exhaustion under my heavy leather coat. The poet is shivering too beneath his old sheepskin-lined cloak, from cold and weakness. He is young, thin and wan, with a sparse, discoloured beard. We strike up an acquaintance. He talks and talks, and I sense that my presence is an event for him, which is true enough: he has been living alone for months in this underground solitude, wondering if he was going to be shot. A kindred restlessness keeps us awake for a long time, and brings us close together, strangely moved, each checking the same outflow of feeling, not knowing what to do for one another. I can do only one thing for him: listen to him and reassure him. I prove to him that they cannot shoot him, that the examining magistrate who threatens him is a ruffian using a professional stratagem; arrests are submitted to the secret Collegium which, however slightly, still does ponder possible repercussions. I am calm and reasonable, and I think I see the poet straighten a little, his confidence restored.

He is a child of highways and famine. Self-trained, he became a schoolteacher, and began to write simple poems—which I found full of charm—because he loves to gaze on the rustle of cornfields, the clouds racing above the country scenes, the brushwood and the roads shining by moonlight. 'A peasant poet, do you follow?' Along with two or three friends, he published a hand-written journal at Dietskoe Selo; a subversive tendency was unearthed in it. Why, they asked him, is there not a single reference to collectivization in your poems? Because you are hostile to collectivization? The worst of it was that he belonged to a literary circle—in no way clandestine—run by the philosopher Ivanov-Razumnik, a former Left Social-Revolutionary. Thus I learn that my friend Ivanov-Razumnik, that great, idea-hungry idealist, is also in jail. 'Say some of your poems to me again, comrade poet, I find them very beautiful. . . .' He recites them in an undertone, eyes ablaze, shoulders huddled for warmth under his fur, neck emaciated. We go to bed at dawn, never to forget this past night.

On the following day I was transferred to Moscow, discreetly, in a passenger compartment, accompanied by two G.P.U. men, one in plain clothes and the other in inconspicuous uniform, both of them comradely and polite. The transfer proved that the case was serious. But what case? There was not and could not be anything against my name except the crime of my opinions, which had been common knowledge for years and could easily have been dealt with on the spot. It is true of course that, where facts are absent, there is a free hand for fiction. An *agent provocateur*'s visit came back to my memory. I reflected too that my message to my friends in Paris could have been intercepted. That would be very serious, but on what passage in it could they lean to justify a heavy charge? Persons corresponding abroad were often charged with espionage (a capital offence). I had written: 'I sometimes begin to wonder whether we are not bound to be murdered one way or another in the end, for there are plenty of ways of going about the job . . .'

Was not that discrediting the régime in a most criminal manner? But then, the letter was only to be published if I disappeared. I thought I had hit on it: I had also written: 'And the lies that one breathes in like the air! The whole Press was proclaiming a few days ago that the fulfilment of the Five-Year Plan was resulting in a 68 per cent. increase in wages. . . . However, the value of the rouble has sunk to about a thirtieth while this increase in nominal wages was being achieved. . . .' In the eyes of the secret Collegium, that could justify a charge of 'economic espionage'. In short, I reached Moscow pretty disturbed, but quite determined to resist unyieldingly.

I was at once driven to the Lubianka, that big building in Dzerzhinsky Square built in the commercial style of the last century. Within the hour I found myself in a minute cell, perhaps in the cellars, windowless but powerfully lit, in the company of a stout-bodied worker with a forceful chin who told me that he had been a G.P.U. car-driver, now arrested for having heard a counter-revolutionary leaflet read out among some friends without denouncing everybody immediately. This suffocating box where we were, two yards long by two across, was driving him to distraction. He finally told me that it was here that prisoners condemned to death waited before being taken off for execution. . . . By about three in the morning there were ten or so of us in this cell, now stuffy and over-hot with our breath. Some of us were on the two iron bedsteads, others were standing on the chilly tiling, others again tucked themselves into the door recess. I had a headache and my heart was paining me. We all behaved very deferentially towards each other, with the affability of undertaker's men. I remember how much we were cheered by an old Jew who recalled having been arrested a year ago to the very day. Now, at last, he was being charged with having allegedly deducted a commission on the sale of a typewriter by one office to another. 'There is no evidence', he said naïvely, 'and besides it is not true; but there is a difference between the two sets of accounts. How do you think *I* can explain that away?' Our little corner of Hell shook in a burst of laughter, with no ill-will.

A few hours later, when it was morning, I was taken into a spacious ground-floor barrack-room which looked like a camp of shipwrecked mariners. About fifteen men had been living more or less at home there for weeks or maybe months, waiting for goodness knows what. Several of them had mattresses, the others made their beds on the cement floor. The atmosphere was heavy with anxiety, and breathed a forced good humour. A young soldier standing near the window talked aloud to himself incessantly; one sentence that he kept obstinately repeating could be heard quite clearly: 'Ah well! Let them shoot me!' followed by a tremendous oath. I found myself a place and asked: 'Citizens, can any of you lend me a haversack or suitcase, anything for me to rest my head on?' A big fellow in Siberian dress, his face flecked with the traces of smallpox, offered me a briefcase covered with a towel, and as he lay down next to me introduced himself—'N——, lecturer in agronomy at Irkutsk. . . .' Another agronomist, this one from Moscow, dressed very smartly and with an expression of extreme distress on his face, joined us as we were talking together. He had been arrested the night before and could not get over the shock; all the leading figures in the People's Commissariat for Agriculture had just been whisked off by the G.P.U., and, a fact that most deeply affected this 'non-Party technician', his Communist superiors were now somewhere in this self-same prison, yes, even Deputy People's Commissar Wolfe, and Konar and Kovarsky! He felt as though he was in the middle of an earthquake.

That day, I was taken up by lift to the floors that constituted the inner prison. A short medical inspection, then my fifth search: absolutely nothing was left on me of those trivial objects that people tend to carry about with them, but this final search was so careful that it disclosed the pencil hoarded away in my lining, and the half razor-blade that I had taken the precaution to conceal in my lapel. And so at last I entered the prison of prisons, which was obviously reserved for prominent persons and those charged with the gravest offences. It was a prison of noiseless, cell-divided secrecy, built barely into a block that had once been occupied by insurance company offices. Each floor formed a prison on its own, sealed off from the others, with its individual entrance and reception-kiosk; coloured electric light-signals operated on all landings and corridors to mark the various comings and goings, so that prisoners could never meet one another. A mysterious hotel-corridor, whose red carpet silenced the slight sound of footsteps; and then a cell, bare, with an inlaid floor, a passable bed, a table and a chair, all spick and span. A big, barred window with a screen masking it from the outside. On the freshly painted walls, not a single scribble or scratch. Here I was in the void, enveloped in a quite astonishing silence. Except that, far away, with a jangle of bells and ironmongery, the trams were passing by in Miasnitskaya Street, which at all hours of the day was full of people. . . . Soldiers of the Special Corps, with the smart style and polish of purely mechanical functioning, shut the door gently behind me. I asked their N.C.O. for books and paper. 'You will present that request to the Examining Magistrate, citizen.'

Here, in absolute secrecy, with no communication with any person whatsoever, with no reading-matter whatsoever, with no paper, not even one sheet, with no occupation of any kind, with no open-air exercise in the yard, I spent about eighty days. It was a severe test for the nerves, in which I acquitted myself pretty well. I was weary with my years of nervous tension, and felt an immense physical need for rest. I slept as much as I could, at least twelve hours a day. The rest of the time, I set myself to work assiduously. I gave myself courses in history, political economy—and even in natural science! I mentally wrote a play, short stories, poems. I bent a great effort of will to avoid going over my 'case' except in a purely utilitarian manner and for a limited time; this as a precaution against becoming obsessed with it. My inner life was most intense and rich, in fact not too bothersome at all. In addition, I did a little gymnastics several times a day, and this did me a great deal of good. My diet—black bread, with wheaten or millet batter, and fish-soup—was tolerable but inadequate, and I had hunger-pains every evening. On 1 May (festival of the world's workers!) I was given an extraordinary meal: mincemeat cutlets, potatoes, and stewed fruit! I got thirteen cigarettes and thirteen matches a day. Out of breadcrumbs I made myself a set of dice and a kind of calendar.

The monotony of this existence was broken up by the investigation. I had half a dozen interrogations, spaced out at intervals. Magistrate Bogin (sharp features, spectacles, uniform) opened the series. Probably an alumnus of the G.P.U. training-school (advanced course, naturally), he had a ready flow of talk, doubtless to try out his little psychological tricks, and I let him go on, being well aware that in a situation like this it is best to speak as little as possible yourself and listen carefully to everything you are told. I was awoken around midnight—'Investigation, citizen!'—and taken via lifts, cellars, and corridors to a floor lined with offices which, I discovered, was just next door to my cell-section. All the rooms along these endless corridors were set aside for the use of inquisitors. The one to which I was taken was numbered 380 or 390. I only met one person on the way: a sort of bishop, most imposing, came out of one of the offices, leaning on a cane. I said to him aloud, just for the pleasure of dismaying our warders, 'Take care of yourself, *batiushka* (Father)!' And he answered me gravely with a motion of his hand. That must have started some pretty reports for them to study.

I went into my first examining session in an aggressive mood. 'So! You are resuming the tradition of interrogations at night! Just as in the worst days of Tsarism. Congratulations!'

Bogin was not put out: 'Ah! how bitterly you speak! If I call you in at night, it is because we work day and night, we people! We have no private life, we people!'

We were smiling now, in excellent wit. Bogin stated that he knew all. 'All. Your comrades are so demoralized—I have their depositions here, you wouldn't believe your eyes. We should like to know whether you are an enemy or, despite your disagreements, a real Communist. You can refuse to answer my questions, just as you please: the investigation will be closed this very day and we shall view you with the esteem befitting an open political adversary.'

A trap! You'd like me to make your job easy by giving you *carte-blanche* to go and cook up all kinds of findings against me with your secret reports—findings which would earn me years in the Isolator at the very least. 'No. I am anxious to reply to the examination. Carry on with it.'

'Well then, let us talk together like the Communists we both are. I am at the post that has been assigned me by the Party. You wish to serve the Party, yes, I quite understand you. Do you admit the authority of the Central Committee?'

A trap! If I admit the Central Committee's authority, I have joined in the game, they can make me say what they like in the name of devotion to the Party. 'Excuse me. I have been expelled. I have not asked to be re-admitted. I am not bound by Party discipline any longer. . . .'

Bogin: 'You are deplorably formalistic!'

Myself: 'I demand to know what I am accused of, so that I can refute the charges. I am sure that no blame in Soviet law can be attached to me.'

Bogin: 'Formalism! So you'd like me to lay my cards out on the table?'

Myself: 'Are we in a card-playing mood?'

Eventually he told me that documents from Trotsky had been found at my home. 'That is not true,' I said. And that I often went to see Alexandra Bronstein; we discussed the number of visits I had paid her.

'You talked Opposition matters with her, admit it!'

'No. We talked about our state of health and about literature!'

'You have been in touch with Andrés Nin, who is a counter-revolutionary, haven't you?'

'Yes, by post, on postcards. Nin is a model revolutionary: you know that he is in jail at Algeciras?'

Bogin offered me cigarettes, and explained that my outlook was visibly that of a hardened counter-revolutionary, which was extremely dangerous for me. I interrupted him:

'Must I conclude that I am being threatened with the death-penalty?' He protested, 'Not at all! But, all the same, you are well on the way to destroying yourself. Your only hope for safety lies in a change of attitude and a complete confession. Think it over.'

I was returned to my cell at about 4 a.m.

After a number of night interviews of this kind, neither of us had got anywhere. All I learnt was that they were trying to link me with some person called Solovian, who was quite unknown to me. This information both puzzled and worried me: it was a door opening on to some conspiracy or other.

Every time I went to an examining session, the electric signals operated all along my route, so efficiently that I did not even see any warder other than my own. One night I noticed that several of the warders were gazing at me in a peculiarly attentive way as I went out. When I returned, at dawn, I found them crowded around the reception-office; they seemed to be looking rather benevolently upon me, and the one who searched me was so friendly as to venture a little joke. I discovered later that on that very night the thirty-five agricultural experts had been executed, along with Konar, Wolfe, and Kovarsky, all of them prominent officials, and including several influential Communists. They had gone off just as I had, down these very corridors, summoned just as I had been 'for the examining session' and the warders knew no more than that they had been shot somewhere down there in the cellars. Doubtless they assumed that I was earmarked for the same end—and so looked upon me with the humane attentiveness that I had noticed. When I came back, the warders were both surprised and pleased to see somebody return from that last 'examining session'. As I went to and from interrogations, I happened to pass in front of the gaping mouth of a cement-lined corridor on the ground floor, which was lit with brutal brilliance. Was that the door to the final descent?

Abruptly, the investigation was cut short. I had a strong sense of danger. I was summoned in the middle of the day and received by some high-ranking person, gaunt, grey, and wrinkled, with a cold little face perched on a bird-like neck, and thin, straight lips. I recognized the examining magistrate for serious Oppositional cases, Rutkovsky, the personal aide to the Head of the Department, Molchanov, and a member of the secret Collegium. (Molchanov was shot in the period of the Yagoda trial.) Rutkovsky was crisp and vicious:

'I can see that you are an unwavering enemy. You are bent on destroying yourself. Years of jail are in store for you. You are the ringleader of the Trotskyite conspiracy. We know everything. I want to try and save you in spite of yourself. This is the last time that we try.'

I was chilled to the bone. I felt I had to gain a few moments and interrupted him. 'I'm very thirsty. Could you get me a glass of water?' There was none there; Rutkovsky had to stand up and call someone. I had time to think, and his effect was ruined. He resumed:

'So I'm making one last attempt to save you. I don't expect very much from you—I know you too well. I am going to acquaint you with the complete confessions that have been made by your sister-in-law and secretary, Anita Russakova. All you have to do is say, "I admit that it is true", and sign it. I won't ask you any more questions, the investigation will be closed, your whole position will be improved, and I shall make every effort to get the Collegium to be lenient to you.'

So Anita Russakova had been arrested! She used to take down quite insignificant translations at my dictation. She was an unpolitical girl whose only interest was in music, innocent in all things as a new-born baby. 'I am listening,' I said.

Rutkovsky began to read and I was terrified. It was sheer raving. Anita related that I had made her send messages and take parcels to addresses which were completely strange to me, to people I did not know at all, notably to a certain Solovian who lived in a 'Red Army settlement'. This heap of impostures, coupled with the address of a 'military settlement' came as an immediate revelation to me. Therefore, they intended to shoot me. Therefore, Anita had been tortured into lying like this. Therefore, she was doomed just as I was. I burst out:

'Stop! Not one more line. You are reading a detestable falsehood, every line is false. What have you done to this child to make her lie like this?'

I was in a rage and I felt that I had to be, that I no longer had anything to gain by discretion. I might as well get myself shot and have done with it.

My inquisitor pretended to be angry, or else really was:

'Do you know that you are insulting me? And that that is another serious offence?'

'Let me calm down and I will answer you more soberly. Out of respect for myself, out of respect for you and for the rank that you hold, I refuse to hear another line of this deposition, which is a pack of lies; I demand to be confronted with Anita Russakova.'

'You're destroying yourself.'

As a matter of fact, I was demolishing the whole case, thereby saving myself and Anita as well. One moment of cowardice meant the triumph of falsehood, and then they could shoot us. I knew that the G.P.U. inquisitors worked under the scrutiny of different committees, especially the Central Committee's Control Commission, and that, before they could bring about the verdicts they wanted, they had to prepare their briefs according to the rules.

Every day I wrote to Rutkovsky demanding a confrontation with Anita so that I might unmask what I called her 'lies'. 'Let her describe the places where she pretends to have gone!' I was aware of being in a dilemma. Clearly I had caught my inquisitors in a flagrant fabrication. I was putting the G.P.U. on trial. After that, could I be allowed to live, whether released or sent to an Isolator where I would meet other comrades and tell them about it, from which I could write to the Government authorities? Rutkovsky stood to lose at the very least his career if he failed to break me (I am convinced that he perished with his superiors Molchanov and Yagoda in 1938). I decided to prepare myself for the worst.

My second examination by Rutkovsky. This time he was a little deflated, and ventured a smile. A brief admonishment for form's sake:

'You would be far better advised, I can assure you, to change your attitude and stop treating us as enemies. I tell you this in your own interest . . .', etc.

I heard him out politely, shaking my head.

'All right then, I can see we can do nothing with you. I am going to close the examination. Too bad for you.'

'As you will.'

Up till now not a word had been written down during the interrogations. Perhaps a shorthand writer was at work, concealed from my view. The inquisitor took out some large sheets of headed paper and began to copy the questions and my replies. There were six insignificant questions and six uninteresting replies. Do you know such-and-such persons? Did you and they take an interest in what happened to the deportees? Yes, of course. We used to meet quite openly, and sent letters and parcels to deported people equally openly. Have you had any subversive conversations with them? Of course not. That will be all. Sign here.

'And my confrontation with Anita Russakova? I want to prove to you that she is innocent. When she lied about me she lied about herself too. She hasn't an Oppositional idea in her head. She is just a child.'

My inquisitor's grey eyes gazed at me with a kind of meaningful smile.

'Will it satisfy you if I give you my word that we attach no importance at all to Russakova's evidence, and that this whole business will have no serious consequences for your sister-in-law?'

'Yes.'

'Good! That's that, then. The investigation is closed.'

I asked for news of my wife and son.

'They are doing well.'

I then asked for books. 'What, haven't they given you any yet? It is a piece of unforgivable negligence!'

'No,' I said quietly, 'it's not negligence. . . .'

'You will have some in a few minutes.'

'And might I have an hour's exercise walking, as in all the prisons of the civilized world?'

Rutkovsky pretended to go into fits of amazement. 'What? Do you mean you haven't had that?'

In the evening a warder brought me a pile of books: a *History of the Moslem World*, an *Economic History of the Directory*, Nogin's *Siberian Memoirs*—riches indeed! The Political Red Cross sent me onions, a little butter, a roll of white bread, and a bit of soap. I knew now that my disappearance had been made known in Paris and that, since they could not wring any signature from me which would have justified a legal condemnation, they wanted to avoid any disagreeable fuss on my account. If I had been only a Russian militant, instead of a French author as well, matters would have taken quite a different turn.

If I have lingered so long in describing my examination this is because it was a great help later on, along with what I know from other sources, in enabling me to understand how the great Trials were fabricated.

Alone and at night, I was taken across Moscow in a prison-van; I found myself in a bare, brightly-lit cell in the old Butyrki jail, a city within the city. I stayed there only for two or three days, provided with books and left untroubled. I reflected that there were plenty more prisons waiting for me to see from the inside. On the second or third day they took me downstairs and locked me in a cell with green-tiled walls, like a bathroom, next to a spacious corridor. A lad from the Moscow streets was there with me for a short while, and told me how his father and brother had certainly been shot, but he himself had been spared—yes, a very complicated case. . . . I could hear people going to and fro in the corridor. A G.P.U. officer bustled in with a little paper slip in his hand. 'Read it and sign!' I read it: '*Counter-revolutionary conspiracy. Condemned by the*

Special Collegium to three years' deportation at Orenburg. . . .' I signed,
angry and glad all at once: angry because I could do nothing, glad
because deportation was, after all, an open-air life, with the free
sky above one's head.

Deportees were forming up in the lobby, in a kind of funeral
procession, Among them I saw a girl, and a young intellectual with
heavy features who shook everyone's hand, introducing himself as
'Solovian' and repeating rapidly: 'I am not in any Oppositional
group: supporter of the General Line. . . .' 'Best of luck with the
General Line,' I told him. I was taken by open car, together with
the girl and several uniformed men, in the direction of a station.
Farewell, Moscow! The city, lit by the spring sun, dazzled my eyes.
The girl was a Moscow worker, the wife of an imprisoned Oppositionist and a Left Oppositionist herself; she was being deported to
the Volga. She gave me news of some of the women comrades locked
up in the female prison, and shared her riches with me: a cube of
compressed tea and twenty roubles. She whispered, 'Oh, so it's you,
Sergo—Sergo for whom we were so afraid! We thought that you
would stay in jail for years!' We parted with a hearty embrace in a
little station in the Tartar Republic.

Several G.P.U. soldiers guarded the compartment; an extremely
stylish, extremely stupid officer, adorned with a pair of superb pince-
nez whose lenses were cut at right angles in the opticians' latest
fashion, sat in various poses on the seat opposite, enticing me into
political conversation; I always let the subject drop, and talked
about the moon. The train shot through the plains of Russia. One
night, in a forest filled with nightingales in song, on the banks of the
Volga, I experienced a momentary thrill of wonder. I traversed
Samara (Kuibyshev) in the small hours, walking through the sleeping streets in the rose-coloured light with a soldier carrying a
lowered rifle behind me, ready to open fire if I looked like running.
At the local G.P.U. headquarters, under the shower—a blessing
indeed—I came across a dark, bearded, emaciated figure who was
frisking about nimbly under the jets of hot water.

'You there, with the intellectual's head—who are you?' he asked
me in jovial tones. He went on: 'I'm a Right Communist myself,
Secretary of the —— District, Stalingrad region, served in the
Civil War, Ivan Yegorovich Bobrov.' I introduced myself in turn.
Bobrov had, as punishment for a cruelly accurate report on the

course of collectivization in his area, practially died of hunger in some hellish prison-cellar where ten of the thirty inmates were at death's door; now he was, like myself, on the way to Orenburg. Our friendship, which was to endure, began in a comfortable cellar furnished with straw.

On the next day a dozen soldiers from the G.P.U. special cavalry, clicking their spurs against the paving-stones, took us to the station and stood guard round us in the middle of the public traffic. I was amused to see my reflection on a glass door. I had an unkempt beard, black-grey and bristling, and I had leather and fur clothing on, though it was the height of summer; Bobrov was the perfect model of a tramp—jacket in holes at the elbows, trousers in tatters and gone at the knees, and lean as a scarecrow. Our eyes were merry and proud. The folk around viewed us with sympathy, and a peasant woman asked our escort to allow her to offer us some wheatcakes. They were delicious.

Orenburg, on the Ural river, is a metropolis of the steppes, solitary under a glorious sky, on the line from Kuibyshev to Tashkent. Although it is geographically situated on the border between Europe and Asia, it belongs to Asia. Up to 1925 it had been the capital of the Autonomous Republic of the Kazakhs (or Khirghiz), a nomadic people of Central Asia, Turkish in origin and orthodox Moslems, who were still divided into three great hordes. Since then Kazakhstan has become one of the eleven federal republics of the U.S.S.R., with its capital at Alma-Ata. Under the Tsars, Orenburg, the central market for the copious livestock of the steppes, had been a wealthy city, crowned with fifteen or so Orthodox churches and several large mosques. There in the Civil War, the working class had undergone battles of legendary ferocity, marked by frightful massacres of the poor, against a Cossack ataman, General Dutov. During the N.E.P., the town had recovered its substantial prosperity, thanks to the steppe from which it drew its life. When we arrived in June 1933, a hideous famine was raging there, in an environment of destruction and decay.

There was hardly any vegetation, apart from a shady wood on the other bank of the Ural, strewn with silvery leaves. It was a lowly town, whose streets were lined with charming little houses built in peasant style. Tall, raw-boned camels trundled along gloomily under their burdens. There were two central thoroughfares of a

European type, the Sovietskaya and the Kooperativnaya, and a number of pretentious buildings in that Imperial style, with massive white pillars, which the governors-general of old times planted everywhere. All the churches, except for one in the near-by Cossack township of Vorstadt (or Orenpossad), had lately been destroyed. The rubble of the dynamited cathedral formed an islet of quaint little rocks in the middle of one of the squares. There was a little old white church on the hill over the river, which had associations with Pugachev's rebellion of 1774; not even this had been spared. All the priests and the bishops had been deported to the north; religion functioned illegally. The synagogue was either closed or demolished; in the absence of a kosher butcher, the Jews were now refusing to eat meat. On the other hand, the mosques had not been damaged, for fear of provoking the Moslem masses, with whom the authorities had quite enough trouble already. The finest mosque had been converted into a Khirghiz high school. One or two Christian churches, their domes split open and their crosses obliterated, were used as goods warehouses by the co-operatives, but there were no goods in them. The vast bazaar of the caravans, which not long ago had been glutted with merchandise, was now deserted, and the caravanserai was empty. Beside these ruins a new city was beginning to grow, with barracks and military schools. Cavalry, tank units, and the Air Force filled the town with well-clad, well-fed young men. Numerous airfields extended far into the adjoining steppe, the Flying School was housed in brand-new buildings of red brick, and if you passed young women in the street with plump cheeks and gaudy silk dresses you knew that they were the wives of airmen. The State retail-trade was at death's door: neither cloth nor paper, shoes nor food was to be found in the shops. In all the three years I spent there, no shoes were sent to Orenburg, except to the co-operatives reserved for the Party and the G.P.U. There were several technical schools for the training of agronomists, vets and teachers; a garment-factory; a railway-repair workshop; a number of prisons, all packed out; and a small concentration-camp. I often saw a great herd of men passing under my windows, ragged and mostly barefoot, surrounded by watchdogs and soldiers with lowered rifles. These were the labour brigades of the penitentiary department; we dubbed them, sarcastically, 'the enthusiasts' brigades', since some of them were actually called by that name and took part in 'Socialist labour emulation'. An immense, flea-ridden market ran out from the town into the steppe, bounded by the Moslem cemetery (now occupied by abandoned children and bandits), the dismal garment-factory, the cavalry school, a maternity hospital and the endless sands.

The G.P.U. issued us with bread-cards, which were valid from the beginning of the current month (a stroke of luck). 'It is forbidden to leave the town, except to go out for fresh air in the woods; from now on you may find any work and lodging that you can; only no employment can be taken up without our authorization.'

We thought that the light from the sky was rich and pellucid as nowhere else; and so it was. The town itself gave the impression of being sun-scorched, exciting, picturesque, and overwhelmed with heat, poverty, and sand. We went on to the barber's and acquired heads of civilized hair again; a dark-skinned urchin stole my three last roubles off me; we hocked my leather-and-fur overcoat at the municipal pawnshop for eighty roubles, and with that our experience of hunger began. The room in the Peasant's Hostelry cost two roubles a night, and the sheets were so filthy that after inspecting them by the light of a match I decided to sleep in my clothes. The inn had an enormous four-sided courtyard, littered with carts, horses, camels, and nomads who slept there, whole families of them, on mats close to their beasts. It was, in the delightful coolness of early morning, a touching spectacle. At that hour the Khirghiz families would have risen, which is to say that they would be squatting in silence or busy at their morning toilet: biblical ancients, mothers with Mongol eyes suckling their babies, children of all ages cleaning themselves of fleas in deep concentration, often cracking the lice between their teeth. It often looked as if they ate them, saying, 'You eat me and I eat you.' A row of crouching Asiatics would be relieving themselves in the latrines and I noticed that several of them excreted blood. Rags, rags everywhere. Some slender girls stood out from the mob, because of their perfect beauty, like Israelite or Persian princesses.

I heard shouting from the street, and then a shower of vigorous knocks on the door. 'Quick, Victor Lvovich, open!' Bobrov was coming back from the bakery, with two huge eight-pounder loaves of black bread on his shoulders. He was surrounded by a swarm of hungry children, hopping after the bread·like sparrows, clinging on his clothes, beseeching: 'A little bit, uncle, just a little bit!' They were almost naked. We threw them some morsels, over which a pitched battle promptly began. The next moment, our barefooted maidservant brought boiling water, unasked, for us to make tea. When she was alone with me for a moment, she said to me, her eyes smiling, 'Give me a pound of bread and I'll give you the signal in a minute. . . . And mark my words, citizen, I can assure you that I don't have the syphilis, no, not me. . . .' Bobrov and I decided to go out only by turns, so as to keep an eye on the bread.

Afterwards the two of us would meander through the town and the woods, as hungry as those children. One rouble was the price of meat-soup in the restaurant, where little girls waited on you so as to be able to lick your plate when you had finished and glean your bread-crumbs. We rationed ourselves strictly, gaining time until work should come our way, or else the relief I hoped to receive from Leningrad or Paris. Twice a week we would buy bunches of unripe onions and some mutton-bones from the market, and make a soup, which smelled delicious, over a wood fire in the courtyard. Then we would lie down and let it digest, in a state of positive bliss. Once we fell ill after the feast. Our usual nourishment consisted of dried bread and sweetened tea made in a samovar; we owed this last to the compressed tea I had been given by the girl-comrade I met at the Butyrki prison. At long last we had some news: Bobrov, that his father had died of hunger in the village; I, that my wife was getting better and would be sending me a parcel. . . .

Among the ruins of churches, in abandoned porches, on the edge of the steppe or under the crags by the Ural, we could see Khirghiz families lying heaped together, dying of hunger. One evening I gathered up from the ground of the deserted market-place a child burning with fever; he was moaning, but the folk who stood around did not dare to touch him, for fear of contagion. I diagnosed a simple case of hunger and took him off to the militia-post, holding him by his frail, boiling wrist. I fetched him a glass of water and a morsel of bread from my place; the effect on the lad was that of a small but instantaneous miracle.

'What do you want us to do with him?' asked the soldiers.

'Take him to the Children's Home.'

'But they're running away from there, because they're starving to death!'

When I returned home, I discovered that someone had stolen my stock of bread that was to last several days.

The Khirghiz folk lay on waste lots in the sun; one could not be sure if some of them were alive or dead; and people passed by without looking their way: the poor people, hurrying and shabby, the functionaries, the military, their bourgeois-looking womenfolk, in brief all those we termed 'the satisfied 8 per cent.' The market, bordered by sky and desert and invaded by the sands, teemed with an incongruous multitude. There people traded back and forth to each other, chiefly in the perpetual bric-à-brac of poverty: lamps patched up a hundred times and still giving out smuts, if no light; precious lamp-chimneys of the wrong sizes; ruined stoves, nomads' garments, stolen watches which went for no longer than five minutes (I knew experts who, out of three watches and a stock of odds and ends, would make four . . .), livestock. The Khirghiz had long arguments around a haughty, regally white camel. Troglodytic old women, their skin so brown as to appear black, practised palmistry. A weird Turkmenian in a turban divined the future by throwing goats' vertebrae upon engravings from an erotic book in French published at Amsterdam in Voltaire's time. Here, even on the worst days, one could find bread, butter, and meat, all at outrageous prices and light-years away from any hygienic regulation. Famished thieves of all ages and all varieties from as far away as Turkestan and Pamir strayed in these crowds, snatching a carrot or an onion from your hands and popping it immediately down their throats. My wife witnessed the following piece of thievery: a housewife had just bought a pound of butter costing fifteen roubles (three days' wages for a skilled worker); an Asiatic smartly nipped it from her hands and made off. He was pursued and caught easily enough; but he curled up on the earth like a ball and for all the blows from fists or stones that rained on him from above, ate the butter. They left him lying there, bloody but full.

For the rest, it was a decently managed town. Three cinemas, and a travelling theatre in the summer, of a fair standard; and an ornamental garden, called *Topoli* (The Lime-trees). About 160,000 inhabitants, a tenth of them unloaded there by the G.P.U. A healthy climate: five months of extremely harsh winter with up to forty-two degrees of frost; five months of extremely hot summer, with hot spells of up to forty degrees. All the year round, violent winds from the steppes, the savage *buran* which in winter whirled the snow around and heaped it into white dunes in the squares, and in summer worked up squalls of warm sand. Among the poor inhabitants at least 70 per cent. suffered from marsh-fever; naturally there was no quinine. I have seen the same ague shaking the grandmother of eighty and the suckling baby; and they did not die of it.

When I first arrived, there were about fifteen political deportees: Social-Revolutionaries, Zionists, anarchists, ex-Oppositional capitulators. Orenburg was considered a privileged spot for deportation. The G.P.U. only used it for leading figures, and for convicts who already had behind them years of imprisonment or exile in other parts. There were in fact a number of grades of deportation. I knew men who had lived inside the Arctic Circle in settlements of five houses; others again at Turgai in the Kazakhstan desert, where the primitive Kazakhs dwelt in hovels of mud, practically without water for five months of the year. In this town of ours L. Gerstein, of the Social-Revolutionary Party's Central Committee, was living out his last years undisturbed; and the G.P.U. was collecting influential 'Trotskyists', those known to be intransigent, for purposes whose very obscurity made us anxious. Soon there was a whole little fraternal group of us, in excellent spirits. An old Georgian Menshevik, Ramishvili, arrived, now in the fourteenth year of his captivity; then another Menshevik, Georgi Dimitrievich Kuchin, a late member of his party's Central Committee; and some ex-Oppositionists of the Right, who, having become supporters of the General Line, had been high in authority only the day before—with these last we never exchanged a word.

Life under deportation was characterized by its instability. The G.P.U. made up exiles' colonies in a fairly homogeneous composition, so as to allow a limited intellectual activity to arise, foment divisions and betrayals and then, under some easily arranged pretext, pack the irreconcilables off to prison or transfer them to regions more squalid and obscure. The deportee, dependent in regard to letters from relatives, work and medical attention, lived literally on the mercy of a few officials. He was obliged to report to the G.P.U. daily, or every three, five or seven days as the case might be. No sooner would he get his life organized a little than it would all be undone by unemployment, prison, or transfer. It was an endless cat-and-mouse game. The deportee who repented and apologized politely to the Central Committee would (though not always) be better treated and find a comfortable job as an economist or librarian; but the others would boycott him. For example, a woman who had been a Trotskyist and was the wife of a capitulator still in jail was given the task of purging the public library, i.e. of withdrawing the works of Trotsky, Riazanov, Preobrazhensky, and a host of others, in accordance with lists that were issued from time to time; the books were not burned after the Nazi pattern, but sent for pulping to provide material for fresh paper.

It was clearly indicated to me that I would receive no work except by seeking the favour of the G.P.U. Once I went to discuss a possible job in the Ural Gold Trust, and had the following fragment of conversation with the local head of the secret police:

'Have you any intention of seeking readmission to the Party?'

'None at all.'

'Or of appealing against your sentence to the Special Collegium of the Interior?'

'None at all.'

Any employment was now out of the question. I was determined to fight back. I had a historical work, three novels, and various other publications on sale in Paris. In Orenburg there was a *Torgsin* shop where, even at the height of famine one could buy, at prices sometimes below the world level, foodstuffs and manufactured goods on which the whole town gazed greedily. The only acceptable payment for them was in gold, silver, or foreign currency. I saw Khirghiz and *mujiks* coming to the counter with ancient necklaces fashioned from Persian coinage or embossed silver icon-frames; these *objets d'art* and rare coins were bought by the weight of metal in them and paid for in flour, cloth or hide. Former bourgeois now in exile brought along their false teeth. On 300 francs a month, the equivalent of about fifteen dollars, I was able both to live myself and to provide a livelihood for some comrade or other who might just be out of prison.

My wife arrived from Leningrad with some books; the G.P.U. gave me back my manuscripts and uncompleted works, as well as my typewriter. I decided to work on, just as though I had some kind of future; which, after all, was still possible. It was an even chance whether I would survive or vanish into the jails. At all costs I would, in opposition to despotism, keep this irrevocable minimum of my rights and my dignity: the right to think freely. I began to write two books at once, one of them an autobiographical work on the struggles of my youth in Paris, and to gather notes on the history of the years 1918–20. I was in the terrain of Chapayev's partisans,[1] and I met some of the survivors of that era. While their glory was being hymned throughout the world in Soviet films, they were just scraping a living, alcoholic and demoralized—but wonderful personalities all the same. I studied that particular phase in the Civil War and the folk-world around me, which, though primitive, had much of human value.

In particular, I was a close observer of a case of banditry, which amounted to no more than the spontaneous violence of a few youngsters who, in a drunken condition, had thought it gallant to have a fight to the death. I saw the most formidable of these youths being tried in a workers' club. He had several deaths on his conscience and had no clear idea of what he was being charged with. His name was Sudakov, and they shot him. Around his name I noted the phenomenon of legend-making. I left the court an hour before the verdict, it being a stifling August night. On the following day several bystanders told me, in great excitement and with all the details, that Sudakov had escaped. He had saluted the audience by bowing, in the old Russian fashion, to the four points of the compass, and then jumped through a window and disappeared in the park outside. People had seen it and the whole town was talking of the affair; only, none of it was true. When they sobered down, people declared that Sudakov had been pardoned; then the G.P.U. sent his clothes to his family.

The dry, scorching summers and the glaring, relentless winters made every hour one of struggle. The first priority was to obtain wood. The stupid regulations of the Soviet, and the G.P.U.'s habit of requisitioning on some pretext or other any peasant homes that were at all comfortable, forced people to abandon the big, well-built houses and build new ones, barely habitable by a single family and so forming no temptation for the military. A big house would be left to rot; permission would then be obtained to demolish it (in view of its condition), and the timber in it was sold for firewood —a brilliant transaction! I followed the smart example of the experts and kept myself warm by this technique. The area covered by

[1] Vassili I. Chapayev (1887–1919): an outstanding Red commander in the Civil War. Fought against the Czechoslovak Legion and Kolchak's troops.

housing diminished regularly, while the town's excess population increased. Through the snow-storms my son and I would drag toboggans loaded with the usual sack of potatoes or drum of paraffin bought on the black market. On some mornings the snow's onslaught on the house would bury it almost completely, and we had to fight it with our shovels to get the doors and windows free. Then too we had to chop and saw the wood, and hide it in case it was stolen. I made wooden barricades which we piled in front of the blocked front door. We had to go and find our bread in the far end of town, sometimes only to push our noses up to a tiny notice: *The bread-ration for the 10th is cancelled.* At the rationing-office a poster announced: 'Grandparents have no right to food-cards.' All the same, people managed to keep those 'useless mouths' alive.

Besides this, we used to go on long ski trips over the frozen Ural and in the woods. The iridescent snow would, every so often, show the tracks of wild beasts, which we proceeded to trail. At the age of thirteen my son had become a first-rate skier, though he had no skis, properly speaking, only old planks fastened to his feet. He was at school, where they had one textbook between three pupils and three exercise books per pupil per session; here the little terrors used to fight one another with knives and go marauding in the market. The little *Frantzuz* (Frenchman) acquitted himself well, without a knife, and was respected by all. As a deportee's son, he was a source of anxiety to the Communist senior staff, who actually upbraided him for not breaking off relations with his father. For a short while he was expelled from school for declaring in the social-science lesson that in France the trade unions functioned freely. The headmaster of the school carpeted me for the 'anti-Soviet activities' which I was encouraging in my son. 'But', I told him, 'it is a fact that trade-union freedom and even political freedom exist in France; there is nothing anti-Soviet about that.'

'I find it hard to believe you', replied the headmaster, 'and in any case it is our duty to impress upon our children that true liberty exists here and not in the capitalist dictatorship of the so-called democratic countries.'

At Orenburg the G.P.U. had gathered (doubtless for the purpose of working up a 'case' at some time) half a dozen deportees from the Left Opposition, together with a few young sympathizers; we were a family circle. They were men and women of a truly wonderful stamp. In my novel *S'il est Minuit dans le Siècle* I have taken some pains to recapture the spiritual atmosphere of deportation. Journeying over the years from prison to prison, from exile to exile, tormented by privation, these comrades kept their revolutionary faith, their good spirits, their sparkling political intelligence. Fanya Upstein, less than thirty years old, was an Odessa intellectual, a devoted student; Lydia Svalova was a worker from Perm, still young, who had been deported to the White Sea coast for raising her voice about wages in a meeting; in the north she had been put to work as a waggoner. Lisa Senatskaya, a kindly and steadfast person, was the wife of Vassili Pankratov, an Oppositionist in jail for the last five years, and had herself been deported for refusing to divorce him, 'a fact which proves her solidarity with her husband'. They were expecting to be reunited here.

The men had all fought in the Civil War. Boris Mikhailovich Eltsin, a Bolshevik since 1903, and a member of the Opposition's 'Leading Centre', was a little man with heart trouble and rheumatism; his powerful head was topped with black hair which stood out in rebellious tufts: black chin-beard and moustache, swarthy skin, deep wrinkles, lively eyes, and a thoughtful, spontaneously sarcastic way of talking. Over fifty-five, he came to us from Suzdal prison, where he had bargained with Stalin. He had been deported at first to Feodossia in the Crimea, along with a son who was dying of tuberculosis; but the climate there had been considered too easy for a man so obdurate. Hegel's *Collected Works* were his constant companion. I used to see him having his dinner, a few potatoes and half a herring; he would then make tea, like the old student he was, and at last smile, bright-eyed, and say: 'Tonight I read a page of Hegel over again: it's a tremendous stimulant for the mind!' He remarked too: 'Our unity is the work of the G.P.U.; in fact we have as many tendencies as there are militants. I don't find this at all objectionable.' His son, Victor Borisovich, was deported to Archangel after being five years in prison.

Vassili Feodorovich Pankratov was sent to us after release from a five years' stay in an Isolator (Suzdal, I think). Aged forty, well-set shoulders and head, in vigorous trim, his features athletic and clean-cut as his nature. Once a sailor in the fighting fleet, he had helped to lead the revolutionary movement at Kronstadt in 1917; after that he was in the Civil War, and headed the G.P.U.

at Vladikavkaz (Northern Caucasus); imprisoned in 1928 for three years; when these three years had expired, the G.P.U. asked him if his ideas had changed, and upon his replying in the negative, added another two years to his term. It was only after the prison-inmates threatened to have a hunger-strike to the death that the secret Collegium stopped doling out increased sentences of this kind, and Pankratov recovered his liberty—by being deported. His wife Lisa had waited for him; in our midst they found happiness together— for a little while.

Chanaan Markovich Pevzner, an economist from the Finance Commissariat, had been seriously maimed in the Manchurian campaign. He had done only four years in the Isolator owing to the pitiable condition of his left arm, which had seven bullets in it and dangled like a rag. The G.P.U. arranged employment for him in the regional treasury, to enable him to deal with an incipient attack of scurvy by eating his fill, or as near as might be. Pevzner was young, lively, a strong swimmer and a pessimist. 'We are in for years of it,' he kept saying; 'I do not believe that the Terror will die down: the economic situation demands it.' He had the sharp, bold features of a fighter from old Israel.

Vassili Mikhailovich Chernykh, lately a high G.P.U. official in the Ural area, had, in bygone days, captured Rostov with a little army of miners, sailors and students. He had come to us from the prison at Verkhne-Uralsk. Tall, the very model of a timberman in the Nordic forests with his powerful arms, toughened face, blond mane, and mocking eyes, he was a warm-hearted warrior with a serious head on his shoulders. He argued that, through the absence of an intelligent and decisive leadership, the Petrograd Soviet had missed the chance of a revolution in February–March 1917 at the time of the autocracy's collapse; and that power should have been seized at that time, thus saving a year of semi-bourgeois Keren-skyism. Chernykh was (like myself) one of the tribe of revisionists, who maintained that all ideas, as well as all recent history, should be reviewed from top to bottom. On this issue the Opposition was divided roughly into two halves: there were the revisionists and there were the doctrinaires, themselves subdivided into the orthodox, the extreme Left, and the followers of the theory that the U.S.S.R. was establishing State capitalism.

Ivan Byk came to us from the concentration-camp on the

Solovietsky Islands. A young man, he had fought in the Ukraine, campaigned for the Workers' Opposition, and undergone confinement at Verkhne-Uralsk: there, he had been one of the organizers of a widespread hunger-strike against the 'doubling' of sentences by administrative decision. The strikers did drink water, which enabled them to hold out for longer; on the eighteenth day the strike committee was carrying on as usual. The formidable Andreyeva, who was in charge of political prisons, came to negotiate with the committee. She began by threatening them with forced labour. Byk answered her, 'If you're afraid of labour, I'm not: I'm a worker.'

In the concentration-camp Byk was informed that, in a short telegram published in the newspapers, Christian Rakovsky had announced his support for the Central Committee 'to stand against the war-danger side by side with the Party'. A conciliator by nature, Byk thought this quite reasonable, and accepted Rakovsky's formulation of 'a united front'. He was flown to the Butyrki prison in Moscow. 'You are in favour of a united front between the Opposition and the Central Committee?' 'Yes.' 'Rakovsky goes further than that. . . . Read this article of his. If you sign it, we release you.' Having read the article, Byk simply asked to be sent back to the concentration-camp. After he had finished his sentence, the G.P.U. passed him to us.

Alexei Semionovich Santalov, a proletarian from the Putilov Works, had been in all the revolutions of Petrograd for twenty years and more. An educated, thoughtful person, but sluggish in outward appearance, he used to defend trade-union rights and factory legislation in whatever workshop he found himself: a serious offence. 'A spineless lot of youngsters, this working class of today!' he would say, 'They've never seen an electric light bulb in their lives—it'll take them ten years or more before they get round to demanding decent lavatories!' The G.P.U. deferred to him, but he eventually landed in trouble. During a revolutionary festival Santalov got a little drunk and wandered into a workers' club, where he stopped short before the Leader's portrait. 'You've got to admit it,' he cried noisily, 'a fine face he has, this grave-digger of the Revolution!' He was arrested and we never saw him again.

I have described these men because I am grateful to them for having existed, and because they incarnated an epoch. Most probably all of them have perished.

Ch——, a history professor at Moscow, had been arrested because it was imagined that certain allusions could be heard in his lectures on the French Revolution (Thermidor!). He was so seriously ill that we asked the G.P.U. to send him to a clinic in Moscow. Our demand was granted. He came back to us far less shaky and brought us news: Trotsky, of whom we had heard absolutely nothing for a long time, was founding the Fourth International. With what forces? What parties? we speculated. Ch——, on behalf of some mysterious 'comrades' whom he had, so he said, managed to contact while in hospital, suggested to me that Eltsin and I should establish an illegal committee of the Opposition: 'We need a brain!' We were sitting on the steps of my house, facing the steppe. I asked him questions about the comrades in Moscow, trying to discover their identity; I looked deep into his eyes, and thought to myself: 'You, my friend, are an *agent provocateur*!' I explained to him that even when shut away in prisons we still embodied a basic principle of life and liberty, and that we had no need to organize ourselves into clandestine committees. His attempt failed, then; but he was pardoned some time later. I had been right. If I had listened to him I should be lying dead at this very hour, with a little hole in the back of my neck.

The winter of 1934–5 was frightful, despite the lessening of the famine towards the New Year, the abolition of bread-rationing and the revaluation of the rouble at the equivalent of a kilo of black bread. For a long while my wife, a victim to crises of insanity, had been away from me for treatment in Leningrad. I was left alone with my son, and the G.P.U. suddenly cut off my supplies. A consignment of money posted from Paris via the *Torgsin* was intercepted and 'lost'. I asked the G.P.U. for work, and the Secret Service ironically offered me a night-watchman's job, adding by the way that it was not certain that I could be given a permit to carry arms and this would be contrary to regulations. I now understood that a directive was out to choke me to death—or else that the protest campaign in France on my behalf was annoying Moscow and so they were trying to break me. Try, try again! Our morale was excellent. We had passionately followed the battles in the Asturias in October 1934; in the talks that I gave in the woods by the River Ural, I proclaimed the Spanish Revolution to my comrades; and I was not wrong. A great popular victory in the West could save us by blowing a gust of fresh air across the U.S.S.R. This news coincided with rumours of a political amnesty; the G.P.U. officials told us that Trotsky was begging to come back, offering to submit to the Central Committee. I learned later that Lozovsky was likewise announcing my own impending submission to my comrades in Paris; this, he said, would mean the end of 'the Victor Serge affair'. Rakovsky had just surrendered, but this did not worry us. We told each other, 'He is getting old, and they've played a classical trick on him, showing him confidential documents about the approach of war. . . .' Meanwhile, most of the comrades were being thrown out of work by the G.P.U.

My son and I rationed ourselves to the limit, so that all we fed on now was a little black bread and 'egg-soup' which I made to last two days with some sorrel and just one egg. Fortunately we did have wood. Soon I began to suffer from boils. Pevzner, famished and homeless besides, came to sleep at our house, bed-ridden by attacks of a strange ague. Later we discovered that he had scarlet fever. An enormous anthrax tumour under my left breast laid me flat on my back, and I saw the abscess devouring me. The G.P.U. refused to send me a physician, and the doctor from the Vorstadt dispensary, a young, overworked little woman, tended us as best she could, with no medicines at her disposal. Rumour grew in the neighbourhood that Pevzner was dying (and indeed he was delirious), and that I was dead. The G.P.U. woke up, since they had to answer for us to the Central Collegium. One morning, the most eminent surgeon in town, a tireless and remarkably talented neurotic, burst into the house, wagged his head, told me, 'Don't worry, I'll save you', and had me conveyed immediately to the hospital. Pevzner was already there, in the huts reserved for contagious patients. This was a little after Kirov's assassination.

I left for the hospital lying in straw on a low sledge, on a day dazzling with sunshine and snow. A bearded, wrinkled peasant would turn round to me every now and then to inquire if I was being jolted too much. My son walked along beside the sledge. I could not move an inch; all I could see was a luminous blue of surpassing purity. Vassili Pankratov had just disappeared; he was arrested obscurely, leaving his young wife pregnant. The comrades thought that my condition would prevent my being arrested, but that I would be imprisoned immediately upon discharge from hospital. Such was the fate of Pevzner, whom we never saw again. Once he was convalescent, policemen waited for him at the exit to the huts and took him away to the cellars of the G.P.U.

Pevzner and Pankratov, in common with many other notable deportees who had recently been let out of Isolators and arrested at this time, were to be enrolled into a 'prison conspiracy', invented in the panic over the Kirov affair. We heard no more of them, except that after several months Pankratov arrived at the prison of Verkhne-Uralsk, which held Kamenev and Zinoviev. His message to us said only one thing: 'The investigation has been frightful. Nothing we have so far experienced can be compared with what is going on. Be ready for anything!' And ready we were.

I no longer know how many weeks I spent in the 'gangrenous' department at Orenburg's surgical hospital, during the bitterest part of winter. The hospital was run as efficiently as the general destitution permitted; what it treated primarily was poverty. It was filled with cases of sickness or accident-casualties whose true sickness or accident lay in chronic undernourishment aggravated by alcoholism. The worker who lived on sour-cabbage soup, without fat content, would acquire an abscess as a result of a simple bruise, the abscess would be followed by septic inflammation and this, since the hospital fed its inmates very poorly, would last indefinitely. Children were covered in cold sores; whole wards were full of peasants with frozen limbs; bellies empty, clothes worn and threadbare, they offered small resistance to the cold.

Disinfectants, anaesthetics, analgesics, gauze, bandages, even iodine, came in inadequate quantities, so that dressings which should have been changed daily were only attended to every three days. In the bandaging-room I heard arguments and bargaining going on among the nurses: 'Give me back the three yards of gauze I lent you the day before yesterday, I've a patient here who can't wait any longer!' 'But you must know, the delivery they promised hasn't come. . . .' The same bandages were washed and used over and over again. I saw gangrenous flesh being torn from the frozen limbs with pincers; indescribable scars resulted. To treat me the doctors had to ask for vaccines and drugs from the G.P.U.'s privileged infirmary, the only one which went short of nothing. True, I was in the hospital for the poor—along with Chapayev's old partisans. Official, technical, and military personnel had special clinics reserved for their use. The medical and ancillary staff, which was generally very underpaid, was extraordinarily conscientious.

In the long winter evenings, the convalescing patients used to gather round a big stove in the passageway, and sing, underhandedly, a tragic ballad of love and brigandage; its refrain was:

> *And money, money all the time:*
> *With no money, you can't live. . .*

I got better, largely I believe because the G.P.U. allowed the next dispatch of money to reach me, and so I was able to buy butter, sugar, and rice at the *Torgsin*. I shall never forget the way in which some of the sick people gazed at me when I was brought such food, or their deference when they took their share of it. Nor, for that matter, shall I forget how on the most wretched of our days of misery we all heard a radio broadcast from a regional meeting of *kolkhoz* workers. Passionate voices went on endlessly thanking the Leader for 'the good life we lead'; and twenty or so patients tormented by hunger, half of them *kolkhoz* workers themselves, listened to it all in silence.

Contrary to all our predictions, I did not disappear, but returned home. This was due to the stubborn battle that was raging around my name in France. Militants and intellectuals were demanding that either I be released or my deportation be justified. They were promised that I would have a proper trial—and the trial never took place; they were promised documentation on the case—and no documents were forthcoming. They were promised that I would be freed forthwith; and I was not. At a time when Soviet policy was seeking the support of left-wing circles in France, it was all rather embarrassing.

I am convinced that at the end of 1934, just at the moment when Kirov was murdered, the Politbureau was entering upon a policy of normality and relaxation. The *kolkhoz* system had been modified so far as to permit the farmers to keep their private property even in the *kolkhoz* itself. The Government was anxious to present the Soviet Union in a démocratic role within the League of Nations and was seeking the support of the enlightened bourgeoisie and petty-bourgeoisie in other countries. The revolver-shot fired by Nikolayev ushered in an era of panic and savagery. The immediate response was the execution of 114 people, then the execution of Nikolayev and his friends, fourteen young folk in all; then the arrest and imprisonment of the whole of the former Zinoviev and Kamenev tendency, close on 3,000 persons as far as I could make out; then the mass deportation of tens of thousands of Leningrad citizens, simultaneously with hundreds of arrests among those already deported and the opening of fresh secret trials in the prisons themselves.

Certain mysterious happenings at the top of the Party have come to light: for example, the Yenukidze case. Aveli Yenukidze, whom I have mentioned a number of times in these reminiscences, was a Caucasian Old Bolshevik, a companion of Stalin's youth and, like Stalin, a Georgian; he had also been Secretary of the Central Soviet Executive since the foundation of the Soviet Union. In the discharge of these high offices he proved himself a man of human feeling, and as liberal and large-hearted as was possible in that age. His honesty was evidently an obstacle to the great settling of political accounts whose preparation was in hand. Relieved of his duties and shifted to a subordinate position, Yenukidze gradually disappeared from view (eventually to be shot in 1937, without 'confession' or trial).

On Nikolayev's crime, the world has seen the publication of a number of successive versions, all of them lavish in improbabilities, but not of the original papers, whether the terrorist's own statements or the documents of the investigation. It was almost certainly an individual act committed by an enraged young Communist. The Left or Trotskyist Opposition was, in all likelihood, represented in Leningrad at that time solely by Alexandra Bronstein; I cannot doubt, with my intimate knowledge of its members, ideas, and general condition, that it had nothing whatsoever to do with the assassination. We still viewed ourselves as the partisans of 'Soviet reform', and reform excluded any appeal to violence. I was too well acquainted with the followers of the Zinoviev tendency, as well as those of the Right Opposition, men tragically cautious and loyal, to suspect them for a single moment. The murder was a spontaneous act, but it confronted the Politbureau with a frightful problem: not only their own responsibility for the years of darkness, but also the existence of a reserve team of government in the persecuted Opposition who, for all the abuse directed so incessantly against them, were more popular among the informed sections of the population than the leaders of the State. 'Just think of it', one official said to me, terrified, 'one of the Party leaders has been deliberately shot by a young Party member who didn't even belong to any Oppositional tendency!'

Throughout the whole of the year 1935, the Politbureau was secretly torn between contrary inclinations, towards normalization on the one hand, towards terror on the other. The first-named tendency seemed to be on the winning side. Executions, jailings, and deportations had long ceased to interest the masses. By contrast, the abolition of bread-rationing made everybody happy. This country, for the sake of a little progress in the direction of prosperity, would walk over any number of corpses without noticing. I told myself that Stalin only had to increase real wages a little, allow the collective farmers room to breathe, wind up the concentration-camps, and shout pardon to any political opponents who were either mere invalids or else interested only in supporting him without loss of face—and he could at once soar into imperishable popularity. I was of the opinion that he was about to enter this course with the new Soviet Constitution, on whose drafting Bukharin was at work.

And so, for what was left of our family of deportees, the year glided past with a deceptive tranquillity. A number of Communist exiles arrived, who all continued to declare their loyalty to 'the General Line'; we avoided their company except for a few of them.

I was finishing my books in a state of uncertainty. What would their destiny be, and mine? There was an autobiographical piece on the French anarchist movement just before the First World War (*Les Hommes Perdus*), and a novel, *La Tourmente*, which followed on from my published novels. In it I reconstructed the atmosphere of the year 1920, the zenith of the Revolution. I had also completed a small collection of poems, *Résistance*, and amassed a great pile of notes for a historical work on War Communism. I finished these writings in two and a half years; they were the only works I have ever had the opportunity to revise at leisure. I wrote in French, in a town where no one understood French; unable to converse in this language myself except with my son. Although I am inured to efforts of will-power, I have to recognize that it was often only an actual hardening of my nature that enabled me to persevere. It is not easy to work without respite, wondering if all one's writing may not tomorrow be seized, confiscated, or destroyed. By one of those strokes of irony that are so frequent in Russia, the Soviet Press was, quite appropriately, commemorating an anniversary of the Ukrainian national poet Taras Shevchenko, who in 1847 had been exiled for ten years to the steppes of Orenburg, 'forbidden to draw or to write'. He did, all the same, write some clandestine poetry which he concealed in his boots. In this report I had an overwhelming insight into the persistence in our Russian land, after a century of reform, progress, and revolution, of the same wilful determination to wipe out the rebellious intelligence without mercy. Never mind, I told myself, I must hold on: hold on and work on, even under this slab of lead.

I made several copies of my manuscripts, and made an arrangement through the post with Romain Rolland to send him my books; he was perfectly willing to forward them to some publishers in Paris. Rolland had no love for me, since long ago I had strongly attacked his doctrine of non-violence which had its inspiration in Gandhism; but he was worried by the repression in the U.S.S.R. and wrote to me in very friendly terms. I posted him a first manuscript in four registered envelopes, not forgetting to inform the G.P.U. that I had done so. All four envelopes were lost. I went to complain to the head of the secret police and he exclaimed, 'Just see how deplorably the Post Office works! And then you say we're exaggerating when we uncover sabotage! Why, my own letters to my wife go astray! I promise you that a proper inquiry will be made and that the Post Office will pay you the lawful compensation without delay!'

He even offered, very kindly, to supervise the transmission, still to Romain Rolland, of another set of manuscripts which the G.P.U. would see were visaed by the literary censors. I entrusted them to his care—and of course they never reached their destination.

While this was going on, my correspondence with abroad was cut off. The head of the secret police shook his head gravely: 'Oh dear! What would you have us do to put the Post Office right?' The Post Office regularly paid me hundreds of roubles for the registered letters that I continued to send at the rate of five a month and which 'went astray'. This afforded me the income of a well-paid technician.

Meanwhile, in France, the 'Victor Serge affair' was proving a troublesome business in working-class and intellectual circles. In its annual conferences the United Teachers' Federation was demanding my release, or else some justification for my confinement. At the 1934 conference of this body the Soviet teachers' delegation had promised that I would be tried before a duly constituted court. At the Rheims conference in 1935, the Russian delegation, which was greeted with chants of '*Victor Serge! Victor Serge!*' raised by the whole hall, provoked a storm of booing by declaring that I was mixed up in the Kirov affair! The League for the Rights of Man published the detailed documentation assembled by Magdeleine Paz. *La Révolution Prolétarienne*, *L'Ecole Emancipée*, *Le Combat Marxiste*, *Les Humbles* (under Maurice Wullens) took up the campaign. Georges Duhamel, Léon Werth, Charles Vildrac, Marcel Martinet, Jacques Mesnil, Maurice Parijanine, Boris Souvarine, and the wavering editorial board of *L'Europe*, all in different ways took an interest in the case. In Holland, Henriette Roland-Holst, in Switzerland Fritz Brupbacher, in Belgium Charles Plisnier lent their support to the protests. Brupbacher was told quite baldly by Helen? Stassova, the secretary of International Class-war Prisoners' Aid in Moscow: 'Serge will never get out.'[1]

In June 1935 an 'International Congress of Writers for the Defence of Culture' took place in Paris, formally upon the initiative of such left-wingers as Alain, Barbusse, Romain Rolland, Elie Faure, André Gide, André Malraux, and Victor Margueritte.[2] The actual initiative came from certain Communist back rooms which specialized in organizing congresses of this kind; their objective was to arouse a pro-Stalinist movement among the French intelligentsia and buy over a number of famous consciences. My friends decided to attend the congress and demand to be heard. Some of them got themselves ejected by the stewards. Aragon and Ehrenburg manipulated

---

[1] Maurice Wullens: 'libertarian veteran' referred to on page 347. Maurice Parijanine: writer, poet, and collaborator with Serge in the translation work of the Communist International's executive; the subject of Serge's memoir, *Deux Recontres*. Fritz Brupbacher (1874–1945): Swiss physician and Socialist over forty years; expelled from the Socialist Party in 1914 for his revolutionary internationalism and from the Communist Party in 1933 for his anti-Stalinism, which was of a semi-anarchist rather than a Trotskyist variety. Charles Plisnier (1896–1952): Belgian novelist and former Communist militant; expelled from the Communist Party in 1928 as a Trotskyist; subsequently turned exclusively to literary work.

[2] Alain (1868–1951): an outstanding French teacher and author in philosophy; formed no system of his own. Elie Faure (1873–1937): nephew of the Reclus brothers; physician, art historian, biographer, and philosopher, of broad progressive sympathies. Victor Margueritte (1866–1942): ex-officer and subsequently anti-militarist writer; prominent pacifist.

the assembly in accordance with secret directives. Barbusse, Malraux, and Gide presided with some embarrassment. Heinrich Mann and Gustav Regler spoke of the persecuted intellectuals of Germany, Gaetano Salvemini of those in Italy and of freedom of thought in general. Salvemini caused a scene by condemning 'all the oppressions' and mentioning my name.[1] Gide, amazed to find that fierce efforts were being made to hush up the dispute, insisted on the ventilation of the matter, and Malraux, who was chairing the session, finally allowed Magdeleine Paz to speak: she spoke harshly, in fighting terms. Charles Plisnier, the novelist and mystical poet, and a Communist militant not long ago, supported her. Henry Poulaille, the author of *Damnés de la Terre*, a true son of the workers' suburbs who did not mince his words, demonstrated in the hall.

The delegation from the Soviet writers included two men with whom I had been on friendly terms, the poets Boris Pasternak and Nikolai Tikhonov, and also a person in the innermost circle of Party confidence, whom I had met in Moscow, the official journalist Mikhail Koltsov, a man as remarkable for his talent as for his pliant docility; besides these there were the successful playwright Kirshon and the hack agitator-novelist Ehrenburg. Pasternak, who is at once the Mallarmé and Apollinaire of Russian poetry, a truly great writer and a victim of semi-persecution besides, kept in the background. The other four fulfilled instructions and declared without a blink that they knew nothing of the writer Victor Serge—these, my good colleagues of the Soviet Writers' Union! All they knew of was a 'Soviet citizen, a confessed counter-revolutionary, who had been a member of the conspiracy which had ended in the murder of Kirov'. As he declaimed this from the platform, Koltsov did not suspect that in 1939 he himself would disappear, in complete obscurity, into the G.P.U. prisons.[2] Kirshon did not suspect that

[1] Heinrich Mann (1871–1950): German novelist and playwright, an exile in France and the United States after the rise of Hitler. Gustav Regler (1898–1963): German novelist and former Communist; political commissar with the International Brigades in Spain; broke with the Party in 1939; a companion of Serge's exile in Mexico. Gaetano Salvemini (1873–1957): Italian historian and independent Deputy (1919–21); in exile after the rise of Mussolini; at Harvard University from 1934 to 1948.

[2] Koltsov was arrested in 1938 after his return from reporting on the Spanish Civil War, and perished in 1942. Kirshon, a friend of Yagoda, and author of *Bread* (1930), a play on the extermination of the *kulaks*, was arrested and shot in 1938. Both men have been officially 'rehabilitated' in recent years.

two years later, he would disappear himself, dubbed a 'terrorist-Trotskyist'—he whose pen had never been anything other than strictly conformist. Ehrenburg forgot his flight from Russia, his banned novels, his accusation against Bolshevism of 'crucifying Russia'. Tikhonov forgot his hymns to Courage, in those splendid epic ballads of his which I had translated into French. Nobody there could foresee the grim tumbrils of the Moscow Trials, but they knew of the 127 executions of innocents; these had been publicly announced the day after Nikolayev's deed and, according to the Soviet Press, were even stoutly approved by humanists such as Jean-Richard Bloch and Romain Rolland. The shameless statement that justified my captivity by a murder committed two years after my arrest sent a shiver down more than one spine. André Gide went to see the Soviet Ambassador, who could give him no enlightenment at all.

Almost at the same time Romain Rolland, who had been invited to Moscow and received by Stalin, spoke to him of the 'Victor Serge affair'. Yagoda, the head of the political police, was consulted, and could find nothing in his files (if he had found the least confession of complicity signed by myself, I should have been lost). Stalin promised that I would be authorized to leave the U.S.S.R., together with my family.

But where could I go? For a moment the battle for visas seemed hopeless. The French Prime Minister Laval refused us the entry-permit into France for which my friends pleaded. Approaches made in London were fruitless. Approaches made in Holland were fruitless. Copenhagen promised. Then Emile Vandervelde, now in the government of Belgium, arranged for us to be granted permission to reside there for three years. If these negotiations had dragged on a few weeks longer, I should never have left the country; I should have been no more than a dead man on bail.

Suddenly I was given three days to get ready to leave for Moscow, and thence for an 'unknown destination' which the G.P.U. Collegium would fix. When the Political Red Cross sent me forms to sign for a Belgian visa, I thought I could understand. Above all, I believed, I had enough standing and support in France to ensure that they would not dare to prolong my confinement. My comrades Bobrov and Eltsin, and others who had just come from Isolators, such as Leonid Girchek and Yakov Belenky, thought that I had fallen victim to unfortunate illusions: 'You'll have a rude awakening when you find yourself in a nice dark prison or some desert in Kazakhstan. . . .'

'It is not to the G.P.U.'s advantage', I replied, 'that I should be in a position to observe its machinery any further. They know quite well that I will never capitulate and that in the end I shall just have to be released, able to write about it all. . . . I would be doomed only if Fascism won in France, and it failed in its *coup* of 6 February 1934.' Old Eltsin, crippled with rheumatism, was living in an icy little room in a house without a w.c.; I asked him, 'Should I start a campaign in the Press abroad to get you out?' and he answered, 'No. My place is here.'

I took the precaution of giving away my household goods only on condition that they be kept at my disposal for a month and sent on to me if, from the heart of some Siberia or other, I asked for them back. All I took with me was papers, useful books, and personal keepsakes. I went off with my son on a freezing day in April. Chernykh, usually so sprightly with his vigorous manner and his wild, Russian plainsman's hair, was gloomy when he said good-bye to me. 'Those of us who are still alive', he told me, 'will be old, forgotten and obsolete on the day that a new liberty is born in Russia. We shall be like that old revolutionary who came back to St. Petersburg after thirty years of exile during the March days in 1917, met nobody he knew in all the chaos and died of neglect in a hotel room. After it was all over, they recognized him . . .!'

My heart was utterly ravaged as I left; I was severing attachments of a unique quality. I should have liked to have those dear faces, that I would never see again, imprinted on my brain, and those landscapes of white countryside, and even some image of our great Russian misery, lived out by this brave, gritty, patient people. If I could have believed in any reasonable chance that I would not ultimately have been obliterated in a voiceless struggle which was already sterile, I should have been content to remain there— even if it were in some little Mongol fishing village inside the Arctic Circle. But we do not live for ourselves; we live to work and fight.

The white plains fled past endlessly in the windows of the train. Two seedy-looking policemen had taken their seats not far from us. At Kuibyshev the Volga was still frozen. Tartar Republic, busy little stations, young women with coloured kerchiefs over their hair, peasant dwellings surrounded by birch-trees and little wooden paddocks. . . . In the station at Syzran a great clang of ironmongery made the passengers jump, and we saw an implausible goods-train slewing to and fro over yielding, dancing metals. It was only a small, unimportant derailment: the ballast gone, the soil dissolved with the early thaw, and a false move. The railwaymen chuckled bitterly about it: 'That's where Stakhanovism gets you, citizen! They still have to learn that the stock gets tired just like people!' In another spot the train slowed down in the middle of the steppe and I saw workmen with iron bars holding together the broken rails over which we were gingerly moving. Our train had to alter its route—and arrived several hours late—because of a serious accident on the line.

Moscow. The bustle of the streets and memories, memories! The luxurious Metro with its granite paving, its walls in Ural stone, its exits, huge underground avenues—but without benches for travellers, and expensive. We know how to build subterranean palaces, but we forget that a working-class woman coming home from work would love to be able to sit down beneath all these rich-hued stones.

At the Political Red Cross, in overcrowded little offices on the Kuznetsky Bridge, a stone's throw from the tall, square tower of the G.P.U. building, we saw Ekaterina Pavlovna Peshkova and her colleague Vinaver, a former Liberal lawyer. Ekaterina Pavlovna still bore the name of Gorky, whose wife she had been and whose devoted friend she still was. Having won Lenin's confidence she was allowed, during the Red Terror, to found a relief organization for political detainees, of whatever kind; it was tolerated, first by the Cheka, then by the G.P.U., with a mixture of respect, trust, and hostility. Peshkova was able to manage the amazing moral feat of retaining the trust simultaneously of victims and inquisitors! For year after year this sad, thin woman, with lovely grey eyes and a style of dress whose very artlessness was elegant, aided by a tiny band of untiring fellow-workers, lavished intervention, intercession, and relief on behalf of all the victims of the various terrors that followed hotfoot upon one another. Nobody else in the whole world during this century, I am convinced, has known, and at such close quarters, so many disasters, deaths, atrocities, and tragedies, some inevitable, some senseless. Peshkova lived in a private hell, the repository of countless secrets, all of them deadly as the strongest poison. She was never too tired, never disheartened, however dark the times were—and for her, only for her, all the times of the Revolution were dark. Pledged to secrecy, she has remained unknown to the great world outside.

Ekaterina Pavlovna informed me that my wife, my poor invalid, was waiting for me, along with Jeannine, the baby that had been been born to us while I was in hospital at Orenburg a little over a year ago. She informed me also that I would not see Anita Russakova, who had just been arrested and deported for five years to Viatka. I immediately understood why: now I should not be able to talk to Anita and resolve the mystery of her lying confessions. I was told that we had to leave for Warsaw that same evening. I asked Ekaterina Pavlovna to request a twenty-four hours delay from the G.P.U. so that I could have an exit-permit for my manuscripts (which had obligingly been promised me for the following day) from the censorship, and for my baggage from the head customs-office. When she came back, Peshkova told me, 'Go this very evening, don't press for anything. The secret-police officer just told me that you were not out of the country yet, and that he was sending Yagoda a fresh memorandum about you. . . .' I demurred no longer. I was never to be given any of my manuscripts although their exit had been authorized by *Glavlit*, the literary censorship. Of our baggage we took away only a few small articles in our attaché-cases. All the rest of it was ultimately seized, or rather stolen, by the G.P.U.

Francesco Ghezzi, gaunt and unbending, now a worker in a Moscow factory and the only syndicalist still at liberty in Russia, came with us to the train. Off we went, travelling third class, alone in our carriage, with a few roubles and ten dollars between four persons. In the smart and empty station at Negoreloye, ornamental uniforms surrounded us and searched us minutely: we were made to undress, and even the soles of my shoes were scrutinized with attention. The train entered the grey no-man's-land of the frontier. Behind us we were leaving the boundless grey fields of the collective farms; now we were crossing a sort of desert laid out for war. We had the feeling that we were the only travellers in this wilderness. Oh, our great Russia of agonies, how hard it is to tear ourselves away from you!

So ended my seventeen years' experience of victorious revolution.

9

DEFEAT IN THE WEST
1936—1941

Once we were over the Polish border we could see charming little houses, newspaper-kiosks selling the journals of Paris, Berlin, London, and New York, decently-clad railwaymen, relaxed faces. By the illuminations of evening, Warsaw was a picture of tall façades, garnished with tasteful arrays of blue electric light. All the clothes in the Marszalkowska seemed elegant, and the very bustle of the street seemed to have an air of nonchalance and prosperity. The shops, full of everything to dream of, were an even greater contrast, compared with our meagre co-operatives. All these comparisons we found heartrending. We did not get out of the train when we were crossing Nazi Germany. I could only manage, from the prominence of a bridge, to glimpse a square that I had known not long ago, near the Silesia Station in Berlin. Germany showed no sign of change to the passing eye: efficiency and neatness everywhere, architecture designed for privacy or sheer size, elaborate garden-plots. Some Jewish travellers whom I questioned told me that they could keep alive, only in fear. I had the impression that, since each of them was looking to his own fortune in a large country in which terror was nothing if not secret, they knew little of the dark side of the régime, and were afraid to speak even of this little, even with a Russian traveller. Still, they regarded the U.S.S.R. as a privileged land.

In Brussels we found refuge in the small home of a syndicalist militant of Russian origin who had lately been in jail at Suzdal, and then expelled from the Soviet Union. He lived off his un-employment benefit and went to the Town Hall for the meals provided at minimum cost to the unemployed. When he offered to give me a share of his dinner, which consisted of a rich soup, stew, and potatoes, I exclaimed, 'Back home over there, this is the kind of meal that a high Party official would eat!' He had three rooms, and possessed a bicycle and a gramophone. This unemployed Belgian lived as comfortably as a well-paid technician in the U.S.S.R.

The day after our arrival, as soon as I got up, I went to explore this provincial scene. The freshly-painted houses still had the look of old Flemish towns, with modern buildings carefully styled to maintain an individual flavour; the square paving-stones were newly-washed. My son and I would stop in front of the shops, moved beyond words. The little windows overflowed with hams, chocolates, gingerbread, rice, and such improbable fruits as oranges, mandarins, and bananas! These riches were within reach, within reach of an unemployed man in a working-class area, without benefit of Socialism or a Plan! It was disconcerting. I had known of all this beforehand, but the reality of it shocked me as if I had been ignorant. It was enough to make one weep in humiliation and grief for our Russia of revolutions.

On May Day we saw these provincial streets full of workers out in their Sunday best with their families; young girls with red-ribboned hair, men with red badges in their buttonholes, all of them with well-fed faces, the women fat at thirty and the men fleshy at forty or so. They were off to a Socialist demonstration, and looked just like the bourgeoisie as pictured by the popular imagination in Russia under the influence of the cinema. Peaceable, content with their lot: I gathered that these workers of the West now had no desire whatsoever to fight for Socialism, or for anything else for that matter.

The city centre, with its commercial opulence, its illuminated signs, its Bourse set solid in the middle of town, was the cause of much astonishment to my son, then in his sixteenth year and a Soviet schoolboy; my answers to his questions seemed incredible, and only confused him the more.

'This big building then, with all these shops and waterfalls of fire on the roof—does it belong to one man, who can do just what he likes with it? Does this shop, with enough shoes for the whole of Orenburg, belong to just one owner?'

'Yes, son: his name is written there in lights. The gentleman probably owns a factory, a country house, several cars. . . .'

'All for him?'

'Yes, you might say.'

It all seemed mad to my Soviet adolescent. He went on:

'But what does he live for, this man? What is his aim in life?'

'His aim', I replied, 'is, broadly speaking, to make himself and his children rich. . . .'

'But he's already rich! Why does he want to get any richer? In the first place it's unjust—and then too, living just to get rich is simply idiotic! Are they all like that, these shop-owners?'

'Yes, son, and if they heard you talking, they would think you were a madman—a rather dangerous madman. . . .'

I have not forgotten this conversation; it taught me more than it taught my son.

I went to Ixelles to see the streets of my childhood once more: nothing had changed there, nothing at all. In the Place Communale I discovered Timmerman's bakery again; there were the same superb rice-tarts, powdered with sugar, so dear to my twelve-year-old self, in the very same shop window. The bookseller in whose shop I bought Redskin tales as a child had prospered: I had known him as an anarchist with a defiantly careless neck-tie, and now he was a Communist sympathizer, white-haired, wearing an artistic cravat, and fat, of course. . . . All those blazing ideas, all those struggles, all the bloodshed, wars, revolutions, civil wars, all our imprisoned martyrs—and all the time in the West here nothing was changing, and the tasty rice-tarts in the baker's window told of the drowsy permanency of things.

The slum districts inspired me with quite different reflections; they *had* changed. La Marolle, Rue Haute, Rue Blaes, and all the wretched alleys near by had become healthy, smart, prosperous streets. This paupers' town, once decked out in rags and saturated in filth, now breathed an air of well-being: wonderful pork-butchers' shops, a fine brand-new hospital, the hovels replaced by working-class flats with flowers lining the balconies. It was the work of reformist Socialism, as splendid as in Vienna.

There I saw Vandervelde, whom we had called 'social-traitor': he was coming back from a demonstration, with several Socialist leaders by him, and a great, loving murmur ran along the street, a sort of whispered acclamation: '*Le Patron! Le Patron!*' I went to see him at his house. His seventy years had spread weight upon him; his voice was weak and he had to listen with a hearing-aid, head bent and eyes set in concentration. His small pointed beard was still dark and his eyes still held the same animated, vaguely sad

expression behind their lenses. Shaking his head to and fro, he asked
me about Russian prisons, about Trotsky, whose 'aggressive manner'
he could not understand—and how could I explain it to him? He
told me, 'This contented Belgium that you see is a positive oasis in
the midst of dangers, terrible dangers.'

Another time, after the execution of the Sixteen in Moscow,
I found him dreadfully depressed, still crushed under the in-
comprehensibility of it all. 'I have read Kamenev's confession:
raving madness. . . . How can you explain it to me? I knew Kamenev: I can see him before me now, with his white hair, his noble
head—I cannot believe that they have killed him after this outburst
of stark lunacy. . . .' How could I begin to explain such crimes to this
old man who, on the threshold of the grave, incarnated half a
century of Socialist humanism? I was dumbfounded, even more than
when my son asked me his questions.

The friends who came from Paris to visit me said, 'Don't write
anything about Russia, perhaps you may be too bitter. . . . We are
just at the start of a tremendous movement of popular enthusiasm.
Oh, if you could see Paris, the meetings, the demonstrations!
Limitless hope is being born. We are allied with the Communist
Party, which is winning over splendid masses of people; for these
Russia is still an unsullied star. . . . Besides, no one would believe
you. . . .' Only Boris Souvarine thought otherwise. 'The truth!'
he said. 'Absolutely naked, as undiluted, as brutal as possible! We
are witnessing an epidemic of highly dangerous stupidity!'

The strikes of May and June 1936 burst suddenly upon France
and Belgium, with their new form of struggle, unplanned by anybody: the occupation of the factories. At Antwerp and in the
Borinage the movement started spontaneously, as soon as the
workers read the newspaper reports of the events in France. My
Socialist friends, some of whom were trade-union leaders, were
surprised, enraptured, and embarrassed. Léon Blum came to
power, announcing social reforms which only the other day nobody
had dreamt of—paid holidays, nationalization of war industries.
The employing class was actually seized with panic.

The Belgian *Sûreté* called me in and accused me, on the lines of
several Press reports, of 'agitating among the Borinage miners'.
I had been 'seen at Jumet'! Most fortunately, I had not gone out
of Brussels, but spent practically every evening there in the

company of influential Socialists. 'The G.P.U. has not forgotten me,' I remarked, 'you can be sure of that.'

For years hence, denunciations were going to rain around me: sometimes public, launched by the Communist Press, which in Belgium demanded my expulsion 'in the name of respect for the right of asylum'; sometimes secret, passed on mysteriously to the police authorities of the West. The welcoming telegram sent me by Trotsky from Oslo got lost—intercepted, no one knew how. A letter from Trotsky's son which mentioned the *agent provocateur* Sobolevicius[1] (Sénine) never reached me. In the house where I lived, the first floor was rented by strangers who kept watch over my comings and goings with no pretence of concealment. When the Spanish Civil War broke out, a police superintendent called on me with a search-warrant, looking even in my baby daughter's cradle for arms intended for the Republicans. 'I know, of course,' he apologized, 'that we can't take it seriously, but you have been denounced.'

Two days after I arrived, a gentleman who seemed over-tanned, overdressed, and over-affectionate, approached me in a café: 'Dear Victor Serge! How good it is to meet you!' I recognized Bastajić, of *La Fédération Balkanique*; he said he was living in Geneva, and pressed me to fix a meeting with him. 'Geneva?' I said to myself, 'You are a secret agent, then', and did not keep the appointment. I learned later that he had been sent by the G.P.U.; he helped to arrange the murder of Ignace Reiss.[2]

All my close relatives in Russia had now been arrested, including two girls and two young men, all of them unpolitical; of these, my brothers-in-law and sisters-in-law, I never heard again. My eldest sister, an intellectual and equally unpolitical, disappeared too. My mother-in-law was torn from her children and deported alone, God knows where.

In 1938 I was living in the outskirts of Paris. Leopold III visited the city, with an entourage of officials which included several Socialists who were friends of mine. Information was laid, and

[1] Sobolevicius later emerged in the United States as an anti-Trotskyist agent under the name of Jack Soble, and was arrested under that name for espionage in 1957.

[2] Pavle Bastajić, a former Young Serb militant before his conversion to Communism, made his return to occupied Yugoslavia in 1940 but was arrested the following year, and later murdered in a concentration-camp.

passed from one department to another at the last moment, accusing me of 'preparing the assassination of the King of Belgium'. A senior Paris police official told me, 'You can guess where that comes from, they're plaguing you and laughing at me!' However, a card classifying me as 'suspected of terrorism' was sent around every police force in Europe, and my dossier swelled, terrifying the officials at the Préfecture. I had no end of trouble as a result.

In the meantime, now that I had made my anguished protest against the first Moscow Trial, the Soviet Legation in Brussels withdrew our passports. Antonov, the First Secretary, informed me that we had been 'deprived of Soviet nationality'.

'My daughter Jeannine too, who is not yet eighteen months old?' I asked ironically.

'That is so.'

Antonov refused me any written certificate of this fact. The Belgian Foreign Ministry received only a verbal confirmation from him, and that after much insisting.

The Communist Press now began a fantastic campaign of slander against me; it was led by a man with whom I had old ties of friendship and who personally, I was to learn, was shocked and sickened by the whole business. For a short while I was the most calumniated man in the world, for in accordance with some directive those scandalous sheets were translated into all languages. Agencies offered to send me all the cuttings at one franc twenty centimes a copy. The Communist cell-organization in the Press and the French reviews was admirably complete. The review *Europe*, to which I contributed, was more or less in bond to them. On the *Nouvelle Revue Française* they were on close terms with Malraux. The left-wing intellectuals' weekly, *Vendredi*, was backed by industrialists doing good business in Russia, and so was 'on the line'. I had to give up my well-paid work on Léon Blum's *Le Populaire*, because of pressures influencing the editorial staff. The publishing-house of Rieder, which had put out my novels, no longer showed them in its window-display, and deleted them from its catalogue. I found myself under a boycott that was practically total; it was impossible for me to live by writing. The only platform I had left was in the Liége Socialist daily, *La Wallonie*, and in extreme left-wing publications with a limited circulation.

I decided to resume one of the crafts of my youth, and become a proof-reader. This was no longer an easy matter since I could not find work in any print-shops where there were Communists. Luckily, the trade union was outside their sphere of influence. I worked in the *Croissant* printing-works; I loved its old-fashioned nineteenth-century buildings, the noise of machines, the smell of ink and dust, and the neighbourhood around—pubs, small hotels catering for the love-life of workers and their girls, houses of Old Paris, the little restaurant where Jaurès was murdered. Cyclists would drink a glass or two, waiting for the last edition. As the 'run' ended, faces would relax, and trade-jokes pass back and forth over the 'stone'. I corrected the proofs of reactionary sheets; and left-wing ones, too, to which I was denied access as a writer, such as *Messidor*, the C.G.T. weekly, which was run nominally by Jouhaux but actually by men who went to Moscow for their instructions, if they did not take them from secret and semi-secret agents.

Bernard Grasset published my books: an essay on Russia (*Destiny of a Revolution*) and a novel (*S'il est Minuit dans le Siècle*). Grasset was something of a reactionary, but of a free-ranging disposition, and he had colleagues who, like himself, loved any book, provided it was good. One knew that really great works would never come near this house. But in it a book retained its whole personality; the publishers never asked any writer to alter a single line.

An expression arose in France which tried to characterize the feeling of strength and confidence in the future generated by the Popular Front: 'euphoria', it was called. Trotsky wrote to me from Norway that it was leading straight to disaster, and I disagreed, wrongly, for at that juncture he saw far and true. For a short while I moved among some of Léon Blum's friends: Blum's brilliance, integrity, deep nobility, and warm popularity gave him such extra-ordinary prestige that people in his circle were afraid that he might be murdered by the Right. 'It would be better', I said, 'if he were also a man of authority—much less of a great Parliamentarian and much more of a leader for militant masses.' They assured me that he was. At this time he was refusing to avail himself of secret funds to manipulate the Press and back his own Party; I observed, from rather close quarters, an instructive piece of negotiation between the head of his Press Office and a large daily newspaper influenced by Mussolini, which only demanded money—which it eventually got —to turn its support to the Popular Front.

I did not share the opinion voiced by several extreme left-wingers who thought that in June 1936 the opportunity for revolution had been lost through a failure of nerve. I regarded the successful strikes as marking the re-emergence of the French working class which, enfeebled by the bloodshed of war, was now managing to recover its strength. It still needed several more years, in my opinion, to reach a fresh maturity, which would come with the passing of twenty or more years after the days of slaughter. For the same reason, I had immense confidence in the working-class movement of Spain; not having been involved in the war, the Spanish populace lived in the sure knowledge of its own brimming energy.

In any case, the 'euphoria' was snapped quite suddenly by two events which had a historical connexion. 18 July 1936 saw the outbreak of the Spanish military uprising, the coming of which was incisively predicted from the tribunal of the Cortes by my comrade Joaquín Maurín. Meanwhile, over the whole of the Soviet Union, arrests were being made—and were publicly reported—of well-known Communist officials. Trotsky sent me a scandalous cutting from *Pravda* proclaiming that 'the monsters, enemies of the people, will be annihilated with a mighty hand'. The Old Man wrote to me: 'I fear that this may be the prelude to a massacre. . . .' For long months, perhaps for years, he had had no first-hand news from Russia, and what I told him shocked him. I began to tremble for all those left behind there. And on 14 August, like a thunderbolt, came the announcement of the Trial of the Sixteen, concluded on the 25th—eleven days later!—by the execution of Zinoviev, Kamenev, Ivan Smirnov, and all their fellow-defendants. I understood, and wrote at once, that this marked the beginning of the extermination of all the old revolutionary generation. It was impossible to murder only some, and allow the others to live, their brothers, impotent witnesses maybe, but witnesses who understood what was going on. 'Why this massacre?' I speculated, in *La Révolution Prolétarienne*, and could find no other explanation except the urge to wipe out all reserve teams of government on the eve of a war now considered as imminent. Stalin, I was convinced, had not specifically planned the trials; but in the Spanish Civil War he saw the beginning of the war in Europe.

I am conscious of being the living proof of the *unplanned* character of the first trial and, at the same time, of the crazy falsity of the charges brought up in all the Trials. I had departed from the U.S.S.R. in mid-April, at a time when practically all the accused were already in prison. I had worked with Zinoviev and Trotsky, I was a close acquaintance of dozens of those who were to disappear and be shot, I had been one of the leaders of the Left Opposition in Leningrad and one of its spokesmen abroad, and I had never capitulated. Would I have been allowed to leave Russia, with my skill as a writer and my firm evidence as a witness whose facts were irrefutable, if the extermination-trials had been in the offing? Then too, not one mad accusation had been made against me in the whole course of the Trials; which proved that lies were being spread only about those with no means of defending themselves. The case of Trotsky is different: his was the most brilliant head, which had to be struck down at all costs.

In Paris we set up a 'Committee for Inquiry into the Moscow Trials and the Defence of Free Opinion in the Revolution', which included the surrealist poet André Breton, the pacifist Félicien Challaye, the poet Marcel Martinet, Socialists like Magdeleine Paz and André Philip, writers like Henry Poulaille and Jean Galtier-Boissière, worker-militants like Pierre Monatte and Alfred Rosmer, Left journalists such as Georges Pioch, Maurice Wullens and Emery, and the historians Georges Michon and Dommanget. I got the Committee's long title accepted through my insistence, ever since the summer of 1936, that we would also have the task of defending, within the Spanish Revolution, those whom Soviet totalitarianism would attempt to liquidate in Madrid and Barcelona by the same methods of lying and murder. We used to meet in café back rooms, first in the Place de la République, then in the Odéon. We had no money at all, and the Popular Front's Press was closed to us. *Le Populaire* reduced its reports on the Trials to a minimum and never published our documents. For years there would be this struggle of no more than a handful of individual consciences against a total suppression of the truth, in the face of crimes which were beheading the Soviet Union and would soon bring about the downfall of the Spanish Republic. Often we felt like voices crying in the wilderness. We were heartened by the formation in the United States of the Commission of John Dewey, Suzanne LaFollette, and Otto Rühle to conduct the same inquiry. (And even now, as I write these lines, I learn of the mysterious murder in New York of one of the great idealists who worked with that Commission, the old Italian anarchist Carlo Tresca. . . .[1])

The most shameless lying conceivable blazed out before our very eyes. But as witnesses we were practically gagged. In *Pravda* I could read the accounts (all of them mangled) of the Trials. I picked out literally hundreds of improbabilities, absurdities, gross distortions of fact, utterly lunatic statements. But it was a deluge of delirium. Scarcely had I analysed one billow of flagrant deceit than another, more violent, would wash away my day's work into futility. The torrent was so overwhelming that one could never find one's bearings. The British Intelligence Service blended with the Gestapo; railway accidents became political crimes; Japan entered the act; the Great Famine of collectivization had been organized by 'Trotskyists' (all of them in jail at the time); crowds of defendants whose trials were pending disappeared for evermore into the shadows; the succession of executions went on into thousands, without trials of any sort. And in every country of the civilized world, learned and 'progressive' jurists were to be found who thought these proceedings to be correct and convincing. It was turning into a tragic lapse of the whole modern conscience. In France the League for the Rights of Man, with a reputation going back to Dreyfus, had a jurist of this variety in its midst. The League's executive was divided into a majority which opposed any investigation, and an outraged minority which eventually resigned. The argument generally put forward amounted to: 'Russia is our ally. . . .' It was imbecilic reasoning— there is more than a hint of suicide about an international alliance which turns into moral and political servility—but it worked powerfully. The Chairman of the League for the Rights of Man, Victor Basch, one of the brave souls of the old battles against the General Staff, gave me an interview lasting several hours; at the end of it, prostrate with melancholy, he promised me that a commission would be called. It never was.

With no resources, with no assistance, I published irrefutable analyses of the three great lying Trials. Events have validated every line of them, even down to certain 'fine points': I announced that Radek, condemned to ten years of imprisonment, would not live for long: he was murdered in prison. The mechanism of extermination was so simple that one could forecast its workings. Months in

---

[1] In January 1943. Tresca's murderers were never discovered.

advance, I foretold the end of Rykov, Bukharin, Krestinsky, Smilga, Rakovsky, Bubnov; Antonov-Ovseyenko, the revolutionary who had led the attack on the Winter Palace in 1917, the wretch who had just had my friend Andreu Nin and the anarchist-philosopher Camillo Berneri murdered in Barcelona, was recalled from his post in Spain to take up that of People's Commissar of Justice, now lying vacant through the disappearance of Krylenko into the shadows; I foretold that he was doomed—and so he was. Yagoda, head of the G.P.U., organizer of the Zinoviev trial, was appointed People's Commissar of Posts and Telegraphs; I foretold that he was doomed—and so he was. One's foresight was absolutely useless. The dreadful machine carried on its grinding, intellectuals and politicians snubbed us, public opinion on the Left was dumb and blind. From the depth of a meeting-hall, a Communist worker shouted at me: 'Traitor! Fascist! Nothing you can do will stop the Soviet Union from remaining the fatherland of the oppressed!' I spoke wherever I could, in Socialist branches, trade-union meetings, at the League for the Rights of Man, in masonic lodges, at receptions held by the *Esprit* group. I could carry a meeting quite easily; contradiction I encountered never, insults and threats rather often. Officials of the Paris police advised me to change my lodgings and take precautions (I had no money, and so could not).

Everywhere, well-intentioned men, troubled to the depth of their souls, would ask me: 'But give us an explanation of the mystery of the confessions.' And when I gave them the threefold Russian explanation, through the selection of defendants, their devotion to the Party, and the terror, they would shake their heads, and appeal to 'the individual conscience which. . . .' They were unable to understand that revolutions and totalitarian systems create quite a different sort of individual conscience, and that we are in an age in which the human conscience is being turned inside out. Sometimes, angry in my own turn, I would shout at them: 'You then, you give me an explanation of the *conscience* shown by the famous intellectuals and Western party-leaders who swallow it all—the killing, the nonsense, the cult of the Leader, the democratic Constitution whose authors are promptly shot!' Romain Rolland had not long ago undertaken, at my request, to intervene if there was any fear of death-sentences. I wrote to him, 'Today in Moscow a trial is opening. . . . No more blood, no more blood upon this poor butchered Revolution!

You alone have a moral authority in the Soviet Union which means that you may—which means that you must—intervene. . . .' Romain Rolland kept his mouth shut and thirteen executions followed.

Georges Duhamel told me, 'I understand this drama. I have been enlightened by a personal experience whose nature I cannot disclose. But I feel that I can do nothing, nothing. . . .' There he was, living in his tranquil study over the Rue de Liége, surrounded by his tall sons (all eligible for the next war), and closeted with his vision of a dying civilization. 'I am a bourgeois, Serge, this world is dear to me because, whatever you may say, it has achieved so much for man, and now it looks as if it is all going to go under. . . .'

Henri Sellier, the Socialist Minister of Health, noted for his efforts in working-class housing, explained to me that the interests of the Popular Front demanded the humouring of the Communists. Around the review *Esprit* I met left-wing Catholics like Jacques Lefranc and Emmanuel Mounier, genuine Christians of fine, honest intellect. They sensed sharply that they were living at the end of an era; they loathed all lying, especially if it formed an excuse for murder, and they said so outright. In their simple teaching of 'reverence for the human person', I felt immediately at one with them. And what teaching could be more wholesome in an age in which civilization itself is cracking like rocks in a volcanic eruption?

On the eve of his journey to Russia I had addressed an open letter to André Gide. In it I said:

'We are building a common front against Fascism. How can we block its path, with so many concentration-camps behind us? Let me say this to you: one can only serve the working class and the U.S.S.R. by seeing absolutely clearly. And let me ask this of you in the name of those over there who have every kind of courage: have the courage to see clearly.'

We met several times in Brussels and Paris. Though well past sixty, he was still surprisingly young in manner and mind. His hairless face, with its tall, bare spread of brow, was austere, as if its contours had been shaped by an unresting inner effort. The immediate impression he gave was of extreme timidity which was, however, mastered by a scrupulous moral courage. I saw him weighing every word of his notes on the Soviet Union. He was full of hesitations, but only as far as concerned the act of publishing; his spirit knew no hesitation, but pronounced sentence, not without hope even then.

His manuscript, entrusted to the printer with instructions for strict secrecy, had nevertheless been read by Ehrenburg: 'These people have their ways and means....' Militiamen on the Madrid front (and how did they know of it?) sent a telegram to Gide begging him not to publish a book which could prove 'a mortal blow' for them. Gide hated all intrigue, but the militiamen of Madrid were infinitely close to his heart. His words had a tone of almost absolute gloom:

'I thought I would be able to do so much in Moscow, for so many victims.... I saw at once that one could do absolutely nothing. They overwhelmed me with banquets—as if I went there to feast! Twice Bukharin tried to get near me, and was stopped. All the same, I do not want there to be the slightest touch of pessimism in my book.... What a flood of abuse I'm going to face! And there will be militiamen in Spain who will believe that I am actually a traitor!' Underlying all his words was the anguish of wondering 'What use can I be now?'

What I was expecting duly happened. In March 1937 (the date has a certain importance), while paying a visit to a friend's house in Brussels, I met a young woman whose eyes were wide with terror. 'I am afraid', she said, 'to believe what I've just heard. A prominent Communist from Spain has been to see my husband. I heard him say that in Barcelona they're getting ready to liquidate thousands of anarchists and P.O.U.M. militants, and that it's going along very nicely....'

At once I warned the comrades of P.O.U.M. The *Partido Obrero de Unificación Marxista*, a minority party of dauntless revolutionaries, had a division of volunteers at the front and a membership of 40,000 or so; its leaders, Maurín (now lost in Franco territory), Juan Andrade, Andreu Nin, Julián Gorkín, Gironella, Jordi Arquer and Rovira, all had some background in the various Communist Oppositions, and had pronounced their judgement, in terms no less clear for being temperate, upon the Moscow Trials. They had serious disagreements with Trotsky, but viewed him with comradely admiration. They published my articles and my pamphlet *Seize Fusillés*. They had a first-rate understanding of the methods of the Comintern, and maintained an uncompromising defence of working-class democracy. Unless it crushed them the Communist Party would be unable to press its concealed authority upon the Spanish Republic.

Julián Gorkín passed through Brussels, and we both went to see the leaders of the Socialist International, Fritz Adler and Oscar

Pollak.[1] Adler had lately published a moving and intelligent pamphlet on the 'Witchcraft Trial' in Moscow. He was the image of despair. Pollak answered us, 'What do you want us to do? Since the Russians are sending arms to Spain, they control the situation!'

From day to day during April, I observed from Paris the preparation of Barcelona's bloody days of May. I scattered my futile warnings in the left-wing Socialist Press, as far as the United States itself. Forces with superior weapons, which could have captured Saragossa, stayed back in Barcelona, for reasons that were obscure—and Catalonia was not sent the arms that Russia had promised. If Franco had begun his attack on that region in the spring of 1937, he would probably have taken it. The Communist provocation came duly at the appointed time, on 4 May. There was a battle in the streets, and rather than begin a civil war behind the lines, the C.N.T. (*Confederación Nacionale del Trabajo*) submitted. A few days went by, and then the P.O.U.M. was outlawed; its leaders were arrested and taken to a secret destination, not by the regular Republican police but by the police force of the Communist Party. I knew that once Andreu Nin fell into Russian hands he would never come out alive: he knew Moscow too well. Fearless, optimistic, and physically weakened by illness, he did not go into hiding. Our Committee in Paris lost no time in sending Magdeleine Paz, Félicien Challaye, and Georges Pioch on a deputation to the Spanish Embassy. There they had an icy reception. An Embassy Secretary gave them guarantees of justice for all the prisoners, but added with a little gesture of despair, 'As for Nin. . . .'

'What do you mean, as for Nin?'

'Nothing, nothing. I know nothing, I can tell you nothing.'

The great flyer Edouard Serre, the head of Air-France and a sincere Socialist with a record of solid service to the Republic and Russia, went to see Suritz, the Soviet Ambassador in Paris.[2] He begged Suritz to save Nin, whose death would lead to

[1] Oskar Pollak (1893–1963): journalist for the Second International and the Austrian Socialist Party (Brussels 1936–8, Paris 1938–40); Executive member, Austrian Socialist Party.

[2] Yakov Suritz (1882–1952): an ex-Menshevik whose sympathies appear to have been genuinely liberal; active in many diplomatic posts abroad; in 1940 recalled, after being declared *persona non grata* by the French Government for an Embassy telegram to Stalin in which Britain and France were denounced as 'war-mongers'; Ambassador to Brazil 1946–9.

repercussions infinitely damaging to the cause of Spain. 'Thank you for coming to see me,' the Ambassador said. 'Draw up a short memorandum on the matter without delay, and I will forward it.' Serre told us of his visit later.

The delegations we had dispatched to Spain managed, after great efforts, to retrace Nin's tracks up to a frontier of darkness where the trail disappeared. Incarcerated in an isolated villa at Alcalá de Henares, just outside Madrid, close to an airfield occupied by Soviet planes, Nin was then kidnapped by uniformed men, and disappeared for ever into the shadows. A Socialist official in the Madrid political police and an examining magistrate opened an investigation, which at once implicated certain leading Communist officials. The police official, Gabriel Morón, had to resign and the magistrate eventually fled. Largo Caballero, the head of the Government, resigned too, and was replaced in office by Negrín. We learnt that old Caballero had refused to outlaw the P.O.U.M., since it was a working-class party, and that the installation of a more docile government had come about through Communist pressure. All we could cry now was: 'The Spanish Republic is doomed!' For indeed it was impossible to defeat Fascism while creating within the Republic a system of concentration-camps and murder directed against the most forceful and reliable anti-Fascists; those methods destroyed the moral standing of democracy.

The Russian Socialist engineer Marc Rhein, the son of the Menshevik leader Abramovich, had gone before Nin into the same obscure graveyard. Kurt Landau, the Austrian Socialist, followed. Erwin Wolf, a student of Czech-German nationality and bourgeois origins, had been Trotsky's secretary in Norway. He came to see me in Brussels and told me that he could not live in peace, studying Marxism, while a revolution was struggling for its life. He was off to Spain. I told him: 'You are going to certain murder.' However, he had all the pugnacious confidence of youth. Tall forehead, fine features, the rigidity of the young theoretician, a mind that was single-track, schematic and keen. He had just married a Norwegian girl, the daughter of the Socialist Knudsen: he was happy and sure of himself. Once in Barcelona, he was of course arrested. The Czechoslovak and Norwegian consulates applied their influence and he was released. A few days later he was kidnapped in the street and disappeared, this time for ever.

Each one of these crimes was enveloped in the thick, suffocating clouds wafted by the Communist Press. The P.O.U.M., the victims of kidnapping, assassination or (as in Mena's case) the firing-squad,[1] the revolutionaries in jail, all were unendingly denounced as 'Trotskyists, spies, agents of Franco-Hitler-Mussolini, enemies of the people' in the undiluted style of the Moscow Trials. The average man, who cannot conceive that lying on this scale is possible, is taken unawares by stupendous, unexpected assertions. Outrageous language intimidates him and goes some way to excuse his deception: reeling under the shock, he is tempted to tell himself that there must, after all, be some justification for this madness, some justification of a higher order passing his own understanding. Success is possible for these techniques, it seems clear, only in epochs of confusion, and only if the brave minorities who embody the critical spirit are effectively gagged or reduced to impotence through reasons of State and their own lack of material resources.

In any case, it was not a matter of persuasion: it was, fundamentally, a matter of murder. One of the intentions behind the campaign of drivel initiated in the Moscow Trials was to make any discussion between official and oppositional Communists quite impossible. Totalitarianism has no more dangerous enemy than the spirit of criticism, which it bends every effort to exterminate. Any reasonable objection is bundled away with shouts, and the objector himself, if he persists, is bundled off on a stretcher to the mortuary. I have met my assailants face to face in public meetings, offering to answer any question they raised. Instead they always strove to drown my voice in storms of insults, delivered at the tops of their voices. My books, rigorously documented, and written with the sole passionate aim of uncovering the truth, have been translated for publication in Poland, Britain, the United States, Argentina, Chile, and Spain. In none of these places has a single line ever been contested, or a single argument adduced in reply: only abuse, denunciation and threats. Both in Paris and in Mexico there were moments when in certain cafés people discussed my forthcoming assassination quite as a matter of course.

Perhaps, for the sake of the reader ignorant of those past dramas, I must press home one example. Andreu Nin had spent his youth

[1] Marcía Mena was a P.O.U.M. member from Lerida, shot on the orders of the Stalinist General Lister after the arrest of the P.O.U.M. Executive.

in Russia, first as a loyal Communist, then as a militant of the Left Opposition. When he returned to Spain he had undergone imprisonment by the reactionary Republic, translated Dostoevsky and Pilniak, attacked the incipient Fascist tendencies and helped to found a revolutionary Marxist party. The Revolution of July 1936 had elevated him to the Ministry of Justice in the Generalitat of Catalonia. In this capacity he had established popular tribunals, ended the terrorism of irresponsible elements and instituted a new marriage-code. He was a scholarly Socialist and a first-rate brain, highly regarded by all who knew him and on close terms of friendship with Companys, the head of the Catalan Government. Without the slightest shame the Communists denounced him as 'an agent of Franco-Hitler-Mussolini', and refused to sign the 'pact against slander' proposed to them by all the other parties; they walked out of a meeting at which the other parties asked them, all calmly, for proofs; in their own Press they appealed continually to the evidence of the Moscow Trials, in which, however, Nin's name had never once been mentioned. All the same, Nin's popularity increased, and deservedly; nothing else remained but to kill him.

We succeeded in opening an international campaign in defence of the persecuted Socialists of Spain. In Britain the Independent Labour Party, including Fenner Brockway, Maxton, McGovern and MacNair, in Holland Sneevliet's Revolutionary Socialist Party gave us their tireless support. In France the revolutionary Left in the Socialist Party was very active; this included Marceau Pivert, Collinet, Edouard Serre, and Paul Schmierer.[1] Only in minority parties and among isolated individuals did conscience still burn. Rossi, an editor on *Le Populaire* and the historian of Fascism, exclaimed to me, 'The conscience of the masses—my friend, it doesn't exist!

[1] Marceau Pivert (1895–1958): prominent revolutionary militant in the Socialist Party and teachers' unions; led the Left of the Socialist Party in the Popular Front era, but founded the P.S.O.P. (see page 347) in 1938 as a breakaway; companion of Serge's exile in Mexico; after the war re-entered the Socialist Party as an Executive Member, but lost his position through his opposition to the Party's complicity in the Algerian war. Michel Collinet (1904–1977): member of the Communist Youth (1925–8) and later of Trotskyist groups; an active member of the Socialist Party from 1935; co-founder of the P.S.O.P.; active in the Resistance movement, especially in journalism; author of a number of important works of sociology and social history from a 'Marxist-revisionist' standpoint. Paul Schmierer (1905–): physician; Socialist militant since 1922; Secretary of the Aid Committee for the Spanish Revolution (1936–9), where he met Serge; as organizer for the *Centre Américain de Secours* in Marseilles (1940–4) assisted in Serge's escape; Resistance leader.

The dirty tricks of a man like Marcel Cachin add up to nothing—
he can supply funds to Mussolini in 1915, slander Lenin in 1917,
worship Lenin in 1920, lament perpetually in private over Moscow's
methods, applaud all the shootings over there at the top of his voice,
call Léon Blum a Social-Fascist yesterday and pledge his friendship
to him today—and the Red suburbs idolize him! We, with our outmoded idealism, are properly blocked!' All this was in order to
explain to me how very difficult it would be to insert, in a Socialist
newspaper, a short note on the trial of the P.O.U.M.

Maxton of the I.L.P. and Sneevliet of the Dutch R.S.P. were at
the head of our deputations to Spain. We briefed our delegates
carefully: 'Trust nobody at their word. If someone points a man out
to you in a prison yard and says that it is Nin, insist on speaking to
him and touching him! If they tell you that Gorkín's prison is a
sanatorium, insist on going there—that same day! If they bring you
a whole cartload of "evidence", insist on an expert opinion for a
single page of it—and without delay!' They harassed Republican
Ministers with their questions and protests, and proceeded to knock
on the doors of the Communist Party's secret prisons. Maxton the
imperturbable, with his angular face and steady grey eyes, pipe in
mouth, heard the Spanish ministers Irujo and Zugazagoitia—
honest Republicans who did their utmost to save the victims—reply
to him: 'These abominable acts are done against our will. Do you
think that we are safe ourselves? And please remember that it is the
Russians who are giving us arms!' Twenty times, if once, we expected to hear it announced that the members of the P.O.U.M.
Executive had been executed summarily in some Communist jail.
Our campaign saved their lives. Their trial, held at the hour when
the Republic was already entering its death-agony, was a real
moral triumph.

Black was the spring of 1937. Hardly were the Barcelona troubles
ended, and the murdered corpses buried or else mysteriously
incinerated when, as I had been able easily to predict, the tragedies
of Russia once more cast their peculiar stupor over the world. The
incessant massacre of an entire revolutionary generation moved
scarcely anybody. Reactionaries were, on the contrary, satisfied with
the sight of a victorious revolution discrediting itself in the extermination of its best men. An Italian Fascist magazine wrote that Bolshevism itself was coming round to the formation of a Fascist style of

State. The Socialist adversaries of Bolshevism, who were of course outraged, emphasized that it was all the irresistible march of History.

The annihilation of the Soviet General Staff—Marshal Tukhachevsky and his companions in ill-fortune—did make a profound impression. 'Just think of it!' one French journalist said to me, 'Every general in the whole world is shocked! Shooting marshals—it just isn't done!' It was, besides, realized that the decapitation of the Red Army High Command could, in the context of a Europe approaching war, have serious consequences. There was no mystery in the logic of these events: impossible to destroy the nucleus of the revolutionary régime without touching that of the army; the army was well aware of this, and perhaps its old leaders would have liked to turn the blow. On 11 June the leaders of the Red Army were executed in the shadows.

Scarcely had the Tukhachevsky case passed from the front pages when I read the report on the crime of Bagnoles-sur-Orne: two men stabbed to death in their car on a country road in Normandy. I immediately recognized the picture of one of them: a splendid comrade, the Italian anti-Fascist Carlo Rosselli, editor of *Giustizia e Libertà*. As in Matteotti's case, the order to kill had come from Mussolini himself. With him fell his brother, the historian Nello Rosselli, who had been allowed to leave Italy (to take a holiday!) so that he could be got rid of in this way. At that very time Mussolini was viewed by all right-thinking folk in Europe and America as 'the enlightened dictator of Latin civilization'. We felt that we were being knifed from two sides at once.

In Russia, writers were disappearing, notably one of the greatest, Boris Pilniak; the P.E.N. Clubs kept a discreet silence. . . . The 'judges' of Tukhachevsky (who had probably been executed without even a faked trial) disappeared too. Generals and leaders of war-industry were followed to the grave by admirals and aeroplane-designers. My unending task of unravelling these tragedies was a nightmare without respite.

September 1937. . . . I had formed a close acquaintance with Hendricus Sneevliet. In the previous year we had spoken on the same platform at evening meetings in Amsterdam and Rotterdam, for solidarity with the Republicans of Spain. Our audiences had been working-class and wonderfully sensible. I was aware of the high calibre of his party. He now informed me that a leading official in the

G.P.U.'s Secret Service, resident in Holland, had been heart-broken by the Zinoviev trial and crossed over to the Opposition: Ignace Reiss was warning us that we were all in peril, and asking to see us.

Reiss was at present hiding in Switzerland. We arranged to meet him in Rheims on 5 September 1937. We waited for him at the station buffet, then at the post office. He did not appear. Puzzled, we wandered through the town, admiring the cathedral, which was still shattered from the bombardment, drinking champagne in small cafés, and exchanging the confidences of men who have been saddened through a surfeit of bitter experiences. Both of Sneevliet's sons had committed suicide—the second out of despair because virtually nothing could be done to help the anti-Nazi refugees in Amsterdam, or prevent them from being turned back at the frontier. Several young men of his Party had just died in Spain. Of what use was their sacrifice? Long ago, Sneevliet had been deported to the Dutch East Indies, where had founded a popular party;[1] the friends of his youth had been sentenced to penal servitude for life and the pleas he had since made on their behalf came to nothing. In his own country, the forces of Fascism were openly growing, although they had the bulk of the population opposed to them. Sneevliet sensed the approach of the war in which Holland, its working class, and its developed culture would be inevitably smashed: doubtless only at the beginning, only to rise again later —but when, how? 'Is it necessary for us to pass through bloodbaths and utter darkness? What can one do?'

All this had aged him a little, so that his face wore a persistent frown amid its close lines, but he never lost heart. 'It is strange', he remarked, 'that Reiss hasn't come. He is such a punctual man. . . .' As we took the train back to Paris we read in a newspaper that on the previous day the bullet-riddled body of a foreigner had been picked up on the road from Chamblandes, near Lausanne. In the man's pocket was a railway ticket for Rheims.

Three days later Elsa Reiss, the widow, told us in a broken voice of the trap that had been laid. A woman comrade named Gertrude Schildbach had arrived. She, like them, had wept in anguish at the news of the Moscow executions. She had known Reiss for fifteen years, and came now to ask his advice. They went out

---

[1] This was the Indies Social-Democratic Union, founded by Sneevliet in 1913, which later became the Indonesian Communist Party.

together; the comrade left chocolates for the wife and child. These were filled with poison. In the convulsed fingers of the murdered man a handful of grey hair was found. . . . The Communist-influenced Press in Switzerland wrote that a Gestapo agent had just been liquidated by his colleagues. Not a single newspaper in Paris would take our disclosures, detailed as they were.

I paid a visit to Gaston Bergery at the office of *La Flèche*. Bergery was running a left-wing movement called *Le Frontisme*, which was directed simultaneously against the monopolies and against Communism. He was an elegant, pugnacious character with open but subtle features, and with talents equally appropriate, it seemed, either for mass-agitation or a Government position. He was also fond of rich living and quite evidently ambitious; we all knew that he could quite easily turn one day either to the Fascist Right or towards revolution.[1] Within the Popular Front he maintained a position of independence. 'We will publish!' he told me. The silence was broken. Our investigation laid the crime open to the light of day. Senior Russian officials, protected by diplomatic immunity, were asked to pack and be out within three days. The inquiry revealed that minute preparations for a kidnapping were being hatched around the person of Leon Sedov, Trotsky's son.

A certain somebody, who was sure that he was about to be killed, telephoned, demanding to see us. Leon Sedov, Sneevliet, and myself met this person in the office of a Paris lawyer, Gérard Rosenthal. He was a little thin man with premature wrinkles and nervous eyes: Walter Krivitsky, whom I had met several times in Russia. Together with Reiss and Brunn (or Ilk) he had headed the Secret Service and was engaged in amassing arms for Spain. Against his wishes he had taken part in preparing the ambush for his friend; he was then ordered to 'liquidate' Reiss's widow before returning to Moscow.

Conversation was painful at first. He told Sneevliet, 'We have a spy in your party, but I do not know his name', and Sneevliet, honest old man as he was, burst out in anger: 'You scoundrel!' He told me that our mutual friend Brunn had just been shot in Russia, like most of those who had been secret agents in the first period of the Revolution. He added that, despite all, he felt very distant from us and would remain loyal to the revolutionary State; the historic

[1] Bergery subsequently served the Vichy Government as Ambassador to Moscow, 1940-2, and Ankara, 1942-4.

mission of this State was far more important than its crimes, and besides he himself did not believe that any opposition could succeed.

One evening I had a long talk with him on a dark, deserted boulevard next to the sinister wall of the Santé prison. Krivitsky was afraid of lighted streets. Each time that he put his hand into his overcoat pocket to reach for a cigarette, I followed his movements very attentively and put my own hand in my pocket.

'I am risking assassination at any moment', he said with a feeble, piqued smile, 'and you still don't trust me, do you?'

'That's right.'

'And we would both agree to die for the same cause: isn't that so?'

'Perhaps,' I said, 'all the same it would be as well to define just what this cause is.'

In February 1938 Leon Sedov, Trotsky's eldest son, died suddenly in obscure circumstances. Young, energetic, of a temperament at once gentle and resolute, he had lived a hellish life. From his father he inherited an eager intelligence, an absolute faith in revolution, and the utilitarian, intolerant political mentality of the Bolshevik generation that was now disappearing. More than once we had lingered until dawn in the streets of Montparnasse, labouring together to comb out the mad tangle of the Moscow Trials, pausing from time to time under a street lamp for one or other of us to exclaim aloud: 'We are in a labyrinth of utter madness!' Overworked, penniless, anxious for his father, he passed his whole life in that labyrinth. In November 1936 a section of Trotsky's archives, which had been deposited in secret a few days previously at the Institute of Social History, 7 Rue Michelet, were stolen in the night by criminals who simply cut through a door with the aid of an acetylene torch. I helped Sedov in his pointless investigation; what could be more transparent than a burglary like this?

Later on he apologized for refusing to give me his address when he went away to the Mediterranean coast for a rest: 'I am giving it only to our contact-man—I really have to become frightened of the least indiscretion. . . .' And we discovered that down at Antibes two of Reiss's murderers had lived near to him; another was in lodgings actually next door to his own. He was surrounded at every turn, and suffered fevers of anxiety each night. He underwent an operation for appendicitis in a clinic run by certain dubious Russians, to which he had been taken under an assumed identity. There he died, perhaps as a result of culpable negligence. . . . We carried his coffin of white wood, draped with the red Soviet flag, to the Père Lachaise cemetery; the inquest revealed no definite findings. He was the third of Trotsky's children that I had seen die; and his brother had just disappeared into Eastern Siberia.

At the cemetery, a tall, thin, pale young man came to shake my hand. His face was downcast, his grey eyes piercing and wary, his clothes shabby. I had known this young doctrinaire in Brussels and we did not get on together: Rudolf Klement, secretary of the Fourth International. In his efforts to infuse some life into this feeble organization he worked at a fanatical pitch, committing in due course gross political blunders which I had many a time rebuked. On 13 July of the same year (1938), I received an express message: 'Rudolf kidnapped in Paris. . . . In his room everything was in order, the meal ready on the table. . . .' Forged letters from him—or genuine ones dictated at pistol-point—arrived from the Spanish border. Then, a headless body resembling Klement was fished out of the Seine at Meulan. The Popular Front Press said nothing, of course. Friends of the missing man identified the decapitated corpse by the characteristic shape of the torso and hands. The Communist daily papers *L'Humanité* and *Ce Soir* joined the argument, and a Spanish officer, actually a Russian who was afterwards nowhere to be found, declared that he had seen Klement at Perpignan on the day of his disappearance. The trail having now been confused, the case was closed.

Shortly after this, Krivitsky left for the United States, where he published his book *I Was Stalin's Agent*. In February 1941 he was found dead in a Washington hotel-room, with a bullet-hole in his head.

The Spanish collapse provoked a catastrophic moral breakdown in France; however invisible this might have been to the superficial observer, it was absolutely clear to the initiated eye. The most deep-rooted Socialist affections, which amount to the same as the noble affections of mankind in general, were almost erased within a few months. Thousands of refugees were crossing the Pyrenees, only to be met by a French constabulary that robbed them, bullied them, and interned them in unspeakable concentration-camps. The C.G.T., which was reasonably prosperous, would not dream of lavishing its funds upon assistance for this flood of heroes and victims. Consumed by discord, governments veered towards the Right, as the Premiership swung from Léon Blum to Daladier, then to Daladier with Reynaud at his elbow. Little by little, merciless legislation (which was never rigorously applied, precisely because it was so merciless) was enacted against the refugees. The masses abandoned the losers of the war, and the issues which they dumbly embodied. It would have been quite easy to accept them in ordinary life, settle them in districts with a declining population, arrange for families to take in the children and youngsters—and even to recruit from their numbers one or two crack divisions for the defence of France, herself under threat of attack. None of these ideas occurred to anybody.

I could see how the psychological mechanism of repression worked. Enjoying so much prosperity themselves, men turned away from so much suffering. Living themselves beneath the shadow of so many dangers, men turned away from the spectacle of so many defeats, inflicted after so many struggles. They were annoyed with the Spaniards for having been beaten. Comrades who had welcomed them at first began to disengage from them, with a kind of anger. Later, on the highways at the time of France's fall, I heard excellent folk speaking contemptuously of the Spanish refugees. I could illustrate factually each line that I am writing; but what purpose would it serve? In the proof-readers' union we had refugees from abroad dying of hunger, and their brothers allowed them to have one or two days' work a week—this at the end of endless, persistent pleading, although most of our members lacked nothing. I battled for months to secure a miserable 300 francs grant to an old man of seventy, one of the founders of the C.N.T., José Negre, who was dying on a wretched bed in a concentration-camp. I roused the 'Elders of the C.G.T.', I had an interview with Jouhaux, all in vain. Several old and devoted friends whom I had known as men full of generous enthusiasm now changed out of all recognition, and we more or less broke off relations. What could we talk about?

Munich was a reflection of this state of mind in the realm of high politics. It was a surrender before Nazi force, a betrayal of our ally Czechoslovakia, a betrayal of the Soviet Union. I knew that

French politicians, reactionaries but (I believe) sincere men, had come back from Berlin and were calling working-class militants in for homilies, saying how afraid they were for France—we must have peace, peace at any price, or ruin would follow. It is a fact that the immense majority of the population welcomed the shameful Munich transaction with inexpressible relief. When Daladier returned from his talks with Chamberlain, Hitler, and Mussolini, his face gloomy as usual (all his photos showed him heavy and downcast—the Prime Minister officiating over the funeral of a political system), he was amazed to find himself acclaimed; he was expecting to be hissed.

I must confess that I too felt a sense of relief at Munich. It was clear to me that this particular French nation, in this particular phase of depression, was incapable of fighting. If they had not fought to save the Republic, if they had not even been able to stop non-intervention from turning into a bloody farce, could one ask them, the day after this disappointment, to go to war for the sake of faraway Czechoslovakia? From this time they would require a period of years, a fresh accretion of energy, before they could recover their full moral integrity.

In the working-class movement, depression becomes expressed and even accentuated by division. As all values begin to be questioned, minorities stiffen into intolerance and majorities lose their bearings. The Socialist Party split at its Royan Congress. The revolutionary Left, now harried by Paul Faure's stupid disciplinary measures, resigned and established the Socialist Workers' and Peasants' Party (P.S.O.P.). By this act it lost its audience in a party of over 300,000 members, isolated its few thousand followers, and started a revolutionary movement just at the time when the working class was retiring into its own demoralization. The split at Royan weakened the Socialist Party and created an unworkable alternative party.

The trade unions were shedding their active membership. Within them pacifism and anti-Stalinism, both negative ideologies, were ranged against warmongering and the blind obedience of the Communists. I had to break off relations with one small review of the far Left edited by a libertarian veteran, usually a most sensible man, because it was invoking the principle of free discussion as an excuse to print apologies for Nazism!

It is from this period, too, that my break with Trotsky can be dated. I had held aloof from the Trotskyist movement, within which I could not detect the hopes of the Left Opposition in Russia for a renewal of the ideology, morals and institutions of Socialism. In the countries I knew at first hand, Belgium, Holland, France, and Spain, the tiny parties of the 'Fourth International', ravaged by frequent splits and, in Paris, by deplorable feuding, amounted only to a feeble and sectarian movement out of which, I judged, no fresh thinking could emerge. The life of these groups was maintained by nothing but the prestige of the Old Man and his great, unceasing efforts; and both his prestige and the quality of his efforts deteriorated in the process. The very idea of starting an International at the moment when all international Socialist organizations were dying, when reaction was in full flood, and without support of any kind, seemed quite senseless to me. I wrote to Leon Davidovich and told him as much. I was also in disagreement with him on certain important issues in the history of the Revolution: he refused to admit that in the terrible Kronstadt episode of 1921 the responsibilities of the Bolshevik Central Committee had been simply enormous; that the subsequent repression had been needlessly barbarous; and that the establishment of the Cheka (later the G.P.U.) with its techniques of secret inquisition had been a grievous error on the part of the revolutionary leadership, and one incompatible with any Socialist philosophy.

In what concerned Russia's contemporary problems, I recognized Trotsky's outstanding vision and his capacity for outstanding insights. At the time when he was writing *The Revolution Betrayed*, I had prevailed on him to include in the Opposition's programme a declaration of freedom for all parties accepting the Soviet system. Blended with the flashes of his superb intelligence I could see the systematic schematizing of old-time Bolshevism, whose resurrection, in all countries of the world, he believed to be inevitable. I understood his inflexibility: he was, after all, the last survivor of a generation of giants. However, convinced as I was that great historical traditions are prolonged only by renewal, I believed that Socialism too had to renew itself in the world of today, and that this must take place through the jettisoning of the authoritarian, intolerant tradition of turn-of-the-century Russian Marxism. I recalled, for use against Trotsky himself, a sentence of astounding vision which he had written, in 1914 I think: 'Bolshevism may very well be an excellent instrument for the conquest of power, but after that it will reveal its counter-revolutionary aspects.'

The only problem which revolutionary Russia, in all the years from 1917 to 1923, utterly failed to consider was the problem of liberty; the only declaration which it had to make afresh, and which it has never made, is the Declaration of the Rights of Man.

I expounded these ideas in an article published in Paris as *Puissances et limites du marxisme* and in the New York *Partisan Review* as *Marxism of Our Time*. The Old Man, true to his habitual stereotypes, was pleased to see nothing in it except 'an exhibition of petty-bourgeois demoralization. . . .' Deplorably misinformed by his acolytes, he wrote a long polemical essay against me—imputing to me an article of which I was not the author and which was totally at variance with my frequently expressed opinions. The Trotskyist journals refused to publish my corrections. In the hearts of the persecuted I encountered the same attitudes as in their persecutors. Contagion through combat has its own natural logic: thus the Russian Revolution proved, despite itself, to be the continuation of certain ancient traditions stemming from the despotism it had just overthrown; Trotskyism was displaying symptoms of an outlook in harmony with that of the very Stalinism against which it had taken its stand, and by which it was being ground into powder. . . . I was heartbroken by it all, because it is my firm belief that the tenacity and will-power of some men can, despite all odds, break with the traditions that suffocate, and withstand the contagions that bring death. It is painful, it is difficult, but it *must* be possible. I abstained from any counter-polemic.

Our Oppositional movement in Russia had not been Trotskyist, since we had no intention of attaching it to a personality, rebels as we ourselves were against the cult of the Leader. We regarded the Old Man only as one of our greatest comrades, an elder member of the family over whose ideas we argued freely. And now, ten years later, tiny parties like that of Walter Dauge in Belgium, which had no more than a few hundred members in a district of the Borinage, termed him 'our glorious leader', and any person in the circles of the 'Fourth International' who went so far as to object to his propositions was promptly expelled and denounced in the same language that the bureaucracy had employed against us in the Soviet Union. Doubtless all this had little importance; but the very fact that such a vicious circle could be set up was a terrible psychological symptom of the movement's inner disintegration.

I came to the conclusion that our Opposition had simultaneously contained two opposing lines of significance. For the great majority of its members it had meant resistance to totalitarianism in the name of the democratic ideals expressed at the beginning of the Revolution; for a number of our Old Bolshevik leaders it meant, on the contrary, the defence of doctrinal orthodoxy which, while not excluding a certain tendency towards democracy, was authoritarian through and through. These two mingled strains had, between 1923 and 1928, surrounded Trotsky's vigorous personality with a tremendous aura. If, in his exile from the U.S.S.R., he had made himself the ideologist of a renewed Socialism, critical in outlook and fearing diversity less than dogmatism, perhaps he would have attained a new greatness. But he was the prisoner of his own orthodoxy, the more so since his lapses into unorthodoxy were being denounced as treason. He saw his role as that of one carrying into the world at large a movement which was not only Russian but extinct in Russia itself, killed twice over, both by the bullets of its executioners and by changes in human mentality.

And war was speeding on its way. I had known a time when the Spanish Republic could almost certainly have won in the space of a few weeks or months. In the days after the military uprising, when it was still based upon Morocco, the Moroccan Nationalists had offered to fight Franco if the Republic would only come to a generous settlement with them. The negotiations (which were conducted by a number of my friends) failed, probably because the chancelleries of Europe intimated some hostility to a reform as daring as this. Everything that had happened subsequently fitted the assumption that the Soviet Union, far from desiring victory for a Republic in which the Communist Party would not have preserved its hegemony, had instead sought to prolong the anti-Fascist resistance merely for the sake of gaining time. Once demoralization had done its work, Franco entered Barcelona in January 1939 without meeting any resistance. Towards the middle of March, the Nazis entered Prague.

It was during that same month of March that I read the *Pravda* report of Stalin's speech to the Eighteenth Party Congress. The

Leader accused Britain and France of trying to 'sow discord between the Soviet Union and Germany'. A speech by Voroshilov confirmed the authenticity of the details of Soviet military power which had been published in a Nazi military review. Through Reiss and Krivitsky we were aware that Soviet agents had been in continual contact with the Nazi rulers. On 5 May Litvinov, the advocate of 'collective security' and of the Politbureau's 'peace policy' within the League of Nations, resigned abruptly. These clues, among others, were a clear indication that Soviet policy would soon switch to collaboration with the Third Reich. Nevertheless, the section of the French Press that was steered by Communist agents was neither willing nor able to understand anything of this; the articles I submitted to journals of the Left were rejected, and the only platform I could find was in the review *Esprit*. It was quite obvious to me that the Politbureau regarded France as beaten before the battle, and was therefore tacking towards finding some accommodation with the strongest side.

An obscure journalist, one Benoist-Méchin, the author of a tolerable *History of the German Army*, asked me to meet him. I asked a left-wing publisher to give me some information about the man, and was told: 'He is a former composer, a good scissors-and-paste man, of no particular political complexion.' We met in a café on the Boulevard St. Michel. This character was young (about thirty-five), featureless, bespectacled, reserved in speech, and most attentive. After ten minutes I was absolutely sure that he must be working simultaneously for the *Deuxième Bureau* and some other organization, probably German. He told me that he was thinking of writing a history of the Civil War in the Ukraine.

'Do you know Russian?' I asked him.

'No.'

'Have you travelled in the Ukraine?'

'No.'

'Have you studied the Russian Revolution?'

'Not particularly. . . .'

Our conversation wandered on to current affairs, and I could see that my interlocutor was primarily interested in the attitude of the Ukrainian peasantry in case of war. I cut the conversation short, and said, 'The Ukraine is disaffected, but will defend itself furiously against any aggression. And besides, what is on the agenda today is not a war between the Soviet Union and Germany, but rather a new partition of Poland.'

I left Monsieur Benoist-Méchin, double agent, in a state of utter perplexity, since nobody in the relevant departments had this hypothesis in mind. (We never met again; in 1942, Benoist-Méchin became a leading figure in the Vichy régime.)

When it came, the war found the mass of the people in the worst possible confusion of feeling and thought. I was ill and utterly alone. I lived in a working-class district, at Pré-St. Gervais; most of my comrades who lived near by had run off to the provinces as soon as mobilization began, terrified of being bombed. I saw practically no one. Every man for himself, that's it—no time for fooling around. Publications ceased appearing of their own accord. On the day of the general mobilization, I found my way to the Socialist Party's headquarters, in a drinking and dancing quarter below the Place Pigalle; the alley, old and bourgeois-looking, was deserted, the building itself empty. I had been the only visitor there the whole afternoon. Séverac,[1] pallid and resigned, was seeing to the routine business. Maurice Paz told me of a surprising statement by Henri de Man: 'Germany does not want a general war, a settlement can be reached while mobilization is still on. . . .'[2] The P.S.O.P. had lost its influence in the Paris region and was in a serious crisis of morale, having been abandoned by its most prominent leaders. Not one group with any life in it was still on the scene.

At the Gare de l'Est the conscripts were departing, without any singing of the 'Marseillaise', in a silence heavy with anxiety and uninspired pluck. The women were not weeping very much. I shall never forget the old worker I saw staggering up a *Métro* staircase, talking to himself: '*Ah! nom de Dieu! Ah! nom de Dieu!* Two wars in one lifetime!' A cartoon in a pacifist paper showed a bill-sticker pasting up posters for the mobilization and explaining to a boozer, 'It's the war, Ben.' 'Which war?' the other was replying in a stunned voice.

This was a war that nobody was keen on. The wealthy classes

---

[1] Jean-Baptiste Séverac (1879–1951): old Socialist and Co-operative activist; editor-in-chief of *L'Humanité* up to 1918; then of *Le Populaire*.

[2] Henri de Man (1885–1953): Belgian Socialist leader, famous for his *Plan du Travail* (1933), advocating planning within a mixed economy. Collaborated (as adviser to Leopold III) with the German occupying authorities during the Second World War. Retired to Switzerland at the end of the war.

had no desire to fight against Fascism, which they preferred to the Popular Front. The intelligentsia judged that a country like France with a low birth-rate, just beginning to recover from its losses of 1914–18, was in no mood for further bloodshed. The pacifism of the Left reflected the same feeling. The workers and the middle-class folk were vaguely conscious of being betrayed, had no confidence in the Government or the General Staff, and could not follow how it was necessary to fight for Poland after having deserted Socialist Austria, Socialist Spain, and our ally Czechoslovakia. Overnight the most forceful elements in the working-class suburbs, namely the Communists, had become pacifists, 'anti-imperialists' and supporters of the new 'peace policy of the Soviet Union'. Maurice Thorez, the leader of the Communist Party, deserted; Duclos, the Vice-President of the Chamber, left for Moscow, a few deputies resigned from the Party, and the rest went to jail. The general opinion was that there would be very little fighting and that everybody would be quite safe behind the impregnable Maginot Line.

Paris waited calmly for the bombing to start: there were black-outs, long wails from the sirens at night and sometimes in broad daylight, the crackle of the anti-aircraft barrage, descents into the cellar shelters, and ridiculous trench-shelters dug in the public gardens. The rich people were taking themselves off to the Mediter-ranean coast. A phoney war indeed.

The walls were covered with posters: '*We will win because we are the strongest . . .!*' A right-wing writer, Thierry Maulnier, denounced the fear of victory which dominated the reactionary parties. They knew the chances of our defeat—not without reason—and 'the defeat of Germany would mean the collapse of the authoritarian systems which constitute the principal bulwark against Com-munist revolution, possibly even the immediate Bolshevization of Europe. . . .' The Royalist *Action Française* remained pro-Italian.

The success of my novel *S'il est Minuit dans Le Siècle* spared me the hazards of internment. I saw Georges Duhamel: he had aged ten years at one stroke, eyelids reddened and voice weak; he was already plumbing the depths of the disaster. I also met Jean Giraudoux; he was unpretentiously elegant, and dejected—his *Appeal to the Workers of France* had, despite his high position in the Ministry of Information, been censored. A great writer, and a member of the Government, wanting to speak 'to the workers'—

what a weird idea! In the same period a comrade of mine who had volunteered for the French Army wrote in a letter that he was 'happy to be fighting for the cause of freedom and democracy'. For this he was severely reprimanded by his commander: 'We are fighting for France and for nothing else!' Jean Malaquais, the author of *Les Javanais*, who was serving on the Maginot Line, told me of the utter passivity of the troops at the front, who had no idea of anything and talked only of women and booze. The most-discussed book of the year was one by Jean-Paul Sartre, an analysis in novel form of a case of neurosis, called *La Nausée*. An appropriate title.

The publishing house of Gallimard had a novel in the press by a young author, dealing with the Spanish Civil War, but decided not to publish it. The subject was too hot: it might upset the Italians. Bernard Grasset were preparing a new edition of my book *L'An Un de la Révolution Russe*, and the Ministry of Information asked them to postpone its appearance until more suitable times; in other words, this was a rather hot subject too. There was an order forbidding too much publicity about my *Portrait de Staline*, which had just appeared. . . . Publishers were refusing any works which were anti-Hitler. There was neither freedom nor intellectual purpose. The war even lacked an ideology.

On the 8th or 9th of May, *Le Figaro* stated that the massing of German forces on the borders of the Low Countries was probably only a bluff. I spent the evening of the 9th at Léon Werth's. He had been an acute and humane romantic chronicler of the last war's aftermath, but he was writing no more; he lived in uncertainty, in ceaseless self-questioning about the values that had disappeared. There Saint-Exupéry, in uniform, stretched his great body on a couch: Saint-Exupéry was still undertaking reconnaissance over enemy territory, and he was devising a new defence-system for aerodromes. He was not sure whether he was of the Left or the Right: reluctant to locate himself anywhere among discredited parties, inhibited by his family name and his relatives, disillusioned by the Spanish tragedy, living out this end of a world with his whole soul, even though his intellect was unable to master its outstanding features. On that particular evening, he was feverishly restless, itching to go and almost silent. I asked him if it was true that for some long months the Allied air force would continue to be inferior to the enemy's. The only answer he gave me was a few despairing words with gestures to match. I went out into the lovely Paris night, literally in agony. On the morning of the 10th, the newspapers reported the invasion of Belgium and Holland.

Within six days the Panzers reached Sedan. Fleeing Belgians told me of the massacre of the French cavalry in the Ardennes: cavalry against tanks and planes! The communiqués invent a new phrase, 'mopping-up operations'. The map shows plainly that the enemy is aiming for the heart of France, and Paris is threatened. On the midday of 3 June the summer sky is filled with the noise of engines: it sounds like an army of the air, but nothing can be seen in the blue above. Then come the dull explosions of bombs bursting, and the crackle of anti-aircraft fire. My wife and I follow this invisible battle from a balcony where the window-panes are trembling. Innocent blood is streaming at this very moment in our midst: at the idea of this, so great a revulsion sweeps over us that everything else is now blotted out of our minds. However, Paris wears no trace of gloom afterwards, but keeps the festive air with which the sun always endows it.

Two factions in the Government begin to clash, almost openly. The clique favouring immediate peace, the clique of reaction and future surrender, demands power for Pétain; the name of the banker Paul Baudouin, unknown up till now, crops up in every conversation. Its opponent is the party favouring resistance, which includes Reynaud, Daladier, Mandel, and Léon Blum. The Socialists are divided, the Paul Faure tendency remaining pacifistic. I hear it said that in certain quarters lists of names have been drawn up for arrest. Mandel, now Minister of the Interior, begins the purge of Paris. Helmeted *Gardes Mobiles*, their rifles loaded, surround the student cafés in the Boulevard St. Michel. Any foreigners whose papers are not in order are packed into lorries which take them to police headquarters. Many of them are anti-Nazi refugees, for the other foreigners' papers are of course quite in order. How can a refugee be in order with this Préfecture of red-tape and petty pestering, a shuttlecock between left-wing influences, right-wing influences, and others more mysterious? The anti-Nazi and anti-Fascist refugees are due to experience yet more prisons: those of the Republic which was their last land of asylum on this continent, which in its death-throes is losing its wits. Spaniards and

International Brigaders who beat back Fascism outside Madrid are treated as if they carried the plague. Meanwhile, with documents in order and purses full, Spanish Falangists, Italian Fascists (still neutrals), and White Russians (and how many actual Nazis were there behind these easy disguises?) walked at liberty through the length and breadth of France. 'Home Defence' is a farce, a horribly symbolic one at that.

Vain appeals reach me from the Belgian frontier. The police are letting the flood of Belgian refugees pass by, but are halting Belgium's anti-Nazi and Spanish exiles in their tracks. The Gestapo is advancing in line with the tanks, but the reply is 'You don't have visas! You can't cross!' A few will get through when the police make themselves scarce. Some of the Spaniards pick up the weapons which the police have abandoned, and start to fight the Nazi tanks. . . . Sneevliet asks me to get him a visa, but in the general stampede there is no one to speak to in Paris. (Sneevliet will be shot, with eight of his comrades, in Amsterdam on 15 April 1942.)

The Press is still making reassuring remarks: 'The Weygand Line will hold fast!'—meanwhile 'German infiltration' has got as far as the Somme, reaching Forges-les-Eaux. . . . Under the sunlight of June, the Champs-Elysées still keeps its smiling face. I am resolved to put off leaving until almost the last train, for I still feel some vague hope that the situation will mend, and I have practically no money. When Paris ends the world ends; useless to see the truth, how could one bear to acknowledge it? On Sunday the 9th, I see Cabinet ministers moving house. Cars, blanketed with mattresses and overloaded with trunks, shoot off towards the city's southern gates. Shops are closed.

On the morning of 10 June, I am in the *Métro* and see men and women on the verge of tears; all one can hear is a murmur of heart-broken rage: 'Oh, the bastards!' Hands, clenched violently, screw up the newspaper which reports Italy's entry into the war; a stab in the back dealt to a man already falling. 'We're betrayed at every turn!' the man next to me says. 'Yes, friend, that is just it.'

Last images of Paris: from the high ground of the Porte des Lilas, the outer suburbs are overshadowed by a strange bluish mist, a suspicious-looking gas or smoke drifting towards Belleville and Montmartre. They say that the petrol tanks at Rouen are burning. The outskirts of the Gare du Nord, empty and pale as evening falls;

the shops with their iron shutters up; people on their doorsteps, listening to the distant moan of shells. All the shopkeepers feel personally threatened: it's the beginning of the end of the world, isn't it? The Boulevard de Sébastopol in complete darkness, practically deserted; underneath, the Réaumur-Sébastopol *Métro* station with its human hotchpotch burdened under an animal despair: the trains are late. . . . Good-bye to all that—let us be off on foot, as best we may. At night, around the Gare de Lyon, we sense violence in the air because, they say, there are no more trains, and in any case no more room in the station. . . . A providential taxi with a one-eyed driver takes us through the Fontainebleau woods, underneath the barrage of shells, along roads thronged with traffic. 'Put your lights out, for God's sake! There's an alert on!' men in steel helmets shout through the darkness, but nobody listens to them. Four of us are making the journey: my wife,[1] my son, a Spanish friend who has joined us at the last moment, and myself. I have raked together 4,000 francs for our escape. (This would be about 100 dollars. . . .)

Our flight is accompanied by a sense of release bordering at times on gaiety. All our possessions have been reduced to a few bundles. Only the other day I was peeved at not being able to find a jotting among my papers; and now, lo and behold, books, personal objects, documents, manuscripts, all disappear at one stroke without effecting any real emotion. (It is true that I am used to it.) A whole segment of old Europe is caving in, events are unfolding in their predestined course. We had been living in a suffocating blind alley. For years now, or so it seems to me, France—and perhaps the whole West—was dominated by the consciousness that 'it could not last'. Nobody believed in anything any more, because nothing in fact was possible any more: certainly not a revolution, with this working class gorged on fresh Camembert, pleasant wine, and ancient ideas which had become mere words—a working class, moreover, ringed on all sides by Nazi Germany, Fascist Italy, Franco Spain, and insular, Conservative Great Britain. And certainly not a counter-revolution either, with this bourgeoisie incapable of daring

---

[1] This is Serge's third wife, Laurette, whom he met in Paris. His Russian wife Liuba had proved to be incurably deranged as a result of the persecution in the Soviet Union, and lapsed into infantilism; Serge had to leave her in a French mental hospital in 1940. She never recovered.

or thinking and, ever since the workers' occupation of the factories, sick with fright as well. Now it is all over: the rotten tooth has been pulled out, the leap into the unknown has been made. It will be black and terrible, but those who survive will see a new world born. There are very few people who have this new sense which modern man is so painfully developing: the sense of history. The folk who are fleeing with us along the highways of France, and on the last trains as defeat sets in, realize all the same that 'it had to happen'.

All at once I re-experience the deepest and most invigorating feeling of my childhood which, I believe, has made a lifelong impression on me. I grew up among Russian revolutionary exiles who knew that the Revolution was advancing towards them, inexorably, out of the depths of the future. In simple words they taught me to have faith in mankind and to wait steadfastly for the necessary cataclysms. They waited for half a century, in the midst of persecution. There is a Spanish friend travelling with us. Between us we can muster quite a fine collection of wrecked régimes. We wake at dawn, in the middle of open country, a thin rain mingled with sunshine falling on our faces, and we decide that, this time, the way forward for the European revolution is already half-clear. Over Nazism, our conqueror, we feel a resounding superiority: we know that it is doomed.

Along with the fleeing army, with the refugees from Paris, Alsace, Lorraine, Champagne, from Belgium, Holland and scores of other places, we invade charming, pious, well-heeled little towns, slumbering around the church and the splendid house of the local rent-collector. Here folk live in the darkness of old houses, skimping on the electricity, never buying a book, but patiently, from the beginning of time, filling out the woollen stocking with cash and amassing their little fortunes. 'Is it really possible?' moan the gossips, 'What's happening? Do you understand anything about it, sir?' The soldiers reply as one man that 'We've been sold out, betrayed, what else?—by the officers who've hopped it with their fancy women, quick as you please; by the General Staff, by the Cagoulards who wanted their revenge on the Popular Front; it's all obvious. . . .' General Staff, militarism, reaction, big bourgeoisie, all have been discredited at one swoop.

We have nothing left now, so we look for some place of sanctuary. Several have been offered or promised to us. It used to be quite the style for people to invite themselves along to Paris: 'Of course you must come and stay with me in Dordogne or Gironde if dear old Paris ever gets too disagreeable for you! You will be able to taste my little stock of wine!' However, my wife is more or less hounded, ever so politely, out of a *château* which is the home of an anarchist well-endowed with worldly goods—this on a day of torrential rain which pours over the dainty slate turrets, the artificial stream and the romantic rock-garden. We enter an abandoned farm in the middle of the woods; a friend, a Socialist journalist, who discloses that he is its owner, begs us to be off at once: 'Take my car, but get out quickly. They're coming this way!' We clear off, and this late Socialist explains to me that he is now a convert to collaboration with Hitler and to strong government, which must inevitably be military rule: the power of the utterly bankrupt, in a word. One sanctuary is still promised me, with a pacifist author. It is a pretty little house surrounded by flowers, but its door is shut and well-guarded; the writer has gone to the hills to meditate. The police arrest us and then let us depart, equally inclined to meditate. These are not simply personal misfortunes, it happens in almost every case. Refugees are suspected as enemies by the inhabitants of the prosperous provinces: they send prices up, gobble the food-supplies, steal bicycles, and among them, just imagine, there are Spaniards, ruffians—God help us! We gladly embrace the peasant-woman (not a wealthy person) who offers us coffee and shelter on a day of teeming rain, and refuses to take our pennies.

It becomes clear that ready money and the sordid influence of prosperity have caused a serious moral deterioration. It never occurs to the syndicalist militants of a certain town to give their adored meeting-hall over to the cause of hospitality. Various town halls, not reactionary ones, refuse to pay the refugees' allowance to anyone from Spain. For people to be refugees twice over is excessive, surely.

The working-class organizations, Socialist Party and C.G.T., have melted into nothing. Old-time Socialists concentrate on keeping their positions in the municipal administrations where they are serving. Fragments of the far Left—schoolmistresses, anarchistic tradesmen, freemasons, and Socialists—still continue to think, and keep solidarity alive. In one small town invaded by the straggling army—actually Agen—we meet some old '*anarchos*' who have known me thirty years and more. In the old days, when I turned to support the proletarian dictatorship they thought I was a careerist; they are happy to realize that they were wrong. We meet together in a secluded spot on the river bank. Moroccan riflemen, idle and sour, wander along by the stream, pondering upon the glory of the Empire. . . .

On a highway of Gascony, amid the chaos of fugitive lorries, some Belgian magistrates, dining on the balcony of a little café, tell me, 'There is going to be a new régime in France—Hitler insists on it.' People weep to hear the loudspeakers announcing the news of the Armistice. Daily I follow the intrigues of the Government at Bordeaux. Some of the Socialists of Agen have returned from there with the latest information. 'Hitler does not want France, now trampled underfoot, to have any more Parliaments. The system of government must be Fascist. That is the unwritten clause in the Armistice. Laval and Baudouin declare that Britain will come to terms within three months. The invasion of the British Isles is well in hand.'

A man can live, and keep his spirits up, in a tent under the rain, as my son and Narciso did. A man can sleep, and sleep well, in a stinking, over-priced hovel next to the slaughter-house, as we did. He can cook his meals in a school and work in cafés; for the Age of Waiting has begun. . . . I go out to work. The problem is to find food for tomorrow or next week. We send S.O.S. messages to Switzerland and across the Atlantic. On our last postage-stamps disappointments and small betrayals rain by the score. Suddenly I become aware of a harsh revelation: that now we political refugees, we cornered revolutionaries, are utterly beaten, because certain of our comrades are no longer our comrades, so demoralized and defeated are they to the quick of their hearts; and among us a squalid battle is beginning for places in the last lifeboat from the sinking ship. However, from Switzerland and America breathtaking replies reach us. These letters, from the poet J.-P. Samson and from Dwight Macdonald—two men I have never seen in my life—seem to clasp my hands in the dark. I can hardly believe it. So then, let us hold on.[1]

---

[1] J.-P. Samson (1894–1964): poet and translator; a socialist militant in the years before the First World War; upon the outbreak of war in 1914 chose exile in Zurich, where he subsequently lived; editor of the independant review *Témoins*. Dwight Macdonald (1906–): American journalist and critic; formerly a Trotskyist, later a pacifist, then an independent liberal; edited the journal *Politics* from 1944 to 1949.

Little towns on the south coast are slumbering peacefully as though nothing was happening. The shock of the earthquake has still not touched here. We reach Marseilles three weeks too late: all seats in the lifeboats are taken. In drawing up visa-lists, both in America and here, the leading figures of the old exiled parties were, it seems, determined to exclude the militants of the far Left, whose very names might be compromising to Ministerial eyes. Besides, everybody is making their escape through the political family-network: groupings are of use now only for that purpose. So much the worse for the man of no Party who has dared to think only in terms of Socialism in all its vastness! All of my party, all of it, has been shot or murdered; and so I am alone, a curiously disturbing figure. People meet, people shake hands, and each one keeps for himself and those close to him the address of the American gentle-man who sees to visas and relief-work. Faces whose strength shone out to me in the old days, in Moscow, Vienna, or Berlin, I now see twitching hysterically. Think of it: the fourth exile, the seventh flight in twenty years!

Marseilles, flushed and carefree with its crowded bars, its alleys in the old port festooned with whores, its old bourgeois streets with lattice-windows, its lifeless wharves, and its brilliant seascapes, is first and foremost a 'Red city', but its exact shade is Off-Red, Dirty-Red or Racket-Red, so to speak. The Vichy régime has sacked the Socialist city council and the key man in the new admin-istration is Sabiani, a real gangster from Doriot's party. The man in the street knows what's what pretty well: 'Nothing one can do while the Nazi occupation lasts. After that, we settle matters with the bastards. That'll be it—a gay time and some faces bashed in!'

How many exiles are there tucked away in small hotels, at the end of their tether? We have the German emigration, the Austrian, the Czech, the Dutch, the Belgian, the Italian, the Spanish, and two or three Russian ones—plus some Rumanians, Yugoslavs, Greeks, and Bulgarians. Not forgetting the Parisians! Rich Jews of all nations are selling, buying and selling back documents, visas, currency, and tasty titbits of information. Little gangs of specialists supply them with perfect forgeries of dollars on the 'Black Bourse'. And the poor Jews of all nations are running through numberless varieties of terror and courage, anticipating every fate they can imagine lying ahead.

Our mob of fugitives includes first-rate brains from all those classes which have ceased to exist through the mere fact of daring to say *No!* (most of them rather quietly) to totalitarian oppression. In our ranks are enough doctors, psychologists, engineers, educationists, poets, painters, writers, musicians, economists, and public men to vitalize a whole great country. Our wretchedness contains as much talent and expertise as Paris could summon in the days of her prime; and nothing of it is visible, only hunted, terribly tired men at the limit of their nervous resources. Here is a beggar's alley gathering the remnants of revolutions, democracies, and crushed intellects. We sometimes tell ourselves that it would be tremendous if only five in a hundred of these forsaken men could manage to cross the Atlantic, and there rekindle the flame of battle in their hearts. If it had not been for Varian Fry's American Relief Committee, a goodly number of refugees would have had no reasonable course open to them but to jump into the sea from the height of the transporter-bridge, a certain enough method.

Those with the most scars take the shock best. These are the young revolutionary workers or semi-intellectuals who have passed through countless prisons and concentration-camps. They are difficult to rescue, because nobody knows them, because the old conformist parties have no sympathy for them, because the governments of the New World are afraid of them (subversives. . . .), because they possess nothing, and because every police force is out to catch them. Our beggars' alley is full of prowlers—the *Sûreté*, the lodging-house patrol, the Gestapo, the O.V.R.A., the Falangist police. Every week people disappear. Hunger is another prowler to reckon with. But we do not panic. Not many of us have very high spirits, but those who are spent come out to coffee exactly as if they still had some spark of life left.

The Frenchmen, whether intellectuals or militants, have no intention of emigrating for some time. Prisoners of habit, they do not realize the full extent of the catastrophe, and have vague hopes of some tolerable way out. Among the intellectuals there is a general tendency to adapt themselves. Various militants tell me, quite simply, 'Our place is here', and they are right. Among the notable writers, the surrealist André Breton is the only one who is anxious to cross the Atlantic; among the painters, André Masson. It is evident that, in the first wave of confusion, many people are fooled by the 'National Revolution' and the personal glamour of the 'Soldier of Verdun', that old man of over eighty who every morning drinks the bitter cup of defeat, retching with disgust but behaving with a repulsive subservience. In the course of the winter these mists melt away: reality is too insistent. The suppression of the Socialist Press, the stupid re-christenings of the streets hitherto named after Rousseau, Anatole France, Jean Jaurès, and Pierre Curie, the official anti-Semitism, the ruthless rationing, all are instructive. In the Rue Saint Ferréol people crowd in front of a *rôtisserie* to see a single chicken being roasted, a prodigious sight! The gulls of the port are so hungry that they come hovering round windows they know to be charitable. This degrading poverty, fastening upon a country so prosperous, does more to open people's eyes than any propaganda that could be devised.

The propaganda of the Allies, lacking as it does any social content, is inferior to the Nazis' demagogy, which is always talking in terms of the New Order and the 'European Revolution'. However, Wavell's victories in Africa fortunately make up for the shortcomings of the London radio. Gaullism is arising spontaneously and fairly generally; Socialist ideas are sprouting unceremoniously everywhere, even as the Socialist Party collapses into silence. Socialist delegates vote in favour of the Vichy régime whilst Blum goes off to prison and Dormoy to house-arrest. One of the Party's most capable brains, Rossi (Angelo Tasca), an old adversary of Mussolini who worked with Léon Blum and who, a month before the fall of Paris, had argued passionately in my hearing for a creed founded on liberty, has joined with Spinasse in supporting the Marshal's 'national revolution'; *L'Effort*, the organ of these Socialist flunkeys, prints the verbiage of the Nazi agent Marcel Déat. The Paul Faure tendency is equally accommodating, and negotiates with the Marshal; not under any illusions, I think, purely to avoid persecution and the mass dismissal of tens of thousands of left-wing officials and teachers. On this point the negotiations are successful.

Our very existence is hanging from slender threads which may break at any moment. Several times the total occupation of France is rumoured to be in the offing. And the long-awaited visas are not here, still not here! This much must be said: because of their reactionary or bureaucratic leanings, most of the American republics have displayed neither humanity nor sense in their immigration policies. Visas were granted in the merest trickle, in a manner so criminally stingy that thousands upon thousands of real victims, all fine human beings, were left to the mercies of the Nazis. People with money and no political commitments got visas, generally speaking, rather easily; a host of anti-Fascist fighters did not get them at all. Visas for practically every American state were habitually sold, at prices more or less exorbitant; and the Vichy officials conducted a trade in exit-permits. A fine trade this, selling lifebelts on a shipwrecked continent! Thanks to my friends in the United States, I was granted a visa for Mexico by President Lazaro Cárdenas, to whom tens of thousands of Spaniards owe their lives.

With some good friends of mine I was living for the moment in a tumbledown *château*, which we nicknamed *Espervisa*. André Breton used to write poetry in the greenhouse there under the November sun. I wrote some pages of a novel, not, however, from any love of literature. For this age must be witnessed; the witness passes, but his testimony manages to endure—and life still goes on. Others, turned rescuers by profession—who included two soldiers from Dunkirk—worked night and day for the American Relief Committee, overwhelmed by work and the appeals from concentration-camps, and in constant peril themselves. As it was, however, this was a shipwreck with too many castaways.

Once I was arrested at home and released afterwards, twice caught in a street round-up, once listed for the concentration-camp, once interned for several days on board ship, with the staff of the American Relief Committee; I was lucky to be a well-known writer—and with pretty powerful support. I lived in a hotel—the *Hôtel de Rome*—where several refugees with a name enjoyed a tranquillity which was only relative, since several Gestapo agents hung around and the *Sûreté* kept a special watch. Both at the Préfecture and among the police, at least half of the officials were pro-British and discreetly anti-Nazi, and this helped matters along. Meanwhile, at this time, the poets Walter Hasenclever and Walter Benjamin[1] commit suicide. Rudolf Hilferding and Breitscheid are carried off

---

[1] Walter Hasenclever (1890–1940): German expressionist poet and playwright, said to have influenced Brecht. Walter Benjamin (1892–1940): German aesthetician and poet; committed suicide when arrested by the Spanish frontier police.

out of our midst and handed to the Nazis.[1] The lawyer Apfel happened to die—of a heart attack—right in Varian Fry's office. In the newspapers: suicide or murder of Krivitsky in Washington. Trotsky murdered in Mexico. Yes, this is just the hour for the Old Man to die, the blackest hour for the working classes: just as their keenest hour saw his highest ascendancy. (Russia is just on the eve of entering the war. . . .)

The morale of my Italian friends is first-rate. These are: a bold-hearted young Marxist, an old Garibaldian, full of Latin saws, and Modigliani, an honest old reformist leader with a keen intellect. They can hear the timber of the whole edifice in their part of the world giving off loud cracks, and explain that the moment has come when Fascism's own profiteers are beginning to realize that their only hope of safety lies in turning traitor promptly enough. An Italian senator has just written that the régime has entered its crisis, and that his circle are thinking in terms of a constitutional monarchy: salvation by putting the clock back a quarter of a century, how very easy. Modigliani—stout, with an impressive beard, his manner most patrician, his blue eyes alert and sad, his words measured, always thoughtful, and burdened with experience—Modigliani, at the age of sixty-three, still likes to keep in his inmost heart the hope that some day he can again be of service. All the same his wife Vera, still at his side, is trembling for his sake. Both of them, with their faultless dignity, incarnate the sober, noble Socialism of an age that has passed. (What has happened to them now? They were still in France at the moment when the Nazis took over the unoccupied zone. . . .)[2]

Some of us whose lives are in danger eventually make our exit. The Battle of the Visas which their friends have had to wage for their sake would stand some description: a single escape would provide material for a book of Balzacian proportions, packed with unexpected incidents and dark happenings behind the scenes. I take the last ship to leave for Martinique. Permission to journey by way of Morocco and the French West Indies has just been refused

[1] Rudolf Hilferding (1877–1944): prominent German economist and Social-Democratic politician; author of important works on imperialism and finance capital. Rudolf Breitscheid (1874–1944): Minister of the Interior in the German Republic, 1918–19, then a leading Social-Democratic Deputy.

[2] Modigliani succeeded in escaping to Switzerland in 1943 and returned to Italy following the liberation. He died in Rome in 1947.

me, but quite suddenly, within two hours, a transit-visa through Martinique is granted me at the Préfecture. . . . So here we are, my son and I, on a cargo boat converted into an ersatz concentration-camp of the sea, the *Capitaine Paul-Lemerle*. I feel no joy at going. I would a thousand times rather have stayed, if that had been possible: but before liberation of some kind comes its way, the chances are ninety-nine out of a hundred that I shall have perished in some filthy prison. Europe, with its bullet-ridden Russias, its crushed and trampled Germanies, its invaded nations, its gutted France—how one clings to it! We are parting only to return.

On board, forty of us are comrades, out of 300 refugees. The rest of them have no thought except for flight, being unpolitical or, in many cases, reactionary. Out in the Atlantic, past the Sahara coast, the stars pitch up and down above our heads. We hold a meeting on the upper deck, between the funnel and the lifeboats. There are a number of appraisals that we can make. We have fresh news, of the kind that does not get into the newspapers, from Germany, Austria, Spain, and Italy. We can see the partnership between Hitler and Stalin drawing to its perilous end. We have witnessed the failure of the Nazi victory and the Nazi-inspired counter-revolution in France. All around us we have seen the growth of fresh ways of thinking, a fresh eagerness to fight, a vague but powerful consciousness of the immense changes that are necessary. In Spanish waters, the fishermen gave us the clenched-fist salute from their little yachts. In Casablanca port, some friends came up to see me, and to tell me that they were looking to the future.

What can I say that is at all essential, to these forty faces gathered together in the twilight between sky and sea, and blending with the stars? I have a faint inkling of what is really essential: that we have not lost after all, that we have lost only for the moment. In the struggles of society we contributed a superabundance of consciousness and will, which greatly exceeded the forces at our command. All of us have behind us a certain number of mistakes and failings, for creative thought of any kind can proceed only with hesitating, stumbling steps. . . . Having made this qualification, in accordance with which each must search his heart—we have been quite astoundingly right. We with our nondescript little journals, we have often seen clearly where statesmen have floundered in ridiculous and disastrous folly. We have caught a glimpse of man resolving his own history. And we have known how to win, we must never forget that. The Russians and the Spaniards among us know what it is to take the world into their hands, to set the railways running and the factories working, to defend bombarded cities, to establish production-plans, to treat the wretched potentates of yesterday according to their deserts. No kind of predestination impels us to become the offal of concentration-camps—and as for the torturers of the prisons, we know very well how they are put against the wall! This experiment of ours will not be wasted. Millions of men who could not hear us are repeating it after us. There are whole armies in the concentration-camps, there are whole peoples in the prisons and under the terror. Yes, we have lost, but our spirit is strong, we are looking ahead eagerly.

In the Western hemisphere, marvellous landscapes open to our eyes. The sun streams down upon every object. In front of the ship's bows little flying fish, the colour of the sky, dart like dragonflies from the sea. The green mountains of Martinique are spread with dazzling riches. On the very edge of the sea, which has all the hues of the rainbow, the coco-nut trees are climbing high. And here we find yet one more concentration-camp, scorching hot, without drinkable water, guarded by tall childlike Negroes, managed by thieves of policemen. Some of them, Vichy officials, are Nazi to the core. (Now for a lesson in the political economy of the West Indies. The island is owned by a few superlatively wealthy families of big rum-distillers and sugar-growers, who maintain a diluted form of slavery on it. We shall see how long that will last; perhaps for quite some time, since here there is the problem of peoples still in their infancy.)

We feel strangely free in Ciudad-Trujillo, the small, spruce capital of the Dominican Republic. This is lit up unassumingly, and filled with flags, well-shaped girls with every conceivable kind of Eurafrican face, and Spanish refugees, comrades of ours, who make us wonder how they manage to live so well. Suddenly, this heavy tropical sky reverberates loud and long with the thunder of a new war, this most evil, most decisive war which the Nazi Empire is now declaring against the Russian people. The Negroes, deeply stirred, gather in crowds before the newspaper posters. Do they too, then, feel unconsciously that they are the citizens of an invisible International? I know the Russian system too well not to expect disastrous reverses. To think that all that has been built, at the cost of

so many sacrifices and injustices, is going to perish under Nazi
cannonfire. . . . I have no doubt that, because of the massacre of the
revolutionary generation (which constituted the Soviet Union's
best-trained nucleus of skill), we are now going to face a horribly
successful advance. For weeks I find it impossible to think of anything else but the nightmare sweeping over Russia. I can guess that,
in these very days, the last of my comrades are being shot in Russian
jails—because they were too discerning and because they might, before
long, acquire too much influence. (Later I learnt that I had guessed
right.) I carry on my work with practically no documentation, in
the tropical heat, anxious for the fate of my wife back in France,
whose painful battle for visas is not ended. This is what I write:

'Those of these men (the persecuted Oppositionists) who are still
alive, if they could battle today for the Russian people, for the
factories built by the Russian people with its own sweat and blood,
for the old red flags of the Ural partisans and the Petrograd workers—these men, in chains for more than a decade, would do battle
with their whole being. And he who is writing these lines, a man who
has come out of the same prisons, would be at their side. For today
the salvation of the Russian people and its revolutionary achievements is indispensable to the salvation of the world.'

I write that the weakness of Russia before industrial Germany
(Russia still being, despite the immense achievements of industrialization, mainly an agricultural nation) would cost her untold
sufferings, extending over years; however 'Russia spells an end to
the effortless victories, an end to the unchallenged butcheries like
Rotterdam—the butchers are now being paid back in kind; an end
to the conquests with immediate booty—real trouble is beginning;
an end to the hope of peace in the near future, since nobody can
really tell any longer when the fighting will end. There are so many
factors tending to material and moral attrition. . . . The Nazi
Empire has been halted in its tracks.'

I predict the stubborn, ever-renewed war of the partisans and
the unconquerable Russian winters. I announce, in July 1941, that
'Stalingrad, a vital strategic point, will be attacked and defended
ferociously'; that Japan will probably refrain from attacking
Vladivostok 'unless the Soviet power disintegrates altogether. . . .
but even in defeat we would judge it far closer to recovery than to
anything that could really be called disintegration. . . .'

Two years of war have not given the lie to this work (*Hitler Contra Stalin*) published in Mexico in September 1941; no publisher in New York would touch it. In the second part I ventured into the future and showed how infinitely probable was the 'resurrection' of Russian democracy from its totalitarian noose. A people as great as this cannot die, still less can it survive such an ordeal without reviving into liberty, suppressing the terror at long last, and asking searching questions which will assign the political responsibility for the past.

My journey to Mexico continues, with a few incidents on the way. The articles I published in Ciudad-Trujillo have excited the attention of the town's Communist cell, which is certainly connected with more powerful organizations in America. I am surrounded by a torrent of filthy denunciations—all over again. The police of Haiti go into a fit of terror at the airport and take us into custody; if we had not greeted the affair with such complete coolness we would have been beaten up there and then. They recover a little composure, only to smile nicely at a Falangist gentleman who is passing through with a pretty passport duly stamped by Franco's consuls. Back in the Dominican Republic, and again in Cuba, our luggage is searched and we are interrogated. But where there is nothing to find, the blackest slander loses its power. Everything is cleared up in a matter of days.

The loveliness of Havana, its sensual delight feeding on electricity —this after our pitifully dark European cities. Meetings with friends hitherto unseen. The heady sensation of being in a free country. We arrive in Havana while the battle of Leningrad is beginning, and we are haunted by mental pictures of the fighting over there.

The aeroplane instructs us in a new vision of the world whose lyrical richness could provide material for a renewed art-form to flourish, whether in poetry or painting.[1] But this semi-bankrupt civilization has made it into a killing-machine; it is used for travel only by the rich, who are dead to any kind of enthusiasm. We see them dozing in the comfortable seats of the Douglas aircraft, and all the while we are winging over the Caribbean Sea, the storm-ridden lands of Yucatan, and then the tablelands of Mexico, covered in

---

[1] Serge is here drawing upon the ideas of a Mexican artist named Dr. Atl, whom he met in the course of his exile. Atl was the theorist and practitioner of *aeropittura*, i.e. of landscapes and scenes as observed from an aeroplane.

heavy clouds which are transfixed by shafts of light. Huge, rose-pink and solid, Tenayuca's Pyramid of the Sun stands out suddenly on its flinty plain.

The first face I see at Mexico Airport belongs to a Spanish friend; it is bespectacled, pensive, vigorous and gaunt—Julián Gorkín. When he was in the jails of Spain we fought for eighteen months to save his life. Now he and other comrades, in New York and Mexico, have just fought over fourteen months to guarantee me this journey, this escape. Without them I should have been doomed, almost hopelessly. My destiny has its privileges: this is the second time in six years that this rational miracle of solidarity has been worked on my behalf. We stick together like this, from one end of the world to the other, few in number but sure of one another—and confident in the march of history.

In the Mexican street, I taste a singular sensation. I am no longer an outlaw, no longer a hunted man, due any minute to be interned or to disappear. Only I am told now: 'There are certain revolvers you must beware of. . . .' That can take care of itself: I have lived too long to live anywhere but in the immediate present. For me, the gracious lights of Mexico are superimposed over the prospect of distant cities, restless, devastated, and plunged into black-out, and in these I see men walking, the most hunted men in the world, whom I have left behind me. I know that not all of them have to leave, that those who can stay have a duty to stay (and, no doubt, they are performing this simple duty exceedingly well); I know that some of them have to be killed, statistics requires it to be so. But there are some of them, too, who cannot stay without being killed and who by reason of their experience, their steadfastness, their idealism, their knowledge, are precious for tomorrow's Europe. If the men who were the backbone of the old European Socialism and the young murdered democracies are not saved, the inevitable revolutions to come will be led by ex-Nazis, ex-Fascists, ex-Communists of the totalitarian stamp, or adventurers devoid of ideas or humanism, or men of goodwill who have lost their bearings. This is a simple and urgent political calculation. Why, then, do the Americas find it so hard to open a chink in their doorways to welcome in a few of these warriors?

10

LOOKING FORWARD

I end these recollections on the threshold of Mexico. Life goes on: the struggle goes on. I know that what I have written is at once too scrappy and too concentrated; I have had too much experience to record. To my regret, for lack of space, I have had to miss many portrayals and many details. I have sought to give only what was typical and essential. The environment of my work has been rather hard, appropriately so for a work of this kind: living with difficulty, surrounded by obscure threats, without knowing when or where the work could be published—but at the same time with the conviction that one day it would find its proper use. Possibly, on some secondary points, I may be guilty of lapses of memory; but I have told only the truth, told it as completely as I can.

It has been observed that I show hardly any interest in talking about myself. It is hard for me to disentangle my own person from the social processes, the ideas and activities in which it has shared, which matter more than it and which give it value. I do not think of myself as at all an individualist: rather as a 'personalist', in that I view human personality as a supreme value, only integrated in society and in history. The experience and thought of one man have no significance which deserves to last, except in this sense. Nevertheless, no one should read into these words any yearning for self-effacement; I am sure that one must be oneself, simply and fully, neither abdicating responsibility nor wishing to diminish others. To sum up, nothing of us is truly our own unless it be our sincere desire to share in the common life of mankind.

Out of a little over fifty years, I have spent ten in various forms of captivity, which have usually been harsh. These confinements have taught me the truth of Nietzsche's paradoxical dictum: 'Whatever does not kill me, strengthens me'. I have never had property, and practically never lived in security. Several times I have lost every material thing that I cherished: books, papers and personal souvenirs. In Brussels, in Paris, in Barcelona, in Berlin, in Leningrad, at the Soviet frontier, in Paris again, I have left nearly everything behind —or it has all been taken away from me. This experience has made me indifferent to material goods, although it has done nothing to discourage me.

My inclinations have always been towards intellectual work. Few satisfactions seem to me as great as those of understanding and expression. Probably my books have been my dearest love, but I have written much less than I could have wished, and then hastily, without opportunity to revise, in the thick of the struggle. My books have undergone a singular fate. In my first fatherland, Russia, and only because I wished to serve my country without lying, every single one was suppressed even before publication; and the political police confiscated the manuscripts of several finished works, the fruit of several years' effort: among these the novel in which I thought I had best conveyed the grandeur of the Revolution. On the other hand, my *History of the first years of the Revolution*, published in Paris and Madrid, is one of the three or four honest and relatively complete works on an epoch whose documents have been destroyed, whose very memoirs falsified, whose witnesses shot. In France and Spain, my books have had a fine reception; in Spain they have been burned, in France I do not know what has become of them. In the United States, with only two exceptions, conservative publishers considered my work too revolutionary, and left-wing publishers too anti-totalitarian, that is, too hard on the Stalin régime. My latest novel, *La Terre Commence à Trembler* . . ., written in my journeyings across the world, with the single passionate motive of giving life to human beings about whom practically nothing has been written up to now, has still not been able to appear, for this double reason. Although their quality has generally been recognized, my books have known a life as hard as my own. I have found that the writer cannot even *exist* in our decomposing modern societies without accommodating himself to interests which forcibly limit his horizons and mutilate his sincerity.

I have outlived three generations of brave men, mistaken as they may have been, to whom I was deeply attached, and whose memory remains dear to me. And here again, I have discovered that it is nearly impossible to live a life devoted wholly to a cause which one believes to be just; a life, that is, where one refuses to separate thought from daily action. The young French and Belgian rebels of my twenties have all perished; my syndicalist comrades of Barcelona in 1917 were nearly all massacred; my comrades and friends of the Russian Revolution are probably all dead—any exceptions are only by a miracle. All were brave, all sought a principle of life nobler and juster than that of surrender to the bourgeois order; except perhaps for certain young men, disillusioned and crushed before their consciousness had crystallized, all were engaged in movements for progress. I must confess that the feeling of having so many dead men at my back, many of them my betters in energy, talent, and historical character, has often overwhelmed me; and that this feeling has been for me also the source of a certain courage, if that is the right word for it.

A political exile since my birth, I have known both the real benefits and the oppressive hardships of the uprooted man. Up-heaval broadens his perception of the world and his knowledge of men; it blows away his foggy conformities and stifling particular-isms; it saves him from that patriotic complacency which really is no more than humdrum self-satisfaction; but, in the struggle for existence, it remains a most serious handicap. I have witnessed the birth of the enormous category of 'stateless persons', that is, of those men to whom tyrants refuse even a nationality. As far as the right to live is concerned, the plight of these men without a country (who are in truth those who are most attached to their own countries and to the country of mankind) can be compared only to that of the 'unacknowledged man' of the Middle Ages who, since he had no lord or sovereign, had no rights and no protection either, and whose very name became a kind of insult. Through their conservative temper, in a time when nothing can any longer be 'conserved' without change, and also through legalistic inertia, most modern states have become accomplices in the persecution of these defenders of liberty. Now at last, when we, the stateless, are beginning to number millions, perhaps things will change. For my own part, I have no regrets at carrying this leaden burden, since I can feel myself to be at one and the same time Russian and French, European and Eurasian, a stranger to no land, despite the law, and recognizing everywhere, in all the diversity of place and person, the unity of the world and of mankind. Even in the earth of Mexico, so profoundly original in its volcanic aridity, I have seen the contours of Russia and Spain; and the *Indio* of this land reveals himself as brother to the toilers of Central Asia.

Early on, I learnt from the Russian intelligentsia that the only meaning of life lies in conscious participation in the making of history. The more I think of that, the more deeply true it seems to be. It follows that one must range oneself actively against everything that diminishes man, and involve oneself in all struggles which tend to liberate and enlarge him. This categorical imperative is in no way lessened by the fact that such an involvement is inevitably soiled by error: it is a worse error merely to live for oneself, caught within traditions which are soiled by inhumanity. This conviction has brought me, as it has brought others, to a somewhat unusual destiny; but we were, and still are, in line with the development of history, and it is now obvious that, during an entire epoch, millions of individual destinies will follow the paths along which we were the first to travel. In Europe, in Asia, in America, whole generations are in upheaval, are involved to the hilt in collective struggles, have become apprenticed to violence and grave danger; endure captivity in its various forms, prove to themselves that the egoism of 'every man for himself' is finished, that private enrichment is no fit aim for life, that yesterday's conservatisms lead to nothing but catastrophe; and they sense the necessity for a fresh outlook tending towards the reorganization of the world.

I give myself credit for having seen clearly in a number of important situations. In itself, this is not so difficult to achieve, and yet it is rather unusual. To my mind, it is less a question of an exalted or shrewd intelligence, than of good sense, goodwill and a certain sort of courage to enable one to rise above both the pressures of one's environment and the natural inclination to close one's eyes to facts, a temptation that arises from our immediate interests and from the fear which problems inspire in us. A French essayist has said: 'What is terrible when you seek the truth, is that you find it.' You find it, and then you are no longer free to follow the biases of your personal circle, or to accept fashionable clichés. I immediately discerned within the Russian Revolution the seeds of such serious evils as intolerance and the drive towards the persecution of dissent. These evils originated in an absolute sense of possession of the truth, grafted upon doctrinal rigidity. What followed was contempt for the man who was different, of his arguments and way of life. Undoubtedly, one of the greatest problems which each of us has to solve in the realm of practice, is that of accepting the necessity to maintain, in the midst of the intransigence which comes from steadfast beliefs, a critical spirit towards these same beliefs and a respect for the belief that differs. In the struggle, it is the problem of combining the greatest practical efficiency with respect for the man in the enemy; in a word, of war without hate. The Russian Revolution, although led by men who were upright and intelligent, did not resolve this problem; the character of the masses had received, from the experience of despotism, a fatal stamp whose effects were imprinted in the leaders themselves. In making this judgement, I do not mean to disown the importance of economic-historical factors; they broadly condition action, but they do not determine its entire quality. There, the human factor intervenes.

Many times I have felt myself on the brink of a pessimistic conclusion as to the function of thinking, of intelligence, in society. Continuously, over a quarter of a century, that is since the stabilization of the Russian Revolution just before 1920, I have found a general tendency to the suppression of percipient thinking. Earlier than that, I was too young to arrive at a fair judgement of the situation in European society before the First World War; but I have the impression that the most daring thinking would have met with a warmer welcome at that period, and consequently found more opportunity to survive.

I do not, after all my reflection on the subject, cast any doubt upon the scientific spirit of Marxism, nor on its contribution, a blend of rationality and idealism, to the consciousness of our age. All the same, I cannot help considering as a positive disaster the fact that a Marxist orthodoxy should, in a great country in the throes of social transformation, have taken over the apparatus of power. Whatever may be the scientific value of a doctri•.e, from the moment that it becomes governmental, interests of State will cease to allow it the possibility of impartial inquiry; and its scientific certitude will even lead it, first to intrude into education, and then, by the methods of guided thought, which is the same as suppressed thought, to exempt itself from criticism. The relationships between error and true understanding are in any case too abstruse for any one to presume to regulate them by authority; men have no choice but to make long detours through hypotheses, mistakes and imaginative guesses, if they are to succeed in extricating assessments which are more exact, if partly provisional: for there are few cases of complete exactness. This means that freedom of thought seems to me, of all values, one of the most essential.

It is also one of the most contested. Everywhere and at every time, I have encountered fear of thought, repression of thought, as an almost universal desire to escape or else stifle this ferment of restlessness. During the dictatorship of the proletariat, when Red posters proclaimed that 'the reign of the workers will never end', no one would admit any doubt as to the eternity of a régime which was quite clearly exceptional, formed in the course of siege. Our great Marxists of Russia, nurtured on Science, would not admit any doubt concerning the dialectical conception of Nature—which is, however, no more than a hypothesis, and one difficult to sustain at that. The leadership of the Communist International classified as a moral lapse, or as a crime, the slightest doubt as to the triumphal future of their organization. Later, in the heart of the Opposition, with all the integrity of its ideals, Trotsky would not tolerate any point of view different from his own. I say nothing of other sorts of men, victims to waves of mob-hysteria, to the blindness of private interest or the inertia of tradition. In 1918 I was nearly torn to pieces by my French workmates because I defended the Russian Revolution at the moment of the Brest-Litovsk negotiations. Twenty years later, I was nearly torn to pieces by the same workers because I denounced the totalitarianism which had sprung from that Revolution.

I have seen the intellectuals of the Left, responsible for editing reputable reviews and journals, refuse to publish the truth, even though it was absolutely certain, even though they did not contest it; but they found it painful, they preferred to ignore it, it was in contradiction with their moral and material interests (the two generally go together). In politics I have observed the appalling powerlessness of accurate prediction, which brings boycott, slander, or persecution on him who predicts. The role of critical intelligence has seemed to me to be dangerous, and very nearly useless. That is the most pessimistic conclusion to which I have felt myself drawn. I am careful not to state it finally; I blame the feeling on my personal weakness, and I persist in regarding critical and percipient thought as an absolute necessity, as a categorical imperative which no one can evade without damage to himself and harm to society, and, besides, as the source of immense satisfactions. Better times will come, and perhaps soon. It is a matter of holding fast and keeping faith until then.

The participant and witness of our epoch's events must be driven to pronounce against historical fatality. It is evident that the broadest outlines of the historical process are the product of factors outside our grasp and control, which we can come to know only after an imperfect, fragmentary fashion. But it is no less evident that the character, and even in certain cases the direction, of historical facts depends to a very large extent on the calibre of individual human beings. When the Central Committee of the Bolshevik Party met in December 1918 to study methods of attacking domestic counter-revolution, it had a conscious choice to make among the weapons it could present to the new régime. It *could have* instituted public revolutionary tribunals (allowing secret trial in certain specified cases) and, within these tribunals, permitted the right of defence, and ensured judicial strictness. It *preferred* to set up the Cheka, that is to say, an Inquisition with secret proceedings, and to exclude from this body any right of defence and any control by public opinion. In doing this, the Central Committee probably followed the line of least resistance; it also followed psychological impulses which are comprehensible to any student of Russian history, but which have nothing in common with Socialist principles.

Was it possible, in the Russia of 1926 and 1927, to foresee the difficulties which would ensue from the combination of industrial backwardness with agrarian revival? We foresaw them; and it would have been possible to remedy them in time, to some degree. But once again, the men in power preferred to follow the line of least resistance, which is also the line of least foresight, but gives the illusion of putting off serious crisis as fearful invalids put off a surgical operation. The difficulties which had been deliberately ignored still kept growing; provoked a kind of panic or blockage of reason, and necessitated solutions which were not only violent, but hideously inhuman and burdensome, those of total collectivization and totalitarian industrialization. In *Destiny of a Revolution* (1937) I concluded: 'The bureaucracy itself could, it seems, have a less disastrous policy without difficulty, if it had displayed more general culture and Socialist spirit. Its infatuation with administrative and military methods, joined to a penchant for panic in critical moments, reduced its real means. In despotic régimes, too many things depend on the tyrant. . . .'; and 'all that was done in the U.S.S.R. would have been done much better by a Soviet democracy. . . .'

The character of the tyrant consequently lends a catastrophic impetus to political conflicts. The Trials of deception and blood were decided upon by the Politbureau, which laid down the sentences and decreed their execution. This means that no more than *ten* individuals deliberated at leisure whether or not to massacre tens of thousands of citizens who were imbued with a spirit of opposition; they could have decided to deprive these adversaries of political rights or to imprison them. Instead, they resolved upon the use of the cruellest and most demoralizing means possible. In another situation, whose significance is incalculable, the same Politbureau, with the choice of collaboration with Hitler and collaboration with the democratic Powers, both solutions implying grave risks of war and invasion, adopted that solution which removed the most immediate danger by increasing the danger post-dated a few months or years, as has now been proved. In all this, the intelligence and character of men play a supreme role; and the observation follows that their rational intelligence, and also their morality—as defined by human feeling and fidelity to principles representing general higher interests—must be at fault.

I take these examples only from facts—and from men whom I know well. Doubtless the same can be said of the most atrocious and tragic crime of our age: the extermination by the Nazis of the Jews of occupied Europe. Nothing at the present can measure the political, social, and psychological consequences of this crime. Even the idea of the human, acquired over thousands of years of civilization, has been put in question. Man's soul will be branded with the fact; and all that was sufficient for it was provided by a decree deliberated by a few individuals. The totalitarian machine, then, functions like a factory to which an engineer comes, turning a lever to make the current run.

It is necessary to conclude against the existence of fatality, and for the immense power of man and for personal responsibility. It is not a pessimistic conclusion. But it stands as a condemnation of systems which concentrate maddening power in a few hands, force a selection of perverted elements, destroy even an imperfect check upon power by the average man, and paralyse the public conscience.

The men of my generation—those born around 1890—above all the Europeans among them, cannot help the sensation of having lived on a frontier where one world ends and another begins. The passage from one century to another was a giddy one. I remember my astonishment as a child when I saw the first 'horseless carriages' pass in the street The motor-car was being born. I was a news-vendor during the first aeroplane rally organized in France; that would be about 1909. Blériot's exploit of crossing the Channel by air provoked mass enthusiasm. I knew domestic lighting by paraffin, then by gas, since electricity still penetrated only into wealthy homes. I waited in the street for that magic character, the lamp-lighter, to pass. . . . The illustrated journals of those distant times were full of the portraits of kings and emperors: the Emperor of Russia, the Emperor of Germany, the Emperor of Austro-Hungary, the Empress of China, the Sultan of the Sublime Porte. . . . Across the screens of the first cinemas, regiments used to parade, rather too rapidly, with jerky steps, and these animated pictures dumbfounded us. There was even some talk of X-rays which allowed one to see right through the human body.

When I was fifteen I was much exercised by the discoveries in the field of energy. A popularizer, dealing with the splitting of the atom, wrote: 'Nothing is created, everything is destroyed. . . .' Anxiously, I questioned my father, a Spencerian positivist. He answered, smiling, 'How do you imagine that could be true over infinite time? Everything would have disappeared billions of years ago!' I was reassured; Mach's book on energy became my bedside reading. The solid idea of matter was now overthrown; the First World War destroyed the idea of the stability of the world. The empires crumpled like houses of cards, the emperors were suddenly only poor devils on the run, who could even be shot. The banknote, that talisman, became no more than a scrap of paper—and we were all millionaires, except that a million would not buy a box of matches. Relativity taught a new—and perplexing—concept of time and space.

I have seen the face of Europe change several times. Before the First World War I knew a buoyant Europe, optimistic, liberal and crudely dominated by money. We reached our twenties as young idealistic workers, and we were angry and desperate, at times, because of the Wall: we could see nothing beyond an eternal bourgeois world, unjust and self-satisfied.

The guns thundered, and Europe was at war, a prey to contending hysterias, bleeding from all her veins, and yet, in the middle of the slaughter, pretty comfortably off. Behind the lines business was good, the world was still solid! Paris, ominous at night, but almost gay in the day-time; Barcelona, full of birds, dancing-girls and *anarchos*, the trains packed with tough, worn-out soldiers . . . without knowing it, the world was sliding towards the maelstrom.

Suddenly the Europe of revolutions was born at Petrograd. Our Red soldiers chased the generals' bands across all Europe and all Siberia. Insurrections and summary executions followed in Central Europe. Among the victorious Powers, there reigned the calm, stupid self-assurance of folk getting back to their profitable affairs. 'It will all quieten down, just wait and see!' Businesses, chancelleries, governments, newspapers, the League of Nations, all were stocked in plenty with competent gentlemen whose bodily nourishment was excellent, and spiritual diet less so, only it was bad taste to talk about that. Post-war 'good time', peace of the victors . . . We saw the cracks in the earth open wide; and when we spoke of it, they called us visionaries.

Meanwhile, totalitarian Europe was growing behind our backs. As to that, we were blind. We revolutionaries, who aimed to create a new society, 'the broadest democracy of the workers', had unwittingly, with our hands, constructed the most terrifying State machine conceivable; and when, with revulsion, we realized the truth, this machine, driven by our friends and comrades, turned on us and crushed us. Maturing into merciless despotism, the Russian Revolution no longer summoned the German masses to give the utmost of their resources and strength. Nazism came to

power, aping the Marxism it loathed. Europe multiplied concentration-camps, burned or pulped books, laid reason under the steamroller and scattered abroad, over all its loudspeakers, intoxicating
lies.

There followed a dream of confused hopes: the Europe of the
Popular Fronts and Moscow Trials seemed convalescent in those
very moments when it was doomed. It became increasingly difficult
to distinguish between revolution and reaction, between democracy
with Fascist trends and Fascism in disguise, between submerged
civil war and the rule of democracy, between open civil war and
war between States, between intervention and non-intervention,
between brands of totalitarianism in opposition but momentarily
allied, between the most criminal impostures and the simple truth.
This confusion sprang from the impotence of men caught up in the
drift towards the cataclysm, and impotence fed in its turn upon
confusion.

The era of huge collapses followed. It seemed that no human value
could survive—only gigantic war-machines whose function was to
establish slavery.

Since I escaped from Europe, other changes have come about.
The prestige and effectiveness of the totalitarian Powers have
declined. Even their victories seem to foreshadow their future defeat.
The horizon begins to clear; the balance-sheet is being drawn up.
For the last thirty years, with the existence of discoveries which
add prodigiously to man's technical knowledge (without proportion-
ately improving his level of consciousness), we have been entering a
cycle of world transformation. In it we are the prisoners of social
systems worn to the point of breakdown. Moulded themselves by a
defunct world, the best and most clear-sighted of us have often been
revealed, in the tempests of the age, as more than half blind. No
doctrine has stood before the shock. There is nothing surprising
about that: such are the limitations of man and of doctrine. Meanwhile, the broad outlines of history now in the course of realization
are breaking clear from the chaos. It is no longer the revolutionaries
who are making the world's tremendous revolution; it is the tyrannies that have set it going, it is the actual technique of the modern
world that is breaking brutally with the past and throwing the
peoples of entire continents into the necessity for starting life afresh
on new foundations. That these foundations must be of social justice,

of rational organization, of respect for the individual, of liberty, is for me a wonderfully evident fact which, little by little, is asserting itself beyond the inhumanity of the present time. The future seems to me to be full of possibilities greater than any we have glimpsed throughout the past. May the passion, the experience and even the faults of my fighting generation have some small power to illumine the way forward!

Mexico, 1942–February, 1943.

APPENDIX

VICTOR SERGE AND GAULLISM

On 31 January 1948 *Le Rassemblement*, the official organ of General de Gaulle's *Rassemblement du Peuple Français* (R.P.F.), published a brief extract from a personal letter written by Victor Serge six days before his death to André Malraux, then as now one of the most prominent figures of Gaullism. (Serge died in November of the year before.) The lines quoted ran: '*I wish to tell you that I judge the political position you have adopted to be courageous and probably reasonable; if I myself were in France, I should be among those Socialists who support collaboration with the movement of which you are a member. The electoral victory of your movement,*[1] *which I foresaw but whose magnitude surprised me, was in my opinion a great step towards the immediate safety of France.*' The extract concluded with a few political generalities.

The publication of those lines came as a tremendous shock to Serge's friends and associates.[2] The Gaullism of 1947 was in several ways even more suspect from a traditional Socialist point of view than the Gaullism of the Fifth Republic; it was a well-drilled anti-Parliamentarian mass-movement with a leader-cult, an ugly proneness to rowdyism, and a corporatist streak in its programme. It was generally held by the Left to be 'soft' towards the ex-Vichyite elements of the population. Any Marxist revolutionary who declared his support for such a movement could be fairly charged with renegacy.

Such a judgement on Serge would be far too harsh; or rather positively misleading. Serge did not, after all, issue any public statement in favour of Gaullism (or, we may add, of any other non-Socialist creed) at any time during his life. The entire evidence in the affair consists of an extract, presented without context, from a

---

[1] In which the R.P.F. had gained 40 per cent. of all votes cast.
[2] See the editorial comments in *La Révolution Prolétarienne*, April 1948.

personal letter which was not intended for publication. According
to his son Vlady,[1] this letter marked a resumption by Serge of
personal relations with Malraux. Despite Malraux's record of
support for the 'Victor Serge campaign' of 1935–6 (including a personal approach by him to Stalin), their last conversation, in Marseilles
before Serge's departure to Mexico, had been of an estranging
character.[2] The phrase in the extract describing the R.P.F.'s success
as 'a great step towards the immediate safety of France' undoubtedly
reflects Serge's deep concern at the post-war strength of the French
Communist Party.

While it is legitimate to wonder if Serge might have worded those
lines rather differently if he had known that they might be quoted as
a political testimonial, the fact remains that he did write them. It
is equally a fact that no other statement with anything like a pro-
Gaullist construction can be found in Serge's writings or in his associates' recollections of him.

Indeed, in a letter (undated but apparently from October 1946)
addressed to the editor of one of the few Paris magazines that was
taking his work, Victor Serge expressed grave chagrin at the Gaullist and pro-Western leanings of the journal's publishing policy: 'I
have been asking myself if you and I still spoke the same language.
What was even more serious is that other articles were flirting with
Gaullism, with Christianity (up to your third issue), endorsing
British foreign policy and—while deploring the collision of the two
blocs—omitting the formulation of any definite critique directed
against American imperialism.'[3] In striking contrast to the complacency with which, in the Malraux letter, Serge views an anti-
Communist electoral stampede, his warning of late 1946 insists that
'We must not play around with an anti-Communist bloc. . . . The
C.P. retains its hold over a large section of the working class. . . .
We cannot adopt a purely negative attitude towards the C.P. We
shall get nowhere if we appear to be more preoccupied with criticizing Stalinism than with the defence of the workers. The reactionary danger is still real, and in practice we shall often have to act
side by side with the Communists.'

---

[1] In *La Révolution Prolétarienne*, May 1948.
[2] M. Malraux has unfortunately been prevented both by the pressure of his
Ministerial duties and by the inaccessibility of his archives from supplying any
further context or background to the extract which has been cited.
[3] *Seize Fusillés à Moscou; Lettres inédites* (Paris, 1972, Spartacus edition), p. 125.

It would be facile to conclude that some kind of deathbed repentance had taken place, simply because Serge died shortly after the date of the Malraux extract. Other revolutionaries have been known to commit doubtful acts which have been forgotten or forgiven simply because their perpetrators have lived to redeem themselves in other ways. If Lenin had died in April 1917 on the sealed train provided for his return to Russia by German imperialism; or if Trotsky had died in December 1939 the instant after consenting to travel to the United States to testify before the House Un-American Activities Committee, it would doubtless be suspected—and not only by their detractors—that two more subversives had made their peace with the old order.

Those six lines or so quoted by Gaullists must be judged, finally, against the whole politico-literary tendency of Victor Serge's last period. In June 1947 he had completed a book-length biography of Trotsky in collaboration with the dead leader's widow. In the following two months he wrote the last essay to be published during his lifetime, a lengthy commemorative piece for the thirtieth anniversary of the Russian Revolution.[1] Like nearly all of Serge's later journalism it was written for an inconspicuous, disestablished, small magazine of the far Left. In it the old combative fire is undiminished:

'*A feeble logic, whose finger beckons us to the dark spectacle of the Stalinist Soviet Union, affirms the bankruptcy of Bolshevism, followed by that of Marxism, followed by that of Socialism. . . . Have you forgotten the other bankruptcies? What was Christianity doing in the various catastrophes of society? What became of Liberalism? What has Conservatism produced, in either its enlightened or its reactionary form? Did it not spawn Mussolini, Hitler, Salazar, and Franco? If we are indeed honestly to weigh out the bankruptcies of ideology, we shall have a long task ahead of us. . . . And nothing is finished yet. . . .*' Here too Serge indulges in a violent invective against the American ex-Marxist James Burnham, who had argued that Stalin was Lenin's authentic continuation:

'*The paradox that he has developed, doubtless out of love for a provocative theory, is as false as it is dangerous. Under a thousand insipid forms it is to be found in the Press and the literature of this age of preparation for the Third World War. The reactionaries have an obvious interest in confounding*

[1] *Trente Ans Après La Révolution Russe*, in *La Révolution Prolétarienne*, November 1947.

Stalinist totalitarianism—exterminator of the Bolsheviks—with Bolshevism itself; their aim is to strike at the working class, at Socialism, at Marxism, and even at Liberalism. . . .'

Whatever else they may be, these are not the words of a man of the Right, or of any variety of ex-revolutionary penitent.

SELECT BIBLIOGRAPHY

HISTORY, POLITICAL ANALYSIS, AND AUTOBIOGRAPHY

1. *Contra la faim*: Paris, Éditions de l'Anarchie, 1911. (A pamphlet written by the young Kibalchich (Victor Serge) under the pseudonym *Le Rétif.*)
2. *Pendant la guerre civile: Pétrograd mai-juin 1909*: Paris, Bibliothèque du Travail, 1921. (Serge's diary during the siege of Petrograd.)
3. *Les Anarchistes et l'expérience de la révolution russe*: Paris, Librairie du Travail, 1921. (An essay on the problems of revolutionary power and the role of anarchists and libertarians within the Socialist state.) Also as Chapter Four of A. Skirda (ed.), *Les Anarchistes dans la révolution russe*: Paris, Éditions de la Tête de Feuilles, 1973.
4. *La Ville en danger: Pétrograd, l'an II de la révolution*: Paris, Librairie du Travail, 1924. (Another piece on the siege in the Civil War.) Reprinted as an appendix to the 1971 Maspero edition of title 9 below.
5. *Les Coulisses d'une sûreté générale: l'Okhrana*: Paris, Librairie du Travail, 1925. (An account of Serge's discoveries in the Okhrana archives and a warning to the Western labour movements of the extent of police infiltration. Also: reissued as *Ce que tout révolutionnaire doit savoir de la répression*: Paris, François Maspero, 1970.)
6. *Lénine, 1917*: Paris, Librairie du Travail, 1925. Also with a new preface as *Vingt ans après*: Paris, Cahiers Spartacus, 1937. (A historical essay on Lenin's ideas and actions in the year of the Revolution.)
7. *La lutte des classes dans la révolution chinoise*: *Clarté* (Paris), Nos. 9, 11, 12, 13, and 14, May to October 1927; reprinted as *La Révolution Chinoise*: Paris, Éditions Savelli, 1977, with introduction by Pierre Naville and the addition of two further articles by Serge, 'Le bolchévisme dans l'Asie' from *Clarté*, No. 7, March 1927, and 'Canton' from *La Lutte des Classes*, No. 1, February–March 1928, the latter first published under the pseudonym 'Paul Sizoff' (see *Memoirs*, p. 239). An English translation by Gregor Benton with a preface by the veteran Chinese Trotskyist Wang Fan-hsi will be published in 1978 by Pluto Press, London.
8. *Vie des révolutionnaires*: Paris, Librairie du Travail, 1930. Mimeographed reprint, Paris, U.C.I. (Union Communiste Internationale), 1961. (A memorial account of some relatively unknown Bolshevik militants.)
9. *L'An I de la Révolution russe*: Paris, Librairie du Travail, 1930. Also: Paris, Éditions de Delphes, 1965; Paris, François Maspero, 1971. (English translation by Peter Sedgwick: *Year One of the Russian Revolution*; New York, Holt, Rinehart, 1972; London, Allen Lane, 1972.)

10. *Littérature et révolution*: Paris, Librairie Valois, 1932. Also: Paris, François Maspero, 1976, and (in a considerably augmented edition) 1978.

11. *Seize fusillés à Moscou*: Paris, Cahiers Spartacus, 1936. (Pamphlet attacking the first Moscow trial.) Also: Paris, Spartacus, 1972, in a volume including unpublished letters by Serge.

12. *De Lénine à Staline*: Paris, *Le Crapouillot*, special issue, January 1937. (English translation by Ralph Manheim: *From Lenin to Stalin*; New York, Pioneer Publishers, 1937; London, Secker and Warburg, 1937. Also in an edition with a selection of articles on Russia by Serge: New York, Monad Press, 1973.)

13. *Vingt-neuf fusillés et la fin de Yagoda*: Paris, 1937, special issue of the review *Lectures Prolétariennes* (No. 3, April 1937).

14. *Destin d'une Révolution: U.R.S.S., 1917–1937*: Paris, Bernard Grasset, 1937. (English translation by Max Schachtman: *Russia Twenty Years After*, New York, Pioneer Publishers, 1937, and Connecticut, Hyperion Press, 1973; *Destiny of a Revolution*, London, Jarrolds, 1937.)

15. 'La Pensée anarchiste': in *L'Anarchie; Le Crapouillot*, special issue, January 1938.

16. *L'Assassinat d'Ignace Reiss*: in *L'Assassinat politique et l'U.R.S.S.*, by V. Serge, M. Wullens and A. Rosmer: Paris, Éditions Pierre Tisné, 1938.

17. *La Révolution Russe: Février–Octobre 1917*: Chapter Six in the collection *Histoire des Révolutions de Cromwell à Franco*: Paris, Éditions Gallimard, 1938.

18. 'Deux rencontres': in *Les Humbles*, Cahiers 8–12, August–December 1938, special issue *A Maurice Parijanine* (Serge's reminiscence of Parijanine, his fellow translator of Lenin, Trotsky, etc). Also in *Témoins* (Zürich), No. 23, May 1960. (English translation under the title 'Twice Met' in *International Socialism* (London), No. 20, Spring 1965.)

19. *Portrait de Staline*: Paris, Bernard Grasset, 1940.

20. *Hitler contra Stalin*: Mexico City, Ediciones Quetzal, 1941. (In Spanish.)

21. *Los Problemas del Socialismo en nuestro tiempo*: Mexico City, *Mundo*, 1944. (A set of essays, published in Spanish, by Julián Gorkín, Marceau Pivert and Serge.)

22. *La Tragédie des écrivains soviétiques*: Paris, Les Égaux, 1947. Also in the 1972 Spartacus reissue of title 11 above. In English translation under the title 'The Writer's Conscience' in *Now* (London), No. 7, March 1947.

23. *Le Nouvel Impérialisme russe*: Paris, Cahiers Spartacus, 1947. Also, with four short articles by Serge, in *Hommage à Victor Serge. Le Nouvel Impérialisme russe*: Paris, Spartacus, 1972.

24. *Vie et Mort de Trotsky*: Paris, Amiot-Dumont, 1951. (A biography written in collaboration with Trotsky's widow Natalia Sedova, whose reminiscences are marked off in the text. Also: Paris, Club

des Amis du Livre, 1961, and (as *Vie et Mort de Léon Trotsky*) Paris, François Maspero, 1973. English translation by Arnold Pomerans: *The Life and Death of Leon Trotsky*; New York, Basic Books, 1975; London, Wildwood House, 1975.)

25. *Le Tournant obscur*: Paris, Les Îles d'Or, 1951. (A fragment of Serge's memoirs which Serge left behind in Paris in 1940 and later incorporated virtually unchanged in the complete *Memoirs*; published separately in error.) Also: Paris, Éditions Albatros, 1972.

26. *Mémoires d'un révolutionnaire, 1901–1941*: Paris, Éditions du Seuil, 1951. Also (with interesting additional material by Julián Gorkín and others): Paris, Club des Éditeurs, 1957. Sections of the *Memoirs* appeared in an English translation by Ethel Libson in *Politics* (New York), June 1944–June 1945. A second version of the *Memoirs*, revised and corrected by Serge, is published by Éditions du Seuil, Paris, Collection 'Points-Histoire', 1978.

27. *Carnets*: Paris, René Julliard, 1952. (Notebooks from the period 1936–1938 and 1942–7. An English translation from Serge's notebooks by James A. Fenwick, overlapping only partially with the *Carnets*, is to be found in *New International* (New York), September 1949–November/December 1950. This is translated from a somewhat separate selection of Serge's diary entries: *Pages de journal* (for 1936–8 and 1945–7) in *Les Temps Modernes* (Paris), Nos. 44 and 45, June and July 1949.)

28. Victor Serge, Leon Trotsky: *La Lutte contre le stalinisme*. Texts from 1936 to 1939 selected and introduced by Michel Dreyfus; Paris, François Maspero, 1977. (Letters between Serge and Trotsky and from Serge to other correspondents, as well as various articles on the themes of Kronstadt, Spain, anarchism and Trotskyism illustrating the different positions of the two revolutionaries; the collection reproduces as a genuine text of Serge the piece referred to on p. 349 of the *Memoirs*, whose authorship Victor Serge repeatedly denied and which was quite out of keeping with his published views.)

NOVELS

29. *Les Hommes dans la prison*: Paris, Éditions Rieder, 1930. (Drawn from Serge's five years in French jails, 1912–17. English translation by Richard Greeman: *Men in Prison*; New York, Doubleday, 1969; London, Gollancz, 1970; Harmondsworth, Penguin, 1972; London, Writers and Readers Publishing Co-operative, 1978.)

30. *Naissance de Notre Force*: Paris, Éditions Rieder, 1931. (Based upon the Barcelona rising of 1917 and Serge's repatriation to Russia. English translation by Richard Greeman: *Birth of Our Power*, New York, Doubleday, 1967; London, Gollancz, 1968; Harmondsworth, Penguin, 1970); London, Writers and Readers Publishing Co-operative, 1978.)

31. *Ville conquise*: Paris, Éditions Rieder, 1932. (Petrograd in 1919.) Also: Lausanne, Éditions Rencontre, 1964. (English translation by Richard Greeman: *Conquered City*; New York; Doubleday, 1975, London, Gollancz, 1976; London, Writers and Readers Publishing Co-operative, 1978.)

32. *S'il est Minuit dans le Siècle*: Paris, Bernard Grasset, 1939. Paris, Hachette, Le Livre de Poche, 1976. (Deals with the life of the Oppositionist political prisoners in the U.S.S.R. English translation by Richard Greeman to be published by Writers and Readers Publishing Co-operative, 1979.)

33. *Les Derniers Temps*: Montréal, Éditions de l'Arbre, 1946; Paris, Bernard Grasset, 1951. (A novel of dispossessed refugees at the time of the fall of France. English translation by Ralph Manheim: *The Long Dusk*; New York, Dial Press, 1946; Toronto, Longmans, 1946.)

34. *L'Affaire Toulaév*: Paris, Éditions du Seuil, 1948. Paris, Hachette, Le Livre de Poche, 1978. (A brilliant novel of the Purges. English translation by Willard R. Trask: *The Case of Comrade Tulayev*; New York, Doubleday, 1950; London, Hamish Hamilton, 1951; Harmondsworth, Penguin, 1968.)

35. *Les Années sans pardon*: Paris, François Maspero, 1971. (A novel of the Second World War, whose characters live the Communist tragedy on the Russian front, in a besieged Berlin and in a final G.P.U. assassination scene in Mexico.)

Le Terre commence à trembler . . ., mentioned by Serge on p. 372, seems to be an alternative title for *L'Affaire Toulaév* (title 34).

Titles 29, 30, 31, 32, and 34 above were published in a single volume under the title *Les Révolutionnaires*, Paris, Éditions du Seuil, 1967.

SHORT STORIES

36. *Le Tropique et le Nord*: Paris, François Maspero, 1972. (A collection planned by Serge which includes two pre-war stories (*Mer Blanche*, 1932, and *L'Impasse Saint-Barnabé*, 1936), a story about a psychiatric clinic, *L'Hôpital de Leningrad*, and a previously unpublished memoir of Mexico, *Le Séisme*.)

POETRY

37. *Résistance*: Paris, Les Humbles, 1938. Reissued as *Pour un brasier dans un désert*, Paris, François Maspero, 1972. (Poems written in the U.S.S.R., confiscated by the Soviet censor in 1936, and re-composed from memory.)

PUBLISHED CORRESPONDENCE

38. Two of Serge's 528 letters from prison to Rirette are given in E. Michon, *Un Peu de l'âme des bandits*, Paris, 1918.

39. Twelve letters to friends in France, describing conditions in Russia (1926–30) are in *La Révolution prolétarienne* (Paris), July–November 1933.

40. *Lettres à Antoine Borie*, Serge's correspondence with a French sympathizer in 1946–7, is in *Témoins* (Zürich), No. 21, February 1959.

41. *De Kibaltchiche à Victor Serge: Le Rétif (1909–1919)*, a series of letters to E. Armand reflecting Serge's evolution from anarchism to Marxism, presented and introduced by Jean Maitron, in *Le Mouvement Social* (Paris), No. 47, 1964.

42. 'Correspondance Emmanuel Mounier–Victor Serge', letters exchanged between Mounier and Serge over 1940–7, is in *Bulletin des amis d'Emmanuel Mounier* (Paris), No. 39, 1972.

Two letters to Mlle Jeanne Saint-Martin in 1940 and eighteen letters over 1945–7, to the publisher René Lefeuvre, are collected in the 1972 Spartacus edition of title 11 above.

Letters between Serge and Trotsky, Marcel Martinet, Andreu Nin, Leon Sedov and Henryk Sneevliet are published in title 28 above.

WORKS CONFISCATED BY THE SOVIET CENSORSHIP

L'An II de la Révolution russe: uncompleted materials for a work on War Communism.

Les Hommes perdus: a memoir of the French anarchist movement.

La Tourmente: a novel on Russia in 1920, 'in which I thought I had best conveyed the grandeur of the Revolution' (*Memoirs*, p. 372).

A complete bibliography of the works of Victor Serge is in preparation by Jean Rière for his major study *Victor Serge, un voix sous la glace et le granit*.

INDEX

Men in Prison
by VICTOR SERGE

Translated by Richard Greeman

(Part One of the Cycle
Victory-in-Defeat, Defeat-in-Victory)

1914. A political activist has been sentenced to five years in prison. The repressive brutality behind bars mirrors a society at war, consuming itself in its own savagery. From its ashes rises a prophecy of revolutionary victory.

Himself imprisoned at the age of 22, Victor Serge found the experience of five years behind bars so intolerable that years later he wrote this novel in an attempt to free himself from this "inward nightmare." Serge's evocation of prison life and its dehumanizing rituals has all the power of recent prison testimonies.

"I know of no other writer with whom Serge can be usefully compared. . . . The truth for Serge was something to be undergone."—John Berger

"A special class of literature that has arisen out of the European political struggle. . . ."   —George Orwell

ISBN   0 904613 50 X

Birth of our Power
by VICTOR SERGE

Translated by Richard Greeman

(Part Two of the Cycle
Victory-in-Defeat, Defeat-in-Victory)

1917. The people of Barcelona rise up in a struggle
which is doomed to failure. In Russia, the revolutionary masses are on the upsurge. Their preliminary victory tastes grimly of defeat, yet their collective power
ensures that no defeat can be permanent.

In this intensely human book, Victor Serge creates a
political novel commensurate to the events he is describing. Like the revolution, the book is made up of
many voices, often dissonant, sometimes unified in
hope, but always part of a resonant, collective WE.

"I can't think of anyone else who has written about
the revolutionary movement in this century with
Serge's combination of moral insight and intellectual
richness."   —Dwight Macdonald

ISBN   0 904613 49 6

Conquered City
by VICTOR SERGE

Translated by Richard Greeman

(Part Three of the Cycle
Victory-in-Defeat, Defeat-in-Victory)

1919–1920. Revolutionary Petrograd sees its darkest days. While Civil War rages, revolutionaries are trapped by their situation into destroying their own comrades. City and Revolution are saved . . . but who or what has conquered?

In this powerful book, Victor Serge—perhaps the greatest writer of political fiction in our century—not only evokes the Russian Revolution (in which he participated), but raises some of the central political questions of our time.

"Facing squarely the antitheses of terror and control, power and humanity, public safety and private agony, Serge's version of Revolution is uncomfortable, savage even, but manages too to be human and honest."   —C.J. Driver *The Guardian*

ISBN   0 904613 51 8

Midnight in the Century
by VICTOR SERGE

Translated by Richard Greeman

This is a book about history's darkest hour: Hitler's triumph in Germany and Stalin's apotheosis in Russia. It is also a book about men and women whose fidelity to the revolution of 1917 brought them to the Gulag of 1934.

First published in 1939, Midnight in the Century conveys—many years before Solzhenitzyn and from within the revolutionary camp—the desperation of those sentenced to deportation in Siberia and trapped in a police state where fear and betrayal make up the texture of life. Yet from these stark, anguished pages, a hope arises in man's ability to change his condition, to live fraternally with his fellows. Serge's heroes—the inarticulate worker, Rodion; the granite-faced old Bolshevik, Ryzhik; the stoical, yet gentle Varvara; even the cynical Elkin—have an appointment with an unknown darkly glimpsed future.

ISBN   0 904613 95 X

The Case of
Comrade Tulayev
by VICTOR SERGE

Translated by William R. Trask

Russia, 1939: the revolutionary fervour of 1917 has given way to the bureaucratic counter-revolution. Defeat in Spain is certain, the Second World War imminent. And Comrade Tulayev, a key party man, has been shot dead on impulse by an unimportant clerk.

But the case goes unsolved: suspicion grows; nobody is safe—even Central Committee men are imprisoned. Dossiers and deportations are followed by forced confessions and executions. Soon all Russia is reverberating with the case of Comrade Tulayev.

Victor Serge's classic novel of Stalin's Russia is an appallingly vivid study of the futility of existence in a totalitarian tyranny. The characters are stripped bare and taken to the end of their tether—and beyond; while the locations—from Siberia to Moscow to Barcelona—serve to trigger their hopelessness and alienation.

ISBN   0 86316 054 9